An American History

Third Edition

Volume II from 1865 to the Present

An American History

Third Edition

Volume II from 1865 to the Present

Rebecca Brooks Gruver

Hunter College of the City University of New York
and
The Institute for Research in History, New York City

ADDISON-WESLEY PUBLISHING COMPANY
Reading, Massachusetts ★ Menlo Park, California ★ London
Amsterdam ★ Don Mills, Ontario ★ Sydney

Sponsoring Editor: Stuart W. Johnson
Development Editor: Kathe G. Rhoades
Production Editor: Barbara H. Pendergast
Designer: Robert A. Rose
Illustrator: Kristin Kramer
Cover Design: Robert A. Rose
Cover Lithograph: The Harry T. Peters Collection,
Museum of the City of New York

Library of Congress Cataloging in Publication Data

Gruver, Rebecca Brooks.
    An American history.

    Includes bibliographies and index.
    CONTENTS: v. 1. To 1877.—v. 2. 1865 to present.
    1. United States—History. I. Title.
E178.1.G9   1981   973   80-22806
ISBN 0-201-05052-8 (v. 1)
ISBN 0-201-05053-6 (v. 2)

TO MY PARENTS
AND
TO MY MENTOR
ARMIN RAPPAPORT

Preface

The narration of America's often complex and chaotic past is a fascinating but demanding task. The many months spent in the preparation of the third edition of *An American History* have given me renewed respect for my predecessors and colleagues who have put their hand to a similar undertaking.

Like most historians who have written such a survey, I have looked for patterns of thought and belief which have lasted or recurred throughout the tumultuous course and sometimes startling changes of direction our history has taken. As a result, this volume, like the second edition, includes references to what I believe are the most important and enduring themes of the nation's past: the desire for individual freedom and equality of opportunity and a humanitarian concern for the less fortunate in society who have not shared equally in that opportunity to create a better life for themselves. These ideals have not been expressed with equal vigor at all times, nor have they always been in harmony. Nevertheless, American history does demonstrate the uneven efforts of a diverse population to maintain and give expression to their ideals as well as to come to terms with the discrepancy between those ideals and reality.

Of course, one of the main purposes of revising any textbook is to bring it up to date. This edition includes three chapters on the dramatic and often disquieting events of the 1960s and 1970s. The political, economic, and cultural events of the administrations of Kennedy, Johnson, Nixon, and Ford have been covered thoroughly; and I have added a completely new chapter which includes an analysis of recent social and cultural trends, a description of the efforts of women and various minorities to obtain a position of equality in American life, and coverage of the domestic and foreign policies of the Carter administration to date.

In response to criticisms and suggestions from fellow historians, I have revised the narrative in numerous places, eliminated material which seemed extraneous, and enlarged the coverage of certain topics which needed greater explanation. For exam-ple, Chapters 8 and 9 of the second edition have been combined in an effort to make the political, economic, and constitutional events of the period 1816–1828 easier to comprehend. The cultural history previously covered in those chapters has been integrated into Chapter 11 which treats American religious and cultural history before the Civil War. Because of its importance in explaining subsequent American political and economic history, I have expanded the discussion of the Progressive Era from one to two chapters. Chapter 22 covers the development of progressivism and the presidency of Theodore Roosevelt. Chapter 23 covers the administrations of Taft and Wilson. Chapter 24 on World War I has been altered slightly by including the debate over American neutrality during Wilson's first term in Chapter 23. The result, I hope, is a clearer presentation in Chapter 24 of American participation in World War I and the American debate over the Versailles Treaty and the League of Nations.

Every effort has been made to bring the text into line with the latest research in the field of American history. For example, the coverage of the history of women and minorities (particularly Indians, blacks, and Hispanics) has been enlarged and updated throughout the book. At the same time I have attempted to show how their role in the nation's past relates to the development of American society as a whole. I have expanded and revised the discussion of such controversial topics as the history of slavery, Reconstruction, and the causes of the Vietnam War. New chapter titles, introductions, and conclusions have been added where it seemed necessary to sharpen the focus of a chapter, clarify the outcome of a controversial period, or interpret a set of events. I am especially indebted to political scientists and the "new" political historians on two counts: for their discovery of the important role played by the ethno-cultural background of voters in the ever-changing course of American politics and for their finding that to date the United States has had five recognizable party systems. I have used their insights on these topics throughout the book.

The bibliographies at the end of each chapter have been brought up to date and a new bibliography accompanies the last chapter.

Finally, this edition includes some brand-new material. There are new feature articles: biographies of John Smith, Margaret Fuller, Susan B. Anthony, and Babe Ruth; and articles on some of the more numerically important ethno-cultural groups which made their way to America: the Irish and German immigrants in the early nineteenth century, and the Italian, Polish, and Jewish immigrants in the late nineteenth and early twentieth centuries. Two short articles have been added discussing the shifting interpretations of populism (Chapter 20) and the cold war (Chapter 28). A list of significant events and dates has been added at the beginning of each chapter as a special aid to students. And several portfolios of photographs have been included at appropriate places to help the student obtain a better feel for a particular period or series of events.

Supplements

The supplementary teaching aids that accompanied the second edition have been thoroughly revised for the new edition of the text. To help instructors in preparing for lectures and discussions, there is an Instructor's Manual with Test Items. A Study Guide is available for student use.

Acknowledgments

I owe a debt of gratitude to Kathe Rhoades, development editor for the third edition, for her efforts to achieve a narrative of the highest standard of accuracy, clarity, and gracefulness of expression. I also appreciate very much the diligence and good advice of Meredith Nightingale, who selected photographs and assisted in the preparation of feature articles.

Special thanks go to the following people for their aid on aspects of the work for this edition: David Smith, who served as project editor during the beginning stages of the work; Barbara Pendergast, who copyedited the final manuscript; LaWanda Cox, Professor Emeritus, Hunter College, CUNY, whose expert advice on the chapter on Reconstruction was invaluable (any errors in my discussion of that thorny topic are, of course, my own); and Jason Berger, whose thorough research in providing new material on American social history has been very useful to me in revising the whole manuscript.

In addition, I would like to thank the following people for their perceptive comments on the manuscript at various stages:

Hugh T. Atkinson, Gainesville Junior College
Francisco A. Balmaseda, San Antonio College
Delmar L. Beene, Glendale Community College
Victor Dahl, Portland State University
Marvin Downing, University of Tennessee at Martin
Melvin W. Ecke, Georgia State University
Mark Gardner, Glendale Community College
Claude H. Hall, Texas A & M
Linda Hastings
Clifford W. Haury, Piedmont Virginia Community College
Donald Higgins
Richard Hunt
Harvey H. Jackson, Clayton Junior College
William B. McCash, Middle Tennessee State University
Roger L. Nichols, University of Arizona
May O'Neal, San Antonio College
James Pohl, Southwest Texas State University
Patricia Presnall, El Paso County Community College
Martha Swain, Texas Women's University
Felix Tejera, El Paso Community College
John Trickel, Richland College
Patricia Wesson Wingo, Jacksonville State University

Finally, I wish to thank my husband, Phil Goodman, for his patience and good humor during the many months of work on this project. He has always had a way of keeping me from taking either myself or my work more seriously than I should.

New York   R.B.G.
September 1980

To the Student

The Study of History

From time to time, Americans are reminded by newspaper quizzes and public-opinion polls that they have a rather limited knowledge of the events that have shaped the nation's past. Some people may not care and others may wonder what difference it makes. But most of us feel a little guilty if we are unable to recall basic information about the history of our own country.

Yet is the knowledge of factual information about the past really a good test of knowing history? Most historians believe that history is much more than a precise recording of facts and dates. While some of us may study the past because it is interesting in itself, most of us also want to know if it can tell us something useful about human experience. We want to know why people did certain things and what the results of their actions were. We want to probe the motives of individuals and groups in earlier times in an effort to comprehend their connection with subsequent history. We wonder what we might have done if we had been confronted with an identical situation.

Can a study of the past tell us anything about ourselves and the nature of our society in general? Have human beings reacted consistently to similar sets of conditions, or are there factors in the historical process that have made them respond differently at different times? What role do economic, ideological, ethnic, and cultural forces play? Is it even possible to isolate the factors that determine how the historical process unfolds? These are some of the questions historians have asked themselves as they examine the record that remains from the past. Often the answers to these questions are contradictory; seldom are they definitive. The lack of a well-defined answer as to what the past means and what it can tell us about ourselves presents historians with an enduring challenge.

Some historians feel that the very complexity of human life prevents us from ever understanding all we can about the past. Others believe that the failure to arrive at a satisfactory solution to the historical puzzle is the result of the fragmentary record that remains to be pieced together. Whereas for many past events (especially those in the recent past) there are voluminous records, for others the information is sparse.

Every good historian, then, must become part detective, part social scientist, part artist, and part interpreter. He or she must locate the documents that will be most useful in creating an accurate picture of a bygone era. Some of the most important primary, or original, sources are government records, including laws, reports, treaties, and diplomatic correspondence; newspapers; and the letters and diaries of the prominent individuals who have participated in events or who have observed them. Such records are invaluable in studying political, constitutional, and diplomatic history. Historians who choose to study the daily lives, working conditions, and political preferences of aggregate groups look to primary sources of a different kind: the masses of data that have been accumulated on the local or community life of the citizenry. We can learn much about various ethnic, racial, religious, or economic groups by examining census records, tax rolls, church records, and voting returns. In addition to primary sources, historians make use of secondary sources—books and articles researched by other historians.

Historical evidence, whether primary or secondary, must be evaluated critically. Historians must determine whether or not their sources are genuine, they must consider what biases or outside influences may have motivated the author of an original document; and they must determine the best source to use when there is conflicting evidence. In addition, they must recognize that their own perceptions shape their interpretation of events.

While scientific objectivity about past human events has been impossible to achieve, many historians have applied the theories of sociologists, economists, and political scientists to their study of the past. Most, however, have not attempted to develop scientific hypotheses about social or political occurrences, for they believe such universal laws do not take into account the variability of human experience. But like the social scientists, they look for patterns of behavior which have recurred under similar circumstances at different times and in different places.

Perhaps the best historians are those who are able to combine careful research with literary artistry; they are good storytellers who can present an engaging narrative that is based on a thoughtful analysis of the motivations behind the flow of events. When they interpret history, however, they seek to convey the complexity of human experience and to render judgments only after careful examination of various sides of an issue.

Historians, like all of us, are influenced in their thinking by the interests and outlook of their own period; consequently, historians living at different times are even more likely to disagree than are contemporaries. For example, many scholars writing about the American past during the relatively complacent period of the 1950s stressed the unifying factors in American history—the ideals that held Americans together as a people. In the turbulent 1960s, however, revisionist historians began to view the American past from a different perspective. Where their predecessors had emphasized mutuality, they stressed the themes of social conflict and violence. The search for a "usable past," as historian Carl Becker has called it, is illustrated by the interpretive controversies labeled "Interpreting American History," which are highlighted throughout this book.

Thus far I have described how historians go about their task. But how can you, the reader of this text, participate in the spirit of historical investigation? Perhaps you will not be studying original documents during the course, and you may be assigned only a few detailed studies of specific events or periods. But you can try to read the text critically. Rather than simply memorizing facts, you, like the historian, can try to isolate the causes and effects of important events, such as the settlement of New England, the Civil War, or Watergate. You might also try to define for yourself the themes that seem to recur during the course of the development of the United States.

Careers in History

Many students enjoy the study of history but question its practical usefulness as preparation for a future career. In the past, the question was easily answered for those who wanted to teach history. After obtaining a degree in the field they sought a teaching position in a high school or college. Today, however, teaching positions are difficult to find, especially at the college level, and this situation is likely to continue for some time.

Does a degree in history prepare an individual for any other kind of work? Recently, several universities have initiated programs to train students for careers in fields which make use of historical knowledge and training. One of these is employment as an historical archivist. Depositories of historical information require efficient management, and the archivist must be adept at finding, collecting, organizing, and restoring documents. In addition, he or she must be capable of directing lawyers, scholars, and journalists to the material they need.

Another career field open to historians is that of "cultural resources management," or, more simply, historical preservation. This type of career primarily involves caring for museum collections, planning exhibits, and handling public relations. It may also include research on the development of a surrounding community and the preservation of historic buildings. Historians interested in working in this field often combine their historical background with training in a related field such as archaeology, anthropology, art history, or architecture.

Finally, a growing number of historians are being employed by corporations and consulting firms and by state, local, and national government agencies in policy planning and applied research. Here again training in related disciplines, such as political science, sociology, and economics, as well as statistics, is of significant value.

Of course only a few of you may decide to pursue a career in history. For the rest, the study of history can still have practical value. If you plunge in enthusiastically, you can be challenged to develop techniques for logical analysis, learn to research a subject with care, and communicate the results of your investigation with clarity and precision. Such training will help provide a background that is useful for success in a variety of careers.

VIEW OF WASHINGTON, 1851.

Contents

Maps and Charts

An American History

Third Edition

Volume II from 1865 to the Present

15 Reconstructing the Union

With malice toward none; with charity for all; with firmness in the right, as God gives us to see the right, let us strive on to finish the work we are in; to bind up the nation's wounds; to care for him who shall have borne the battle, and for his widow and his orphan—to do all which may achieve and cherish a just, and a lasting peace, among ourselves, and with all nations.

Abraham Lincoln, *Second Inaugural Address*
March 4, 1865

Significant Events

Lincoln's Proclamation of Amnesty and Reconstruction (Ten-Percent Plan) [December 1863]

Wade-Davis Bill [July 1864]

Thirteenth Amendment to the Constitution (ratified December 1865) [January 1865]

Freedmen's Bureau established [March 1865]

Lincoln dies [April 15, 1865]

Johnson's Proclamation of Amnesty and Pardon [May 1865]

Black Codes [1865 and 1866]

Civil Rights Act [April 1866]

Fourteenth Amendment (ratified July 1868) [June 1866]

Military Reconstruction Act [March 1867]

President Johnson impeached [February 1868]

Fifteenth Amendment (ratified February 1870) [February 1869]

Enforcement Acts [1870 and 1871]

Amnesty Act [1872]

Economic panic [1873]

Civil Rights Cases [1883]

Atlanta Compromise [1895]

Plessy v. *Ferguson* [1896]

Williams v. *Mississippi* [1898]

Guinn v. *United States* [1915]

RICHMOND, VIRGINIA, AFTER THE CIVIL WAR.

The Civil War preserved the republic and abolished slavery, but it left a nation bitter and divided. Of the tasks remaining to be accomplished, none was more critical than the need to restore the South to the Union without sacrificing the newly won freedom of the slaves.

In the North a great and stormy debate developed over the nature of the settlement to be imposed on the South. This debate, which largely determined the character of the postwar period, involved power struggles between the legislative and executive branches of government and between a triumphant Republican party and a resurgent Democratic party.

In the South the war and abolition left a society in disarray. During the Reconstruction period lingering Southern bitterness against the North was compounded by the efforts of many Northerners to prescribe the political and economic structure of the postwar South.

The options open to the North in reconstructing the defeated states of the Confederacy were circumscribed by the fact that the powers ascribed to the federal government under the Constitution were limited, and by the related awareness that any regulation of the social and economic life of the citizenry should be a state and local responsibility. The armies of both sides were disbanded and the men returned to civilian life with no further support than pensions for their services. In the South private companies financed by the states and foreign and Northern capital gradually rebuilt railroads and other facilities. Only in regard to the freedmen did the national government reluctantly become involved in a piecemeal approach to easing their transition to a new life.

Presidential Reconstruction Plans

The South at War's End

At the war's end the South was in disarray and its economy was in ruins. Charleston and Richmond had been almost completely leveled, and entire sections of Atlanta, Mobile, Vicksburg, and Galveston lay in ashes. Sherman's armies, following their commander's scorched-earth policy, devastated much of the Georgia and Carolina countryside on their march to Savannah. Transportation was a hopeless shambles. Roads were impassable, rivers were unnavigable, bridges were down, and wagons, horses, and steamboats had all but disappeared. The destruction of countless schools disrupted education; many teachers who had gone off to war would never return. Even more calamitous than the physical destruction was the huge loss of life. Out of an army of one million, some 260,000 Southerners died (Northern losses were no less consequential— 360,000 Northerners dead out of an army of 1.5 million).

The war also had severe economic effects on the South. Runaway inflation closed Southern banks and drove businesses into bankruptcy. Many large plantations were producing far below capacity, land values dropped dramatically, and little capital or credit was available for rebuilding or reinvesting.

The freeing of the slaves created an immediate labor shortage, since many freedmen were traveling from place to place in search of their families or moving into the towns in search of work. Plantation owners were alarmed by persistent rumors that the victorious North intended to carve up Southern plantations and distribute the land among the newly freed blacks. If all this were not enough, Southern whites looked upon the freedom of their slaves as a threat of unknown proportions to the future social and political order of the South.

Lincoln's Reconstruction Program

While the war was in progress President Lincoln began to lay the groundwork for rebuilding the nation. His primary goal for the immediate postwar period was to enable the Southern states to resume their rightful place in the Union while at the same time taking measures to ensure the "ultimate extinction" of slavery. On the question of the status of the South, Lincoln reasoned that because secession was an illegal act, the Confederate states had never really left the Union. All that was necessary was to remove the illegitimate rebel authorities and replace them with newly constituted, loyal state governments.

Lincoln believed there was some support for the republic in every Southern state, and he intended to make it as easy as possible for the former Confederate states to resume proper "practical relations" with the Union. Therefore, in December 1863 he issued his Proclamation of Amnesty and Reconstruction. Popularly known as the Ten-Percent Plan, the president's Reconstruction blueprint stipulated that all citizens of a Confederate state (with the exception of highly placed officials of the Confederacy) would be granted amnesty and would be returned all property lost in the war upon taking an oath of loyalty to the Constitution and to the laws and proclamations regarding slavery passed by Congress and the president during the war. When a number of voters in a state equal to 10 percent of those who had voted in the 1860 presidential election had taken this oath, those voters could write a new constitution creating a loyal government. The state could then resume its proper functions in the Union.

The loyalty oath was the only part of the plan that dealt with the abolition question. Lincoln made no provision for enforcing the oath, but instead called upon Southern leaders to bring about the permanent freedom of the slaves. Moreover, early in 1865 he stated publicly that he wished to see the suffrage extended at least to those blacks who were educated, who owned property, and "who serve our cause as soldiers." The federal government began almost immediately to carry out the provisions of the Ten-Percent Plan in the occupied states of Louisiana, Arkansas, and Tennessee. Lincoln installed military governors who began organizing the support of the loyal minority of citizens in preparation for establishing new state governments.

Many Republicans in Congress were willing to accept Lincoln's plan, but leading Radical Republicans considered it too lenient. Some Radicals did not share Lincoln's view that the Confederate states had not left the Union, and they wanted to punish the South by making the requirements for reentry more stringent. Radical Republicans also insisted that steps be taken to ensure that black people would be granted equality before the law and all the civil rights that entailed. Finally, all Republicans believed that as the representatives of the people it was their proper legislative function, and not the function of the president, to decide the terms on which the former states could be recreated.

The issues of which branch of government should have authority to formulate Reconstruction policy and what the nature of that policy should be became bound up in a struggle for power between the executive and the legislature. During the course of the war President Lincoln had strengthened the executive enormously at the expense of Congress. Now that the conflict was drawing to a close, Congress began to reassert its constitutional authority, using its legislative powers as the instrument.

In July 1864 Congress countered Lincoln's Ten-Percent Plan with the harsher Wade-Davis bill. The bill required that a majority of a state's voters, instead of just 10 percent, swear allegiance to the Union before being readmitted; it limited political participation to those who had been loyal to the Union during the war; and it required that the new state constitutions contain provisions repudiating all debts contracted by the Confederacy, abolishing slavery, and denying the vote to all ex-Confederate officials. Like Lincoln's plan, the Wade-Davis bill left to the states the determination of black civil rights. The bill was passed by Congress, but Lincoln, concerned that the Reconstruction process that was already well under way in Louisiana would be nullified by the bill and believing that the rights of freedmen could be better ensured by a constitutional amendment than by an act of Congress, let it die by pocket veto.

Radical Republicans, led by Thaddeus Stevens in the House and Charles Sumner in the Senate, were enraged. They responded with the Wade-Davis Manifesto, which censured the president and accused him of an "outrage on the legislative authority." Aware that he would have to make some concessions to the Radicals in order to proceed with Reconstruction, Lincoln began to formulate a new plan. But his efforts to devise a compromise with Congress were sidetracked by the resistance of conservative members of Congress to inclusion of a Radical proposal for universal black male suffrage. In January 1865, under pressure from Lincoln, Congress passed and later that year a majority of states ratified the Thirteenth Amendment to the Constitution prohibiting slavery or involuntary servitude in the United States. This was the first time the federal government had undertaken a nationwide reform in the area of domestic institutions, and it did so with a full awareness that the social consequences of freeing the slaves would still have to be worked out.

ONLOOKERS MOURN AS THE BODY OF PRESIDENT LINCOLN ARRIVES AT THE CITY HALL IN NEW YORK, 1865.

The Assassination of Lincoln

On April 9, 1865, with Lee's surrender to Grant at Appomattox Court House in Virginia, the restoration of the Union was no longer in doubt. But the North's triumph was shadowed by the tragedy that struck on Good Friday, April 14. That evening Lincoln and his wife drove to Ford's Theater in Washington to attend a play. Just after ten o'clock, John Wilkes Booth of Virginia, a young actor and pro-slavery fanatic, slipped unnoticed into the corridor behind the president's box while the one guard assigned to protect the president had stepped out for a drink. Through a hole he had bored earlier in the day Booth watched his victim, and at an amusing moment in the play, while the audience was laughing, he entered the box and shot the president in the head. Then, springing to the stage of the theater, he cried dramatically, *"Sic Semper Tyrannis!* The South is avenged!"* and dashed through the wings to a waiting horse. The president, mortally wounded, was carried across the street to a private home. Early the next morning he died. Booth was hunted down and cornered in a barn in Virginia. The barn was set on fire and Booth was shot dead.

The news of Lincoln's death stunned the North. Grief-stricken mourners stood silently by the railroad tracks as his funeral train carried their leader home to Springfield. Lincoln's death suspended hopes for an early reconciliation between North and South. Whether the new president would be as compassionate to the defeated South remained to be seen.

Reconstruction under Andrew Johnson

The leadership of the divided nation now fell to Andrew Johnson. As a senator from Tennessee, Johnson had opposed secession and had continued to sit in Congress even after his state had withdrawn from the Union. For this action he became a hero to many Northerners, and his loyalty did not go unrewarded. When Tennessee fell to Union forces in 1862, Lincoln appointed Johnson military governor of the state. Two years later, Lincoln selected him as his running mate, and five months after the election Andrew Johnson was president.

Because Johnson detested the wealthy Southern aristocracy, the Radical Republicans at first thought they had an ally in the White House. Their optimism was short-lived, however. Johnson was no Radical, but a democrat who represented the interests of the small farmer. Moreover, his opposition to secession was a reflection of his reverence for the Constitution and the Union, not of a concern for racial justice.

It was Johnson's belief that the Constitution did not give to Congress the authority to dictate the terms by which the Confederate states could rejoin the Union. The new president therefore decided to direct the Reconstruction of each state himself, actively carrying out his policy "to restore said state to its constitutional relations to the Federal government" for seven months while Congress was not in session. He began by recognizing the new state governments of Louisiana, Arkansas, Virginia, and Tennessee that had been reorganized under Lincoln's Ten-Percent Plan. Next, in a Proclamation of Amnesty and Pardon, he set forth his own plan to be implemented in all Confederate states not already reorganized under the Ten-Percent Plan. Johnson's design was similar to Lincoln's in that it offered to pardon most ex-Confederates who would pledge their loyalty to the Union except that it excluded high-ranking Confederate officials and those owning property worth more than $20,000. These groups would be required to petition the president himself for pardon.

The plan provided for presidential appointment of a provisional governor in each state, election of delegates to state constitutional conventions, and the reorganization of the state governments. However, Johnson stipulated that before a state could be restored to the Union it must nullify its ordinance of secession, ratify the Thirteenth Amendment, and repudiate the Confederate debt.

Unfortunately, Johnson was not willing to move decisively to enforce the plan. Lincoln had believed that the Confederate South should not be given a strong voice in deciding on terms for resuming its role in the Union, but should be required to accept them as a consequence of defeat. As a Republican, Lincoln's goals had been similar to those of the congressional majority, and he had come to realize that the terms of Reconstruction had to be tough enough on the issue of the treatment of the freedmen to be acceptable to the people of the North. The North wanted to know that slavery was, indeed, dead and that the power of the former slaveholders was at an end. Johnson's enforcement of Reconstruction policy was not reassuring to Northerners. He did not attempt to enforce compliance with Northern demands, and in an attempt to create loyal regimes in the former Confederate states which would give him political support, he even implied that the South could ignore them. As a result, the South soon began to reassert its independence. Mississippi refused to ratify the Thirteenth Amendment, and Alabama refused to ratify part of it. South Carolina and Mississippi refused to repudiate their Confederate debts. Some states only "repealed" their secession ordinances, and some newly reorganized states actually sent as their representatives to Congress highly placed Confederate leaders and military men. As if this were not enough, the South moved to place restrictions on black people.

The Freedmen

The status of the freedmen in American life was the central issue in the aftermath of the Civil War. Although at the end of the war the Thirteenth Amendment was on its way to the states for ratification, the legal status of the freedmen as citizens had not yet been established. In Johnson's plans for Reconstruction, the welfare of the newly freed slaves had been subordinated to the reunification of the nation. Although only a few Radicals believed in absolute equality between the races, and although moderate Republicans were divided concerning the exact degree of suffrage that should be granted to blacks, in general the party thought blacks should be recognized as citizens with all the rights of free people. This view set them apart from the Democrats

TO DEAL WITH THE FOOD SHORTAGE THAT
PLAGUED LOCAL AREAS AFTER THE WAR,
STOREKEEPERS INSTITUTED A RATIONING
SYSTEM. IN THIS PRINT GENTLEWOMEN,
FREED BLACKS, AND POOR WHITE FARMERS
HAVE GATHERED TO COLLECT THEIR AL-
LOTMENT.

and from President Johnson, and it laid the groundwork for a power struggle between Congress and the president, between the parties within Congress, and between the North and the South.

The Freedmen's Bureau and the Black Codes By the war's end homeless former slaves were crowding into shantytowns often built by the Union army, moving into Southern cities to find jobs, and migrating to the Texas frontier in search of land. So intolerable were conditions that in 1865 alone an estimated one hundred thousand blacks reportedly died from starvation and disease. In March 1865, while Lincoln was still president, the Union government passed a bill establishing the Freedmen's Bureau to provide relief to freed slaves and white refugees and to facilitate the transition from slavery to freedom. The bureau distributed food and helped blacks reestablish employment on the plantations on the basis of agreements with planters. It cooperated with private agencies and individuals in setting up schools and providing teachers for black people of all ages. Under its auspices, Atlanta University, Fisk University, and Howard University were established, and a Freedmen's Bureau study in 1866 found that black children in the South were attending school more regularly than were whites. In addition the Bureau performed thousands of marriage ceremonies legalizing black family life.

Meanwhile, in the absence of a unified Northern policy on the rights of the freedmen, the former

Confederate states began enacting measures designed to keep the ex-slaves in a position of economic, social, and political inferiority. Collectively called the Black Codes, these measures, passed in 1865 and 1866, reflected the widespread Southern view that blacks were innately inferior and must be kept in their appropriate subordinate position. At the same time that enactment of the codes granted the former slaves a legal status—including the right to make contracts, to sue and to be sued, and in some states to acquire property without restrictions—it limited their freedom of employment and generally prohibited them from voting, holding office, testifying against white people, serving on juries, or bearing arms. Of all the provisions of the Black Codes, the most repressive were vagrancy laws which authorized local authorities to arrest unemployed black people, fine them for vagrancy, and hire out those who could not pay the fine, their wages going to pay the fine. Some states even provided that black people who jumped their labor contracts could be dragged back by white "negro-catchers" who would be paid by the mile for their efforts.

President Johnson neither condemned nor condoned the Black Codes. He did suggest to Mississippi that Northern advocates of black suffrage would be disarmed if blacks who could read and write and owned property were enfranchised. But he did not object when this was not done, nor did he repeat the suggestion to other Southern states. Suffrage remained a privilege reserved for whites only, a situation that could be justified by pointing to the fact that outside of New England and New York blacks could not vote in Northern states either.

Agriculture: Sharecropping and Crop-Lien Systems One of the provisions of the act establishing the Freedmen's Bureau involved the distribution of confiscated and abandoned Southern land to freedmen and poor white farmers. The land was to be rented for three years and then sold to the holder at its 1860 appraised value (although the law recognized that the government could not give a clear title under the wartime confiscation act). However, the black dream of "forty acres and a mule" was never realized. President Johnson quickly pardoned many previous owners and restored them to their land, thereby leaving very little land available for the freedmen. Moreover, the idea of confiscation was unpopular, since it ran counter to the firmly held American belief in the sanctity of private property and since it would impede the process of healing the bitter divisions between North and South. For a limited time Congress did open to former slaves some forty-six million acres of federal lands in the South, but most of the land was undesirable or difficult for black homesteaders to reach.

In the absence of a viable federal policy for providing the freedmen with land, the rural South began resolving the issue of the freedmen's role in the economy in its own way. With Southern agriculture in a state of total confusion at the end of the war, the planters had to change from being lords to being landlords, as historian James L. Roark has described it. Slowly, white landowners and black farm workers came to an accommodation. Impoverished plantation owners could not pay wages to their newly freed slaves, and freedmen wanted to escape from the gang labor and discipline of slavery. Through persuasion and sometimes under duress, many blacks signed annual labor contracts prepared by agents of the Freedmen's Bureau. Within a few years they generally became sharecroppers or in some cases sharetenants on small plots on the old plantations. Under the sharecropping system the plantation owner provided the sharecropper with land, shelter, seeds, tools, and animals and each agreed to share equally the profits of the forthcoming crop. The sharetenant owned his own mule and plow, and received a larger share of the crop.

Many plantation owners had been so devastated by the war that they could not even afford to advance to sharecroppers the food and other supplies they needed. In such instances owners often turned to local merchants for help, and as a result, both planters and sharecroppers became indebted to the merchants, who would demand that the most marketable crop—cotton or tobacco—be planted. The merchant's interest was secured by a lien on the crop. Although this crop-lien system revived Southern agriculture, it was inefficient and helped keep the Deep South a one-crop economy. With a limited supply of credit and an abundance of black labor that was increasingly subjected to legal restrictions, the introduction of technological advances in farming was retarded. Seventy-five percent of the black population endured submarginal economic conditions. Although some 20 percent of Southern black farmers owned their own land in 1880, like sharecroppers and tenant farmers, most were poor.

Nevertheless, the sharecropping system, which lasted into the twentieth century, did have some advantages for both the planter and the black farmer. At a time when there was a shortage of cash in the South, planters did not have to pay wages to sharecroppers and could feel secure in share labor through the harvest. For their part, croppers had obtained the use of a plot in exchange for work. They had some freedom in deciding how much time to spend cultivating, and harvesting the crop, and the return from the effort. It has been estimated that the income of a typical black family in 1879 was percent greater than that received by slaves. Most important, blacks at last could units in the privacy of their own cabins.

Congressional Reconstruction plans

While efforts were under way to revive Southern agriculture, every former Confederate state except Texas had generally met the terms of either the Tennessee Johnson's plan. Most had accepted amendment, and all had organized Percent governments and elected new senators and representatives. When Congress met in December 1865, the new Southern representatives arrived in Washington with the support of President Johnson. Congress, however, rebuffed them. The process of Reconstruction had gone ahead too fast, and the North did not find the terms of reconciliation acceptable.

Republican Views on Reconstruction

The Republicans were enraged by the Black Codes and by the reluctance of the Southern states to repudiate the ordinances of secession. They were further angered that Southern congressional delegations included many former top-ranking officers of the Confederacy, and that the delegations contained almost all Democrats, who would threaten the hard-won Republican majority in Congress. All Republicans were united in their belief that as the party that had saved the Union they must do everything possible to prevent the Democrats from gaining control of the government. Consequently, in what amounted to a rejection of presidential Reconstruction formulas, they flatly refused to seat the newly elected delegations and they immediately appointed their own Joint Committee on Reconstruction, which became a forum for many different points of view.

A few Radicals believed that the victorious North should change the entire power structure in the Southern states and force them to grant equal sta blac to blacks. According to Thaddeus Stevens, nomic ffrage was the goal and far-reaching economic fiscate uges were the means. He proposed to con- up, dist nd of all former slaveholders, carve it the rest. Some of it to former slaves, and sell the politica Sumner was more interested in lieved that t struction of the South. He be- and enjoy all dmen should become citizens the right to be fits of citizenship including to vote and to h the courts and the rights soned, would prou. The suffrage, he rea- economic opportunit blacks freedom and ensure to assert that education even went so far as grated public Repu rticipate in inte- The moderate gress, however, did not sh the reorganization of Sout rity in Con- they disliked Johnson's Recon ng views on Even so, ram be-

cause it did not require a strong enough guarantee of Southern loyalty and gave no protection to black people. Although they did not believe in racial equality, they agreed with the Radicals that freedmen should be recognized as citizens. The future of the freedmen was not their sole concern, however. Well aware that if left to its own devices the South would rapidly become a Democratic stronghold, both moderate and Radical Republicans sought to ensure that their party would maintain a strong influence in the former Confederate states. Moderate Republicans began to fear that excluding blacks from the vote might result in a coalition of former rebels and Northern antiwar Democrats gaining control of the country. Thus, Republicans arrived at a commitment to black suffrage both in order to safeguard their own control of the national government and to give blacks the political power necessary to ensure racial justice in the South.

The Fourteenth Amendment

In 1866 Congress passed a bill to protect the rights of blacks by continuing and broadening the powers of the Freedmen's Bureau, which had originally been intended to operate for only one year. The Bureau was to continue its present activities and, in addition, was granted authority to protect blacks from discrimination by law or by custom and to inaugurate a modest land program. Johnson vetoed the bill and his veto was sustained. Some months later, however, a revised bill became law.

Next Congress passed a Civil Rights Act (over Johnson's veto) which guaranteed citizenship to blacks and prohibited discrimination against citizens on the grounds of race or color. Faced with a hostile president and a recalcitrant South, Congress sought to give the new act constitutional protection by incorporating its provisions into an amendment to the Constitution. In taking this step, Congress was guarding against the annulment of the Civil Rights Act by a future Congress or by the Supreme Court.

The proposed Fourteenth Amendment was in effect a congressional plan for Reconstruction. Based on compromises between moderate and Radical Republicans, it was the final effort by the Congress to find a solution that would be acceptable to the South and that would at the same time guarantee the rights of the freedmen.

In an effort to prevent a state from denying political rights to any citizen, the amendment provided that anyone born in the United States was a citizen. This was the first time that American citizenship had been clearly defined. The amendment also stipulated that no state could deny any citizen the equal protection of the laws or deprive any citizen of life, liberty, or property without due process of law. Although not directly conferring suffrage on every citizen, the amendment declared that if a state denied the vote to any of its citizens, that state's representation in Congress and in the electoral college would be proportionately reduced. Finally, the Fourteenth Amendment disqualified from federal office all those who had at one time pledged loyalty to the Constitution and then had broken that oath to support the Confederacy. Such persons could hold office only if pardoned by two-thirds of the Congress.

From the congressional point of view, the Fourteenth Amendment was a fairly lenient proposal. The Southern states did not have to enfranchise the freedmen as long as they were willing to give up seats in Congress. Moreover, the amendment did not legislate the freedmen's economic independence at the expense of Southern whites. Yet it did affirm the constitutional rights of black people and it brought them under federal jurisdiction. It avoided the problem of black suffrage nationwide and at the same time kept former Confederates out of national office.

Had President Johnson been willing to accept the Fourteenth Amendment and to warn the South either to accept it or face harsher terms, the real difficulties of Reconstruction probably would have been over. But Johnson was no longer in touch with political reality. He believed that the Southern states were already reconstructed—that is, that they were valid states—and that a Congress operating without their participation was not a legitimate Congress. He overlooked the fact that the South had lost the Civil War and that the North was in a position to dictate its own terms. He advised the South to reject the amendment and to rely on a Republican defeat in the upcoming congressional elections.

The lines of opposition were clearly drawn, and the president decided to make the Fourteenth Amendment the major issue in the congressional elections of 1866. Laying his prestige on the line, Johnson embarked on a nationwide tour, campaigning hard for candidates who opposed the amendment. His two-fisted speaking style proved to be highly inflammatory in many parts of the country. When hecklers hurled insults at him, he responded in kind with his choicest homespun Tennessee epithets. The tour was a dismal failure. The mood of the North was against him. The election gave the Republicans a two-thirds majority in both houses of Congress, large enough to override any presidential veto. But even with the overwhelming Republican victory, ten of the eleven Southern states followed the president's advice and rejected the amendment. Furious at continuing Southern defiance, the new Congress was now in a position to enforce its will.

Radical Reconstruction

Although moderates wanted little more than to force the South to accept the Fourteenth Amendment, they united with Radical Republicans to dictate much harsher terms to the defeated states. The first Reconstruction Act, passed by Congress in March 1867 over Johnson's veto (and supplemented by three more Reconstruction Acts passed in 1867 and 1868), declared all existing state governments in the South to be illegal. This action enabled Congress to create new Southern state governments while avoiding the delicate constitutional issue of states' rights. Since no state governments legally existed, their rights could hardly be violated.

The Southern states (excluding Tennessee, which had ratified the Fourteenth Amendment and been readmitted to the Union in July 1866) were divided into five military districts under the control of the United States Army. A major general in each district was to supervise the registration of all male citizens without regard to color, except for those former public officeholders disfranchised by their participation in the rebellion. This new electorate would then choose delegates to state constitutional conventions and members of new state governments. The act further stipulated that each new state constitution be required to provide for male black suffrage and that each state be required to ratify the Fourteenth Amendment. After the states had met these conditions, and after the Fourteenth Amendment had become part of the federal Constitution, Congress would then readmit them to the Union and military occupation would end.

By July 1868 all the Confederate states except Mississippi, Texas, and Virginia had fulfilled these terms, the Fourteenth Amendment had become part of the Constitution, and Congress had seated the new delegations. Delays by the three recalcitrant states postponed their return to the Union until 1870, and Georgia, already readmitted, was removed for expelling black members from its legislature and not readmitted until 1870. In order to be readmitted these four states had to meet an additional requirement: they had to ratify the Fifteenth Amendment to the Constitution, which provided that "The right of citizens of the United States to vote shall not be denied or abridged by the United States or by any state on account of race, color, or previous condition of servitude."

Because the terms of the Military Reconstruction Act were a compromise between moderates and Radicals, they pleased no one completely. The Radicals were frustrated in their desire to provide land and education at federal expense to the freedmen and to end racial inequality. On the other hand, the president and the state governments already elected in the South were outraged by the provisions for military rule and black suffrage. Historians continue to disagree over the reasons behind the Republicans' interest in civil rights for black people. Some maintain that they were concerned with securing simple justice; others believe they were more concerned with securing votes for blacks in the expectation that blacks would vote Republican.

The Impeachment of Andrew Johnson

The Republicans were fully aware that military Reconstruction was abhorrent to Johnson, and they

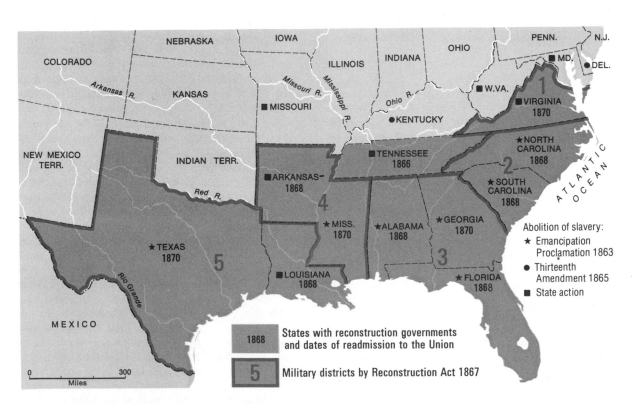

Reconstruction of the South • 1865 to 1877

THE SMELLING COMMITTEE, AN 1868 CARTOON, COMMENTS ON THE RADICAL REPUBLICANS' EFFORT TO IMPEACH PRESIDENT ANDREW JOHNSON.

feared that he would try to curb it. In their zeal to prevent presidential interference with the Reconstruction process, they began to overreach themselves. In 1867—over Johnson's veto—Congress passed two bills limiting the president's power. The Army Appropriations Act restricted his control of the army by preventing him from issuing military orders except through the general of the army who could not be removed without the consent of the Senate. The Tenure of Office Act prohibited him from removing federal officials, including his own cabinet members, without the consent of the Senate.

Believing the Tenure of Office Act to be unconstitutional, and confident that the Supreme Court would overturn it, Johnson decided in February 1868 to create a test case by removing without Senate consent the only Radical member of his cabinet, Secretary of War Edwin M. Stanton. The struggle between Congress and the president soon reached the point of no return. Radicals had been searching unsuccessfully for grounds which would

enable them to impeach the president, and his flouting of the Tenure of Office Act gave them the ammunition they needed. Within a few days the House of Representatives passed articles of impeachment against President Johnson for his deliberate violation of a federal law.

For the first time in American history, a president was tried in the United States Senate. The proceedings were heated and bitter, focusing on the question of what constituted an impeachable offense. Johnson's lawyers argued that the Constitution called for removal of a president only upon conviction of "high crimes and misdemeanors" and that none of the charges brought against Johnson could be so characterized. Clearly Johnson had not violated the Tenure of Office Act in removing Stanton, because Stanton was a Lincoln appointee who had served beyond Lincoln's term. The real issue was whether a president could be removed simply for being unacceptable to Congress. If the Senate voted to remove him, it would seriously undermine executive independence. The prosecution contended that officials could be removed for other than criminal offenses, such as actions or even intentions "against the public interest." Impeachment was the only way to get rid of an incompetent official. If the Senate had voted with the prosecution, it would have established a precedent for using impeachment as a means of expressing "no confidence" in an offcial. When the count was finally taken, the prosecution failed by only one vote to muster the two-thirds majority needed to remove Johnson from office.

Seven Republican senators joined the Democrats in voting to clear Johnson. They supported him because they considered the Tenure of Office Act unconstitutional and the president therefore innocent of the criminal offense they believed necessary for conviction. The outcome of the trial discouraged the future use of impeachment as a political weapon.

Although he completed his term, the beleaguered president was unable to secure the Democratic nomination in 1868. He returned to Tennessee where he failed in a number of attempts to be elected to local offices. Finally, in 1874 he was elected again to the United States Senate from Tennessee. He died the following year.

Thus the Radicals, at the height of their influence, impeached the president but they could not convict him. The effect of this case was to damage the Radicals' power irreparably. Thaddeus Stephens had died and Sumner never regained his former influence. The election of 1868 shifted congressional power into the hands of moderate Republicans who, along with the newly elected president, Ulysses S. Grant, were in disagreement with the harshness of Radical Reconstruction policy.

The South under Radical Reconstruction

For all the difficulties it produced, there were some solid achievements under Radical Reconstruction. The new constitutions produced by Southern constitutional conventions were distinct improvements over those they replaced. They provided for more equitable apportionment of representation; they further extended women's property rights and in some states provided divorce laws; they provided for penal-code reform; and they made many appointive offices elective. A system of state-supported educa-

tion was created throughout the South in an attempt to close the educational gap between the South and the rest of the nation. In addition, the reorganized governments encouraged the development of new industry.

From the perspective of most Southern whites, however, Radical Reconstruction had little to recommend it. For one thing, it upset the political balance by depriving large numbers of whites of the right to participate in the political process and hold public office. Although the number of disfranchised whites has often been exaggerated (it never exceeded 150,000), the fact remains that Northern Republicans played an inordinately large role in Southern politics during the Reconstruction era. In 1869 Northerners occupied four Southern governors' mansions, held ten Southern senate seats, and represented twenty Southern congressional districts. Opponents of Reconstruction called them "carpetbaggers," suggesting that they were moneyless opportunists who arrived with all their possessions in a carpetbag (a kind of valise) to plunder the South. Although some Northerners were indeed primarily interested in power and wealth, the majority were either idealistic reformers who went South to work for racial equality or Union veterans who had returned South hoping to build a future as planters or in business.

As bitterly as Southerners resented the presence of the Northern Republicans, they hated Southern Republicans even more. These "scalawags," as they were scornfully called, some of whom were small farmers or wealthy former Whigs, were held in contempt by their fellow Southerners who regarded them as unprincipled maneuverers who supported the enemy in order to advance their own interests. In fact, some among the wealthy Southern Republicans were men of previous political experience who had opposed secession; others were eager to control black voters in order to attain political office; still others were genuinely devoted to achieving equality for the freedmen. Among the small farmers, most were attracted to the Republican party because its program to improve internal transportation would help them get their crops to market.

Equally offensive to many Southerners was the part blacks began to play in the political process. Republican organizations called "Loyal Leagues" organized black voters, and in 1868 seven hundred thousand blacks voted for Grant, contributing heavily to his victory. Once the Republicans realized how important the black vote would be, they took steps to protect it by proposing the Fifteenth Amendment, which became part of the Constitution in March 1870.

Blacks also began to serve in public office. Between 1868 and 1875 two blacks served in the Senate and fifteen in the House of Representatives. A black man, Jonathan Jasper Wright, was appointed to the Supreme Court of South Carolina. Yet for the most part, black officeholders served at the state and local levels, and, considering the proportion of blacks living in the South, their participation in Southern politics must be considered extremely limited. They were a majority in only one state constitutional convention (South Carolina) and were never a majority in both houses of any state legislature. They never elected a state governor and seldom raised the issue of land confiscation.

Despite the achievements of Radical Reconstruction, some historians have alleged that it failed to create a new South because of the large-scale corruption, extravagance, and waste that characterized Reconstruction governments. In South Carolina, for example, the legislature voted to reimburse one of its members for $1000 he lost betting on the horses, and payments were made for at least three times as many militia as were actually serving in the state force. In Louisiana the annual cost of running the state government skyrocketed from $100,000 to $1 million under Reconstruction. Public funds were commonly squandered on furniture, homes, jewelry, and liquor for public officials, often plunging the states into debt.

It should be noted, however, that corruption in the South was due in part to the fact that many legislators lacked experience and lacked education. Moreover, political corruption existed in all parts of the country in the 1860s as a by-product of the lax moral climate following the war. In fact, the level of corruption in the Reconstruction governments was less than that in the national government.

The End of Reconstruction

From the very beginning of Reconstruction, Southerners bitterly resented the attempt to alter the political and social fabric of their region. Southerners' anger over the participation of blacks in the Radical governments was at the core of their efforts

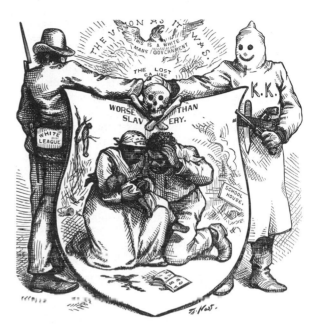

THIS 1870 ENGRAVING DEPICTS THE PLIGHT OF THE BLACK PEOPLE AFTER THE CIVIL WAR.

to wrest leadership away from the reconstructed governments.

Former Southern political leaders were determined to "redeem" the South and restore themselves to power. In Virginia, Tennessee, and North Carolina, large white majorities were able to regain control of the governments through elections. Sensing a growing opposition in the North to Radical Reconstruction, President Grant made no move to prevent a peaceful return to white supremacy. In other states, however, white citizens resorted to terrorism. Thousands of white Southerners banded together in secret organizations such as the White Brotherhood, the Knights of the White Camelia, and the Ku Klux Klan. Best known of all the societies, the Klan was based mainly in the Deep South. Founded in 1866 as a social club, the Klan soon turned its attention to driving blacks out of Southern politics, depriving them of the franchise, and restoring white supremacy. Garbed in white hoods and long robes, Klansmen at first tried to intimidate blacks and so prevent them from voting by surrounding their cabins at night, making frightening noises, and firing guns in the air. Harassment quickly turned to violence, as black homes were burned, blacks were beaten or lynched, and both white and black Radical leaders were attacked. President Grant was deeply angered by the activities of the Klan, and Congress responded by passing the Force Acts of 1870 and 1871, which placed elections under federal jurisdiction, gave the President the right to impose martial law, and imposed fines and sentences on those convicted of interfering with any citizen's right to vote.

Despite these laws, white supremacists began to take more direct action to gain control of Southern governments. Although the president used his power under the Force Acts to institute martial law to quell rebellions in South Carolina, Louisiana, and Arkansas, paramilitary organizations such as the South Carolina Redshirts continued to terrorize blacks even more openly than the Klan had done. Other armed groups, such as the Rifle Clubs and the White Leagues, used coercion and even violence to ensure election victories. White men were faced with a choice of joining the Democratic party or being driven out of the community; black men were deprived of the right to vote unless they voted Democratic. Those who persisted in their loyalty to the Republican party were denied employment or fired from the jobs they already had. Thus by means of violence and economic pressure blacks began to stay away from the polls and white supremacists welded the South into a solidly Democratic voting bloc.

While Southerners were growing more determined to restore their old political and social system, Northerners were losing interest in enforcing Reconstruction policies. They were growing less willing to bear the costs of defending the freedmen and of maintaining Republican regimes and an army in the South. The Northern business community wanted stability in the South so that normal cotton production and trade would be restored. The Republicans in the South could not accomplish this, but the white Southerners could.

Republican politicians also were beginning to realize that they could win national elections by

OF COURSE HE WANTS TO VOTE THE DEMOCRATIC TICKET COMMENTS ON THE POLITICAL PRESSURE BROUGHT TO BEAR ON BLACKS DURING RECONSTRUCTION. FIVE YEARS AFTER THE EMANCIPATION PROCLAMATION, EX-SLAVES HAD BECOME A SIGNIFICANT FORCE BACKING THE REPUBLICAN PARTY, AND WHITE SUPREMACISTS WERE DETERMINED TO RETURN POWER TO SOUTHERN DEMOCRATS.

INTERPRETING AMERICAN HISTORY

RECONSTRUCTION It was not until the 1890s that the first important historical perspectives on Reconstruction appeared. In *Reconstruction, Political and Economic*, William A. Dunning argued that Reconstruction had deprived Southern whites of their rightful control of Southern life and had given it instead to ignorant freedmen and unscrupulous carpetbaggers and scalawags. Central to Dunning's interpretation was his belief, much in vogue at that time, in the biological inferiority of blacks.

By the 1930s a new school of historians had emerged which rejected Dunning's perspective. Historians such as Francis B. Simkins, Robert Woody, and C. Vann Woodward contended that blacks had played a relatively minor role in Reconstruction politics. They argued, moreover, that the Radical Reconstruction governments in the South were set up mainly to ensure Republican control of the national government. But corruption under Radical Reconstruction regimes was no worse than in the North at the same time and was less prevalent in the Southern conservative regimes that followed. The real struggle of Reconstruction, these revisionist historians claimed, was the economic conflict between the business and financial interests of the North represented by the Radicals and the old agrarian interests of the South.

In the 1950s and 1960s a third historical interpretation of Reconstruction developed, attuned to the Civil Rights movement. This neorevisionist interpretation emphasized the moral issue of racial discrimination as the central theme of the Reconstruction struggle. Its proponents included R. P. Sharkey, Eric L. McKitrick, La Wanda and John Cox, and Kenneth M. Stampp. In general, these historians held that the Reconstruction era was a tragedy. McKitrick argued that Reconstruction was a failure because efforts to achieve racial equality created intense hostility in the white South. Stampp, on the other hand, maintained that if white Southerners had been forced to accept racial equality long enough, they ultimately would have acquiesced in it. The Coxes stressed that protection of the freedmen's civil rights was central to the conflict between Johnson and the Republicans.

In the 1970s historians continued to debate the impact of Reconstruction legislation. Some historians, such as Louis S. Gerteis and C. Peter Ripley, held that the Union Army and the Freedmen's Bureau tried to establish stability rather than to ensure real economic and political reform. In other words, their goal was to provide an orderly, cheap labor force of freedmen. Racism in the North was as strong as in the South and limited the effective enforcement of Radical Reconstruction. On the other hand, Herman Belz in *A New Birth of Freedom* (1976) has argued that before the war the definition of citizenship was determined by the individual states. The achievement of the war and the Republican party was to ensure through the Thirteenth, Fourteenth, and Fifteenth Amendments that citizenship and equal rights before the law would be uniform throughout the nation.

carrying the North and the West alone and that the Southern black vote was expendable. Reconstruction was now considered largely a failure, and as the 1872 presidential election drew near, Republicans wished to shed political liability. That year Congress passed an Amnesty Act which had the effect of restoring political participation to most white Southerners. As a result of an increased white vote, as well as infighting among Republicans who controlled the Reconstruction governments, these regimes began to topple. By the end of 1875 only Louisiana, Florida, and South Carolina still had Reconstruction governments. A year later, the disputed presidential election of 1876 was settled by a compromise that brought Reconstruction to an end. The last federal forces were withdrawn from the South in April 1877. The nation had been reunited but not reconciled.

As extreme as Radical Reconstruction seemed at the time, it did not change the basic structure of Southern life. Blacks were unable to achieve economic independence and so were unable to retain their political equality when Reconstruction ended. The machinery established to protect their right to vote proved inadequate. All that remained as a posi- tive, enduring legacy of Reconstruction were the Fourteenth and Fifteenth Amendments to the Constitution.

Grant's Presidency

The Election of 1868

In 1868 the Republicans nominated General Ulysses S. Grant, an extremely popular war hero with few known political views, as their presidential candidate. The party continued to seek the support of Northern manufacturing interests by adopting a platform that supported a high tariff and encouraged cheap labor through a liberal immigration policy.

The Democratic nominee was Horatio Seymour, an opponent of Radical Reconstruction. Unlike the Republicans, the Democrats aimed their campaign at Western farmers and other indebted voters with a "cheap money" platform. During the war Congress had issued a large amount of paper money (greenbacks) that was not backed by gold. At the end of the war Congress gradually began withdrawing the greenbacks, against the wishes of debtors—Western bankers, farmers, and railroad pro-

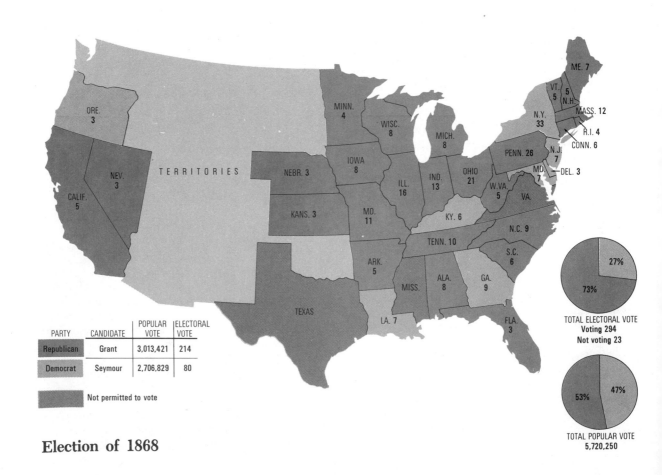

PARTY	CANDIDATE	POPULAR VOTE	ELECTORAL VOTE
Republican	Grant	3,013,421	214
Democrat	Seymour	2,706,829	80

Not permitted to vote

TOTAL ELECTORAL VOTE
Voting 294
Not voting 23

TOTAL POPULAR VOTE
5,720,250

Election of 1868

moters—who wanted to repay their debts with cheap money. Creditors—largely Eastern bankers and financiers—wanted to receive full value for the money they had lent and consequently favored withdrawing the greenbacks from circulation. The Democratic platform of 1868 supported the continued circulation of greenbacks.

Despite these clear economic differences between the parties, the decisive issue in the campaign proved to be the war that had ended three years earlier. The Republicans presented themselves as the party that had saved the Union and the Democrats as the party of rebellion. Grant's candidacy reinforced this view, and although the popular vote was close, the Republicans swept the electoral college 214 to 80.

Grant's Political Style

With his limited political experience, President Grant had no plans to initiate policies. He believed that the primary duty of the president was to execute the will of Congress. Those who hoped that he would be a firm and wise leader who would control the Radicals and raise the tone of public life were soon disappointed. Influenced by his military background, Grant ran the presidency along military lines, issuing commands and discouraging debate of the issues. At the same time, his lack of political experience and his receptivity to flattery made him an easy target of self-seeking politicians and business leaders. When he did act on his own initiative, as he did in choosing his advisors, the results were uneven. For example, his White House staff, which also controlled federal patronage appointments, was dominated by old army colleagues with no political experience; they dispensed jobs to friends, relatives, and those with the money to pay for their positions.

Economic Policies

One of the central domestic issues facing Grant was the need to formulate a policy on greenbacks. Grant wanted to please the Eastern financiers who had supported him, but feared that retiring the greenbacks would alienate those in debt. He finally settled on a compromise that would leave the greenbacks in circulation but make it possible to back them with gold in the future. Because the compromise was not especially popular with the large mass of voters, Grant supported the highly popular congressional measures aimed at eliminating the wartime income tax and excise duties.

Another economic issue was the high tariff Congress had enacted as an emergency wartime measure. When the war ended, manufacturing and industrial interests favored retaining the duties to keep out foreign competitive products. These interests had supported Grant in the election, and their lobbyists had little trouble convincing him that the high tariff should be retained. Some advisers claimed that high tariffs merely enriched Eastern industrialists at the expense of many consumers, especially Western farmers. But the president supported the protectionists in Congress, who raised duties on many products in 1870.

Corruption in Washington

The major issue of Grant's administration was misconduct in the federal government. During the eight years of his presidency, a number of those holding high political office used their power and influence to amass personal fortunes at the expense of the voters who had elected them. Other public officials were naive victims of businesspeople who exploited them and their offices. The result was a great loss of public confidence in government.

The corruption of the Grant years was largely the result of the relaxed moral climate in all segments of society following the Civil War. The growth of industrialization (to be described in Chapter 17) and of business enterprise related to the war effort encouraged the rise of a wealthy class of businesspeople and entrepreneurs. Americans worshipped wealth as never before, and the acquisition of material possessions became an obsession. A pattern of bribery and favoritism in government-business relations that had developed during the war years continued into the era of postwar politics.

Given this climate of corruption many politicians were unable to resist bribes for favors they could dispense freely. Others, including Grant himself, did not intentionally abuse their offices or gain personally from corruption, but were unwitting accomplices in scandal because of their naiveté and negligence. Infatuated by the startling successes of American business and possessing only a limited understanding of the complex postwar economic

THIS 1876 CARTOON ILLUSTRATES THE FOLLOWING "CONVERSATION" BETWEEN UNCLE SAM AND PRESIDENT GRANT. UNCLE SAM: "THIS IS THE RESULT OF YOUR INEFFICIENCY. CAPTAIN ROBINSON SAYS YOU HAVE KNOWN FOR FOUR YEARS THAT THIS MAN HAS BEEN DEFRAUDING, YET YOU HAVE KEPT HIM IN OFFICE." PRESIDENT GRANT: "HAVEN'T I A RIGHT TO DO AS I PLEASE? DIDN'T I COME HERE TO HAVE A GOOD TIME?" UNCLE SAM: "YES, IT APPEARS SO. IF I DIDN'T KNOW HOW AVERSE YOU ARE TO RECEIVING PRESENTS, I MIGHT HAVE SUSPECTED THAT THERE WAS A LITTLE DIVVY SOMEWHERE."

situation, Grant allowed incompetence and corruption to invade his entire administration.

The boldest incident of corruption during Grant's first term was the Fisk-Gould scandal. Jim Fisk and Jay Gould, two speculators, conceived a plan to corner the nation's gold supply. They would buy up all the available gold, hold it until its price soared, and then dump it on the market, reaping enormous profits. Working through Grant's brother-in-law, Gould managed to convince the president to withhold the government's gold from sale, a necessary part of the plan. The gigantic gamble came to a head on "Black Friday" (September 24, 1869), when a panic occurred at the New York Stock Exchange because the price of gold had soared too high. Finally realizing what was happening, the president released $4 million in gold to stabilize the market. But his action came too late to prevent serious damage to the business community.

That same year Grant was duped again, this time by a group of American fortune hunters who wished to exploit the economic potential of the Dominican Republic. The speculators convinced Grant that the island was of strategic importance to the United States and should be annexed. Annexation, they argued, would lead to enormous business profits. Only the opposition of the Senate, led by Charles Sumner of Massachusetts, prevented the annexation proposal from being accepted.

The Election of 1872: A New Party

Toward the end of Grant's first term, a group of disillusioned Republicans and Democrats formed the Liberal Republican party. Angered by Radical Reconstruction, scandal, and Grant's lack of interest in civil service reform, the new party's members included an impressive number of reformers. Though solidly united in their opposition to Grant, members of the new party agreed on little else. Some favored a low tariff; others were ardent protectionists. Some wanted to circulate more greenbacks; others wanted all greenbacks withdrawn. Some of the former Democrats opposed military Reconstruction; others wanted to avoid causing the party to be associated with the Confederacy.

The candidate they nominated and the platform they formulated reflected the new party's internal conflicts. While the platform favored amnesty for all former Confederates and the withdrawal of troops from the South, it also approved Radical Reconstruction. On the tariff and greenback issues the Liberal Republicans were unable to reach agreement and took no stand at all. The platform did, however, voice strong support for civil service reform.

When the Liberal Republicans nominated Horace Greeley to oppose Grant in the 1872 election, they ensured their own defeat. Although well known as a newspaper editor and greatly respected for his years of crusading against slavery, Greeley was widely regarded as an eccentric. Nonetheless, the Democrats realized that their only hope of unseating Grant was to align themselves with the Liberal Republicans and endorse Greeley for president.

In contrast to the confusion surrounding the platforms of the Liberal Republican and Democratic parties, the regular Republican party stood on its record of high tariffs and Radical Reconstruction. Industrialists and bankers poured large sums of money into Grant's campaign. In the end, Grant won by a larger margin than he had before, and the Liberal Republican movement disintegrated.

The Crédit Mobilier Affair and the "Whiskey Ring" Scandal

During Grant's second term even worse scandals involving the government were exposed. There was corruption in the Bureau of Indian Affairs, and bribery of internal revenue officials was discovered. One of the worst scandals was the Crédit Mobilier affair, in which a construction company involved in building the transcontinental railroad bribed congressmen and other high government officials to prevent investigation of its fraudulent drain of profits from construction contracts. Grant's previous and current vice-presidents were both among the recipients.

Another scandal, the "Whiskey Ring" conspiracy, involved hundreds of distillers who bribed internal revenue officials to falsify reports that defrauded the government of millions of dollars in excise-tax revenue. When Grant's own private secretary, General Orville Babcock, was exposed as one of the conspirators, Grant unquestioningly defended him and even sent a written character deposition to his trial. Babcock was acquitted and the president allowed him to resign quietly.

Corruption was not confined to the federal government. In large cities such as Chicago and Philadelphia politics was becoming dominated by political machines that maintained power by giving and taking bribes in return for favors. Perhaps the most notorious example was New York's Tweed Ring. Led by William Tweed, boss of the Democratic Tammany Hall machine, the ring, over a period of a few years, took some $200 million from the city through fraud and bribery, and gained control of the police and the courts. While he did work for improved urban services, "Boss" Tweed bribed the New York State legislature in 1869 into passing a new municipal charter which would have entrenched the machine in power. When the activities of the machine threatened to drive the city into bankruptcy, the ring finally was exposed by means of articles in the *New York Times* and through the political cartoons of Thomas Nast in *Harper's*

THE SCATHING CARTOONS OF THOMAS NAST EVENTUALLY LED TO THE DOWNFALL OF THE TWEED RING. ONE OF HIS MOST FAMOUS CARTOONS, *THE TAMMANY TIGER LOOSE—WHAT ARE YOU GOING TO DO ABOUT IT?* WAS PUBLISHED SEVERAL DAYS BEFORE THE CITY ELECTION OF 1871. IN RESPONSE THE VOTERS OUSTED THE RING'S OFFICIALS, AND TWEED WAS INDICTED FOR GRAND LARCENY.

Weekly. A committee led by Samuel J. Tilden secured Tweed's indictment, and in 1871 he was convicted and sent to prison.

The Panic of 1873

In addition to being plagued by scandal and corruption, the nation faced a disastrous economic decline culminating in the Panic of 1873. Since 1850 the economy of the North and West had grown steadily. Following the Civil War the growth rate had accelerated: thousands of new businesses were started, and railroads were built to link the various regions. By 1871, however, the new businesses and railroads had overexpanded and found themselves without the markets they needed to prosper. At the same time the nation's gold reserves were drained by a rapid increase of imports over exports. In Sep-

tember 1873 the foremost banking firm in America, Jay Cooke and Company, declared bankruptcy, triggering a chain reaction of over five thousand additional business failures. One-half million workers were soon out of jobs. The hard times that began in 1873 continued almost until the end of the decade.

The Compromise of 1877

The scandals of the Grant years had cost the Republicans control of the House of Representatives in the 1874 congressional elections. President Grant's popularity also had been badly eroded by corruption (now known as "Grantism") and the depression, but many Republicans still supported him for a third term in 1876. The president's supporters, known as the "Stalwarts," were opposed by the

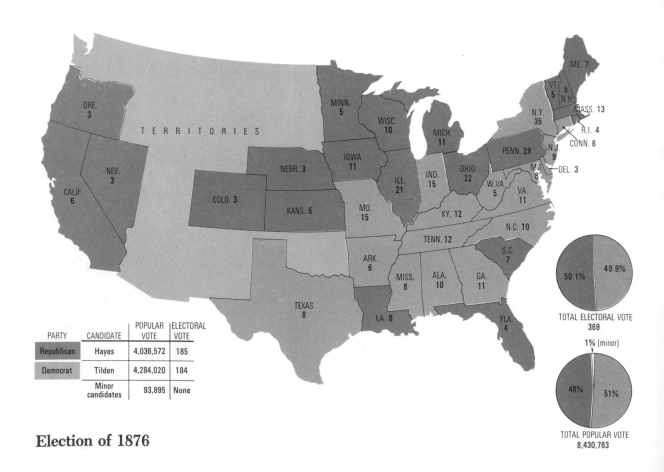

PARTY	CANDIDATE	POPULAR VOTE	ELECTORAL VOTE
Republican	Hayes	4,036,572	185
Democrat	Tilden	4,284,020	184
	Minor candidates	93,895	None

TOTAL ELECTORAL VOTE
369

TOTAL POPULAR VOTE
8,430,783

Election of 1876

"Halfbreeds," Republicans who claimed to be reformers although they had remained loyal to the party in 1872. At the Republican convention the Halfbreeds supported the nomination of Speaker of the House James G. Blaine of Maine. Blaine, however, had been among those accused of dispensing favors to several railroads, and the Republicans finally decided to avoid all hint of scandal by nominating the untarnished Rutherford B. Hayes, three-time governor of Ohio.

The Democrats, also reacting against corruption in government, nominated Governor Samuel Tilden of New York, who had been instrumental in breaking up the Tweed Ring in 1871.

No clear issues divided the candidates. Both called for an end to Reconstruction, still in force in three Southern states. Both avoided taking a stand on the tariff issue. And both called for civil service reform to end corruption in government.

The vote was so close that on the morning after the election, the outcome was still undecided. Although Tilden had a popular majority and had carried many states, twenty electoral votes (the returns from Florida, South Carolina, Louisiana, and one electoral vote from Oregon) were in dispute. Nevertheless, Tilden had 184 of the 185 electoral votes he needed to win; if he could obtain only one of the twenty disputed electoral votes, a Democrat would occupy the White House for the first time since 1856.

Voters were surprised and concerned to learn that there was no means provided by the Constitution for determining the validity of disputed returns. On the question of the counting of electoral votes, the Constitution stated simply that "The President of the Senate shall, in the presence of the Senate and House of Representatives, open all the certificates and the votes shall then be counted." The problem was, who would do the counting? The Senate and its president were Republican, and the House was Democratic. Thus, no matter who did the counting, the process would not be impartial. To resolve the dilemma, Congress appointed a special commission to investigate the disputed returns and award them to the rightful winner. The commission was initially made up of five congressional Democrats, five congressional Republicans, and five Supreme Court justices (two Republicans, two Democrats, and an Independent). But at the last minute the Independent was disqualified (he was elected to the Senate and resigned his seat) and replaced by a staunch Republican. In a straight party vote the commission awarded all of the disputed electoral returns, and therefore the presidency, to Hayes. But it took further negotiation and compromise before Hayes could take office.

Although they had lost the battle for the disputed presidency, the Democrats still had a strong card left to play. Threatening a filibuster in the Senate to prevent the commission from reporting its findings, the Democrats in secret negotiations secured a Republican promise to (among other things) remove all remaining federal troops from the South. The Republicans knew that when the Reconstruction government fell, they could no longer count on the Southern black vote, and the South would be lost to the Democrats. They therefore abandoned the freedmen and tried to attract white Southerners to their camp by agreeing to end the military occupation of the South, to return control of federal patronage in the South to Southerners, to work for federal support for a projected transcontinental railroad (the Texas and Pacific), and to include at least one Southerner in Hayes's new cabinet. In return for these concessions, the Democrats agreed to support the election of a Republican Speaker of the House, even though they now controlled the chamber, and to uphold the rights of black people.

The compromise reached, Hayes moved into the White House without opposition, and the last federal troops were withdrawn from the South in April 1877. Hayes, however, reneged on his support for funds for the new Southern railroad, and the Democrats did not elect a Republican Speaker and did not uphold their promise to protect the rights of blacks. Thus in a quest for national reconciliation the political parties had worked out the Compromise of 1877 which brought a formal end to Reconstruction. Both parties left black Americans to fend for themselves.

Disfranchisement and Segregation of Blacks

With the end of Reconstruction, control of Southern politics was returned to the old planter aristocracy and the equally conservative new business class. This new ruling elite immediately took steps to ensure its continued political, social, and economic dominance.

Although the conservatives believed in white supremacy, they made no immediate attempt to disfranchise blacks. Having incited racist passions in order to regain control of their state governments, they now tried to quiet them. They were eager to gain the support of black voters for their efforts to industrialize the South, and they recognized the usefulness of the black vote in offsetting the opposition of poor whites to political dominance by the wealthy. Moreover, conservative Democrats tried to help blacks assert their influence in the Republican party against its white leadership. While often coerced to support conservative candidates, some 70 percent of black voters throughout the South continued to exercise their right to the franchise until the late 1880s.

By then, however, agricultural depression and unrest had changed conservative strategy. Poor white farmers always had objected to black suffrage because they understood that the black vote was being used against them to ensure economic dominance of the ruling wealthy elite. They therefore demanded that blacks be deprived of the franchise. The conservatives now complied, in part because they hoped to appease the poorer whites, and in part because they were aware that growing agrarian problems were causing white farmers to court the black vote. The idea of competition for the black vote was alarming to whites—rich and poor alike. Thus, in order to ensure white supremacy the wealthy conservatives formed a new coalition with poor farmers.

Now that the black vote was no longer useful, white Southerners moved to disfranchise their former slaves. Southern legislatures enacted a host of technical qualifications for voting. The new requirements were designed to prevent blacks from voting without violating the Fifteenth Amendment. Many states still used the poll tax, which had been instituted in the 1870s as a weapon against black voters, and several states enacted literacy requirements whereby voters had to demonstrate an ability to read and interpret the Constitution. Other states passed "grandfather laws" guaranteeing the right to vote only to those whose ancestors had voted in 1866. In addition to disfranchising black voters, this legislation reduced the overall turnout at election time and made the South a one-party region.

The resurgence of racist politics led to a more rigid segregation of the races in the South. Blacks had founded their own churches after the war, and black children attended separate public schools under the system established during Radical Reconstruction. Although transportation and some public services had not yet been segregated in the late nineteenth century, by 1900 legal measures to assure segregation, popularly called Jim Crow laws, had been enacted throughout the South. These statutes typically provided for separate railroad cars and in some states for segregated railroad stations, street cars, and other public services.

The efforts of Southern state governments to maintain white supremacy and then to bring about segregation of the races were aided by a number of decisions of the United States Supreme Court. In the *Civil Rights Cases* of 1883 the Supreme Court declared unconstitutional an 1875 Civil Rights Act which had guaranteed all citizens "full and equal enjoyment" of public places, ruling that Congress had no jurisdiction over discrimination by private individuals and private organizations. In *Plessy* v. *Ferguson* (1896) the Court further declared that it was not a violation of the Fourteenth Amendment, nor did it imply that black people were inferior, to

BLACK EDUCATOR BOOKER T. WASHINGTON.

Plessy v. Ferguson

"A statute which implies merely a legal distinction between the white and colored races . . . has no tendency to destroy the legal equality of the two races, or reestablish a state of involuntary servitude. . . .

Laws permitting, and even requiring, their separation in places where they are liable to be brought into contact do not necessarily imply the inferiority of either race to the other, and have been generally, if not universally, recognized as within the competency of the state legislatures in the exercise of their police power. The most common instance of this is connected with the establishment of separate schools for white and colored children, which has been held to be a valid exercise of the legislative power even by courts of states where the political rights of the colored race have been longest and most earnestly enforced. . . .

If the two races are to meet upon terms of social equality, it must be the result of natural affinities, a mutual appreciation of each other's merits and a voluntary consent of individuals. . . . If one race be inferior to the other socially, the Constitution of the United States cannot put them upon the same plane. . . ."

The United States Supreme Court, 1896

Plessy v. Ferguson: Dissenting Opinion

"Every one knows that the statute in question had its origin in the purpose, not so much to exclude white persons from railroad cars occupied by blacks, as to exclude colored people from coaches occupied by or assigned to white persons. . . . The fundamental objection, therefore, to the statute is that it interferes with the personal freedom of citizens. . . . If a white man and a black man choose to occupy the same public conveyance on a public highway, it is their right to do so, and no government, proceeding alone on grounds of race, can prevent it without infringing the personal liberty of each. . . .

In the view of the Constitution, in the eye of the law, there is in this country no superior, dominant, ruling class of citizens. There is no caste here. Our Constitution is color-blind, and neither knows nor tolerates classes among citizens. In respect of civil rights, all citizens are equal before the law. The humblest is the peer of the most powerful. The law regards man as man, and takes no account of his surroundings or of his color when his civil rights as guaranteed by the supreme law of the land are involved. . . ."

Justice John Marshall Harlan, 1896

---

enforce separate facilities for each race, so long as the facilities provided for blacks were "equal" to the facilities for whites. This decision provided the constitutional rationale for separating the races in many areas of life and particularly for maintaining the segregation of Southern schools for the next fifty years.

The Supreme Court upheld the literacy tests and poll taxes in *Williams* v. *Mississippi* (1898), declaring that since these laws did not "on their face discriminate between the races," they did not violate the Fifteenth Amendment. Sometime later, in *Guinn* v. *United States* (1915) the court invalidated the "grandfather laws," reasoning that their only possible purpose was to disfranchise black people and that they therefore violated the Fifteenth

Amendment. By this time, however, the discriminatory laws had already accomplished their purpose.

Many blacks at this time felt their best course of action was to accept their second-class status in exchange for the right to pursue economic security. In 1895 black educator Booker T. Washington called for an emphasis on self-help through manual labor, vocational education, and subsistence farming in a speech that became known as the Atlanta Compromise. "The wisest among my race," said Washington, "understand that the agitation of questions of social equality is the extremest folly. . . . It is important and right that all privileges of the law be ours, but it is vastly more important that we be prepared for the exercise of these privileges. The opportunity to earn a dollar in a factory just now is worth infinitely more than the opportunity to spend a dollar in an opera-house." Many white Southerners—recognizing in Washington's position support for the status quo—applauded the concepts embodied in the Atlanta Compromise. Some blacks, however, strongly opposed compromising their demands for the rights of full citizenship for possible economic advancement. In 1903 black intellectual W. E. B. DuBois asked, "Are we going to induce the best class of Negroes to take less and less interest in government, and to give up their daily right to take such an interest, without a protest? . . . Daily the Negro is coming more and more to look upon law and justice, not as protecting safeguards, but as sources of humiliation and oppression."

Conclusion

The Reconstruction of the nation lasted from 1863 to 1877. It began with the Emancipation Proclama-

tion and ended with the compromise that settled the disputed election of 1876. In the process blacks were freed from slavery, granted political equality, and then abandoned as the price paid for national reconciliation. Further, the antebellum domination of national politics by an agrarian South was replaced by a Northern-based political coalition closely attuned to the needs of an increasingly industrial economy, national in scope. Profound economic changes transformed American life by the end of the nineteenth century. Just as the course of Reconstruction had thwarted black hopes for economic opportunity, so the magnitude of the changes in the American economy would threaten the economic opportunity of countless other Americans. The varied responses to these economic developments ultimately transformed American politics as well.

Readings

General Works

Belz, Herman, *Reconstructing the Union.* Ithaca, N.Y.: Cornell University Press, 1969.

Buck, Paul H., *The Road to Reunion, 1865–1900.* Boston: Little, Brown, 1937.

Cash, Wilbur J., *The Mind of the South.* New York: Knopf, 1960.

Cruden, Robert, *The Negro in Reconstruction.* Englewood Cliffs, N.J.: Prentice-Hall, 1969.

Donald, David, *Liberty and Union.* Lexington, Mass.: D. C. Heath, 1978.

———, *The Politics of Reconstruction.* Baton Rouge: Louisiana State University Press, 1965.

Du Bois, William E. B., *Black Reconstruction in America, 1860–1880.* New York: Atheneum, 1969.

Fairman, Charles, *Reconstruction and Reunion, 1864–1888.* New York: Macmillan, 1971.

Franklin, John H., *Reconstruction After the Civil War.* Chicago: University of Chicago Press, 1961.

Gillette, William, *Retreat from Reconstruction, 1869–1879.* Baton Rouge: Louisiana State University Press, 1979.

Hyman, Harold M., *A More Perfect Union: The Impact of the Civil War and Reconstruction of the Constitution.* New York: Knopf, 1973.

Patrick, Rembert W., *The Reconstruction of the Nation.* New York: Oxford University Press, 1967.

Randall, James G., and David Donald, *The Civil War and Reconstruction.* Boston: D. C. Heath, 1961.

Stampp, Kenneth M., *The Era of Reconstruction 1865–1877.* New York: Knopf, 1965.

Trefousse, Hans L., *The Radical Republicans: Lincoln's Vanguard for Racial Justice.* New York: Knopf, 1969.

Wright, Gavin, *The Political Economy of the Cotton South.* New York: Norton, 1978.

Special Studies

Belz, Herman, *A New Birth of Freedom.* Westport, Conn.: Greenwood, 1976.

Benedict, Michael L., *A Compromise of Principle: Congressional Republicans and Reconstruction, 1863–1869.* New York: Norton, 1974.

Bentley, G. R., *A History of the Freedmen's Bureau.* New York: Octagon, 1970.

Cox, LaWanda, and John H. Cox, *Politics, Principle and Prejudice, 1865–66.* New York: Free Press, 1963.

Gerteis, Louis S., *From Contraband to Freedman.* Westport, Conn.: Greenwood, 1973.

Gillette, William, *The Right to Vote: Politics and the Passage of the Fifteenth Amendment.* Baltimore: Johns Hopkins Press, 1965.

James, Joseph B., *The Framing of the Fourteenth Amendment.* Urbana: University of Illinois Press, 1956.

Litwack, Leon F., *Been in the Storm So Long: The Aftermath of Slavery.* New York: Knopf, 1979.

Logan, Rayford W., *The Negro in American Life and Thought: The Nadir 1877–1901.* New York: Macmillan, 1965.

McCrary, Peyton, *Abraham Lincoln and Reconstruction.* Princeton, N.J.: Princeton University Press, 1978.

McKitrick, Eric L., *Andrew Johnson and Reconstruction.* Chicago: University of Chicago Press, 1960.

McPherson, James M., *The Abolitionist Legacy: From Reconstruction to the NAACP.* Princeton, N.J.: Princeton University Press, 1976.

_____, *The Struggle for Equality: Abolitionists and the Negro in the Civil War and Reconstruction.* Princeton, N.J.: Princeton University Press, 1964.

Meier, August, *Negro Thought in America, 1880–1915.* Ann Arbor: University of Michigan Press, 1963.

Nolen, Claude H., *The Negro's Image in the South: The Anatomy of White Supremacy.* Lexington: University Press of Kentucky, 1967. (Paper)

Roark, James L., *Master Without Slaves: Southern Planters in the Civil War and Reconstruction.* New York: Norton, 1977.

Trefousse, Hans L., *Impeachment of a President: Andrew Johnson, the Blacks & Reconstruction.* Knoxville: University of Tennessee Press, 1975.

Trelease, Allen W., *The White Terror: The Ku Klux Klan Conspiracy and Southern Reconstruction,* Kenneth B. Clark (Ed.). New York: Harper & Row, 1971.

Wharton, Vernon L., *The Negro in Mississippi, 1865–1869.* New York: Harper & Row, 1965.

Williamson, Joel, *After Slavery: The Negro in South Carolina During Reconstruction, 1861–1877.* Chapel Hill: University of North Carolina Press, 1965.

Woodward, C. Vann, *Reunion and Reaction: The Compromise of 1877 and the End of Reconstruction.* Boston: Little, Brown, 1966.

_____, *The Strange Career of Jim Crow.* New York: Oxford University Press, 1966.

Primary Sources

Cox, LaWanda, and John H. (Eds.), *Reconstruction, the Negro and the New South.* Columbia: University of South Carolina Press, 1973.

Current, Richard N. (Ed.), *Reconstruction, 1865–1877.* Englewood Cliffs, N.J.: Prentice-Hall, 1965.

Reid, Whitelaw, *After the War: A Tour of the Southern States, 1865–1866.* New York: Harper & Row, 1965.

Shenton, James P., *The Reconstruction, A Documentary History: 1865–1877.* New York: Putnam, 1963.

Washington, Booker T., *Up from Slavery.* New York: Bantam, 1970.

Biographies

Brodie, Fawn M., *Thaddeus Stevens: Scourge of the South.* New York: Norton, 1959.

Donald, David, *Charles Sumner and the Rights of Man.* New York: Knopf, 1970.

Hesseltine, William B., *Ulysses S. Grant: Politician.* New York: Ungar, 1957.

McFeely, William S., *Yankee Stepfather: General O. O. Howard and the Freedmen.* New Haven, Conn.: Yale University Press, 1968.

Van Deusen, Glyndon, *Horace Greeley: Nineteenth-Century Crusader.* Philadelphia: University of Pennsylvania Press, 1953.

Fiction

Faulkner, William, *Go Down, Moses.* New York: Random House, 1942.

_____, *The Hamlet.* New York: Random House, 1940.

The First Civil Rights Movement

RECONSTRUCTION AND EDUCATION

On a quiet morning in April 1865, a tall, dignified gentleman in a gray uniform handed his sword to a short, rumpled man in a blue uniform, and the shooting stopped in America's bloodiest war ever.

However, as one Civil War historian has pointed out:

The American Civil War did not end at Appomattox. Lee's surrender only marked the abandonment of armed resistance in a struggle that had been going on . . . for a generation or more. *

The next stage of that struggle was Reconstruction, a time when half the country ruled the other half as occupied territories, complete with military government and military supervision of the reconstruction process. Now the focus shifted from civil war to civil rights. The war confirmed that black

*Avery Craven, *Reconstruction: The Ending of the Civil War* (New York: Holt, Rinehart and Winston, Inc. 1969), p. 1.

people deserved the same freedoms as white people, but whether they deserved equality was another matter.

The issue of equality was felt strongly in the area of education. In fact, the structure of the present American educational system was set in place during the Reconstruction era.

After the war, millions of black people were thrown unprepared into a society whose rules and customs few of them understood, and many of them believed that education was their only hope. Most of the former slaves were illiterate, and their freedom was irrelevant if they could not read the wage contracts offered them by their new employers (who were, in many cases, their former owners).

Southern whites felt less pressure. Before the war, schooling and other matters of social welfare had been considered private affairs. Plantation owners had sufficient income to educate their children as they pleased, and poorer farmers generally distrusted education as an "upper class" extravagance. Immediately after the war, these attitudes were still widespread among people in the white community. Thus it was Southern blacks who took the lead in creating pressure for a

THE MISSES COOKE'S SCHOOL ROOM WAS A FREEDMEN'S BUREAU SCHOOL IN RICHMOND, VIRGINIA, 1866.

new approach to education in the South, leaving most whites to oppose or ignore their efforts.

The education of Southern blacks had already begun, even before the war had ended. In Louisiana, for example, fifteen thousand pupils attended 126 schools that had been set up by the military government before Lee's surrender at Appomattox. Northern philanthropic groups assisted the military effort, with the Freedmen's Aid Society taking the lead. By 1867 the society had enrolled eleven thousand pupils in schools throughout the South.

These early schools were open to all children, and were some of the first truly integrated schools in the United States. However, white resistance to the whole idea of black education can be measured by the fact that only 1 percent of all pupils were white. Many white Southerners were opposed to these schools, for not only were they mixed, but their Yankee teachers were also rumored to be preaching racial equality.

Over time, however, black enthusiasm for the new educational opportunities had a more positive impact on Southern whites. Edward Pollard, a South Carolinian who originally supported slavery, wrote a remarkable article about emancipation in an 1870 issue of *Harper's* magazine. Pollard declared that he had been wrong about black people and how they would use their new freedom. Among other reasons for his changed attitude, he noted, "I have witnessed the zeal with which the black people are availing themselves of the schools and means of education. . . ."

Other whites saw that a modern school system might benefit the South as a whole even though the idea was being urged primarily by blacks and Northern Reconstructionists. When new constitutions were written for the

THIS "EXTRACT FROM THE RECONSTRUCTED CONSTITUTION OF THE STATE OF LOUISIANA" CITES ARTICLE 135: "ALL CHILDREN OF THIS STATE SHALL BE ADMITTED TO THE PUBLIC SCHOOLS OR OTHER INSTITUTIONS OF LEARNING SUSTAINED OR ESTABLISHED BY THE STATE IN COMMON, WITHOUT DISTINCTION OF RACE, COLOR, OR PREVIOUS CONDITION. THERE SHALL BE NO SEPARATE SCHOOLS OR INSTITUTIONS OF LEARNING ESTABLISHED EXCLUSIVELY FOR ANY RACE BY THE STATE OF LOUISIANA."

states of the old Confederacy, every one contained provisions for establishing a public school system. It was white support which ensured this.

The question of school integration was not raised at this time, and most of the new systems provided separate facilities for black and white children from the very beginning. But this was not really surprising. Even as late as the 1850s, most Northern states provided no public education for black children, and where they did, the schools were usually segregated.

In general, Northerners were as uncertain as Southerners about the notion of racial equality. The idea seemed especially threatening to laborers during the periods of economic decline in the decades after the Civil War. And, following a pattern that has persisted into modern times, Northerners were able to avoid the issue because so much of the nation's attention was focused on the more visible problems in the South.

Thus, perhaps it is not surprising that some Northern philanthropies, organized specifically to assist black educational development, refused to provide aid to integrated schools and colleges in the South. Integrated education, these charities believed, was a hopeless illusion, and would not be encouraged by their support.

Given this attitude in the North, Southern resistance to the idea could hardly be expected to decrease. In Louisiana, the only state where integration was practiced to any extent, the state school superintendent once remarked: "There is probably no other state in the Union where the work of popular education is conducted under the disadvantages which are encountered in Louisiana." The evidence indicates that the superintendent was not exaggerating. In 1874, for example, a mob attacked a mixed high school in New Orleans, and drove out all stu-

LOOKING TOWARD FREEDOM: TWO EMANCIPATED SLAVE CHILDREN, NAMED SIMPLY ISAAC AND ROSA, STAND DRESSED IN SPANKING NEW CLOTHES FOR THIS PICTURE TAKEN IN 1863, EMANCIPATION YEAR.

dents who were black or even suspected of having mixed blood.

Hostility to the public school systems was not limited to integrated schools, however. Even where facilities were segregated, white opposition sometimes flared into violence. In 1870, farmers in Mississippi were incensed over the high taxes they were paying to support public schools. They burned down a number of buildings, intimidated teachers, and forced schools to close in a number of counties.

As long as Reconstruction lasted, however, the new approach to education was never in any real danger. Blacks, sympathetic whites, and

Northerners controlled the state governments thoughout the South, and this coalition was enough to keep the schools from being dismantled by their opponents.

In addition, opposition to the public schools lessened in the later phases of Reconstruction. As the South prepared to reenter the Union and began to build an economy less dominated by agriculture, the competitive advantages of a good education became more and more obvious.

Unfortunately, this late-blooming interest worked to the disadvantage of blacks, now that the school systems had been firmly established on a segregated basis. The South lagged behind the North economically and did not possess the resources to support separate schools that were truly equal.

As the Reconstruction period ended, politicians dedicated to retrenchment began taking over state governments throughout the South. Many of them were pledged to end the fiscal excesses which they claimed had been perpetrated by the Reconstruction governments. And "economy moves" were often aimed at the schools. Moreover, segregation made it possible to manipulate budgets so that cutbacks could fall most heavily on black schools. Over time, this practice would provide strong ammunition for opponents of segregation. It was also one of the factors leading to the Supreme Court's 1954 decision.

The school issue is a good example of how the country handled basic problems during the Reconstruction period. It also illustrates how decisions made in the past can affect the present. While Reconstruction fulfilled its goal of restoring the Union, it allowed slavery to be replaced by segregation. Just as slavery had generated a demand for black freedom which led to civil war, segregation produced a demand for equality which led to the civil rights movement.

16 The Conquest of the Great West

Once we were happy in our own country and we were seldom hungry, for then the two-leggeds and the four-leggeds lived together like relatives, and there was plenty for them and for us. But then the white men came, and they have made little islands for us and other little islands for the four-leggeds, and always these islands are becoming smaller, for around them surges the gnawing flood of the white man; and it is dirty with lies and greed.

Black Elk, Sioux holy man, 1890

Significant Events

National Indian policy: concentration [1849–1853]

Comstock Lode discovered in western Nevada [1859]

Homestead Act [1862]

Sand Creek Massacre [1864]

National Indian policy: large reservations [1867–1868]

General Custer's defeat at Little Big Horn [1876]

Timber Culture Act [1873] 40

The Desert Land Act [1877]

Timber and Stone Act [1878]

"Long drive" by cattlemen [1866–1888]

Drought strikes Great Plains [1886]

Dawes Severalty Act [1887]

"Battle" of Wounded Knee [1800]

WHEAT HARVESTING IN THE DAKOTAS.

The preservation of the Union had revived Americans' belief in their country's special destiny to expand successful self-government over an entire continent. Nationalizing trends, which had been intensified by a wartime economy, gained momentum during and after Reconstruction. By the 1880s the American economy, which had once been predominantly local and diverse, had been transformed into one that was national in its scope. Various states and regions still maintained social and economic characteristics particular to themselves. Now, however, the most important economic developments were caused by industry on a large scale catering to a national market and by the conquest of the trans-Mississippi West.

During the 1850s the Great Plains and the region beyond the Rocky Mountains had been inhabited by a variety of wildlife, including great herds of buffalo, and by several hundred thousand Indians. Then in the space of twenty years, six million white settlers poured into the area, and by 1890 America's last landed frontier was gone. The conquest of the Far West and its incorporation into the Union was precipitated by discoveries of gold and silver during the 1850s. In 1869 the completion of the transcontinental railroad set the stage for the long cattle drives from Texas across the Great Plains and for the eventual conversion of this vast grassland to large-scale farming of grain. By 1912 all of the nation's remaining Western territories had become states.

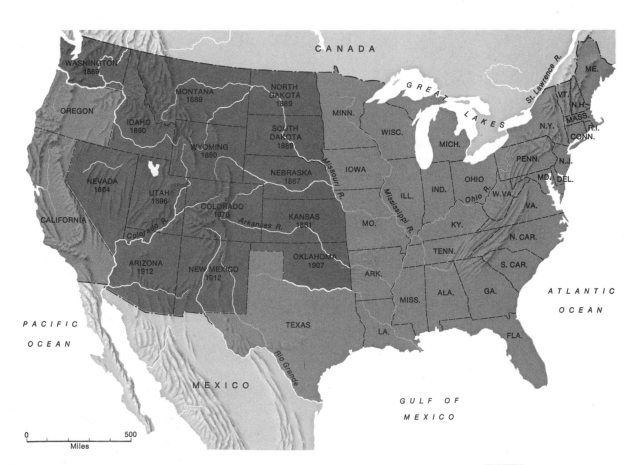

United States • 1861 to 1912

New states admitted

Lured by promises of greater personal freedom and opportunities for economic improvement, miners, cattle ranchers, and farmers joined in a fierce competitive struggle with nature and each other. Some attained great wealth, but many more failed to strike it rich, or they saw their crops and livelihood destroyed by the harsh climate. The gap between their hopes and the reality of frontier existence inspired one homesteader from Greer County, Oklahoma, to adapt a Kansas folk song to his experiences:

Hurrah for Greer County! The land of the free,
The land of the bedbug, grasshopper, and flea;
I'll sing of its praises, I'll tell of its fame,
While starving to death on my government claim.

If settlers from the Eastern and Southern regions of the United States were frequently challenged in their attempt to achieve economic success, the native inhabitants, the Plains Indians, found their very survival threatened. Cattle raisers and farmers moving westward disrupted the nomadic life of these tribes, and many bloody battles were fought between the Indians and the settlers, who were sometimes aided by federal or local troops. Ultimately, the Indian way of life was destroyed, and most of their hunting grounds were seized. The federal government forced the remaining tribes to sign treaties which provided for their relocation to isolated reservations.

Coercion of the Indians

Despite reports of friendly trade agreements between the Plains Indians and settlers moving westward, increased hostility between the two groups was inevitable. This confrontation was the culmination of a struggle that had begun with the first advances of European settlers into North America. The two cultures—one eager to extend its system of government and way of life, the other seeking only to preserve an ancient heritage—were diametrically opposed. Consequently, each time they came into contact, conflict resulted.

The native Americans had always existed on the fringe of the country's constitutional system. They were not citizens, not taxed, and not counted in apportioning representatives. The Constitution had granted Congress the power to regulate commerce with the Indian tribes, and for a time the federal government dealt with them as "domestic dependent nations" under its treaty-making powers. In exchange for promises of food, clothing, and other provisions, and guarantees that their way of life would remain undisturbed, Indian leaders ceded vast areas of fertile land to the national government. Unfortunately, treaty promises were regularly ignored, both by corrupt federal officials and by land-hungry settlers who encroached on land still legally held by the Indians.

During the 1830s most of the Indians of the Southeast had been removed to a section of present-day Oklahoma under the pretense of reducing their contact with whites and thereby avoiding conflict. The real reason was the desire of white Americans for valuable Indian lands. Only the smallest and least aggressive tribes were allowed to remain east of the Mississippi.

White settlers were excluded from the area in Oklahoma set aside for the Indians, and traders were supposed to be rigidly licensed. Despite these policies, during the 1840s whites were determined to move through Indian territory—with or without government permission—in their march to settle the Far West. On reaching California, miners and settlers eliminated some seventy thousand Indians they scornfully called "Diggers." These Indians were a peaceful people whose simple way of life caused the whites to consider them primitive.

In addition to the tribes that had been resettled in Indian territory after 1830, there were numerous tribes native to the West: the Pueblo groups, including the Hopi and Zuni tribes—peaceful farmers and herders in the Southwest; the Ute, Nez Percé, and Shoshones—small, scattered bands living in the harsh desert and mountain regions between the Sierra Nevadas and the Rockies; and the many tribes collectively known as the Plains Indians—among them some of the most warlike bands in North America. Wresting the land from these Indians was no easy matter, even with the assistance of the

THE GREAT HERDS OF BUFFALO THAT GRAZED THE PLAINS WERE THE MAINSTAY OF INDIAN LIFE, PROVIDING NOT ONLY FOOD BUT MOST OTHER NECESSITIES. BY 1885, WITH THE ELIMINATION OF THE BUFFALO BY GREEDY WHITES, THE PLAINS INDIANS THEMSELVES FACED VIRTUAL EXTERMINATION.

United States Army. Between 1869 and 1876 soldiers and Indians fought some two hundred pitched battles in the area west of the Mississippi River.

Culture of the Plains Indians

In 1860, approximately two-thirds of America's three hundred thousand Indians lived on the Great Plains. The principal tribes were the Sioux of Minnesota and the Dakotas, the Blackfeet of Idaho and western Montana, the Cheyenne and Arapaho of the central Plains, the Pawnee in western Nebraska, the Osage in western Kansas, and the Apaches and Comanches of Texas and New Mexico.

The nomadic, warlike culture of the Plains Indians had evolved from their dependence on the buffalo and the horse. During the sixteenth century, Spanish explorers had introduced the modern horse to the New World. Eventually some of these animals broke loose and wandered northward onto the prairies. Once they had domesticated the descendants of these wild horses, the Plains Indians achieved a new mobility which changed their pattern of life. They became superb horsemen who ranged far and wide in pursuit of the great buffalo herds. Equipped with French and English guns instead of bows and arrows, they found it far easier to

kill buffalo. Although braves sometimes hunted for sport or for sale to traders, normally they relied upon the buffalo as their main source of food and for most other necessities of life. Buffalo skins were used to make tepees as well as clothing, moccasins, blankets, and robes. The hide was fashioned into pouches, workbags, and cosmetic kits. Buffalo bones were shaped into knives and the horns and hooves were boiled into glue. Tendons became bowstrings, strips of hide served as lariats, and the dried manure was used as fuel. were all used greatly

Rivalries between tribes competing over territory and the buffalo herds encouraged the development of a fierce and skillful warrior class. While large-scale warfare was uncommon, raids and skirmishes were a normal part of life. Through combat a warrior could achieve status, win social recognition, and obtain material rewards. Bravery was a much-stressed ideal, and warriors sought membership in "soldier societies" which valued the accomplishment of bold deeds. Many Plains tribes taught boys that it was more glorious to be killed in battle as a youth than to die peacefully as an old man. Yet, despite strong emnities between tribes, factors such as trade and the common danger of white advancement tended to unite the Indian nations. Another common bond was their ability to communicate with one another, for although the various Plains tribes spoke different languages, they shared a highly developed sign language.

Equal to bravery in battle in the Indian's moral code was generosity, expressed by the liberal bestowal of gifts on relatives and friends. The Plains Indians reserved their highest praise for two classes of people: those who "had given to the poor on many occasions and had invited guests to many feasts" and those who "had killed several of the foe and had brought home many horses." Theft among members of a tribe was prohibited, although it was completely acceptable to acquire property through raids on enemy villages.

Because of their migratory way of life, Plains Indian tribes were relatively small, the average tribe in the 1850s numbering three to four thousand. Men engaged in hunting, trade, and ceremonial activities; women performed hard camp work, packed the horses, farmed vegetables, and gathered berries and roots. Because Indians had no written records, oral storytelling became an important means of keeping historical accounts. Elderly historians passed on sacred stories and rituals to carefully chosen young men, and in this way the traditions of the tribe were handed down.

Concentration

With the acquisition of Oregon, Texas, California, and the Southwest, white Americans increasingly coveted the land in these areas used by the Indians. As a result, the government attempted to establish a national Indian policy and eventually decided to segregate the tribes of the Plains, the Southwest, and the Far West on large reservations under federal supervision. Between 1849 and 1855 a series of treaties were concluded for the resettlement of the major tribes in these areas. The government was determined to prevent the rise of an Indian confederacy, such as the one led by Tecumseh before the War of 1812, and under the new policy the Plains Indians were to receive payment and gifts in return for agreeing to observe definite boundaries to each tribe's hunting grounds. In this manner, the government hoped to reduce tribal warfare and keep the tribes under control.

Putting this policy of concentration into effect was not easy. The new treaties were difficult to enforce, and army troops were constantly being called

on to halt conflicts between Indians and settlers who were moving into or through Indian territory. Serving with the army in the West were several all-black infantry and cavalry units. Many of these black troopers intended to make the army their career. Their enlistment rate was high, they established a record for bravery in battle, and they won the grudging admiration of several white commanders.

Despite government promises to stop white encroachment, miners and settlers moved onto Indian lands. The Indians were devastated by their wanton destruction of the buffalo and the grasslands and by the spread of contagious diseases such as smallpox and cholera. In Colorado the Cheyenne and Arapaho had been guaranteed perpetual possession of their native lands, but in 1858 the discovery of gold attracted thousands of prospectors to the region. In 1861, barely ten years after pledging the land to them, the government purchased most of Colorado from the Indians. The two tribes were removed to barren territory in southeastern Colorado where they faced near starvation, for the land lacked moisture, and tools promised by the government had not been provided. In 1864 the Indians gave vent to their anger by attacking settlers' wagons and stagecoaches. While the local militia and the army fought back, the governor sent word that all friendly Indians should report to army posts to seek protection from the fierce guerrilla warfare.

The Sand Creek Massacre Reassured by promises of official protection and government rations to help them survive the winter, a group of Arapahos and Cheyennes under the leadership of Black Kettle set up camp at Sand Creek, forty miles from Fort Lyon. Then, late in November, Colonel J. M. Chivington, who had been tracking Black Kettle's group under military orders to make the Indians "suffer more," arrived at the fort with seven hundred Colorado militia. The young commander of the fort told Chivington that Black Kettle had not been promised protection and urged him to attack at once. Chivington held the view that "the Indians were an obstacle to civilization and should be exterminated" and ordered a surprise attack on Black Kettle's camp. In the ensuing massacre, the militia killed many of the unsuspecting Indians, scalping and bludgeoning women and children as well as warriors.

Although miners in the West congratulated Chivington on his "brave" action, many Easterners

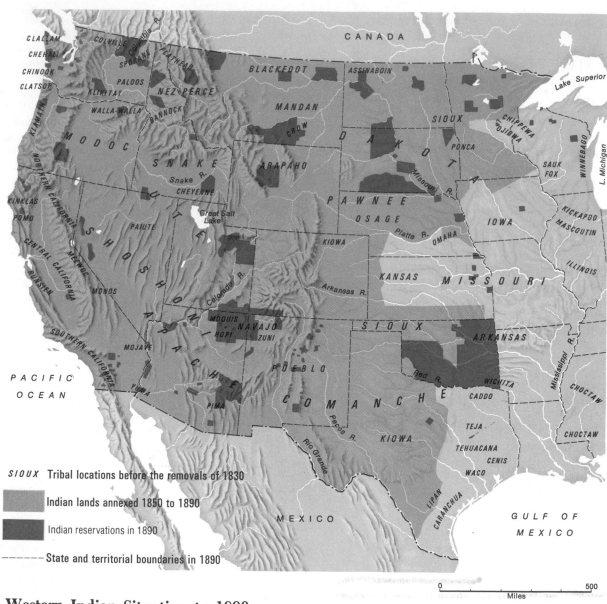

Western Indian Situation to 1890

Map legend:

SIOUX Tribal locations before the removals of 1830

Indian lands annexed 1850 to 1890

Indian reservations in 1890

-------- State and territorial boundaries in 1890

0 ___ 500 Miles

condemned him. The commissioner of Indian affairs denounced the attack as outright murder, and in 1865 Congress appointed an investigating committee. Later a treaty with the Arapaho and Cheyenne tribes condemned "the gross and wanton outrages" and ordered reparations for the surviving Indian widows and children; however, the treaty was never ratified by the Senate. Thus the old story of broken promises was repeated. The Cheyennes and Arapahos were forced to relocate to even poorer land than before. When the young warriors broke out in rebellion, soldiers set fire to their village.

The Sioux Uprising Another slaughter took place a few years later in Montana, but this time the victims were white settlers. When gold was discovered in the Montana Territory in the early 1860s, miners flocked into the area in blatant violation of Indian treaty rights. To provide transportation to and from the mines, miners began construction on a road running from Wyoming through southern Montana and cutting directly through the heart of Sioux hunting grounds in the Big Horn Mountains. Responding to this invasion, more than two thousand Sioux led by Chief Red Cloud ambushed and wiped out a force of 81 soldiers under Colonel William J. Fetterman.

In its eagerness to get tribal chiefs to sign treaties granting passage for roads and railroads through their territory, the government actually strengthened the ability of the Indians to wage war. In return for signatures, the Bureau of Indian Affairs issued rifles and ammunition which the Indians then used to defend their lands. These weapons, combined with the Indians' intimate knowledge of the terrain, good marksmanship, and superb horsemanship, turned small bands of warriors into extremely dangerous guerrilla fighters.

The United States Army, on the other hand, had the advantage of greater numbers and the use of the railroad and telegraph. Information sent by telegraph enabled the army to keep close watch on Indian movements, and when reinforcements were needed, troops could be sent relatively quickly by train. The Indians, however, soon learned to bend rails and pull down telegraph wires.

New Plans for Confinement

The failure of its concentration policy to prevent conflicts forced the government to reconsider its Indian policy. In 1867 a report by a congressional committee blamed the miners for the confrontations and claimed that the encroachment of gold prospectors onto Indian lands invariably led to violence.

An Indian Peace Commission was created to study ways to end the conflicts. It proposed that the Plains Indians be confined to two large reservations, one to the north in the Black Hills of the Dakota Territory and one to the south in the Oklahoma Territory. In 1867 and 1868 the leading chiefs agreed to give up their nomadic ways and become sedentary, peaceful farmers on these reservations.

The recommendations of the commission were ineffective in reducing Indian uprisings over the next few years, largely because they were based on the mistaken notion that tribal chiefs could sign away lands without the agreement of their people. Moreover, since the goal of white Americans to possess a continent was foreign to Indian tradition, the Indians found little meaning in treaties that handed over exclusive ownership of landed property from one party to another. Army troops would drive the Indians onto a reservation, but as soon as they left, the Indians would drift back into the open countryside. The Indians did not want to give up hunting buffalo, and when the herds moved to their summer feeding grounds, the tribes followed them.

In return for the Indians' cooperation, the government promised liberal supplies, but these promises went largely unfulfilled. The bitterness of the Indians was further intensified by corruption and ineptness in the Department of the Interior's Bureau of Indian Affairs. During the Civil War, military demands caused frequent delays and failures in the delivery of annuities and food to the Indians. The withdrawal of Union troops from Western posts left tribes free to continue their traditional wanderings, and the officers left to staff Western posts were often inexperienced or second-rate.

In 1871, at the recommendation of reformers, Congress decided to treat the Indians as dependents, or wards, who would be given supplies, annuities, and agricultural training on the reservations in preparation for their assimilation into American society. Despite these official policy changes, however, the government continued to use the army to enforce treaties, and the Indian Bureau was far from being the sympathetic guardian that reformers had envisioned. Although there were some honest federal agents, others distributed moth-eaten blankets and spoiled beef to their Indian "wards" and pocketed most of the government funds appropriated for these goods. One agent who earned a yearly salary of $1500 was able to retire with $50,000 after four years.

In an effort to curb corruption, the federal government gave the major churches authority to nominate new agents and to direct educational and other activities on the reservations. Humanitarian reformers believed the churches would be more effective

The White Man's Attack

"The American public does not know the meaning of the phrase, Indian atrocity—not its true meaning. For their sakes I am glad they do not, but for the sake of the small but not insignificant number of Americans whose homes are darkened through their knowledge of it, I wish the American public did know it.

The whites on our frontier are suffering the tyranny of a democracy. The Indian question is a local question, and the treatment of it by representatives of the people at large is naturally careless and defective. The people of Arizona and New Mexico are not allowed to settle their Indian troubles themselves, and the national government will not settle them for them."

John Bigelow, Jr., 1885

Geronimo's Defense

"I would like to know now who it was that gave the order to arrest me and hang me. I was living peaceably there with my family under the shade of the trees, doing just what General Crook had told me I must do and trying to follow his advice. . . . I was praying to the light and to the darkness, to God and to the sun, to let me live quietly there with my family. . . .

I have several times asked for peace, but trouble has come from the agents and interpreters. I don't want what has passed to happen again. Now, I am going to tell you something else. The Earth-Mother is listening to me and I hope that all may be so arranged that from now on there shall be no trouble and that we shall always have peace. . . .' "

Britton Davis, *The Truth About Geronimo*, 1929

than the military in protecting the Indians and in helping them assimilate to American life. Again, the policy failed. The churches quarreled among themselves over jurisdiction, gave inadequate support to the project, and sent agents who were just as corrupt and unsympathetic as the previous agents had been. The policy was abandoned in the late 1870s.

Sioux Resistance   In 1874 miners discovered gold in the Black Hills region of South Dakota, land sacred to the Sioux and part of their reservation. Thousands of prospectors swarmed into the region, and the government, finding it impossible to keep them out, finally decided to restore the Black Hills to the public domain. But the Indians refused demands to give up their land. Angered by the presence of prospectors and crews building the Northern Pacific Railroad, the Sioux went on the warpath, winning several minor clashes with the army along the Big Horn River in southern Montana. The government responded by ordering all tribes to return to their reservations by the end of January 1876; however, the order reached the Indians too late for them to comply even had they wished to do so. Subse-

quently, a government campaign was launched to clear the disputed territory for white occupation. By the summer of 1876, three columns of troops were in pursuit of the Sioux, who were led by the great war chief, Crazy Horse, and the powerful medicine man, Sitting Bull.

In June 1876 a large gathering of Sioux and their Cheyenne and Arapaho allies had encamped near the Little Big Horn River for the annual sundance ritual. One member of the three-prong military offensive moving toward them was a flamboyant and fiercely ambitious young cavalry officer, Colonel George Armstrong Custer. Custer was on President Grant's blacklist for having recently exposed corruption in the War Department and was eager to regain favor through his exploits as an Indian fighter. Recklessly ignoring orders to reconnoiter only, Custer split his seventh cavalry into three units and ordered an attack on the Indian camp. Not only did the soldiers fail to take the Indians by surprise, but they were vastly outnumbered. The two supporting wings were turned back, leaving Custer and some 264 men to face the majority of the camp's twenty-five hundred warriors. Although the troopers fought bravely, the entire battalion was wiped out. The massacre caused a nationwide demand for revenge on the Sioux, thus contributing in the long run to the Indians' ultimate defeat.

The following year, another great Indian leader, Chief Joseph of the Nez Percé, led his people in an heroic attempt to outrun the army and escape to Canada. For over a thousand miles Chief Joseph and his followers evaded and outfought their pursuers before being brought to bay some thirty miles below the Canadian border. The weary chief voiced the feeling of many Indians when he said, "I am tired of fighting . . . My heart is sick and sad. From where the sun now stands, I will fight no more for-ever." The remnants of his tribe were put on a reservation where many grew sick and died.

Destruction of Tribal Life

The army's most effective campaigns took place during the winter when Indian bands were immobilized by severe weather and the scarcity of food. By pressing the Indians at this time, the military hoped to turn the very structure of the Indians' nomadic way of life against them. Nevertheless, the Indians were never successfully defeated by military force alone. It was the disappearance of their chief re-

SITTING BULL, MEDICINE MAN OF THE SIOUX.

A SIOUX DRAWING OF THE BATTLE OF THE LITTLE BIG HORN. THE GREAT WAR CHIEF CRAZY HORSE IS SHOWN AT CENTER, WEARING HIS PROTECTIVE HAILSTONE MEDICINE PAINT.

APACHE PRISONERS AND THEIR UNITED
STATES ARMY GUARDS. THE THIRD MAN
FROM THE RIGHT IN THE FRONT ROW IS
GERONIMO. (Smithsonian Institution)

source, the buffalo, which by the 1880s had sapped their strength and destroyed their unique pattern of living.

Buffalo had been pushed to the brink of extinction by white hunters, encouraged by those who believed wiping out the herds was the best way to end the Indian problem. During the 1860s sportsmen traveled across the plains by rail and shot the animals from train windows. William F. Cody, better known as Buffalo Bill, claimed to have killed 4280 of the animals in eighteen months. Buffalo meat proved to be tasty and popular, and buffalo bones were ground up and used as fertilizer. In a two-year period the railroads shipped East 1.5 million hides, almost seven million pounds of meat, and thirty-two million pounds of bones.

Even after the destruction of the buffalo herds, some tribes refused to accept the authority of the United States government. In the Southwest most Apache bands had been either coaxed or coerced onto reservations by the mid-1870s. However, one of their fiercest war leaders, Geronimo, carried on the desperate struggle until his surrender in 1886.

The Sioux, bewildered and humiliated by the threat of losing their cultural identity, became caught up in a new religion that spread like wildfire through the Plains tribes. The new cult foretold an approaching cataclysm during which all whites would be removed from the earth, dead Indians would return, and the buffalo would roam the plains as before. Fearing this movement would renew the Sioux's sense of power, the federal government sent army troops to ban the cult and its frenzied "ghost dancing." Sitting Bull was killed during an escape attempt on his reservation. Then in December 1890, some 350 Sioux fleeing through the Dakotas were arrested and escorted to Wounded Knee Creek. A scuffle arose when the Indians refused to surrender their weapons. In the confusion, soldiers opened fire, cutting down between 150 and 200 men, women, and children. The next month the last of the Sioux surrendered.

"Assimilation": The Dawes Act

The destruction of the buffalo left the Indians without resources to sustain them and robbed them of their independence. In the 1870s public indignation over the treatment of the Indians led to new plans to improve their conditions. The idea that achieved widespread acceptance was that the "Indian problem" could best be resolved by "civilizing" them; that is, by assimilating them into white society. To achieve this would require bringing an end to tribal organization.

In 1887 Congress enacted the Dawes Severalty Act, which was intended to accomplish Indian assimilation. This legislation gave the president the authority to dissolve tribal units and to divide reservation lands into farms of 160 acres for each family, with less acreage delegated to unmarried adults, orphans, and dependent children. Of the 137 million acres in the reservations, only 47 million were needed to make the farm allotments. The remaining 90 million acres, almost always the most fertile, were made available to new settlers. Revenue from the sale of this land was to be used to educate the Indians, often in the form of vocational training.

To ensure that the Indians would not be tricked out of possession of their property, the Dawes Act stipulated that their land could not be sold for twenty-five years. At the same time, however, the act permitted leasing the land. As a result, by the 1930s more than half the land given to the Indians under the act had passed out of their hands by means of quasi-legal manipulations by land-hungry whites. The Dawes Act also made the Indians legal citizens of the United States. Nevertheless, the federal and state governments continued to deny native Americans basic civil rights and to suppress their religions, customs, languages, and social organization.

Hispanics: Conflict and Accommodation

Texas

The Indians were not the only minority group whose culture was threatened by contact with Anglo-Americans during the post–Civil War period. In Texas cultural conflict arose between American settlers and *tejanos*, as descendants of the original Spanish colonists were called north of the Rio Grande. Most Americans who settled in Texas regarded the *tejanos* as racially inferior. Some *tejanos*, in their turn, eventually intermarried with Americans and looked down on the Mexicans who migrated to Texas to meet the need for agricultural labor. Sometimes, however, the intermingling of different cultures proved beneficial. After the Civil War, Texas became the center of the cattle boom, and cowboys from Texas to the Rocky Mountains copied the skills and techniques of Mexican *vaqueros* who herded Texas cattle. In addition, the American demand for beef provided a boon to the cattle industry in northern Mexico. And as the demand for lamb and wool expanded, many Mexicans found employment as sheepherders.

California

Although freedom of religion, equal citizenship, and equal property rights had been guaranteed to *Californios* under the Treaty of Guadalupe Hidalgo (1848), the ink on the treaty was hardly dry when *Californios* found themselves competing with fortune-hunters from all over the country for gold discovered in California. Within a short time, the Hispanic population had been reduced to a minority which faced harsh discrimination. Moreover, tensions were heightened when there was an influx of Mexican miners from Sonora. Not only did the *Californios* heartily dislike these new immigrants, but Anglo-Americans resented everyone of Spanish ancestry and tried to drive them off their lands. Despite the conflict between these factions, when the territory sought statehood in 1848, *Californio* representatives were included at the constitutional convention, and it was provided that laws should be printed in Spanish as well as in English.

As more settlers moved into California, however, the *Californios* began to lose economic and political influence. Anglo-Americans seized many of their land holdings, and, consequently, there was much violence during the 1850s and 1860s, especially in northern California. Some *Californios* even resorted to banditry in order to restore their lost wealth. By contrast, the Spanish-speaking population of southern California remained a majority and evolved into a prosperous agricultural community. Then during the 1870s and 1880s American railroad interests took control of more and more land. Once again, although new jobs were created for Hispanic workers, the influence of the *Californios* was reduced.

New Mexico

The history of the Territory of New Mexico illustrates recurring trends in the lives of Hispanics from Texas to California. The *ricos*, a small group of wealthy New Mexican merchants and landowners, wanted no connection with Mexico and supported the 1850 constitutional convention which petitioned Congress for statehood. When Congress made New Mexico a territory instead, the *ricos* played an important role in territorial government. They seldom intermarried with Anglo-Americans and maintained their *haciendas* (ranches) as self-sufficient cultural units in which they dominated the religious and secular lives of their Mexican farm workers.

Most Spanish-speaking people in the territory found it difficult to understand American concepts of government, taxation, and land-holding. When the transcontinental railroad was under construction during the 1870s, more Anglo-Americans moved in and invested in timber, cattle, minerals, and cotton. As had happened in Texas and California, these large enterprises provided employment for many Hispanics although at the same time they gradually acquired land from both Hispanic and Anglo-American farmers. Additional land was lost when the federal government set aside millions of acres for national forests in 1891. Nevertheless, even though the Spanish-speaking people became more culturally isolated, they were powerful enough politically to obtain an article in the Constitution of New Mexico providing for the legal equality of the English and Spanish languages when New Mexico entered the Union in 1912. The document also restated the guarantees of the Treaty of Guadalupe Hidalgo.

Gold Fever

Prospectors infected with gold fever poured into the Far West. With them they brought picks, shovels, and pans to remove gold from "placers," the surface deposits of sand, earth, or gravel containing eroded bits of precious metals. Placer mining quickly exhausted the supply of surface gold. The remaining ore was locked in quartz crystals beneath the upper layers of earth, and expensive equipment was required to extract it. Only large companies financed by Eastern investors could afford equipment for hard-rock mining.

Most of the leading mining entrepreneurs were of lower- to middle-class backgrounds and came from the South and Midwest. For the most part, they had little formal education or mining experience, but they did have business experience, a background appropriate to the risky operation of buying and selling at the right time. The original prospectors either remained and worked for company wages or drifted off in search of new sites of surface gold. After the California Mother Lode petered out, many of them followed the yellow metal to the Rocky Mountains, but few found the fortunes they were seeking. Although more than $500 million worth of ore came out of the West between 1848 and 1858, most of the profits went into the pockets of the East Coast financiers.

The mining companies tunneled and shafted mines and crushed tons of quartz, drawing out the gold through a complex refining process. Finally, when even the gold beneath the surface was exhausted, many company workers turned to farming or ranching.

Major Lodes

Colorado enjoyed a mining boom which lasted almost half a century. In July 1858 gold was discovered along Dry Creek, near present-day Denver, and new lodes were subsequently discovered in the mountains west of Denver near Central City. Later, silver mining near Leadville and Aspen added to Colorado's wealth. By the turn of the century, however, most of Colorado's precious metals had been extracted, and farming and ranching became the basis of the state's economy.

In 1859 the Comstock Lode, the most fabulous silver strike in the West, was discovered in western Nevada, and within a year ten thousand inhabitants had settled Virginia City on the mountain side above the mining site. Soon Nevada was producing more silver than all other sites combined. Between 1860 and 1880 $306 million was earned from the Comstock. The infusion of such large amounts of precious metals into the American economy aided the financing of the Civil War and provided needed capital for the country's postwar industrialization.

The mining frontier also extended to Idaho, Montana, the Dakotas, and Arizona. In 1864 gold prospectors struck pay dirt at Last Chance Gulch in Montana; there, however, gold was soon replaced in importance by copper, essential to newly invented electrical equipment. In 1874 the discovery of gold on the Sioux reservation in the Black Hills of the Dakota Territory produced the last great gold rush. In Arizona the biggest boom town was Tombstone, which produced millions of dollars' worth of silver between 1880 and 1900.

Life in the Mining Towns

Flamboyant camps which mushroomed near the big strikes mirrored the get-rich-quick attitudes of their inhabitants. Mark Twain described Virginia City during its boom period in *Roughing It:*

Joy sat on every countenance, and there was a glad, almost fierce intensity in every eye, that told of the money-getting schemes that held sway in every heart. Money was as plenty as dust; every individual considered himself wealthy, and a melancholy countenance was nowhere to be seen. There were military companies, fire companies, brass-bands, banks, hotels, theaters, "hurdy-gurdy houses," wide-open gambling palaces, political powwows, civic processions, street-fights, murders, inquests, riots, a whiskey-mill every fifteen steps . . . a dozen breweries, and half a dozen jails and station-houses in full operation, and some talk of building a church. The "flush times" were in magnificent flower. .

A MINING CAMP IN COLORADO.

INTERPRETING AMERICAN HISTORY

THE ROLE OF THE FRONTIER IN AMERICAN LIFE In 1890 the superintendent of the census announced that for the first time in American history, there was no longer a discernible frontier line. Although millions of acres remained open to homesteading until the 1930s, most of this acreage was desert or grazing land of marginal value.

Three years after the frontier line was consigned to history, a young professor from the University of Wisconsin, Frederick Jackson Turner, wrote a provocative paper titled "The Significance of the Frontier in American History" in which he presented the bold thesis that it had been the frontier, rather than the country's European heritage, which had shaped the national character. American nationalism, democracy, and individualism, he said, were the legacy of tough, heroic settlers who for decades had moved westward. "Now," he concluded, "four centuries from the discovery of America, at the end of a hundred years of life under the Constitution, the frontier has gone, and with its going has closed the first period of American history."

It was Turner's contention that most of the cultural habits and institutions of Europe had been lost in the American wilderness. Settlers had discarded old patterns and sunk into a primitive society, devoid of complex government institutions, class distinctions, and cultural refinements. As an increasing number of settlers arrived, the frontier gradually changed. The development of frontier towns represented the evolution of human history from simple to complex forms, but the entire European heritage was not repeated. There was no well-defined class system, no autocratic government, and no Old World etiquette and prejudice. Instead, argued Turner, the frontier produced such distinctively American traits as mobility, optimism, a ready acceptance of new ways, and, on the negative side, materialism and a wasteful exploitation of natural resources. In their desire to take advantage of America's vast natural riches, frontier people came to dislike government intervention, particularly economic controls. In addition, the leveling influence of frontier conditions and the need to solve common problems as a group produced in frontier people a respect for majority rule. Thus, Turner concluded, the frontier was the seedbed of democracy.

Criticism of the Turner Thesis One recent commentator has written that Turner's frontier thesis "was the most widely influential idea conceived by any American historian." A brilliant and persuasive teacher, Turner attracted many disciples, and although he published little himself, his ideas were disseminated widely by his followers. His theory was perfectly adapted to the spirit of early twentieth-century America, stressing as it did a strong sense of patriotism and optimism and emphasizing success gained through individual effort.

After Turner's death in 1932, previously unexpressed criticism of his thesis came into the open. Most criticized were his statements that: (1) the existence of cheap, available frontier land made it possible for settlers to move repeatedly from complex to simple forms of civilization, refreshing and reshaping the national spirit through a series of new beginnings; (2) the frontier served as a "safety valve of discontent" in older parts of the country by permitting disgruntled Eastern factory workers to pull up stakes and seek their fortunes in the West; (3) the frontier allowed democratic ideas and institutions to grow and nurture the principle of rugged individualism in America; (4) the frontier served as a melting pot, a place where European immigrants could shed national customs and adopt those of their new country; and (5) the frontier produced a people with unique characteristics.

When Turner died, the United States was in the middle of its worst depression. At the time, the optimism of Turner's thesis struck historians as an inadequate explanation for American development. Writers with Marxist leanings stressed the influence of class conflict on the American character, rather than the geographic forces which Turner emphasized. The importance Turner gave to the individualism that grew out of the frontier experience conflicted with the trend in the 1930s toward collective action and government regulation as solutions to the country's problems. An urban, industrialized nation did not look to the agricultural frontier for explanations of its development and character. American life seemed too complex to be explained by a single factor.

Several modern historians such as Robert E. Riegel and Fred Shannon have admitted that the frontier may well have influenced the shape of American history but have expressed doubts about aspects of Turner's thesis. They question Turner's emphasis on the importance of free land. According to Riegel, "Certainly farmers wanted cheap land, but they took surprisingly little advantage of the free land provided under the Homestead Act of 1862." Turner had overlooked the fact that much of the free land had not passed into the hands of poor farmers, but instead became the property of land speculators. Riegel questioned the logic of comparing frontier development with the concept of evolution and echoed a common complaint when he said, "Most present authorities feel that Turner's point of view led him to oversimplify the whole frontier process and to place undue emphasis on physical environment and on uniformity of result."

Modern historians also have disagreed with the theory of the frontier as a "safety valve of discontent." Turner suggested that hard times caused factory workers to migrate to the West, but the greatest movements to the West were during periods of prosperity, and relatively few of the settlers came from the more industrialized parts of the East. They pointed out that a great deal of capital was needed to move West, to buy farm equipment, and to live until the first crops were harvested. Industrial workers were unlikely to possess much money at any time, and few people were likely to have extra cash in time of depression.

Historians also have attacked Turner's claim that the frontier was the seedbed of democracy and political innovation. They argue that on the American frontier, the freedom to experiment actually resulted in an expansion of the same type of representative government which had already been provided for in federal and state constitutions. According to this line of reasoning, the frontier environment did not of itself create a democratic political system.

Although Turner's critics concede that during the early settlement of the West all pioneers were equally poor, they point out that any absence of social and economic distinctions did not last long. Moreover, the West did not vote as a bloc in favor of innovations; the region was divided over most political issues. For example, the old Northwest opposed slavery, whereas the old Southwest favored it. According to Riegel, Jacksonian democracy won no more support in the West than in the East: "Popular Presidents such as Jefferson, Jackson and Lincoln, noted for their love of the common man, were elected more by eastern than by western votes." Riegel has commented that although "western support in the years around 1900 of such democratic measures as the direct primary, popular election of Senators, votes for women, the initiative, referendum and recall" has often been cited in arguments linking the frontier with the shaping of democracy, "in every case, however, the idea came from Europe, while the support was largely eastern, with the West itself divided."

Regarding Turner's point that the frontier served to Americanize European immigrants, some historians contend that Turner's idea "that each new frontiersman shed his old customs, started anew, and became a real American" appears to have been more a hope than a fact. Several historians have shown clearly the extent to which national characteristics were retained in Western settlements.

Turner's view that the frontier environment in America produced unique characteristics in people who lived there has been challenged by studies of frontier settlers in other parts of the world which have shown that these settlers developed attitudes and approaches to problems similar to those of America's pioneers. In every instance, frontier people were crude, tough, individualistic, and inventive.

Historical research has now determined that the American West, which Turner and many others identified with rural life, actually had a strong urban tradition. The growth of cities often preceded the settlement of the countryside.

(Continued on next page.)

INTERPRETING AMERICAN HISTORY (Cont.)

St. Paul, Kansas City, Denver, Omaha, Los Angeles, San Francisco, Seattle, Portland, and Tacoma were developed long before rural areas nearby. Several of these cities had over a hundred thousand inhabitants by 1890 and were often the cause, rather than the consequence, of their area's growth and settlement.

A Defense of Turner Turner's defenders, such as Ray Allen Billington, while conceding that Turner's thesis was wrong in many details and oversimplified in general, have nevertheless insisted that the frontier theory pointed to an essential truth: "The recurring rebirth of society in the United States over a period of three hundred years did endow the people with characteristics and institutions that distinguished them from the inhabitants of other nations. It is obviously untrue that the frontier experience alone accounts for the unique features of American civilization; that civilization can be understood only as the product of the interplay of the Old World heritage and

New World conditions. But among those conditions none has bulked larger than the operation of the frontier process."

These historians contend that the frontier, though it did not invent democratic theory and institutions, tended to make them, in practice, even more democratic. In every new territory along the frontier, pioneer "constitution-makers" adopted the most liberal features of older frames of government with which they were familiar. They credit two factors with strengthening democratic attitudes: the widespread ownership of land and the absence of any prior leadership structure. The first factor gave each member a stake in the community; the second meant that the community did not simply inherit leaders, but had to choose them.

Even if the Turner thesis was flawed in many particulars, these historians regard as unassailable his general contention that "frontiersmen did develop unique traits and that these, perpetuated, form the distinguishing characteristics of the American people today."

Mining towns such as Virginia City, Nevada; Deadwood, South Dakota; and Tombstone, Arizona teemed with gamblers and were notorious for their lawlessness. Twenty-five saloons had opened in Virginia City before its population reached four thousand. Deadwood was the home of such free-wheeling characters as professional gambler and gunman "Wild Bill" Hickok, his hard-drinking girlfriend, "Calamity" Jane, and black cowboy Nat Love. A rough sort of law and order was maintained by citizens' vigilance groups and by sheriffs, some of whom were well-known gunmen themselves. Former buffalo hunter Wyatt Earp, who became Deputy Marshall of Tombstone and participated in the infamous shoot-out at the O.K. Corral, may have spent more time as a gambler and troublemaker than as an officer of the law.

The mining property itself was governed in every town by a miners' association. This group established the size and number of claims each person could hold and arbitrated water rights and questions relating to absentee ownership and land tenure. While the miners indulged in drinking and

gambling, they also formed debating groups and literary societies and erected churches and public libraries. Eventually, as communities grew in population, vigilance committees and miners' associations gave way to more traditional forms of government.

Before railroad lines reached the mining centers, mining towns were connected to the outside world by horse or stagecoach. In April 1860 the Pony Express began carrying mail between San Francisco, California, and St. Joseph, Missouri. The company employed about two hundred riders who changed ponies at more than 150 relay stations along the two-thousand-mile route. Mail sometimes reached San Francisco after only eight days, an amazing record for swiftness on horseback through rough country. The work was exhausting and dangerous. A company ad published in San Francisco read: "Young skinny wiry fellows, not over eighteen. Must be expert riders willing to risk death daily. Orphans preferred." The initial charge for mail delivered this way was five dollars per half-ounce; later it was reduced to one dollar. In October 1861, the transcontinental telegraph ended the brief, colorful career of the Pony Express. The biggest of the stagecoach lines after 1866 was Wells, Fargo & Company, which carried passengers, gold, and miscellaneous freight. The completion of the first transcontinental railroad in 1869 ended Wells, Fargo's long-distance hauling, although animal-drawn vehicles continued to serve small communities in the West for decades.

Cattle Fever

While mining towns were booming in the Western mountains, ranchers discovered that the Great Plains, long believed to be infertile, offered a valuable resource: buffalo grass. This vast grassland was capable of feeding cattle, even in winter, just as it had nourished the thriving buffalo herds. The discovery prepared the way for the emergence of a great cattle kingdom stretching across the Plains from Texas northward to the Canadian border and from the Rockies eastward to Kansas. For twenty years after 1865 cattle ranching dominated this region.

The Long Drive

In 1866 and 1867 Texans opened the era of the "long drive." Dairy cattle bred with rugged Texas longhorns produced heavy, easily marketed beef, and cattle raisers discovered that herds could be driven from their home grounds to shipping points in Kansas, Nebraska, or Wyoming. Instead of losing weight during the journey, cattle actually fattened up on the nourishing Plains grass. As yet there were few farms on the Great Plains, and after 1867 the Indians were more effectively confined to reservations. Since there were fewer buffalo to compete for the grass, cattle raisers could feed their herds on millions of acres of free pasturage.

Between 1866 and 1888 some ten million cattle were driven to market. Between 1878 and 1885, when the open-range cattle business was at its peak, cattle raisers were earning a yearly profit of 40 percent on their investment. Cattle-raising became such a profitable business that in just one year twenty corporations, with a combined capital of $12 million, were chartered in Wyoming alone. Such companies controlled millions of acres of ranchland.

Stories about the men who rode herd on the long drives for $25 to $30 a month fired the American imagination. With their broad-brimmed hats and gaudy neckerchiefs, forty-pound saddles and eighteen-foot lassoes, cowboys became the new national folk heroes. Their independent way of life attracted thousands of blacks who migrated from the South in search of new opportunities. But if independence and adventure were elements of the cowboy's life, the reality included loneliness, danger, and hard work as well. Every spring cowboys rounded up the new calves and branded them with the distinctive insignia of their employer. Twelve to fifteen cowboys would then drive between two thousand and five thousand steers to market, moving the herd about fifteen miles a day. Eventually, after weeks in the saddle, the drovers would reach their destination at a cow town where the cattle would be sold and shipped by rail. The invention of the refrigerator car in the 1870s made it possible to transport beef from the slaughterhouses of Chicago and Kansas City to the industrial cities in the East.

DINNER-ON-ROUND-UP. A GROUP OF COWBOYS GATHER AROUND THE CHUCK WAGON FOR SOME HOT FOOD DURING A BREAK IN THE ROUND-UP.

There an ever-growing urban population provided a huge market for fresh meat.

The Cattle Towns

Abilene, Kansas, an insignificant stop along the route of the Kansas Pacific Railroad, became the first of the big cattle towns. During the mid-1860s Joe McCoy, a cattle-buyer's agent, began building vast cattle pens in Abilene for the purpose of providing a more accessible depot to which ranchers could drive their herds and from which buyers could ship stock east. Abilene prospered. As the railroads extended their lines, new cattle towns sprang up: Ellsworth, Wichita, Ogallala, and Dodge City.

In these colorful towns cowboys just off the trail squandered their meager wages on fancy clothes and high times. During profitable years the cattle towns attracted an assortment of raffish visitors, such as buffalo hunters, gamblers, gunmen, and camp followers. Nevertheless, the cow town's reputation for violence was somewhat exaggerated.

Often the increased cattle trade stimulated the organization of local government and law enforcement. Respectable citizens were willing to tolerate only a limited amount of mayhem. In order to attract the free-spending visitors and still encourage permanent businesses, local officials permitted a variety of rowdy saloons, dance halls, and brothels which they controlled through a system of lucrative fines.

In time, as the number of wives and children in these rough towns increased, so did the impulse toward moral reform. However, it was the expansion of the agricultural frontier that eventually ended the long drives and changed the cattle towns' unique character.

End of the Open Range

Since the mid-1860s, longhorns had been recognized as carriers of "Texas" fever (a disease caused by a parasite and transmitted by a tick). Although practically immune to the disease themselves, these animals spread the infection to other areas of the coun-

A SOD DUGOUT IN NEBRASKA, 1892. FARMERS ON THE PLAINS FACED BLIZZARDS, TORNADOES, AND DROUGHTS. MANY GAVE UP IN DESPAIR AND MOVED BACK HOME.

try. By the mid-1880s Kansas farmers with rifles were blocking the cattle trails, forcing drovers to seek new shipping centers farther west.

The open range was threatened from other quarters, too. No longer satisfied with sharing the public domain, large operators had begun to claim exclusive rights to grazing lands and watering places. In so doing, they helped prevent overgrazing but also created new conflicts among ranchers. Stock-growers' associations were formed to bring order to the cutthroat competition for control of land. The rules worked out by these associations for governing the range had the force of law in some Western territories. Such regulations tended to restrict competition in the cattle business by keeping out newcomers; however, they never completely prevented new ranchers from entering this lucrative enterprise.

The cattle boom years came to a close when homesteading farmers began fencing their property with barbed wire. Joseph F. Glidden had started manufacturing the wire in 1874, and it proved a valuable commodity in treeless country where rail fences could not be built. By 1883 the American Steel and Wire Company was turning out six hundred miles of wire a day.

Another challenge to the cattle raiser's unhindered use of lush public grasslands came from sheep ranchers. Although over half of the sheep were raised in the mountains, the remainder were being grazed across the Plains. Cattle could not forage where sheep had grazed, since the sheep destroyed pasturage by grazing down to the roots, and waterholes were tainted after sheep had used them. As a result, sheepherders and cattle ranchers engaged in hundreds of bitter skirmishes.

Overproduction drove the price of beef down at the same time that cattle raising became more expensive. In the summer of 1886, drought struck the Great Plains. The herds, which were forced to feed on the sparse vegetation of a diminished range, were in weakened condition when winter set in, and the winter of 1886–1887 was the worst in memory. By springtime nine out of every ten range cattle were dead.

After this disaster many small cattle ranchers sold out to big corporations which partitioned the open range into enclosed ranches. Cattle breeding, like mining before it, ceased to be a spirited, individualist enterprise and became an efficiently managed business. More and more cattle ranchers fenced their land and laid up a supply of hay to see their herds through the winter. Thoroughbred Aberdeen Angus and Hereford bulls were introduced into the herds, and scientific hybrid breeding began. The railroads were building lines into the Southwest, so there was no longer any need to drive cattle hundreds of miles to a railroad terminal. Trains brought in cattle feed and carried away thousands of pounds of dressed beef every week.

The Farmer's Last Frontier

Neither mining nor cattle ranching brought large numbers of settlers to the Great Plains, but farming caused the area's population almost to triple between 1870 and 1890. This was due in part to the enormous population growth throughout the entire country during these years—30 percent in the decade between 1866 and 1876 alone.

Farmers from Scandinavia, eager for cheap land, poured into the Northwest after 1865. A significant number of Irish, Scottish, English, German, and Russian immigrants settled the Great Plains during the 1870s. Some newcomers came to escape military duty; others were lured by the bright promises of railroad agents; still others fled Europe during the poor wheat-growing years of the 1870s. Most settlers, however, were poor American farmers from the Midwest who had moved westward in search of a better life.

Many women also found their economic position improved when they moved from the East or the South to Western territories. First in Oregon and then in other parts of the West, women were allowed to homestead and faced no obstacles in owning property. In fact, women often were given preferential access to credit, and a number became entrepreneurs.

The railroad was crucial to the settling of the Great Plains. Miles of track linked the prairie states to the East, and railroad companies actively encouraged immigration from Europe in order to sell excess land. The railroads had received some 180 million acres of land as subsidies from the federal and state governments. Some tried to hold out for the highest possible prices for this land when they sold it, but most let it go at low rates because every farmer who settled along the track was a potential freight customer. Indeed, by the end of the nineteenth century, far more land had been sold to settlers by the railroads than was settled under the Homestead Act.

The Homestead Act

The Homestead Act of 1862 provided that anyone who wanted a free 160-acre farm had only to live on it for five years, improve it, and pay a fee of $10. This act was intended to help those of limited economic means, in the expectation that America would once again become a land of small, independent property holders.

Although about four hundred thousand families had received free homesteads by 1900, this ideal-istic scheme actually did little to further economic democracy. Poor industrial workers usually did not know how to farm, and few truly poor farmers could afford to transport their families to the Great Plains and purchase farm machinery necessary for raising crops there. Western soil and weather conditions were utterly foreign to anything in most Eastern farmers' experience. In the winter, blizzards bringing temperatures of sixty and seventy degrees below zero swept across the land. There were only approximately fifteen inches of rainfall per year, and during the summer droughts often destroyed crops. Tornadoes struck unexpectedly, and in the summer of 1874 a plague of grasshoppers attacked the vegetation. Many farm families, exhausted from living in drafty sod houses, tilling dusty fields, carting water from wells miles away, and listening to the everpresent wind, gave up in despair and returned to their former homes.

The act's provision of 160 acres was also a serious flaw because that amount of land was not prac-

EVEN POWERFUL LOCOMOTIVES WERE STOPPED BY THE ARMIES OF GRASSHOPPERS THAT PERIODICALLY SWEPT ACROSS THE GREAT PLAINS.

AGITATION FOR FERTILE LAND FORMERLY OCCUPIED BY THE INDIANS PAID OFF WHEN THE UNITED STATES GOVERNMENT OPENED THE OKLAHOMA TERRITORY TO WHITE SETTLEMENT. AT NOON ON APRIL 22, 1889, A BUGLE CALL SET LOOSE A STAMPEDE OF WOULD-BE SETTLERS HOPING TO STAKE A CLAIM. MOST OF THE "SOONERS"—THOSE WHO SNEAKED IN AHEAD OF THE STARTING TIME—LOST THEIR CLAIMS BUT GAVE OKLA-HOMA ITS NICKNAME: THE "SOONER STATE."

tical for Western farming. In the Midwest a 160-acre farm was considered adequate, but in the West, where water was scarce, an area of 160 acres was too large to irrigate and grow vegetables and too small for cattle grazing and growing grain. One alternative was dry farming, or tilling the land with a plow, disc, and harrow to create a blanket of finely compacted particles of soil. This dirt cover retarded the evaporation of rainwater from the soil bed beneath the crops and pulled subsurface water up to the plants' roots.

Corrupt practices also blighted the success of the Homestead Act. Wealthy land speculators frequently obtained large tracts by bribing poor people to file claims for homesteads and then deed the property rights to them. These large landholders then resold the land to farmers at a profit.

Other Land Laws

Public protests over the flaws in the Homestead Act led Congress to pass a number of supplementary land laws, but like the earlier act, these were of little help to small farmers. The Timber Culture Act of 1873 provided that a homesteader who planted trees on a minimum of 40 acres could obtain an additional 160 acres. This legislation was impractical, since it was impossible to grow trees in an arid region, and the act was later repealed. The Desert Land Act of 1877 awarded temporary title to 640 acres for $160. After three years the farmer could obtain permanent title by paying an additional $640 and by proving that at least one-eighth of the tract had been irrigated. Few farmers, however, could afford to irrigate in desert areas, and the main beneficiaries were cattle raisers who bought more land for grazing their herds. The third attempt to remedy the inadequacies of the Homestead Act was the Timber and Stone Act of 1878. This measure offered 160-acre tracts of valuable forest land to individual buyers for $2.50 an acre. Again, few small farmers benefited. Large corporations hired dummy buyers to file claims and bought up most of the available good land. Such abuses permitted a few big lumber companies to gain control of the forests covering the Rocky and Sierra mountains at a low price.

Solving the Problems of Plains Farming

Despite land grabbing by corrupt speculators and the awesome hardships of farming on the Plains, large areas of the West were quickly populated between 1865 and 1890. Those who stuck with their claims were aided by a growing number of inventions which enabled them to better cope with the hostile environment.

The most persistent problem encountered by new arrivals was the shortage of water. Wells had to be machine drilled thirty to three hundred feet deep and the water raised by windmill. Windmills were introduced to the West in the 1870s, but they were not cheap enough to be generally available for two decades. Although by the turn of the century almost every farm had its own windmill and deep-drilled well, not until the federal government sponsored dam projects during the twentieth century did large-scale irrigation of dry regions begin. Previously, the federal government had left the problem of irrigation to the states, but the states lacked the resources to tackle such ambitious projects. Before irrigation dams were built, lack of moisture in the Plains soil was partially compensated for by the use of a new strain of cold- and drought-resistant wheat from Russia and by allowing each section of land to stand uncultivated every other year.

The invention of new equipment helped to meet the special problems of Western farming. A particular problem had been the resistance of the hard soil to ordinary plows. In 1869 James Oliver of South Bend, Indiana, invented an unusually sturdy plow of chilled iron. Several of these plowshares could be mounted on a single horse-drawn sulky, enabling the farmer to cut several furrows at once. In the 1870s John F. Appleby invented a twine binder which facilitated quick harvesting of wheat before it could be destroyed by unpredictable weather. During the 1880s large farms began to use the combine, pulled by twenty to forty horses, to reap, thresh, and bag grain in one operation. Other machinery such as the grain drill, hay baler, and new mowers permitted Plains farmers to sow and reap their crops more efficiently.

Such equipment was expensive, and huge farms were required to ensure a profitable investment. By 1890 many farms on the Plains extended over a thousand acres, and farmers increasingly abandoned self-sufficiency in favor of growing a single cash crop, usually wheat. To survive on such a large scale they had to ship their grain to international markets, where they competed with wheat growers from Russia, Argentina, and other countries. Issues concerning farmers became an important factor contributing to widespread political and economic unrest during the latter part of the nineteenth century.

Readings

General Works

Bartlett, Richard A., *The New Country: A Social History of the American Indian Frontier, 1776–1890*. New York: Oxford University Press, 1974.

Billington, Ray A., *America's Frontier Heritage*. New York: Holt, Rinehart and Winston, 1966.

_____, *Westward Expansion*. New York: Macmillan, 1967.

Clark, Thomas D., *Frontier America: The Story of the Westward Movement*. New York: Scribner's, 1969.

Hayter, Earl W., *The Troubled Farmer: Rural Adjustments to Industrialism, 1850–1900*. DeKalb: Northern Illinois University Press, 1968. (Paper)

Machado, Manuel A., Jr., *Listen Chicano!, An Informal History of the Mexican American*. Chicago: Nelson Hall, 1978.

Peterson, Richard H., *The Bonanza Kings: The Social Origins and Behavior of Western Mining Entrepreneurs, 1870–1900*. Lincoln: University of Nebraska Press, 1977.

Savage, William W. (Ed.), *Indian Life: Transforming an American Myth*. Norman: University of Oklahoma Press, 1978.

Smith, Henry N., *Virgin Land*. Cambridge, Mass.: Harvard University Press, 1950.

Turner, Frederick J., *The Frontier in American History*. New York: Holt, Rinehart and Winston, 1963.

Webb, Walter P., *The Great Plains*. New York: Grosset & Dunlap, 1957.

Special Studies

Andrist, Ralph K., *The Long Death*. New York: Macmillan, 1969. (Paper)

Atherton, Lewis, *The Cattle Kings*. Bloomington: University of Indiana Press, 1961.

Choate, Julian E., and Joe B. Frantz, *The American Cowboy: The Myth and the Reality*. Norman: University of Oklahoma Press, 1955.

Dick, Everett, *The Sod-House Frontier, 1854–1890*. Lincoln, Neb.: Johnsen, 1954.

Fite, Gilbert C., *The Farmer's Frontier, 1865–1900*. New York: Holt, Rinehart and Winston, 1966.

Fritz, Henry E., *The Movement for Indian Assimilation, 1860–1890*. Philadelphia: University of Pennsylvania Press, 1963.

Gard, Wayne, *The Great Buffalo Hunt*. Lincoln: University of Nebraska Press, 1959.

Greever, W. S., *The Bonanza West: The Story of the Western Mining Rushes, 1848–1900*. Norman: University of Oklahoma Press, 1963.

Hagan, William T., *United States Comanche Relations: The Reservation Years*. New Haven: Yale University Press, 1976.

Katz, William Loren, *The Black West*. Garden City, N.Y.: Anchor Press/Doubleday, 1973.

King, Joseph E., *A Mine to Make a Mine: Financing the Colorado Mining Industry, 1859–1902*. College Station: Texas A&M University Press, 1977.

Mardock, Robert W., *The Reformers and the American Indian*. Columbia: University of Missouri Press, 1971.

Osgood, E. S., *The Day of the Cattleman*. Chicago: University of Chicago Press, 1957.

Paul, Rodman W., *Mining Frontiers of the Far West 1848–1880*. New York: Holt, Rinehart and Winston, 1963.

Shannon, Fred A., *The Farmer's Last Frontier: Agriculture 1860–1897*. New York: Holt, Rinehart and Winston, 1945.

Thompson, Gerald, *The Army and the Navaho*. Tucson: University of Arizona Press, 1976.

Utley, Robert M., *Last Days of the Sioux Nation*. New Haven: Yale University Press, 1963.

Primary Sources

Adams, Andy, *Log of a Cowboy*. Lincoln: University of Nebraska Press, 1964.

Jackson, Helen H., *A Century of Dishonor*. New York: Harper & Row, 1960.

Smith, Duane A., *Colorado Mining: A Photographic History*. Albuquerque: University of New Mexico Press, 1977.

Twain, Mark, *Roughing It*. New York: New American Library, 1962.

Biographies

Debo, Angie, *Geronimo: The Man, His Time, His Place*. Norman: University of Oklahoma Press, 1976.

McCracken, Harold, *George Catlin and the Old Frontier*. New York: Dial, 1959.

Sandoz, Mari, *Old Jules*. Lincoln: University of Nebraska Press, 1962.

Stegner, Wallace, *Beyond the Hundredth Meridian: John Wesley Powell and the Second Opening of the West*. Boston: Houghton Mifflin, 1954.

Stewart, E. I., *Custer's Luck*. Norman: University of Oklahoma Press, 1955.

Vestal, Stanley, *Sitting Bull, Champion of the Sioux: A Biography*. Norman: University of Oklahoma Press, 1972.

Fiction

Cather, Willa, *My Antonia*. Boston: Houghton Mifflin, 1918.

———, *O Pioneers!* Boston: Houghton Mifflin, 1913.

Rolvaag, Ole, *Giants in the Earth*. New York: Harper & Row, 1927.

17 Becoming a Great Industrial Power

Assuming that you have all obtained employment and are fairly started, my advice to you is "aim high." I would not give a fig for the young man who does not already see himself the partner or the head of an important firm. Do not rest content for a moment in your thoughts as head clerk, or foreman, or general manager in any concern, no matter how extensive. Say to yourself, "My place is at the top."

Andrew Carnegie, *The Road to Business Success*, 1885

Significant Events

On the Origin of Species, Charles Darwin [1859]

Union Pacific Railroad joined to Central Pacific Railroad to complete the first transcontinental line [1869]

Alexander Graham Bell transmits first telephone message [1876]

Munn v. *Illinois* [1877]

Standard Oil Trust formed [1882]

Wabash, Saint Louis and Pacific Railroad Company v. *Illinois* [1886]

Interstate Commerce Act [1887]

Sherman Antitrust Act [1890]

United States v. *E. C. Knight Company* [1895]

United States Steel Corporation formed [1901]

At the same time that the nation's Far Western frontier was rapidly disappearing, the American economy was experiencing phenomenal industrial growth. Between 1865 and 1900 a variety of interdependent factors made possible this remarkable industrial expansion. An abundance of private capital provided by the more highly developed economy of the North as well as by foreign investors was used to exploit an apparently inexhaustible supply of natural resources. The challenge of competition and the promise of great wealth impelled ambitious entrepreneurs to seek out new ways of producing more and producing it faster. Scientists and inventors helped to develop the technologies necessary to make America a competitive industrial power. The expansion of the railroad system opened up a nationwide marketplace for goods and fostered the growth of new markets by transporting settlers to far-flung localities. A booming population—both native-born and immigrant—provided the labor needed to produce an astonishing variety of goods and services. Finally, the benevolent attitude of the government toward industrial growth meant that few laws restricted and many advanced the activities of the powerful corporate giants that influenced—for good and for ill—the nature of life in America.

The Shift toward an Industrial Society

In the pre–Civil War years the United States was still primarily an agricultural nation. The typical American worker was a farmer who either grew cash crops for national or European markets or worked for someone who did. Despite the commercialization of agriculture and the beginnings of industrialization, the United States still resembled Jefferson's ideal of an agrarian society living close to nature, away from the corruptions of urban life. After 1865, however, the emphasis in the economy shifted rapidly from agriculture to industry. Factories and machines became the new symbols of American life. By 1890 the value of industrial goods and services produced surpassed that of agricultural goods for the first time. By 1914, the United States had become the foremost industrial nation in the world.

Economic opportunity unfettered by government restraint enabled entrepreneurs who had the talent, vision, and willingness to take risks to achieve wealth and power unprecedented in American life. One historian has written:

The next generation after Lincoln was to produce no great statesmen, few novelists and poets of stature, and but two or three artists of world eminence; but produced more business genius than any country in the world had yet seen.

During the 1890s, the term "American millionaire" came into common use, for more than four thousand Americans estimated their wealth in at least seven figures. They made their fortunes in industry, trade, railroads, and banking—in fact, wherever a commodity or service responded to an extensive public demand. Never before had so much money been made so quickly by so many individuals.

A belief in progress infused the spirit of the times. Money and the display of material wealth became the hallmarks of success, and most Americans approved of the acquisitive instinct that made such achievement possible. They believed that competition would protect American society and promote economic growth. But the American laissez-faire economy also led to the concentration of power in the hands of an aggressive few, who exploited the rest of society.

The intense competition among developing industries and the subsequent creation of monopolies hurt many small businesspeople and wiped out many thousands more. The federal government had always shied away from regulating business, but because of public protest over the unfairness of uncontrolled monopoly, it made its first tentative efforts to check cutthroat business practices. Yet the first acts of regulatory legislation were of little benefit to the mass of Americans, since many legislators and judges looked on any government restraint of business as an unwarranted interference with individual freedom.

Factors in Industrialization

A major factor in America's industrialization was its abundance of natural resources: coal and oil from

THE INDUSTRIAL REVOLUTION WAS SPEEDED BY ALL MANNER OF INVENTIONS. BETWEEN 1860 AND 1890 OVER HALF A MILLION PATENTS WERE REGISTERED IN THE UNITED STATES. THE HUGE ALLIS-CORLISS ENGINE MADE AN AWESOME DISPLAY AT THE 1893 CHICAGO WORLD'S FAIR.

Pennsylvania; oil from Texas; iron ore from the vast Mesabi Range in Minnesota; deposits of gold, silver, lead, zinc, and copper from the Rockies and Sierra Nevadas; and forest ranges stretching from the Rocky Mountains to the Pacific Coast and Alaska. But the wealth of its natural resources alone did not account for the rapidity of industrialization after 1865.

Developments in technology contributed significantly to transforming the American economy. The steam engine, which had been employed in water transportation since early in the century, was now harnessed to power factories as well as huge railroad locomotives. Americans had a head start on mechanization, which had been necessary at the beginning of industrialization to make up for the small labor force. The arrival of large numbers of immigrants from 1840 on provided an added boon to manufacturers who were already familiar with machinery and who had developed systems that could be operated by unskilled workers. As machines continued to replace muscle power and as the labor force grew, the number of goods and the efficiency with which they were produced increased rapidly.

Innovations in transportation and communication also helped bind the nation together and tie it to the outside world. The railroads (discussed in the next section) soon dominated internal transportation. The development of the submarine cable in 1866 accelerated international communication; the Suez Canal (completed in 1869) opened a route to the East Asian markets; and improved ships carried goods farther, faster, and more cheaply. These developments opened up a vast market for all types of goods.

In addition, everyone with a new or better gadget hoped to patent it and become wealthy in what seemed to be an inventor's market. Between 1860 and 1890 Americans registered nearly half a million patents, and some of the inventions created new industries. Christopher Sholes's invention of the typewriter in 1868 facilitated the rapid flow of business information and attracted women to industry. Alexander Graham Bell's telephone, introduced in 1876, was a further enticement to women to work outside the home; thousands obtained work as switchboard operators. By the 1890s the American Telephone and Telegraph Company had installed nearly half a million phones in homes and businesses. William S. Burroughs contributed to the speed of doing business with his invention of the adding machine in 1891.

Undoubtedly the most productive inventor of all was Thomas Alva Edison, the "Wizard of Menlo Park," who held more than a thousand patents on such innovations as the electrical storage battery (based on an explanation of electromagnetism provided by the Englishman Michael Faraday), the phonograph, and the motion-picture camera. But it was his invention of the electric light bulb that most changed the way Americans lived and worked. Edison's invention created an inexpensive system of lighting that soon made the more costly gas illumination obsolete. In addition, he and others designed electric generating stations and power plants that could supply electricity to large factories and office buildings as well as to private homes. George Westinghouse and Hungarian immigrant Nikola

Tesla further improved on Edison's limited range, low-voltage, direct-current motor with their superior alternating-current motor. High-voltage alternating current could be transmitted cheaply over long distances where it could be converted by the new motor to mechanical power. Even though electric power was slow to replace steam in factories, America's twentieth-century electrical industry was the result of these inventions.

The tremendous expansion of American industry was aided by several other factors as well. After the Civil War the agrarian South had lost its influence on national politics, and the North obtained federal support for its industrial projects. In addition, a population that was expanding in size while declining in self-sufficiency provided a market for the greater number of manufactured goods. Finally, the United States had access to European, especially English, capital for investment. By 1900 foreign investment in railroads, mines, and municipal bonds amounted to almost $3.5 billion. American money, as a result, went mainly into manufacturing.

The Railroad Era

When the Civil War ended, the United States had only 35,000 miles of railroad track. By 1880 this figure had tripled, and by 1890 the country had 166,000 miles of track, more than all of Europe and Russia combined.

Between 1865 and 1914 the railroad did as much to change American life as the sailing ship had done to change life in ancient times. Travelers could now arrive at their destinations in a matter of hours or days instead of weeks or months. Communication, too, became more rapid, as the railroad reduced the time required to carry mail, and as the use of the telegraph expanded along with the railroad.

An industry in itself, the railroad brought hinterland communities out of isolation and provided jobs for the workers who laid the rails and handled the switches. Local stores in towns along the lines profited from trade brought in by the trains. Giant steel, copper, wood, and coal industries flourished from the production of rails, ties,

cars, and fuel for the locomotives. New bridges strong enough to support the weight of the trains had to be built. And George Pullman founded a new business that specialized in building and leasing sleeping cars. The vast reach of the railroads did much to contribute to mass production. Sales were no longer limited to local markets. As unfamiliar items appeared on store shelves—Arkansas pork in Cleveland, Milwaukee beer in Denver—consumers developed new purchasing habits, which in turn stimulated production.

The railroads helped build new markets by moving settlers, both native-born and immigrant, to new localities. Scandinavians came by train to Minnesota, Germans to St. Louis, Slavs and Irish to Chicago. Were it not for the Iron Horse, much of the West might have remained open expanse for many more years. The railroad drew the nation together economically as well. By 1890 there was a transcontinental network of rails, all interconnecting. Transportation charges decreased, and distant economies enjoyed prosperity based on a single enterprise, with the railroad linking buyer and seller. For example, Pittsburgh relied on iron from the Mesabi Range for use in its steel mills, and Minnesota's economy was in turn dependent on Pittsburgh's purchases of iron. Whole areas rich in natural resources could not have been exploited without the railroads.

Transcontinental Routes

America's railroad lines had scarcely reached across the Mississippi before the Civil War. But during the war pressure from Northerners hoping to bolster the Union by linking the West to the East prompted Congress to support the building of a transcontinental line. The government offered the railroad companies substantial long-term loans and grants of up

to twenty square miles of land instead of the usual ten for every mile of track laid along the right-of-way.

This lucrative challenge was taken up at the war's end by the Union Pacific Railroad whose crews laid lines westward from Omaha, Nebraska, and the Central Pacific Railroad whose crews worked east from San Francisco for an attempted linkup west of the Rockies. The companies overcame formidable costs, rugged terrain and weather, and Indian attacks to build the road. Driven by a spirit of competition, the Irish immigrants working for the Union Pacific and the Chinese and Mexican laborers brought in by the Central Pacific raced to the meeting point. On May 10, 1869, they joined the rails at Promontory Point, Utah. As Leland Stanford, one of the directors of the Central Pacific, drove a golden spike to symbolize the linkup, railroad workers and directors alike cheered wildly in

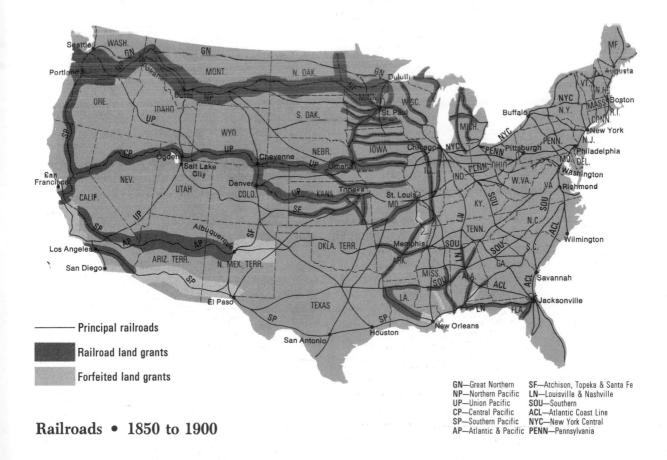

Principal railroads
Railroad land grants
Forfeited land grants

Railroads • 1850 to 1900

GN—Great Northern SF—Atchison, Topeka & Santa Fe
NP—Northern Pacific LN—Louisville & Nashville
UP—Union Pacific SOU—Southern
CP—Central Pacific ACL—Atlantic Coast Line
SP—Southern Pacific NYC—New York Central
AP—Atlantic & Pacific PENN—Pennsylvania

JOINING OF THE UNION PACIFIC AND CENTRAL PACIFIC RAILROAD LINES AT PROMONTORY POINT, UTAH, MAY 10, 1869.

THIS ADVERTISEMENT FOR THE UNION PACIFIC RAILROAD BOASTS AN OMAHA-TO-SAN FRANCISCO RUN "IN LESS THAN FOUR DAYS, AVOIDING THE DANGERS OF THE SEA!" (Smithsonian Institution)

the most dramatic scene in the history of American railroading.

Other transcontinental lines followed. The directors of the Central Pacific established the Southern Pacific, originating at San Francisco and terminating at New Orleans. The Atchison, Topeka and Santa Fe was extended from Atchison, Kansas, to San Diego, California, and linked up with the Southern Pacific in New Mexico. In 1883 the Northern Pacific began carrying passengers and freight between the Twin Cities, Minneapolis–St. Paul, and Portland, Oregon. And in 1893 the Great Northern line crossed the continent from Duluth, Minnesota, to Seattle, Washington.

Financing the Railroads

Railroad building consumed enormous amounts of money. The long construction period brought no financial return and, once completed, the lines were expensive to operate and maintain. In 1890 America's railroads were worth more than $8 billion, owed more than $5 billion, and took in revenue exceeding $1 billion. To fund such a monumental enterprise the railroad companies sold shares to private individuals and institutions, including banks. So many foreign investors put money into United States railroads that by 1907 over one-fourth of their entire value was held by Europeans.

Government policies also aided railroad development. State and local governments offered money, land, and sometimes tax-exempt status to railroad companies in exchange for connecting their lines with the major rail arteries. Railroad builders also received millions of dollars in interest-free cash loans from the federal treasury and approximately 135 million acres in land grants. Companies that received the usual grants of ten square miles, alternating in checkerboard pattern on either side of each mile of track, did more than just build railroads across the free land. They upped their profits by logging some of their forest land and selling off other acreage.

Railroad Tycoons and Abuses

Such enticements lured the ambitious and sometimes the unscrupulous. The notorious speculator and swindler, Jay Gould, for example, was a railroad tycoon who had no interest in building railroads. Instead, Gould approached railroading as he had other enterprises (such as cornering the gold market in 1869), with the goal of amassing a fortune by whatever means it took. In one instance, he even cheated his own line, the Erie Railroad, out of millions of dollars. Gould and his piratical partners, Daniel Drew and flashy "Jubilee" Jim Fisk, were supposed allies of steamboat millionaire and railroader "Commodore" Cornelius Vanderbilt. But Vanderbilt, owner of the New York Central Railroad and a ruthless operator himself, was eager to obtain control of Gould's line and began buying up Erie stock. Gould and his cohorts kept him from gaining a controlling interest by making available for sale several times more stock than the railroad was worth—a maneuver called "stock watering." Vanderbilt bought huge quantities of Erie stock but never managed to obtain control. Eventually the two sides fought it out in court and Gould was finally forced into the position of having to make huge

payoffs to state legislators in order to legitimize the printing of the watered stock. The railroad, however, was the real loser. Left high and dry with millions of dollars of watered stock, it never recovered.

Gould next acquired the Kansas Pacific Railroad simply for its nuisance value. Because the Kansas Pacific competed with the Union Pacific, Gould improved his line and announced his intention of extending it farther into Union Pacific territory. The Union Pacific was forced to pay Gould a high price for the line to end this threat. Gould then spent the next several years building branch lines which tied into the Union Pacific and buying up lines which extended through the Southwest into California. By 1890 he controlled nine thousand miles of track. The system was poorly constructed and charged shippers outrageous rates for its use.

James J. Hill, by contrast, was probably the best example of a public-spirited railroad builder. He too made a fortune, but not at the expense of the line he headed. Hill not only extended his Great Northern Railroad from Minnesota to the West Coast, he took personal pride in its performance. He even directed his work gangs as they laid the tracks. Once, when aboard a train stopped by a snowdrift, he jumped out of his car and wielded a shovel along with his hired hands. Concerned for the welfare of the people along the Great Northern route, he lent money to farmers, imported British bulls to improve native cattle, and paid experts to give free demonstrations of farming methods.

Despite his integrity and civic-mindedness, Hill was drawn by the unregulated competition of the time into condoning the use of violence. Challenged by railroad builder Edward H. Harriman over the right to run tracks along the Columbia River, Hill ordered his lawyers and workers to resist. Violent battles erupted on the banks of the Columbia, wild melées fought with picks, shovels, and crowbars. The confrontations ended only after the courts decided in Hill's favor.

The struggle between Hill and Harriman typified one of the chief problems of the railroad era: too many railroads were built, creating conflicts as various lines competed for the same trade. Overexpansion often ended in bankruptcies. During the 1870s some 450 failures spread economic disaster not only among railroad owners and investors, but also among railroad workers thrown out of jobs, as well as among businesspeople and farmers.

Struggling desperately to survive in an overcrowded industry, many railroad directors resorted to discriminatory practices. The most notorious tactic was the use of the rebate, by which a railroad would return ("kick back") part of a large company's shipping costs in exchange for receiving all of its freight business. In 1869, for example, the Lake Shore Railroad agreed to give John D. Rockefeller rebates on shipments of oil to Cleveland. The Lake Shore line immediately began to prosper, while the Cleveland refineries competing with Rockefeller declined. This pattern was repeated over and over throughout the country by other industries.

Another sort of practice took place where a railroad had no nearby rival line. Thus unchallenged, it would charge as much as the traffic would bear. Hence the so-called long- and short-haul abuse: a short journey where no competition existed would cost more than a long one where two or more lines competed for the same business.

During the 1870s and 1880s railroad interests, fearful that the bitter rivalry between various lines would lead to their ruin, tried to regulate their industry by forming pools in which a number of companies agreed to share the traffic rather than to compete for it. But such agreements had no binding force. Some companies did not want to give up the system of kickbacks; others preferred to continue to charge as much as they could regardless of the hardships this caused shippers and competing railroads. Even when pools were in effect, agreements by the railroads to charge high rates made the practice unpopular. Many people also were opposed to pools as an undue restraint on trade.

Railroads also were caught up in graft. Construction companies controlled by the same people who ran the railroads often voted themselves large contracts. As a result, some lines were so heavily laden with debts that they went bankrupt. Stock watering was a common way for railroads to pay their expenses and camouflage their earnings. So much stock was issued without being backed by an equivalent amount of equipment that by 1890, less than one-half the country's railroad stocks paid dividends. These practices not only hurt the public and the railroads, they also led to corruption in public

THE GRANGE AWAKENING THE SLEEPERS, AN 1873 CARTOON, SHOWS THE GRANGE ATTEMPTING TO ROUSE THE PUBLIC TO THE DANGERS OF THE ONCOMING "CONSOLIDATION TRAIN."

life, for officials were routinely bribed to ignore abuses. The silence of many influential people was bought with free train passes.

The Public Protests The public eventually lost patience with such practices. Shippers attacked the discriminatory charges and rebates. Farmers resented their helplessness against railroad abuses when there was only one line available to them. The depression of the 1870s prodded farmers into using their social organization, the Grange, as a means of mobilizing farm sentiment against railroad policies. Farmers called on state governments to establish a schedule of maximum rates, prohibit greater charges for short hauls than for long ones, forbid the consolidation of parallel lines, and eliminate free passes for public officials. To secure these demands the Grangers turned out in large numbers on election days to vote officials into office who were favorable to their cause. Several states appointed commissions to examine railroad practices, and Illinois, Wisconsin, Minnesota, and Iowa passed "Granger laws" to protect the public interest.

The Supreme Court Response The railroads counterattacked by challenging state regulatory legislation in the courts, with several cases reaching the Supreme Court. The Court at first upheld the Granger laws. In *Munn* v. *Illinois* (1877), for example, the Court ruled that an Illinois law that put a ceiling on warehousing rates for grain was a constitutional exercise of the state's police power to regulate business that involved "a public interest." In the absence of federal legislation on the subject, the state had a right to act. Within a decade, however, the Court had become dominated by justices who, like the business community, believed in a laissez-faire economy. The Granger laws went against the prevailing idea that government control of business was an improper interference with the laws of economics. In *Wabash, St. Louis and Pacific Railroad Co.* v. *Illinois* (1886) the Court reversed itself and ruled that state governments could not prohibit long- and short-haul practices, because only the federal government had the authority to regulate interstate commerce.

Over the next few years the Supreme Court handed down other rulings that further hampered state regulation of business. It broadened the interpretation of the Fourteenth Amendment to include corporations by declaring that a corporation was legally a "person" and could not be deprived of its property without due process of law. The Court contended that state regulatory legislation might so limit the use of a business or railroad's property as to be unreasonable. In such cases, it asserted, due process would have been denied. Thus, state regulations pertaining to corporations would require review by the courts when they involved the question of denial of property under the Fourteenth Amendment; the state legislatures alone could not decide matters of social and economic policy.

The Interstate Commerce Act Despite Supreme Court rulings against state regulation of the railroads, public pressure mounted for some kind of national supervision of what was considered a public utility. Under pressure, Congress began to investigate the possibility of legislating national control of the vital rail transportation network. In 1887 it passed the Interstate Commerce Act, under which all rates were to be reasonable and trains crossing state lines were prohibited from giving rebates or charging higher fares for short hauls than for long ones. Pools were also declared to be illegal. Power to enforce the act was given to a five-member Interstate Commerce Commission (ICC).

This was the first time the federal government had attempted to regulate business practices. But all ICC orders were subject to review by the courts, and fifteen out of the first sixteen cases brought to the Supreme Court under the law from 1897 to 1906 were decided in favor of the railroads.

Industrialization and Consolidation

An indispensable contribution to the country's great industrial growth was made by a few individuals possessing shrewd vision, business genius, and driving ambition who consolidated small businesses until they largely overshadowed their competition. There were outstanding leaders in the steel and oil industries and also in banking, as the large financial concerns moved into the area of directing business consolidation as well as supplying capital for it.

Unlike the mining entrepreneurs in the West, few of these wealthy industrialists rose from humble origins. Many of them liked to tell themselves that this was the case, but more often the industrial and financial giants had the advantage of comfortable beginnings. In the late nineteenth century, of fifty-one railroad magnates, twenty-one had attended college, and all but six had attended high school; of three hundred business leaders in all fields, most were native-born Americans whose fathers had been businessmen. The majority came from homes of above-average income, and most never worked before they were eighteen years old.

Rockefeller and the Rise of Trusts

When drillers in Pennsylvania struck the first oil gusher in 1859, thousands of Americans rushed to the petroleum-bearing areas of the state hoping to strike it rich. A shrewd young man by the name of John D. Rockefeller was one of those who went into the oil fields to see whether the find was worth exploiting commercially. Although the new industry was highly unstable, Rockefeller, influenced by geological reports of immense underground oil reservoirs,

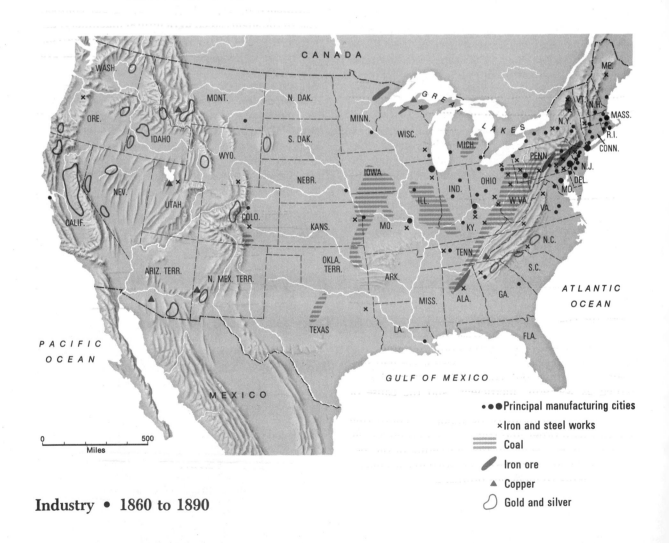

Industry • 1860 to 1890

Legend:
- ●●● Principal manufacturing cities
- × Iron and steel works
- ≡ Coal
- ⟋ Iron ore
- ▲ Copper
- ◯ Gold and silver

returned to his Cleveland home convinced that here was a splendid new business opportunity. He was already earning healthy profits in a thriving produce business, but he persuaded his two partners to add their capital to his to start a new venture: an oil refinery. In 1870 they founded Standard Oil of Ohio.

From the outset Rockefeller was determined to outmaneuver his competitors by keeping ample money reserves to use whenever an oil company wanted to sell out. Moreover, in an effort never to be at the mercy of banks, he made himself and his partners their own bankers, able to act instantly to finance their undertakings. This policy paid off to an astonishing degree. When the Panic of 1873 forced other oil companies into bankruptcy, Standard Oil bought them out with cash made available through Rockefeller's foresight. Those who struggled to survive were usually forced out of business by Rockefeller's strong-arm tactics. He raised the rebate system to a fine art, forcing the railroads to carry crude oil to his refineries at a much lower rate than anyone else was charged, and even getting them to pay him rebates on his competitors' freight! Before long, Rockefeller had completely taken over the oil business in the Cleveland area and massive parts of it elsewhere. In addition he gained control of everything his business depended on, including pipelines. As one historian pointed out, "In 1879, the Standard Oil interests were the only bona-fide buyers, the only gatherers, and the only refiners of all but 10 percent of the petroleum of the country."

Rockefeller put the capstone on his financial empire in 1882 by drawing into the huge Standard Oil trust some thirty-nine separate oil-refining concerns. The "trust" was a new corporate arrangement that placed the stock of a number of businesses under the control of a single board of trustees. By forming the Standard Oil trust Rockefeller dominated 95 percent of the production, refining, and marketing of oil in the United States. He had succeeded in wiping out competition, which he regarded as wasteful, inefficient, and the cause of higher prices. He maintained that he had greatly improved the oil industry by replacing conflicting interests with order and stability. To his credit, he did increase efficiency in the marketing of oil, cut production costs, and lower the price to consumers. While making tremendous profits, he also provided a pension system for his employees. However, Standard Oil made no further important technological improvements in petroleum production before the turn of the century.

In an era of laissez-faire capitalism, Rockefeller was not disturbed by the fact that he had built a business empire by mercilessly ruining competitors who stood in the way of ever-higher profits. A devout Baptist who regularly contributed 10 percent of his wealth to his church, he explained his phenomenal rise by stating that "The good Lord gave me my money."

The oil business was not the only industry moving toward consolidation. By 1900 large corporations dominated American enterprise, with two-thirds of all manufactured goods being produced by giant companies. Small businesses had grown to prominence by expanding or buying out competitors. In the sugar, steel, agricultural machinery, and meat-packing industries as well as in oil a single concern controlled 50 percent or more of the total production. Many large businesses owned their own sources of raw materials and transportation and marketing facilities. Tobacco, leather, and sugar followed Rockefeller's lead and organized as trusts. The reasons for this trend are perhaps obvious. A

A FIRM BELIEVER IN THE THEORY OF SURVIVAL OF THE FITTEST, ROCKEFELLER EXPLAINED "THE AMERICAN BEAUTY ROSE CAN BE PRODUCED IN THE SPLENDOR AND FRAGRANCE WHICH BRING CHEER TO ITS BEHOLDER ONLY BY SACRIFICING THE EARLY BUDS WHICH GROW UP AND AROUND IT.

consolidated enterprise could better exploit the enormous market created by the railroads and growing urban areas and could claim to bring about greater efficiency. Finally, most important to the trust, they could effectively eliminate competition.

The Morgan Influence

Rockefeller's financial self-sufficiency was the exception in the world of big business. The heavy capital demands of railroad and industrial expansion created a need for more sophisticated methods of financing corporate enterprise. Many industries came to depend on bankers for marketing their securities. By 1900 about one dozen investment banking firms dominated the money market.

At the outbreak of the Civil War, the House of Morgan, an American investment banking firm, was already a leader in the international money market. Junius S. Morgan had made a fortune in London handling funds for businesses that needed an astute banker in what was then the financial capital of the world. His son, John Pierpont, soon demonstrated that he had inherited his father's ability to make money grow. In an era of unprecedented concentrations of liquid capital, Morgan became the master of high finance, ultimately dominating banking as well as a number of other businesses.

J. P. Morgan pioneered the movement of finance capital into the country's basic industries and public utilities in the 1890s. He sold stocks and bonds and helped his clients run their businesses. To promote market stability, Morgan often advised businesses to form trusts, which he viewed as a remedy for inefficiency.

It was these ideas that prompted him to enter the highly competitive railroad business. Starting with several small bankrupt lines, he became an expert in reorganizing railroads to promote cooperation. He stopped a feud between the Central and Pennsylvania lines by persuading each to sell the other a subordinate competing line. Such arrangements earned him the title "Doctor of Wall Street" to the "sick" railroad industry. Eventually, he led a systematic and general reorganization of the industry in order to end the ruinous competition with which it was plagued. In 1889 he summoned a group of railroad magnates to New York, where he had them form a committee to regulate their dealings with one another. Any line that defied commit-

tee decisions would find that it could not get bank loans from any of the Morgan banks.

The Morgan group did not take over the railroad industry, but its members controlled enough lines to bring stability to the system as a whole. Management improved because the bankers who moved onto the boards of directors aimed to make the lines profitable through sound financial methods. Passengers were offered higher standards of service, and shippers found that they could depend on promised rates and schedules. Thus, changes within the railroad industry came not from government regulation, but from self-regulation under the direction of bankers.

But the immense power of the major financiers created new cause for public alarm. In addition to financing the mergers or reorganizations of businesses, the House of Morgan and rival investment houses, such as Kuhn, Loeb and Company, saw to it that the banking house had a representative on the boards of directors of these new organizations. A small group of financiers thus obtained vast power in determining the policies of America's great corporations.

The Steel Monopoly

While Morgan was becoming the most powerful banker in the country and Rockefeller was taking over the oil industry, a small, dapper Scottish immigrant named Andrew Carnegie was making a similar impact on the production of steel.

Andrew Carnegie was a young boy when his family immigrated to America. He first found work as a bobbin boy in a cotton mill and then as a telegraph messenger. From there he rose to the position of train dispatcher and then private secretary to the president of the Pennsylvania Railroad. At twenty-eight he became a divisional superintendent of the railroad. With the profits from his investments in Pullman stock, he founded a bridge-construction company and then gained control of the Union Iron Mills. Although he was now earning $50,000 a year, Carnegie switched his investments to the new steel industry, opening his first steelworks in Pennsylvania in 1873. Always looking for ways to cut his costs, Carnegie recognized the value of the new Bessemer process of producing steel cheaply by blowing hot air through molten iron ore. When the more efficient open-hearth system was developed,

Rockefeller as Robber Baron

"Very often people who admit the facts, who are willing to see that Mr. Rockefeller has employed force and fraud to secure his ends, justify him by declaring, "It's business." That is, "it's business" has come to be a legitimate excuse for hard dealing, sly tricks, special privileges. . . . Now if the Standard Oil Company were the only concern in the country guilty of the practices which have given it monopolistic power, this story never would have been written. . . . But it is simply the most conspicuous type of what can be done by these practices. The methods it employs with such acumen, persistency, and secrecy are employed by all sorts of business men, from corner grocers up to bankers. If exposed, they are excused on the ground that this is business. . . . "

Ida M. Tarbell, *The History of the Standard Oil Company,* 1904

Rockfeller as Innovator

"The life of Rockfeller, we can say again, is not one which invites swift and dogmatic judgments. The lessons which men draw from it will vary according to the preconceptions with which they approach the subject. Some will give a heavier weight to the debit items in the ledger than others. But it can safely be said that the prime significance of Rockefeller's career lies in the fact, that he was a bold innovator in both industry and philanthropy; that he brought to the first a great unifying idea, which he insisted should be thoroughly tested, and to the second a stronger, more expert, and more enduring type of organization. . . . "

Allan Nevins, *John D. Rockefeller,* published 1959

he quickly adopted it. He held down labor costs by mechanizing as much of the operation as possible, working his employees twelve hours a day, seven days a week, and making his subordinates accountable for every penny spent. Eventually he bought out eight of his rivals and consolidated them into his Carnegie Steel Company. He further strengthened his position in the industry by gaining control of his product from the mining to the marketing. He leased part of the iron-rich Mesabi Range and bought coal fields for fuel and railroads and steamers to carry the iron ore from Minnesota to his Pennsylvania steel mills. His became the largest and wealthiest concern in a booming industry.

Ready to retire in 1901 at the age of sixty-five, Carnegie devised a shrewd plan to sell his steelworks to J. P. Morgan. Knowing all the while that he planned to retire, Carnegie threatened to intrude on Morgan's territory, steel pipe tubing, unless Morgan offered him the right price. Fearing possible ruin from such a formidable competitor, many investors connected with Morgan's Federal Steel Company appealed to him to make a deal with Carnegie. After exhaustive negotiations, Morgan finally agreed to buy out Carnegie for over $400 million.

Carnegie retired to his castle in Scotland and turned to philanthropic work.

Morgan began incorporating the Carnegie Steel Company into the mighty United States Steel Corporation, which controlled 70 percent of the country's steel industry and included the Federal Steel Company and numerous banking and railroad interests. With Carnegie out of the picture, Morgan dominated Wall Street and through it the business life of the United States as no one had ever done before. According to a joke then current, God created the world in 4004 B.C. and J. P. Morgan reorganized it in A.D. 1901 when he formed United States Steel.

Views of Big Business

The attitudes of Americans toward big business were almost always ambivalent. On the one hand, people wanted to invest and see their investments succeed. They needed, indeed demanded, services and conveniences that could be provided cheaply only by large concerns. They admired the efficiency afforded by industrial and financial consolidation and recognized the benefits the public derived in the long run. Moreover, they looked upon the fabu-

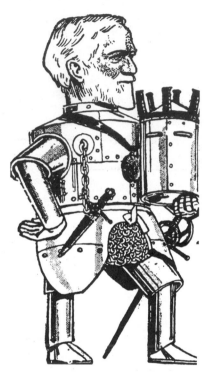

ANDREW CARNEGIE, STEEL KING, AS SEEN
BY A CARTOONIST IN 1903.

JOHN D. ROCKEFELLER PASSING OUT PENNIES TO A SUNDAY SCHOOL CHILD.

lously wealthy industrialists as models of what could be achieved under capitalism. On the other hand, there were those who criticized the leaders of big business as ruthless exploiters who were undermining free competition and whose methods would not bear close examination. Historian Matthew Josephson called them the "robber barons," a term that has become part of the American lexicon.

The industrialists themselves believed that their success and their methods were appropriate. They were deeply committed to the system of laissez-faire capitalism which they viewed as rewarding their individual initiative and unique talent. They saw themselves motivated not by greed, but by the desire to achieve success and to impose their wills on a specific environment. When criticism of his business tactics mounted in the late nineteenth century, John

D. Rockefeller was puzzled. "There has been nothing in my life," he said confidently, "that will not bear the utmost scrutiny." Big business was the great game of the late nineteenth century. A few individuals gradually dominated the game while continuing to talk about an era of open and equal competition that was long since past.

Aside from the challenge of the game and the lure of increased profits, the economic realities of the times encouraged the trend toward monopoly. Extreme competition was ruining all but the biggest and hardiest. Rate wars in the railroad industry had led to the failure of many companies. The increasing costs of machinery and plants for large-scale production meant heavy capital investments, which could only be met by the large entrepreneur. The overhead costs of labor and advertising were more easily met by large companies. Finally, the utilization of manufacturing byproducts, as in the slaughtering of beef, required the resources of large companies.

The Gospel of Wealth

Since the success of a few individuals was creating considerable social and economic inequality, the wealthy went to some lengths to justify their position. In 1901 Andrew Carnegie published his philosophy of the rights and obligations of millionaires in a book called *The Gospel of Wealth*.

Carnegie attempted to justify the possession of vast wealth by identifying it with traditional American moral values. He defined liberty as the right to accumulate an unlimited amount of private property through thrift and hard work. However, he did not challenge the position of those wealthy individuals who demanded high protective tariffs, free land grants, or government loans to further their own business ventures. He defined equality as equal opportunity for gain, but tended to oppose any effort made by the state to curtail monopolies. To him, the idea of progress meant ever-increasing production and thus ever-increasing wealth.

Although Carnegie recognized the gulf between the wealthy few and the rest of society, he praised corporate enterprise for raising the economic well-being of the nation as a whole. To his credit, Carnegie also believed that the accumulation of wealth brought with it certain obligations toward society. The successful businessman, he asserted, should set an example of modest living, provide for those dependent on him, and dispense his fortune to better the community.

After he retired, Carnegie began living up to his assertion that money was essentially worthless unless put to work on behalf of humanity. He proceeded to give away most of his fortune funding libraries and universities and establishing numerous foundations and other charitable enterprises. His gospel of wealth was generally accepted by most business interests, big and small. This philosophy was behind much private charity in Carnegie's era and in the years that followed. Part of the wealth of the great industrialists was spent on universities, art galleries, and private foundations for medical and social research.

Social Darwinism

Further justification for laissez-faire capitalism was extracted from the leading scientific thought of the time. English naturalist Charles Darwin's controversial work *On the Origin of Species* was published in 1859, but its influence in the United States was delayed until well after the conclusion of the Civil War. Darwin expounded the theory that animals had evolved through a process of natural selection in which those species best able to adapt to their environment survived and less adaptable species eventually disappeared. This idea has been described as "the survival of the fittest."

The English social philosopher Herbert Spencer, drawing on Darwin, argued against government intervention in business and efforts at social reform. Spencer concluded that competition among humans was a further example of the natural evolutionary process. According to the laws of nature, each person must rely on his or her own capabilities. Those who are naturally strong will inevitably prevail; those who are weak will be pushed aside. Eventually, if natural forces are allowed to hold sway, a better society will emerge. Spencer insisted that state regulation to protect or guide society was a violation of the law of nature. The state existed only to keep order and protect property.

Professor William Graham Sumner of Yale studied the theories of Darwin and Spencer and became America's foremost exponent of what was called Social Darwinism. Sumner roundly condemned any effort at social reform. He even opposed factory legislation and child labor laws on the grounds that they were artificial, "against the constitution of nature." The strong, self-reliant individual would succeed in the natural world of competition for survival. Millionaires were the product of natural selection, and trusts were the outgrowth of the competitive evolution of business enterprise. If these institutions were not interfered with, society would move rapidly toward perfection. People in big business, ignoring the fact that government support had helped them prosper, gratefully accepted the theory of Social Darwinism. They believed that it validated their most cherished convictions. Rockefeller told his Sunday school class:

The growth of a large business is merely a survival of the fittest. . . . The American Beauty rose can be produced in the splendor and fragrance which bring cheer to its beholder only by sacrificing the early buds which grow up around it. This is not an evil tendency in business. It is merely the working out of a law of nature and a law of God.

The Success Myth

A more optimistic concept—the success story—was introduced in fiction for young boys. Unlike Social Darwinism, the success story suggested in the spirit of the Gospel of Wealth that any boy could rise from humble origins by hard work, thrift, honesty, and a generous measure of luck. The most successful creator of this kind of story was Horatio Alger, whose formula in books such as *Pluck and Luck* became a commonplace. Virtue was invariably rewarded by lucky coincidences. The old lady the hero helped across the street would turn out to be a wealthy widow. Recognizing his sterling merit, she would send him to college. Or the infant the hero saves from toppling off a cliff would turn out to be the son of the local banker. The Alger hero would promptly be given a job at the bank, with the chance of becoming a banker himself one day.

Alger informed his juvenile audience that the rich might properly help the poor, echoing a sentiment expressed by both Carnegie and Rockefeller, who felt that they would be judged for the good deeds they performed with their wealth. But although Alger painted the miseries of victims of an urban and industrial society—the newsboys and the widows' children—he taught a generation of young people not to consider social welfare a state or federal responsibility. This idea was generally acceptable because it upheld the traditional American belief that the less fortunate in society were the responsibility of their families or of private charity.

The Sherman Antitrust Act

Despite theoretical and fictional approval of a laissez-faire economic system, there was widespread public protest against the unprecedented concentration of economic power. Under the pressure of public opinion the federal government gradually became concerned that state laws against monopolies were inadequate. In 1890, Congress passed the Sherman Antitrust Act which made it illegal to monopolize trade or to conspire to restrain trade. It declared: "Every contract, combination in the form of trust or otherwise, or conspiracy, in restraint of trade or commerce among the several states, or with foreign nations, is hereby declared to be illegal." The act authorized private persons to go to court to obtain damages for injuries suffered from a trust.

Even with the passage of the act, most of the large trusts continued their operation. In part this was because the law was broadly written and therefore difficult to enforce. Moreover, at the time, government officials were disinclined to use the powers that the act granted them. Corporation lawyers interpreted the phrase "restraint of trade" to their clients' advantage in courts sympathetic to big business. In 1895 the Supreme Court ruled in *United States* v. *E. C. Knight Company* that although the sugar trust controlled virtually the entire production of that commodity, production could not be construed as restraining *trade*. In other words, since the Knight Company's monopoly over the production of sugar had no direct effect on commerce, the company could not be controlled by the federal government.

Since the Supreme Court refused to recognize a connection between manufacturing and commerce, the federal government could not use its powers under the interstate commerce clause of the Constitution to control a monopoly over production.

As a result of the *Knight* case, monopolistic practices in business went on practically unhampered. Even though the Ohio courts managed to break up the Standard Oil Trust in 1892 and put a damper on further trust formation, big business devised a new means of maintaining monopolistic control: the holding company. This involved the creation of a new company which would own enough stock in a number of operating, subsidiary companies to control their policies but which performed no operating functions in its own right. Standard Oil was soon transformed into a holding company, enabling Rockefeller to guide the decisions of the executive boards of his former subsidiaries and to ensure that their policies were favorable to him. Between 1897 and 1903, 234 new business monopolies were formed, including the giant United States Steel Corporation. Not until 1914, with the establishment of the Federal Trade Commission and the passage of the Clayton Antitrust Act, were more rigorous efforts made to end predatory business practices.

Industrialization in the New South

Whereas Northern industry grew rapidly after the Civil War the Southern economy recovered slowly. The antebellum plantation owners had not favored an industrialized South, fearing that it would disrupt their way of life. But the conservative Democrats who came to power after the war felt otherwise. Although agriculture remained of major importance, the South began to realize its industrial potential as well. Henry Grady, editor of the *Atlanta Constitution* and one of the most eloquent representatives of the "New South," declared, "We have sowed towns and cities in the place of theories and put business above politics."

The South possessed an abundance of raw materials that had never really been developed. Now the possibilities of a large logging industry in the Appalachians and of factories drawing their power from the rivers of Tennessee and the Carolinas began to be realized. Geologists discovered coal and iron in Alabama. An economic revival based on these resources seemed promising.

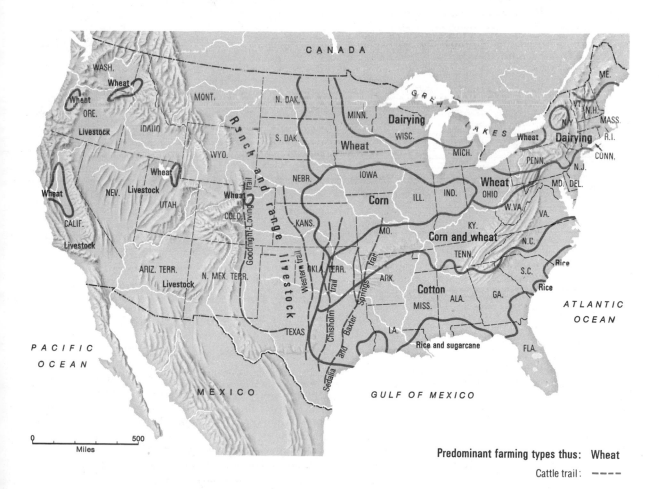

Predominant farming types thus: Wheat

Cattle trail: ----

Agriculture • 1860 to 1890

AT THE TURN OF THE CENTURY SOUTHERN COTTON MILLS OFFERED MUCH-NEEDED EMPLOYMENT TO POOR FAMILIES. PICTURED HERE, SPINDLE BOYS IN A GEORGIA COTTON MILL.

Economic Recovery

Despite newly discovered industrial possibilities, enterprises based on the land were the first to reach prewar levels. Although cotton was no longer the absolute monarch of the South's economy, the cotton fields were flourishing. By 1880 production surpassed the levels reached in 1860. Cotton continued to climb to a record 10 million bales in the mid-1890s. Cotton-based industries grew at the same time. Cotton seed, once thrown away, was discovered to have marketable value in the forms of oil and fertilizer. In the 1890s, Southern cotton mills also multiplied, challenging the cloth manufacturers of New England.

The tobacco industry developed in a spectacular manner under the leadership of such individuals as James B. Duke of Durham, North Carolina. Duke, who understood thoroughly the trust concept worked out by Rockefeller and Morgan, gained control of the tobacco industry in the South and opened an office in New York City to channel his cigarettes, cigars, and pipe and chewing tobacco into the Northern market. He followed the Northern giants' example so closely that in 1911 the federal government brought an antitrust suit against his American Tobacco Company, compelling it to restore independence to two subsidiaries, Reynolds and Lorillard.

Mining gained considerable importance in the South, as Appalachian coal and iron began to be exploited; fifteen years after Appomattox, Southern mines accounted for approximately one-eighth of the nation's coal output. Iron worth $25 million per year was produced by some two hundred foundries. Among the most important were the Tredegar Iron Works in Virginia and the iron industry in Birmingham, Alabama, which by 1890 became known as the "Pittsburgh of the South" because of its easy access to coal and oil.

As was true in the North, the railroads were fundamental to the pattern of Southern industrial development. Alabama iron production could not have expanded so rapidly had it not been for the Louisville and Nashville Railroad and other lines. The revival of Georgia cotton production depended on the rebuilding of the rail network ruined during the Civil War. Between 1865 and 1880 the railroad mileage of the South doubled and doubled again before the turn of the century.

Southern Problems: Lack of Capital and Northern Control

Even with its new industries, the South still lagged far behind the rest of the country in its economic development. As late as 1914, the income of the individual Southerner was only about half the national average. Of all the problems that beset the New South, the self-perpetuating and extremely widespread sharecropping system was perhaps the worst. Once tenant farmers mortgaged their crops in advance, they saw little chance of ever paying off their debts and saving money for their own farms. The large number of such poverty-stricken farmers provided a poor market for a high-powered industrial economy.

Nor was the growth of Southern industry a completely accurate indication of the region's financial health. Much of the money made in the South went to Northern and British investors who had underwritten development costs. Factories, textile mills, steel mills, warehouses, coal mines, railroads, and ships had to be paid for, and the cost was far too high for the Southern states to finance themselves. In order to meet its debts the South avidly courted Northern capital investments. By 1890 Northern investments in the Southern cotton industry were seven times greater than they had been in 1880. Federal lands in the South had been sold to Northerners in large tracts during Reconstruction, and the Southern states continued to sell land at wholesale prices to Northern lumber syndicates and land speculators.

Despite its short-term value as a revenue-raising device, Northern investment created serious problems for the South. Most of the railroads, industries, and banks belonged to absentee owners more interested in earning profits than in improving conditions for the local population. Northern businesses also saw to it that Southern business activity was limited to the handling of raw materials or involvement in the initial stages of processing, so that the final steps in the manufacturing process could take place in the North. Many Southern businesses found that if they tried to produce finished goods, they had trouble borrowing money from Northern banks.

Southern railroads could not adopt a systematic policy to aid their own region, because they depended on Northern funds and took their orders from Northern directors. Freight differentials sometimes openly discriminated against the South. Shippers of raw materials received favorable rates, but those with manufactured goods to sell had to pay more to ship them than did their competitors in the North.

The fact that the South was late in industrializing put the region at a real disadvantage in a national economy controlled by Northern big business. Businesses in Boston, New York, Philadelphia, Cleveland, and Chicago had simply expanded after the Civil War. Those in Richmond, Charleston, Mobile, and New Orleans had to be founded or rebuilt. An Alabama steel company could hardly hope to make a real dent in a national market already controlled by Carnegie. A Louisiana banker could not realistically hope to rival J. P. Morgan. To their credit, Southern businesses were undaunted by this challenge, although they knew that they were cast for a subordinate role in the country's industrial life for some time to come.

The Southern Achievement

In 1900 the Southern states were still essentially agrarian, their urban population amounting to less than 10 percent of the total. Yet cities had been built or rebuilt, and hundreds of settled localities had expanded under the pressure of economic need. The establishment of cotton mills in the cotton-growing areas created much-needed jobs. Impoverished families desperately seeking work came into the mill towns. The men did the heavy work, such as lifting bales onto wagons; the women ran the looms; and the children did whatever odd jobs were available for as little as a dime a day. To many such people, a seventy-hour week, however brutalizing, came as a welcome relief from the grinding poverty of unemployment.

Few people became fabulously wealthy in the South, but some who migrated to the financial capital of the country, New York, achieved notable success. For instance, John H. Inman of Tennessee, a former Confederate soldier, penetrated the inner circle of Wall Street. He was "at thirty-six worth a million and a half," according to Southern journalist Henry Grady. And Adolph Ochs of Chattanooga, Tennessee, transformed the *New York Times* into the nation's leading newspaper.

Readings

General Works

Chandler, Alfred D., Jr., *The Visible Hand: The Managerial Revolution in American Business*. Cambridge, Mass.: Harvard University Press, 1977.

Cochran, Thomas C., and William Miller, *The Age of Enterprise*. New York: Macmillan, 1942.

_____, *200 Years of American Business*. New York: Basic Books, 1977.

Fine, Sidney, *Laissez-Faire and the General Welfare State*. Ann Arbor: University of Michigan Press, 1964.

Fogel, Robert W., *Railroads and American Economic Growth: Essays in Econometric History*. Baltimore: Johns Hopkins, 1970. (Paper)

Higgs, Robert, *The Transformation of the American Economy, 1865–1914*. New York: Wiley, 1971.

Hofstadter, Richard, *Social Darwinism in American Thought*. Boston: Beacon, 1955.

Josephson, Matthew, *The Robber Barons*. New York: Harcourt, Brace, 1934.

Kirkland, Edward C., *Dream and Thought in the American Business Community, 1860–1900*. Ithaca, N.Y.: Cornell University Press, 1956.

_____, *Industry Comes of Age. Business, Labor, and Public Policy, 1860–1897*. New York: Holt, Rinehart & Winston, 1961.

Mitchell, Broadus, and G. S. Mitchell, *The Industrial Revolution in the South*. Westport, Conn.: Greenwood, 1968.

Noble, David F., *America by Design: Science, Technology, and the Rise of Corporate Capitalism*. New York: Knopf, 1977.

Porter, Glenn, *The Rise of Big Business*. Northbrook, Ill.: AHM, 1973.

Wiebe, Robert H., *The Search for Order, 1877–1920*. New York: Hill and Wang, 1966.

Woodward, C. Vann, *The Origins of the New South*. Baton Rouge: Louisiana State University Press, 1951.

Special Studies

Benson, Lee, *Merchants, Farmers and Railroads*. Cambridge, Mass.: Harvard University Press, 1955.

Burns, Rex, *Success in America: The Yeoman Dream and the Industrial Revolution*. Amherst: University of Massachusetts Press, 1976.

Cochran, Thomas C., *Railroad Leaders, 1845–1890: The Business Mind in Action*. New York: Russell, 1966.

Gaston, Paul M., *The New South Creed: A Study in Southern Mythmaking*. New York: Knopf, 1970.

Grodinsky, Julius, *Transcontinental Railway Strategy*. Philadelphia: University of Pennsylvania Press, 1962.

Hidy, Ralph W., and Muriel E. Hidy, *Pioneering in Big Business*. New York: Harper & Row, 1965.

Hughes, Jonathan, *The Vital Few: American Economic Progress and its Protagonists*. New York: Oxford University Press, 1973. (Paper)

Hurst, James W., *Law and the Conditions of Freedom in the Nineteenth-Century United States*. Madison: University of Wisconsin Press, 1956.

Kolko, Gabriel, *Railroads and Regulations, 1877–1916*. Princeton, N.J.: Princeton University Press, 1965.

Lewis, Oscar, *The Big Four*. New York: Knopf, 1938.

McCloskey, Robert G., *American Conservatism in the Age of Enterprise*. Cambridge, Mass.: Harvard University Press, 1951.

Miller, George H., *Railroads and the Granger Laws*. Madison: University of Wisconsin Press, 1971.

Moody, John, *The Truth About the Trusts*. Westport, Conn.: Greenwood, 1960.

Weiss, Richard, *The American Myth of Success*. New York: Basic Books, 1969.

Primary Sources

Adams, Charles F., Jr., and Henry Adams, *Chapters of Erie*. Ithaca, N.Y.: Cornell University Press, 1956.

Chandler, Alfred D., Jr. (Ed.), *The American Railroads*. New York: Harcourt, Brace, 1965.

Diamond, Sigmund (Ed.), *The Nation Transformed: The Creation of Industrial Society*. New York: Braziller, 1963.

Kirkland, Edward P. (Ed.), *The Gospel of Wealth and Other Timely Essays by Andrew Carnegie*. Cambridge, Mass.: Harvard University Press, 1962.

Twain, Mark, and C. D. Warner, *The Gilded Age*. Indianapolis, Ind.: Bobbs-Merrill, 1970.

Biographies

Allen, Frederick Z., *The Great Pierpont Morgan*. New York: Harper & Row, 1949.

Conot, Robert, *Streak of Luck: The Life and Legend of Thomas Alva Edison*. New York: Simon & Schuster, 1979.

Josephson, Matthew, *Edison*. New York: McGraw-Hill, 1959.

Livesay, Harold C., *Andrew Carnegie and the Rise of Big Business*. Boston: Little, Brown, 1975. (Paper)

Martin, Albro, *James J. Hill and the Opening of the Northwest*. New York: Oxford University Press, 1976.

Nevins, Allan, *Study in Power: John D. Rockefeller, Industrialist and Philanthropist*, Vols. I–II. New York: Scribner's, 1953.

Nixon, Raymond B., *Henry W. Grady*. New York: Russell, 1969.

Wall, Joseph F., *Andrew Carnegie*. New York: Oxford University Press, 1970.

Fiction

Dreiser, Theodore, *The Financier*. New York: New American Library, 1967.

———, *The Titan*. New York: New American Library, 1968.

Hay, John, *The Breadwinners*. Upper Saddle River, N.J.: Gregg, 1967.

Howells, William D., *The Rise of Silas Lapham*. New York: Macmillan, 1962.

James, Henry, *The American*. New York: Dell, 1900.

18 The Social and Economic Response to Industrialism

A common argument used by the opponents of the radical industrial reformation . . . is that the condition of the working classes in this country is better than it was a generation or so ago. This, it is argued, ought to be enough to satisfy reasonable workingmen and teach them contentment. As we have often before remarked, this sort of logic entirely misses the point of the industrial reform agitation. It does not turn on the question whether the lot of men is better or worse than it once was, but whether it is as satisfactory as it might be made under entirely new conditions. The workers of the world have at last reached the point of believing and declaring that the best the world can be made to yield is none too good for them.

Edward Bellamy, *The New Nation*, 1891

Significant Events

National Labor Union [1866]

Knights of Labor [1869]

Railway strikes [1877]

American Federation of Labor [1881]

First act to restrict immigration [1882]

Haymarket riot [1886]

Homestead strike [1892]

Pullman strike [1894]

Department of Commerce and Labor [1903]

Dillingham Commission Report [1907]

ITALIAN IMMIGRANT WORKERS BUILDING A TUNNEL IN NEW YORK CITY AT THE TURN OF THE CENTURY.

The revolution in transportation and industry that took place between 1865 and 1900 had a profound effect on millions of Americans. The nationwide railroad system brought new and improved products to people all over the country, and the urbanization which accompanied industrial growth created new economic and cultural opportunities for the middle class. Yet millions of new immigrants who flocked to the United States to escape economic uncertainty and religious oppression in Europe and Asia were all too often exploited anew by American business, victimized by antiforeign bias, and feared by native workers who felt their jobs were being threatened. The new industrial economy also undermined the traditional view that every American had unlimited opportunity for upward mobility. In an attempt to begin to share in the economic abundance of America, workers began to forge the structure of a labor union movement which developed increasing power by the beginning of the twentieth century. If labor unions were the instruments of reform for a growing number of workers, it was social workers and church leaders who made the first efforts to confront the problems that accompanied the growth of America's urban centers—poverty, illiteracy, overcrowding, and political corruption.

The New Immigration

Between 1865 and 1910, twenty-five million immigrants arrived in the United States. The need to escape poverty and persecution was the most important factor behind the mass movement out of Europe that began in the 1860s. Repeated crop failures, low prices, and depressed economies led farmers and farm workers in England, Ireland, the Scandinavian countries, and Germany to come to America. They accounted for almost 90 percent of the newcomers during that decade. Many were attracted by the cheap land available in the West. The Germans and Scandinavians usually settled on farms in the Midwest and the northern Plains and in cities such as Milwaukee, Chicago, and Cincinnati. The British and Irish tended to settle in the cities of the Eastern seaboard. These immigrants were generally easy to assimilate, since their backgrounds were similar to those of most Americans.

By the early 1880s, however, immigration from northern and western Europe began to decline. The growth of industrialization in these nations and a decreasing birthrate coupled with a rising demand for labor encouraged many to stay at home. At the same time, conditions in southern and eastern Europe created a new source of immigrants. Economic changes in parts of Italy and in the Austro-Hungarian Empire created hardships for peasants and farm workers in those areas. Italy was plagued by poor soil, an absence of coal, and a scarcity of manufac-

HESTER STREET ON NEW YORK'S LOWER EAST SIDE WAS HOME TO MANY NEWLY ARRIVED JEWISH IMMIGRANTS.

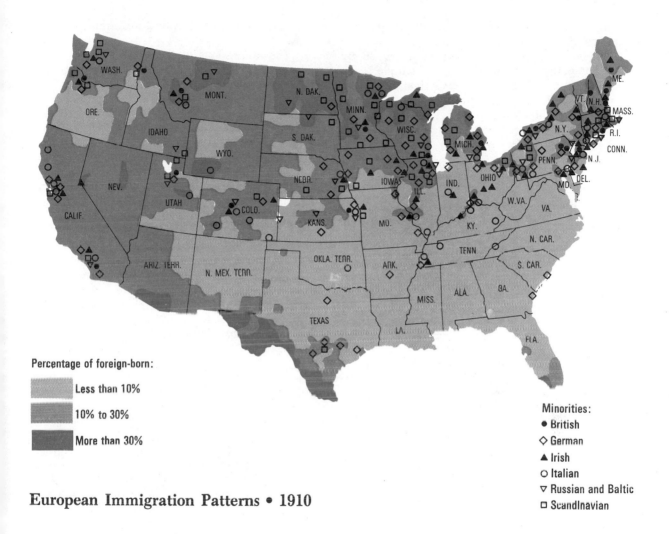

Percentage of foreign-born:

Less than 10%

10% to 30%

More than 30%

Minorities:

● British

◇ German

▲ Irish

○ Italian

▽ Russian and Baltic

□ Scandinavian

European Immigration Patterns • 1910

turing; taxes were high, there was little opportunity for education, and few farmers owned the land they worked. The Slavic peoples of the Austro-Hungarian Empire and Russia also faced poverty and illiteracy. In addition, many people left Russia and eastern Europe to escape persecution for their religious or political beliefs. Russian Jews were harassed by a violent anti-Semitic campaign of pogroms and restrictive laws that began in the 1880s.

Powerful forces in America also encouraged immigration. In the late nineteenth century the country had an increasing need for labor in farming, mining, and manufacturing. Railroads wanted to sell their large landholdings, which meant encour-

aging people to settle the areas they serviced. These industries and the immigration bureaus of the Western states created great advertising campaigns in Europe. American steamship lines cooperated with the advertisers so that they might fill their returning cargo ships with people.

The newcomers had to find jobs as soon as they arrived. Most were of working age, and their desperate financial condition forced them to take low-paying jobs offered by industries that needed cheap labor. Some, known as contract laborers, were even hired in Europe by representatives of American companies. These workers were given their passage over and then paid it back out of payroll deductions during the years they worked for the company, a practice finally outlawed in 1885.

Some immigrant workers were recruited by their compatriots in America. One example is the Italian and the Greek *padrone* system. *Padrones* were ethnic leaders who organized "immigrant banks," or groups of unskilled workers, in their homeland. They arranged passage and provided jobs and housing for a price that would be profitable.

Thus, although most immigrants had come from rural areas, in America they became city dwellers because that was where the economic opportunities were. An exception were the Russian-Germans from the Ukraine, many of whom settled in Nebraska, Kansas, and the Dakotas. But few recent arrivals had the capital to invest in farmland, which was no longer cheap or plentiful. By the early twentieth century the new workers had taken over most of the jobs in the textile and steel mills, the mines, oil refineries, and the manufacturing plants.

Another continuing source of immigrants was nearby Mexico. Cowboys, sheepherders, miners, farm hands, and political refugees arrived steadily, searching for better wages and safety. The long rule of Porfirio Díaz (1876–1911) brought great hardship to Mexico's poor farmers and Indians. Subjected to economic and racial discrimination, thousands left Mexico for the American Southwest. Some Mexican exiles also used the United States as a base for planning a revolution against the Díaz dictatorship, and during the revolution (1910–1920) as many as one million may have fled to the United States to escape the terror and bloodshed. Although some were middle-class businesspeople, most were farm workers who easily found jobs on the expanding cotton and sugar-beet farms in the Southwest and seasonal work in other parts of the country.

The Revival of Nativism

The antiforeign feeling, usually called nativism, that had arisen in the 1840s and 1850s in response to the influx of Irish and German Catholics resurfaced in the 1880s and 1890s. In the pre–Civil War years nativism had several causes. Americans of English Protestant ancestry had a deep-seated fear of the Roman Catholic church. Many Americans had also associated immigrants with radical attacks on government authority, since some of the pre–Civil War immigrants had been involved in European revolutions.

The immigrants of the 1880s and 1890s provoked even greater fear and hostility. In contrast to earlier immigrants, many of these new aliens were swarthy, dark-haired, and strangely costumed. Because of their different appearance and customs it was easy for native-born Americans to brand them as illiterate and dirty and to look down on them for being poor, for living together in slum communities, and for preserving strange customs. Their higher birthrate made some people fear that old-stock Americans would soon be outbred and outvoted.

Fear of foreign radicalism and subversion was another powerful force in creating prejudice. Many of the new immigrants had come from countries that did not have representative governments, leading some Americans to suspect that they were radicals or subversives who wanted to overthrow the capitalist economy. Many employers claimed that the immigrants were "anarchists and communists," thus reinforcing the hostility already felt by other Americans.

Native-born workers often greeted the new immigrants with hostility. They regarded the newcomers, who usually were willing to work for whatever wages they were offered, as a threat to their efforts to secure higher pay. The fact that nearly half of the male immigrants who came to the United States in the late nineteenth and early twentieth centuries returned to their native land after earning some money also aroused the resentment of native American laborers. Labor union leaders felt that immigrants were difficult to organize, because most did not speak English. By the 1880s, however, aliens were joining forces with other workers in labor unions to demand better pay and improved working conditions.

Nativist associations similar to those that had sprung up in the 1840s and 1850s (such as the Know-Nothing party) now began to reappear. Among the most prominent was the American Protective Association (APA), formed in 1887 and soon boasting a million members. The APA's efforts were directed particularly against Catholics and other immigrants from southern and eastern Europe, whom they accused of being clannish, unable to assimilate, and racially inferior. The APA urged voters not to elect Roman Catholics to office. But both the Republicans and the Democrats repudiated the association and leading politicians and the clergy defended the loyalty of American Catholics. Plagued by internal dissension, the APA broke up by 1896.

By the 1890s the popular theory of Social Darwinism was being used to rationalize prejudice by claiming to show that the economic and political success of the United States was the result of the superior mentality of people of Anglo-Saxon background. Writer Henry Pratt Fairchild in his book *The Melting Pot Mistake* maintained that the aliens belonged to "races in a more primitive stage of evolution." He argued that the country must beware "the effects of race mixture," which would be to mongrelize the "superior" Nordic "races." Such diatribes enabled prejudiced people to believe that their bias was the product of clear, scientific thinking.

Early Exclusionary Measures

Early regulation of immigration had been left to the states, but it was no simple matter to check the flow of immigrants, since they could be smuggled in through Mexico or Canada. Eventually antiforeign feeling moved the federal government to act. In 1882 Congress forbade the entry of "undesirables": they included "lunatics, convicts, idiots, and those who might readily become public charges," categories that were expanded by later legislation. In a further effort to discourage immigration, the 1882 law levied a head tax of 50 cents on every person admitted to the country. That same year Dennis Kearney and his Workingmen's party directed a campaign against the Chinese, accusing them of being immoral and of taking jobs from the native-born by working for lower wages than American workers. This hate campaign resulted in the Chinese Exclusion Act of 1882, cutting off all Chinese immigration for ten years. The provisions were extended periodically until 1902, when they became permanent.

Even these two measures were not enough for the extreme exclusionists, who demanded a literacy test that they hoped would exclude further immigration from eastern and southern Europe. Congress obliged in 1897, but President McKinley vetoed the bill, believing that it undermined the ideal of America as a land of opportunity and that the test provided a measure of education, not of intelligence. Pressures in favor of the literacy test intensified,

however, and in 1917 Congress passed a law, over President Wilson's veto, denying admittance to aliens over age sixteen who were unable to read in any language.

The rising tide of feeling against immigrants also prompted Congress to appoint a commission to investigate demands for immigration restriction. The resulting Dillingham Commission Report of 1907 read like a list of the popular complaints against the "new immigration." The charges, now given official government sanction, were nonetheless based on popular fallacies and a biased perspective. The accusation that the immigrants tended to

THE CHINESE WERE AMONG THE EARLIEST VICTIMS OF NATIVIST EXCLUSIONARY MEASURES. THIS 1880 ILLUSTRATION SHOWS A MOB IN DENVER, COLORADO, HARASSING CHINESE WORKERS AND RANSACKING THEIR HOMES.

Immigration: The Prospect

"Praised by Jesus Christus. . . . I inform you that I intend to emigrate to America where I have many friends, for the most part relatives, who write that I can come to them and they will find work for me. . . . I know only one handicraft, carpenter's. I practiced with a country carpenter, but at the present time it is very difficult to find material, and therefore difficult to earn. . . .

I know how to read and I read many books and papers, *Gios Ludu, Lud Bozy* and others [popular religious papers]. I also know something about writing, as you can see from this letter. I have been to some monthly agricultural courses in Lublin, where I learned a little about the science of agriculture and model farming. . . . I hope if I live to try with all my strength to organize a model farm but now, because of lack of money and because my father has still a debt, it is difficult to make practical improvements in any way or to buy agricultural machines, which are very dear."

Thomas and Zuanieki, *The Polish Peasant in Europe and America, 1918–1920*

Immigration: The Reality

"It is mainly the immigrant and the children of the immigrant who swell the ranks of [the] indigent element in our great cities. Those who are poverty stricken are not necessarily parasitic. . . . If through continued poverty they become truly parasitic, then they pass over to the ranks of the criminal, the pauper, the vicious, the indolent and the vagrant, who, like the industrial class, seek the cities.

The dangerous effects of city life on immigrants and their children cannot be too strongly emphasized. This country can absorb millions of all races from Europe and can raise them and their descendants to relatively high standards of American citizenship in so far as it can find places for them on the farms. . . ."

John R. Commons, 1904

congregate in clans in the cities overlooked the fact that except for the few who became farmers, they had no choice. Discrimination in jobs and housing made it impossible for them to move out of their city ghettos. The assertion that many were unskilled could also have been made concerning the earlier immigrants. Moreover, the charge that they were unassimilable has not been borne out by the facts. In the 1870s the Irish, Germans, and Scandinavians actively began to influence American politics, challenging the dominance of those of Anglo-Saxon ancestry. Later, Italians, Poles, and Jews all took their place in America's political, economic, and social life.

Japanese Exclusion The Japanese began immigrating to the United States in 1885. By 1910 there were seventy-two thousand Japanese living in the United States, most of whom were concentrated in the Pacific Coast states. Nativists, who had already successfully excluded the Chinese, were alarmed at this new influx of Orientals and determined to prevent any more Japanese from entering. Like the Chinese, Japanese laborers were accused of taking jobs from Americans by their willingness to work for low wages. Japanese success in farming was another source of antagonism. The Japanese had bought some of the richest farmlands on the West Coast. In fact, although they owned less than 2 percent of the land in that area, Japanese farmers dominated the production of tomatoes, spinach, strawberries, celery, onions, and cantaloupes. They incurred further animosity for refusing to give up their Japanese citizenship.

The crisis came to a boil in the aftermath of the San Francisco earthquake and fire of 1906. The San Francisco school board took advantage of the unrest and dislocation of the economy caused by the disaster to order that because of space problems, Japanese children must attend special schools. The Japanese were outraged by this insult to their children, and irresponsible rumors of war splashed the newspaper headlines in both countries. President Theodore Roosevelt, eager to resolve the issue because Japan was a rising world power, made an arrangement with Japan in 1907–1908 known as the Gentlemen's Agreement, under which Japan would voluntarily restrict the emigration of its nationals to the United States. In the meantime, the California school authorities were persuaded to drop their discriminatory rule. Despite the fact that the Japanese government scrupulously observed the "Gentlemen's Agreement," a number of Japanese laborers illegally entered the United States by crossing the Mexican and Canadian borders. Americans on the West Coast continued to harass the Japanese, whom they considered to be unassimilable and an economic threat. By 1920 the Japanese were legally prohibited from leasing or buying land in California.

Labor Conditions

The steady arrival of huge numbers of immigrants and the continuing high birthrate among native-born Americans fueled the nation's industrial labor force in the second half of the nineteenth century. Both immigrant workers and farm laborers flocked to the cities—the immigrants, because they were too poor to move on, the farm workers because the increasing mechanization of farming decreased the number of jobs available to them and because they wanted to escape the tedium and isolation of farm life. By the end of the nineteenth century only about one-third of the country's workers remained on the farms. More women joined the labor force than ever before, supplying cheap labor for factories and working as clerical staff in business offices. The number of working children under the age of fifteen also increased rapidly as the demand grew for workers in textile mills, coal mines, and meat-packing houses.

As the American economy became increasingly industrial, workers had to adjust to the tempo of a factory system run by huge corporations. Whereas smaller businesses had been based on personal relationships between employer and employee, the growth of giant corporations put an end to this kind of contact. The ability of laborers as individuals to improve their wages, hours, and working conditions through face-to-face negotiations with their employers was all but destroyed. Laborers, looking to one another for assistance, began forming unions to strengthen their position. Ultimately they challenged powerful employers by using strikes and boycotts, as well as by pressuring legislators for improved labor laws.

Wages and Working Conditions

The prevailing attitude of management toward labor in the Age of Big Business is summed up in the remark: "I regard my work people just as I regard my machinery!" Employers assumed that it was their right to decide how labor should be used. They viewed labor as a commodity to be bought at the cheapest price and maintained at minimal expense. They encouraged competition among workers in an effort to prevent them from joining together, and they blacklisted troublemakers so that they could not gain employment elsewhere.

Management's high-handed attitude was probably the strongest incentive toward unified action among workers. Workers began to realize that their profit-minded employers were indifferent to their needs and that it was becoming increasingly difficult for workers to rise in the organization or to earn enough money to go into business for themselves. Organized labor therefore began to concentrate its efforts on solving workers' immediate problems: low wages, the long workday, and unsafe conditions.

To gain a clear picture of the economic position of the American wage earner in the late nineteenth century, it is important to make certain distinctions. Statistics show that the average non–farm worker's yearly income was rising steadily; by the early twentieth century, it had reached $700, with some workers earning over $1000 a year. These figures generally apply to white, male, native-born skilled workers, who probably comprised nearly one-half the urban labor force. This group of workers usually owned their own homes and possessed some addi-

CHILD LABORERS WORKING THE NIGHT SHIFT (5 p.m. TO 3 a.m.) IN A GLASS FACTORY. MOLDER BOYS REPLACED
ADULT MALE WORKERS WHO COMPLAINED THAT THE WORK WAS TOO HOT.

tional comforts. At the same time, they worked long hours at jobs that were often dangerous and subject to layoffs.

The Unskilled Worker Unskilled workers, new immigrants, women, and blacks faced harsher working conditions and subsistence-level wages (approximately $500 a year). Women were paid about half as much as men, and blacks earned lower wages and had less job security than white workers—male or female—in both the North and South. Recent immigrants were paid even less than native-born unskilled workers. As a result, whole families, including children, were forced to work. Nevertheless, recent research on the Jewish and Italian immigrants in New York City between 1880 and 1915 shows that because of the city's expanding economy about 32 percent of these immigrants were able to move from unskilled to skilled jobs. For all these less privi-

leged groups, food was simple and monotonous, clothes were cheaply made, and furniture consisted of the bare necessities. It was virtually impossible for people in these circumstances to accumulate savings and pensions were unheard of. After years of toil workers frequently were left with a few hundred dollars and a small piece of property. Many older workers eventually were forced to move in with their children.

Black Americans faced special hardships. Hampered by poor educational backgrounds and discrimination in hiring and promotion, most blacks were relegated to a low economic position. Although 56 percent of the over three million employed black people were Southern sharecroppers or poorly paid farm laborers, another 31 percent were domestic servants, waiters, cooks, porters, launderers, and barbers. Only 12.7 percent of black Americans were employed in factories, in trade, or in one of the professions such as law or medicine. While women and children were a significant percentage of the work force in low-paying jobs, working black women and children outnumbered their white counterparts. For example, in 1890 46 percent of white Americans ten years of age or older were employed while the number of blacks in this category was 57 percent. And while 36 percent of black women had jobs, only 15 percent of white women were working.

Before the industrial revolution reached its height most white women who did work outside the home served as domestics in the homes of those with higher incomes. By the early twentieth century, however, black women had come to dominate this occupation, as more factory work became available to white native-born and immigrant women. Large numbers of women were hired as factory workers because of the scarcity of labor and because they could be hired for less than men. Thousands of unskilled immigrant women worked long hours for low wages in New England textile mills and the sweatshops of New York and Philadelphia.

Factory Conditions For men and women alike, the conditions in factories were deplorable. Safety precautions were few, regulations were rarely enforced, and compensation for accidents was almost nonexistent. Most employers could avoid paying damages for accidents that occurred on the job by claiming that the accident was the result of the worker's own negligence. Many workers were constantly exposed to chemicals, dust, and other pollutants. In 1860 the average workweek was sixty-six hours long. By 1910, although the national average had declined to fifty-five hours a week, workers in many industries still labored seventy hours a week; at that time there was no sick leave and no paid vacations.

Moreover, as the Industrial Revolution took hold in post–Civil War America, the preference of work over leisure which had characterized an earlier, more egalitarian era began to decline. Despite Horatio Alger stories and Sunday sermons, the drudgery and monotony of factory life gradually undermined the belief that work in itself was noble. While American society has continued to be work-oriented, the concept of leisure—and the desire for more of it—was a consequence of the transformation of the American economy in the late nineteenth century.

Union Movement

Despite the obvious need for organized efforts to protect their interests, workers often quarreled about objectives and how to achieve them. Yet as they became increasingly angry over their small share of America's great wealth, they became convinced that solidarity was the only way to fight the industrial giants. Most workers did not belong to unions, but more and more began joining.

Although in small towns the people and press knew the workers and their grievances and often were sympathetic to them, in large cities the workers were unknown and usually viewed with hostility. Opponents of labor unions looked on them as a conspiracy which interfered with laissez-faire capitalism and hampered the country's economic growth. The business community and the public were both impatient with strikes, which occurred with increasing frequency after a secret organization of workers known as the Molly Maguires led violent strikes in the coalfields of Pennsylvania in the early 1870s. The public was usually unsympathetic to the complaints of workers, arguing that they were, after all, among the highest paid in the world. In addition, the public often applied its prejudice against foreigners to people in the labor movement, accusing organizers of being radicals who used the strike to undermine American economic and political stability. At the same time, ethnic and racial prejudices among native-born white workers were intensified when businesses used immigrants and blacks as strikebreakers.

The National Labor Union

The first national union of industrial workers was formed—despite many difficulties—in 1866. The National Labor Union (NLU) attempted to organize the members of various unions made up of skilled craft workers and reform groups into a giant federation. By the early 1870s the NLU had some three hundred thousand members whose goals included the organization of producer and consumer cooperatives, the improvement of society through education, temperance, and women's rights, and the establishment of an eight-hour workday. The NLU's leaders tried to include blacks in their membership, but the white workers' hostility prevented black people from joining. In response, blacks formed the Colored National Labor Convention.

Despite its contribution to the successful effort to secure the eight-hour workday for federal employees in 1868, the NLU encountered a number of setbacks. It never really encouraged its members to develop a sense of solidarity, so many workers soon lost interest in the union. Attempts to form cooperative stores also failed. In 1872 the NLU entered politics as the National Labor Reform party, but the depression following the Panic of 1873 led to its collapse.

Effects of Depression: 1873–1878

Labor was badly hurt by the depression of the 1870s. Although unskilled immigrants were hardest hit, all workers were forced to compete for jobs at very low wages, and union activity dwindled. Whole communities were thrown out of work in the small, single-industry mill and mining towns. And although the diversity of jobs available in the city

forestalled widespread urban unemployment, the depression was soon felt everywhere. It was this situation that eventually led workers to organized protest.

In 1877 the depression prompted railroad workers to take action to protest wage cuts of as much as 10 percent in a series of bitter strikes. The first was instigated against the Baltimore and Ohio Railroad at Martinsburg, West Virginia. Railroad workers had been handed a 10-percent wage cut, and they refused to let the trains move until full pay was restored. Almost completely spontaneous and non–union-inspired, railroad strikes spread from West Virginia as far as St. Louis. In Pittsburgh federal troops were ordered in to clear the tracks. When the workers refused to move, rioting, burning, and looting followed. Twenty-six people died, and property damage was estimated at $5 million. The railroad strike continued to spread until some two-thirds of the country's rail lines were shut down. In cities where railroad workers lived, frightened business people demanded that the state militias be called out to patrol the streets.

The violence of the 1877 strikes was unprecedented in American history. Governors of the affected states appealed to the federal government for assistance, and President Hayes responded by dispatching federal troops to restore order. Faced with the prospect of federal intervention, the strikes collapsed.

VIOLENCE ERUPTED IN 1877 WHEN FEDERAL TROOPS FIRED ON THE RAILROAD WORKERS DURING THE STRIKE AGAINST THE BALTIMORE AND OHIO RAILROAD IN MARTINSBURG, WEST VIRGINIA.

Violence sparked by antiforeign sentiment erupted within the ranks of labor as well. In 1877 Dennis Kearney's Workingmen's party charged the Chinese with taking jobs from American workers because of their willingness to work for lower wages. Violent attacks on the Chinese broke out in San Francisco and within a few days angry workers had destroyed more than $10,000 worth of property.

The Noble Order of the Knights of Labor

The Noble Order of the Knights of Labor was formed in 1869 as a secret society in order to protect its members from retaliation by employers. Led by Uriah S. Stephens, a group of skilled garment workers from Philadelphia comprised its earliest membership. The organization was designed to draw together all workers into one great union. Anyone who worked for wages was welcomed, "without regard to sex, color, race, or position"; lawyers, liquor dealers, and professional gamblers were the only exceptions. The Knights of Labor made a successful attempt to recruit women and black members. Some ninety thousand blacks eventually joined. However, its ability to attract skilled workers was much less successful than its ability to attract the semiskilled and unskilled. Stephens emphasized that organizing was the only effective way for workers to protect their welfare, but because of the depression of the 1870s the growth of the union was slow.

The goals of the Knights of Labor included the creation of favorable public opinion for the labor movement and support for legislative programs to improve working conditions. At the First National Assembly of the Knights of Labor in 1878, the union called for the abolition of contract labor, enforcement of the eight-hour day, establishment of a federal bureau of labor statistics, and the distribution of public lands to those who wished to settle on farms.

When Terence V. Powderly stepped into Stephens's place as "Grand Master Workman" in 1879, the Knights of Labor entered a new and more aggressive phase. Labor was to lead the fight for social reform. The establishment of labor cooperatives would ensure that the nation's wealth would be distributed equitably. "There is no reason why labor

cannot, through cooperation, own and operate mines, factories, and railroads," Powderly proclaimed.

Between 1884 and 1887 workers started many cooperative enterprises, including mines and foundries. But these ventures were short-lived. The lack of capital and managerial experience made the cooperatives vulnerable to challenge by larger private corporations. This was the last time that the formation of workers' cooperatives was a major objective of organized labor.

Beginning in 1884, the Knights of Labor staged a series of strikes against several railroads. The first strikes were successful and the Union was suddenly flooded by new members. By 1886 the organization had swelled to over half a million, most of them unskilled workers. In March 1886, however, a Knights of Labor strike against Jay Gould's southwestern railroad lines proved that management still wielded the greater power. Gould refused to negotiate with the workers and brought in strikebreakers to put down the "insurrection" by force. As food shortages spread across the country, people turned against the strikers, who were soon forced to give up their fight and return to work, a major setback for the organization.

In 1886 the Knights of Labor had had seven hundred thousand members, but by 1890 membership had dropped to one hundred thousand. Along with unsuccessful strikes, the organization's preoccupation with social reform was a major factor in its downfall, since most Americans at the time equated social reform with radicalism. In addition, the union had suffered from a lack of solidarity from the beginning. The nation's skilled workers never really supported the Knights of Labor, and the unsuccessful southwestern railroad strike took a heavy toll. Finally, the concurrent rise of an anarchist movement intensified the public's fear of violent disorder.

The Haymarket Square Riot In May 1886 some two hundred thousand laborers went on strike in various parts of the country in support of an eight-hour day. In Chicago, one of the major centers of the eight-hour-day movement, a small group of anarchists joined the cause. The goal of these radicals was to destroy the capitalist system of wages and private property. When a striker was accidentally killed in a scuffle at the McCormick Harvester Company, the anarchists, led by August Spies, seized the opportunity to rouse the workers by printing inflammatory circulars calling wage earners to arms. On May 4 a crowd of three thousand gathered at Haymarket Square. The gathering was smaller than Spies had hoped and the demonstration was relatively calm. Following the meeting police stepped in to disperse the small group that remained. At this point someone hurled a bomb into the ranks. Seven policemen were killed and seventy injured in the ensuing melée. Public response bordered on hysteria, since the riot was thought to have been caused by wild-eyed radicals. Seven anarchists were sentenced to death, four were executed, and three were imprisoned, although there was no evidence that they were involved in the bombing. The Knights of Labor, by extension, were accused of being in-

volved, but a connection between them and the bombing was never established. Even so, the union and the movement for an eight-hour day had acquired the stigma of violence and subversion. In many states laws were rushed through restricting the rights of workers to organize, and employers engaged in repressive actions against union members. As a result, workers began to desert the organization, and during the 1890s the much weakened Knights of Labor was disbanded.

The Knights of Labor did succeed in effecting some measure of progress for labor. It was largely through their efforts that the federal Bureau of Labor Statistics, which collected information of all types on the American work force, was set up in 1884 and that Congress passed legislation outlawing contract labor in 1885.

AS A BOMB EXPLODES IN THEIR RANKS, CHICAGO POLICEMEN FIRE WILDLY ON THE ANARCHISTS GATHERED IN HAYMARKET SQUARE.

The American Federation of Labor

As the Knights of Labor declined, a more conservative labor movement emerged under the leadership of Samuel Gompers. Gompers, a friendly, earthy man, was born in London and raised in New York among German and Hungarian cigar makers. While he and his friends worked they educated themselves in philosophy and economics. Gompers developed into a brilliant administrator. He organized the International Cigar Makers Union, shaping it into a model of efficiency and mutual aid. Gompers was strongly opposed to the political orientation of the National Labor Union and to the "indiscriminate" admission of unskilled workers to the Knights of Labor. He also rejected cooperatives and socialist reforms that were designed to replace the wage system. It was his belief that labor should enlarge its bargaining power within the capitalist framework by strengthening trade unions composed of skilled workers (for example, stonemasons or carpenters). In 1881 a number of trade unions founded the American Federation of Labor (AFL), and in 1886 it was reorganized and Gompers was elected president.

The federation, as its name suggests, was composed of independent, self-governing unions. The function of the AFL was to determine general goals, but individual workers did not join the overall organization. Gompers remained the driving force behind the organization until his death in 1924. His approach to the problems of labor was deceptively simple. When asked to identify the goal of the AFL, he said, "More!" Under his leadership the federation became the vanguard of the modern labor movement, emphasizing the workers' basic needs —higher wages, shorter hours, and improved working conditions—and finally establishing the strike as labor's most potent weapon. Although the AFL rejected alliances with political parties, it did not reject the use of political pressure. Labor legislation was another important demand, and the AFL urged its members to voice their interests through the ballot.

Although it sought to enlarge its membership, the AFL began to control entry into its ranks and ignored the vast pool of unskilled laborers. A major reason for this was the growing fear of skilled workers that their crafts would be taken over by unskilled labor. The invention of new machines that could be operated by anyone and the militancy of unskilled workers were perceived as serious threats. Experienced craft workers believed that they must band together or lose everything—higher wages, shorter hours, even their jobs. In its early years the federation had opposed the practice of barring blacks in its affiliated unions, but by the end of the century the AFL was admitting unions whose constitutions contained exclusionary clauses. Although the AFL usually ignored women, they joined trade unions in large numbers and at times carried out strikes on their own. The garment, tobacco, and laundry unions were largely made up of women workers; even so, the union officers were invariably men.

By 1900 the AFL had more than half a million members, although one-third of organized workers still were not affiliated. By 1914 its membership numbered two million. By excluding "divisive" elements, the leaders built a structure that could survive, though it was narrowly based. As a result of union efforts, Congress established the Department of Commerce and Labor in 1903 (split into two departments in 1913) which represented the interests of American labor in the national government.

The Homestead Strike

The steady growth of organized labor and its willingness to use the strike led to some bitter clashes in the late nineteenth century. One of these occurred at Homestead, Andrew Carnegie's steel plant near Pittsburgh. In 1892, at the time of the strike, Carnegie was in Scotland. He had left the management of the company to Henry Clay Frick, along with instructions to operate the plant on a nonunion basis even though the workers were unionized.

Trouble broke out when Frick instituted a new wage scale that would mean a cut in pay for a small number of workers. When the employees struck, three hundred guards from the Pinkerton Detective Agency, whose specialty was strikebreaking, were called in to restore operations. On July 6, 1892, the hated Pinkertons traveled by barge to the docks near the plant where they were met by strikers wielding guns. In the violence that followed, three guards and ten strikers were killed, scores were injured on both sides, and the Pinkertons were forced to surrender.

As in the earlier Haymarket riot, the bitterness of the strike—especially an attempted assassination of plant manager Frick by a revolutionary anarchist—turned public sympathy away from the strikers. The state militia was called in to restore order, and the strike was broken on company terms.

The Pullman Strike

A second clash occurred two years later. The Pullman Palace Car Company, founded by George M. Pullman, was in the business of leasing sleeping cars to railroads. Near its Chicago manufacturing plant Pullman had built a town where the company rented dwellings to its employees. When a nationwide depression during the winter of 1893–1894 reduced company revenues, the management severely cut employees' wages and fired several workers who were serving on a grievance committee to protest this action. To make matters worse, the company refused to reduce rents in the town, which were substantially higher than other rents in the area.

The vast majority of the workers at the Pullman plant were members of the powerful American Railway Union founded by Eugene V. Debs. When union members at the company voted to strike, they were locked out. In retaliation the American Railway Union voted to refuse to handle Pullman cars. Workers who refused to handle the cars were fired, as a large number of railroad companies banded together to help Pullman fight the strike. Whenever a firing occurred, the railway union directed its entire membership to stop work. Within a month train tieups had shut down rail lines all the way from Chicago to the West Coast.

Ordinarily a company facing a strike appealed to the state governor for help, but the Pullman Company did not. The governor of Illinois, John P. Altgeld, had pardoned the Haymarket anarchists who were serving prison terms and the Pullman Company did not expect him to be sympathetic to them. The company instead looked to the federal government for help. President Cleveland, who was being flooded with complaints from postal authorities that the strike was interfering with the move-

FOR HIS PART IN THE PULLMAN STRIKE OF 1894 EUGENE V. DEBS WAS AWARDED A TIN CROWN BY *HARPER'S* AND A SIX-MONTH JAIL TERM.

ment of mail on the rail lines, complied with the Pullman request and ordered federal troops to Chicago. In the meantime, government lawyers drafted an injunction which would in effect restrain Debs from continuing the strike. Based on the Sherman Antitrust Act, the injunction declared that the strike was illegal: as a "combination in restraint of trade" the strike interfered with the mails and therefore with interstate commerce. Debs, however, ignored the injunction and attempted to continue the strike. As a result he was tried for contempt of court (without benefit of a jury) and sentenced to six months in jail. This experience embittered Debs. He left prison a confirmed socialist who helped to form the Socialist party in the United States in 1901. With federal troops on the scene, the strike was quickly crushed.

The United States Becomes an Urban Nation

When the first census was taken in 1790, a mere 3 percent of the population lived in towns of eight thousand people or more. In 1860, 20 percent were

living in towns, and by 1910, the number of city dwellers had risen to nearly 50 percent. New York was growing at an unprecedented rate with over a million inhabitants in 1880 and more than 4.7 million by 1910. Chicago passed the one million mark in 1890 and had over two million inhabitants by 1910. Other cities with outstanding growth were Buffalo, Detroit, Milwaukee, Minneapolis, St. Louis, and Denver.

Urbanization did not take place at a uniform rate. The move to the cities was strongest in the North Atlantic states and in the Midwestern states around the Great Lakes. The Pacific Coast states, too, experienced rapid urbanization. The South lagged behind the rest of the country, with only 20 percent of its population living in cities by 1910. Cities also were few and far between in the Western mountain and Plains states.

The Lure of the Cities

The movement of farming people to the cities was a major factor in urban growth. Many farmers had become tired of the monotony and drudgery of country life. In addition, the nation faced a severe agricultural depression during the last twenty years of the nineteenth century; harvests were poor, and it was increasingly difficult for farmers to meet their mortgage payments. The most drastic abandonment of farms took place in New England and the Midwest. Entire villages were deserted as rural workers migrated to the cities, lured by the promise of high wages in a variety of new mechanized industries. Stories of sudden fame and fortune were so much a part of the popular literature that many came to the city with unrealistic dreams of future success.

A flood of new immigrants also nurtured urbanization. To a greater degree than the farmers, these newcomers had an immediate need for income. Their settlement in the cities was almost unavoidable because they lacked the resources to move on. In 1890 four out of every five residents of New York City were either foreign-born or children of immigrants.

In addition to economic opportunities, the cities offered conveniences that made the rural areas seem backward by comparison. City dwellings had central heating and indoor plumbing. Power stations were built as gaslight gave way to electric power, and by 1884 the entire city of Chicago had electric lighting. Improved lighting made the cities safer at night and enabled factories and schools to remain open longer and theaters to operate with

greatly reduced risk of fire. By 1880 there were telephone exchanges in eighty-five American cities. By 1900 a large part of the country was connected by a vast network of telephone wires.

The enormous influx of people necessitated improved modes of transportation. The electric trolley car, introduced in 1887 in Richmond, Virginia, quickly replaced the slower street railways and led to the development of overhead railways and subways. New York's Brooklyn Bridge, dedicated in 1883, was the first of numerous giant bridges spanning the urban waterways.

The development of industrial technology required a better educated work force. As a result, educational opportunities expanded in the cities; free secondary education was instituted by the 1870s, and some cities built colleges and business schools which residents provided their tax dollars to support.

City life also had a far-reaching effect on family structure and the home environment. Urban conveniences helped give many American women a new sense of independence. Middle-class married women who could afford to purchase ready-made clothing and prepared foods were freed from some of the tasks of homemaking. Single women found they could support themselves in clerical positions in the cities' businesses. Poorer women became a mainstay of the factory system.

Urban Problems

Despite the many attractive features of urban life, problems abounded. Public services, such as water systems and sewage disposal, were inadequate. Water was impure and often several families had to rely on a single outlet for their water supply. Garbage was dumped into rat-infested alleys or left in open ditches within the city limits. These conditions resulted in severe outbreaks of smallpox, diphtheria, and other contagious diseases.

City leaders had to decide whether to turn over control of water and sanitation to private businesses or furnish them as municipal services. If the cities granted a franchise to a private agent, the franchise would, in effect, become a monopoly. Even though the results were not always efficient, many cities decided to construct, own, and operate their own central water systems. Garbage was burned and water-treatment plants were introduced. Sewage remained a problem, polluting lakes and rivers.

Eventually boards of health were organized to oversee the regular collection and disposal of garbage, the construction of reservoirs, and the implementation of water-purification programs. Medical advances, such as the discovery of bacteria, the development of vaccines and antitoxins, and the pasteurization of milk contributed significantly to improved health and increased longevity.

Most cities grew quickly and haphazardly, without design or even the most rudimentary planning. Rich people lived well and the middle class found comfortable lodgings. But the poor, especially immigrants, were packed into tenements designed to yield maximum financial return to the landlord. These four- to six-story-high wood buildings, built in large numbers after the 1880s, contained several small units on each floor. The rooms were dark, cramped, and poorly ventilated. With large families crowded into close quarters, tuberculosis became widespread. By the end of the nineteenth century there were 430,000 tenements in New York City alone, housing 2.5 million people. In his book *How the Other Half Lives*, published in 1890, New York reporter Jacob Riis exposed the grim facts of tenement life:

. . . the hall is dark and you might stumble over the children pitching pennies back there. Not that it would hurt them; kicks and cuffs are their daily diet. . . . All the fresh air that ever enters these stairs comes from the hall door that is forever slamming, and from the windows of dark bedrooms. . . . The sinks are in the hallway, that all tenants may have access—and all be poisoned alike by their summer stenches. . . .The gap between dingy brick walls is the yard. That strip of smoke-colored sky up there is the heaven of these people.

Although cities tried to regulate tenements through building codes, standards were low at first. In 1867 in New York City it was considered sufficient for each sleeping room to be ventilated by a transom to another room and to have a single toilet for every twenty occupants. By 1901 the law required an opening for every room and running water and a private toilet in each apartment. In order to enforce these requirements New York City established a Tenement House Department in 1901. Fires were a common hazard in the cities,

CITY ATTRACTIONS INCLUDED COMFORTABLE ELECTRIC TROLLEYS, WHICH PERMITTED MANY TO TAKE HOLIDAY EXCURSIONS AT LOW RATES. AS THIS BRIGHTLY LIT CAR DEPARTS ON AN OUTING, THE BAND PLAYS, THE PASSENGERS SING, AND AN EVENING BREEZE TEMPERS THE SUMMER HEAT.

DUMPING BARGES CREATE HAVOC AT CONEY ISLAND DURING THE LATE 1800S. NEW YORK EMPTIED MOST OF ITS GARBAGE INTO THE CITY'S SURROUNDING WATERWAYS, AND MUCH OF THE REFUSE DRIFTED TOWARD THE SHORELINE.

especially in wooden slum dwellings. As late as the 1880s many big cities were still using volunteer fire departments. Fortunately, new products introduced in the late nineteenth century—fire-alarm systems, sprinkler systems installed in buildings, and such construction materials as steel and brick—somewhat reduced the destructiveness of fires.

The problem of crime was widespread, particularly as the urban population burgeoned between 1880 and 1900. Cities tried to reduce the number of incidents by passing vagrancy laws, but authorities could do little about constant gang warfare or about prostitutes, gamblers, and liquor dealers who regularly paid corrupt police departments for protection. Corruption was rampant in city politics as well. Good government seemed to decline as cities grew. In his book *The American Commonwealth* (1888) James Bryce, the English writer and observer of the American scene, called the government of its cities "the one conspicuous failure of the United States." The boss-controlled political machine dominated city politics. Vested business interests—many of whom willingly bribed politicians to secure building contracts—faulty city charters, and the purchased vote of large numbers of immigrants unfamiliar with representative government helped maintain the machines in power. The ward bosses did act as friends to the newly arrived immigrants, however, often giving them a job, coal, or groceries in exchange for a vote.

Urban Reform

The social, economic, and physical ills of the city did not go unchallenged. The churches and social-work groups began making efforts to improve urban conditions. Other reformers organized civic federations that sought to institute competitive civil service exams to curtail the appointment of unqualified persons to city governments.

The Churches and Social Reform

In the late nineteenth century churches joined with private agencies and philanthropic organizations in an effort to bring about social reform. Traditionally the Protestant leadership had taken the view that only individual salvation, not church intervention,

would overcome the sufferings of the poor. Supported by wealthy industrialists such as John D. Rockefeller, the churches grew wealthy and attracted large numbers of thriving middle-class worshippers. However, church tardiness in addressing the needs of the poor threatened to drive away the working people. As a result, the emergence of a new approach to Christianity, the Social Gospel, gained wide appeal among those clergy eager to be perceived as compassionate humanitarians. The Social Gospel stressed concern for humanity through good works and social reform. One of the most influential exponents of this doctrine was Washington Gladden, whose book *Applied Christianity* infused the theology of many Protestant denominations by the 1890s. Churches turned to organizing charitable services for the poor and established schools and youth organizations. The Episcopal church formed the Christian Social Union to aid labor. In 1908 thirty-three denominations took an important step toward social awareness when they formed the Federal Council of Churches of Christ in America to fight social ills.

A large percentage of the new immigrants were Roman Catholic and the Catholic clergy was sympathetic to their needs. Cardinal Gibbons, the liberal archbishop of Baltimore, supported the trade-union movement and praised the public school system. In 1891 Pope Leo XIII's encyclical *De Rerum Novarum* recognized labor unions and social legislation as ways to improve the conditions of the poor. Catholic charitable institutions and schools were established to offer poor immigrants religious training and to introduce them to American life. Church leaders even worked among Protestants to overcome traditional anti-Catholic prejudice, but Catholic demands for public funds for church schools antagonized many Protestants.

The practical implications and obligations of the Christian ethic were particularly prominent in the activities of the Salvation Army and the theology of the Christian Science church. The Salvation Army, founded in London by William Booth, was exported to the United States in 1879. Using revivalist methods to attract followers, recruiters supplemented their sermons with practical social service to the urban poor.

The Christian Science movement, founded by Mary Baker Eddy in 1879, also appealed primarily to city dwellers. Christian Science was closely linked to transcendental thought in its emphasis on the omnipotence and omnipresence of God and to the philosophy of pragmatism in its emphasis on the idea that theology must be practical in order to be true. A distinctive aspect of Christian Science is its emphasis on the healing of physical disease and other human problems by absolute trust in divine power.

With the influx of immigrants from eastern Europe and Russia at the end of the nineteenth century, Jews for the first time became a significant religious minority in the United States. Before 1880 the small group of Jews who had emigrated to the United States were of German background and were generally prosperous. Most practiced Reform Judaism, which abandoned the idea of the return to Palestine and permitted full commitment to America. With the coming of some three and a half million eastern European Jews in the late nineteenth and early twentieth centuries, however, Orthodox Judaism became an important religion in the big cities. Many of these Jews wanted to participate in American life, yet retain Orthodox beliefs and practices that separated them from the mainstream. They therefore formed a compromise form of faith, Conservative Judaism, which they felt was more suited to the American environment. Like the Protestants and Catholics, the Jews established welfare agencies to care for Jews in need.

The Social-Work Movement

A new approach to social service emerged with the concept of the social worker. Middle-class women, operating from an established center in the slums called a settlement house, gave assistance, direction, and encouragement to the poor. By the 1890s the Social Justice movement had developed; its purpose was to study carefully the poverty problem in a given area and develop plans to alleviate it. The settlement houses in major American cities provided nurseries and playgrounds for poor children as well as libraries and instruction in a variety of subjects for youngsters and adults alike.

The model for settlement houses was Toynbee Hall, founded in London in the early 1880s. After visiting Toynbee Hall, the American social worker Jane Addams was inspired to set up Hull House in Chicago. Hull House offered classes in music and art, developed a theatrical group, and provided a gymnasium and day nursery. Addams also worked for improved public services and social legislation. She even maneuvered to be appointed garbage inspector of her ward so that she could pressure landlords and garbage contractors for better collection services.

New York City's Henry Street Settlement, founded by Lillian Wald, was as famous as Chicago's Hull House. Lillian Wald was the first social-service worker to propose a federal children's bureau. She wrote concerning the aims of her settlement-house staff: "We were to live in the neighborhood . . . identify ourselves with it socially, and, in brief, contribute to it our citizenship."

The activities of churches and social workers on behalf of the poor, together with that of labor unions, represented a new concern in America for the effects of industrialization and urbanization. The social and economic problems of industrialization became a major concern of America's thinkers, artists, and writers as well, as the following chapter demonstrates.

Readings

General Works

Commons, John R., et al. *History of Labor in the United States*, Vols. I–II. New York: Macmillan, 1918–1935.

Dinnerstein, Leonard, and David M. Reimers, *Ethnic Americans: A History of Immigration and Assimilation.* New York: New York University Press, 1977.

Glaab, Charles N., and A. Theodore Brown, *History of Urban America.* New York: Macmillan, 1967. (Paper)

Green, Constance M., *The Rise of Urban America.* New York: Harper & Row, 1965.

McKelvey, Blake, *The Urbanization of America.* New Brunswick, N.J.: Rutgers University Press, 1962.

Rodgers, Daniel T., *The Work Ethic in Industrial America, 1850–1920.* Chicago: University of Chicago Press, 1978.

Schlesinger, Arthur M., *The Rise of the City, 1878–1898.* New York: Macmillan, 1933.

Seller, Maxine, *To Seek America: A History of Ethnic Life in the United States.* Englewood, N.J.: Ozer, 1977.

Taft, Philip, *Organized Labor in America.* New York: Harper & Row, 1964.

Warner, Sam Bass, Jr., *The Urban Wilderness: A History of the American City.* New York: Harper & Row, 1972. (Paper)

Wittke, Carl, *We Who Built America.* Cleveland: Press of Case Western Reserve, 1964.

Yellowitz, Irwin, *Industrialization and the American Labor Movement, 1850–1900.* Port Washington, N.Y.: Kennikat, 1977.

Special Studies

Abell, Aaron I., *American Catholicism and Social Action.* Notre Dame, Ind.: University of Notre Dame Press, 1960.

Bremner, Robert H., *From the Depths: The Discovery of Poverty in the United States.* New York: New York University Press, 1956.

David, Henry, *History of the Haymarket Affair.* New York: Macmillan, 1964.

Davis, Lawrence B., *Immigrants, Baptists, and the Protestant Mind in America.* Urbana: University of Illinois Press, 1973.

Erickson, Charlotte, *American Industry and the European Immigrant 1860–1885.* New York: Russell, 1967.

Handlin, Oscar, *The Uprooted.* Boston: Little, Brown, 1951.

———, *A Pictorial History of Immigration.* New York: Crown, 1972.

Higham, John, *Strangers in the Land: Patterns of American Nativism 1860–1925.* New York: Atheneum, 1963.

Hopkins, C. H., *The Rise of the Social Gospel in American Protestantism, 1865–1915.* New Haven, Conn.: Yale University Press, 1940.

Howe, Irving, *World of Our Fathers.* New York: Harcourt, 1976.

Kessner, Thomas, *The Golden Door: Italian and Jewish Immigrant Mobility in New York City, 1880–1915.* New York: Oxford University Press, 1977.

May, Henry, *Protestant Churches and Industrial America.* New York: Octagon, 1963.

Mindel, Charles H., and Robert W. Habenstein, *Ethnic Families in America: Patterns and Variations.* New York: Elsevier, 1976.

Rischin, Moses, *The Promised City: New York's Jews, 1870–1914.* New York: Harper & Row, 1970. (Paper)

Solomon, Barbara, *Ancestors and Immigrants.* Cambridge, Mass.: Harvard University Press, 1956.

Taft, Philip, *The AF of L in the Time of Gompers.* New York: Octagon, 1970.

Taylor, Philip, *The Distant Magnet: European Emigration to the United States of America.* New York: Harper & Row, 1971. (Paper)

Thernstrom, Stephan, *The Other Bostonians: Poverty and Progress in the American Metropolis, 1880–1970.* Cambridge, Mass.: Harvard University Press, 1973.

Warner, Sam Bass, Jr., *Streetcar Suburbs, The Process of Growth in Boston, 1870–1900.* Cambridge, Mass.: Harvard University Press, 1962. (Paper)

Wertheimer, Barbara Mayer, *We Were There: The Story of Working Women in America.* New York: Pantheon, 1977.

White, Ronald C., Jr., and C. Howard Hopkins, *The Social Gospel: Religion and Reform in Changing America.* Philadelphia: Temple University Press, 1976.

Wolff, Leon, *Lockout.* New York: Harper & Row, 1965.

Primary Sources

Diamond, Sigmund (Ed.), *The Nation Transformed: The Creation of Industrial Society.* New York: Braziller, 1963.

Gompers, Samuel, *Seventy Years of Life and Labor,* Vols. I–II. New York: Kelley, 1925.

Handlin, Oscar (Ed.), *Immigration as a Factor in American History.* Englewood Cliffs, N.J.: Prentice-Hall, 1959.

Powderly, Terence U., *Thirty Years of Labor.* New York: Kelley, 1962.

Riis, Jacob, *How the Other Half Lives.* New York: Dover, 1970.

Biographies

Levine, Daniel, *Jane Addams and the Liberal Tradition.* Madison: State Historical Society of Wisconsin, 1971.

Livesay, Harold C., *Samuel Gompers and Organized Labor in America.* Boston: Little, Brown, 1978.

Peel, Robert, *Mary Baker Eddy,* 3 Vols. New York: Holt, Rinehart and Winston, 1966–1977.

The New Immigrants

Give me your tired, your poor,
Your huddled masses yearning to
breathe free,
The wretched refuse of your teeming
shore.
Send these, the homeless, tempest-tost
to me,
I lift my lamp beside the golden door!

THESE words from Emma Lazarus's poem *The New Colossus* were engraved in bronze on the base of the Statue of Liberty, a gigantic figure erected on an island in New York harbor to symbolize America, the land of freedom and opportunity. Dedicated in 1886, the copper-sheathed maiden faced the harbor entrance with a lawbook cradled in one arm and the broken shackles of slavery at her feet. The torch in her upraised hand offered a silent welcome to millions of homeless immigrants who poured into the United States after 1880. Of course immigration had been going on throughout the nation's history. What made this new mass of immigrants different was their numbers—15 million between 1890 and 1920; their background—families from Eastern Europe and the Mediter-ranean bringing unfamiliar customs and languages; and their new expectations—many had worked in industrial centers in their homelands and were seeking employment in the cities of the Northeast and Midwest. Among the major groups of new immigrants who passed through the golden door were the Italians, the Poles, and the Jews.

Although Americans associated Italy with its classical past, travelers to the Italian peninsula during the nineteenth century were quick to note the area's poverty, political instability, and slow economic development.

A FAMILY OF IMMIGRANTS PAUSE ON ELLIS ISLAND TO LOOK BACK AT THE HUGE STATUE WHICH WELCOMED NEWCOMERS TO NEW YORK'S HARBOR.

Throughout the country the rapidly growing population, coupled with famine and drought, was forcing young men to travel long distances in search of work. The exodus to America began in the north among people in the professions and skilled workers and spread south where small tenant farmers were being forced off their land. For the most part the young men who set out for America planned to earn just enough money to return home and buy their own farm. Some three to five million of those who came to the United States worked for varying intervals before returning home. Native-born Americans resented these "birds of passage" who reaped the wealth of the New World without sharing the responsibilities of its citizens. Many more young Italians remained in America and only dreamed of returning home some day.

The first loyalty of the young Italian immigrant was to the family, and as soon as he could a young man sent for his kin. Although large extended families were common, the nuclear family, which centered around an authoritarian father and a warm, emotional mother, was the major source of intimacy and trust. Nonrelatives were admitted into the family circle through the ritual kinship of godparenthood.

The Italian's second loyalty was to his home town in Italy. Even in America, intense loyalty was associated with locality, and families sacrificed other luxuries in order to buy a home in a neighborhood where they would be surrounded by old-country relatives and customs. Large cities, including Boston, Chicago, and New York, contained densely settled neighborhoods where families took in boarders, and three-room apartments housed as many as fourteen people. These crowded conditions bred crime and violence and spread disease; yet they also encouraged community coopera-

IN ORDER TO SUPPORT THEIR FAMILIES, MANY ITALIANS ENTERED SERVICE OCCUPATIONS BECOMING WAITERS, ICEMEN, OR BARBERS AS IN THE PICTURE ABOVE

tion. Because living quarters were cramped, people spent much of their time on the street where they learned the necessity of mutual tolerance and support.

Although the majority of Italian immigrants had been farmers, many gravitated to large American cities where they worked as laborers in excavation and construction jobs. Their familiarity with the ways of Americans was facilitated by the *Padrone*, a middleman who acted as employment agent, interpreter, banker, grocer, and landlord. Although he provided these useful services, he also conspired with contractors to exploit his fellow countrymen.

The need for a stable job in order to support one's family led many immigrants to labor in the mines or factories. Others offered their services as barbers, icemen, and waiters. The few

upper-class northern Italians who had emigrated found it difficult to retain their professional status and were often reduced to performing manual labor in addition. Because they resented the peasants, they offered neither leadership nor tutelage to their countrymen.

Because of their poverty and unfamiliar customs, the Italians encountered the prejudice of native-born Americans. Lower-class southern Italians were denounced by labor groups as strike-breakers and stereotyped as gangsters. Their fierce need to guard the family honor and protect the chastity of the women often resulted in bloodshed. Personal vendettas and the Black Hand, a secret society dealing in extortion under threat of death, flourished in Chicago and Boston just as they had in Naples and Palermo.

Conscious of the poor image of Italians, a group of professionals formed an organization to ban scavenging, organ-grinding, and begging. Mutual-aid societies were created to provide relief for the sick and funds for elaborate funerals and to sponsor social events, such as feast day in honor of a patron saint. In general, however, there were no philanthropic organizations to serve the Italian community as a whole.

Another source of support lay in the Catholic church which assisted schools, hospitals, and orphanages. Most southern Italians, however, remembered the church in their homeland as an oppressive landlord and the clergy as greedy and immoral. Magic and superstition dominated their lives in America as they had in Italy.

The wave of immigrants from Poland, like that from Italy, consisted initially of young men seeking employment. They left a homeland dominated by the great empires of Russia, Germany, and Austria. Throughout eastern Europe the mass of peasants lived in poverty under a small ruling class of landowners. Suppression of their culture and population increases forced many Polish laborers, miners, and farmers to emigrate. Many found industrial work producing metals and machines in Chicago, Milwaukee, Pittsburgh, Detroit, and Buffalo. Eventually over one million Poles came to America.

Low wages and harsh working conditions relegated the Poles to shanty towns and urban tenements. It was the strength of family ties that enabled them to begin to build viable communities. When an immigrant found a good job, he sent for relatives and friends living in Poland or other Polish-American settlements. Often the first step in creating a settlement was the establishment of a Polish boarding-house. When the population of a colony numbered between one hundred and three hundred, its members

formed a Polish Society to offer mutual aid in cases of emergency and to provide information to newcomers. In addition to sponsoring balls, picnics, lectures, and theater presentations, the society arranged religious services, thus serving as the foundation for the establishment of a parish church.

While the majority of Poles were Catholic and wished to retain their traditional affiliation to the Roman Catholic church, they were alienated by the influence of the Irish, Germans, and Italians in existing parishes. Eventually extremists created the Independent Polish National Church, which was free of ties to Rome.

With the establishment of parish churches, community activities expanded, and many cultural and economic organizations sprang up. These organized activities were meant to attract more members and to open avenues to social prominence within the community. Schools were established for the purpose of instilling respect for national history and values; among the best known was the College of the Polish National Alliance in Cambridge Springs, Pennsylvania.

Another unifying factor in Polish-American life was the strong nationalist sentiment that had sprung from the fight for independence in the old country. Bound together by common language, customs, and religious practices, Polish-Americans successfully retained their national identity and withstood the prejudice directed against most foreign laborers.

The Jews, a third major group of "new immigrants," made their own distinctive contributions to America. The small group of Jewish-Americans who had emigrated from Germany and Spain early in the century had dispersed throughout the country and successfully adjusted to American society. The majority of new Jewish immigrants, by contrast, came from Russia,

Poland, Hungary, and Rumania. Speaking Yiddish, bizarrely dressed, these Orthodox Jews were generally small shopkeepers or semiskilled laborers fleeing oppression in the region of Russia known as the "Pale."

Over 70 percent of the three and a half million Jews who came to the United States by 1920 remained within the shadow of the Statue of Liberty, settling in strictly separated enclaves in the lower East side of Manhattan. By 1914 New York was the home for more Jews than any city in the world. Despite the miserable living conditions in the slums, families and neighbors offered mutual support. Although not welcomed by the established Jewish community, the new immigrants nevertheless were helped to make the transition to American life. Orphanages, hospitals, and homes for delinquents were set up. The Jewish Theological Seminary was founded to train Rabbis in the Conservative religion, a compromise between rigid old-world orthodoxy and the Americanized Reform Synagogue. In addition, the Industrial Removal Office was formed to help disperse the newcomers from the ghettos.

Few Jews desired to remain within the working class. From street peddlars they became shopkeepers and then owners of large emporiums. They taught each other the mass-production methods which were transforming the garment industry and sought out opportunities in the manufacturing and building trades. Often they were exploited in sweatships run by the established German Jews. Poor working conditions led to unionization efforts: the International Ladies' Garment Workers and the Amalgamated Clothing Workers sought better working and living conditions through the development of auxiliary services and social reforms. An extraordinary number of Jews went into the entertain-

MANY EASTERN EUROPEAN IMMIGRANTS, INCLUDING THE ORTHODOX JEWS, FACED
DISCRIMINATION BY NATIVE-BORN AMERICANS, WHO FOUND THEIR APPEARANCE AND
CUSTOMS DISTASTEFUL.

ment business. By 1905 half the actors in New York were Jewish, and from the theater they moved into radio, movies, and television. Two professions which offered status and enabled educated Jews to escape working for anti-Semitic employers were medicine and law, and Jews entered these fields in large numbers.

The culture of eastern European Jews flourished in New York City. Avid patrons of the arts and literature, Jews frequented the numerous cafes and theaters. Between 1885 and 1915 they founded over 150 Yiddish-language newspapers. Unlike the Italians, the Jews did not cling to the original neighborhoods (the average stay on Hester Street in the heart of the ghetto was only about ten years), but moved uptown and later to the new suburban areas. Education played an important

role in achieving social mobility, for parents were willing to sacrifice in order to educate their children for professional advancement. The Jews took advantage of New York's remarkable public school system, and by 1915 85 percent of the students attending the City College of New York were Jewish. This emphasis on education contrasted sharply with the attitude held by the Italians and the Poles, who either distrusted education or established their own parochial schools.

In spite of the efforts by German Jews to assimilate the eastern Europeans, the newcomers' worst fears were realized when anti-Semitic feeling among native-born Americans rose in response to the flood of new immigrants. Private schools and clubs established quotas or outright restrictions regulating membership, and Jews

found themselves excluded from resorts that they had formerly patronized. Although the Anti-Defamation League of B'nai B'rith was established to combat anti-Semitism in 1913, it was not until after World War II that significant new educational and economic opportunities again became available to the Jews.

The United States has been called a "melting pot" for various cultures, yet the new immigrants did not simply blend into the American cauldron. Each ethnic group retained a sense of identity through the preservation of traditions and values that had characterized their lives in Europe. Past the waiting new colossus they streamed, strangers from distant lands, bringing with them the unique qualities that were their contribution to the complex society called America.

19 The Intellectual and Cultural Response to Industrialism

TOM SAWYER DETECTIVE a new story by MARK TWAIN begins in this number

HARPER'S AUGUST

EDWARD PENFIELD

With the laying of the Union Pacific rails in the late sixties the destiny of America as a self-sufficient economic unity was fixed. Henceforth for an indeterminate period the drift of tendency would be from the outlying frontiers to industrial centers, and with that drift would come far-reaching changes in the daily routine of life. The machine would reach into the remotest villages to disrupt the traditional domestic economy, and the division of labor would substitute for the versatile frontiersman the specialized factory-hand. . . . A new urban psychology would displace the older agrarian, and with the new psychology would come other philosophies in response to the changing realities.

Vernon Louis Parrington

Significant Events

Chautauqua movement [1874]

Phonograph invented [1877]

Progress and Poverty by Henry George [1879]

American Historical Association formed [1884]

American Economic Association formed [1885]

The Principles of Psychology by William James [1890]

The Theory of the Leisure Class by Thorstein Veblen [1899]

An Economic Interpretation of the Constitution by Charles Beard [1913]

COVER OF *HARPER'S*, ONE OF NUMEROUS MAGAZINES FOUNDED DURING THE LATE NINETEENTH CENTURY TO SATISFY THE DESIRE OF MIDDLE-CLASS AMERICANS FOR LEISURE READING.

The two main currents of thought in late nineteenth-century American intellectual life were Darwinism and pragmatism. It is difficult to underestimate the impact that Darwin's theory of biological evolution had on people of that time. Whereas most thinkers accepted the idea of scientific evolution, many regarded Social Darwinism, the application of Darwin's deterministic theory of nature to human social development, as a direct challenge to the American ideals of individual initiative and opportunity for economic advancement. If "survival of the fittest" applied to human society, what could be done to alleviate the host of social and economic problems that accompanied the rapid industrialization of America? Some reformers resolved this dilemma by offering new interpretations of Darwin or by adopting instead the new philosophy of pragmatism which countered the Darwinian perspective, emphasizing free will over determinism. The pragmatic view received practical application in the social sciences as well as in the law and education.

As the nation entered the new industrial age, the emphasis in literature and art changed from a romantic to a realist perspective. Naturalist writers began to examine the darker side of human experience and realists in painting turned to everyday events for their subject matter. Although the mass of Americans had little interest in serious intellectual pursuits, many people did try to better themselves through educational societies, libraries, and newspapers. An increase in leisure time made possible by urbanization and industrialization gave rise to a multitude of popular pastimes in which workers eagerly took part. By the early twentieth century Americans were increasingly doing the same things and to some extent even thinking the same things.

The Philosophy of Pragmatism

As discussed in Chapter 17, Social Darwinism was used to justify the excesses of laissez-faire capitalism. Wealthy industrialists gratefully embraced the doctrine because it enabled them to rationalize the acquisition of great wealth and power as the natural consequence of the laws of evolution. Thoughtful critics were quick to point out that government support had a great deal to do with the success of such business leaders. They perceived in Social Darwinism the poison that would destroy individual initiative. If the strong would inevitably prevail and the weak be cast aside, what place remained for individual striving or for efforts to better the lot of the unfortunate?

In their quest for greater social justice and in their desire to preserve the American spirit of individual initiative, some reformers looked to new philosophical concepts which challenged the determinist perspective of Social Darwinism. Perhaps the most important of these was pragmatism.

William James: The Pragmatic View

The individual who did the most to shape the philosophy of pragmatism was William James. Perhaps the foremost American intellectual of the late nineteenth century, James studied art, took a medical degree, helped to pioneer the new field of psychology, and advanced the study of philosophy. In 1890 he published his first great work, *The Principles of Psychology*, which was instrumental in establishing the discipline as a modern science. Turning his attention to philosophy and religion, he wrote *The Varieties of Religious Experience*, in which he attempted to reconcile religious faith with new discoveries about the physical universe. His short work entitled *Pragmatism* was published in 1907.

As a budding thinker James had been disturbed by the determinist attitudes that were becoming widespread as a result of Darwin's theory of evolution. While he accepted the idea of the scientific evolution of living things, he rejected absolutely the notion that biology alone shaped human nature and human destiny. He believed instead that humans possessed free will. They were constantly interacting with their environment, influencing events as well as being influenced by them; they were not simply buffeted about by forces beyond their control. Whereas Darwinian theory proposed that existence was a reflection of universal, unbreakable laws, James saw life as relative, indeterminate, ever-changing, diverse—much like industrial America itself.

William James's pragmatism was not so much a philosophy as a method of seeking truth. He coined the phrase "cash value" to describe his test for deter-

WILLIAM JAMES, THE PRIMARY EXPONENT OF PRAGMATISM, WAS PROBABLY THE FOREMOST AMERICAN INTELLECTUAL OF THE LATE NINETEENTH CENTURY.

mining the truth in any given case. An idea has "cash value" when it works, when it produces results. The truth of any idea was to be tested by experimentation—gathering the facts, constructing and testing hypotheses, and discarding explanations if they did not work. But James felt that the truth is more than just observable facts. It is also a person's beliefs about those facts. James introduced the idea that "the will to believe" affects the outcome of events. The effectiveness of an idea can be increased by believing in the possibility that it will work. Conversely, doubt is likely to produce failure. From James's perspective, then, truth is relative. It does not exist in some abstract sense, but is the product of an individual's perception of a particular set of circumstances.

James also asserted that ideas or beliefs did not have to be provable by the scientific method to have reality in the human mind. For example, if believing in God gives meaning to a person's life, then God truly exists for that person.

James's idea that knowledge comes from experience, not from abstract theory, emphasized the spontaneity of the universe, the sudden, unpredictable events that upset predictions based on so-called natural laws. In so doing it countered the views of followers of Darwin who held that events in the universe were controlled by unassailable laws.

The Impact of Pragmatism

The pragmatists' emphasis on the power of human will and other creative faculties was behind much of the reform spirit of the late nineteenth and early twentieth centuries. Pragmatic reasoning encouraged people to believe that they could shape their own destiny and led those who were dissatisfied with society to work for change. It has been characterized as a natural extension of the Enlightenment emphasis on experimentation to ensure social progress. An expression of the country's optimistic outlook, pragmatism prepared America for the discoveries of modern science in the twentieth century. It was a short step from William James's relative values to Albert Einstein's relative physics.

Yet pragmatism also created problems for thinking Americans. With its emphasis on results rather than on values, pragmatism was accused of reflecting the materialism of American life. A more important charge was that it put an end to the search for absolute values. Without faith in unchanging religious principles or in natural law, how could Americans defend a concept of natural rights or even a democratic form of government?

New Ways of Thinking in the Social Sciences

Pragmatic philosophy, with its insistence on an ever-changing universe with limitless possibilities, was a liberalizing and creative new outlook. As such it provided a favorable climate for the burgeoning of reformist ideas in the social sciences. The Darwinian perspective also influenced reformers, who incorporated as well as challenged the evolutionary view of life.

Reform Thinkers

Lester Frank Ward and Reform Darwinism The founder of American sociology, Brown University professor Lester Frank Ward, reacted against the Social Darwinists who had described human interaction in terms of unending competition and who viewed institutions as operating outside of human control.

In his two most important books, *Dynamic Sociology* and *Applied Sociology*, Ward set forth the outlook known as Reform Darwinism. He insisted that nature offers numerous examples of cooperation as well as of competition. He also suggested that it was unnecessary to wait for natural law to produce movement in society. Deeply influenced by the philosophy of pragmatism, Ward believed that the human mind can intervene to speed up the process of change through rational choices, since people are part of nature and can participate in their own development.

Ward favored "artificial means of accelerating the spontaneous processes of nature." By this he meant that intelligence, especially scientific intelligence, can give direction to human life. He regarded education as fundamental to social change and argued for the training of sociologists and their employment at every level by the government. Ward welcomed government intervention to help bring about reforms. His ultimate vision was of a "sociocracy," a society moving toward worthwhile, scientifically selected goals through social planning.

Henry George and the Single Tax Ward's attack on the laissez-faire aspect of Social Darwinism was reinforced by the popular writer and reformer Henry George. George despised the fatalistic outlook that denied people an active role in ordering the direction of society. He focused on the unequal distribution of wealth as America's basic problem, and he expounded his solution in *Progress and Poverty*. Published in 1879, it is one of the few texts on economics ever to become a best-seller.

Neither a trained economist nor college-educated, George based his observations on broad experience rather than academic learning. The dreadful condition of the poor in Eastern cities and the huge tracts of land granted to the Central Pacific Railroad prompted him to ask, How could so much national economic progress be accompanied by so much individual poverty? He concluded that given the existing system of land ownership, progress and poverty naturally went together. His theory started from the premise that material progress depends on the productive use of land, which fluctuates in value. The problem was that most of the available land in America had fallen into the hands of a small number of landlords who charged rent to the rest of the population. This meant that all land—coal mines and oil fields as well as urban developments—produced rent as unearned income. When a highway was built, for instance, the value of certain property would double or triple. Yet the owner of that property had performed none of the labor that produced the increased value. The owners had not really earned the additional dollars. On the other hand, the people whose toil was making the land values rise were slipping down the economic ladder. With too many workers for too few jobs, wages fell and unemployment rose. At the same time, renters continued to hand over what they earned to landlords who had done no work to earn this income. The situation created the paradox of progress for the (useless) landlord and poverty for the (useful) tenant.

According to George, landlords should no longer be permitted to exploit the public. If rent is the root cause of social ills, then abolishing rent will do away with those ills. He proposed to accomplish his reform in one stroke—by taxing the unearned income on land that resulted from desirable locations and community development. No other taxes would be necessary, because the government would be able to pay its own way from tax returns on land. George wanted to make it unprofitable to leave land undeveloped and to reduce the size of landed estates, thereby creating more landholders. The extremes of wealth and poverty in America would thereby be eliminated.

Henry George's theory of the single tax helped to undermine support for Social Darwinism by suggesting an alternative view of the laws of nature. He argued that because nature had given the land such a decisive influence on human society, the public deserves to enjoy the wealth derived from the land. Although he provided some scientific analysis of his ideas, he was essentially defending a theory of social justice that he believed would create a better world. He traveled throughout the United States and Europe to spread his theory of the single tax. Single-tax societies were established and single-tax communities were formed.

In the long run, however, the single-tax idea failed. George had neglected to consider other factors in the complex industrial economy of the United States. Economists have pointed out that taxing rent out of existence would affect not only a few large landholders, but a large number of small investors in land enterprises as well. Yet George's influence continued into the twentieth century, modified according to place and circumstance. Many of the existing tax structures that give a special emphasis to the tax on land reflect the single-tax theory put forward in *Progress and Poverty*.

Edward Bellamy and Utopian Socialism Whereas Henry George was preoccupied with the subject of land ownership, journalist Edward Bellamy examined the broader question of unrestricted capitalism. In his best-selling novel *Looking Backward, 2000–1887*, Bellamy argued for a moral reformation of society and the state. He believed that human beings were naturally good but that they were trapped in evil circumstances brought about by an unnatural system of competition that dominated American life. He urged all classes to join in a general uplifting of society for the good of all. The nationalization of industry with the citizenry organized into armies of industrial labor and paid equal wages was his formula for dealing with economic and social ills.

The hero of Bellamy's novel falls asleep in 1887 and awakens in the year 2000. Looking around at the society of the twenty-first century, he is astounded at the transformation. Regulated labor is universal, and cooperation has supplanted competition. No citizens are rich, none are poor, and all have whatever they need for a comfortable existence. The profit motive has been removed from the social order, and incentive consists of the honor to be earned by serving the state. In Bellamy's utopia, the role of government is limited. Fewer elected officials are needed, and the behaviors that made police forces and armies necessary are outmoded. "All these wonders, it was explained, had very simply come about as the results of replacing private capitalism by public capitalism, and organizing the machinery of production and distribution, like the political government, as business of general concern to be carried on for the public benefit instead of private gain."

Bellamy supported the ideas in his utopian novel with direct social criticism of the American scene in his book *Equality*, published in 1897. Although his work gained some supporters, most Americans were strongly attached to a competitive capitalist system. As a result, no efforts were made to implement his theories.

The Economists

By the 1880s some economists were beginning to challenge Herbert Spencer's theory that unalterable economic laws operated without regard to time or place. Richard T. Ely, one of the leaders of this group, disregarded economic theory and concentrated on an investigation of specific economic developments. He argued that human beings could use the power of the state as an instrument for the improvement of society. He helped to form the American Economic Association in 1885, an organization dedicated to using "the state as an agency whose positive assistance is one of the indispensable conditions of human progress."

Thorstein Veblen Another economist, Thorstein Veblen, while influenced by the concept that society was always in a process of evolution, did not believe that there was any law which proved that the wealthy business interests were the "fittest" members of society. In fact, he focused his attack on the behavior of wealthy industrialists. Much of his career was spent at the University of Chicago, where he published *The Theory of the Leisure Class* in 1899 and *The Theory of Business Enterprise* in 1904.

Veblen had a first-hand look at the leisure class in Chicago, which was the focus of a gigantic railroad system, the center of the meat-packing industry, and a metropolis where the immensely rich lived off the laboring poor. From his observations he concluded that if people earned a lot of money, their labor was considered dignified; if they earned little money, their labor was considered undignified. Pure work was no longer considered honorable. Wealth was admired and poverty despised. To display their wealth, persons with means indulged in "conspicuous consumption," ostentatious spending that was not required for comfort, but for the purpose of showing the world that they belonged to the leisure class. It gained them the admiration of all the other classes, and the desire to emulate the rich bound society together in spite of class distinctions.

Veblen believed that the very rich are neither socially useful nor the result of "the survival of the fittest." He distinguished between the technicians who are involved in production and the accumulators of great wealth who are concerned solely with finance. Veblen saw business and industry as rivals, not partners. The recent past had shown many examples of business leaders who had lacked genuine concern for the industries they dominated. Jay Gould's ownership and destruction of the Erie Railroad for his own profit was only the most notorious case. To Veblen's way of thinking, the Erie should have been placed under the control of its engineers, who would have taken pride in its operation. More generally, he outlined a technocracy in which the technicians would oust the business leaders and assume the direction of industry for the good of society.

The Historians

The intellectual ferment of the late nineteenth century transformed the study of history. American historians, such as Herbert Baxter Adams of Johns Hopkins University, introduced their students to German methods of historical research. With their emphasis on careful documentation and the objective presentation of the facts, these methods raised the standards of historical scholarship. Now thinking of themselves as professionals, a group of historians formed the American Historical Association in 1884. In addition, a number of historians sought to combine German research methods with current theories in science and philosophy, particularly Darwinism and pragmatism. Some were convinced that history could throw light on how society actually evolved, while others sought ways to apply the lessons of history to the reform of society.

The Germ Theory of History Leading historians such as Adams and John Fiske were involved in a serious reexamination of the historical process and believed that American political institutions were the outcome of the evolutionary process. They traced America's political institutions all the way back to the Germanic tribes that had overthrown the Roman Empire. In what became known as the "germ theory" of history, they claimed that "seeds" planted by these Teutonic tribes had flowered into free institutions, first in England and then in the United States. Bringing biological evolution together with the development of political institutions, they believed that the Anglo-Saxon peoples have a natural inclination toward freedom and against tyranny.

Frederick Jackson Turner, while accepting the idea of historical evolution, challenged the germ theory: "Too exclusive attention has been paid by institutional students to the Germanic origins, too little to the American factors. The frontier is the line of most rapid and effective Americanization. The wilderness masters the colonist. . . . Little by little he transforms the wilderness, but the outcome is not the old Europe. . . . The fact is, that here is a new product that is American." For Turner, the evolutionary process on the American frontier provided the most accurate explanation of the development of American mores and institutions.

The Historian and Reform Shortly after the turn of the century, James Harvey Robinson of Columbia University urged yet another new direction for the historical profession. He held that the historian's primary consideration should be to seek the meaning in events, not merely to rehearse the facts. As a Reform Darwinist, Robinson believed that human beings are part of the historical process and can use their interpretations of history to effect social change. Robinson himself chose to help the lower classes by emphasizing their role in the historical drama, instead of confining himself to writing about kings and generals.

Two twentieth-century historians, Charles A. Beard and Carl L. Becker, also saw the study of history as relevant to contemporary needs. Beard, in particular, supported Robinson's view of history as a tool for social reform. For example, in his book *An Economic Interpretation of the Constitution*, published in 1913, he claimed that many of the Founders had favored adopting the Constitution because they were creditors of the federal government and believed that a stronger national government would establish a fiscal policy which would include payment of the government debt. While his interpretation has been partially discredited in recent years, at the time the book was published the arguments it presented were used by reformers, who were trying to curb the influence of the business interests on government.

Becker was more preoccupied with the pragmatists' concept of the constant evolution of nature and human beings and their influence on each other. He concluded that there are no absolute values in the universe and that there is no way to determine with certainty the truth about the past. Thus historians' interpretations of past events can never be truly objective; their outlook on the past is always influenced by their view of the present.

Pragmatism and the Law

The influence of pragmatic philosophy was profoundly felt in the law. Before the 1880s legal theory had been viewed as a science dependent on a fixed body of logical rules. The emphasis was on searching in books for legal precedents and applying those precedents to current cases. Justice Oliver Wendell Holmes, Jr., who served for thirty years on the Supreme Court, challenged the conception of law as unchanging and unrelated to contemporary events. He interpreted the law and the court system as living adjuncts to the country's social and economic life. Applying pragmatic philosophy, Holmes viewed legal changes as responses to practical needs. "The life of law has not been logic: it has been experience," he wrote in his book *The Common*

Law. Similarly, he perceived th[...] living instrument whose meanii[...] terpretation by judges and which [...] unchangeable theory. While he did not reject the idea of looking to legal precedent, he gave greater attention to practical conditions in society that related to legal cases. He believed that government regulation of the economy should not be overruled on the ground that it conflicted with laissez-faire economic theory unless such regulation was incompatible with a specific clause of the Constitution.

Holmes's views were extremely controversial, even among his colleagues on the Supreme Court. He often found himself in the position of writing dissenting opinions; it was a matter of decades before his pragmatic approach to the law gained widespread currency.

Roscoe Pound, dean of Harvard Law School for many years, was another strong advocate of "sociological jurisprudence." Like Holmes he challenged the view that there were fixed and absolute legal principles. He called for a pragmatic philosophy of law which adjusted legal doctrines to the human conditions they were to govern.

Reform in Education

Pragmatists believed that education should help children adapt to the demands of a constantly changing society. Gradually, educational reform came to be seen as central to the problem of reforming society itself. "We are impatient," wrote Jane Addams, "with the schools which lay all stress on reading and writing." She claimed that traditional methods of education failed "to give the child any clew to the life about him." The most important figure in developing and applying new ideas in the field of education was the noted pragmatist and follower of William James, John Dewey.

John Dewey and Progressive Education

John Dewey began his career as a teacher of philosophy at the University of Minnesota. In 1894 he moved to the University of Chicago, where he became interested in Francis W. Parker's remarkable experimental school, organized as "a model home, a complete community and an embryonic democracy."

In 1896 Dewey and his wife founded the Laboratory School in Chicago as a place where they could develop and test their own theories of education. Three years later, Dewey published *The School and Society*, a description and defense of his innovative ideas. The book's popularity immediately advanced him to the forefront of the movement that would later be called "progressive education." He was a prolific writer whose many books and articles have had a lasting influence on the philosophical thought of the twentieth century.

Dewey accepted William James's concept of a universe characterized by growth, change, flexibility, and diversity. Dewey believed, moreover, that experience and education could teach people how to deal with change. The human mind, like the rest of the universe, is in a state of evolution, and the interplay between the mind and the environment shapes the goals and movement of society. Moreover, through philosophy people can reflect on experience, make fundamental value judgments, and choose from the options open to them. Dewey had an optimistic faith in progress, based on the human ability to transform the environment while being subtly shaped by it at the same time.

Understandably, Dewey has been called "the philosopher of freedom." In his form of pragmatism, ideas were instruments for dealing with practical problems. Their chief function was to help people explore social issues, using "social" in the broad sense to cover science and all other human enterprises. Ideas were "plans of action" rather than mere reflections of external reality. Having also termed ideas "instruments," Dewey called his philosophy "instrumentalism." It was the most fully articulated statement of pragmatism.

Dewey believed that adults have to make choices from the alternatives presented to them and that to do so wisely, they have to be properly trained. Therefore, education is all-important. Dewey's Laboratory School became celebrated for

JOHN DEWEY'S IDEAS ON PROGRESSIVE EDUCATION HAVE HAD A PROFOUND AND LASTING INFLUENCE ON THE SCHOOLING OF AMERICAN CHILDREN.

its method of progressive education; children learned by doing instead of by rote.

When Dewey's methods were attacked as being too permissive, he retorted that he was training his pupils to make choices as citizens of a democratic social order. Dewey believed that it is as important to build character and teach good citizenship as it is to transmit knowledge.

The Growth of the Public School System

The rapid urbanization that followed the Civil War gave impetus to the movement toward mass public education in the United States. The tremendous increase in productivity brought about by industrialization also generated huge sums of money which helped make universal education possible. However, opponents of public schools contended that it was unconstitutional to use tax dollars for education. A landmark legal decision in settling this issue came out of the *Kalamazoo* case of 1874, which concerned the city's right to build a high school. The Michigan Supreme Court's ruling in favor of the right to build was a sweeping defense of free public education from kindergarten to college. Other states referred to this ruling when they established their own public school systems.

While school attendance beyond the elementary grades was still voluntary, by the turn of the century the United States had more than six thousand high schools, compared with only a few hundred at the end of the Civil War. The number of pupils had jumped from fewer than one hundred thousand to more than one-half million. In elementary education the kindergarten, developed in Germany in the 1830s, caught on rapidly. The first public kindergarten in America opened in 1873 in St. Louis. By the 1890s many public school systems had adopted the idea.

Much of the growth of public schools resulted from the expectation that they would assume many of the functions of parents, police, and ministers. Furthermore, it was hoped that public schools would take up the task of "Americanizing" immigrants. To accomplish these goals, public expenditures for education quadrupled between 1870 and 1900. During this same period, the national rate of illiteracy was reduced from 20 percent to 10 percent. By the turn of the century all but two states

ONE OF THE INSTRUCTORS AT TUSKEEGEE INSTITUTE WAS GEORGE WASHINGTON CARVER, WHO LATER WON
FAME FOR HIS DEVELOPMENT OF AGRICULTURAL BY-PRODUCTS, INCLUDING MEDICINES AND FERTILIZERS.

outside the South had laws making elementary education compulsory.

Education in the South Public education in the South lagged behind that of the rest of the country. Although every Southern state had appropriated funds for a free public school system during Reconstruction, with the restoration of conservative, elitist rule public education was scorned. Opposition to state-planned educational systems, the belief that even elementary education was not necessary for a rural population, and the argument that the section was too poor to afford it were all significant factors leading to a decline in expenditures. By 1897 a quarter of the white South was still unable to read, many teachers were poorly trained and earned less than hired convicts, schools were run down, and the school year never exceeded three months. With attendance voluntary, fewer than 60 percent of Southern children were enrolled in school. Yet, new efforts by intellectuals and educators to improve the Southern educational system began to make some headway, and by the early twentieth century, teacher training and elementary education were beginning to improve.

Education for Blacks A number of privately financed vocational and normal schools for black youths in the South had been created following the Civil War. With the end of Reconstruction, many of these schools closed or were forced to limit their offerings to vocational training. Many Southerners believed that education was unnecessary for black people, since they were expected to continue doing menial tasks. Northern philanthropic groups such as the Peabody Fund did support some black schools after 1876, including Booker T. Washington's famous Tuskegee Institute. Unfortunately, these vocationally oriented schools were able to survive only by adopting an "accommodationist" outlook. They emphasized farming or crafts and avoided academic subjects which would have challenged Southern beliefs about the inferiority of blacks. For instance, in setting up the Tuskegee Institute in 1881, Washington stressed that for the present it was only important for black people to learn agricultural skills or a trade. In effect, he was telling black youths to settle for second-class citizenship. Within a short time, however, his willingness to accept an inferior status for black Americans came under sharp attack by more militant black leaders.

Parochial Schools Some groups were opposed to public schools. Many Roman Catholics, for example, favored universal education, but wanted to see it permeated with a religious point of view. They objected to being taxed for schools to which they could not in good conscience send their children. In 1884 the Third Plenary Council of American Bishops made it an obligation of each pastor to establish a parochial school in his parish.

Methods of Instruction

Before the late nineteenth century, learning was equated with rote memorization. By the early 1900s, however, the situation was changing, in large part due to the influence of John Dewey. Schools began teaching subjects they believed necessary for adapting successfully to the new urban age. Dewey felt that the school should be a miniature urban community, and his goals were furthered by advanced methods of instruction being used in Europe.

A German educator, Johann Herbart, emphasized instructing children in terms compatible with their natural interests; new information should be related to what the child already knew. Another new system of this period was "object teaching," developed by the Swiss educator Johann Pestalozzi. According to this method, the use of books and writing was subordinated to physical activity. Mathematics, for example, was taught by giving children objects to handle instead of making them write numbers on a slate. Increasingly, traditional methods were being challenged by these new approaches.

Higher Education

The passage of the Morrill Act of 1862 provided much of the impetus for the rapid growth of higher education in America. This legislation gave generous grants of public lands to states for the establishment of educational institutions that would teach improved agricultural methods and allied vocational subjects. Several states quickly took advantage of the Morrill Act, building "land-grant" colleges which subsequently developed into some of America's finest state universities. Private universities also flourished during this period thanks to the generosity of rich industrialists. The University of Chicago, Cornell, Vanderbilt, Stanford, Johns Hopkins, and Carnegie Institute were just a few of the new schools founded by wealthy businessmen.

Both the private and the land-grant universities began to expand the range of academic offerings. As late as 1865 the classical languages, mathematics, and philosophy had formed the core of higher education. In the late nineteenth century, English, the modern languages, the natural sciences, and the social sciences became part of the concept of liberal education. By 1900 history, political science, and economics had made strong inroads as academic disciplines, and sociology was making an entrance. As a result of the efforts of William James, psychology was beginning to gain recognition as a discipline independent of philosophy. Laboratory experiments became an integral part of chemistry and physics courses, as did field study in geology courses. Gradually, the subject of education itself came to be viewed as a serious academic discipline. By 1911 a majority of states had passed teacher-certification laws, and requirements for certification included instruction in the latest teaching methods.

The founding of America's first graduate school, Johns Hopkins University, in 1876 gave impetus to specialized advanced studies. Before the Civil War advanced scholarship had been available only in Europe. The success of Johns Hopkins did not completely halt the flow of American scholars to Europe, but it did encourage a number of wealthy individuals to endow other universities so that they too could offer advanced studies. By the early twentieth century the quality of American scholarship compared favorably with the best in Europe.

Popular Culture

Advances in education offered a great boon to America's children; yet its benefits did not extend to the mass of adult Americans. In response to this need there arose a mass market for books, magazines, and lectures aimed at the average citizen.

Educating Adults

The increased opportunity for public education was partly attributable to the growth of public libraries. The American Library Association was founded in

1876, and five years later Andrew Carnegie launched a program of private donations to support a system of Carnegie Libraries. By the turn of the century the United States boasted of more than nine thousand public libraries, offering more than forty-five million volumes.

The rise of the Chautauqua movement also helped to satisfy the mass desire for information. The movement was started in 1874 at Chautauqua Lake in western New York as a summer program to train Sunday school teachers. The idea spread quickly so that instruction in such subjects as literature, science, government, and economics was eventually available to thousands of people. The success of the original Chautauqua Institute produced many imitations. By 1900 more than two hundred Chautauqua-type organizations had been established all over the United States. However, the intellectual standards in these programs were low, and entertainment often overshadowed enlightenment. Nevertheless, this method of spreading information provided the opportunity for millions of Americans to improve themselves.

Mass Journalism

In attracting and influencing the mass of Americans, no other printed matter could compete with the newspaper. In 1871 a British observer commented: "America is the classic soil of newspapers; everybody is reading; literature is permeating everywhere; publicity is sought for every interest and every order; no political party, no religious sect, no theological school, no literary or benevolent association is without its particular organ; there is a universality of print."

In the field of mass journalism, the major impetus for growth and change was supplied by technological advances. One important mechanical improvement in the craft of printing was the invention of the web press, which could print both sides of a page simultaneously. Another time- and labor-saving development was a device capable of gathering, folding, and cutting each copy of an edition. Machines for making paper out of wood pulp reduced the cost of newspaper production. The crowning achievement was the invention in 1885 of the linotype machine, which allowed lines of type to be cast in a single operation, replacing the laborious business of casting each piece by hand. One worker at a keyboard could now handle large quantities of type rapidly. The telephone, the telegraph, and the transoceanic cable vastly increased the rate at which information was collected and disseminated.

The enormous cost of machinery increased the need for advertising revenue. One unfortunate result was that editors began to avoid printing material that might offend advertisers. Controversial editorials were replaced by lurid headlines promising titillating scandal, as efforts to increase circulation intensified. Joseph Pulitzer, a Hungarian immigrant, revolutionized the newspaper business through his efforts to reach an ill-educated mass audience. Before the Civil War no newspaper had exceeded a circulation of fifty thousand. In 1884 Pulitzer's *New York World* was selling one hundred thousand copies daily, and by 1898 its circulation had climbed to over one million.

Pulitzer's successful formula was to offer something for everyone—human-interest stories, hard-hitting editorials, and crusades as well as exposés, rumors, and comic strips. In 1895 William Randolph Hearst purchased the *New York Journal* and challenged Pulitzer to a circulation war. Hearst ran a freewheeling paper often criticized for sensationalism. A colored comic feature in the *Journal* called "The Yellow Kid" gave rise to the term "yellow journalism," which has since come to mean Hearst-style journalism, no matter who practices it. With its emotional appeal, the *Journal* gradually surpassed the *World* in circulation. Although both newspapers provided useful services in crusading for various social reforms, their desire to attract more and more readers often overshadowed their commitment to inform the public. The formation of press associations and the rise of syndication helped to advance more responsible methods of newsgathering and reporting.

Magazines

The periodical press generally offered somewhat better fare than the newspapers. Within a few decades after the Civil War, a small group of magazines became vehicles for crusading reformers. One of the most influential journals was the *Nation*, which led the way in exposing the laxity of the Grant administration and the corruption of Washington politics in general. The efforts of investigative journalism were aided by the campaigns waged

ZOLA'S "WIFE BEATERS"----READ IT TO-DAY.

NIGHT SPECIAL.

NEW YORK JOURNAL

EVENING s

NO. 5,566—P. M.　　　　NEW YORK, FRIDAY, FEBRUARY 11, 1898.

EXTRA

BABIES KILLED BY SCORE

Twenty Bodies Have Been Recently Found in the Streets of Harlem.

POLICE AFTER SLAYERS.

Direct Attention to Midwives and Already One Arrest Has Been Made.

SHE IS HELD WITHOUT BAIL.

Harlem is to-day confronted with such another grewsome mystery of dead babies as recently puzzled the Hoboken police.

Hardly a day in the last thirty has gone by that a dead baby has not been found in some doorway or alley.

Ever since the appalling accusation of wholesale baby murder were made against Mrs. Augusta Nack, the ex-slayer of Wm. Guldensuppe, by her husband, Herman Nack, the police have been suspicious of the practice of midwives.

An Important Arrest.

They consider as highly important the arrest and arraignment to-day of Mrs. Eva Gaguel, a midwife of No. 249 East the Hundred and Tenth street, who was held, without bail, to await the result of injuries to Mrs. Mary Ethel Gardner, upon whom she operated three weeks ago.

Mrs. Gardner is dying at her home, No. 523 West Thirty-seventh street. A consultation of physicians has been held, and at their instance Coroner Zucht has taken the woman's ante-mortem statement. She has

ALLOWS $605,237 FOR THE TEACHERS.

Board of Estimate Fixes the Amount for Salaries and Other Expenses for January.

The Board of Estimate and Apportionment this afternoon allowed $605,237 for the Board of Education, covering expenses and salaries for January.

The Board heard Colonel Kearny on a proposition to renovate the brownstone building in City Hall Park for the use of the City court. He agreed to put in new floors and elevators and to make other improvements for $15,000.

The bid was accepted.

THE DE LOME QUESTION.

Washington, Feb. 11. — Will Hale sail?

BELIEVED TO BE TROLLEY ROBBERS.

Four Men Arrested on Suspicion of Having Murdered a Philadelphia Motorman.

Detectives Cronin and Brown this after-

THE POLICE KEEP BRINGING THEM IN.

ABANDONED IN THE RAILROAD YARDS.

FOUND IN LONELY PLACES

AND DISCOVERED IN DARK DOORWAYS.

The Harlem police are convinced that a baby farm is in operation within their district. Twenty bodies of slaughtered babes have been found within the last month in doorways, alleys and secluded spots. A mysterious woman was seen at Park avenue and Ninety-eighth street carrying a small wooden box, which she threw under the "L" road. A policeman picked up the box and found it contained the body of an infant two days old. The scenes in the sketch show some of the discoveries of dead babies by the police.

LIGHT ON DREYFUS PLOTTING

Colonel Picquart Tells of Disregarded Evidence Against Esterhazy.

HANDWRITING RECOGNIZED

Zola Feelingly Replies to a Reflection of General Pellieux Amid Great Excitement.

WHAT M. BERTILLON DISCOVERED.

Paris, Feb. 11.—Colonel Picquart, while waiting in the corridor of the Assize to-day to be called as a witness in the trial of Emil Zola, created an immense sensation by declaring that he had decided to disclose the whole Dreyfus mystery in the witness box, regardless of consequences to himself, the army and the country.

Pettenson's Shaft at Zola.

General Pellieux, who was the first witness of the day, testified that General

THIGH OF THE BODY FOUN

NEW CLEW TO THE EAST RIVER

$1,000 REWARD FOR

Evening Journal Will Pay This for the Clearing Up of the Crime.

Questions to be answered and detective clews up to date:

WHO WAS HE?

Jean Lemerct?　George Farrell?
C. Swantzchild?　Peter Smith?
P. Abrahamson?
Wm. McCaright?

WHY WAS HE SLAIN?

For Money?　　By a Woman?
For Revenge?　In a quarrel?
For Jealousy?　By a Maniac?
WHO KILLED HIM?

Nothing Known of the Identity of the Murderer.

HOW WAS HE KILLED?

Choked?　　　Crushed?
Shot?　　　　Dismembered?

WHERE WAS HE KILLED?

Not more than a week ago. No one knows, but somewhere in the limits of New York.

PORTION ORIGINALLY FOUND

PORTION FOUND TO-DAY

A man's thigh was found floating in the East River at the foot of Pacific street, Brooklyn to-day.

Careful measurements taken by the Evening Journal showed at once that the limb was a part of the body of the murdered man whose trunk was at the Morgue.

These measurements were confirmed by Coroner's Physician Donlin and other experts when the thigh was brought to the Morgue this afternoon.

About thirty contusions were found, proving beyond doubt that the murdered man had engaged in a fierce struggle.

The body had apparently been disjointed by the use of a hatchet, pounded with a hammer.

The bone in the thigh was complete. The joints were disarticulated. The flesh was hacked. Then the joints were twisted and torn from the sockets.

The finding of the thigh has added a new and thrilling interest to the great murder mystery. For information

leading to its solution the Evening Journal will pay $1,000 reward.

The right thigh of the murdered man whose trunk floated into the Roosevelt street ferry slip last Monday was found in the East River, at the foot of Pacific street, Brooklyn, to-day.

The thigh reached the Morgue at 1:35 o'clock. It was brought from Brooklyn in a baby's coffin and wrapped in a canvas covering.

It was placed in a closet in the dissecting room to await an examination by Coroner's Physician Donlin. No effort was made to fit the limb upon the body until Dr. Donlin had arrived.

DISCOVERY DRE WA CROWD.

At 7:30 o'clock this morning Joseph Morgan, a boatman, living at No. 76 Pacific street, saw an object bobbing up and down on the water near the shore. He drew it in with a boathook and found it was a man's thigh well preserved.

Morgan notified Policeman Ross.

The thigh was taken to the Fifteenth Precinct police station, at Emmett and Amity streets, Captain Michael Campbell at once notified Police Headquarters in this city, and detectives were sent over to con-firm the suspicion that the thigh was a part of the body of the murdered man.

EXT

BY WIRE TO THE EVE

DANGER OF

PARIS, Feb. 11.—At 4 o'clock blocked all the neighboring street closed by the police.

It became evident that a class of the session, and a large barracks. After the interruption testimony. "The interests of my I was sent away on a secret reflec-ts pursuing the investigation dec attitudes of my superiors."

Then there followed several Picquart was confronted with an did not agree with him in certain dience giving loud expression to

REDMOND AMENDMENT

LONDON, Feb. 11.—In the H debate on the Address, Mr. John lodge, with not having moved a Nationalist cause was sacrificed b

Mr. James O'Kelly, Parn-onded Redmond's motion. Sir V that Mr. Redmond had asked th the Imperial Parliament which home rule bills with the consent ment was rejected by a vote of 2

EDGEMONT SMELT

TRENTON, Feb. 11.—A re-mont and Union Hill Smelting C ated in New Jersey with a capita in which Cashier Quinlan is said Bank of New York. The receiver

MR. ASTOR GET

John Jacob Astor got his po-to-day from $2,000,000 to $250,00 million dollars' worth of propert $250,000 worth on his hotel.

MORE MEN

Thirty-six employes of the P were dismissed this afternoon.

by several brilliant political cartoonists. *Harper's* featured the work of Thomas Nast, who is credited with being instrumental in the downfall of the notorious Tammany Hall leader Boss Tweed. Similarly, Joseph Keppler helped make *Puck* the best satirical publication of the late nineteenth century, with his political cartoons attacking the evils of business monopoly. While these periodicals appealed primarily to intellectuals, others were read avidly by middle-class men and women looking for practical advice and leisure reading. *The Ladies' Home Journal, Good Housekeeping, Collier's,* and *Cosmopolitan* offered feature articles and stories by the finest contemporary writers.

Popular Pastimes

As the industrial revolution took hold in late nineteenth-century America, the enjoyment of work which had characterized an earlier, more egalitarian era, began to decline. Despite Horatio Alger success stories, most urban workers found themselves locked into lives of drudgery and monotony. City dwellers—native-born and immigrant alike—looked forward eagerly to their leisure hours which they filled with a variety of amusements.

A favorite urban pastime was spectator sports. Baseball had been played since before the Civil War, and with the formation of professional leagues beginning in 1876, it soon attracted paying spectators in droves. In 1903 the Boston Red Sox beat the Pittsburgh Pirates in the first World Series. Football was slower to capture a mass audience, although it was played on many college campuses. Boxing satisfied the public's appetite for violent excitement. Originally boxers traded punches bare-knuckled, but in 1892 "Gentleman Jim" Corbett donned gloves to defeat the famous, hard-drinking John L. Sullivan. In Springfield, Massachusetts, the new game of basketball was introduced in 1891. It caught on rapidly as a participant sport and later became enormously popular as a spectator sport.

BOYS DISCUSS WHETHER TO GO THE NICKELODEON. IN 1907 NICKELODEONS IN NEW YORK CITY WERE DRAWING TWO HUNDRED THOUSAND VIEWERS A DAY, ONE-THIRD OF WHOM WERE CHILDREN.

Americans enjoyed numerous other amusements as well. Barnum and Bailey's three-ring circus enthralled children and adults alike with its wild animals, bulb-nosed clowns, and high-flying trapeze artists. Vaudeville shows featuring pratfalls and acrobatic tricks sold many more tickets than symphony concerts or legitimate theater.

The introduction of the motion picture near the turn of the century heralded a new era in entertainment. The early moviehouses, called nickelodeons because of the nickel admission, showed crudely made five-minute films of dancing girls or boxing matches. Little more than a decade later, D. W. Griffith's *Birth of a Nation* elevated the film to a serious art. Recorded music—classical and popular—came into American homes within a few years of Thomas Edison's invention of the phonograph in 1877.

The entertainments available to urban dwellers not only helped them to forget the frustrations of lives in thrall to industry, but drew Americans of many different backgrounds together in similar ways of living and thinking.

Cultural Landmarks

Literature: The Emergence of Realism and Naturalism

Immediately after the Civil War, American literature was still dominated by the mood of romanticism. Most of the popular fiction of the decade after 1865 was purely sentimental and patently unrealistic. It catered to the "genteel" preconceptions of the middle class and imposed sentimental stereotypes of the family, children, women, blacks, and the poor. The version of reality implied in what Walt Whitman referred to as "ornamental confectionary" and "copious dribble" did not disappear even by the turn of the century. At the same time the dishonesty of much contemporary fiction caused a strong reaction among writers concerned with "real human life."

Realism By the 1880s realism had become the prevailing trend in serious literature. Whereas early nineteenth-century romanticists had attempted to portray life as it should be, realists sought to portray life as it was. The most important forces behind this shift were the same factors that were changing every other aspect of American life: industrialism and the complexities that accompanied it, evolutionary theory with its concern for the effects of the environment on human development, and the pragmatic approach with its insistence on the relativity of values.

One early type of realist literature was the regionalist school, composed of writers who turned to a specific area they knew well in their effort to describe real situations. Bret Harte, for example, found his best story ideas in his native California. Harte's eye for local color, his ear for the dialect of mining camps and waterfronts, and his ability to write both dramatic and humorous scenes accounted for his popularity. Of the many memorable characters he created, probably the best known type was the Western gambler John Oakhurst of "The Outcasts of Poker Flat."

The other prominent regionalist connected with the West, Mark Twain, was America's most outstanding realist writer. Born Samuel Langhorne Clemens, Twain grew up along the Mississippi River in Hannibal, Missouri. As a young boy he had often watched the riverboats coming into port, and he took his pen name from a riverman's term he had heard many times—"mark twain," that is, two fathoms. All of his works, including *Life on the Mississippi*, *A Connecticut Yankee At King Arthur's Court*, *Tom Sawyer*, and *Huckleberry Finn*, draw on his own experience. *Huckleberry Finn*, considered his masterpiece, is one of the greatest portrayals of character in all of American literature. Both humorous and dark, it is a study of "innocents" cut off from the trappings of society, as well as an attack on hypocrisy, greed, and social injustice. His use of common speech rather than formal literary language began a revolution in American prose style.

William Dean Howells, for ten years the editor of the *Atlantic Monthly* in Boston, wrote about the genteel middle class he knew best. At first, Howells was content to write about what he called the "smiling aspects of life," but gradually he began to develop an awareness of the problems being created by

MARK TWAIN ON THE LECTURE CIRCUIT. ALTHOUGH HE HATED LECTURING, TWAIN WAS A POPULAR SPEAKER AND SET OUT TO MAKE HIS TALENTS PAY.

industrialization. His most widely read novel was *The Rise of Silas Lapham,* the story of a self-made man who attempts to make himself acceptable to the upper crust of Boston society. The novel explores the moral conflicts Howells detected in the competitive world of business.

One of the greatest novelists of the period was Henry James, brother of the philosopher William James. James left America in 1875, spending most of his adult life in England writing novels, short stories, plays, and literary criticism. A realist in his subtle portrayals of ladies and gentlemen of social standing, James is perhaps the foremost analyst of the behavior and moral dilemmas of upper-class society. The naive American confronting sophisticated Europeans was a theme he returned to again and again.

Naturalism Another group of American writers took realism to the extreme. Exploring a Darwinian universe in which human fate is determined by a merciless environment, many of these "naturalist" writers took for their subjects the lower classes and the netherworlds of crime and degradation. Stephen Crane described the evils bred by poverty in *Maggie, A Girl of the Streets* and showed the horrors of war in *The Red Badge of Courage.* Frank Norris attacked the corruption resulting from the unchecked growth of big business in two powerful novels, *The Octopus* and *The Pit.* Theodore Dreiser, foremost of the naturalist writers, portrayed a dark world in which humans are at the mercy of forces beyond their control. His most important work, *An American Tragedy,* explores the downfall of a young man in the grip of an obsessive passion. An earlier novel, *Sister Carrie,* had been denounced as immoral for its frank portrayal of sex, an accusation Dreiser faced many times before his works were accepted by the reading public. In *The Titan,* a book strongly influenced by the doctrine of Social Darwinism, he sketched the portrait of a man whose rise to success is achieved by pushing aside all those who stand in his way. Jack London was an adventurer who put his experiences into dramatic novels and short stories. His fascination with the power of nature over civilized society is exemplified by such tales as *The Sea Wolf,* about the violence of life at sea, and "The Call of the Wild," about a sled dog that chose to revert to the primitive life of the wilderness rather than remain with human beings.

Literature for the Masses While the works of such writers as Mark Twain and Bret Harte gained wide appeal, this was not the case with most of the realist and naturalist writers. The novels of Henry James, for example, were read primarily by well-educated members of the upper class. The general reading public was still attached primarily to sentimental literature. By 1900 nearly 90 percent of the American public could read, but their tastes did not call for portrayals of "real life." For the middle class there were overdone romances, cloak-and-dagger tales, and stories of exotic lands. For the working classes there were Horatio Alger stories, sentimental love dramas, and, above all, Western adventure stories. Technology had made possible the publication of ten-cent thrillers, and this sort of fiction outsold realistic novels four to one. In the late nineteenth century the realists and the popular romanticists carried out a form of literary warfare. One side tried to point out the realities of American life; the other was satisfied to "foster agreeable illusions."

Trends in Art

American painting after the Civil War tended to be more conservative than American literature. With few exceptions, artists still took the lead from the European academic tradition. Even so, some American painters were influenced by the movement toward realism.

Albert Pinkham Ryder remained rooted in romanticism, but his art was not completely untouched by actual events. In *Death on a Race Track* he combined elements of the fantastic with elements from real life to work out a theme which had come to him after hearing about a man who had committed suicide after losing his money at a horse race. Ryder depicted Death as a ghostly apparition galloping, scythe in hand, around the track.

Regionalism The themes chosen by regionalist painters in this period resembled those of the local colorists of American literature. Winslow Homer painted scenes from his native New England, particularly the rocky shores and the pounding surf of the coast. A dramatist of the sea, Homer's trademark was high color and swirling movement. His paintings carried such descriptive titles as *The Hurricane* and *Breaking Storm*. Another regionalist, Frederic Remington, recorded the life of the cowboys, the Plains Indians, and the open range. Charles Marion Russell was similarly drawn to character studies and scenes from Far Western life. A self-taught artist who had worked as a trapper and a cowboy, Russell settled in Great Falls, Montana, in 1897 to record the West he had known as a youth. His paintings and illustrations made a significant impact on the New York market, and his mural *Lewis and Clark Meeting the Flathead Indians* was commissioned by the state of Montana for display in its House of Representatives.

Realism and Naturalism Thomas Eakins, often considered America's most outstanding nineteenth-century painter, pursued artistic realism. Many were dismayed by his refusal to beautify a scene or soften a likeness to please his sitter. For instance, his portrait of President Hayes working in his shirt-sleeves horrified many people. Determined to show life as it was, Eakins gained admittance to hospitals and medical schools and sketched exactly what he saw. Out of this experience he painted two magnificent group studies, *The Surgical Clinic of Professor Gross* and *The Clinic of Professor Agnew*.

Eakins's realism was followed by an even more extreme expression in the naturalism of the Ashcan school. This style, best represented by John Sloan, received its name from its emphasis on sordid scenes, usually taken from city life. Painters of the Ashcan school depicted subjects considered excessively ugly or ordinary by the general public and the artistic establishment: prizefighters and chorus girls, bars, back alleys, and ashcans. Their work paralleled the literary themes of Crane and Dreiser and dominated the art scene until World War I.

Expatriate Artists Two major American painters lived so long in Europe that they may be considered international figures. James McNeill Whistler, whose painting of his mother (which he called *Arrangement in Grey and Black*) is probably the most famous canvas ever painted by an American, produced many fine works in which he subordinated subject matter to "an arrangement of light, form, and color." John Singer Sargent was a virtuoso portrait painter whose work captured the elegance of the late Victorian and Edwardian eras. A third important expatriate artist was Mary Cassatt, America's greatest woman painter. Cassatt became associated with the impressionist movement in Paris during the 1880s. She painted many sensitive studies of mothers with their children.

Trends in Architecture

As in the fine arts, nineteenth-century architecture was dominated by conservatives. Yet two designers made a dramatic break with tradition. "Form follows function," one of the most-quoted statements about modern architecture, was made during this period by the American architect Louis Sullivan. It expressed his desire to rid architecture of pretentious styles that failed to consider in the designing process the use to which a building would be put. Sullivan believed that a house calls for one type of architecture, an office another, a store yet another. The original American contribution to architecture, the skyscraper, was in danger of being turned into an

THE BLOCK-LONG TOWNHOUSE OF MILLIONAIRE CORNELIUS VANDERBILT, LOCATED ON 5TH AVENUE IN NEW YORK. DURING THE LATE NINETEENTH CENTURY, A NUMBER OF SHREWD, AMBITIOUS MEN MADE INCREDIBLE FORTUNES BY GAINING CONTROL OF AMERICA'S VITAL INDUSTRIES. UNHAMPERED BY GOVERNMENT RESTRAINTS OR A FEDERAL INCOME TAX, VANDERBILT, STEAMBOAT KING AND PRINCIPAL OWNER OF THE NEW YORK CENTRAL RAILROAD, AMASSED $94 MILLION IN A LITTLE OVER A DECADE. LIKE THE OTHER HARD-DRIVING MONEYMAKERS WHO RAN THE UNITED STATES BETWEEN 1865 AND 1900, VANDERBILT BRIBED GOVERNMENTS AND BOUGHT PUBLIC OPINION. "LAW?" HE COMMENTED TO ONE OF HIS ASSOCIATES, "WHAT DO I CARE ABOUT LAW? HAIN'T I GOT THE POWER?" (Culver Pictures)

AT THE TURN OF THE CENTURY, NEW YORK CONSTRUCTED A PUBLIC
TOBOGGAN RUN 42 FEET HIGH AND SOME 1200 FEET LONG. CLUBS
WERE ESTABLISHED FOR "SCIENTIFIC AND FASHIONABLE" TOBOGGAN-
ING, AND A CONTEMPORARY NEWSPAPER REPORTED: "THE PROBLEM
OF HOW CHILDREN OF MATURE YEARS MAY SLIDE DOWN-HILL AND
MAINTAIN THEIR DIGNITY IS NOW HAPPILY SOLVED IN NEW YORK."
(The Bettmann Archive)

CHILDREN FROM THE BIRNEY PUBLIC SCHOOL RECEIVE A DEMONSTRATION FROM THE LOCAL ICEMAN. (Reproduced from the collections of the Library of Congress)

A DOCTOR PERFORMS AN OPERATION IN HIS KANSAS OFFICE WHICH BOASTED A PLUSH CARPET, A CANOPIED BED, AND A NURSE AND ANESTHETIST. THE SUSPENDED BOTTLES WERE USED TO IRRIGATE WOUNDS. (The Kansas State Historical Society, Topeka)

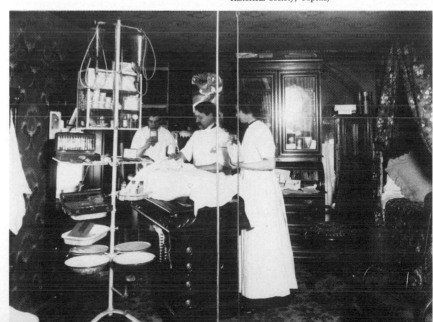

IN 1904 TWO DRIVERS DROVE AN AUTOMOBILE
FROM SAN FRANCISCO TO NEW YORK IN FORTY-
THREE DAYS, THUS BEATING THE CONTINENTAL
RECORD BY EIGHTEEN DAYS. (Culver Pictures)

FOLLOWING THE CIVIL WAR, THE INTRODUCTION
OF GERMAN AND SWEDISH GYMNASTIC PROGRAMS
INTO THE UNITED STATES STIMULATED A STRONG
INTEREST IN PHYSICAL FITNESS. HERE A GROUP OF
WOMEN PARTICIPATE IN A PHYSICAL-EDUCATION
CLASS AT THEIR LOCAL GYMNASIUM. (The Byron
Collection, Museum of the City of New York)

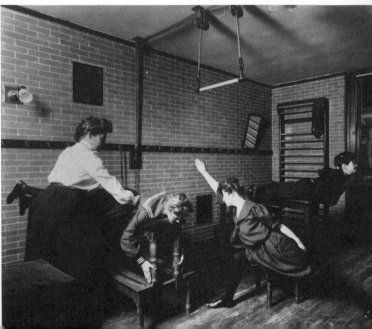

BETWEEN ROUNDS BY THOMAS EAKINS, 1899, SHOWS THE INFLUENCE OF REALISM ON AMERICAN PAINTING BY THE END OF THE NINETEENTH CENTURY.

ornate wedding cake. Sullivan stripped away classical ornamentation to reveal the true function of the building.

To Frank Lloyd Wright, Sullivan was "the master." Yet during a career that spanned over sixty years, Wright left a deeper imprint than any other American architect. Born in 1869, Wright was still influencing the direction of architecture at the time of his death in 1959. Calling his style "organic architecture," Wright designed buildings that seem to grow out of the landscape around them. Both he and Sullivan developed their theories in the years before World War I, when so many thinkers were

applying the concepts of evolution and pragmatism to their fields of study. Their architectural concepts broke with the ideas of the past much as did thought in philosophy, law, sociology, economics, and history.

Conclusion

The swift transformation of the United States into a great industrial power in the late nineteenth century had changed the geographic distribution of the population from rural to urban and had greatly limited the economic horizons of most American laborers. As we have just seen, the social inequities accompanying industrialization also set the stage for a revolution among American intellectuals. Many of the country's best-trained minds sought new ways to ensure that opportunities would be available for people to realize their full potential. But the political process, itself undergoing a transformation in this period, was slow to respond to the demands of farmers, workers, and intellectuals for curbs on the power of America's industrial elite. It was not until the 1890s that a new movement for reform emerged in national politics with the goal of alleviating the inequities that had been created by industrialization.

Readings

General Works

Aaron, Daniel, *Men of Good Hope*. New York: Oxford University Press, 1951.

Bellot, H. H., *American History and American Historians*. Norman: University of Oklahoma Press, 1952.

Commager, Henry S., *The American Mind*. New Haven, Conn.: Yale University Press, 1950.

Cremin, Lawrence A., *The Transformation of the School: Progressivism in American Education, 1876–1957*. New York: Knopf, 1961.

Cubberly, Ellsworth P., *Public Education in the United States*. Boston: Houghton Mifflin, 1919.

Hofstadter, Richard, and Walter P. Metzger, *The Development of Academic Freedom in the United States*, Vol. II. New York: Columbia University Press, 1955.

Kazin, Alfred, *On Native Grounds*. New York: Harcourt, Brace, 1942.

Larkin, Oliver W., *Art and Life in America*. New York: Holt, Rinehart and Winston, 1960.

Martin, Jay, *Harvest of Change: American Literature 1865–1914*. Englewood Cliffs, N.J.: Prentice-Hall, 1967.

Morgan, H. Wayne, *New Muses: Art in American Culture, 1865–1920*. Norman: University of Oklahoma Press, 1978.

Russett, Cynthia Eagle, *Darwin in America: The Intellectual Response, 1865–1912*. San Francisco: Freeman, 1976.

White, Morton G., *Social Thought in America*. Boston: Beacon, 1957.

Wish, Harvey, *Society and Thought in Modern America*, Vol. II. New York: David McKay, 1962.

Special Studies

Andrews, Wayne, *Architecture, Ambition and Americans*. New York: Free Press, 1964.

Bleyer, Willard G., *Main Currents in the History of American Journalism*. New York: Plenum, 1969.

Carter, Everett, *Howells and the Age of Realism*. Hamden, Conn.: Shoestring Press, 1954.

Hofstadter, Richard, *The Progressive Historians: Turner, Parrington, Beard*. New York: Knopf, 1968.

Mott, Frank L., *A History of American Magazines 1885–1905*. Cambridge, Mass.: Harvard University Press, 1957.

Rudolph, Frederick, *The American College and University, a History*. New York: Knopf, 1962.

Smith, Henry Nash, *Democracy and the Novel: Popular Resistance to Classic American Writers*. New York: Oxford University Press, 1978.

Spivey, Donald, *Schooling for the New Slavery: Black Industrial Education, 1868–1915*. Westport, Conn.: Greenwood, 1978.

Tunnard, Christopher, and Henry H. Reed, *American Skyline: The Growth and Form of Our Cities and Towns*. New York: New American Library, 1956.

Veysey, Laurence R., *The Emergence of the American University*. Chicago: University of Chicago Press, 1965.

Primary Sources

Hofstadter, Richard, and Wilson Smith (Eds.), *American Higher Education, A Documentary History*, Vols. I–II. Chicago: University of Chicago Press, 1961.

Lerner, Max (Ed.), *The Mind and Faith of Justice Holmes*. New York: Random House, 1954.

Miller, Perry, *American Thought: Civil War to World War I*. New York: Holt, Rinehart and Winston, 1954.

Veblen, Thorstein, *The Theory of the Leisure Class*. New York: New American Library, 1964.

Biographies

Barker, Charles A., *Henry George*. New York: Oxford University Press, 1955.

Brooks, Van Wyck, *Howells: His Life and Works*. New York: Dutton, 1959.

Edel, Leon, *Henry James*. Minneapolis: University of Minnesota Press, 1960.

Hook, Sidney, *John Dewey*. New York: John Day, 1939.

Kaplan, Justin, *Mr. Clemens and Mark Twain*. New York: Simon & Schuster, 1966.

Perry, Ralph B., *The Thought and Character of William James*. Cambridge, Mass.: Harvard University Press, 1948.

Porter, Fairfield, *Thomas Eakins*. New York: Braziller, 1959.

Scott, Clifford H., *Lester Frank Ward*. Boston: Twayne, 1976.

20 Politics in the Gilded Age

The man who is employed for wages is as much a business man as his employer; the attorney in a country town is as much a business man as the corporation counsel in a great metropolis; the merchant at the cross-roads is as much a business man as the merchant of New York; the farmer who goes forth in the morning and toils all day—who begins in the spring and toils all summer—and who by the application of brain and muscle to the natural resources of the country creates wealth, is as much a business man as the man who goes upon the board of trade and bets upon the price of grain. . . .

William Jennings Bryan

Significant Events

Bland-Allison Act [1878]

Texas Farmers' Alliance [1880]

Northwestern Alliance [1880]

President James A. Garfield assassinated [July 2, 1881]

Pendleton Act (Civil Service Reform Act) [1883]

Mongrel Tariff [1883]

McKinley Tariff [1890]

Sherman Silver Purchase Act [1890]

Populist party organized [1892]

Depression [1893–1897]

Gold Standard Act [1900]

THE BOSSES OF THE SENATE, BY POLITICAL CARTOONIST JOSEPH KEPPLER, SATIRIZES THE INFLUENCE OF THE BLOATED TRUSTS ON CONGRESS DURING THE GILDED AGE.

The Gilded Age (1873) was the title of a novel by Mark Twain and Charles Dudley Warner which satirized the shallow materialism of industrial America in the late nineteenth century and the "shameful corruption" which had crept into American politics. The term came to be applied generally to the last few decades before the turn of the century. Many historians agreed with the view set forth by Twain and Warner. Henry Adams, for example, quipped: "The progress of evolution from President Washington to President Grant was alone evidence enough to upset Darwin." Some thinkers, however, have viewed the period not as "gilded" but as "golden," perceiving in the hectic politics of the era an expression of the American commitment to political democracy.

While the ethical standards of late nineteenth-century politicians were never again as low as they had been during the Grant administration, members of Congress continued to be held in low esteem. While there were probably few out-and-out rogues, there was widespread corruption. Washington teemed with lobbyists who maneuvered to protect their interests and obtain favorable legislation by every means from persuasion to bribery. It was standard practice for legislators to be allowed to win easily at card games and to be fêted with lavish parties and provided with female companionship. Members of Congress regularly received free passes from railroad leaders and advice on investments as well as shares of stock from business leaders. Most politicians experienced no ethical conflict in retaining investments in businesses whose interests they were required to vote on in the legislature. By the end of the century, however, these practices gradually decreased in response to demands by the public for higher standards of conduct in government.

Yet despite the influence of business in politics, the great majority of politicians at the national level were neither businesspeople nor simply the tools of business interests. Most of them had risen through years of hard work in state and local politics and by accepting the discipline of the party organization. Politics was considered a profession, and party loyalty was rewarded with increases in patronage and choice committee assignments. The resulting party cohesion made it necessary for the business interests to compete with each other for the ear of prominent politicians, which to some extent constrained their political influence.

During the Gilded Age politics on the state level became a full-time occupation for many men. While some of them were interested in obtaining wealth, most were more interested in gaining influence. Thomas Platt, boss of the Republican party organization in New York, rose to prominence through unswerving loyalty to the party and availability for consultation with local politicians and newspaper reporters. Like other bosses of state machines, he controlled the nominations for elective offices, influenced legislation, and distributed federal patronage. Summing up the role of the political boss in this era, James Bryce wrote: "The aim of a boss is not so much fame as power, and power not so much over the conduct of affairs as over persons."

The strong emphasis on maintaining efficient party organization as well as the general climate of acquisitiveness contributed to a reluctance to deal with the inequities created by industrialization. The Gilded Age witnessed a resurgence of long-held beliefs in local control, individualism, and laissez-faire economics, accompanied by hostility to strong government. Politicians at all levels—reflecting the attitudes of a majority of their constituents—responded ambivalently to the idea of increased government regulation. The result was the creation of a third political party, the Populists, which strove to supply answers to the economic plight of many farmers and workers. The upsurge of populism in the 1890s failed, but not before bringing back to center stage the continuing quest for a balance between industrial growth on the one hand and a humanitarian concern for the less fortunate on the other.

Politics in the Late Nineteenth Century

Though politial partisanship was intense during the late nineteenth century, in actuality few issues distinguished one party from the other. For example, the Republicans traditionally favored a high tariff and the Democrats a low one, but within each party there was debate on the question. Not until 1888 was the tariff a key issue in a national election. On other economic issues such as expansion of the money supply and government regulation of business the party positions also were similar. The Interstate Commerce Act of 1887 and the Sherman Anti-Trust Act of 1890 were supported by majorities in both parties.

The absence of issue-oriented politics was due in part to the delicate balance of power that existed from 1876 to 1892. Presidential elections were close, although with the exception of Grover Cleveland, all the presidents elected during this period were Republicans. State allegiances were stable. Republican officeholders generally outnumbered Democrats throughout the country and dominated the United States Senate. Even so, the Democrats, with strong support in the North and solid control of the South, narrowly remained the majority party until the 1890s and usually controlled the House of Representatives. Only between 1889 and 1891 did the Republicans control both houses of Congress as well as the

presidency. This situation contributed to the reluctance of politicians to take positions that might alienate voters. With no clear-cut distinctions between the parties on issues, party affiliation was based on other criteria. Sectional divisions, family tradition, local issues, race, religion, and ethnic identity were the most influential factors.

Factors in Party Affiliation

Sectionalism The Republicans drew most of their support from the Midwest, the Far West, Pennsylvania, and New England. Though the interests of these areas often conflicted, memories of their common effort to preserve the Union generally kept them in the party. The Republicans tried to ensure this loyalty (especially among Northern blacks and Union army veterans) by "waving the bloody shirt"; that is, by pointing to the Democrats as the party of

THE REPUBLICANS TRIED TO ENSURE PARTY LOYALTY BY "WAVING THE BLOODY SHIRT"—STIGMATIZING THE DEMOCRATS AS THE PARTY THAT BETRAYED THE UNION. NOTE THE VARIOUS SYMBOLS OF DEMOCRATIC WRONGDOING.

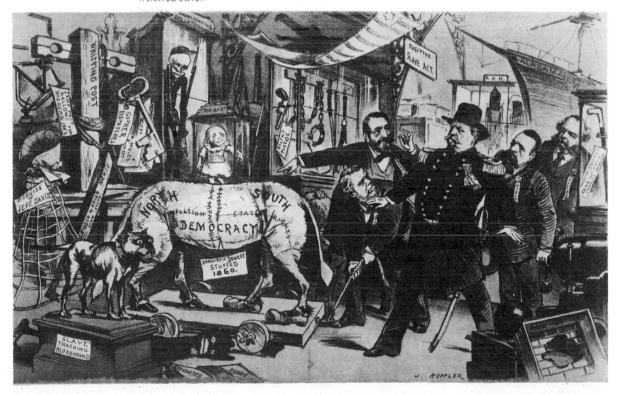

rebellion against the Union and by supporting high pensions for former Union soldiers. Party leaders continued making intermittent efforts to attract the Southern black vote until the 1890s, abandoning these efforts only when Republican control of the national government was absolutely secure.

Because of the conflicting interests of its membership, Republican party unity was threatened whenever real issues arose. The most serious rift was between Eastern business and Western farming interests. The business community favored a sound currency backed entirely by gold, a high tariff to protect them from foreign manufacturers, and government support for industrial and railroad interests. Most farmers, by contrast, opposed the gold standard, favoring instead an inflated currency they believed would help increase the money supply, make it easier to pay their debts, and raise the price of farm goods. They also opposed the high tariff, which benefited manufacturers but increased the cost of farm machinery. Finally, they detested the railroads for their high freight rates and their widespread influence in politics. The party tried to soft-pedal these and other issues to prevent the coalition from splintering.

The two great Democratic strongholds were the South and the machine-dominated cities of the Northeast. The South had been heavily Democratic since the Civil War. Even poor whites, victimized by the South's conservative Democrats, remained loyal out of fear that a weakened Democratic party would return the Republicans and their black allies to power. In the urban areas of the Northeast, the party was supported largely by industrial workers, most of whom were Catholic immigrants. Finally, there was a wing of the party composed of a mixture of conservative Eastern and Midwestern business interests that favored a lower tariff and sound money, as well as small farmers and small businesspeople who resented the leadership by the conservatives but were traditionally Democrats.

Religious and Ethnic Differences Religious and ethnic differences were also crucial in determining party affiliation. Most Episcopalians, Lutherans, Jews, and Roman Catholics—whose churches emphasized church supremacy in matters of morality and denied the state the right to define proper moral conduct—were Democrats. On the other hand, except in the "Solid South," most Methodists, Con-

gregationalists, Quakers, and many Presbyterians and Baptists—whose churches wanted the government to play a role in the moral reform of society—were Republicans.

These preferences emerged for pragmatic as well as religious reasons. The Democratic city machines encouraged the support of immigrant groups such as the Germans and the Irish by helping them to find jobs and by supplying necessities when they were in need. Moreover, since the Jeffersonian era, the Democratic party (at least in the North) had taken a tolerant view of the diversity in American ethnic and religious life. It was natural that Catholic immigrants from Germany and Ireland would be attracted to the party that sympathized with their demands for parochial schools supported by public funds and understood their opposition to restrictions on the purchase or consumption of alcoholic beverages and "blue laws" which curbed recreation on Sundays.

On the other hand, the Republicans, like the Whigs before them, resisted endorsing practices that offended the religious preferences of most party members. Mostly native-born old-stock Americans drawn mainly from Protestant denominations, they wanted a party dedicated to creating a nation of hardworkng and pious individuals, and they believed it was the proper role of government to help establish standards of virtue and morality. Now that the crusade against slavery had succeeded, they turned to passing laws on the local and state level banning work and recreational activities on Sunday, restricting the sale and consumption of liquor, and opposing state support of parochial schools.

Although sectional, religious, and ethnic issues were the major determinants of party affiliation, they were addressed at the state and local rather than the national level. Indeed, only during a national campaign did party leaders try to mobilize voters across the country with emotional appeals to party ideology. While listening to political speeches during presidential and congressional elections was almost as much a national pastime as watching a baseball game, it was the party organizations in each state, operating full time, that consolidated control in local communities by giving representation to the ethnic, religious, class, and regional interests of their members. Because the parties devoted attention to local needs, their followers loyally supported party candidates for every office from local judgeships to congressional seats and the presidency. Voter turnouts were high (usually over 80 percent) except in the South where blacks were effectively deprived of the vote and the domination of politics by the Democrats limited voter choice.

The Decline of the Presidency

Another important factor in late nineteenth-century politics was the decline in the power and prestige of the presidency and the concurrent resurgence of the legislative branch.

The balance of power had begun to shift after the Civil War when Congress successfully asserted itself in the battle over Reconstruction. The impeachment proceedings against Andrew Johnson further weakened executive authority, and Grant's inefficient administration and lack of initiative allowed Congress to increase its power even more. When Grant's successor, Rutherford B. Hayes, tried to exert presidential authority, he found his efforts opposed by a firmly entrenched congressional leadership.

Other factors also contributed to the eclipse of the presidency. Isolationism in foreign policy limited the opportunity to exert executive leadership in the conduct of diplomacy. Furthermore, no president during this period commanded majorities in both houses of Congress for a sustained period of time. Presidents therefore lacked the support necessary to enact any programs they might formulate. Finally, the prevailing interpretation of the Constitution held that it was the function of Congress to make the laws and the function of the president to execute them. The late nineteenth-century presidents took the conservative view that they should not attempt to exert strong initiative in generating policy.

Efforts to Curb Corruption

Although the large-scale political corruption and abuse of political power that characterized Grant's administration declined in the late nineteenth century, abuses were still evident in urban political machines, state government, the federal patronage system, and the influence of business in politics. For their part, politicians at all levels of government continued to demand payoffs for favors or for closing their eyes to corrupt business practices. Corruption also persisted as a result of opportunities for shrewd and unscrupulous individuals to acquire great wealth and power and to use it to gain favors from politicians. On the national level, the president's declining ability to counterbalance congressional power encouraged abuses by the legislative branch. Various reform groups called for an end to these abuses, but the political bosses usually succeeded in blunting their efforts.

Republican Reformers Before the 1890s a group of liberal Republicans, tagged "Mugwumps" by party regulars (supposedly from an Indian word suggesting self-righteousness), were the leading advocates of political reform. Many Mugwumps believed that industrialization had deprived responsible and honest people of leadership and given it to a corrupt class of business leaders. The reform Republicans included such refined and well-educated leaders as the German-born intellectual Carl Schurz; Henry Adams, grandson of President John Quincy Adams; George Curtis, editor of *Harper's* magazine; and E. L. Godkin, editor of *The Nation*. Horrified by the excessive influence of business in politics and its attendant corruption, they wanted the "best men" to enter government service and put an end to dishonest election practices such as the stuffing of ballot boxes. They also called for civil service reform to curb the spoils system and to limit business influence in government. At the same time they advocated a laissez-faire economic policy whereby government regulation would be limited to lowering the tariff. This position set them apart from farm and labor reformers, who wanted more government regulation of business, and it effectively prevented the establishment of a unified force for political and economic change.

Conservative Control

When Rutherford B. Hayes became president in 1877, the nation was in the middle of a worsening depression, the spoils system dominated American politics, and reformers were making little headway. Hayes, who sported a full reddish beard and had a high forehead, was a conservative politician who had helped found the Republican party in Ohio and had served three terms as governor of the state. His integrity and considerable administrative skill were attractive qualities, but unfortunately he possessed an aura of small-town morality that had little appeal to the new ethnic minorities and working-class people. His wife earned the nickname "Lemonade Lucy" by banning alcohol from White House social events.

Once in the White House, Hayes intended to continue the policies of efficient administration and civil service reform that had won him respect as governor of Ohio. However, he almost immediately encountered stiff opposition from the leaders of his own party. Furthermore, the party leaders remembered that he had been a compromise candidate and that his victory over Tilden had not been clear-cut. Senator Roscoe Conkling, New York's corrupt Republican boss, derisively called him "His Fraudulency." Many party regulars shared Conkling's opinion and scoffed at Hayes's intention to bring reform to national politics.

Determined nevertheless to create a reform administration, the new president began selecting his cabinet on the basis of talent rather than party loyalty. He appointed other reformers including Senator John Sherman of Ohio as secretary of the treasury and Carl Schurz as secretary of the interior. But when he named former Confederate David M. Key to head the United States Post Office, the party bosses finally exploded. Led by Conkling, they persuaded the Senate to refuse to confirm the president's cabinet nominations. Within a few days, however, public outrage at this obvious political maneuver forced the Senate to reverse its stand.

Despite opposition within his party Hayes continued to pursue reform. His efforts finally culminated in a showdown with Conkling. At issue was the New York Customs House, a longstanding bastion of corruption controlled by Conkling. Some two-thirds of the nation's customs revenues passed through the Customs House, and its officials regularly embezzled sizable amounts of these funds. Hayes, determined to eliminate this source of graft, called for the resignation of two Customs House officials, Conkling appointees Alonzo Cornell and Chester A. Arthur. Conkling fought the dismissals in the Senate, but Hayes produced records documenting the corruption and won his case. In spite of this sensational case, there was very little support for curb-

ing the spoils system. When Hayes left the White House in 1881, patronage abuses were still widespread.

Hayes and Labor

The depression that began with the Panic of 1873 worsened as the decade progressed. Large numbers of workers were unemployed, and unions could do little to improve the situation of those who did have jobs, since employers could easily replace troublesome workers. Hayes had genuine sympathy for the hardship of the workers, but his conservative philosophy placed him squarely with employers. When the railroad workers went on strike in 1877 to protest wage cuts, Hayes dispatched federal troops to maintain order but not to move the trains. The strikes were eventually broken. The president's personal conflict was reflected in his diary: "The strikes have been put down by *force,* but now for the *real* remedy. Can't something be done by education of the strikers, by judicious control of the capitalists, by wise general policy to end or diminish the evil? The railroad strikers, as a rule are good men sober intelligent and industrious."

Hayes faced a similar dilemma on the issue of Chinese immigration. A treaty had been concluded with China in 1868 permitting unlimited immigration of Chinese laborers to the United States. Employers welcomed this provision, since it guaranteed a plentiful supply of very cheap labor. American workers, on the other hand, feared competition for their jobs. As the depression worsened and jobs became more scarce, sentiment against Chinese immigration grew. In 1879 Congress passed a bill restricting immigration. Hayes, although concerned about the depression, vetoed the bill, believing it to be "inconsistent with our treaty obligations." His solution was to negotiate a new treaty with China, which would enable the United States to restrict immigration. Thus the president's action preserved the United States' relationship with China and accomplished the objective of keeping out more Chinese workers. It was too late for Hayes, however. His popularity already had been damaged by his veto of the bill.

The Election of 1880

Hayes declined to seek a second term, and the Republican presidential nomination provoked a bit-

THE CINDERELLA OF THE REPUBLICAN PARTY AND HER HAUGHTY SISTERS BY KEPPLER SATIRIZES THE ELECTION OF 1880. THE HARDWORKING REFORMER HAYES (LEFT) IS IGNORED, WHILE GRANT (CENTER) LED BY CONKLING TRIES FOR A THIRD TERM.

ter struggle between the two factions of the party. The Stalwarts, led by Roscoe Conkling, opposed reforming the patronage system and wanted to nominate Grant again. The Halfbreeds, followers of James G. Blaine, Conkling's political rival, claimed to be reformers but were in fact only slightly less aggressive in their pursuit of the spoils of office than the Stalwarts were. The differences between the factions concerned power more than policy. A deadlock at the convention finally resulted in the nomination of a Halfbreed compromise candidate, James A. Garfield of Ohio. Garfield, an orphan, had served in the Army, eventually rising to the rank of major general, and had served for a number of years in Congress. In an effort to heal party wounds he selected as his running mate Chester A. Arthur, a Stalwart and one of the men President Hayes had dismissed from the New York Customs House.

The campaign lacked substantive issues. The Democrats, who had nominated a former Union general, Winfield Scott Hancock, charged the Republicans with fraud in the 1876 election and reviewed for the electorate the Crédit Mobilier scandal, in which Garfield had been implicated (though later cleared). Claiming credit for recent improvements in the economy, the Republicans withstood the Democratic charges and emerged victorious. In a close contest, Garfield was elected president and the Republicans won control of both houses of Congress.

Once in the White House, Garfield demonstrated an independence in making appointments that infuriated the Stalwarts. The new president appeared to be planning to continue Hayes's battle for reform, but it is unclear whether he genuinely wanted reform or was merely trying to strengthen the Halfbreed faction of his party. To the dismay of Conkling, he appointed Halfbreed Blaine as secretary of state. Shortly thereafter he appointed another Halfbreed as collector of the Port of New York, a post Conkling had long coveted. The ensuing battle between Conkling and the president created intense bitterness between the two factions. Both Conkling and New York's junior senator, Thomas Platt, resigned from the Senate, confident that the New York state legislature would reelect them as a slap at Garfield. The legislature failed to do so, however, and Conkling's senatorial career was over.

Amid this political animosity, on July 2, 1881, Charles J. Guiteau, a demented loner who had been disappointed in his efforts to secure a diplomatic appointment, shot the president at the Washington railroad station. Garfield lay dying for over two months, finally succumbing on September 19. When apprehended, Guiteau declared: "I am a Stalwart and Arthur is president now," apparently a reference to his belief that under Arthur, Stalwarts would secure the choice appointments. Guiteau was tried for murder, found guilty, and hanged. James A. Garfield had been president for only four months.

President Chester A. Arthur

Thrust unexpectedly into the nation's highest office, Arthur was widely regarded as unworthy of occupying it. A worldly, handsome man who favored fine food and sported expensive clothing, Arthur had never held elective office. Although he had begun his career as an abolitionist, after the war his interests turned to the spoils of office. During the Garfield-Conkling feud, Arthur had sided with his Stalwart patron against the president. Once he took office, he began replacing a number of Garfield's Halfbreed appointees with Stalwart friends of Grant and Conkling, mostly men of mediocre ability.

Nevertheless, as time went on, it became apparent that Arthur was not the spineless party hack that many had expected. Stunned by Garfield's assassination, he seemed to awaken to the moral and political responsibilities of the presidency. He defied the Stalwarts by refusing to fire all the Halfbreed appointees. He advocated civil service reform and vetoed "pork barrel" legislation—projects or appro-

priations enacted only for the benefit of a specific legislator's constituents.

Civil Service Reform The number of government employees had grown rapidly in the late nineteenth century, mostly as a result of the spoils system. Whereas there had been 20,000 people on the federal payroll under Jackson, by 1884 there were 131,000. Political leaders who accepted the time and money of supporters during a campaign were then beseiged for reward in the form of patronage appointments after the campaign was won. Garfield expressed the sentiment of other presidents in this era when he lamented that office seekers were "lying in wait" for him "like vultures for a wounded bison." Yet presidents also knew that Congress would be more likely to support an administration which supplied their friends with postmasterships, clerical jobs, and positions in the customs and diplomatic services. Describing the importance of the spoils system to the running of the political process, no less a practitioner than Roscoe Conkling remarked that parties "are not built up by deportment, or by ladies magazines, or by gush."

Civil service jobs were eagerly sought because wages were better than for many jobs in private industry and because federal workers usually worked an eight-hour day (a goal as yet unrealized by most factory workers). Bribes to secure these jobs were common. The result was that many positions were filled by individuals whose only qualification was that they supported the party in power.

Garfield's assassination by a disappointed office seeker finally compelled Congress to do what a decade of protest by reformers had failed to make it do. In the wake of the president's death, demands for reform swept the Congress, resulting in the Pendleton Act, also called the Civil Service Reform Act of 1883. The act created the Civil Service Commission to administer a new merit system for filling public offices. Competitive examinations would determine qualifications and ensure that parties did not extort money from public officials or discharge qualified officeholders for political reasons. At first the commission's jurisdiction extended to only 10 percent of federal offices. Presidents were empowered, however, to enlarge the list of offices coming under the commission's jurisdiction, and 90 percent of all federal employees were under the merit system by 1950.

Virtues of Civil Service Reform

"The perversion of the Civil Service to a mere party machine is pitilessly cruel. . . . how many lives are hanging at this moment in agony of terror by that single thread of patronage. It is unspeakable cruelty. I do not hold the immediate appointing power responsible for this tragedy. It is the crime of the system. . . .

The Civil-Service Reform therefore begins with the assertion that there is no reason in the nature of things or of our form of government that the United States should not manage its affairs with the same economy, ability, and honesty that the best private business is managed; and that to do this it must take the most obvious means not incompatible with the Constitution, with a popular government, with experience and common-sense. It therefore proposes a system of examinations and probations open to all citizens; the appointments to the subordinate offices to be made from those proved to be best qualified. . . ."

George W Curtis, 1883

Evils of Civil Service Reform

"This Civil Service Law is the biggest fraud of the age. It is the curse of the nation. There can't be no real patriotism while it acts. How are you goin' to interest our young men in their country if you have no offices to give them when they work for their party? Just look at things in this city to-day. There are ten thousand good offices, but we can't get at more than a few hundred of them. How are we goin' to provide for the thousands of men who worked for the Tammany ticket? It can't be done. These men were full of patriotism a short time ago. They expected to be servin' their city, but when we tell them that we can't place them, do you think their patriotism is goin' to last? Not much. They say: 'What's the use of workin' for your country anyhow? There's nothin' in the game.' And what can they do? I don't know, but I'll tell you what I do know. I know more than one young man in past years who worked for the ticket and was just overflowin' with patriotism, but when he was knocked out by the civil service humbug he got to hate his country and became an Anarchist."

George W. Plunkitt, 1883

Although the Pendleton Act made a small dent in patronage appointments, it by no means eliminated them. Bosses of city machines, national party managers, and members of Congress continued to wield enormous power over appointments, using their influence to assist those large business interests that had money to buy the politicians they wished to control.

The Treasury Surplus Another problem demanding Arthur's attention was a treasury surplus. The Republican party generally supported a high tariff to stimulate economic development. The problem was that high tariffs were bringing revenue into the treasury faster than the government could spend it, and many people believed that the money should be put into circulation to stimulate the economy. The Democrats opposed a high tariff, claiming that the surplus represented the high rates consumers paid to support a small number of manufacturers.

Arthur proposed two separate measures to reduce the surplus. First, he asked for an across-the-board tariff reduction of 20 percent. This was violently opposed by the manufacturing interests, which used all their influence to pressure Congress into defeating it. In response, Congress returned to Arthur an amended tariff that offered no real reduction and in fact increased certain rate schedules. The president reluctantly signed the so-called Mongrel Tariff of 1883 because in principle he believed in the protective tariff and he knew that the general public was indifferent to the issue. Arthur's second proposal was to inject the treasury surplus into the economy by increasing government spending; specifically, he called for modernizing the badly outmoded United States Navy. This would not only reduce the surplus, Arthur argued, but would also make the nation's decrepit fleet more competitive with the superior iron and steel European navies. Congress reluctantly passed the necessary legislation, thus taking the first steps toward building a modern American fleet.

The Election of 1884

Arthur's independence had offended the Republican leadership and they refused to nominate him in 1884. Instead the party gave the nod to the "Plumed Knight," James G. Blaine, whose charismatic style had won him the most enthusiastic and loyal following of any politician of the era. Unfortunately, Blaine's otherwise formidable political assets were tainted by charges that he had abused his position as Speaker of the House between 1869 and 1875 to secure favors for railroad interests and by unresolved questions about his complicity in the Crédit Mobilier scandal. Disdainfully observing that Blaine had "wallowed in spoils like a rhinoceros in an African pool," Mugwump leader Carl Schurz led a defection of reformists, who threw their support to the Democrats.

With a strong chance of winning the presidency for the first time since the Civil War, the Democrats nominated portly Grover Cleveland, who had a reputation as a reformer and as an enemy of the Tammany Hall machine. As mayor of Buffalo, Cleveland had eliminated graft in munici-

ANOTHER VOICE FOR CLEVELAND SHOWS CANDIDATE CLEVELAND'S CONSTERNATION OVER THE ISSUE OF HIS ILLEGITIMATE OFFSPRING.

pal sewerage and street-cleaning projects. As governor of New York he had enhanced his reputation for integrity and at the same time won the favor of conservative business interests by upholding their contract rights and vetoing a few articles of poorly conceived reform legislation.

The election of 1884 was one of the dirtiest in American history. Instead of being centered on political issues, the campaign was fought over the personal morality of the two candidates. During the campaign it was revealed that Cleveland, a bachelor, had accepted responsibility for an illegitimate child. It was not clear whether Cleveland was in fact the father, but he had granted the possibility and gallantly agreed to support the child. Shortly thereafter Blaine's knightly armor was tarnished with the release of a letter implicating him in the Crédit Mobilier scandal and ending with the phrase, "Burn this letter." The presidential campaign soon degenerated into a shouting match between Republicans chanting "Ma! Ma! Where's my pa? Gone to the White House Ha! Ha! Ha!" and Democrats answering with "Blaine, Blaine, James G. Blaine, The Continental liar from the State of Maine. *Burn this letter!*"

As the campaign entered its last few days the election was too close to call. At this point Blaine made two mistakes that seriously hurt his chances in the key state of New York. Tammany Hall, which controlled the Irish-American vote, was supporting Blaine because of his Irish background and his support for Irish independence from England. When a Protestant minister and supporter of Blaine referred to the Democrats as the party of "rum, Romanism, and rebellion," an obvious slur against the Irish, Blaine failed to repudiate the remark, and this cost him much Irish support. Blaine's second mistake was to attend a fund-raising banquet with wealthy business leaders in New York. The next morning's New York *World* headlined the event and implied that Blaine was an ally of the wealthy and an enemy of the poor.

When the returns were in Cleveland had won by less than twenty-five thousand popular votes and 219 electoral votes to Blaine's 182. Blaine's loss of New York was costly; had he been able to carry that pivotal state, he would have won the election. In the congressional contest, the Democrats gained control of the House of Representatives, and the Republicans retained their majority in the Senate.

The Cleveland Administration

President Cleveland faced three major problems: relations between the North and the South, reform, and the tariff.

In keeping with the attitude of his party, Cleveland wanted to complete the reintegration of the South into national affairs. Problems arose when he appointed two former Confederate officers to his cabinet, and they multiplied enormously when he began returning captured Confederate flags to Southern states as a symbolic gesture of conciliation. In 1887, he vetoed the Dependent Pension bill, which would have awarded exorbitant sums of money to Union veterans. Cleveland's veto incensed the veterans and appeared to lend credence to the Republican contention that a Democratic presidency would be the handmaiden of Southern interests.

On the issue of civil service reform, Cleveland attempted to steer a middle course. Although he was committed to reform, Cleveland felt obliged to fill some of the jobs held for so long by Republicans with office-hungry Democrats. He therefore dismissed some forty thousand Republican postmasters and replaced them with Democrats. This, however, was not enough to satisfy his own party, and it alienated the Mugwumps, who were committed to eliminating politics from the civil service.

On the issue of business influence in government, Cleveland recognized that some kind of government regulation was called for. Thus he undertook investigations into the practices of the railroads, lumber companies, and cattle interests and supported the Interstate Commerce Act. He also concluded that a high tariff was no longer needed and that the treasury surplus should be eliminated by lowering the tariff. When both Democrats and Republicans failed to respond to his gentle prodding, Cleveland took the extraordinary step of devoting his entire 1887 State of the Union message to Congress to the tariff question. He argued that the high tariff created unnecessarily high prices and imposed a special "burden upon those with moderate means and the poor, the employed and unemployed."

The president's speech was both denounced and applauded. Republicans accused him of promoting a "free-trade" policy, when in fact he was only asking for a moderate reduction in rates. Mug-

TO AMEND BUT NOT DESTROY.
UNCLE SAM. "How much o' that dew ye calkelate ter take off?"
G. C. "The rough edges, merely."

ALTHOUGH CLEVELAND ASKED FOR ONLY A MODERATE REDUCTION IN TARIFF RATES, REPUBLICANS ACCUSED HIM OF ADVOCATING A "FREE-TRADE" POLICY.

wumps and other reformers hailed him, calling the speech an act of great courage. At the president's urging, a lowered tariff bill was introduced in Congress, but the Republicans blocked it in the Senate. The tariff therefore became an issue in the 1888 election.

The Election of 1888

Though some Eastern Democrats grumbled about Cleveland's low tariff policy, most Democrats favored it, and he was renominated by acclamation in 1888. The Republican nominee was Senator Benjamin Harrison, a lawyer, churchman, and Union army brigadier general. Though neither a strong leader nor at five feet six of commanding physique, Harrison had served one term in the Senate and was honest, dignified, and competent. He was also the grandson of President William Henry Harrison and came from Indiana, a pivotal state which the Republicans had to carry if the election was a close one.

In contrast to the extraverted Cleveland, Harrison was a reserved and quiet man. To Harrison's advantage, Cleveland felt that campaigning was beneath the dignity of a president, and he failed to use the campaign to project his personality. Harrison, on the other hand, ran a successful "front porch" campaign, delivering more than eighty speeches to groups that came to hear him at his Indianapolis home.

Harrison focused on Cleveland's veto of the veterans' pension bill as a key issue in the campaign. He capitalized on the veterans' dissatisfaction by "waving the bloody shirt" and asserting that "It was no time to be weighing the claims of old soldiers with apothecary's scales." The veterans were delighted to have an alternative to Cleveland and they organized extensively on Harrison's behalf. Ignoring Harrison's attacks, Cleveland campaigned on the tariff issue. With Harrison supporting the continuation of a high tariff, most businesspeople joined veterans behind his candidacy.

Harrison's managers established a highly efficient and systematic method of collecting campaign funds. Civil service reform had diminished the likelihood of reward through patronage so officeholders had become less willing to donate time and money to campaigns. As a result, the parties had to rely increasingly on the business community for financial support. Industrial and business interests who favored the retention of a high tariff contributed an unprecedented $4 million. These contributions proved to be very important, enabling the Republican party to spend large sums buying votes in closely contested states, especially Indiana. This money may also partly explain why the election of 1888 was among the most corrupt in history.

As the campaign progressed, both candidates moderated their statements on the tariff issue in order to attract as many voters as possible. But in the last days of the campaign Cleveland lost the critical Irish vote when a Republican posing as a naturalized Englishman wrote the British Ambassador in Washington, Sir Lionel Sackville-West, asking his advice on how to vote in the election. The ambassador foolishly sent back a letter expressing his support for Cleveland. When gleeful Republicans made the letter public, it drove many Irish voters,

who were bitter against Britain over the issue of Irish independence, into Harrison's camp.

Although Cleveland received more popular votes than Harrison, he lost the electoral contest 233 to 168. The loss of the crucial states of New York and Indiana because of election frauds and Irish and veteran opposition cost Cleveland the presidency.

The Harrison Administration

Soon after Harrison took office, it became apparent that his campaign promises of civil service and election reform had been mere rhetoric. Republican politicians were quick to reclaim the spoils of office. And although the young Theodore Roosevelt, an advocate of civil service reform, was appointed to the Civil Service Commission, he was able to accomplish little and soon became frustrated with the Harrison administration.

The Republicans did keep their promise to the veterans by passing the Dependent Pension Act of 1890, essentially the same bill that Cleveland had vetoed. Hailed by veterans as "the most liberal pension measure ever passed by any legislative body in the world," the act authorized the distribution of $160 million a year to veterans, a staggering sum for that time. The Harrison administration also enacted the McKinley Tariff of 1890, the highest peacetime tariff in the nation's history. The tariff shielded American manufactures from foreign competition, raised the duties on such farm products as potatoes, eggs, barley, and corn, and placed certain raw materials such as sugar, coffee, and tea on a free list as a means of disposing of a surplus of these goods. However, the protectionists had to make concessions to Western Republicans to secure passage of the bill.

Western Republicans had gained new power when six Western states joined the Union in 1889 and 1890. Western farmers traditionally opposed a high tariff because protective tariffs generally benefited manufacturers and discriminated against farmers. This time, however, their representatives voted for the McKinley Tariff on two conditions: first, that some farm products be included under its protection, and second, that the tariff's supporters vote for the Sherman Silver Purchase Act, a bill intended to increase the amount of money in circulation and drive up farm prices. Unfortunately, the tariff and the Silver Purchase Act did little to help the farmers, and farm prices continued to fall.

The Politics of Agriculture

Mid–nineteenth-century industrialization brought great changes in farming which at first glance seemed to benefit the farmer. The revolution in transportation and communication opened up foreign markets for American farm products. Technological advances promised to ease the farmers' burden and at the same time increase production. Yet during the late nineteenth century the farmers' economic situation grew worse.

As the nation industrialized and more farming people were drawn to the city, fewer farmers were producing more food for the growing number of urban dwellers. Small farmers were being ruined by large commercial farmers who produced crops to feed a nation.

The settling of the West doubled the amount of available farmland. This, together with industrialization and scientific advances, increased productivity far beyond America's needs. Farmers had originally assumed that foreign markets would absorb the surplus, but this proved to be a false hope. Agricultural production abroad was increasing as well, and American farm produce was forced to compete with foreign produce both at home and overseas. The high tariff on manufactured goods meant that American farmers had to pay more for equipment and supplies than their foreign counterparts did. Since there was an agricultural surplus, the tariff, which protected only certain American agricultural produce, had little effect. American farmers were therefore caught in an economic squeeze. If their produce was priced high enough to cover their costs and make a respectable profit, consumers would buy the cheaper foreign produce. If it was competitively priced, farmers could barely break even.

Between 1887 and 1890 the price of a bushel of wheat fell by almost 50 percent. During this same period a series of droughts in the Plains states destroyed the harvests. But even with crop shortages, farm prices did not rise, because world food production was more than adequate to meet market demands. These conditions resulted in an increase in the number of mortgaged farms and reduced almost 35 percent of American farmers to tenancy.

The farmers' most visible enemy was the railroads. Granted some 135 million acres of public land, the railroads offered it to farmers for what they claimed was easy, long-term credit. The credit was indeed long term, but far from easy. By the last quarter of the century large numbers of Western farmers were deeply in debt to the railroads—and not just for land. The railroads' monopoly over transportation enabled them to charge exorbitant rates for transporting agricultural commodities to market.

The farmers often blamed wealthy Eastern manufacturing interests for the high tariff that victimized them. But the tariff was not the only tax

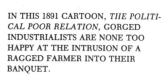

IN THIS 1891 CARTOON, *THE POLITICAL POOR RELATION,* GORGED INDUSTRIALISTS ARE NONE TOO HAPPY AT THE INTRUSION OF A RAGGED FARMER INTO THEIR BANQUET.

that discriminated against farmers. Business and railroad interests commonly concealed their holdings in order to pay lower taxes. But farmers had no way of hiding their land and were often forced to pay the entire tax on mortgaged land that was actually owned by a railroad or some other absentee owner.

As if all this were not enough, the quality of life for farmers was inferior to that of city dwellers. Rural education, roads, and sanitation were inadequate, and there was no free rural mail delivery until the 1890s. Farmers increasingly came to look upon themselves as honest, hardworking people who fed the nation and in exchange were victimized by the Eastern industrial, railroad, and banking interests.

The Farmers' Alliances

The farmers' first real political organization, the National Grange, was founded in the 1860s to educate poor farm people and to provide a sense of community for those who lived in isolated areas. Admitting women on an equal basis with men, the Grangers held rallies, outings, and discussions and distributed books and farm journals.

In the 1870s, as the depression worsened and farm prices fell, the Grange became more political and membership soared. By 1876 the Grangers were demanding lower freight rates, lower interest rates, and government regulation of monopolies. Their most innovative measure was the formation of cooperatives, which would buy goods directly from a wholesaler and distribute them at lower than retail cost to Grange members. By the late 1870s, however, the Granger movement had faded. Farmers who had joined the organization during hard times left just as rapidly when prosperity returned.

In the late 1880s, as agrarian discontent resurfaced, new agricultural organizations sprang up. In the Plains states, farmers joined the Northwestern Alliance. This relatively small organization, founded in 1880 by Milton George, sought to revive the Grangers' political program by uniting farmers "for their protection against class legislation and the encroachments of concentrated capital and the tyranny of monopoly."

The much larger Southern Alliance had its roots in the Texas Farmers' Alliance formed in 1874 to protect farmers against horse thieves. Under the

leadership of Dr. C. W. Macune, the movement spread throughout the South; by 1888 it claimed to have a membership of several million. The Southern Alliance was loosely affiliated with an organization of over one million black farmers called the Colored Farmers' National Alliance and Cooperative Union.

Although Southern Alliance leaders wanted to ensure that blacks could vote in their section, they, like the conservative Democrats, believed in white supremacy and had no program to aid poor black farmers. Initially, efforts to merge the Northern and Southern Alliances failed because leaders of the Northern Alliance opposed a separate organization for blacks and believed that a nationwide movement would be dominated by the larger Southern Alliance. In 1889, however, the Southern farmers movement, reorganized as the National Farmers' Alliance and Industrial Union, gained the support of the organizations in Kansas and the Dakotas.

Although the Farmers' Alliances sponsored educational and social programs similar to those of the Grange, their main interests were economic and political. They established cooperative grain elevators, marketing associations, and retail stores that transacted millions of dollars' worth of business each year. When many of the cooperatives failed due to lack of funds and poor management, the Alliances turned increasingly to political activity. Their political objectives included an inflated currency, lower tariffs, easier credit, more equitable taxation, and government ownership of the railroads.

Although the Alliances agreed on their goals, they disagreed on the best way to get their program enacted. Farmers in the Northwestern Alliance favored creating independent third parties to oppose Republicans and Democrats. But leaders of the Southern Alliance opposed such a plan, believing that in the South it made more sense to try to work within the firmly entrenched Democratic party.

Third parties emerged in many of the Plains states and the Midwest in 1890. Farmer desperation was reflected in the success of Alliance candidates in the congressional elections of that year. Seven Alliance candidates were elected to the House of Representatives, and Kansas and South Dakota elected Alliance candidates to the Senate. In the Plains states the Alliance cut deeply into the Republican vote. In the South, forty-four congressmen and three senators, the majority of them Democrats, were elected with Alliance support. Even though many of the

Democrats later proved to have a stronger allegiance to the Democratic party than to the farmers, the 1890 elections were nevertheless a stunning victory for the farmers—now a political force in twelve states—a severe defeat for Republicans in the Plains states, and a warning that the farmers were becoming a powerful force.

The Election of 1892

Although cheered by the results of the 1890 congressional elections, the farmers' movement still lacked a national political organization. The "people's parties," under whose banners many of the Alliance candidates had run, comprised a loose coalition, each state having its own party name and organization. Yet renewed attempts to unite all the people's parties into a national third party failed at first, largely because of the allegiance of poor Southern farmers to the Democrats. In time, however, worsening economic conditions increased militancy and solidarity among farmers. Mary Elizabeth Lease, a farm leader known as the "Kansas Pythoness," exhorted farmers "to raise less corn and more hell!" In 1892 the new mood of unity was formalized with the creation of the People's (Populist) party. The first Populist convention was held later that year in Omaha, Nebraska, in an atmosphere of tumultuous excitement. The Populists nominated former Union general James B. Weaver of Iowa for president and former Confederate general James G. Field for vice-president.

The Populist Platform The platform, written by Ignatius Donnelly, a fiery journalist, declared that the nation was on the verge of "moral, political, and material ruin" that only drastic change would be able to prevent. Charging that the two major parties were dominated by greed, corruption, and wealth, the platform proposed specific economic reforms that would improve the condition of both workers and farmers: an inflated currency and free coinage of silver; control of the supply of currency by the government instead of private banks; restriction of immigration to protect the American labor market; government ownership of railroads, the telegraph, and telephone; a graduated income tax; and a shorter workweek. The platform also favored political reforms to eliminate corruption and increase popular participation in government: the use of

secret ballots in all elections, the use of the initiative and referendum to make government officials more responsible to the people, the direct election of senators, and a one-term presidency.

The Populist platform seemed alarmingly radical to many people. Most disturbing of all was the Populist notion that the government should assume some responsibility for the economic well-being of its citizens. "We believe," the platform stated, "that the power of government—in other words, of the people—should be expanded . . . to the end that oppression, injustice, and poverty shall eventually cease in the land." Believing that all poor people were oppressed and victimized by the same forces and should work together, the Populists attempted to rally industrial workers as well as farmers to their cause. Some Southern Populists even tried to break down the hostility of poor white farmers toward poor blacks. This effort had little success, however.

Cleveland Reemerges Out of office for four years, Grover Cleveland was once again nominated by the Democrats to oppose Benjamin Harrison. Harrison had alienated labor by supporting a high protective tariff and by using federal troops to break a silver miners' strike in Idaho. Western Republicans who wanted an increase in silver coinage also opposed the president. Cleveland, on the other hand, was still an extremely popular public figure, and during the past four years he had become more conservative and had drawn a good deal of business support away from Harrison.

Since neither the Democrats nor the Republicans would take a firm stand on the silver issue, the only issue they debated was the high duties imposed by the McKinley Tariff. Having lost the support of both business and labor, Harrison and the Republicans were badly beaten in the election, losing to Cleveland in the electoral college 271 to 145. Populist candidate Weaver did well in the Plains states, winning twenty-two electoral votes and 8.5 percent of the popular vote; moreover, with the election of five Populists to the Senate and ten to the House of Representatives, it looked as if populism might be a force to reckon with in future elections.

Yet in spite of this impressive showing, the Populist party was unable to sustain political momentum, largely because many Southern Populists still preferred to work through the Democratic

INTERPRETING AMERICAN HISTORY

POPULISM Whereas political opponents of Populism in the 1890s unanimously condemned its program as radical and unsound, twentieth-century historical interpretations of the movement have been characterized by great diversity. In *The Populist Revolt* (1931) John D. Hicks described Populism as a popularly based agrarian movement which had formulated a comprehensive legislative program to eliminate many of the inequities and injustices created by an industrialized economy. Hicks believed that the Populist program had anticipated many of the political and economic reforms of the twentieth century. Over twenty years later Richard Hofstadter in *The Age of Reform* (1955) argued that the character of populism was more complex. While it had a progressive side, it also was a regressive movement in that it responded to the social crisis of industrialization by trying to turn back the clock to a mythical agrarian past. Too, there was an irrational strain in populism evidenced in such proto-fascist and nativist tendencies as lashing out at Jews, blacks, immigrants, and the British "money conspiracy" as the causes of the nation's problems. While it was true that most Populists were antagonistic to allowing large numbers of new immigrants into the country, in *The Tolerant Populists* (1963) Walter T. R. Nugent showed that in Kansas, at least, Populists were not anti-Semitic and that they even favored women's suffrage. It is also a fact that in most Southern states the Populists denounced the convict lease system and lynching and supported political rights for blacks.

While recent historians have disagreed on the exact goals of the Populist movement, they have once again seen its proposals as constructive and farsighted. Norman Pollack rejected Hofstadter's interpretation in his analysis of Midwestern populism, *The Populist Response to Industrial America* (1962). According to Pollack the Populists were a

progressive group which was receptive to modern technology and the mechanization of agriculture. They had concrete plans to remedy existing political and economic problems and were optimistic about forming a farmer-labor coalition to reform society. "Populism was more than a protest movement," wrote Pollack, "it was a glorious chapter in the eternal struggle for human rights." In *Populism: Reaction or Reform* (1968) Theodore Saloutos found large areas of agreement with Pollack's interpretation. He defined populism as a middle-class, rural movement whose aim was to preserve the agrarian way of life in industrial America. Its advocates did not challenge the concept of private property but wished to protect the family farm as the mainstay of the economy. They wanted to see more farmers and wage earners enter politics in order to break the hold of business corporations on the economy and restore economic competition. In short, Saloutos believed the Populists wanted the federal government to undertake reforms within the framework of democratic capitalism. Taking issue with this interpretation, Lawrence Goodwyn in *Democratic Promise: The Populist Movement in America* (1976) has described populism as a truly radical movement growing out of the Southern Alliance. Its real goal was not the free coinage of silver but the development of a socialized economy based on cooperatives, a subtreasury system which would take control of the economy from commercial bankers, and an inflated currency to meet the farmers' financial problems.

It is quite likely that, given the diversity of its manifestations, populism will continue to undergo varying interpretations. As historian James Wright has written: "Populism grew from disparate needs, and in its various state and local manifestations it reflected sharply different cultural, economic, and political realities" (*Reviews in American History*, Vol. 6, No. 3, September 1978, p. 369).

party in order to maintain the policy of white supremacy. Moreover, the Populists were unable to attract a broad base of support, particularly among

labor and middle-class Americans who feared the inflationary consequences of unlimited coinage of silver. This meant that the party's strength was limited to the Plains states and parts of the South, the major seats of agrarian discontent. The lasting contribution of the movement proved to be in the adoption of many of its proposals by other reformers and in the eventual enactment of these proposals during the next half century.

The Gold and Silver Controversy

The controversy over the coinage of silver was the most critical and complex domestic issue of the decade. Both political parties were divided on the question, and it involved monetary theories about which historians and economists still disagree.

Since gold was the international monetary standard, "hard-money" advocates such as businesspeople and wage earners argued that the amount of currency in circulation should reflect the amount of gold in the treasury. A currency backed by gold would be "sound"—respected at home and abroad—and would not fluctuate in value. Accordingly, "hard-money" people believed that the government should print only as much paper currency as it could back with its gold reserves.

Debtor farmers, workers, and mining interests, on the other hand, viewed money in radically different terms—as a form of credit. These "soft-money" people believed that currency should represent the quantity of goods in a society relative to the population. Therefore, the currency supply should not be limited to the amount of gold in the treasury, but should increase as productivity and population increased. The fact that the currency supply had not kept pace with the expansion of population and production, they argued, was a major cause of the country's economic problems. It had created a situation in which there was not enough money to pay wages and buy the available goods. They wanted to put more money into circulation to improve the average American's well-being. This could be done either by allowing silver, as well as gold, to stand behind the currency or by letting Civil War greenbacks circulate, even if they were not completely backed by gold.

Agitation for Free Silver

Silver had been used as a monetary standard until 1873, when it was demonetized by the Coinage Act. Within a few years a great increase in silver produc-

tion drove down the market price, and silverites began to demand its free and unlimited coinage. It would be cheaper to pay debts with silver than with gold, they argued, and the abundance of silver would increase the country's money supply and have the inflationary effect of raising prices. Nevertheless, in 1875 supporters of the gold standard successfully engineered the passage of the Specie Resumption Act, which provided that all currency would be redeemable in gold by 1879. Even though the act left most of the greenbacks in circulation, the fact that greenbacks were now backed by gold prevented the inflation of currency the silverites desired.

As the depression of the 1870s continued, farmers and workers exerted pressure to increase the money supply by again allowing the free and unlimited coinage of silver. In 1878 monetary conservatives and silverites in both parties passed a compromise agreement, the Bland-Allison Act, which required the government to purchase $2-$4 million of silver each month and to put sixteen ounces of silver in a silver dollar in comparison to one ounce of gold in a gold dollar. However, because the act did

IN THIS CARTOON UNCLE SAM PLEADS FOR SOMEONE TO SEE HIM THROUGH THE SILVER CONTROVERSY.

not permit the "free and unlimited" coinage of silver, the amount of currency in circulation did not increase greatly and every dollar was still backed by gold. To change this, silverites from both parties sponsored the Sherman Silver Purchase Act of 1890. It provided for government purchase of 4.5 million ounces of silver per month, thus raising the amount of silver the government would buy and use to back new silver certificates added to the nation's money supply. Even so, prices did not rise significantly because the act still did not provide for the unlimited coinage of silver, and the treasury's supply of gold was so large that every silver dollar and certificate was still redeemable in gold.

Depression Years: 1893–1897

Only a few months after Cleveland took office, the Panic of 1893 unglued the shaky Democratic coalition. By the end of 1895 more than 160 railroads, tens of thousands of businesses, and countless banks had collapsed. The Panic of 1893 was the beginning of the worst depression the country had yet experienced, and its effects lingered on until 1897.

The depression was fueled by several problems. The treasury surplus of $190 million in 1890 was gone by 1892, in part because less revenue was being collected under the McKinley Tariff and in part because of increased expenditures for veterans' pensions and purchases of silver under the Sherman Silver Purchase Act. In the early 1890s depressions in Europe and Australia severely harmed American foreign trade. The call for "free and unlimited" coinage of silver to help expand the currency supply made foreign investors uneasy, and many of them began selling their American stocks. At home, the agricultural depression continued to reduce the farmers' purchasing power. The financial instability of the railroads, which had overextended themselves during the industrial boom, became apparent. Finally, a series of labor strikes stalled production and undermined public confidence in the nation's economy.

The number of unemployed during the depression years is estimated to have been between 2.5 and 4 million, nearly 25 percent of the labor force. Relief expenditures in the big cities ran into millions of dollars. Destitute people wandered across the country, hitching rides on freight trains, looking for work in city after city. "Never within my memory have so many people literally starved to death as in the past few months," declared a New York clergyman.

Some efforts were made to combat the suffering of the unemployed. The New York *World* distributed bread, the *Herald* gave away clothing, and some cities paid subsistence wages to people for sweeping the streets and working on other improvement projects. Yet private charity efforts were undertaken on too small a scale to make much headway, and many people agreed with the governor of New York that it was "not the province of government to support the people." With nowhere to turn for help, some people organized into ragtag "armies of the unemployed" for mutual assistance in finding employment. The movement culminated in the formation of "Coxey's Army."

Jacob S. Coxey, a wealthy man who had risen from the working class, proposed that the government spend $500 million on public work projects, thus providing work for the unemployed. When Congress showed no interest in his idea, Coxey conceived a plan to send an army of the unemployed to Washington as "a petition with boots on." One hundred people began the march from Ohio in the spring of 1894. By the time it reached Washington, Coxey's Army had swelled to some four hundred. Their arrival was unceremonious to say the least. Coxey and his assistants were arrested for trampling the Capitol grass, and the idea of public works projects was widely ridiculed.

Cleveland's Remedy

Cleveland was convinced that purchasing silver with federal gold reserves had caused the depression. He therefore asked Congress to repeal the Silver Purchase Act and to increase the treasury's gold reserves. In a battle that crossed party lines silverites in Congress argued that repeal of the act would decrease the amount of currency in circulation and worsen economic conditions. In the end, Cleveland prevailed, but it was a costly victory that caused a split in the Democratic party.

In addition, contrary to Cleveland's expectations, repeal of the Sherman Silver Purchase Act did not bolster the sagging economy by raising the treasury's gold reserves. In fact, it did precisely the opposite. To withdraw the silver-backed currency from circulation, the government had to redeem it with gold, which dangerously depleted the treasury's gold reserves. Furthermore, Congress (which would have preferred a standard based on gold *and* silver) refused to give the president the authority to shore up reserves with long-term borrowing. Left to solve the problem as best it could, the administration decided to float a bond issue in January 1894. Public confidence was so low, however, that less than 10 percent of the bonds were sold. Desperate now, Cleveland and Secretary of the Treasury John G. Carlisle persuaded New York bankers to take the issue. This move confirmed the silverites' suspicions that the government and the "Eastern money interests" were conspiring to maintain the gold standard at the expense of the indebted farmers and workers. When the New York banks failed to dispose of the bonds, there were more complex negotiations between the bankers and the administration. In the end the administration made an arrangement with a group of bankers headed by J. P. Morgan who agreed to supply gold to the treasury. This transaction stabilized the treasury's gold reserves, but silverites pointed to the enormous profit (estimated at between $1.5 and $7 million) realized by Morgan and his colleagues. The silverites viewed this as further proof that the Eastern money interests, with the cooperation of the government, were making fortunes in gold at the expense of the public.

Just how politically costly it was to maintain the gold standard became even more apparent to Cleveland when he tried to secure congressional approval for a lower tariff. His leadership weakened by the fight with the silverites, he could not control even the probusiness Democrats. The McKinley Tariff was so high that it was keeping foreign goods out of the country, causing a drastic decline in customs revenues. Together with increased spending on veterans' pensions, it had resulted in a deficit of $60 million by 1894. Cleveland believed that the increased customs revenues that would be generated by a lower tariff would aid the depressed economy, yet he was not sure he had the congressional support necessary for its enactment. A lower tariff did pass the House, but it was revised upward by protectionists in the Senate. In the end, Cleveland accepted the Wilson-Gorman Tariff of 1894 which provided a modest 8-percent reduction in the tariff rates.

The Silverites Find a Home

By 1895 the "silver craze" had become a crusade to cure the depression and end the victimization of the poor by the wealthy. The two major parties remained officially committed to the gold standard, however, and the silverites were without a political party to call home.

As the depression continued, Cleveland's policies became increasingly unpopular. The Democrats were rebuffed in the 1894 congressional elections, and the president lost most of his support within the party. Aware of Cleveland's vulnerability, the silverites threatened to bolt the party and join the Populists unless the party made major concessions on the silver issue. But by the time the Democratic convention opened in Chicago, it was apparent that the silverites would not have to leave the party: the momentum of the silver issue had put them in control.

At the convention the policies of the party's incumbent president were defiantly and openly condemned. At the end of the platform debate on the silver issue, a thirty-six-year-old congressman from Nebraska already well-known in the party as an orator rose to address the convention. Beginning quietly and without attacking Cleveland, William Jennings Bryan eloquently explained the silverite position. As he continued, a quality of religious fervor crept into his voice. Extolling the poor, especially the farmers, as the backbone and lifeblood of America, his voice rose: "Burn down your cities and leave our farms, and your cities will spring up again as if by magic; but destroy our farms and the grass will grow in the streets of every city in the country. . . ." Moving to the climax of his speech, Bryan told the gold advocates: "You shall not press down upon the brow of labor this crown of thorns, you shall not crucify mankind upon a cross of gold." When he finished there was silence at first, and then havoc—a silverite demonstration that led conservative Democrats to label Bryan a demagogue and caused many of them to leave the party. Yet the silverites now had a party, a spokesman, and a candidate. Largely because of his so-called Cross of Gold speech, Bryan became the Democratic presidential nominee.

These events created a dilemma for the Populists. The depression had infused the movement with renewed determination to see their platform realized. They had increased their support in the 1894 congressional elections by 42 percent, doing especially well in the South. At the same time, however, they lost control of a few Western states to candidates who stressed only the issue of free silver. Western Populists who wanted to make free silver the key issue in the 1896 campaign called for fusion with the Democrats. The more radical Populists wanted to remain separate to work for a more thorough reform program. At their convention in St. Louis, the fusionists won out, and the Populists nominated Bryan. Many reformers left the convention believing that the Populist movement had sealed its own doom.

The Republicans Nominate McKinley

To oppose Bryan in 1896, the Republicans nominated Governor William McKinley of Ohio, sponsor of the McKinley Tariff. The wealthy Marcus Alonzo Hanna, who dominated Ohio's Republican party, engineered McKinley's nomination. McKinley was a clever politician and an attractive candidate, since he was sympathetic to the demands of labor. Hanna had orchestrated the convention so as to leave the monetary question in the background. Even so, it was impossible to avoid the issue completely. When finally forced to take a position, McKinley declared his support for the gold standard, and a small number of silverites walked out.

The Election of 1896

Because of the explosive nature of the silver issue, the campaign was charged with emotion. Rumors spread that the East would secede from the Union if Bryan won. A conservative clergyman asserted that Bryan's platform was "made in hell."

The campaign styles of Bryan and McKinley were as far apart as their views on silver. Young, energetic, and passionately dedicated to reform, Bryan traveled almost twenty thousand miles and gave more than six hundred speeches. In urgent terms he pleaded his case to countless Americans. Cool and cautious, McKinley conducted a low-key "front porch" campaign designed by Hanna. Hanna's strategy was to win the critical labor vote

A DEPICTION OF BRYAN SHOWS THE SILVERITE CANDIDATE AS A DEMAGOGUE FOR HIS CROSS OF GOLD SPEECH.

by convincing workers that the silver standard would inflate the currency and lower the real value of their wages. While McKinley spoke from his front porch, Hanna engineered a last-minute effort to convince the public that Bryan represented the forces of anarchy. The party sent speakers and disseminated literature around the country in support of the high tariff and the gold standard. The effort was made possible in part by $7 million in campaign funds that were raised by playing on the business community's fears of Bryan and free silver. Some employers even warned workers that the election of Bryan might mean factory layoffs. (By contrast, the Democratic campaign treasury contained a paltry $300,000, less than 5 percent of the Republicans' campaign chest.)

When the votes were counted, McKinley had defeated Bryan by six hundred thousand popular votes and nearly one hundred electoral votes. Bryan swept the Deep South and the Far West except for Oregon and California, but McKinley carried the more populous states of the Northeast and the Midwest.

The Democratic attempt to forge a coalition of farmers and workers was a serious miscalculation. The farmers of the Midwest were generally self-sufficient and secure, and they could not identify with Bryan's portrait of them as an exploited class. Urban workers on fixed incomes feared that the free coinage of silver would raise the cost of living. The moralistic flavor of Bryan's crusade also alienated many Catholics and Lutherans. And finally, many white-collar workers and professionals also were creditors, who would naturally be opposed to cheap money.

The Republicans, on the other hand, could now appeal to both urban workers and middle-class farmers as defenders of American prosperity. Although many reformers left the party, attracted by Bryan's crusade to reform society through government legislation, the Republicans gained new support by putting aside some of their nativist inclinations, thereby attracting a broader ethnic and religious base. Although the Irish remained in the Democratic fold, German Lutherans switched to the Republican party. Thus in the election of 1896 the Republicans solidified their hold on Protestant America outside the South. The party was established as the majority coalition between 1894 and 1896 and maintained that position until the early 1930s.

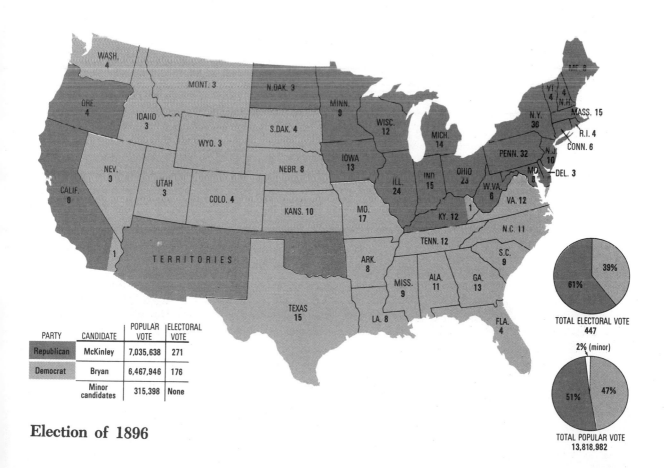

PARTY	CANDIDATE	POPULAR VOTE	ELECTORAL VOTE
Republican	McKinley	7,035,638	271
Democrat	Bryan	6,467,946	176
Minor candidates		315,398	None

TOTAL ELECTORAL VOTE 447

TOTAL POPULAR VOTE 13,818,982

Election of 1896

Prosperity Returns

The final blow to the agrarian movement and the silver issue occurred with the return of prosperity in 1897. Wheat prices, boosted by increased European demand, climbed for the first time in a generation and the agricultural depression was brought to an end. At the same time, new discoveries of gold in Alaska and South Africa produced the inflationary effect that free silverites had wanted. Thus at the turn of the century large numbers of workers and farmers were optimistic about the country's economic condition, and when America's commitment to the gold standard was formalized in 1900 with the passage of the Gold Standard Act, they made little protest.

Readings

General Works

DeSantis, Vincent P., *Republicans Face the Southern Question: The New Departure Years, 1877–1897.* Westport, Conn.: Greenwood, Reprint of 1959 edition.

Garraty, John A., *The New Commonwealth 1877–1900.* New York: Harper & Row, 1968.

Goldman, Eric F., *Rendezvous with Destiny.* New York: Random House, 1956.

Grantham, Dewey, *The Democratic South.* Athens: University of Georgia Press, 1963.

Hofstadter, Richard, *The Age of Reform.* New York: Random House, 1955.

Howe, Daniel Walker (Ed.), *Victorian America.* Philadelphia: University of Pennsylvania Press, 1976.

Josephson, Matthew, *The Politicos.* New York: Harcourt, Brace, 1938.

Keller, Morton, *Affairs of State: Public Life in Late Nineteenth Century America.* Cambridge, Mass.: Harvard University Press, 1977.

Kleppner, Paul, *The Third Electoral System, 1853–1892: Parties, Voters, and Political Cultures.* Chapel Hill: University of North Carolina Press, 1979.

Marcus, R. O., *Grand Old Party: Political Structure in the Gilded Age, 1880–1896.* New York: Oxford University Press, 1971.

Merrill, Horace S., *Bourbon Democracy of the Middle West.* Seattle: University of Washington Press, 1969.

Morgan, H. Wayne (Ed.), *The Gilded Age.* Syracuse, N.Y.: Syracuse University Press, 1963.

Morgan, H. Wayne, *From Hayes to McKinley.* Syracuse, N.Y.: Syracuse University Press, 1969.

Rothman, David J., *Politics and Power: The United States Senate 1869–1901.* Cambridge, Mass.: Harvard University Press, 1966.

Tomsich, John, *A Genteel Endeavor: American Culture and Politics in the Gilded Age.* Stanford, Calif.: Stanford University Press, 1971.

White, Leonard D., *The Republican Era.* New York: Macmillan, 1958.

Special Studies

Durden, Robert F., *The Climax of Populism.* Lexington: University of Kentucky Press, 1965.

Glad, Paul W., *McKinley, Bryan and the People.* Philadelphia: Lippincott, 1964.

Goodwyn, Lawrence, *Democratic Promise: The Populist Movement in America.* New York: Oxford University Press, 1976.

Grantham, Dewey, *The Democratic South.* Athens: University of Georgia Press, 1963.

Grossman, Lawrence, *The Democratic Party and the Negro: Northern and National Politics, 1868–92.* Urbana: University of Illinois Press, 1976.

Hackney, Sheldon, *Populism: The Critical Issues.* Boston: Little, Brown, 1971. (Paper)

Hicks, John D., *The Populist Revolt.* Lincoln: University of Nebraska Press, 1961.

Hirshson, Stanley P., *Farewell to the Bloody Shirt.* Bloomington: Indiana University Press, 1962.

Hollingsworth, J. Rogers, *The Whirligig of Politics.* Chicago: University of Chicago Press, 1963.

Hoogenboom, Ari, *Outlawing the Spoils.* Urbana: University of Illinois Press, 1961.

Jensen, Richard, *The Winning of the Midwest: Social and Political Conflict, 1888–1896.* Chicago: University of Chicago Press, 1971.

Jones, Stanley L., *The Presidential Election of 1896.* Madison: University of Wisconsin Press, 1964.

Kleppner, Paul, *The Cross of Culture: A Social Analysis of Midwestern Politics, 1850–1900.* New York: Free Press, 1970.

Nugent, Walter T. K., *The Tolerant Populists.* Chicago: University of Chicago Press, 1963.

Pollack, Norman, *The Populist Response to Industrial America.* Cambridge: Mass.: Harvard University Press, 1962.

Saloutos, Theodore, *Farmer Movements in the South.* Lincoln: University of Nebraska Press, 1964.

Unger, Irwin, *The Greenback Era.* Princeton, N.J.: Princeton University Press, 1964.

Weinstein, Allan, *Prelude to Populism, Origins of the Silver Issue, 1867–1878.* New Haven, Conn.: Yale University Press, 1970.

Williams, R. Hal, *Years of Decision: American Politics in the 1890s.* New York: Wiley, 1978.

Primary Sources

Bryce, James, *The American Commonwealth,* Vols. I II. Louis Hacker (Ed.). New York: Putnam, 1959.

Tindall, George B. (Ed.), *A Populist Reader.* New York: Harper & Row, 1966.

Biographies

Barnard, Harry, *Rutherford B. Hayes and His America.* New York: Russell & Russell, 1967.

Coletta, Paolo E., *William Jennings Bryan,* Vols I–III. Lincoln: University of Nebraska Press, 1964–1969.

Morgan, H. Wayne, *William McKinley and His America.* Syracuse, N.Y.: Syracuse University Press, 1963.

Nevins, Allan, *Grover Cleveland.* New York: Dodd, Mead, 1932.

Peskin, Allan, *Garfield: A Biography.* Kent, Ohio: Kent State University Press, 1978.

Reeves, Thomas C., *Gentleman Boss: The Life of Chester Alan Arthur.* New York: Knopf, 1975.

Ridge, Martin, *Ignatius Donnelly: Portrait of a Politician.* Chicago: University of Chicago Press, 1962.

Woodward, C. Vann, *Tom Watson: Agrarian Rebel.* New York: Macmillan, 1938.

Fiction

Donnelly, Ignatius, *Caesar's Column.* Cambridge, Mass.: Harvard University Press, 1960.

Garland, Hamlin, *Main-Travelled Roads.* Columbus, Ohio: C. E. Merrill, 1970.

21 The Road to Imperialism

The commercial supremacy of the Republic means that this Nation is to be the sovereign factor in the peace of the world. For the conflicts of the future are to be conflicts of trade—struggles for markets—commercial wars for existence. And the golden rule of peace is impregnability of position and invincibility of preparedness. . . . We cannot fly from our world duties; it is ours to execute the purpose of a fate that has driven us to be greater than our small intentions. We can not retreat from any soil where Providence has unfurled our banner; it is ours to save that soil for liberty and civilization.

Senator Albert J. Beveridge
September 16, 1898.

Significant Events

Treaty of Washington [1871]

The Influence of Sea Power Upon History, 1660–1783 by Alfred Thayer Mahan [1890]

Venezuela boundary dispute [1895]

Cuban rebellion begins [1895]

de Lôme letter [February 1898]

Sinking of the battleship *Maine* [February 1898]

Congressional resolution declaring the freedom of Cuba from Spain [April 19, 1898]

Hawaiian islands annexed [July 1898]

Treaty of Paris ending Spanish-American War [December 19, 1898]

Acquisition of part of Samoan islands [1899]

Open Door Notes [1899–1900]

Platt Amendment [1903]

Jones Act [1916]

Philippine independence [July 4, 1946]

CARTOON ON AMERICAN IMPERIALISM FROM THE DENVER *ROCKY MOUNTAIN NEWS*, 1900. THE CAPTION READS: "BY GUM, I RATHER LIKE YOUR LOOKS."

By 1860 Americans had pushed their way across the continent, bringing the whole area between the Atlantic and the Pacific under their control. Although this expansion was achieved at the cost of a bitter war with Mexico and the coercion and displacement of tens of thousands of Indians, Americans nevertheless looked upon their conquest of the frontier as the march of progress.

During the decades following the Civil War social, political, and economic disruptions subdued expansionist tendencies. Indeed, until the 1880s Americans were overwhelmingly isolationist, as people turned their attention to reconstructing the Union, settling the West, and building the nation's economy. By the last decades of the nineteenth century, however, the United States had reached a turning point in its relations with the rest of the world. With no land frontier left on the continent and with vast economic potential, the nation began once again to look outward.

While some such as Andrew Carnegie urged the development of new internal markets, other Americans were looking abroad. Many business leaders and farmers were impressed by the fact that the depressions of the 1870s and 1890s had lifted only when exports increased. They concluded from this that expanded world markets would solve economic problems at home. Bryan's followers and the Populists also were interested in new markets. They maintained that free silver, their favorite economic panacea, would inflate the currency and reduce the price of American goods abroad, thus increasing the volume of American exports. Thus vast numbers of Americans wished to expand American power by acquiring new territories and to ensure new markets. These pressures helped bring on the Spanish-American War.

As a result of the conflict with Spain, the United States acquired more than some additional territory; it also acquired new influence, responsibilities, and problems in the Caribbean and the Far East. Territorial and economic expansion were the result of an aggressive foreign policy which initially had widespread support among the American people. But after 1900, Americans' imperialistic interests waned rapidly, and presidents after McKinley were left with the task of maintaining the country's overseas commitments without the use of armed force.

American Diplomacy in the Mid-Nineteenth Century

By the mid-nineteenth century the United States had established economic ties around the world. Europe provided a major market for American agricultural products, and Latin America and the Orient offered potentially vast markets. A trade pact with China had been concluded in 1844 and Commodore Perry had penetrated the economic isolation of Japan ten years later.

In the area of diplomacy the Monroe Doctrine committed the nation at least nominally to maintaining the security of the entire Western Hemisphere. The United States was very cautious in its dealings with the European powers, particularly England and France. From the early days of the republic it had been American policy to avoid political links with Europe. Mistrust of Great Britain as the former mother country had persisted since Revolutionary times, and numerous conflicts throughout the nineteenth century had refueled American antipathy. During the Civil War, for example, many Americans were enraged when the British government declared its official neutrality yet permitted the use of English shipyards to build sea raiders for the Confederacy. At the same time the French dictator Napolean III attempted to establish a puppet monarchy in Mexico. These actions further convinced many Americans that the Western Hemisphere should quarantine itself to avoid infection from European politics.

Conflicts with Great Britain

Until the end of the century baiting Great Britain was a popular sport for politicians and the American press. In addition to the bitterness generated by Britain's indirect aid of the Confederacy, other factors contributed to American animosity. Silverites, for instance, were suspicious of the English because they associated them with the gold standard and the banking interests. The fact that Americans came from diverse ethnic backgrounds also helped perpetuate anti-British sentiment. For example, Populist dislike of the English may have been furthered by the German, Scandinavian, and Dutch ancestry of many farmers. The great majority of Irish, a large and crucial voting bloc, were anti-British. The Fenians, a group of Irish-Americans who supported Irish independence from Great Britain, even carried out small-scale raids on Canada in 1866 and 1871. The band hoped to conquer Canada and hold it hostage until Ireland was liberated from oppressive British rule.

Ironically, during these decades the British were becoming friendlier toward the United States. The British foreign office gradually came to realize that its behavior during the American Civil War was setting a dangerous precedent. Britain wanted to ensure that if it went to war with another power, a neutral United States would not feel entitled to sell ships to the enemy as the British had sold them to the South during the Civil War. A related issue was the concern of Americans for recovery of damages inflicted by the British-built raiders. When the Liberals, headed by William Gladstone, came to power in Britain the new government was friendlier to the United States than its Tory predecessors and eager to put British-American relations on a sound footing. At last, in 1869 Great Britain agreed to submit to arbitration the disputes that had grown out of the Civil War.

The negotiations were difficult. The Senate rejected the first agreement because Britain did not admit its guilt in prolonging the war by supplying the Confederacy with sea raiders. Such an admission would have meant making huge payments to the United States for indirect war damages. However, thanks to the patient diplomacy of Secretary of State Hamilton Fish, the two countries worked out the Treaty of Washington signed in 1871. The treaty provided for the establishment of a tribunal to arbitrate the *Alabama* dispute. The tribunal, meeting in Geneva, Switzerland, awarded the United States $15.5 million. A longstanding quarrel over ownership of the San Juan Islands south of British Columbia was referred to the German emperor, who awarded the territory to the United States. For its part, the United States agreed to compensate Great Britain almost $2 million for attacks on Canada by the Fenians and to pay more than $5 million to secure extensive fishing rights in Canadian waters. Both nations agreed that neutral countries would not build or arm vessels for any country if there

were reasonable grounds to believe that they could be used against a friendly power. Finally, they agreed not to allow their ports to be used against a friendly power. The treaty thus established a valuable precedent for arbitration, set the tone for a relatively long period of improved relations between the United States and Britain, and foreshadowed a new era of American importance in world politics.

French Designs on Mexico

The United States also had its problems with France. During the Civil War Napoleon III had invaded Mexico, supposedly to collect unpaid debts. His real purpose was to consolidate French control in Mexico by installing a puppet emperor, Ferdinand Maximilian of Austria.

William Henry Seward, secretary of state from 1861 to 1869, made no formal protest for fear of provoking the anti-Union French into using their superior naval fleet to break the Northern blockade of the Confederacy. Instead, the United States recognized the Mexican leader, Benito Juarez, as the legitimate ruler of the country. Once the Civil War was over, Seward began to push diplomatically for French withdrawal. In the meantime, Juarez had defeated the French forces, and France was aware that the United States had a large, battle-hardened army which now could be dispatched to Mexico. Faced also with Prussian hostilities in Europe, the French abandoned Maximilian in 1866. He died before a Mexican firing squad the next year.

The Purchase of Alaska

In spite of the fact that during the post–Civil War period American interest in expansion was subordinated to domestic preoccupations under President Andrew Johnson, the United States successfully negotiated the purchase of the huge landmass of Alaska.

Secretary of State Seward championed the idea of economic and territorial expansion, claiming that it was in the interests of both business and agriculture. Like later expansionists he sought to control the Caribbean and spread American influence across the Pacific.

Seward's greatest success was the purchase of Alaska from Russia. The vast territory called Russian America boasted fur trade, fisheries, and even,

A BRITISH CARTOONIST'S VIEW OF THE
AMERICAN PURCHASE OF ALASKA.

it was rumored, gold. On the other hand, the so-called "Icebox" was costing the Russians a great deal to oversee, and the czar feared that in the event of war between his nation and Britain, the Russians would lose their undefended possession. In order to create a barrier against English encroachment, the Russians were eager to sell the province to the United States.

Seward was so anxious to close the deal that he negotiated a treaty late one night, agreeing to pay more than $7 million for Alaska. When news of the treaty reached the public, there was widespread astonishment. The icy landmass, physically separate from the rest of the states, seemed worthless to most Americans. But Seward, in his campaign to get the treaty ratified, stressed Russo-American friendship, the potential value of Alaskan resources, and the territory's strategic importance for Far Eastern trade and as a barrier to British encroachment in North America. He finally won the support of the influential Senator Charles Sumner, and the treaty was ratified by the Senate in 1867. This purchase marked the beginning of a revived American interest in expansion.

The Pan-American Movement

The idea of a league of American states was suggested by Henry Clay as early as 1820, and in 1826 Simon Bolivar, the Latin American revolutionary leader, summoned the Panama Congress, the first concrete step in the creation of such an organization. Unfortunately, the meeting ended without providing for any practical steps to establish a union of the nations of the Western Hemisphere. The idea, however, did not die, and during the 1880s Garfield's secretary of state, James G. Blaine, became its advocate.

Blaine was interested in Latin America for two reasons: to increase American trade south of the border and to maintain peace in the area in order to prevent European intervention in the affairs of the Western Hemisphere. When his efforts to act as a peacemaker in two Latin American territorial disputes were unsuccessful, he prevailed upon the president to call an inter-American conference in hopes that it would establish the principle that the American states should cooperate with each other in matters of peace and trade.

Almost a decade passed before Blaine's proposal was realized. After Garfield was assassinated, his successor, Chester A. Arthur, replaced Blaine in the State Department and the Pan-American idea was shelved. It was revived in 1888 when Congress asked President Cleveland to call such a meeting to discuss the creation of an American customs union and work for an agreement on free trade in the Western Hemisphere. Happily for Blaine, by the time the conference met, he was again secretary of state and welcomed the delegates of seventeen Latin

American states to the first Inter-American Conference on October 2, 1889, in Washington. Although the conference rejected the idea of a customs union, it did adopt a plan for the arbitration of disputes among its members. It also established a bureau, later called the Pan-American Union, for the exchange of economic, scientific, and cultural information. Most important, it was the first of many conferences to discuss issues of common interest to the American republics.

American Imperialism in the 1890s

The extension of the power of a nation through acquisition of foreign territories or through exclusive economic or political influence over the population of another area is known as imperialism. The United States in the 1890s was part of a movement among the industrialized nations to extend their dominance at each other's expense. Although many of the ingredients of American imperialism were similar to those that had spurred Manifest Destiny in the 1840s, a complex of additional factors—economic, social, and political—fired the drive for American dominance abroad.

Economic Factors in Imperialism

In 1900 the United States, with a population of forty-five million people in rural areas and only thirty million in urban areas, was still an agricultural nation. Because many farmers produced a surplus of products for export they were interested in acquiring new foreign markets. In 1880 the *American Agriculturist* dramatized the role of exports when it estimated that over 1.5 million wagons would be needed to haul the grain that left New York Harbor; lined up, the wagons would stretch fifteen thousand miles.

These statistics explain why McKinley, when he toured the West during the 1898 debate over the Philippines, found that farmers favored annexation. The pressure of agricultural surpluses in wheat, cotton, and tobacco drove American farmers to seek outside markets and to support aggressive policies that would provide these markets.

Economic expansionism also had the strong support of business. In the 1880s Secretary of State Blaine, a supporter of the business interests, promoted reciprocal-trade agreements as a means of securing wider markets for American goods. Concern about the growing surplus of American manufactured goods was also reflected in the reciprocal-trade clause of the McKinley Tariff of 1890. Furthermore, the depression of 1893 had clearly shown that the domestic market alone could not absorb all of the goods manufactured in the country. In fact, both political parties began sponsoring a search for new foreign markets for industrial products. And in 1895, the business interests themselves formed the National Association of Manufacturers specifically to work for increased foreign trade.

Statistics for the period 1870 to 1900 support the increasing involvement of industry in the export trade: while total exports increased from $392 million to $1.5 billion, manufactured exports increased from $21 million to $805 million. At the beginning of the period agricultural goods accounted for more than two-thirds of all exports; by 1900 manufactured goods accounted for more than one-half the total.

Support for increased foreign trade came from other quarters as well. Beyond the profits to be generated, many government leaders believed that exporting a surplus of goods could help alleviate social unrest caused by overproduction and unemployment. Advocates of a strong international role for the nation viewed foreign trade as an indication of American economic power that could lead to political influence abroad. Finally, the missionaries of some churches were eager to export their religious beliefs and, in the process, to lift up less developed areas overseas.

Social and Political Factors in Imperialism

Yet demands for a more aggressive search for overseas markets do not in themselves explain the rise of American imperialism of the 1890s. Historian Richard Hofstadter has suggested that the 1890s were a time of upheaval and uneasiness for the American people. The Panic of 1893, the rise of populism, concern about the development of trusts, the decline of the ideal of a competitive economy, the end of the American frontier, strikes, and even the influx of masses of new immigrants—all helped produce a state of anxiety in America. This led some public figures to argue for a foreign policy of aggressive nationalism to divert the American people from their preoccupation with domestic problems.

Another force that gave impetus to imperialist strivings was the doctrine of Social Darwinism. Just as the powerful industrialists justified their dominance in business as the inevitable consequence of their natural superiority, so a small group of imperialists believed that it was the destiny of America to extend its influence throughout the world. The popular writer and historian John Fiske, for example, spoke of the superiority of the Anglo-Saxon race. The historian John W. Burgess argued that it was the obligation of civilized nations to "force organization" on the uncivilized. The Reverend Josiah Strong envisioned a "final competition of races" in which the Anglo-Saxons would emerge victorious, since they "represented" the virtues of civil liberty and spiritual Christianity. Some members of the clergy adopted this argument, seeing in it possibilities for making converts to Christianity through territorial expansion. Their attitudes became known as the "imperialism of righteousness."

The doctrine of Social Darwinism was supplemented by sophisticated assessments of the world-wide competition for territorial possessions by the European powers. By far the most important was Admiral Alfred Thayer Mahan's *The Influence of Sea Power Upon History, 1660–1783*, published in 1890. Arguing that if the United States did not want to fall behind in the struggle for survival among the great powers, it should "cast aside the policy of isolation which befitted [its] infancy" and look outward. Tracing the history of sea power from the seventeenth century to show that it has been the decisive factor in the success of great nations and empires, he stressed that the United States must develop a powerful navy. Victory in war as well as success in expanding foreign trade had depended on a nation's command of the seas. To sustain a strong navy the country needed an improved merchant marine, overseas naval bases, and even colonial possessions. Mahan's work combined the popular concepts of Anglo-Saxon superiority and a moral mission to uplift the less fortunate with a clear statement of America's self-interest in a competitive world.

Mahan's book was the culmination of a decade of successful efforts in Congress to expand American naval power. Politicians and the Navy Department supported appropriations for a Naval War College in 1884 and for the construction of vessels. By 1889 thirty-four new ships had been built, and in 1890 and 1896 respectively three new battleships were authorized by Congress.

Among the influential supporters of Mahan's views were politicians Theodore Roosevelt, Henry Cabot Lodge, Albert J. Beveridge, and John Hay, publishers Whitelaw Reid and Walter H. Page, and writers Henry and Brooks Adams. They called for heroism, courage, and a defense of American honor among nations by expanding American naval power. Mahan's views were read with interest, too, by leaders of other expansionist-minded nations. Consequently, Germany, Japan, and Great Britain were stimulated to embark on a race for naval supremacy that began to take shape by 1900.

Expansionism in the Pacific

Samoa American involvement in Samoa illustrates the quickening American interest in overseas possessions. The Samoan islands, three thousand miles south of Hawaii in the mid-Pacific, had long provided a coaling and repair station for American ships en route to the Far East. In 1878 the United States had gained special rights to use Pago Pago Harbor as a naval station.

Soon after the American treaty was signed, Britain and Germany, the other powers with interests in Samoa, made treaties confirming their own sphere of influence. Although Germany was the dominant commercial power in the islands, Americans had acquired substantial property, and a large proportion of imports consisted of American goods.

In 1887 and 1888 tensions grew. The Germans disposed of the Samoan king and set up a puppet ruler. When the natives rebelled, the Germans established martial law in their portion of the islands. Ready for hostilities to begin, American warships confronted German vessels in Apia Harbor. At this point nature intervened in the form of a furious hurricane, and all the German and American warships went down. The mutual tragedy made the squabble seem trivial and facilitated negotiations for setting up a three-way protectorate.

In 1899, after the American victory in the Spanish-American War and the acquisition of the Philippines, the need for the Samoan naval base seemed more urgent. New negotiations divided the islands between the United States and Germany; Britain was compensated with the Gilbert and Solomon islands in the South Pacific.

Hawaii Even more important to the United States for trade and possibly a military base were the lush Hawaiian Islands in the central Pacific. American merchant and whaling ships had been stopping in Hawaii since the early nineteenth century, and Protestant missionaries, eager to spread their faith and to "civilize" the natives, began flocking to the islands in 1820. The missionary families established strong roots, eventually becoming prominent in island life. By the 1840s Americans looked upon Hawaii as a virtual territory and the government even warned foreign powers that any undue interest in the island paradise would not be looked upon kindly. A commercial treaty signed in 1875 brought Hawaiian sugar cane into the United States duty free. With the renewal of the treaty in 1887 the United States gained a valuable strategic advantage: the exclusive use of Pearl Harbor as a naval base. That same year American planters and investors in a bid for political control forced King Kalakaua to accept a constitution that provided for protection of private property, personal liberty, and a legislature under their direction.

Thus by 1890 Americans—even though constituting a small minority of the population—were the dominant influence in the Hawaiian Islands. Three-fourths of the islands' imports came from the United States, which in turn bought virtually all Hawaiian exports. Trade thrived until the McKinley Tariff gave a two-cents-per-pound bounty to American sugar growers. At this point sugar production dropped sharply, property values declined, and workers lost their jobs. American planters and investors, eager to protect their interests, began to agitate for annexation. The Harrison administration was openly sympathetic to the annexation movement.

When King Kalakaua died in 1891, his sister, Queen Liliuokalani, ascended the throne. An advocate of control by native Hawaiians, her slogan was "Hawaii for the Hawaiians." Among her chief opponents were plantation owner Sanford Dole and John L. Stevens, the United States minister in Honolulu,

a fervid annexationist. In 1893 when the queen moved to abolish the constitution and restore the rights of the monarchy, the planters engineered a coup and enlisted Stevens's support. Without official authorization, Stevens summoned United States Marines stationed in Honolulu Harbor on the pretext that American lives and property were in danger. The military coup was successful, and Queen Liliuokalani was deposed. Stevens conferred recognition on a new government propped up by American planters and proclaimed Hawaii a protectorate of the United States. He wrote the State Department enthusiastically that the "Hawaiian pear is now fully ripe, and this the golden hour for the United States to pluck it."

A treaty of annexation was drawn up hastily and sent to the Senate. Republicans on the whole favored it, for they saw Hawaii as a key to American economic penetration of the Far East, and they feared Japanese control of the islands if the United States did not take them first. Democrats opposed it, partly because they believed that it was wrong to control territory and people who were not to be in-

QUEEN LILIUOKALANI.

corporated into the republic and partly to oppose the Republicans, who were in office.

Cleveland, a strong anti-imperialist who felt the United States had dealt unfairly with Queen Liliuokalani, withdrew the treaty when he became president again, and he sent James H. Blount to Hawaii to determine the sentiment of the Hawaiian people. Blount reported that the people were against annexation, and he ordered the marines who had aided the coup to withdraw. But the queen was not returned to power. Such an action would have required military intervention, which the American public would not have accepted. The leaders of the coup proclaimed Hawaii an independent republic and continued to work for annexation for the next four years.

During the Spanish-American War, with expansionist sentiment at its peak, imperialists called for the annexation of Hawaii ostensibly because of its importance as a stopping-off point for American naval forces. Although the islands could have filled this role without being annexed, in July 1898 Congress made Hawaii a United States territory.

Incidents in Latin America

Chile America's aggressive new foreign policy was also seen in its actions toward Latin America. Relations with Chile, for example, had been strained for some time because of American friendship with Peru, Chile's long-standing enemy. During a Chilean revolt in 1891, American authorities detained a rebel steamer, the *Itata*, with a cargo of arms. The American minister clearly favored the losing faction and gave asylum to people fleeing the revolutionaries. Despite these actions the revolution was successful, and Chilean public sentiment became heatedly anti-Yankee.

President Harrison, during whose administration these events occurred, was a strong supporter of the military and of American naval expansion. When a drunken brawl between Chileans and Americans in Valparaiso, Chile, resulted in the death of two American sailors and the injury of some twenty United States citizens, Harrison was enraged. Calling the incident "an insult to the uniform of the United States sailors," he demanded both an apology and reparations to support the families of the dead. Chile in turn demanded that the American ambassador be recalled, and it looked as

though a military confrontation would occur. In the end, however, thanks to the patient negotiations of Secretary of State Blaine, Chile finally backed down and paid the United States an indemnity of $75,000. The excessive reaction of the American government to the incident left a long-standing bitterness on the part of Chile.

Venezuela The boundary between Venezuela and British Guiana had been in dispute since the 1840s. It came to a head when gold was discovered around the disputed area in the 1870s and Venezuela sought United States support, invoking the Monroe Doctrine. The United States offered to arbitrate the dispute but Great Britain turned down the offer. In 1894 a former American minister to Venezuela wrote a pro-Venezuelan pamphlet that was widely circulated in the United States and resulted in a congressional resolution again calling for arbitration of the dispute. President Cleveland was caught between peace advocates and strong anti-British politicians such as Republican Senator Henry Cabot Lodge and the Irish bloc in his own party who claimed that the Monroe Doctrine was being tested by outrageous British demands.

Although an anti-imperialist, Cleveland was no friend of Britain. He realized that failure to defend the applicability of the Monroe Doctrine would give Britain the advantage in trade with Venezuela and hurt him politically. He therefore decided to take a strong stand by reasserting the doctrine.

On July 20, 1895, Secretary of State Richard Olney sent a pugnacious note to the British prime minister, stating that British efforts to acquire more territory in the disputed area were a violation of the Monroe Doctrine. The fact was that Venezuelan claims were more excessive than those of Britain. After four months' delay, the prime minister replied that the Monroe Doctrine was not applicable to the situation and was not internationally accepted. His response created a surge of war hysteria in the United States, even though the American navy was no match for the British fleet. "Mad clear through," Cleveland sent a message to Congress proposing that he be authorized to appoint a commission to determine the boundary. He threatened that the United States would use force to support its findings if necessary. Although the British were irritated, they were unwilling to become further embroiled in a conflict with the United States. The situation in

Europe was dangerous, since France and Russia were unfriendly and the German navy would soon be as mighty as that of England. Moreover, American raiding vessels could create problems for the British merchant fleet. British sentiment in favor of a peaceful settlement became overwhelming when a British raiding party of six hundred was captured by the Boers in South Africa, and the German leader, Kaiser Wilhelm II, sent a congratulatory message to the Boer victors. At this point the British agreed to submit the issue to an arbitration board (from which Venezuela was excluded), and in October 1899 they were awarded 90 percent of their original land claim. American imperialists, forgetting their earlier assertion that the British claim was a viola-

tion of the Monroe Doctrine, were now satisfied that the doctrine had been upheld. Actually, the doctrine had been reinterpreted to mean that the United States could interfere in almost any crisis in the Western Hemisphere involving territorial disputes. Anglo-American relations improved after the arbitration, but the assertions of American power in the issues concerning Chile and Venezuela frightened many Latin Americans. For their part, Americans were proud of their government's handling of these crises, and the Monroe Doctrine gained new stature in international politics. The Venezuelan incident in particular set the stage for major American expansion in the next few years.

The Spanish-American War

Cuban Rebellion

In the last years of the nineteenth century a movement called *Cuba Libre* ("free Cuba") came to maturity. From 1868 to 1878 Cuban insurgents had fought a bloody war for independence from Spanish rule, but the United States, preoccupied with its own problems, took little notice. Spain had put down the revolutionaries, but a government-in-exile set up headquarters in New York, and Cuban journalists began publicizing the rebels' cause.

Meanwhile, Cuban-American trade grew until Cuban exports of tobacco and sugar to the United States became the mainstay of the island's economy. When depression struck the United States in 1893 Congress passed the Wilson-Gorman Tariff, which placed a high duty on sugar and withdrew a special sugar agreement with Cuba. This plunged the island into a depression: between 1889 and 1897 Cuban sales to the United States dropped from $89 million to $56 million.

As a result of these economic difficulties and Spanish mismanagement of Cuban affairs, a new revolution broke out in 1895. Using "scorched earth" tactics, the insurgents intended to burn the cane fields to destroy any economic benefits Spain might squeeze from the colony and to bring about United States intervention. They were confident that American and Cuban businesses eager to protect their investments in the island would support any action that would end the conflict and restore

order. They therefore circulated propaganda in the United States to persuade the public of the rightness of their actions.

The Spanish countered Cuban terrorism with a brutal policy called *reconcentrado*. General Valeriano Weyler arrived in Cuba in 1896 and proceeded to set up concentration camps. Virtually the whole island was spotted with camps of dislocated civilians, now supposedly isolated from the revolutionaries and thus prevented from aiding them. The strategy, aimed at starving out the resistance movement, instead starved the people in the camps. Some fifty thousand Cubans, mostly women and children, died in the Havana province alone.

The American Reaction

President Cleveland, who believed American intervention would be wrong, tried to keep the United States out of the conflict by proclaiming American neutrality in 1895. But a number of things about the Cuban crisis made it a subject of great interest to the American people. Cuba was geographically very close to the United States, American business holdings on the island were significant, and the oppression of the people by the Spanish monarchy offended the Americans' democratic idealism. In 1896 Congress adopted a joint resolution calling upon the president to recognize the existence of a state of war in Cuba. Cleveland, however, refused to do so. At this point the 1896 elections intervened. With an astute politician and expansionist, William McKinley, in the presidency, hopes for a more assertive foreign policy and overseas expansion now were centered in the Republican party.

The sensationalist press, especially Hearst's New York *Journal* and Pulitzer's New York *World*, vied for readership by printing exaggerated and sometimes fabricated stories of Spanish atrocities. Hearst allegedly told one of his illustrators to furnish sketches of atrocities even though things looked quiet, adding "I'll furnish the war." Tales of the atrocities of the *reconcentrado* policy stirred public indignation throughout the country.

Spanish Provocations

By the end of 1897 it appeared that the Spanish had almost crushed the rebellion. They had made two concessions to Cuba: they had tendered a promise to extend a form of self-government and they had removed the hated General Weyler. But two episodes in February 1898 aroused American demand for intervention to a fever pitch.

The de Lôme Letter The first incident involved a letter written by the Spanish minister in Washington, Dupuy de Lôme, which was stolen from the mails and delivered to Hearst. In it de Lôme called McKinley "weak and a bidder for the admiration of the crowd . . . who tries to leave a door open behind himself while keeping on good terms with the jingoes of his party." The Spanish government apologized for the letter, but the American people felt insulted, and McKinley, who had been moving prudently in this volatile situation, was undermined in his efforts to prevent intervention.

The *Maine* The second incident involved the explosion of the American battleship *Maine*. McKinley had stationed the ship in Havana Harbor early in 1898 to protect Americans in Cuba should hostilities resume. Its presence may have hardened Cuban resistance to any settlement. The Spanish, eager to avoid conflict with the United States, received it as diplomatically as possible. On February 15, 1898, the *Maine* sank after "a terrible and mysterious explosion," as the New York *Journal* called it. Two hundred and sixty navy men died, and the yellow press reported the incident in terms calculated to arouse unprecedented public hysteria. An American investigation of the explosion reported that a mine had destroyed the battleship. A second investigation undertaken by Spanish authorities (who were not allowed near the wreck) correctly determined that the explosion had been internal. The Spanish sought to have the incident submitted to arbitration, but the American public was so enraged that the United States refused the Spanish request.

IN THIS CARTOON PRESIDENT McKINLEY IS SHOWN TRYING TO HUSH THE YELLOW NEWSPAPERS WHOSE TALK OF WAR IS UPSETTING THE GOOSE THAT LAID THE GOLDEN EGG OF PROSPERITY.

A LITHOGRAPH PUBLISHED IN 1898 GIVES A DRAMATIC RENDERING OF THE EXPLOSION OF THE *MAINE*.

Public opinion was aroused further when on March 17 the respected Senator Redfield Proctor of Vermont returned from Cuba to report that even the yellow press did not accurately reflect the dire situation on the island. Of the people in the camps he said, " . . . one-half died and . . . one-quarter of the living are so diseased that they cannot be saved." Mass meetings around the country called for intervention.

The Move toward War

Although the attitude of the general public was bellicose, until early 1898 the business community had mixed feelings about intervention. Support for war came primarily from those with direct ties to the Cuban economy. Most other business leaders viewed the idea as a threat to the new and fragile prosperity the nation was enjoying after the depression of a few years before. When the United States had teetered on the brink of war with Britain over the Venezuelan crisis, the stock market had fallen drastically; during the Cuban crisis, every threat of war with Spain drove the market down. Business sentiment began to shift toward a more aggressive policy in the early spring of 1898. With renewed violence in Cuba, many business leaders began to believe that a protracted threat of war might be as damaging to prosperity as war itself would be. Perhaps it was time to "get it over with." There had always been certain key industries that would profit from a war: mining interests, the steel industry, and the railways; and agricultural prices would be likely to soar during wartime.

The pressures on McKinley for a declaration of war were mounting. The president had been exerting quiet pressure on Spain to declare an armistice to end hostilities, put an end to the *reconcentrado* policy, and ultimately grant Cuba its independence. By early April the Spanish had given in to the president's first two demands, but they refused even to consider the idea of Cuban independence. On April 11 McKinley asked Congress for authority to use armed force in Cuba to free Cuba.

It is unclear what finally convinced the president that war was his only remaining alternative. Although the yellow press had aroused the emotions of the general public, McKinley was not much influenced by its stories. The sinking of the *Maine* was another important factor in shaping a war mentality among the citizenry, but McKinley did not ask for intervention until two months after the incident. The president was closely allied to the imperialists in his own party and to the business interests, and their combined influence was no doubt considerable. Refusal to heed the wishes of the leaders of his party could spell defeat in the fall elections. As an astute politician loyal to the party that favored hard money, McKinley preferred to oversee the end of Spain's South American empire than to see the Silverites swept into office on a platform of free silver and free Cuba. Moreover, he knew that he could not persuade the Spanish to leave Cuba, and that the American people were demanding action to force them out. But only when Congress had appropriated money for possible military intervention and he was fully convinced that the Spanish concessions in early April were too limited to gain popular acceptance did he finally decide to request armed intervention.

On April 19, 1898, Congress reinforced McKinley's reluctant request with a resolution equivalent to a declaration of war. It declared Cuba independent and demanded that Spain withdraw completely. The president was to use the army and navy to oust Spain if necessary.

There was, however, one note of apparent restraint. Although many Americans had been eyeing Cuba hungrily for decades, the Teller Amendment to the congressional resolution vowed that the

DEWEY'S DEFEAT OF THE SPANISH IN MANILA BAY MADE A DRAMATIC HEADLINE IN PULITZER'S NEW YORK *WORLD*, MAY 2, 1898. ▶

United States had no interest in annexing the island. This was to be a war to liberate Cuba, not to gain territory. The amendment stated that at the close of the war, the United States might station troops on the "said Island" only so long as they were necessary for "pacification." To what extent the amendment would be honored remained to seen.

Dewey Takes Manila Bay

Good spirits and popular support marked the very brief conflict that followed after Spain declared war on the United States on April 24. The first and most

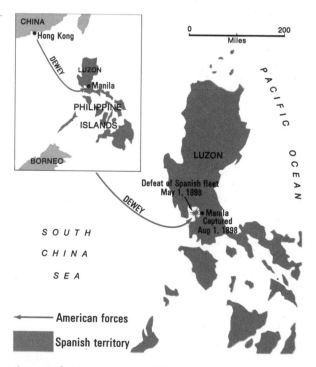

← American forces

Spanish territory

Spanish-American War Pacific Theater

 1,011,068

Per Work-Day April Average.
GAIN in One Year - - 338,748

"Circulation Books Open to All."

 The

 World.

1,011,068

Per Work-Day April Average.
GAIN in Three Years - 461,205

"Circulation Books Open to All."

VOL. XXXVIII. NO. 13,494.
NEW YORK, MONDAY, MAY 2, 1898.
PRICE ... TWO CENTS.

DEWEY SMASHES SPAIN'S FLEET

VICE-ADMIRAL MONTOJO.

The Defeated Commander of the Spanish Fleet.

Great Naval Battle Between Asiatic Squadron and Spanish Warships Off Manila.

THREE OF THE BEST SPANISH VESSELS WIPED OUT, OTHERS SUNK.

The Damage Done to the American Boats Engaged Only Nominal---Hundreds of the Enemy Slain in the Encounter.

COMMODORE DEWEY.

Winner of First Great Victory for New American Navy.

LISBON, Portugal, May 1, 11 P. M.----The Spanish fleet was completely defeated off Cavite, Philippine Islands, according to trustworthy advices received here.

WASHINGTON, May 1, Midnight.---President McKinley expresses entire satisfaction over the reported battle between Commodore Dewey's squadron and the Spanish fleet. He accepts the news as true, but believes it is worse for the Spanish than they will admit. There has been no official confirmation of the news. Nothing official is expected for forty-eight hours.

THE THREE SPANISH CRUISERS COMPLETELY DESTROYED.

CASTILLA.

DON JUAN DE AUSTRIA.

SPANISH FLAG SHIP
"REINA MARIA CRISTINA."

FLYING SQUADRON STRENGTHENED.

PORT MONROE, May 1.--The rumor of increased naval forces, in charge of Lieut.-Commander Harris, joined the Flying Squadron in Hampton Roads at 7 P. M. to-day after a quiet trip from New York. The Secretary's arrival practically doomed Commodore Schley, as the squadron will now be heavier fighting ships. It went to work, lighthouses

Chaplain Jones, the "fighting parson" of the Texas, preached a red-hot sermon to-day on the officers and men of the battleship. He took his text from the thirty-second chapter of Deuteronomy, reading from the eighteenth to the forty-third verse, inclusive.

"As each of these verses had been written in order to set admonition to Spain, their appropriateness might not have been more apparent.

"As said I will tell you my face from them; I will see what their end shall be: for they are a very froward generation, children in whom is no faith...

"I will heap mischiefs upon them; I will spend mine arrows upon them.

"...there are some that I may as if they may apprehend...

"...the sword without, and terror within, shall destroy both the young man and the virgin, the suckling also with the man of gray hairs.

Pennsylvania Railroad Commission

ADMIRAL MONTOJO ADMITS HIS UTTER ROUT.

In His Report to Spain He Says Many Ships Were Burned and Sunk and the Losses in Officers and Men "Numerous."

MADRID (via Paris), May 2.--The time of the retreat of the American squadron behind the merchantmen was 11.30 A. M. The American squadron forced the port before daybreak and appeared off Cavite. Night was completely dark.

The Naval Bureau at Manila sends the following report, signed "Montojo, Admiral:"

"In the middle of the night the American squadron forced the forts, and before daybreak appeared off Cavite. The night was completely dark. At 7.30 the bow of the Reina Christina took fire and, soon after the poop also was burned.

"At eight o'clock, with my staff, I went on board the Isla de Cuba. The Reina Maria Christina and the Castilla were then entirely enveloped in flames.

"The other ships having been damaged retired into Baker Bay. Some had to be sunk to prevent their falling into the hands of the enemy. The losses are numerous, notably Capt. Cadarso, a priest, and nine other persons.

The Spaniards fought splendidly, the sailors refusing to leave the burning and sinking Don Juan de Austria. There is the greatest anxiety for further details.

MADRID'S FORLORN HOPE.

LONDON, May 2.--The Madrid correspondent of the Financial News, telegraphing this morning, says:

"The Spanish Ministry of Marine claims a victory for Spain because the Americans were forced to retire behind the merchantmen. Capt. Cadalso (or Cadarso), in command of the Reina Maria Christina, went down with the ship.

MADRID OFFICIAL REPORT ADMITS DISASTROUS DEFEAT

(Despatch Sanctioned by Spanish Government and Passed by the Censor.)

MADRID, May 1, 8 P. M.--The following is the text of the official despatch from the Governor-General of the Philippine Islands to the Minister of War, Lieut.-Gen. Correa, regarding the engagement off Manila:

"Last night, April 30, the batteries at the entrance to the fort announced the arrival of the enemy's squadron, forcing a passage under the obscurity of the night.

"At daybreak the enemy took up positions, opening with a strong fire against Fort Cavite and the arsenal.

"Our fleet engaged the enemy in a brilliant combat, protected

(Continued on Second Page.)

significant victory took place not in Cuba, not even in the Caribbean, but halfway across the world in the Spanish Philippines. The American people may have agitated for a war to free Cuba, but imperialists in strategic positions in the government had other goals in mind. Several months before the war began, when Secretary of the Navy John D. Long was away for the weekend, Assistant Secretary Theodore Roosevelt secretly instructed Commodore George Dewey in Hong Kong to "keep full of coal." Should war be declared Dewey was to head south and attack Spanish ships in the Philippines. The order was discovered and Roosevelt was mildly reprimanded for his action, but President McKinley allowed the strategy to be carried out.

On the night of May 1, Dewey sailed a fleet of six steel warships into Manila Bay. The following morning he blasted the ten antiquated Spanish vessels out of the water, in the process killing or wounding 381 Spanish sailors but losing not a single American life. In spite of his widely applauded victory, Dewey was left in a predicament; he could not take Manila without ground troops, and he was forced to wait two months for them to arrive.

In the meantime, warships from other imperialist nations, notably Germany, steamed into Manila Bay. The five-ship German force was supposedly needed to ensure the safety of German nationals. However, the German admiral proceeded to ignore Dewey's blockade rules and the outraged American admiral threatened war. Fortunately for the Americans, the situation cooled; the German fleet was superior to their own.

Ground troops finally arrived, and reinforced by Filipino *insurrectos*, they captured Manila on August 13, 1898. On August 17 the United States officially declared a military occupation of the Philippines.

The War in Cuba

In Cuba the war was characterized by inefficiency and confusion. The American army was disorganized and undersupplied. Because no lightweight uniforms were available, many soldiers wore hot winter uniforms to fight in this semitropical island. The troops suffered debilitating illness from eating canned meat they derisively dubbed "embalmed

COLONEL THEODORE ROOSEVELT AND HIS ROUGH RIDERS ON SAN JUAN HILL.

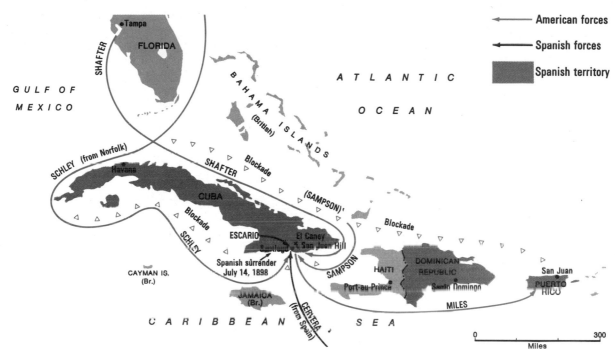

**Spanish-American War
Caribbean Theater**

beef," and often they had no rifles, blankets, or tents. Fortunately, they were confronted by an equally disorganized Spanish army low on morale. While only four hundred Americans died in battle, five thousand others succumbed to such diseases as dysentery and malaria.

American strategy was to bottle up the Spanish fleet under Admiral Cervera by a blockade of Santiago Harbor and to dispatch land forces to push out Cervera from the rear. The leader of the ground troops was the obese General William R. Shafter. Regular forces were joined by the volunteer Rough Riders, a mixed bag of cowboys, polo players, ex-convicts, and other adventurers led by Theodore Roosevelt. Roosevelt, who was so nearsighted he could never have passed a military physical, had used his political position to finagle a military commission. Convoys to Cuba were so crowded that most of the Rough Riders had to leave their horses at

home. Even then, some of them found it difficult to obtain transportation.

Shafter's seventeen thousand American troops, poorly trained and equipped with archaic artillery, encountered an even more disorganized Spanish army of only two thousand men near Santiago. American forces took the city easily. Bloodier fighting occurred at El Caney and San Juan Hill. Roosevelt, hungry for glory, joined his cavalry-without-horses in a wild and dangerous charge up San Juan Hill, assisted by two well-trained regiments of black troops. A large number of Americans were killed or wounded in what the regular soldiers called a "schoolboys' charge." Even so, the Rough Riders' sheer bravado added to Spanish bewilderment and helped the Americans win the hill.

Ultimately it was a naval battle that determined the outcome of the war. With Santiago in danger of falling, the Spanish fleet was trapped in

Santiago Harbor and had to choose between surrender or attempted escape. Although Admiral Cervera preferred surrender to virtual suicide, he was ordered to stand and fight. In a four-hour battle on July 3 all his ships were destroyed. Some five hundred Spanish lost their lives; only one American was killed. The Spanish surrendered formally in Santiago two weeks later and signed an armistice on August 12.

Before the war was over American annexationists sped to Spanish-owned Puerto Rico. A United States expeditionary force was welcomed warmly, for most Puerto Ricans viewed the Americans as liberators of Cuba. Consequently there was little protest when the island, which was not protected by the Teller Amendment, was claimed for the United States.

America's New Empire

After a ten-week war, Spain and the United States signed a preliminary peace agreement on August 12 and met at the conference table in Paris in October 1898 to negotiate a formal peace treaty. Spanish negotiators had already granted independence to Cuba and ceded Puerto Rico to the United States in August. Now they formalized these concessions and, in addition, ceded the western Pacific island of Guam to the United States. American superiority in the Caribbean, part of the planning for an isthmian canal, was now assured.

The war also had resulted in Spain's defeat in the Philippine Islands. After his victory at Manila Bay Dewey had brought Emilio Aguinaldo, the charismatic, part-Chinese leader of the Filipino *insurrectos*, out of exile in Asia to help American forces take Manila. Aguinaldo was led to believe that after the war the Philippines would be granted independence; but a resolution to this effect in Congress was narrowly defeated. Aguinaldo, fearing that the islands might be annexed by the United States, organized his armies, set up a government, and called upon foreign powers to recognize Philippine independence. All over the islands posters proclaiming the nationalist position should have warned Washington that acquisition would be no simple matter. However, American envoys failed to perceive, or else to communicate, the extent of Filipino opposition. McKinley apparently continued to believe that native opposition was mild and scattered and that the goodwill of American administrators would soon pacify the islands.

The Debate over Annexation

Debate over the matter grew rapidly, and each side had its moral as well as practical justifications. McKinley later described his decision to take the islands as a religious crisis. He told members of the General Missionary Committee of the Methodist Episcopal Church that night after agonizing night he "prayed Almighty God for light and guidance . . . . And one night it came to me this way—I don't know how it was, but it came . . . that there was nothing left for us to do but to take them all . . . and Christianize them. . . . And then I went to bed, and went to sleep, and slept soundly, and the next morning I sent for the chief engineer of the War Department (our map-maker) and I told him to put the Philippines on the map of the United States." This alleged religious motive for extending the American map halfway round the globe was more than a little suspect. Most of the Filipinos had converted to Christianity long before. One historian, pointing to American trading interests in the area, noted that McKinley's policy came down to "God directs us—perhaps it will pay." In any case, a speaking tour around the country in the fall of 1898 had given McKinley a clear impression that public opinion strongly favored annexation.

Business leaders were tantalized by the prospect of the Philippines becoming a base for American trade in the Far East. Commercial journals began to speak openly of America's economic destiny and need for markets. In 1900 Henry Cabot Lodge defended acquisition thus: "We make no hypocritical pretense of being interested in the Philippines solely on account of others . . . we regard the welfare of the American people first . . . we believe in trade expansion."

In addition to economic interests, the belief in the superiority of Anglo-Saxon institutions inspired by Social Darwinism played a part in much expansionist propaganda. Rudyard Kipling's phrase "take up the white man's burden" was used to urge the United States to take on the task of civilizing "backward" nations. Senator Beveridge, a vocal imperialist, spoke more bluntly. "They are not capable of self-government," he said. "How could they be? They are Orientals, Malays, instructed by Spaniards . . ." It was, or so the argument ran, the manifest duty of a "higher" civilization to uplift a "lower" one.

Among the antiimperialists who opposed these ideas were Grover Cleveland, Andrew Carnegie, Carl Schurz, William James, and Mark Twain. They argued that American trade expansion was not dependent on holding colonies and that the Philippine Islands were not contiguous and would be difficult to defend. They held that it was contrary to the spirit of the Declaration of Independence for the United States to acquire sovereignty over another country and keep it in a subordinate position. Also influenced by Social Darwinism, they argued that it would be difficult to bring people of such "inferior" cultural background into the Union.

In the midst of this heated debate, McKinley boldly instructed the Paris conference that "cession must be of the whole archipelago or none." Even the American negotiators were stunned. Spain resisted, rightfully claiming that the islands had still been under Spanish control when the preliminary peace agreement was signed in August. But in the end Spain, not strong enough to resist American pressure, was coerced into giving up the Philippines in exchange for a $20 million war indemnity. The Treaty of Paris ending the Spanish-American War was signed on December 19, 1898.

When the treaty came up for ratification, the antiexpansionist William Jennings Bryan unexpectedly advised his Democratic colleagues in Washington to approve it. He believed that it would be better to fight imperialism in the elections a year and a half later than in the Senate now. Even while the vote was being taken, on February 6, 1899, news came that a Filipino insurrection against the United States had begun. Nevertheless, the treaty squeaked through with a bare two-thirds majority, fifty-seven to twenty-seven.

Subjugation of the Philippines

When the United States began efforts to put down the insurrection, it was under the impression that the *insurrectos* were a small minority. In fact, however, Aguinaldo had raised an army of some eighty thousand soldiers. Major General Ewell Otis, commander of the American forces, conducted a conservative campaign, and by summer the United States had still not crushed Filipino resistance. Otis requested more troops, and by early 1900 there were sixty-five thousand American soldiers on the islands.

The Filipinos pursued a strategy of guerrilla warfare. General Otis's more conventional strategy of "capturing" villages ignored the fact that enemy soldiers rarely were caught by such tactics: they merely vanished into the jungle and returned to the villages as soon as the American force had departed. The brutality of guerrilla war also spurred racial hatred, with horrible atrocities committed by both sides. Ironically, United States involvement in the Philippines had begun in part because of American outrage at Spanish atrocities in Cuba.

With little progress being made, General Otis was replaced by General Arthur MacArthur (father of the famous World War II general). Finally, in March 1901, Emilio Aguinaldo was captured, thus seriously weakening the *insurrectos*. He submitted to an oath of allegiance to the United States, and the war ended, although sporadic outbursts of guerrilla activity continued for four years.

President McKinley was genuinely disturbed by the bloodshed on the islands and in 1899 sent several missions to study how the Filipinos should be governed. The commissioners, led by the competent William Howard Taft, concluded that the Filipinos required a form of government that would both respect their culture and Americanize them politically. After the hostilities ceased, the United States, while extending its rule throughout the islands, spent millions of dollars building schools and roads and improving sanitation and public health.

Such efforts did not put an end to demands for political independence, however, and in 1916 Congress finally passed the Jones Act, setting up a democratically elected Philippine legislature and providing for eventual independence. But it took almost two more decades of Filipino agitation before the United States guaranteed in 1934 that freedom would be granted at the end of a ten-year period. Delayed by World War II, Philippine independence was finally proclaimed on July 4, 1946.

American Governance in Puerto Rico

The Teller Amendment had guaranteed Cuban sovereignty once the island was liberated from Spanish rule, but it did not forbid annexation of other former Spanish colonies in the Caribbean. After the well-received American occupation, there was no real question about the annexation of Puerto Rico. A Senate committee drew up a plan for governance which was approved in 1900. It provided for American domination of the government through a powerful executive council appointed by the president of the United States. Puerto Ricans had more voice in the selection of the lower House of Delegates, but this branch had no power to legislate without the council's consent.

Puerto Ricans agitated for more autonomy, and in 1917 they won United States citizenship and their own elective upper house. In 1952 Puerto Rico became a self-governing commonwealth, electing all of its own officials.

Cuba under American Occupation

Despite the Teller Amendment, the United States did not withdraw immediately from Cuba; instead, it set up a military government to pacify the island and restore order. Cuban nationalists protested that this was a betrayal, but Washington replied that it could not abandon the island, whose economy and political organization had been ruined by years of warfare.

Between 1898 and 1902 the United States established a rural police force, public schools, sound government finance, and a public health program. An outstanding success of the occupation was the work of Dr. Walter Reed and his colleagues in isolating the *stegomyia* mosquito as the carrier of yellow fever during a particularly severe epidemic. The United States also freed political prisoners, distributed food, and arranged for the import of cattle to restock Cuban herds.

But this constructive record was marred by the tensions of occupation. Although some landowners sought annexation because they feared their own local poor more than the Americans, most of the Cuban population wanted independence. Thus in 1900, under orders from Washington, an elected Cuban assembly was asked to draft a constitution to take effect when American troops were withdrawn.

Unwilling to grant the complete autonomy suggested by the draft, the United States insisted on inclusion of a rider, the Platt Amendment, which limited Cuba's ability to make treaties by providing an American veto over agreements that might impair Cuban independence. It also guaranteed to the United States the right to buy or lease "naval stations" on the island and to intervene to preserve Cuban independence and American lives and property. Cubans deeply resented the Platt Amendment, but reluctantly accepted its provisions in 1903. The intervention clause was more than symbolic. By 1917 the United States had already intervened three times in Cuban affairs.

The Open Door Policy

European Imperialism in China

The acquisition of the Philippines brought the United States new commitments in the Far East. Americans' attention turned toward their own economic interest in China. After its defeat in the Sino-Japanese War of 1895 China was forced to cede territory to Japan. Korea, traditionally a buffer state, came increasingly under Japanese influence. In the next few years European imperialist powers—Russia, France, Great Britain, and Germany—took advantage of China's weakened condition to consolidate territorial and economic concessions on the Chinese mainland and in Chinese ports,

THIS SELF-CONGRATULATORY CARTOON FROM 1900 SHOWS UNCLE SAM STANDING BEFORE THE NEWLY UNLOCKED DOOR TO THE COMMERCIAL RICHES OF CHINA. THE KEY IN HIS HAND IS MARKED "AMERICAN DIPLOMACY."

setting up so-called spheres of influence. With the Russians established in Manchuria, the Germans in the Shantung Peninsula, the British in numerous ports and the Yangtse Valley, and the French in Southern China, the United States began to fear that the old Chinese Empire would be partitioned and that the Europeans would monopolize the China trade.

British Interest in Alliance

The commercial interests of Great Britain were growing alarmed over rising German power which they believed posed an ominous threat to free trade in China. Thus they looked to the United States, which had no leases in China, as an ally against partition. In March 1898, in a move that presaged the improvement of Anglo-American relations in the coming century, the British approached the United States with a proposal whereby they would acknowledge United States' dominance in the Western Hemisphere in exchange for a cooperative alliance in the Far East. Secretary of State John Hay rejected the British advance; such an open alliance with Britain would have been extremely unpopular in the United States, where there was still an ample reserve of anti-British sentiment. America's acquisition of Hawaii and the Philippines had enlarged public interest in trade and investment in the Orient, but an Anglo-American alliance to achieve these ends probably would have meant political suicide for the Republicans.

Formulation of the Open Door Policy

A look at two American industries involved in Far Eastern trade reveals some of the commercial motives behind what was to be called the Open Door policy. The America-China Development Company had plans for railroad construction in China, and partition would make such plans impractical. Perhaps more important was the increase of American cotton exports to China. Though Britain still had a larger cotton trade, American exports had grown by 120 percent in ten years, whereas British exports had declined. When the Russians began expanding their influence in Manchuria, Americans began to fear that they might close the area, which was the center of American cotton trade in the Orient. The Cotton Spinners' Association therefore actively supported a policy that would keep the China trade open, as did the American Asiatic Association, created in 1898 and supported by many important corporations and industrialists. While the amount of American trade in China was small, there was widespread, if unfounded, optimism about its future prospects.

The policy of keeping the door open in China was bolstered too by American missionaries and, of course, imperialists. In 1899, fifteen hundred American missionaries were in China, and their denominational leaders in America viewed China as a vast area for converts. Ardent imperialists in Washington believed that the United States, as a great power, must have influence in the Far East. Ironically, Americans demanded an Open Door in China at the same time they were excluding Chinese immigration, a policy which did little to endear the United States to the Chinese.

McKinley, under pressure from all of these groups—as well as being advised of the imminent partition of China by the European powers and Japan—finally decided to take a stand. In a bold move, Secretary of State John Hay sent the so-called Open Door notes to the major powers involved to try to ensure fair competition among all foreign traders in China.

The first Open Door note sent on September 6, 1899, asked the powers with interests in China to allow equal commercial opportunity in their sphere of influence, not to interfere with or impede collection of Chinese customs duties in the treaty ports (sixteen Chinese ports opened to foreign trade and residence under previous treaties with the European powers), not to charge discriminatory railroad rates or harbor dues, and to cooperate with the United States in establishing the principle of the Open Door.

Although the United States was not prepared to back the note with force, the American military presence in the Philippines lent it some authority. Not surprisingly, the great powers were less than enthusiastic about being asked to endorse such a magnanimous policy. Even so, Britain, France, Germany, and Japan accepted the Open Door principle provided that all the others would agree as well. Russia, however, seeing that the Open Door would prevent it from closing off Manchuria, gave no clear-cut answer. Secretary of State Hay nevertheless interpreted what in essence was a refusal as an acceptance and declared that all of the interested parties had given their "final and definitive" consent.

The Boxer Rebellion

A few months after the announcement of Hay's first note, the Boxer Rebellion broke out in China. The Boxers were a militant nationalist group that could endure neither the "foreign devils" who were devouring their country nor the weak Chinese government that was permitting it. In May 1900 the Boxers launched a fanatical war on foreigners and Christian Chinese, murdering hundreds. In June they laid siege to Peking, putting the capital out of contact with the Western world for a month.

Japan, Russia, Britain, France, Germany, and the United States hastily sent a combined force of eighteen thousand troops to recover the besieged city. This concerted international effort endangered what was left of China's sovereignty, since it could have encouraged the foreign powers to demand new concessions that could lead to China's complete partition.

With this danger in mind, and while the international forces were still in China, Hay formulated the second Open Door note in July 1900, to "preserve Chinese territorial and industrial entity . . . and safeguard for the world the principle of equal and impartial trade with all parts of the Chinese Empire." Clearer and more comprehensive

UNITED STATES MARINES DEFEND THE AMERICAN LEGATION IN PEKING DURING THE BOXER REBELLION IN CHINA.

than its predecessor, the second note included all parts of China and emphasized the principle of "Chinese entity," or sovereign wholeness. This time Hay did not request formal acceptance of the policy.

Alone, the United States would not have been able to enforce acceptance of the principle and prevent partition. But American policy was guided by the realization that the European powers feared one another more than they wanted new concessions. Excessive competition in the Orient or a scramble for Chinese territory might lead to a general war. So, without much enthusiasm, the other powers accepted the new policy, and an extended invasion was avoided. Instead of territory the powers took huge indemnities from China, totaling some $333 million. The United States eventually realized that its own share, $25 million, was exorbitant, and about $18 million was returned to the Chinese. This demonstration of American goodwill did not go unnoticed. The Chinese used the money to fund the education of Chinese students in American colleges and universities.

Conclusion

An examination of late nineteenth-century American foreign policy in the Pacific and in the Caribbean has illustrated the paradoxical nature of American imperialism. The perception of economic and strategic needs was coupled with the philosophical ideal of a civilizing mission. The self-interest of businesspeople and naval officers was united with that of missionaries in a drive to develop both the natural and the human resources of new areas. Few expansionists realized that there was only a thin line between economic development and exploitation, between intervention to assist and intervention to dominate. Actions by the United States which were usually viewed by the recipients as aggressive and selfish were seen by a majority of Americans as altruistic and protective. Moreover, blinded by the ease with which America had acquired new territory, most Americans assumed that the superiority of American institutions and ideals would secure the nation's position of leadership in the world without further troublesome commitments and responsibilities. Only a few politicians, such as Theodore Roosevelt, understood that the expansion of American power carried with it long-range commitments.

Readings

General Works

Beisner, Robert L., *From the Old Diplomacy to the New: 1865–1900.* Northbrook, Ill: AHN, 1975.

Bemis, Samuel F., *The Latin American Policy of the United States.* New York: Norton, 1967.

Campbell, Charles S., *The Transformation of American Foreign Relations, 1865–1900.* New York: Harper & Row, 1976.

Crapol, Edward P., *America for Americans: Economic Nationalism and Anglophobia in the Late 19th Century.* Westport, Conn.: Greenwood, 1973.

Griswold, A. Whitney, *The Far Eastern Policy of the United States.* New Haven: Yale University Press, 1938.

Healy, David, *United States Expansionism: The Imperialist Urge in the 1890s.* Madison: University of Wisconsin Press, 1970.

Kennan, George R., *American Diplomacy: 1900–1950.* New York: New American Library, 1952.

LaFeber, Walter, *The New Empire.* Ithaca, N.Y.: Cornell University Press, 1963.

May, Ernest R., *American Imperialism: A Speculative Essay.* New York: Atheneum, 1968.

Millis, Walter, *The Martial Spirit.* Boston: Houghton Mifflin, 1931.

Morgan, H. Wayne, *America's Road to Empire.* New York: Wiley, 1965.

Perkins, Dexter, *The Monroe Doctrine, 1867–1907.* Gloucester, Mass.: Peter Smith, 1966.

Pratt, Julius W., *Expansionists of 1898.* Chicago: Quadrangle, 1964.

Young, George B., and John A. Grenville, *Politics, Strategy, and American Diplomacy.* New Haven, Conn.: Yale University Press, 1966.

Special Studies

Beisner, Robert L., *Twelve Against Empire.* New York: McGraw-Hill, 1968.

Campbell, Charles S., Jr., *Anglo-American Understanding, 1898–1903.* Baltimore: Johns Hopkins Press, 1957.

Campbell, Charles S., Jr., *Special Business Interests and the Open Door Policy.* Hamden, Conn.: Shoe-string Press, 1968.

Cohen, Warren, *America's Response to China.* New York: Wiley, 1971.

Coletta, Paola E. (Ed.), *Threshold to American Internationalism: Essay on the Foreign Policies of William McKinley.* Jericho, N.Y.: Exposition, 1970.

Cosmas, Graham A., *An Army for Empire: The United States Army in the Spanish-American War.* Columbia: University of Missouri Press, 1971.

Foner, Philip S., *The Spanish-Cuban-American War and the Birth of American Imperialism.* New York: Monthly Review, 1972.

Healy, David F., *The United States in Cuba: 1898–1902.* Madison: University of Wisconsin Press, 1963.

Jenson, Ronald J., *The Alaska Purchase and Russian-American Relations.* Seattle: University of Washington Press, 1975.

May, Ernest R., *Imperial Democracy.* New York: Harcourt, Brace, 1961.

Pletcher, David M., *The Awkward Years.* Columbia: University of Missouri Press, 1962.

Thompkins, E. B., *Anti-Imperialism in the United States: The Great Debate, 1890–1920.* Philadelphia: University of Pennsylvania Press, 1972. (Paper)

Wolff, Leon, *Little Brown Brother.* Garden City, N.Y.: Doubleday, 1961.

Young, Marilyn Blatt, *The Rhetoric of Empire: America's China Policy, 1895–1901.* Cambridge, Mass.: Harvard University Press, 1968.

Primary Sources

Gardner, Lloyd (Ed.), *A Different Frontier.* Chicago: Quadrangle, 1966.

Mahan, Alfred T., *The Influence of Sea Power Upon History.* New York: Hill & Wang, 1957.

Biographies

Dennett, Tyler, *John Hay.* Port Washington, N.Y.: Kennikat Press, 1963.

James, Henry, *Richard Olney*. New York: Da Capo Press, 1969.

Leech, Margaret, *In the Days of McKinley*. New York: Harper & Row, 1959.

Morgan, H. Wayne, *William McKinley and His America*. Syracuse, N.Y.: Syracuse University Press, 1963.

Seager, Robert, II, *Alfred Thayer Mahan: The Man and His Letters*. Annapolis, Md.: Naval Institute Press, 1977.

Swanberg, W. A. *Citizen Hearst*. New York: Scribner's, 1961.

Mr. President, I have talked in vain if I have not made plain the thought that there is just one issue before the country today. It is not currency. It is not tariff. It is not railroad regulation. These and other important questions are but phases of one great conflict.

Let no man think he is not concerned; that his State or his constituency is not interested.

There is no remote corner of this country where the power of Special Interests is not encroaching on public rights.

Let no man think this is a question of party politics. It strikes down to the very foundation of our free institutions. The System knows no party. It is supplanting government.

Senator Robert M. La Follette
Speech in Senate, March 1908

Significant Events

National American Woman Suffrage Association [1890]

Newlands Act [1902]

Northern Securities Company v. *United States* [1904]

Hay-Bunau-Varilla treaty [1904]

Roosevelt corollary [1904]

Russo-Japanese War [1904–1905]

Treaty of Portsmouth [1905]

Lochner v. *New York* [1905]

Hepburn Act [1906]

Meat Inspection Act [1906]

Pure Food and Drug Act [1906]

Root-Takahira agreement [1908]

Muller v. *Oregon* [1908]

National Association for the Advancement of Colored People [1910]

Triangle Shirtwaist Company fire [1911]

Ratification of the Nineteenth Amendment [1920]

THEODORE ROOSEVELT SPEAKING AT GRANT'S TOMB IN 1911
WHILE MEMBERS OF THE PRESS, IN THE FRONT ROW, TAKE NOTES.

The Progressive Profile

At the same time that it was beginning to flex its muscles as a world power, the United States also went through a period of significant domestic reform. The reform spirit that emerged at the turn of the century—which historians have called progressivism—was not an organized movement. Rather, it represented a diversity of prescriptions for trying to solve the political, economic, and social ills that were undermining American life.

The first manifestations of progressivism were evident in the urban-reform movement that occurred in the 1890s. This was the culminating response to the economic and political abuses that had grown out of unregulated industrialization and urban expansion in the late nineteenth century. Many Progressives focused on eliminating political corruption; others worked for regulation of big business. Some were deeply concerned about social justice and supported women's rights, the prohibition of child labor, temperance reform, and in a few cases the prohibition of racial discrimination. Regardless of their specific goals, the Progressives were seeking to preserve the opportunity for individual self-fulfillment they believed was part of the national heritage.

This ideal confronted the reformers with a dilemma. They realized that in a complex industrial society, some decisions formerly left to the individual now had more far-reaching implications. One solution was to shift policymaking on certain matters to the state. Although some Progressives feared paternalism in government as much as in big business, most were willing to enlarge public authority to deal with some of the more pressing problems of industrialization and to promote general welfare and social justice. Above all, most wanted to change the machinery of government to make it possible for the people's will to be felt at all levels.

The Reform Heritage

The Progressives built on the late nineteenth-century tradition of intellectual reform, endorsing the view advanced by advocates of Reform Darwinism such as Lester Ward and Henry George and pragmatists such as William James that human beings are part of the unfolding historical process and can therefore influence its development. They particularly responded to George's ideas that the welfare of a majority of Americans was being undermined by monopoly control and that the government's power to tax could be used to redistribute wealth fairly. They believed that the fortunate had a moral obligation to aid the less fortunate.

Progressivism derived important ideas from populism. Both movements opposed control of the economy by industrial and financial monopolies; both opposed corrupt machine politicians; and both were committed to economic individualism while calling for some government intervention in the economy. Yet being predominantly city dwellers, the Progressives reflected the growing importance of America's urban centers and were considered more moderate and respectable than the Populists.

Urban reformers appropriated another strand of late nineteenth-century thought as well—an emphasis on economical and efficient management to establish orderly national development. These reformers advocated a reorganization of city bureaucracies. They believed that government by an elite of experts would be honest, efficient, and frugal. Some even went so far as to suggest that uninformed citizens be deprived from voting. Most Progressives, however, sought to replace corrupt politicians with public officials who combined expert training in management with adherence to the popular will.

The missionary spirit of the Social Gospel movement of the late nineteenth century also influenced Progressive thinking. Many of the clergy called upon their congregations to join a Christian crusade to reform society as well as improve the conditions of the poor.

As a group, most of the early Progressives came from the urban middle class. Most were native-born, Protestant, self-employed professional people active in civic affairs. Among social reformers many were women, who were usually under thirty, well-educated, single, and from comfortable homes. Their desire to help others attracted them to the settlement houses. Not only were these houses laboratories for social reform but they served as centers for contact between social workers and highly trained professionals such as economists, sociologists, political scientists, and tax reformers who staffed commissions investigating urban problems.

By the second decade of the twentieth century, the composition of the Progressive movement changed. Now, a significant number of political reformers came from working-class, Roman Catholic, and recent-immigrant backgrounds. Active primarily in the state legislatures of New York and Massachusetts, these political Progressives were strong advocates of economic reform. They called for the regulation of big business, and succeeded in getting enacted legislation protecting women and children in factories, limiting working hours, and enforcing industrial safety regulations. They even managed to obtain passage of some pension laws.

Even though most Progressives were strongly biased against big business, not all business leaders opposed reform. Some small business interests joined reform politicians and academic experts in supporting such bureaucratic reforms as the city commission or city-manager plan (adopted by 420 cities by 1915). Supporters of the city commission plan believed that an elected commission of trained administrators could govern the cities better than the frequently corrupt elected mayors or city councils. When some of the commissions did not prove to be expert managers, reformers tried a modification of the concept called the city-manager plan. Under this scheme an expert, responsible to a mayor and council, was hired to administer the city government. Most of these reformers were not trying to achieve more democratic government, but rather to concentrate decision making into the hands of a smaller number of responsible officials who would represent their interests and improve city life. Even some leaders of big business favored more government regulation in order to ensure against a return to the chaotic competition of an earlier era.

The Social-Justice Movement

Between 1898 and 1903 so many business mergers were concluded that by 1910 control of America's basic industries was in the hands of a small number of bankers and industrialists. Two percent of the population controlled 60 percent of the nation's wealth. Not only did monopolies have the power to corrupt government officials for their own ends, but big business was not accountable to consumers for the quality of its products. A steady rise in prices between 1897 and 1913 eroded the buying power of the poor and middle class, a situation the Progressives also blamed on the monopolies.

The worst inequities could be seen in the extremes of wealth and poverty in the country's growing urban centers. The class and social differences and the squalor of the slums aroused Progressive indignation, as did the plight of women and children who worked in factories ten to sixteen hours a

A SETTLEMENT HOUSE ON NEW YORK'S LOWER EAST SIDE.

day for meager wages. The prime movers behind the social-justice movement were the clergy and settlement house workers. Jane Addams and Florence Kelley of Hull House in Chicago and Lillian Wald of the Henry Street Settlement in New York made careful studies of the extent of poverty and how to alleviate it. Believing that environmental, not personal, problems lead to social disorder, they concentrated their efforts on securing the passage of state laws to prohibit child labor, protect women in industry, improve public education, and provide industrial accident insurance for workers. Along with various women's clubs, the settlement houses also supported the work of reform mayors.

In March 1911, a tragic fire at the Triangle Shirtwaist Company in New York dramatically focused attention on the unsafe working conditions prevalent in the factories. Two hundred seamstresses struggled to escape as flames raced through the building. Some suffocated or burned to death; others died when they panicked and jumped from the windows. The death toll reached 146. No longer could anyone pretend that working conditions in the United States were satisfactory. The Triangle Shirtwaist fire provided support for the Progressives in their movement to reform the unsafe working and living conditions of poor urban workers, and it led to an increase in the membership of the International Ladies' Garment Workers Union (ILGWU).

Muckrakers and Social Thinkers

The Progressive movement was given important direction by a group of magazine writers, who set out to expose the political and economic evils of the day. Dubbed Muckrakers by Teddy Roosevelt, some of them specialized in sensationalism, but many penned responsible and accurate descriptions of such abuses as graft and corruption in public office, industrial monopoly, patent-medicine fraud, and adulteration of food. In 1902 two of the most famous muckraking series ran in *McClure's:* Ida Tarbell's reports on the Standard Oil Trust and Lincoln Steffens's articles on municipal corruption. These stories whetted the public's appetite, and for the next several years the magazines were full of exposés on a wide variety of social, economic, and political topics. Books that advocated reform also gained a wide audience. Jacob Riis's investigation of New York City's slums resulted in his moving social document *How the Other Half Lives* (1890).

In *The Promise of American Life* (1909), Herbert Croly argued that Americans had always believed that an individual's profits were indistinguishable from social gain, but the development of business monopolies made it necessary to abandon laissez-faire economics. He proposed a platform for Progressive reform that would recognize the important role of the big corporations in the economy and at the same time invest in the government the power to regulate big business. Another writer who influenced Progressive thinking was Walter Lippmann. In *Drift and Mastery* (1914), written early in his long career, he suggested a similar approach, arguing that the problems created by laissez-faire capitalism could be solved by cooperation between government and business to promote the constructive use of America's natural resources.

Progressivism Enters Politics

City and State Reform

Many Progressives won their political spurs as city reformers before the turn of the century. Voters organized good-government groups to bring about tax reform, regulation of public utilities, better health regulations and transportation, and an end to the corrupt alliance between political bosses and the business interests. Unlike the academic reformers who wanted a commission to run the cities, many politicians who ran for city office sought to assure the independence of mayors and introduce a system whereby civil servants would be chosen by competitive examination, not by the spoils system. As a result of Progressive efforts, reform mayors were elected into office in one city after another. One of the most famous was Samuel L. Jones of Toledo. Jones announced that he intended to run his administration by the Golden Rule, thus acquiring the nickname "Golden Rule" Jones. He attacked political corruption and took a personal interest in the welfare of the city's young people. He attended juvenile court to ensure that delinquents were being judged fairly. In an effort to instill a feeling of collective pride in the environment, he even had park signs changed from KEEP OFF THE GRASS to CITIZENS PROTECT YOUR PROPERTY.

Most municipal reformers stressed both efficient city government and the need to wrest power from the business-dominated politicians and return it to the people. Progressive mayors undertook to arouse their citizens through educational campaigns. Through public speeches and newspaper articles they helped to awaken the public to the fact that it was directly affected by local issues such as crime, juvenile delinquency, and sanitation. Cities throughout the country established parks, juvenile courts, and progressive public schools; and they enacted local tax reform and put utilities under public control.

La Follette Since many state legislatures had some fiscal control over cities within their states, the Progressives were interested in reform at the state level as well. Many state legislators and governors were in the pay of the railroads and business corporations and as a result had long ignored the public interest. With the increasing influence of the Progressives this situation began to change.

The most important figure in bringing about reform on a statewide level was Robert "Battling Bob" La Follette. Intense, humorless, vastly self-assured, and an orator of high style, La Follette was greatly admired for his honesty and uncompromising approach. He entered politics as a Republican in the depression years of the 1890s, organizing a coalition of farmers and workers that eventually helped him win the governorship of Wisconsin over the opposition of party leaders who were controlled by railroad and lumber interests. He served as governor of Wisconsin from 1901 to 1906 and then was elected to the United States Senate. During his years as governor, La Follette formulated and implemented what came to be known as the "Wisconsin Idea," a plan that included such reforms as a state primary which allowed the people more voice in choosing candidates, a railroad tax, state regulation of railroad rates and of industries, new banking laws, workers' compensation, and conservation of natural resources. La Follette's use of experts and advisory commissions to evaluate proposed legislation and make recommendations served as a model

for future government policymaking. Many states throughout the country followed his lead in adopting regulations to control railroad rates and bringing suits against utilities and other businesses for monopolistic practices.

Labor Legislation

Many Progressives opposed trade unions because they feared concentrations of power in any sector of American life, but they shared the unions' concern about protecting America's workers. The plan for workers' compensation introduced by the Wisconsin Idea was quickly imitated, and most states had similar laws on the books before the end of World War I. By 1907 two-thirds of the states had passed labor legislation barring factories from hiring children under the age of fourteen. Many states also raised minimum wages, lowered maximum working hours, and improved factory conditions. However, rising prices in the first decade of the twentieth century soon negated the wage victories; more money in pay envelopes did not necessarily mean greater purchasing power.

State legislation regulating hours and working conditions was soon challenged by employers. Between 1900 and 1937 the Supreme Court wavered between ruling against all regulatory legislation on the grounds that it interfered with an individual's freedom to form a contract and accepting the fact that without such regulation workers would continue to be exploited. In *Lochner* v. *New York* (1905), for example, the Court ruled unconstitutional a New York law preventing bakers from working more than ten hours a day. The Court argued that under the Fourteenth Amendment it was unreasonable for the state to limit the bakers' freedom to contract for any amount of work they wished.

In dissent, Justice Oliver Wendell Holmes argued that the Court had no right to invalidate a law unless it conflicted with a specific provision of the Constitution. He contended that the Court was using its own economic theory to interpret the Constitution. Three years later in *Muller* v. *Oregon*, the Court reversed itself and upheld a law providing for a ten-hour day for women factory workers. In this case it argued that women had a special "structure of body" that required more protection and thus merited less freedom than men.

Freedom to Make Contracts

It is manifest to us that the limitation of the hours of labor as provided for in this section of the statute . . . has no such direct relation to and no such substantial effect upon the health of the employee, as to justify us in regarding the section as really a health law. It seems to us that the real object and purpose were simply to regulate the hours of labor between the master and his employees . . . in a private business, not dangerous in any degree to morals or in any real and substantial degree, to the health of the employees. Under such circumstances the freedom of master and employee to contract with each other in relation to their employment, and in defining the same, cannot be prohibited or interfered with, without violating the Federal Constitution.

Lochner v. *New York* (1905)

Government Responsibility for Social Welfare

The two sexes differ in structure of body, in the functions to be performed by each, in the amount of physical strength, in the capacity for long continued labor, particularly when done standing, the influence of vigorous health upon the future well-being of the race, the self-reliance which enables one to assert full rights, and in the capacity to maintain the struggle for subsistence. This difference justifies a difference in legislation, and upholds that which is designed to compensate for some of the burdens which rest upon her. . . .

For these reasons, and without questioning in any respect the decision in *Lochner* v. *New York*, we are of the opinion that it cannot be adjudged that the act in question is in conflict with the Federal Constitution, so far as it respects the work of a female in a laundry, and the judgment of the supreme court of Oregon is Affirmed.

Muller v. *Oregon* (1908)

"Returning the Government to the People"

One of the most popular proposals contained in the Wisconsin Idea was the direct-primary method of choosing political candidates. Until La Follette's tenure as governor, political candidates had been chosen by the party bosses. But now, in most states, ballot boxes began replacing political caucuses or party conventions, thus promoting competition within a party for a nomination.

Other kinds of reform legislation, too, began to gain support. South Dakota and Oregon adopted initiative and referendum measures. The initiative enabled private individuals to propose legislation; the referendum enabled citizens to approve or veto laws by registering an opinion on the election-day ballot. These practices spread, and a few other states also adopted a recall measure, enabling voters to remove elected officials before the completion of their terms if these officials were believed to be corrupt or incompetent. The use of the secret ballot which listed the candidates for all parties was put into effect in response to demands that voters be

able to decide privately which candidates to vote for rather than having to ask openly for a specific party ticket to mark.

Although the Constitution provided for the election of United States senators by the state legislatures, many Progressives had come to believe that the state legislatures, vulnerable as they were to political pressure, could not fairly choose the most qualified candidates. Since this position had extensive popular support, a number of states decided the public should demonstrate its preference. Eventually, Congress submitted a constitutional amendment to the states providing for the direct election of senators. It was adopted in 1913 as the Seventeenth Amendment.

Reform of the political process had some unexpected consequences. While reform measures were instrumental in ending the corrupt alliance between political party bosses and powerful business interests, they also had the effect of weakening the political parties in general. Moreover, contrary to the hopes of reformers that the populace would become more directly involved in the political process, the declining power of the political parties in choosing the candidates and in defining and dramatizing the issues led to diminished voter interest and participation. The number of voters in the South was already low: only about 40 percent of the electorate voted in 1900 because blacks had been effectively denied the vote and because there was no party competition. In national elections in the early twentieth century voting outside the South also gradually fell off.

The Search for Equality in the Progressive Era

The Changing Status of Women

The national mood for reform was reflected in the changing status of women. The number of women in the work force was growing rapidly; with women comprising about one-fifth of factory and office workers by 1910, they began to press for labor reforms along with men. The Women's Trade Union League attempted to attract female workers into the trade-union movement, but because of ethnic animosities within the union, it met with limited success.

At the same time, large numbers of young, middle- and upper-class women began to take advantage of greater educational opportunities. By 1900, five thousand women were being graduated from American colleges each year, and more of these women were taking up careers in the professions. Jane Addams and other social workers called for ways to develop and use the inherent capabilities of this independent "New Woman." The radical feminist Charlotte Perkins Gilman wrote in *Women and Economics* (1898) that the inequalities and inefficiencies of marriage were the basis of the economic subordination of women. She argued that women as well as men found satisfaction in creative work and that true social progress could come only from altering the roles played by men and women in the nation's economy.

Demonstrating a growing self-confidence, many women devoted themselves to furthering various Progressive causes. The National Consumer's League, led by Florence Kelley, championed legislation to protect working women and children. In addition, women worked in urban slums and for civic improvement, and organized to fight pornography and prostitution and to promote world peace.

Women also were active in the temperance movement, which had been revived in 1873 when Eliza Trimble Thompson led a protest against a liquor vendor in Hillsboro, Ohio. In 1874 delegates from seventeen states met in Cleveland and formed the Women's Christian Temperance Union (WCTU). Its leader, Frances Willard, was as interested in women's rights and the expansion of labor unions as she was in temperance, but her attempts to broaden the scope of the prohibition movement were unsuccessful. In 1893 the Anti-Saloon League, whose membership included both men and women, was formed in Washington, D.C. Militant temperance reformer Carrie Nation gained widespread notoriety by waging a one-woman war on saloons in her home state of Kansas.

Urbanization, industrialization, and new educational opportunities also produced changes in traditional marriage practices. With other options open, more women chose not to marry or not to marry as early as had been the norm. As birth-control knowledge and devices became more widely available through the courageous efforts of Mar-

THIS 1901 CARTOON POKES FUN AT THE FORMIDABLE CARRIE NATION, A TEMPERANCE REFORMER WHO USED A HATCHET TO SMASH UP SALOONS IN HER HOME STATE OF KANSAS. NATION'S HUSBAND HAD DIED OF ALCOHOLISM.

THE SUFFRAGISTS WERE NOT THE ONLY WOMEN TO ORGANIZE. HERE MEMBERS OF A WOMEN'S TRADE UNION
DEMONSTRATE FOR FAIR TREATMENT.

garet Sanger, some women chose to have fewer children or not to have children at all. Many more marriages were ending in divorce, probably because more women resisted being tied to lives characterized by self-denial and domesticity.

The Suffragist Movement The most powerful force for changing the status of American women came from the drive for women's suffrage which dated back to the first women's rights convention held in Seneca Falls, New York, in 1848.

During the late nineteenth century the women's suffrage movement had expanded. Susan B. Anthony helped found the National Woman Suffrage Association in 1869, and along with Elizabeth Cady Stanton she welcomed women of all backgrounds into the organization. The only requirement for joining was a commitment to the cause of women's suffrage. A rival, New England-based organization, the American Woman Suffrage Association, was highly selective, granting membership only to women of sufficient prestige and propriety. In 1890, after three years of negotiations, the two groups merged to form the National American

Woman Suffrage Association. Stanton was elected the first president. She withdrew, however, when the national convention opposed a book she had written in which she claimed that the Bible contained a derogatory view of women. Susan B. Anthony succeeded her in 1892.

The suffragist movement encountered formidable problems, both internal and external. It was divided on the issue of whether to concentrate on state or on federal legislation. It was opposed by powerful liquor interests, which believed that it was linked to the prohibition movement. And it had to face the hostility and ridicule of men as well as the apathy or disapproval of many women.

When Carrie Chapman Catt followed Susan B. Anthony as president of the National Association in 1900, progress at the state level was disappointingly slow; as a result the organization began to focus on federal legislation. Wyoming had granted women the right to vote in 1869 when it was still a territory. Colorado, Utah, and Idaho followed in the 1890s. By 1914, the number of states granting women's suffrage totaled only eleven, and all but one of these were the more liberal Western states.

Catt and Anna Howard Shaw, a social worker who became president in 1904, joined forces with Alice Paul and Lucy Burns, founders of another women's rights organization, the Congressional Union. Paul and Burns had been active in the suffragist movement in Britain and they helped create interest in an amendment to the United States Constitution. They were, however, more militant than their sisters in the National Association: they engaged in disruptive and sometimes destructive activities such as picketing, smashing windows, or interrupting public meetings in order to gain attention. They even picketed the White House in 1917. Such behavior created a rift between the English radicals and the more moderate Americans who favored political action. Catt, again serving as president of the National Association, was pressured into disavowing any connection between the Congressional Union and her organization.

In spite of the divisions in the movement, the suffrage drive began to succeed. Support came from Progressives who believed that giving women the vote would raise the moral level of the political process and from temperance reformers who thought that enfranchised women would support their cause. Opposition came from liquor dealers and men calling for war preparedness, who argued that women were too tenderminded to vote rationally on the question of war. Nevertheless, the 1912 Progressive party platform included a plank supporting women's suffrage, and in 1918 the movement celebrated its first major victory. The "Anthony Amendment," which provided that "the right of citizens of the United States to vote shall not be denied or abridged by the United States or by any State on account of sex," gained the support of President Wilson and passed in the House of Representatives. This was a glorious moment for the movement, but much work remained. There was widespread involvement in the war effort by women before the Nineteenth Amendment to the Constitution was passed in the Senate and finally ratified by the states in 1920.

Black Americans

Given the Progressives' emphasis on reform, it is ironic that the situation of black people saw little improvement during the Progressive Era. The imposition of Jim Crow laws to disfranchise blacks in the South was supported by those Progressives whose overriding concern was political, not social, reform. Many, influenced by the widely held racist views of that period, believed that reform in the South would never be possible if blacks could vote. If Progressives tried to help blacks exercise the franchise, antireform leaders would argue that they were facilitating Negro domination of Southern politics. It was during the Progressive Era, too, that the use of lynch mobs became widespread in the South as a means of keeping blacks passive and that bloody race riots broke out in both the North and South.

Perhaps because of these worsening conditions a new movement toward racial equality did emerge. This new departure was led by W. E. B. DuBois, an historian and sociologist who was the first black to receive a Ph.D. from Harvard. An advocate of complete equality for black people, DuBois challenged the leadership of Booker T. Washington as the primary spokesman for black Americans. DuBois was a

W. E. B. DuBOIS DEMANDED COMPLETE ECONOMIC AND SOCIAL EQUALITY FOR BLACKS AND CRITICIZED BOOKER T. WASHINGTON FOR HIS ACCOMMODATIONIST VIEWS. DuBOIS WAS AMONG THE FOUNDERS IN 1910 OF THE NATIONAL ASSOCIATION FOR THE ADVANCEMENT OF COLORED PEOPLE.

severe critic of Washington's position that blacks should strive for economic advancement through self-help programs but should not agitate for civil rights. Whereas DuBois believed in the self-help aspects of Washington's program, he opposed gradualism and accommodation, which he viewed as reinforcing the status quo. DuBois was unsuccessful in persuading the majority of blacks to his view, for most black people agreed with Washington that acceptance of their current political and social status, hard work, and time would eventually make possible a better life.

DuBois therefore built his program around the small nucleus of well-educated blacks whose economic and cultural standing put them in the position of being leaders in their communities. In 1905 DuBois founded the Niagara Movement, a loosely knit group of black and white reformers who met on occasion to agitate against school segregation and to place responsibility for racial discrimination in the white community. The movement reflected the frustrations felt by those who rejected Washington's gradualism. Whereas Washington discouraged higher education for blacks, DuBois believed that blacks should have the opportunity to attend college, to enter the professions, and to exercise full political rights.

An incident in 1908 led to the formation of a more cohesive, nationwide organization for black civil rights. In Springfield, Illinois, a race riot erupted at the time the city was planning for the 1909 centennial of Abraham Lincoln's birth.

Spurred by this incident, members of the Niagara Movement met on Lincoln's birthday in 1909 with a small group of Progressives including Oswald G. Villard (grandson of William Lloyd Garrison), John Dewey, Jane Addams, and others to form a permanent organization to help black Americans attain political and social equality. In 1910 they founded the National Association for the Advancement of Colored People (NAACP).

While most of the offices of the NAACP were held by whites, DuBois was named as head of research and publicity and edited *Crisis*, the organization's publication, for many years. Beginning with a campaign against lynching, the NAACP brought its cases to the courts, winning several important Supreme Court decisions including the 1915 ruling in *Guinn* v. *United States* that declared unconstitutional the grandfather clause in an Oklahoma law. It also pushed for the complete integration of American society. By 1921 there were four hundred branches throughout the country.

In 1911 the Urban League, devoted primarily to helping blacks find jobs and adjust to life in the cities, was organized. With the outbreak of World War I, black migration from the rural South to the nation's cities accelerated as blacks flocked to fill jobs created by the war economy. The growth of black urban ghettos provided a base for the development of black newspapers, shops, and banks. At the same time a new black consciousness began to develop in the working class.

The Roosevelt Administration

By 1900 Progressive leaders like La Follette had achieved considerable success in restructuring the machinery of government on the state level. Now Progressives hoped for nationwide economic and political change under the leadership of a reformer who was able to use the political party system to bring about Progressive legislation.

Teddy Roosevelt

The answer to the Progressives' hopes, by all political odds, should never have made it to the White House. Theodore Roosevelt, governor of New York and a political maverick, received the 1900 vice-presidential nomination on the McKinley ticket because New York Republican party boss Thomas C. Platt wanted to get him out of state politics. What Platt and his cohorts termed his "unsound and unreliable" ideas about society, politics, business, and economics made Roosevelt a nuisance to the party councils. At this time, the vice-presidency was considered "the graveyard of political ambition," not a springboard to the presidency. Mark Hanna, McKinley's campaign manager, called Roosevelt "that damned cowboy," and hoped that the office of the vice-presidency would make Roosevelt harmless.

Theodore Roosevelt was the decendant of a well-to-do New York family of Dutch ancestry. An

THEODORE ROOSEVELT'S ENERGY AND ZEST FOR LIFE SHINE THROUGH IN THIS PHOTOGRAPH.

asthmatic, nearsighted child teased mercilessly by his peers, he was motivated to build up his body with special exercises. As a young man he was of medium height, muscular, with small eyes and a set of teeth that later became the delight of political cartoonists. Energetic, boyish, adventuresome, always delighted with life, he became an avid sportsman and even spent a short period as a rancher and cowboy. As energetic mentally as he was physically, he graduated Phi Beta Kappa from Harvard and in his early twenties published the first of dozens of volumes of history. He studied law at Columbia University, but then sidestepped a legal career to go into politics. He joined the Republican party, worked on the precinct level, and won election to the New York state legislature where he soon discovered the strong connections between members of the legislature and business leaders. But the reform-minded Roosevelt refused to make deals with the vested interests.

In 1895 the mayor of New York appointed Roosevelt president of the city's Police Board, a posi-tion which brought him into national prominence. With writer Jacob Riis he investigated New York's gambling dens, houses of prostitution, and the places where payoffs were made to corrupt members of the Police Department.

Roosevelt's subsequent rise in national politics was meteoric. He served as assistant secretary of the navy in McKinley's first administration, became a popular hero after his reckless ride up San Juan Hill, and was elected governor of New York. He persuaded the legislature to impose heavier taxes on railroads and utilities, appropriate money for the renovation of New York City tenements, and enact conservation legislation, trust regulations, and an eight-hour day for state employees.

The Election of 1900

In 1900 the Democrats again nominated William Jennings Bryan for president. But the country was no longer interested in the issues of free silver and antiimperialism, and McKinley was reelected with the largest popular majority since Grant's landslide victory in 1872. Six months later McKinley was assassinated in Buffalo, New York, by a self-proclaimed anarchist who had the urge to kill "a great leader." Roosevelt took the oath of office as America's twenty-sixth president in September 1901.

Roosevelt's Domestic Policy

The new chief executive—at 42 the youngest ever to hold the office—came well-prepared for his job. A man of strong social conscience, he was bent on reform; at the same time he was an astute politician and realist who was willing to compromise rather than achieve nothing at all. Although he despised the maneuvering of the firmly entrenched party bosses and conservative office-holders, known as the Old Guard, he believed it was necessary to find a way to work with them.

Roosevelt intended to be a forceful, aggressive leader. He considered Congress incapable of leading and thought that the judicial process moved too slowly. He believed that the Constitution gave him the right to exert executive authority, and he interpreted the document in broad terms as an instrument to better the lot of the nation's people. He believed that as president he could do anything that was not specifically forbidden by the Constitution.

Roosevelt was the individual most responsible for convincing Americans that efficient government administration coupled with the creation of independent commissions run by experts could solve the nation's problems.

Because Roosevelt inherited a Congress dominated by conservatives he was politically cautious at first, retaining McKinley's cabinet and maintaining fairly good relations with the Republican Old Guard. The Progressives, led by La Follette, were not powerful enough to challenge party leadership until after Roosevelt left office. The Democrats, still divided between the Bryan and Cleveland wings, caused Roosevelt little concern.

Curbing Abuses of Business and Labor Although Roosevelt was not opposed to bigness in business per se, his experience in New York had convinced him that the public was being exploited by the monopolies. As president, he felt he must challenge trust abuses, and he directed his attack first against the railroad trusts. In 1902, using the authority of the Sherman Anti-Trust Act, Roosevelt ordered the attorney general to begin proceedings to dissolve the Northern Securities Company, a holding company formed by J. P. Morgan in 1901, on the grounds that it controlled "practically the entire railway system in the Northwest—possibly as the first step toward controlling the entire railway system of the country." Company lawyers fought back, and the case dragged through the courts for two years. Then, in 1904 the Supreme Court ordered the Northern Securities Company dissolved under the Sherman Anti-Trust Act. The president had won his first big battle with the trusts. In 1905 the government won a second important antitrust case, against Swift and Company, the giant of the meat-packing business. In all, Roosevelt initiated action against forty companies and secured twenty-five indictments.

Despite Roosevelt's reputation as a "trust buster," his record was not spectacular. Many powerful corporations that were apparently dissolved simply took other forms and continued business as usual. Moreover, Roosevelt's belief in the ability of big business to contribute efficiently to the development and management of the economy led him to favor regulation over dissolution. As it turned out, more big-business combinations came into being under Roosevelt than under either McKinley or Roosevelt's successor, Taft; and under Taft the government

ALTHOUGH SHOWN HERE WIELDING HIS BIG STICK AGAINST THE TRUSTS, ROOSEVELT'S RECORD AS A TRUST BUSTER WAS NOT AS IMPRESSIVE AS THAT OF HIS SUCCESSOR, WILLIAM HOWARD TAFT.

won more big antitrust victories than under Roosevelt. Nevertheless, Roosevelt's role in initiating action against the abuses of corporations facilitated the job of his successors.

Roosevelt was generally sympathetic to labor's demands for better working conditions. In 1902 workers in the anthracite coal mines of Pennsylvania struck to protest exploitation, particularly a high accident rate, excessively long hours, and low pay. They demanded, among other concessions, a 20-percent wage hike and a shorter nine-hour working day. The mine owners refused to negotiate, and as the weather turned cold, businesses, factories, and schools had to shut their doors. The president was infuriated by the stubborn refusal of the mine operators to deal fairly with the strikers. Knowing that if the strike was not settled soon the country would face a major crisis, he threatened to send in federal troops to seize and operate the mines. At this point, the mine operators, pressured by J. P. Morgan, backed down and accepted binding arbitration. In a compromise settlement the workers received a 10-percent wage increase and a nine-hour day, but no official recognition of their union. In the wake of this incident the president persuaded Congress in 1903 to create the Department of Commerce and Labor to assist in resolving some of the problems between management and labor. The new department included a Bureau of Corporations to keep an eye on businesses involved in interstate commerce.

The Square Deal

Having worked diligently behind the scenes to secure the support of both conservatives and Progressives in the Republican party, Roosevelt was nominated easily in the election of 1904. A rousing and indomitable campaigner, enormously popular with the people, he swept to victory over his Democratic opponent, conservative Alton B. Parker, by more than two million votes. Roosevelt returned to the White House with large Republican majorities in both houses of Congress.

Railroad Regulation With a broad mandate from the public, Roosevelt was determined to secure a package of far-reaching reform legislation that he referred to as the Square Deal. In terms of practical politics this meant preventing the rich and powerful from exploiting the weak and poor. By 1900 there were well over a million workers employed by the railroads, and unrest over working conditions occasionally flared into strikes. Consumers resented the lack of uniform standards for establishing fares and freight rates. Progressive newspapers condemned the railroads' use of free passes to reward politicians who favored them.

The Interstate Commerce Act of 1887 had proved to be largely ineffective in curbing railroad abuses and Roosevelt urged Congress to enact a law that was specific enough to have real teeth in it. In response to his demands, the House passed the Hepburn Act by an overwhelming majority; but it took the president's considerable political skill to steer the bill through the conservative Senate, where the railroad lobby had worked assiduously for its defeat. The Hepburn Act of 1906 gave the Interstate Commerce Commission the right to inspect once closely guarded railroad-company books, nullify unreasonable rates, fix maximum rates, stop rebates, and cur-

tail free passes. It also assigned to the commission the responsibility for evaluating conditions under which perishable goods were transported and extended ICC jurisdiction over express and sleeping-car companies and railroad terminals. Furthermore, the act declared that when railroad cases came to court, the commission did not have to prove that the law was being violated. Instead, it would be up to the railroads to prove that they were obeying the law.

Pure Food and Drugs For a number of years the Agriculture Department had been conducting tests that showed the harmful effects of a variety of canned and prepared foods adulterated with chemical preservatives and dyes. In 1906, with the publication of *The Jungle*, Upton Sinclair's widely read novel describing the filthy conditions that prevailed in the slaughterhouses, action finally was taken to remedy the situation. At the same time the public was aroused by muckraking articles exposing the sale of harmful and mislabeled patent medicines. After securing passage of the Hepburn Act, Roosevelt turned his full attention to pressuring Congress to protect American consumers against harmful meat and drugs. He ordered an investigation of the so-called Beef Trust which revealed "scandalous abuses" that in Roosevelt's words would have to be "remedied at once." As a result, Congress passed the Meat Inspection Act of 1906, laying down binding rules for sanitary meat packing and government inspection of meat products crossing state lines. The Pure Food and Drug Act was passed at the same time, forbidding the manufacture or sale of mislabeled or adulterated food or drugs in interstate commerce.

Conservation Roosevelt's strong personal interest in protecting America's lands, forests, rivers, and wildlife led him to champion the careful development and conservation of natural resources. Conservation had become a national issue during Cleveland's administration. Concern over the destruction of vast forest ranges in the West had resulted in the enactment of the national Forest Reserve Act of 1891 which set aside millions of acres of forest land. While experts in forest management, particularly Gifford Pinchot who became the head of the Federal Forestry Service in 1898, wanted a program of planned forest management, many ranchers, lumbermen, and other Westerners were eager to exploit forest resources and keep them out of government hands. A third faction, led by John Muir, one of the founders of the Sierra Club in California, called for complete preservation of the American wilderness rather than planned management. Pinchot's views won out, and Congress passed the Forest Management Act in 1897.

When Roosevelt took office he became a strong ally of Pinchot, enabling him to expand the activity of the Forest Service to preserve the forests from exploitation. Under Roosevelt the Western area set aside for forest reserves was more than tripled. The president also used his influence to secure passage of the Newlands Reclamation Act of 1902 which provided for large irrigation projects. He supported the establishment of the Inland Waterways Commission in 1907 to protect waterways and forests as well as coal, oil, and natural-gas lands, and called a National Conservation Congress the next year to study the nation's conservation problems. As an outgrowth of the conference forty-one states established their own conservation commissions and a National Conservation Commission was created which drew up an inventory of the country's natural resources.

Evaluation of Roosevelt's Domestic Policy

Despite Roosevelt's accomplishments, he did encounter criticism for some of his domestic policies. A brief business panic occurred in 1907 for which the president was widely blamed. Some claimed that he had caused business leaders to lose confidence in the economy; others condemned him for not fighting openly with party conservatives in an effort to lower the tariff. In a message to Congress in 1908 Roosevelt proposed many advanced progressive reforms, but could not attract progressive support because he was not seeking reelection.

Nevertheless, Roosevelt was one of the country's most outstanding chief executives, and as a reformer he set many important precedents for his successors. He instituted an attack on trusts that was carried forward after he left the White House. He was aware of conservation problems and called for the protection of natural resources long before ecology became a national issue. He sponsored the idea of independent commissions run by experts to regulate the concentrations of economic power in American society for the public interest. Of course, time has shown that such commissions can only be successful when their powers are not abused and when they are truly independent of the interests they are supposed to regulate. Finally, Roosevelt reasserted the concept of a strong presidency. During the last decades of the nineteenth century a series of weak chief executives had left most of the initiatives in government to the Congress. Roosevelt demonstrated that the presidency could be used to initiate and gain acceptance of national policy and could be effective in providing moral leadership for the nation.

Big-Stick Foreign Policy

More clearly than any other public figure of the Progressive Era, Teddy Roosevelt expressed the thrust of American foreign policy after 1898. Aware of the growing rivalries among the great nations for territory and influence, he believed that an expanding foreign trade would ensure American economic strength and a strong navy would ensure the protection of the nation's imperial interests and help maintain world order. "I have always," he stated, "been fond of the West African proverb, 'Speak softly and carry a big stick, [and] you will go far.'" In Roosevelt's view the American nation could be persuasive in foreign diplomacy only if it had military strength and the willingness to use it. He swung the big stick in several areas of foreign policy.

The Panama Canal

Once the United States had annexed the islands of Guam and eastern Samoa in the Pacific and acquired the Philippines in addition, the nation suddenly discovered that it had two-ocean interests but only a one-ocean navy. Thus the conclusion of the Spanish-American War reinforced the importance for Americans of constructing an isthmian canal. There were, however, diplomatic, political, and financial obstacles to its construction.

First, it was necessary to abrogate the 1850 Clayton-Bulwer treaty with Great Britain, which provided that the two countries would construct an isthmian canal and would not fortify it or try to maintain exclusive control over it. The Clayton-Bulwer treaty was eventually replaced by the 1901 Hay-Pauncefote treaty, giving the United States the right to build an isthmian canal without any restrictions on fortification. It stipulated only that the canal be open to all shipping on an equal basis.

The second obstacle, obtaining rights to a route, was more difficult to overcome. Some wanted to build the canal through Nicaragua, others through the isthmus of Panama, which was controlled by Colombia. Both routes had complications. The Nicaraguan route was longer, but it would be much easier to build. The Panama route was favored by the French. The French Canal Company had begun work on a canal across Panama in 1883 but had failed, suffering a huge financial loss. Its agent, the New Panama Canal Company, was aided in its vigorous efforts to sell its assets to the United States by a representative, Philippe Bunau Varilla, and by its American legal advisor, William Nelson Cromwell. When thirty thousand people died in a volcanic eruption in Martinique in 1902, the Panama lobby encouraged public concerns about possible volcanic danger in Nicaragua. Then it abruptly dropped the price of its Panama rights to $40 million, about one-third its original asking price. At this point, Congress passed a bill approving the Panama route. In January 1903 the United States and Colombia prepared a treaty leasing territory for construction of a canal, but Colombia's senate, hoping for slightly more money from the New Panama Canal Company as well as from the United States, and fearing possible infringement of its national sovereignty, refused to ratify it.

Believing that Colombia had negotiated in bad faith and influenced by his friendship with Bunau-Varilla, Roosevelt was impatient to secure the Panamanian route for the canal. In later years he explained, "The Canal was for the benefit of the entire world. Should the blackmailing greed of the Bogota ring stand in the way of civilization? . . . I determined that I would do what ought to be done

without regard to them." They were standing in the way of not only "civilization" but of Roosevelt's political ambitions. He wanted to be elected in his own right in 1904, and he believed that the canal would dramatize the success of his presidency.

Panamanians had long resented Colombian control and had rebelled against it many times before. Now, fearful that the prosperity that would surely follow the construction of the canal was but a fading dream, they were primed for another revolution. Bunau-Varilla, believing that Colombia's refusal of the lease meant that the assets of the New Panama Company would be wiped out, was eager to assist the Panamanians and plotted with a small group to raise an "army" consisting largely of paid Colombian troops and Panamanian firemen. Roosevelt and Secretary of State John Hay were informed of the plot and, while not committing the United States government to any action, they did not oppose it.

The revolution took place on November 3, 1903, one day after the naval vessel U.S.S. Nashville, on order of President Roosevelt, had arrived on the scene. Although some Colombian troops landed in Panama to put down the rebellion, their general was bribed to send them home and United States troops seized the Panama railroads to bar other Colombian troops from the isthmus. The United States officially recognized the new regime led by the Frenchman Bunau-Varilla, only to encounter widespread indignation in the world press. Latin Americans condemned the American action as another instance of "Yankee imperialism."

Undaunted, the United States met with Bunau-Varilla in Washington and concluded the Hay-Bunau-Varilla treaty. Bunau-Varilla did not bother to consult with Panamanian leaders during negotiations. The treaty gave the United States a lease in perpetuity on a canal zone ten miles wide at a rental fee of $250,000 per year and gave Panama a guarantee of independence. It was signed on November 18 and ratified in February 1904. Bunau-Varilla never returned to Panama. Roosevelt defended his actions throughout, insisting that if he had used "traditional, conservative methods," the canal never would have been built. "I took the Canal Zone," he said, "and let Congress debate; and while the debate goes on, the Canal does also." It opened in August 1914.

TEDDY ROOSEVELT USES THE BIG STICK TO ENFORCE THE MONROE DOCTRINE IN THE CARIBBEAN.

The Roosevelt Corollary

During his presidency Theodore Roosevelt expanded the policy of intervention in Caribbean affairs. The small Caribbean republics tended to be unstable and were often in debt to European countries. In 1902, for example, Venezuela's iron-fisted dictator, Cipriano Castro, reneged on government debts to banking houses in Great Britain and Germany. The European powers resorted to blockade, bombardment, and seizure of customs houses. Though Roosevelt despised Castro and believed that Britain and Germany had a right to collect their debts, the American public was incensed over the European military action. As a result, Roosevelt dispatched a naval force under Admiral Dewey to the Caribbean, and Germany and Great Britain agreed to international arbitration of the dispute.

The possibility of other such European interventions, particularly in the strife-torn Dominican Republic, prompted Roosevelt to declare in 1904 that "chronic wrong-doing or an impotence which results in a general loosening of the ties of civilized society . . . may force the United States . . . to the exercise of an international police power." In 1905,

during a debt crisis in Santo Domingo, Roosevelt clarified the meaning of this so-called Roosevelt corollary to the Monroe Doctrine. The island, indebted to Europeans and Americans, asked the United States for assistance. Roosevelt set up a company to oversee Dominican customs revenues and make sure that 55 percent of those revenues went to the island's creditors. The principle was clear: to prevent European use of force or control of territory in the Caribbean, the United States would use its "international police power" and intervene to maintain order and fiscal responsibility. The policy worked well in Santo Domingo, keeping out Europeans and restoring the republic to financial health. New interventions to stabilize the island's economic and political life occurred in 1914 and from 1916 to 1924. But Congress would never ratify a treaty that was negotiated to legalize these actions. Roosevelt acted alone, as Wilson did later on, boldly asserting executive authority in interpreting the Monroe Doctrine.

Controversy surrounded the Roosevelt corollary for the next quarter century. Most Republicans and nationalists approved the theory as an appropriate extension of the Monroe Doctrine, while most

Democrats and antiimperialists condemned it as an American effort to achieve complete domination of the Western Hemisphere. Because it was used to justify American influence in Central America and the Caribbean, the Roosevelt corollary has been called a perversion of Monroe's original idea of preventing intervention in the Western Hemisphere by the European powers. Some scholars see Roosevelt's doctrine as nothing more than a cover for the extension of American imperialism cloaked in the mantle of a time-honored statement of American foreign policy.

The Russo-Japanese War

Russia's continuing efforts to obtain Manchuria were perceived by the Japanese as an intolerable threat to their security. They feared that once the Russians had acquired Manchuria, they might then move to take Korea. In 1904 Japan attacked the Russian naval fleet at Port Arthur, thus sparking the Russo-Japanese War.

Most people in the United States sympathized with the Japanese. Reports of Russian atrocities under the czar shocked Americans; magazine descriptions of pogroms carried out against Russian Jews were especially horrifying. Moreover, the American public regarded the Japanese as underdogs. American business leaders had economic motives for supporting Japan; Russian control of Manchuria would threaten America's China trade. Roosevelt's main concern, however, was with the balance of power in Asia. He believed that it was to America's advantage to keep the powers evenly matched.

Japan, after a series of impressive victories, became economically depleted and uncertain that it could win the war. The Japanese therefore secretly requested that Roosevelt mediate a truce. In 1905 Russian and Japanese delegates met in New Hampshire, with Roosevelt using his influence behind the scenes.

Japan demanded an indemnity from Russia as well as the entire Russian island of Sakhalin, the accessway to the Amur River in Siberia. After difficult negotiations Japan finally agreed to lesser concessions. The Treaty of Portsmouth (1905) gave Japan the southern half of Sakhalin, made Japan the dominant influence in the southern half of Manchuria, and reaffirmed Japan's hold over Korea.

The president won the Nobel Peace Prize in 1906 partly for his role in mediating the conflict.

The treaty, though recognizing Japan's new influence in Asia, increased Japanese-American tensions. Roosevelt was reviled for thwarting the Japanese demand for an indemnity from Russia. Many Japanese took to the streets to riot against Roosevelt and their own negotiators. These demonstrations in turn caused the American public to begin to feel less friendly toward Japan. Relations between the United States and Russia also deteriorated. The Russians, claiming they could have won the war, denounced Roosevelt for his interference.

The American Fleet Goes on Tour

Japanese-American relations were strained, too, by the San Francisco school incident of 1906 (described in Chapter 18). Although the Gentlemen's Agreement had cooled the flames somewhat, Roosevelt was concerned that his efforts to resolve the dispute had been viewed by the Japanese as evidence of weakness and he therefore set out to impress Japan with American military might. In a dramatic ges-

ROOSEVELT AS PEACEMAKER IN THE RUSSO-JAPANESE WAR. HIS EFFORTS HELPED SECURE HIM THE NOBEL PEACE PRIZE OF 1906.

ture he sent the American fleet on a world tour (1907–1909), the high point of which was to be a visit to Japan. To his great pleasure, the Japanese greeted the American ships with tremendous enthusiasm. The goodwill generated by the president's bold initiative resulted in the Root-Takahira agreement of 1908 whereby both nations agreed to respect each other's territories in the Pacific and to uphold the Open Door in China.

Evaluation of Roosevelt's Foreign Policy

More than any other political leader of his generation Theodore Roosevelt had an astute grasp of international politics and the role that power plays in determining the fate of nations. An aggressive imperialist, he wanted the United States, now one of the world's preeminent economic powers, to assume an important role in international affairs. Accurately assessing the rising power of Japan, he extended American friendship through his efforts to mediate in the Russo-Japanese war and in the Root-Takahira agreement. At the same time he used the dramatic

world cruise of the American fleet to impress the Japanese with American naval might. Yet, impatient and moralistic by nature, Roosevelt did not hesitate to bully weaker countries if he believed they stood in the way of America's national interest. Determined to have a canal built through Central America so that the United States fleet would have quick access to both the Atlantic and the Pacific Oceans, he created long-lasting ill will between the United States and Latin America by the highhanded manner in which he obtained the canal zone. The Roosevelt corollary to the Monroe Doctrine, while protecting the Western Hemisphere from European intervention, also angered Latin Americans by providing the justification for United States' dominance of Central America and the Caribbean. In short, in pursuing his foreign policy Roosevelt demonstrated a clear understanding of international politics and the potential role of the United States among nations. Moreover, he demonstrated a willingness to use the country's military and economic might for arguably beneficial ends. Unfortunately, he had few scruples regarding the means used to secure these ends.

Readings

General Works

Davis, Allen F., *Spearheads for Reform: The Social Settlements and the Progressive Movement, 1890–1914*. Richard C. Wade (Ed.). New York: Oxford University Press, 1967. (Paper)

Ekirch, Arthur A., Jr., *Progressivism in America*. New York: Watts, 1974.

Hays, Samuel P., *The Response to Industrialism*. Chicago: University of Chicago Press, 1957.

Hofstadter, Richard, *The Age of Reform*. New York: Random House, 1955.

Iriye, Akira, *From Nationalism to Internationalism: United States Foreign Policy to 1914*. London: Routledge & Kegan, 1977.

Kolko, Gabriel, *The Triumph of Conservatism*. New York: Macmillan, 1963.

Merrill, Horace S., and Marion G. Merrill, *The Republican Command, 1897–1913*. Lexington: University Press of Kentucky, 1971.

Mowry, George, *The Era of Theodore Roosevelt*. New York: Harper & Row, 1958.

Munro, Dana G., *Intervention and Dollar Diplomacy in the Caribbean: 1900–1921*. Princeton, N.J.: Princeton University Press, 1964.

Newby, Idus A., *Jim Crow's Defense: Anti-Negro Thought in America, 1900–1930*. Baton Rouge: Louisiana State University Press, 1965.

Nye, Russel B., *Midwestern Progressive Politics*. East Lansing: Michigan State University Press, 1959.

O'Neill, William L., *The Progressive Years: America Comes of Age*. New York: Dodd, Mead, 1975.

Unger, Irwin, and Debi Unger, *The Vulnerable Years: The United States, 1896–1917*. New York: New York University Press, 1978.

Special Studies

Beale, Howard K., *Theodore Roosevelt and the Rise of America to World Power*. Baltimore: Johns Hopkins Press, 1956.

Blum, John M., *The Republican Roosevelt*. Cambridge, Mass.: Harvard University Press, 1954.

Buenker, John D., *Urban Liberalism and Progressive Reform*. New York: Scribner's, 1973.

Chalmers, David M., *The Social and Political Ideas of the Muckrakers*. New York: Citadel Press, 1964.

Esthus, Raymond A. *Theodore Roosevelt and International Rivalries*. Waltham, Mass.: Blaisdell, 1970. (Paper)

Forcey, Charles B., *The Crossroads of Liberalism*. New York: Oxford University Press, 1961.

Grimes, Alan P., *The Puritan Ethic and Woman's Suffrage*. New York: Oxford University Press, 1967.

Gusfield, Joseph R., *Symbolic Crusade: Status Politics and the American Temperance Movement*. Urbana: University of Illinois Press, 1966. (Paper)

Henri, Florette, *Black Migration: Movement North, 1900–1920*. Garden City, N.Y.: Anchor, 1975.

Israel, Jerry, *Progressivism and the Open Door: America and China, 1905–1921*. Pittsburg, Pa.: University of Pittsburg Press, 1971.

Kellogg, Charles F., *NAACP: A History of the National Association for the Advancement of Colored People, 1909–1920*. Baltimore: Johns Hopkins University Press, 1970.

Lubove, Roy, *The Progressives and the Slums*. Westport, Conn.: Greenwood, 1974.

Meier, August, *Negro Thought in America, 1880–1920*. Ann Arbor: University of Michigan Press, 1963.

Morgan, David, *Suffragists and Democrats: The Politics of Woman Suffrage in America*. East Lansing: Michigan State University Press, 1971.

Neu, Charles E., *An Uncertain Friendship: Theodore Roosevelt and Japan, 1906–1909*. Cambridge, Mass.: Harvard University Press, 1967.

Nielson, David Gordon, *Black Ethos: Northern Urban Negro Life and Thought: 1890–1930*. Westport, Conn.: Greenwood, 1977.

O'Neill, William L., *Everyone Was Brave: The Rise and Fall of Feminism in America*. New York: Quadrangle, 1969. (Paper)

Perkins, Bradford, *The Great Rapprochement: England and the United States, 1895–1914*. New York: Atheneum, 1968.

Rice, Bradley Robert, *Progressive Cities: The Commission Government Movement in America, 1901–1920*. Austin: University of Texas Press, 1977.

Schiesl, Martin J., *The Politics of Efficiency: Municipal Administration and Reform in America, 1880–1920*. Berkeley: University of California Press, 1977.

Thelen, David P., *The New Citzenship: Origins of Progressivism in Wisconsin, 1885–1900*. Columbia: University of Missouri Press, 1972.

Wiebe, Robert H., *Businessmen and Reform*. Cambridge, Mass.: Harvard University Press, 1962.

Primary Sources

Addams, Jane, *Forty Years at Hull House*. New York: Garrett Press, 1970.

Croly, Herbert, *The Promise of American Life*. New York: Bobbs-Merrill, 1965.

Du Bois, William E., *Auto-Biography of W.E. Burghardt Du Bois: A Soliloquy on Viewing My Life from the Last Decade of Its First Century*. Herbert Aptheker (Ed.). New York: International, 1968. (Paper)

Lippman, Walter, *Drift and Mastery*. Englewood Cliffs, N.J.: Prentice-Hall, 1961.

Steffens, Lincoln, *Autobiography of Lincoln Steffens*. New York: Harcourt, 1931.

Biographies

Burton, David H., *Theodore Roosevelt: Confident Imperialist*. Philadelphia: University of Pennsylvania Press, 1969.

Chessman, G. Wallace, *Theodore Roosevelt and the Politics of Power*. Boston: Little, Brown, 1969. (Paper)

Harbaugh, William H., *Power and Responsibility*. New York: Macmillan, 1963.

Levine, Daniel, *Jane Addams and the Liberal Tradition*. Madison, Wis.: State Historical Society, 1971.

Morris, Edmund, *The Rise of Theodore Roosevelt*. New York: Coward, 1979.

Pringle, Henry, *Theodore Roosevelt*. New York: Harcourt, Brace, 1956.

Thelen, David P., *Robert M. LaFollette and the Insurgent Spirit*. Boston: Little, Brown, 1976.

Fiction

Doctorow, E. L., *Ragtime*. New York: Random House, 1975.

Susan B. Anthony

BATTLE FOR THE BALLOT

AMONG the lights of the nineteenth century women's rights movement, Susan B. Anthony shone with extraordinary brilliance. With singular devotion she labored for most of her life to achieve equality for women. Her most cherished dream, universal suffrage, was denied her in her lifetime. On her deathbed she cried out: "Just think of it. I have been striving for over sixty years for a little bit of justice—and yet I must die without obtaining it. Oh, it seems so cruel!" Yet she could also look back on her work with satisfaction. "These have been wonderful years . . . . It's too bad that our bodies wear out while our interests are just as strong as ever."

Susan B. Anthony was born on February 15, 1820, in the small town of Adams, nestled in the Berkshire hills of western Massachusetts. Her father, Daniel, was an enterprising Quaker businessman who owned his own cotton mill. Her mother, Lucy, was a Baptist homemaker who had given up an active social life to adopt the Quaker's simple life-style. In the Quaker church men and women were encouraged to work and speak as equals, and during these early years Susan Anthony developed a respect for fair-mindedness and industry. Her father had a reputation as an independent thinker who was firmly opposed to slavery and just as strongly in favor of education for women and men alike. Her mother often wondered aloud at the justice of society's decree that a woman should make the accommodations in marriage, changing name, customs, and religion to suit her husband.

One summer after a new baby was born to the family, Susan Anthony was surprised to hear her father request that eleven boarders be added to the already busy household. Surprise turned to dismay when Lucy agreed and then proceeded to turn the money *she* had earned over to her husband. It was the law, Lucy explained. Married women couldn't own anything. Besides, their husbands gave them everything they needed. But Susan suspected that all husbands were not as kind as Daniel Anthony, and she vowed to

SUSAN B. ANTHONY.

keep her own money when she grew up, even if it meant not marrying.

At seventeen Susan Anthony entered a women's seminary in Philadelphia, only to withdraw the following year when her father's business failed. During the next few years she taught school in order to help her family pay their debts. Unable to rescue his business, Daniel Anthony relocated to a pleasant thirty-two acre farm in Rochester, New York. There Susan Anthony lived, teaching and helping at home until 1846 when she accepted a position at Canajoharie Academy. She moved in with her cousin Margaret Read Caldwell and, surrounded by lively new acquaintances, finally gave up her austere Quaker conduct and dress.

Anthony became caught up in the nation's growing interest in social reform and decided to join the Daughters of Temperance in Canajoharie. Elsewhere in the state, efforts were being made to bring to an end legal, social, economic, and educational discrimination against women. Anthony was amused to learn that a former teaching colleague, Lucretia Mott, was attending a women's rights convention in Seneca Falls. But when members of her family went to a second convention and earnestly supported the Declaration of Sentiments and the impressive speakers, her good-natured ridicule turned to interest.

After the death of her cousin Margaret, Anthony resolved to put teaching behind her, and she returned to the farm to decide on a meaningful life's work. Inspired by the *Liberator*, she became involved with abolitionists and the eloquent free black, Frederick Douglass. It was through her antislavery activity that Anthony chanced to make the acquaintance of Elizabeth Cady Stanton, a forthright and level-headed champion of abolition, temperance, and women's rights. When

the two women met, Mrs. Stanton was wearing her notorious "bloomer costume," consisting of a pair of long trousers beneath a short, mid-calf length skirt, a fashion she enthusiastically recommended to all busy housewives and mothers. Anthony was impressed by Stanton and her colleague, Lucy Stone, and began to consider what she herself might do to further the national temperance and antislavery movements. Eventually a strong friendship developed among the three women, and in time they formed a formidable feminist triumverate.

A Sons of Temperance convention in Albany exposed Anthony to her first major rebuff because of her sex. Eager to share the work of the Daughters of Temperance, she rose to speak, only to be told: "The Daughters of Temperance were asked here not to speak but to listen and learn." Anthony and several other women left indignantly and soon arranged a meeting of their own. Subsequently the Women's State Temperance Society was formed with Stanton as president and Anthony as secretary. A year later, a similar rebuff occurred in Syracuse, but this time the Daughters brought most of the men with them from the main convention. In the New York *Tribune*, Horace Greeley chastized the good men gathered to oppose strong drink who "spent the entire first day crowding a woman from the platform, the second day gagging her, and the third day shouting that she should stay gagged."

Anthony's experiences in social reform brought to her attention more and more of the inequities experienced by women: limited educational opportunities, unequal pay for equal work, and limitations by custom and law on women's free speech and participation in the political process. Eventually she came to view universal suffrage as the pivotal issue in the struggle for human rights, and she made that cause her

major life's work. When the 1853 World Temperance Convention rebuffed the women delegates, Anthony's mission became clear. Without a vote women could exert neither significant influence on government policy nor any real control over their own lives. Although generally better treated, women had no more rights than slaves.

In December 1854 Anthony began campaigning for women's rights in New York state. Every other night she held a meeting in a different town, often to a hostile reception. Many women attending the meetings were timid or indifferent, tied down with children and housework. The men, who had the power to change the law, came to be entertained. Some ridiculed and condemned her for threatening the sanctity of the home, but a few asked intelligent questions and even encouraged their wives to join the movement. Weary and suffering from rheumatism, Anthony still managed to canvas fifty-four counties before returning home in May. In 1856 she set out on another campaign, determined to gather more signatures on her petitions for amending the state's property laws governing women's civil rights. Unfortunately the legislature's only response to her efforts was a derisive report issued by the judiciary committee which treated the entire matter as a joke.

During the late 1850s the abolitionist crusade reached fever pitch. Although Anthony devoted most of her energy to freeing the slaves, she did not abandon her fight for women. She spoke publicly on the controversial subject of coeducation and offered a bold resolution proposing that all educational institutions open their doors to women. In 1860 she and Mrs. Stanton scored a stunning victory. Their address before the joint session of the New York legislature resulted in passage of the Married Woman's Property Bill, which gave women the right to make contracts, to sue, to own property, and to assume joint guardianship of their children.

After the Civil War broke out, Anthony and Stanton formed the Women's Loyal League for the purpose of gathering support for a Fourteenth Amendment enfranchising all adults. Having worked with abolitionists for years, Anthony was thunderstruck when Wendell Phillips and Theodore Tilton led the opposition to linking women's suffrage to the antislavery program. She declared angrily: "I would sooner cut off my right hand than ask for the ballot for the black man and not for woman." From that time on feminists drew farther and farther apart from their male allies. When Negro suffrage was approved on July 28, 1868, the rank injustice of denying women the vote became obvious. It was no longer possible to pretend the vote was reserved for the nation's intellectual elite; sex alone stood out as the basis for denying women this right.

In 1866 the Women's Rights Society gathered ten thousand signatures, petitioning Congress to secure the vote for women. The following year Lucy Stone and her husband, Henry Blackwell, Elizabeth Stanton, and Susan Anthony began a campaign that would last beyond Susan Anthony's lifetime—the drive to obtain suffrage on a state-by-state basis. They went first to Kansas. Little assistance was offered by the abolitionists, however, and Kansas Republicans withdrew their support of women's suffrage.

While Anthony was seeking ways to win over the Democrats, unexpected help arrived in the form of the wealthy eccentric George Francis Train. Together he and Anthony toured the state, and Train drew large crowds with his flashy dress, his mimicry, and

ELIZABETH CADY STANTON DEVISED THE BLOOMER COSTUME FOR THE CONVENIENCE OF WORKING WOMEN AND MOTHERS. THE TROUSERS AND RELATIVELY SHORT SKIRT WERE INTENDED TO MAKE IT EASIER TO GET ABOUT. ALTHOUGH STANTON AND SOME OF HER FEMINIST COLLEAGUES WORE THE BLOOMER COSTUME, THEY LATER ABANDONED IT BECAUSE IT ATTRACTED WIDESPREAD RIDICULE.

his dramatic oratory. As their strenuous campaign was drawing to a close, he offered to underwrite the cost of a newspaper devoted to the cause of women's suffrage. Thus, the *Revolution* was born. To Anthony's dismay, her association with Train and the Democrats and the *Revolution's* forthright approach to controversial topics alienated many of her former supporters. The paper, which first appeared in 1869, eventually folded, but not before it had produced two years of insightful commentary, not only on suffrage but on fair employment, equality in marriage and divorce, and sensible health practices for women.

In 1869 the first women's suffrage law passed without fanfare in Wyoming, but it was the movement's last success for almost a decade. After the *Revolution* folded, Anthony returned to the lecture circuit with Mrs. Stanton. Tired of the dissension and rivalry splitting the Equal Rights Association, she and a group of forward-looking women from nineteen states had formed the National Woman Suffrage Association. With their backing, Anthony continued to push for universal suffrage through passage of a Sixteenth Amendment and to speak out on behalf of women's rights.

In 1872, she put into practice her belief that women had been granted the right to vote under the Fourteenth and Fifteenth Amendments by registering and voting in Rochester, New York. Two weeks later she was arrested. At her arraignment, Anthony conceded that she had, in fact, voted, but concluded: "We ask the juries to fail to return verdicts of 'guilty' against honest, law-abiding, tax-paying United States citizens for offering their votes at our elections . . . remembering that 'the true rule of interpretation under our national constitution, especially since its amendments, is that anything for human rights is constitutional, everything against human rights unconstitutional.' And it is on this line that we propose to fight our battle for the ballot . . . through to complete triumph, when all United States citizens shall be recognized as equals before the law."

The subsequent trial, held in June 1873, was a travesty. Judge Hunt, reading from a written document prepared before the trial, proclaimed the defendant's guilt and directed the jury to bring in that verdict. Against the objections of Anthony's counsel, the jury was then dismissed. National outrage at this denial of a fair trial actually furthered the cause of universal suffrage. The $100 fine and court costs Anthony was assessed were never paid.

Following the trial, Anthony continued her lecturing circuit in the West and after six long years paid off the last of the debt left by the *Revolution*. At fifty-six she began her massive *History of Woman Suffrage*, which she came to regard as her most satisfying life's work. Eventually the history was expanded to four volumes, the last appearing when she was eighty-three years old.

The National Woman Suffrage Association was holding annual conventions in Washington to lobby for a Sixteenth Amendment, and members of congress began to take notice. Each year after 1878, Anthony presented a federal woman-suffrage amendment to the Congress, and each year it was turned down. However, the opponents of the bill laughed with increasing nervousness. Early in 1887 the bill came up for a vote, only to be defeated by a two-to-one margin. It did not come up again for twenty-five years.

Between 1890 and 1896, Anthony had the satisfaction of seeing nineteen states extend local school suffrage to women and the states of Utah, Idaho, and Colorado join Wyoming in giving women the vote. At the age of seventy-six she began another cross-country campaign to assist her sisters in California who were supporting an amendment to the state constitution enfranchising women. For eight months she made speeches at political rallies, churches, women's clubs, and men's clubs, in pool rooms, schoolhouses, and wigwams. It was a valiant battle, resulting in more than 110,000 favorable votes. The defeat, brought about by last-minute efforts of liquor dealers, was a crushing blow.

Anthony returned East, visiting family and friends along the way, but her work was by no means over. In 1889 she attended the International Council of Women in London where she was received by Queen Victoria. The following year, approaching eighty, she resigned as president of the National Association but continued to divide her time between her work and the writing of her *History*. Although her health and strength were deteriorating, she continued speaking out, traveling at age eighty-six to Oregon, California, and Kansas. Her final gift to the movement was the donation of her birthday money to the Oregon Campaign Fund. Three weeks later, still following the campaign's progress from her bed, she died, having ensured in her will that her modest fortune would go in its entirety to the cause of women's suffrage.

Tributes poured in from all over the world. Ten thousand people passed by her bier, and politicians outdid themselves in flowery rhetoric. But the monument that would have pleased her most eluded the movement. The Oregon campaign failed. Not until 1910 was suffrage again expanded to include women, this time in Washington. Within the next three years Arizona, Kansas, and Illinois followed suit.

Women would wait seven more years before receiving the right to vote in every state in the Union. In 1920, Susan B. Anthony's Centennial Year, the Nineteenth Amendment to the Constitution was finally ratified, a fitting tribute to the vigorous, determined woman who spent her life striving for justice and equality under the law. "Failure is impossible," had been her message to those dedicated to carrying on her work.

and the Challenge of Neutrality

The Nation has been deeply stirred, stirred by a solemn passion, stirred by the knowledge of wrong, of ideals lost, of government too often debauched and made an instrument of evil. . . . We know our task to be no mere task of politics but a task which shall search us through and through, whether we be able to understand our time and the need of our people, whether we be indeed their spokesmen and interpreters, whether we have the pure heart to comprehend and the rectified will to choose our high course of action.

President Woodrow Wilson
First Inaugural Address
March 4, 1913

Significant Events

Socialist party organized [1901]

Payne-Aldrich Tariff [1909]

Mann-Elkins Act [1910]

Underwood Tariff [1913]

Federal Reserve Act [1913]

Federal Trade Commission Act [1914]

Clayton Anti-Trust Act [1914]

Outbreak of war in Europe [July 28–August 3, 1914]

Wilson proclaims American neutrality in European war [August 1914]

Sinking of *Lusitania* [May 1915]

Sinking of *Sussex* [March 1916]

Sussex pledge [May 1916]

National Defense Act [1916]

Federal Farm Loan Act [1916]

Lansing-Ishii agreement [1917]

WOODROW WILSON CAMPAIGNING FOR THE PRESIDENCY.

Following his sweeping victory in the 1904 election, Roosevelt impulsively announced that he considered the three and a half years he had already spent in office as his first term and that after serving his current term he would step down. Yet when it became time to plan for the 1908 election, he was still wildly popular with the people and not looking forward to leaving the White House. Thus, although he honored his earlier commitment, he insisted on hand-picking his successor.

His choice was the genial, 350-pound secretary of war, William Howard Taft of Ohio, a lawyer-judge who had proved himself a capable administrator at home and abroad. Taft had made a particularly favorable impression as governor-general of the Philippines, where he demonstrated a genuine concern for the Filipinos, whom he fondly called his "little brown brothers." Roosevelt believed that Taft would continue "my policies," and his support assured Taft of the nomination as well as victory in the general election. Taft ran against Bryan, whom the Democrats nominated for the third time. The Republican platform was dictated by the party's conservative leadership, and the Democratic platform adopted Progressive planks. The Democrats called for curbing the trusts and opposed the use of injunctions in labor disputes—a plank which gained Bryan the support of the AFL. But Taft still won handily by garnering 321 electoral votes to Bryan's 162 and polling over a million more popular votes than Bryan.

The Taft Administration

While the Republicans had won the presidency for the fourth time in a row, the split between the Old Guard and the Progressive wing was growing wider. The party's hold on both houses of Congress had been weakening since 1906, and the Republicans had lost control of several governorships in 1908. It remained to be seen whether the new president could resolve the growing division in the party. The new chief executive faced a special problem. It was common knowledge that he owed the office to Roosevelt, and both the former president and his partisans expected Taft to follow closely in Roosevelt's footsteps. Some of Taft's actions apparently did conform to Roosevelt's pattern, notably his efforts to bring antitrust cases to court. But Taft ultimately decided issues as he saw them, and being basically conservative he did not always see them through Roosevelt's eyes. Moreover, since he was a lawyer by nature as well as by training, he meticulously examined the legality of policies which he proposed and was generally acquiescent in his dealings with Congress. Indeed, he had little real interest in the art of politics, his dream being to serve on the Supreme Court.

The Payne-Aldrich Tariff

Reformers had been pressing hard for a reduction of the Dingley Tariff of 1897. They favored lowering rates to make imported goods cheaper on the American market, and they argued that the high tariff was contributing to a rise in the cost of living and to the consolidation of corporate control over American life. Although Roosevelt had nimbly sidestepped a tariff fight within his party, the Progressives had grown stronger. They succeeded in securing a plank in the 1908 Republican platform calling for tariff revision. During his campaign Taft promised to work for a significant tariff reduction.

In 1909 the House approved the Payne Bill, which provided for a moderate tariff reduction. The Senate, however, led by the powerful protectionist Nelson W. Aldrich of Rhode Island, made literally hundreds of changes in the bill. The net effect was to ensure that there would be no effective tariff reduction. A bloc of senators from the grain-producing Midwestern states, spurred on by their angry constituents, unsuccessfully fought to prevent passage of the gutted bill. Although defeated, they did succeed in attaching a rider calling for a 1-percent tax on corporate profits and in helping to further a drive for a constitutional amendment providing for a graduated income tax.

Taft agonized over whether to sign or veto the Payne-Aldrich Bill, knowing that whatever choice he made would be an unpopular one. Eventually, he signed; then, he stated in a political speech, "This is the best tariff bill that the Republican party has ever passed." This ill-considered action helped create a serious rift between the president and the Progressive wing.

AT AN AMPLE 350 POUNDS, PRESIDENT TAFT MADE AN AMUSING
FIGURE ON THE GOLF COURSE. HERE HE ADDS UP HIS SCORE.

TO A GREAT EXTENT TAFT OWED HIS ELECTION TO TEDDY ROOSEVELT, WHO ▶
HANDPICKED HIM FOR THE PRESIDENCY. A CARTOON FROM *PUNCH* SHOWS TR
HELPING TAFT VAULT OVER THE ELECTION HURDLE.

The Ballinger-Pinchot Dispute

Like Roosevelt, Taft was a firm conservationist. He
established the Bureau of Mines to ensure conservation of mineral resources. In addition, he worked
with Congress to protect valuable water-power sites
and coal lands from rapacious private developers.

Unfortunately, these efforts were quickly forgotten as a result of Taft's clumsy handling of the
Ballinger-Pinchot dispute that began in 1909.
Richard A. Ballinger, the secretary of the interior,
was a legalist, much like Taft. Disturbed by Roosevelt's liberal interpretation of the law in implement-
ing his plans to preserve America's resources, Ballinger opened Alaskan coal and timber lands for private
development as well as mineral and water-power
areas in Wyoming and Montana which under Roosevelt had been excluded from public sale. Conserva-
tionists, led by Pinchot of the Forestry Service,
responded angrily. They accused Secretary Ballin-

ger of failing in his duty to keep mineral and water-
power sites out of private hands and of undermining
Roosevelt's conservation policies by allowing private
developers to obtain control of Alaskan coal and
timberlands. Taft sided with Ballinger, sharing his
view that Roosevelt had exceeded his legal authority
in withdrawing federal lands from public sale. To
put an end to the administrative infighting the president dismissed Pinchot for insubordination. When a
congressional committee found Ballinger not guilty
of selling public lands to private interests, the Roosevelt Progressives were convinced there had been a
whitewash and protested angrily. Taft loyally stood
behind Ballinger, who despite heavy criticism
remained in his administration for another year and
a half.

Roosevelt was deeply angered by the treatment
of his old friend Pinchot. In fact, the Ballinger-
Pinchot affair helped drive a wedge between Roosevelt and his successor. Roosevelt believed that Taft

had not only deserted his program but was also tearing apart the Republican party.

The Progressives Bridle "Uncle Joe"

The rift between Taft and the reform bloc of the Republican party widened further in 1910. When Taft became president, the Speaker of the House was Joseph Gurney Cannon, an Old Guard conservative who had used the considerable powers of his office to make himself virtual master of the House. His dictatorial use of power was popularly known as "Cannonism." Fed up with Cannon's autocratic rule, particularly his consistent blocking of reform legislation, a coalition of Progressives, led by George Norris of Nebraska, rose up against "Uncle Joe." By courting Democratic support, they gained enough votes to strip Cannon of his power to appoint the Committee on Rules, which determined which bills would reach the floor for debate. Committee membership was made elective, and the Speaker was barred from participation. Although Cannon remained as Speaker, this action dealt a deathblow to his power. Progressives across the country applauded the move as a significant step toward the reform of national politics.

Taft remained aloof from the Cannon fracas on Capitol Hill, and his seeming indifference further alienated the Progressives. He later lamented, "I thought of encouraging a movement to beat Cannon, but I found that he was so strongly entrenched . . . it was impossible." Taft now found himself allied even more closely with party conservatives and began an unsuccessful effort to defeat Progressive Republicans in the 1910 elections.

Progressive Victories under Taft

Despite the rift with the Progressive bloc in Congress, Taft did support some Progressive legislation and had considerable success in curbing the trusts. In response to demands for further regulation of the railroads, he pleased the public by signing the Mann-Elkins Act of 1910. This act gave the Interstate Commerce Commission the right to suspend fare increases pending an investigation into the need for the increase. It also stipulated that all shipping charges had to be based on the same rates. In 1913 the Physical Valuation Act gave the ICC the right to establish the proper relationship between the value of railroad properties and the amount the railroads could charge for them.

Although many more antitrust suits were brought to court under Taft than under Roosevelt, Taft's most impressive victories—notably against Standard Oil and the American Tobacco Company—were initiated by Roosevelt. In 1911 Standard Oil and the monopolistic American Tobacco Company were ordered dissolved as combinations in restraint of trade under the Sherman Antitrust Act. These were landmark cases, for the Court in handing down its decisions reinterpreted the Sherman Antitrust Act by establishing the "rule of reason." According to this principle, large business combinations per se were not unlawful, only those that were engaged in unreasonable restraint of trade. The rule of reason was necessary because the original law could be applied indiscriminately, thus endangering the very structure of American business.

Taft threw his personal support behind some other important Progressive measures. The Publicity Act of 1910, aimed at preventing business interests from buying political favors, compelled congressional candidates to reveal campaign contributions. The graduated income tax, long demanded by Progressive reformers who believed the poor should not be taxed at the same rate as the rich, was ratified during Taft's term in office as the Sixteenth Amendment to the Constitution.

Taft's Dollar Diplomacy

In foreign relations as in domestic policy, Taft's views diverged from those of his predecessor. While Taft sought to protect America's position abroad, he believed the way to accomplish this was through economic investment rather than through brandishing the Big Stick. Thus, instead of advocating military readiness he encouraged American businesses to invest their dollars abroad to increase United States influence. Taft attempted to carry out this policy, which his enemies in Congress dubbed "dollar diplomacy," in the strategic Caribbean area and the Far East.

In 1909 a revolution in Nicaragua, located very close to the Panama Canal, resulted in the expulsion of that country's dictator. In the aftermath, the United States drew up a treaty with the new ruler which provided for American bankers to take over direction of Nicaragua's finances and to supply the forces that would guarantee collection of the debts as well as political stability. Although the Senate rejected the treaty, by 1911 American bankers were supervising Nicaraguan finances and in 1912 the marines were sent in to quell another uprising. Financial aid also was poured into Haiti and Honduras in hopes of preventing investment in these countries by other foreign powers.

In the Far East, Taft directed his attention to Manchuria. After the Russo-Japanese War the former antagonists, now less friendly to the United States, jointly controlled the Manchurian railways. Fearing that this situation could result in the closing of America's Manchuria trade, in 1909 Secretary of State Philander C. Knox conceived a plan whereby American and foreign business interests would purchase the railroads and put them under Chinese control. Russia and Japan rejected this idea and Taft was blamed at home for a diplomatic failure. When Roosevelt returned home in 1910 from a trip abroad, he also expressed disapproval of "dollar diplomacy" in China because it aroused the antagonism of the Japanese.

The Roosevelt-Taft Split

The president was overwhelmed with political problems a year before he had to face reelection. The public, angered by the Payne-Aldrich Tariff and demanding more social reforms, had thrown its support to the Democrats in the congressional elections of 1910. The Republicans, seriously divided after the Cannon episode, lost control of the House and faced a greatly reduced majority in the Senate. Taft had proven himself to be politically inept, unable to hold his party together or to maintain broad public support.

When Roosevelt returned to New York in 1910, he was already being touted as a presidential candidate for 1912. Many people began calling themselves "Roosevelt Republicans" to distinguish themselves from Taft's supporters. Roosevelt, his ire thoroughly aroused by reports of Taft's cozy relationship with the Republican Old Guard, soon abandoned his stance against seeking a third term. In fiery public statements, he began espousing the platform he later called the "New Nationalism." He demanded that the national government be strengthened to defend the people against the "malefactors of great wealth," he called for reform

of the courts because they often ruled in favor of the monopolies, and he advocated sweeping social reforms.

In the meantime, Progressives in the Republican party had formed their own group to oppose Taft's renomination. The National Progressive Republican League was established in 1911 with La Follette as its recognized leader. La Follette campaigned all over the country, but lost support as Roosevelt threw himself into the fray. When La Follette suffered a physical breakdown from exhaustion in 1912, the movement toward Roosevelt accelerated. By this time the former president, believing that the people wanted him and that La Follette could not win, had definitely decided to run again. La Follette, for his part, felt that the Progressives had betrayed him.

Taft, angered and bewildered by Roosevelt's attack, fought back. When Roosevelt won overwhelming support in the thirteen presidential primaries, Taft used his strength to woo Republican conservatives in the South, traditionally a Democratic stronghold. At the nominating convention in Chicago, the Taft-controlled conservative bloc took the reins, deciding disputes over the seating of contested delegates in the president's favor. Their maneuvering secured the nomination for Taft. Roosevelt, in no mood to quit the fray, then bolted the Republicans and hastily organized the Progressive party, made up of social reformers and some businesspeople attracted to Roosevelt's views. With great fervor and unanimity the new party's convention nominated him as its presidential candidate. Declaring himself "fit as a bull moose," Roosevelt gave the party its colorful nickname.

The Socialist Party

The reformist trend of the Progressive Era was further evidenced in the formation of the Socialist party. Founded in 1901, its numbers grew steadily during the next ten years. Its membership included muckraking author Upton Sinclair, reform journalist Edward Bellamy, many Populists, and some labor-union members. Its platform called for government ownership of transportation and communications, natural resources and production, and banking and finance; the eight-hour day, a minimum wage, safety regulations, and other measures to protect labor; the graduated income tax; and the

ROOSEVELT'S PROGRESSIVE "BULL MOOSE" PARTY CHALLENGES THE COWERING REPUBLICAN
ELEPHANT AND THE DEMOCRATIC DONKEY IN THE ELECTION OF 1912.

adoption of the initiative, referendum, and recall. Pledging to gain power through the democratic process, the Socialist party attacked capitalism as the source of social injustice.

There was considerable support for the Socialists in 1912, but the party never had a chance of winning a national election. Few Americans could accept the idea of state control of the economy, because it conflicted with their belief that there was a strong connection between political liberty and capitalism. Many were put off by the Socialists' belief in class struggle as the means of bringing about social reform. Samuel Gompers told the Socialists: "Economically, you are unsound; socially, you are wrong; industrially, you are impossible." Roosevelt was another harsh critic: "The immorality and absurdity of the doctrines of Socialism . . . are quite as great as those of . . . absolute individualism."

The Election of 1912

The Democrats were elated over the split in the Republican ranks. They had not elected a president since Grover Cleveland in 1892, and now the time

seemed ripe. The public was demanding reform, and the Democratic party responded by nominating Woodrow Wilson, the successful Progressive governor of New Jersey. Wilson was a compromise candidate. The party selected him when William Jennings Bryan, realizing he could not win a fourth nomination, gave his support to Wilson against the leading contender, Champ Clark of Missouri, the candidate of the New York political machine.

Taft and Roosevelt seemed bent on committing political suicide. Once fast friends, they now shouted epithets at each other. Taft accused Roosevelt of being a demagogue and a radical, and Roosevelt countered that Taft was a "fathead" and a reactionary. Taft fell far behind in the competition for public attention as Roosevelt toured the country drawing crowds and generating enthusiasm with his vigorous style. At one point Roosevelt was wounded by a would-be assassin, but he paused only for medical treatment and then gamely finished his speech as scheduled. After this episode, however, he left the campaign briefly to recuperate.

Wilson took a middle path, winning crowds with his calm, assured manner and moderate, reasoned arguments. In general, public opinion held that the divided Republicans would destroy their chances and Wilson would win the election.

Personalities aside, the contest centered around the question of reform. Each of the party platforms was progressive to an extent, but there were important differences. Roosevelt's program, the New Nationalism, stressed that business consolidation was not only inevitable but in many ways beneficial; however, a strong central government was needed to regulate big business in order to protect the American public from potential corporate abuses. His Progressive party platform, titled "A Contract with the People," also advocated the need for comprehensive social reform, including workers' compensation, minimum-wage standards, prohibition of child labor, popular primaries, direct election of senators, women's suffrage, and recall of judicial decisions.

The major theme underlying the Democratic platform, which Wilson called the New Freedom, was a distrust of big government and a belief in the continuing viability of a freely competitive economy. Declaring that business monopolies were the enemy of free enterprise, Wilson argued that they should not merely be regulated but broken up in order to decentralize the economy and restore competition. If such an action were combined with a lower tariff, greater business opportunities would become available to small proprietors and to disadvantaged Americans, thus obviating the need for government intervention to cure social ills. Wilson's platform reflected the agrarian thinking of William Jennings Bryan as well as the ideas of the nation's leading Progressive lawyer, Louis Brandeis.

When the election returns were in, Taft and Roosevelt had polled over one-half the popular vote,

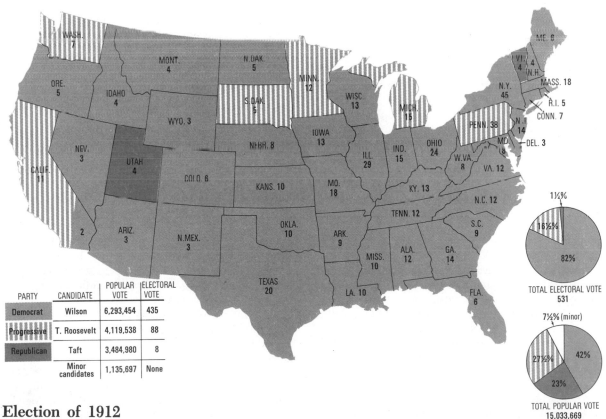

PARTY	CANDIDATE	POPULAR VOTE	ELECTORAL VOTE
Democrat	Wilson	6,293,454	435
Progressive	T. Roosevelt	4,119,538	88
Republican	Taft	3,484,980	8
	Minor candidates	1,135,697	None

Election of 1912

with Wilson receiving only a little over 41 percent. The Socialist party demonstrated considerable popular support as well. Its candidate, labor leader Eugene V. Debs, accumulated over nine hundred thousand popular votes, 6 percent of the total. Nevertheless, Wilson emerged victorious, garnering 435 electoral votes to 88 for Roosevelt and a mere 8 for Taft. Labor was moving toward the Democrats, and new voters from Eastern and Southern Europe were joining the Democratic camp. The Democrats also gained control of both the House of Representatives and the Senate, setting the stage for the Democratic party under Wilson to become the vehicle for the national Progressive program.

Wilson's First Term

Before he became governor of New Jersey, Woodrow Wilson had been a professor of political science, an author, and the president of Princeton University. During his years at Princeton, he worked unceasingly for reforms in higher education. As governor of New Jersey he drove out the entrenched political bosses and instituted sweeping reform measures. Highly intelligent, an eloquent speaker, and a devout Presbyterian, Wilson had a strong commitment to moral duty. He believed that the president must be a firm and forceful leader. Convinced that God had called him to the office, he was determined to rally the Congress and the American people to a high purpose. Wilson's idealism at times proved a handicap since it made it difficult for him to compromise. When faced with political opposition he sometimes became dictatorial and stubborn, allowing differences over issues to deteriorate into personal animosity. Nevertheless, during his first term in office his domestic measures received wide popular support and he was very successful in dealing with Congress.

Reform Legislation

The Underwood Tariff Wilson made good on his promise of securing a lower tariff. He worked closely with Oscar Underwood, his manager in the House, against party factions supporting high duties to protect those industries with which they had connections. Long an advocate of a freer trade policy, Wilson persuaded American business leaders that high tariffs at home could lead to retaliation abroad. He used his personal influence to outmaneuver lobbyists who opposed the measure and appealed directly to the American people for support of the bill. He finally succeeded in shepherding the Underwood Tariff Bill through the Senate. The new measure reduced rates on many foreign goods and completely removed them from other items.

Banking and Currency Reform Another of Wilson's goals was to reform the outmoded banking and currency system which had been in effect since the Civil War. The country had no central banking system to coordinate banking activity, and although national bank notes were in circulation the currency was so inelastic that it was difficult to obtain credit for investment purposes. Most bankers wanted to return to a privately controlled central banking system. The Progressives and Bryan Democrats, however, called for a decentralized banking system under strong federal government jurisdiction, and Wilson was won over to their point of view.

The result was the Federal Reserve Act of 1913, establishing the Federal Reserve System. Under this system the country was divided into twelve regional districts, each of which had a Federal Reserve bank that was owned by member banks. The Federal Reserve banks functioned as bankers' banks, serving only commercial customers, not private individuals. The new system included among its members all nationally chartered banks—which were required to join—as well as state-chartered banks that were willing to comply with Federal Reserve regulations. This arrangement facilitated closer supervision of the activities of much of the American banking community. The system as a whole was supervised by a Federal Reserve Board of seven members located in Washington.

A new federal currency, Federal Reserve notes, was issued to member banks. The new currency was backed by the amount of money (including commercial paper such as mortgages) in circulation at the time as well as by a 40-percent gold reserve and government bonds which made the currency supply more flexible and thus more adequate to the needs of the economy.

The Federal Reserve Act centralized American banking, stabilized finance (especially in the Western and Southern states where conditions had been precarious) by allowing the Reserve banks to borrow money within the system, and enabled the federal government to help control financial ventures.

Just as the Federal Reserve Act was passed to stabilize commerce and banking, the Federal Farm Loan Act of 1916 was designed to stabilize agriculture. American farmers had been seriously disadvantaged by the high mortgages they had been required to pay with short-term loans. The Federal Farm Loan Act made it possible for farm loan associations to secure long-term loans at lower rates of interest from twelve new Farm Loan Banks, using their lands and buildings as security.

Another Wilson measure to aid farmers provided federal aid for an agricultural extension program under which federal agents would conduct educational programs in every rural county in the nation. Money also was made available to match state allocations for commercial, industrial, and domestic science programs in schools, and for the building of rural roads.

WOODROW WILSON READS THE "DEATH WARRANT" OF THE BLOATED MONEY TRUSTS.

Anti-Trust Legislation Wilson's New Freedom included among its goals the breaking up of the trusts. Many corporations were still expanding monopolistic control by using loopholes in laws or reorganizing under new names. Wilson ordered his attorney general to take action and pressed for legislation which would give the federal government increased regulatory power over big-business interests.

The Federal Trade Commission Act of 1914 made Wilson the champion of small business. The act sought to encourage competition by extending the government's powers to regulate the activities of big business. The five bipartisan members of the Federal Trade Commission (FTC), appointed by the president, were empowered to investigate businesses involved in questionable practices (such as bribery, false advertising, or mislabeling of products) in interstate commerce and issue "cease and desist" orders against them when appropriate. But the act also provided for judicial review of the orders, which limited the commission's effectiveness.

A companion measure, the Clayton Anti-Trust Act of 1914, was intended to supplement the Sherman Anti-Trust Act. It outlawed price discrimination, the purchase of stock by one corporation in

other, competing corporations, and interlocking directorates involving two or more businesses or banks if it was discovered that they intended to diminish competition or create a commercial monopoly. The act also extended to labor the right to strike, picket, and boycott and limited the use of restraining orders and injunctions in labor disputes to situations involving irreparable property damage. Furthermore, requests for restraining orders or injunctions had to be submitted in writing, sworn by the applicant or a representative attorney. No longer could employers obtain court orders against their employees simply by saying that there was danger of a strike. The unions called the Clayton Anti-Trust Act "Labor's Magna Carta." Unfortunately, this assessment proved to be overly optimistic.

Evaluation of Wilson's Domestic Program

Wilson's efforts to curb big business were partially realized in the antitrust legislation of 1913–1914. Although the FTC did take action against certain abuses and dissolved some monopolistic combinations, its sympathies were with business, and it preferred to advise rather than to issue directives. The Federal Reserve Board, too, was under the control of business interests.

The mood of the country continued to favor strong government leadership in enacting far-reaching social reforms, and the congressional elections of 1914 brought more Progressives into the legislative branch. As a result, Wilson reluctantly abandoned his belief in laissez-faire economics and accepted the need for more government regulation. The labor and agricultural wings of the party pushed hard for reforms, and in order to keep the Democrats in power and improve his own chances for reelection, Wilson had to adopt their views. He therefore lent his support to such programs as agricultural banks, child-labor legislation, workers' compensation for federal employees, and an eight-hour day for workers on interstate railroads. Legislation in all these areas was enacted in 1916.

World War I interrupted Wilson's domestic program, diverting his attention from domestic reform to foreign policy and undermining some of his achievements in the years 1913 to 1916. The Underwood Tariff was a casualty of the war, and federal regulation of business also was sidetracked, though the antitrust laws remained on the books.

Wilson perceived the presidency as a "moral office" from which to lead the nation toward humanitarian goals. He believed in a strong leadership role for the chief executive, and by the end of his first term he was the recognized leader of American progressivism. Having expanded the role of the federal government more than he had originally intended, his domestic program during his first term may be described as combining elements of the New Freedom with the New Nationalism.

Progressivism in Perspective

While a number of progressive reforms had been achieved by the beginning of Wilson's second term, further efforts were brought to an end by America's entrance into World War I. Some of the most ardent Progressives opposed America's involvement in the war, considering it an interference with domestic reform. This cost them public support and after the war ended, the mood of most Americans was not congenial to reform legislation. While the spirit of reform was not completely dead, it was overshadowed by other concerns until the 1930s.

It should be stressed that even at its peak, between 1910 and 1916, the progressive movement was never radical and did not seek to overthrow the capitalist economy. Few Progressives were interested in a redistribution of wealth or efforts to strengthen organized labor. Indeed, for the most part Progressives feared class conflict and social turmoil. And while initially many Progressives thought of themselves as representing the mass of American consumers being exploited by big business, as reform activity evolved it most frequently took the form of interest groups or lobbies working for their own protection within the capitalist system. The Progressives believed that expanding political democracy and improving the efficiency of government would end corruption. Whereas the removal of some political machines, the institution of the initiative and the referendum, and the efforts to streamline administration were useful measures, they clearly did not end corruption in government.

Progressivism was to a great extent a protest against economic monopoly and political corruption that appealed to many Americans of diverse backgrounds and party affiliations. Many Progressives who believed that they were involved in the political and economic improvement of the nation did not fully understand the trend toward business consolidation. They clung to the ideal of a smaller-scale economy in which trusts did not exist, believing that competition among innumerable small entrepreneurs would regulate the economy. In the end, the movement made a stab at, but by no means solved, the problems of poverty, injustice, and big-business domination of American life.

Although many Progressives in politics called vigorously for many social and economic reforms, they made few efforts to aid black Americans or other racial minorities. To his credit, Roosevelt met with Booker T. Washington and made a few political appointments of blacks in the South. Wilson, on the other hand, showed no concern for the welfare of black people, believing that if the economy could be decentralized there would be no need for government programs to cure social ills. He even maintained segregation in federal government departments. Intense protests by some Progressives and black activists brought only a slight modification in this policy. Yet, despite these obstacles black activists and their white allies, along with the advocates of social justice in the cities and the crusaders for women's rights, added an important if sometimes overlooked egalitarian strain to the reform ideology of the era.

Despite its deficiencies, the progressive movement had a strong impact on the future of America. Progressive laws and constitutional amendments did much to improve the nation's political and economic life. Such innovations as workers' accident insurance, safeguards for working women, restrictions on child labor, and wage and hour legislation were permanent contributions. The important principle of government regulation of railroads, businesses, and banks was established on the national level. The Federal Reserve System evolved into an effective system of fiscal control. The income tax remained in force and was eventually extended. And the Progressives took steps toward federal protection of natural resources.

Wilson's Foreign Policy: Latin America and the Far East

Intervention in Mexico Relations between the United States and Latin America had deteriorated seriously by the time Wilson became president in 1913. Although the United States had participated in three Pan-American conferences, Yankee intervention in the Caribbean undermined diplomatic initiatives at these international gatherings. Hostility to American foreign policy was rampant in the Latin American press and among students and intellectuals.

In 1910, to further complicate the relations between the United States and its neighbors to the south, Mexico's urban workers and rural peasants precipitated a far-reaching economic and social revolution. For thirty-four years under the autocratic dictator Porfirio Díaz, the wealth of Mexico had been concentrated in the hands of a small, privileged native elite and foreign investors. American investments in Mexico were enormous, amounting to 40 percent of the nation's property. In addition, some fifty thousand Americans were comfortably settled in Mexico. The great majority of Mexicans, on the other hand, including 95 percent of the rural population, owned no land, and workers' wages were very low. The discontented masses rallied behind revolutionary leader Francisco Madero, who succeeded in driving out Díaz in 1911.

But Madero was totally unprepared for the violent upheaval that followed the outbreak of revolution. In February 1913 he was overthrown in a coup engineered by General Victoriano Huerta with the backing of American investors in Mexico who opposed Madero's call to halt foreign investment. A few days later he was murdered, apparently on Huerta's orders, and Huerta seized power.

Wilson assumed office only weeks after Huerta gained control. He was immediately urged by American business interests to recognize the new Mexican regime. At that time it was the policy of the United States to extend diplomatic recognition to governments that were clearly in control, regardless of how that control had been achieved. The bloody Huerta regime was repugnant to the idealistic new president, however, and Wilson refused to do anything that gave even the appearance of condoning it. It was his view that the Mexican government did not have the support of the people, and he aimed to use American foreign policy to force Huerta from office and pave the way for a freely elected government.

In October 1913 Huerta declared himself dictator. The British government, wishing to court American friendship at a time when German power was growing in Europe, decided to withdraw recognition and support from Huerta. Wilson now lifted an earlier embargo on the sale of American arms to Mexico in order to supply anti-Huerta forces led by Venustiano Carranza.

Despite this action, Wilson was not eager to involve the United States militarily. He abhorred the use of violent tactics and believed it morally wrong to intervene. Republicans in Congress assailed him for being weak and for vacillating, and the public mood turned bellicose when American citizens were killed in various incidents. The president's wait-and-see policy was not to last. In April 1914 a group of American sailors was arrested at the Mexican seaport of Tampico and taken from an American vessel, but soon released. The American officer in charge, strongly overreacting, demanded a formal apology from the Mexican government and a twenty-one gun salute to the flag, both of which Huerta contemptuously refused. Although this incident was in itself of minor import, Wilson, under strong pressure from some business and political interests, used it to reach a quick showdown with Huerta.

After obtaining congressional authority, the president in April ordered the seizure of the port city of Veracruz on the east coast of Mexico, hoping thereby to cut off arms and import revenues being used to support the Huerta regime. To Wilson's dismay, the Mexican people were furious over the American action, viewing it not as an effort to save Mexico from Huerta and prepare the way for a democratic government, but as blatant aggression. The seizure of Veracruz cost the lives of nineteen Americans and over 120 Mexicans. Both Huerta and Carranza protested this violation of Mexican sovereignty. Wilson, seeing that he had gone too far, accepted the offer of the ABC powers—Argentina, Brazil, and Chile—to mediate the dispute. The conference, held in Niagara Falls, left the problems unsettled, but Huerta, now under heavy pressure from the faction in Mexico calling for constitutional

government, abdicated in July and Carranza assumed power.

Wilson's problems with Mexico were not over, however. An illiterate bandit-general, Francisco (Pancho) Villa, broke with the Carranza government and captured Mexico City. After much internal fighting in Mexico during which Villa massacred a number of Americans in a town in northern Mexico, many in the United States called for intervention. Villa now tried to involve the Carranza regime in war with the United States, and Wilson found that the United States had to fend off attacks by Villa's marauding bands in southern New Mexico. In March 1916, Villa's forces killed seventeen Americans in the town of Columbus.

In retaliation, United States forces under General John J. "Black Jack" Pershing chased Villa deep into Mexico, severely punishing Villa's band

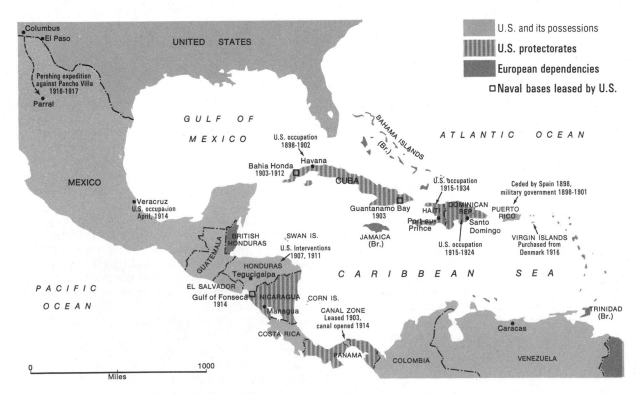

The United States in Central America and the Caribbean • 1898 to 1947

GENERAL JOHN J. PERSHING WAS
DUBBED "BLACK JACK" DURING THE
SPANISH-AMERICAN WAR WHEN HE
WAS AN OFFICER WITH THE BLACK
10TH CAVALRY.

but failing to capture Villa himself. American troops remained in Mexico, infuriating Carranza and soon becoming embroiled in clashes with Carranza's forces. President Wilson did not withdraw the Pershing expedition from Mexico until January 1917 when war with Germany was imminent. A constitutional government was finally set up in Mexico with Carranza as its first president, and the United States extended formal recognition in August 1917.

Caribbean Policy Despite his controversial handling of the situation in Mexico, Wilson initially made a slightly better impression in Latin America than had Roosevelt or Taft, because he spoke as an idealist and an antiimperialist. He assured Latin America that the United States sought no territorial gains in the Western Hemisphere and added that his country wanted to work with Latin American nations as an equal partner.

Although Wilson wanted the Caribbean countries to develop self-government, his sense of the moral superiority of United States' institutions led him to try to impose his concept of democracy on them. The result was that Wilson's Caribbean policy was more interventionist than that of his immediate predecessors. To keep order in the strife-torn region, he not only encouraged American investment—although he was opposed in principle to Taft's "dollar diplomacy"—but, ironically, his administration usually found itself supporting the forces of reaction instead of reform. Wilson sent troops to Santo Domingo in 1916, which remained until 1924; and to Cuba in 1917, which stayed until 1922. He continued the American presence in Nicaragua, and in 1916 the Senate ratified a treaty giving the United States the right to build naval bases there. Unrest in Haiti brought American intervention in 1914; and under a 1916 treaty the United States remained in control of customs, the army, and the island's foreign policy until 1934.

Maintaining the Open Door In outlining his New Freedom, Wilson had demonstrated his distrust of corporate power by calling for the breakup of business monopolies. This opposition to big business was also reflected in his repudiation of Taft's policy of "dollar diplomacy" in the Far East. He announced that he would not stand behind the efforts of American bankers to finance a Chinese railroad because such a project might infringe upon the sovereignty of China and put the United States in a potentially dangerous diplomatic position. At the same time, he called for maintaining the Open Door policy. The president, naively believing that the overthrow of the Manchu dynasty in 1912 was the precursor to the emergence of democracy in China, recognized the new Chinese republic under Sun Yat-Sen in 1913.

The Japanese, taking advantage of the unsettled situation in the Far East during World War I, openly defied American pleas to maintain the Open Door policy. They took over the German conces-sions in north China and in May 1915 presented the Chinese government with the so-called Twenty-one Demands, which included Japanese dominance of Manchuria, north China, and all of the Chinese coast, plus the right to develop the interior of the country. The United States made two protests, but American preoccupation with the war in Europe prevented any action. In 1917, in the Lansing-Ishii agreement, the United States reluctantly recognized Japan's "special interests" in China in return for a vaguely worded recognition by the Japanese of the Open Door policy.

The Outbreak of War in Europe

During the first fourteen years of the twentieth century, despite the continuing involvement of the United States in the politics of Latin America and the Far East, Americans' concern for domestic reform had to a great degree eclipsed their interest in international politics. A few Americans understood their nation's potential as a world power, and there existed a small movement which advocated the establishment of world peace through disarmament and arbitration treaties. But most Americans were uninterested and uninformed about political developments outside the United States. Although war scares flared periodically, it was commonly believed that modern nations were too civilized to engage ever again in mass bloodshed and destruction. Thus, when World War I broke out, Americans on the whole were astounded. When it was finally over, Europe was devastated, millions lay dead or were starving, and the Communist revolution unleashed in Russia foreshadowed a period during which totalitarian rule threatened to spread across the globe.

The war had its roots in tensions among the European powers that had been increasing rapidly since the late nineteenth century. Fear of the rise of German power in Central Europe precipitated a new arms race and a new system of alliances as each nation sought to protect itself and to maintain the balance of power. Germany, Austria-Hungary, and Italy formed the Triple Alliance in 1882. France and Russia became formally allied in 1894. Britain had traditionally remained aloof from European alliances, relying on its superior navy and geographical isolation for protection, but the rise of German naval power finally prompted Britain in 1907 to join with France and Russia in the Triple Entente.

The political situation in the Balkans was especially unstable. Both Russia and Austria-Hungary sought to dominate the area, which was torn by internal warfare between 1912 and 1913. Serbia was seething with antagonism toward Austria, and members of a Serbian nationalist society plotted to assassinate Archduke Francis Ferdinand, heir to the Austrian throne. The plot was carried out successfully in June 1914.

The series of events that followed plunged Europe into the most devastating war the world had yet seen. One after another, the European powers were drawn into the conflict as a result of their alliances. The Central Powers—Germany and Austria-Hungary, and later Bulgaria and Turkey—lined up against the Allied Powers—France, Britain, and Russia, and later Italy and Japan. In one week, from July 28 to August 3, 1914, Austria-Hungary declared war on Serbia, and Germany came to Austria's support. Russia, assuming leadership of the Slavic peoples of Europe, mobilized to help neighboring Serbia. Germany declared war on Russia and on France, Russia's ally. Finally, Britain, France's ally, declared war on Germany.

The American Reaction

The United States' first reaction was to stay out of the struggle. Geographically isolated from Europe and free of "entangling alliances," most Americans felt smug and secure. President Wilson promptly issued a proclamation of neutrality. This was not to be America's war.

Emotionally, however, the situation was more complex. In 1914 over 32 million Americans—one-third of the population—were either foreign-born or the children of foreign-born parents. One-quarter of them were Germans or Austrians, and many were sympathetic to their old homeland. They were joined by another large minority, the Irish-Americans, who favored any nation hostile to their long-time enemy, Great Britain.

Most Americans, however, were strongly anti-German. The clash with Germany over Samoa, the incident in Manila Bay during the Spanish-American War, and German efforts to gain a foothold in the Far East were unsettling evidence of German expansionism and militarism. In addition, the German navy was superior to that of the United States and the well-disciplined, battle-seasoned German army was considered the finest in Europe. Finally, the Germans posed an economic threat by their practice of underselling their competitors, including the United States, in world markets.

There were also strong reasons for Americans to favor the Allies. Franco-American friendship dated from the eighteenth century, when France helped the fledgling nation in its fight for independence. Antagonism toward England was gradually being replaced by appreciation of a shared political and cultural heritage. Britain's diplomatic concessions to the United States after 1895, such as negotiation of the Venezuela boundary dispute, acceptance of America's sole right to build an inter-oceanic canal, and support of the Roosevelt corollary to the Monroe Doctrine contributed significantly to improved relations. President Wilson, who had long admired British culture, personally favored the Allies, although he did not express these feelings during the early part of the war. His sympathies toward the Allies were reinforced by his longtime key advisor, Colonel Edward M. House.

American suspicion of Germany deepened when, in its first aggressive action of the war, the German army overran neutral Belgium. Faced with enemies on both sides, the Germans moved swiftly, hoping to defeat France before the Russian czar had time to mobilize his huge army. In carrying out the plan to strike at France through Belgium, the Germans not only violated an international treaty to

CARTOONS SUCH AS THIS ONE, ENTITLED *WHAT WILL YOU GIVE FOR HER?* HELPED ROUSE AMERICAN SUPPORT FOR THE ALLIES AND ANTAGONISM TOWARD GERMANY.

respect Belgian neutrality, but displayed their arrogance by later claiming that neutrality was "just a word" and that the treaty was only "a scrap of paper."

Propaganda Efforts France and particularly Britain shrewdly exploited American sympathy for tiny Belgium by spreading propaganda about German atrocities against Belgian civilians. Accounts of babies impaled on the bayonets of murderous German Huns and factories where human fat was made into soap, although blatantly false, nevertheless found a receptive audience in the United States. In addition to generating propaganda, the British provided the major source of war news received in the United States; reports originated from the London bureaus of the American news services. The books, articles, movies, and speakers sent over from Britain repeatedly emphasized German atrocities and German war guilt. Americans were moved by the suffering of the Belgians. When they learned that the Belgians were facing starvation, they responded generously. An American mining engineer in London, Herbert Hoover, organized a superb relief effort which was gratefully received by the victims.

Not surprisingly, German propaganda efforts met with little success. Any support Germany might have gained among Americans who had not already made up their minds was effectively eliminated when the Germans executed an English nurse, Edith Cavell, who had aided the escape of dozens of Allied soldiers from Belgium. This action was viewed among Americans as intolerably barbaric.

The Problem of Neutral Rights

Despite their strong sympathy for the Allied cause, the majority of the American people still wanted desperately to avoid becoming involved in the war. The United States was the richest neutral country and the largest neutral transoceanic shipping country in the world. Under the traditional rules of international law, neutrals had the right to sell non-contraband goods in any belligerent ports not under blockade. Thus as long as the United States remained neutral it retained the right to continue its economically important foreign trade. The problem in the first stages of the war was to make England, which commanded the seas, acknowledge America's rights as a neutral carrier.

From the start of the war the British used their superior sea power to cut Germany off from foreign supplies. Their first action was to declare the North Sea a British military area and to plant it with mines. Neutral ships approaching the area were stopped for inspection, and if they carried contraband, they were not allowed to proceed. The British definition of contraband included almost everything that could aid Germany, including food. The British also instituted a highly unconventional type of blockade. Traditionally, to blockade meant to close enemy ports by surrounding them with warships just outside the three-mile limit. But because long-range guns and submarines made such techniques risky, British warships roamed the high seas, intercepting neutral ships sailing to Germany and forcing them into Allied ports to search for contraband.

These tactics were clearly not in accord with international law and evoked strong protest from American shippers. It was said that Britain "ruled the waves and waived the rules." Since American friendship was considered essential for an Allied victory, Britain tried to soothe American resentment of its high-handed policy by paying for confiscated cargoes, and by 1915 Wilson let it be known that maritime disputes would be settled after the war.

Although British naval tactics exasperated both Wilson and the American shippers whose cargoes were being seized, it was economically impossible to maintain true neutrality by cutting off trade with Britain. When the war began, the United States was in an economic recession. Huge orders placed by the Allies with American munitions makers and other businesses suddenly reversed this trend. An abrupt halt in Allied purchasing might have caused another serious economic slowdown. Although American trade with Germany was reduced to almost nothing by the British blockade, the loss was more than offset by vastly increased trade with the Allies. England had long been America's best customer, and the demands of wartime simply bolstered the relationship.

A few months after the war began, it became clear that the Allies were running out of cash and would have to borrow from the United States to pay for their enormous orders. President Wilson had initially banned loans to belligerents, believing that such loans were inconsistent with neutrality. But, faced with growing American sympathy for the Allies and not wanting to handicap the lucrative trade, he overrode the objections of Secretary of State William Jennings Bryan and relaxed the restrictions. In October 1914 he allowed bankers to float a loan of $500 million in the form of French and British bonds. Over the next year and a half the Allies borrowed an astounding $1.7 billion more. During the period that America remained neutral, private American bankers loaned the Allies some $2.3 billion. Loans to the Central Powers, on the other hand, totaled only about $27 million, a situation that drew an angry response from the Germans.

Submarine Warfare

Since the Germans had a powerful army, they were not particularly troubled during the first months of the war about neutral rights, American trade, or even a blockade of their supply routes. But American munitions shipments to the Allies and the British blockade began to take their toll, and when the land war reached a stalemate in northeastern France, the Germans sought ways to counteract the British blockade. They began using a new weapon: the submarine, better known as the U-boat. The U-boat was a formidable commerce raider because it could discharge its torpedoes before the enemy knew it was in the area, and it could then turn and race for safety. It could not, however, observe maritime law, which insisted that a warship could not lawfully capture or sink a merchant vessel without first boarding it to learn whether it was a belligerent or was transporting cargo to a belligerent. The submarine was a small vessel, and if it surfaced near warships or armed merchant ships to examine them, it presented an easy target for deck guns. It could even be sunk by ramming. Thus its military operations were necessarily irregular and, according to maritime tradition, illegal. *soon*

In February 1915 Germany announced that it intended to establish a war zone around Britain and that U-boats would sink without warning any enemy ship sailing into the area. The world was shocked. Although the British blockade had violated the rules of the sea, no citizen of a neutral state had been killed as a result. Announcing the war zone, Germany informed the American government that although it would not intentionally destroy neutral ships, it could not guarantee the safety of the people or the cargoes of neutrals. In giving this warning the Germans hoped to deter neutral vessels and effect a counterblockade of the British Isles. President Wilson, standing up for the traditional rights of neutrals, immediately informed the Germans that the United States would hold them to "strict accountability" if American ships were destroyed or American citizens were harmed.

Crisis over the Lusitania In May 1915 a tragedy occurred which illustrated exactly how difficult it would be, given the new techniques of warfare on the high seas, to uphold the traditional neutral maritime rights. The British steamship line, Cunard, advertised the sailing of its luxury passenger liner, the *Lusitania*, in American newspapers. In the same papers, the German government published a warning that "travellers sailing in the war zone on ships of Great Britain do so at their own

risk." This notice was highly irregular; under international law, passenger ships were not subject to attack by warships. The British were using the *Lusitania* to carry not just passengers but also contraband—4200 cases of small arms, ammunition, and other munitions. Despite the warning, the British said the ship was safe and the State Department refused to intervene. The ship sailed on schedule. On May 7 it was proceeding slowly along the coast of Ireland when the commander of a German U-boat on patrol, with orders to sink British vessels, saw the large ship and fired a torpedo at it. In eighteen minutes the ship sank, taking with it 1198 people, including 128 Americans. The American public was outraged. "It is a colossal sin against God and it is premeditated murder," declared one well-known clergyman. Some prominent leaders, including the saber-rattling Theodore Roosevelt, clamored for war. The *New York Times* proclaimed, "The Germans shall no longer make war like savages drunk with blood." Despite their emotional response, most Americans continued to prefer peace to war. Wilson, seeking a peaceful solution, chose to respond to the incident with diplomacy, demanding in a series of notes that Germany make reparations and take immediate steps to ensure that passenger ships would not be attacked again. The tone of the president's second note was so militant that Secretary of State Bryan, seeing it as an abandonment of his policy of strict neutrality, resigned rather than sign it. His successor, former State Department lawyer Robert Lansing, was strongly pro-British and wholeheartedly supported Wilson's strong stand.

After a year of diplomatic correspondence, the German government secretly ordered its naval officers not to attack passenger liners. In February 1916 Germany apologized for sinking the *Lusitania* and offered reparations. Nevertheless, despite the German government's desire to appease the United States, another British liner, the *Arabic*, was sunk in August 1915, and two American lives were lost. Responding to Washington's protests, the German government again apologized and promised that no unarmed passenger ship would be sunk without warning unless the ship resisted German search efforts.

There were good reasons for Germany to try to placate the United States. By 1915 the pivotal factor in the European struggle was American shipment of

TORPEDOED BY A GERMAN U-BOAT, THE
ENGLISH LUXURY LINER *LUSITANIA* WENT
DOWN IN EIGHTEEN MINUTES, TAKING WITH
IT 1198 PEOPLE.

OCEAN STEAMSHIPS.

CUNARD

EUROPE VIA LIVERPOOL
LUSITANIA

Fastest and Largest Steamer
now in Atlantic Service Sails
SATURDAY, MAY 1, 10 A. M.
Transylvania, Fri., May 7, 5 P.M.
Orduna, - - Tues., May 18, 10 A.M.
Tuscania, - - Fri., May 21, 5 P.M.
LUSITANIA, Sat., May 29, 10 A.M.
Transylvania, Fri., June 4, 5 P.M.

Gibraltar—Genoa—Naples—Piraeus
S.S. Carpathia, Thur., May 13, Noon

NOTICE!

TRAVELLERS intending to
embark on the Atlantic voyage
are reminded that a state of
war exists between Germany
and her allies and Great Britain
and her allies; that the zone of
war includes the waters adja-
cent to the British Isles; that,
in accordance with formal notice given by the Imperial German Government, vessels flying
the flag of Great Britain, or of
any of her allies, are liable to
destruction in those waters and
that travellers sailing in the
war zone on ships of Great
Britain or her allies do so at
their own risk.

IMPERIAL GERMAN EMBASSY

WASHINGTON. D. C., APRIL 22. 1915.

munitions and food to the Allies, who otherwise would have been helpless. Although the Germans resented this trade, they were still trying to observe neutral rights in an effort to prevent the United States from actually entering the war on the side of the Allies.

President Wilson was sure that Germany would disregard America's neutrality if defeat seemed imminent. He believed that the United States could remain neutral only if the war ended quickly. Therefore early in 1915 he sent Colonel House on a secret mission to Britain, France, and Germany in an effort to persuade each government to let the United States mediate the conflict. House was rebuffed by all three parties, each believing itself one step away from a clearcut victory. Britain also rejected Wilson's suggestion that the Allies stop arming merchant vessels in return for a German pledge to warn Allied merchant ships before attacking them.

The Sussex Incident Congress was not satisfied that Wilson's efforts to force the Germans to comply with international maritime law would be sufficient to keep the United States out of war. In order to reduce the likelihood of incidents in the future, the Gore-McLemore Resolution was introduced in February 1916, declaring that American citizens would henceforth travel on armed belligerent ships at their own risk. Wilson, who considered the resolution an admission that the United States was surrendering its neutral rights, succeeded in having it shelved.

On March 24, 1916, after a six-month period during which Germany honored its agreement not to sink unarmed passenger vessels, a U-boat torpedoed an unarmed French liner, the Sussex, injuring several Americans. President Wilson, seething over this apparent treachery, angrily warned Germany that if another such incident occurred, the United States would break off diplomatic relations between the two nations. Again, Germany backed down and on May 4—in the so-called Sussex pledge—promised to spare all lives in any future U-boat attacks on all merchant ships whether neutral or belligerent. The Sussex pledge was a fragile promise, however. The German government attached to it an impossible condition: the United States must convince the Allies to respect accepted maritime law in carrying out their blockade. Clearly, Wilson was in no posi-

tion to do this. And if the Allies continued their illegal blockade—which they almost certainly would do—the Germans could choose to renew their attacks on merchant ships and the United States would find itself on the brink of war.

Military Preparedness

The American public was growing increasingly alarmed by Germany's war policies. Taking advantage of the U-boat crisis, skillful British propagandists swamped Americans with constant lurid accounts of German intrigues and war guilt. While the mood of the nation still did not favor going to war, it had reached the point of approving measures to ensure the national defense. Peace groups that had opposed increased armaments on the grounds that they would lead to war were losing support.

Although the United States had a strong navy, its army was so small and so poorly equipped that it probably could not have defended itself against a German invasion. At one point in 1915 the army had only a two-day supply of ammunition for artillery, and the artillery itself was largely obsolete. From the beginning of the war, military leaders, notably Theodore Roosevelt and General Leonard Wood, strongly urged the government to strengthen the armed forces. At first Wilson opposed new armaments. Like most Americans, he did not believe that the United States was threatened by the European conflict. But the submarine menace gradually convinced him that preparedness was necessary. In November 1915 Wilson asked Congress for massive appropriations to enlarge the navy and build up the army, which now numbered between one hundred thousand and four hundred thousand men.

Wilson, hoping to arouse popular support for his defense program, made a series of speeches throughout the country. But Congress, responding to the pacifist West and the Progressive element in the South, refused his request. The president then substituted a smaller compromise program, which was passed by Congress. The National Defense Act of 1916 made provision for an army of 175,000 men and a National Guard of 450,000 men; in addition, Congress appropriated $500 million for a three-year program designed to make the American navy —now ranked third internationally—the most powerful in the world.

ALTHOUGH PRESIDENT WILSON STILL HOPED TO KEEP THE NATION OUT OF THE EUROPEAN WAR, HE
BECAME INCREASINGLY CONVINCED OF THE NEED FOR AMERICAN PREPAREDNESS. HERE HE LEADS A
PREPAREDNESS PARADE IN 1916.

To finance the preparedness program, Wilson suggested raising taxes, a proposal opposed by conservatives and Progressives. Conservatives wanted to issue bonds instead, whereas most Progressives feared that rearmament would lead to American intervention in the European war. Southern and Western Progressives argued that the proposed taxes would end domestic reforms, burden people in the middle- and low-income brackets, and serve only to enrich the business and banking interests. When they finally accepted the popular demand for rearmament, the Progressives sought to finance military expenditures through new income and inheritance taxes that were frankly aimed at the rich. When the Revenue Act of 1916 became law, tax levies fell heavily on the wealthy for the first time in American history.

Readings

General Works

Gould, Lewis L. (Ed.), *The Progressive Era*. Syracuse, N.Y.: Syracuse University Press, 1974.

Graham, Otis L., Jr., *The Great Campaigns: Reform and War in America, 1900–1928*. Englewood Cliffs, N.J.: Prentice-Hall, 1971. (Paper)

Gregory, Ross, *The Origins of American Intervention in the First World War*. New York: Norton, 1972. (Paper)

Iriye, Akira, *From Nationalism to Internationalism: United States Foreign Policy to 1914*. London: Routledge & Kegan, 1977.

Link, Arthur S., *Woodrow Wilson and the Progressive Era.* New York: Harper & Row, 1954.

Merrill, Horace S., and Marion G. Merrill, *The Republican Command, 1897–1913.* Lexington: University Press of Kentucky, 1971.

Munro, Dana G., *Intervention and Dollar Diplomacy in the Caribbean: 1900–1921.* Princeton, N.J.: Princeton University Press, 1964.

Seymour, Charles, *American Neutrality.* Hamden, Conn.: Shoestring, 1967.

Shannon, David A., *The Socialist Party of America.* Chicago: Quadrangle, 1967.

Unger, Irwin, and Debi Unger, *The Vulnerable Years: The United States, 1896–1917.* New York: New York University Press, 1978.

West, Robert Craig, *Banking Reform and the Federal Reserve, 1863–1923.* Ithaca, N.Y.: Cornell University Press, 1977.

Wiebe, Robert H., *The Search for Order, 1877–1920.* New York: Hill & Wang, 1967.

Special Studies

Gardner, Lloyd C. (Ed.), *Wilson and Revolutions, 1913–1921.* Philadelphia: Lippincott, 1976.

Haley, P. Edward, *Revolution and Intervention: The Diplomacy of Taft and Wilson with Mexico, 1910–1917.* Cambridge, Mass.: MIT Press, 1970.

Israel, Jerry, *Progressivism and the Open Door: America and China, 1905–1921.* Pittsburgh, Pa.: University of Pittsburgh Press, 1971.

Schmitt, Karl M., *Mexico and the United States, 1821–1973.* New York: Wiley, 1974.

Primary Sources

Sullivan, Mark, *Our Times*, Vols. I–VI. New York: Reprint House International, 1960.

Biographies

Blum, John, *Woodrow Wilson and the Politics of Morality.* Boston: Little, Brown, 1956.

Currie, Harold W., *Eugene V. Debs.* Boston: Twayne, 1976.

Link, Arthur S., *Wilson*, Vols. I–V. Princeton, N.J.: Princeton University Press, 1947–1965.

Mulder, John M., *Woodrow Wilson: The Years of Preparation.* Princeton, N.J.: Princeton University Press, 1078.

Pringle, Henry, *The Life and Times of William Howard Taft.* Hamden, Conn.: Shoestring, 1965.

24 The United States and World War I

The right is more precious than peace, and we shall fight for the things which we have always carried nearest our hearts—for democracy, . . . for the rights and liberties of small nations, for a universal dominion of right by such a concert of free peoples as shall bring peace and safety to all nations and make the world itself at last free.

Woodrow Wilson
Message to Congress
April 2, 1917

Significant Events

Wilson's "Peace Without Victory" address [January 22, 1917]

Germany announces resumption of unrestricted submarine warfare [January 31, 1917]

United States declares war on Germany [April 1917]

Espionage Act [June 1917]

Russian Revolution [November 1917]

Wilson's Fourteen Points Speech [January 1918]

Treaty of Brest-Litovsk [March 1918]

Sedition Act [May 1918]

Battle of the Argonne [September–November 1918]

Armistice signed [November 11, 1918]

Treaty of Versailles [June 1919]

Senate rejects Treaty of Versailles [March 1920]

America's Decision for War

Shortly after Wilson's reelection in 1916, the momentum of the European conflict swept the United States into the war. The president's words set the tone for the war effort: "The world must be made safe for democracy. Its peace must be planted upon the tested foundations of political liberty." The American people, knowing little of European politics, were easily persuaded that the war was a struggle between one group of nations dedicated to these democratic ideals and another group of nations bent on extending autocratic government by the most brutal means. In their first involvement in a total war effort, most Americans responded with remarkable dedication and bravery.

Unfortunately, the fervor of government propaganda not only oversold the war's idealistic purpose, it encouraged those who supported American participation to silence those who opposed it. Suppression of the civil liberties of critics of the war during the conflict was followed at war's end by public disillusionment with the terms of the peace treaty negotiated in Paris. Within a short time, most Americans became convinced that the country's departure from its traditional policy of isolation from the politics of Europe had been a mistake.

The Election of 1916

At the Democratic convention, which renominated Wilson for a second term, it became obvious that many Americans approved of his policy of opposing Germany with words instead of bullets. "He kept us out of war" became the Democratic slogan. Yet Wilson did not pledge to preserve neutrality at any cost. "I can't keep the country out of war," he stated. "Any little German lieutenant can put us into war at any time by some calculated outrage."

Theodore Roosevelt was renominated for president by a remnant of the Progressive party. But Roosevelt was so enraged at Wilson's refusal to join the war on the side of the Allies that he was determined to do whatever was necessary to ensure Wilson's defeat. To avoid splitting the Republicans as he had done in 1912, he declined the nomination, promising to back the regular Republican candidate and campaign together against the president. The Republicans chose Charles Evans Hughes, a Supreme Court justice, former governor of New York, and a mild Progressive who was also acceptable to conservatives. The Republican platform stressed preparedness, and Roosevelt promptly led his supporters back into the Republican fold.

Hughes proved to be an unexciting candidate whose campaign was badly managed. Such phrases as "America first and America efficient" sounded so cautious that some wags said he had left the bench for the fence. Roosevelt, goading him from the sidelines to make strong prowar statements, complained to newspaper reporters that instead of taking advice, Hughes just "withdraws into his whiskers." As Hughes reluctantly gave in to this pressure, he began to sound like a war candidate, which frightened many voters and alienated others. Still, on election night the early returns indicated that Hughes would be swept into office. Although Wilson had been cultivating the Progressives and warning that a Republican victory would lead to American involvement in the war, returns from the East and Midwest indicated a near landslide for Hughes. But late returns from California, where Hughes's campaign had been hurt by political blunders, were decisive. Hughes, who had gone to bed thinking he was to be the next president, awoke the next morning to learn that Wilson had narrowly won a second term, polling 277 electoral votes to 254 for Hughes and receiving 9.1 million popular votes to Hughes's 8.5 million.

Wilson's Efforts at Mediation

Bolstered by reelection, Wilson made a final attempt to mediate an end to the war. In December 1916 he sent identical notes to all the belligerents, asking for a clear statement of their goals as a preliminary step to a negotiated settlement. This was a useless gesture, however; both sides felt that they had fought too long to compromise their terms for peace. The Germans, believing they could win the war, made sweeping demands and called for direct negotiations between the powers. Britain and France rejected this proposal.

Unwilling to give up, President Wilson made a dramatic attempt to win world opinion to his view. Speaking before the Senate on January 22, 1917 he declared prophetically that the only lasting peace would be a "peace without victory," a "peace

A WOODROW WILSON CAMPAIGN TRUCK, 1916.

between equals." A solution arrived at after more bloodshed "would leave a sting, a resentment, a bitter memory upon which terms of peace would rest . . . as upon quicksand."

War Becomes Inevitable

The German response to Wilson's efforts was to embark on an all-out effort to win the war. On January 31, one week after Wilson's speech, Germany declared that its U-boats would attack all merchant ships sailing toward Allied ports. One clearly marked American liner would be allowed through to the British port of Portsmouth once a week, provided it carried no contraband. As to other ships, Germany was returning to unrestricted submarine warfare.

The German declaration came at a time when relations between the United States and Germany were relatively stable, but British actions were caus-

ing intense irritation. Ever since the *Sussex* ultimatum the Germans had refrained from sinking merchant ships without warning. At the same time, the British had been trying American patience by searching United States mail for correspondence with Germany and blacklisting those American and South American firms they suspected of employing German workers. The German announcement therefore came as a severe blow and, keeping to his *Sussex* ultimatum, Wilson broke diplomatic ties with Germany three days later. Nevertheless, the president still hoped to resist the relentless pressures that seemed to be pushing the United States into the conflict.

This hope faded in February 1917, when the British delivered to the United States government a German dispatch to Mexico which they had intercepted. The note, sent by German foreign secretary Zimmerman, proposed a secret alliance between Germany and Mexico if and when America joined the Allies. In return for attacking the United States, Mexico would recover its lost provinces of Texas, New Mexico, and Arizona. Japan also was to be included in the alliance. When the note was released to the press, it created a great furor. The West and Southwest, previously the region in which opposition to the war had been most vocal, now began to fear for their security.

After the disclosure of the Zimmerman note, American entry into the war seemed inevitable. Wilson asked Congress to vote to arm American merchant ships; and while the Senate, led by a small antiwar faction, tried to stall, he began arming American vessels on his own authority as commander in chief.

In March German U-boats sank four American vessels. That same month the autocratic Russian czar was overthrown and replaced with a democratic provisional government. This made Russia, the ally of England and France, more appealing to the United States as a potential ally. These events increased the popular call for intervention.

On April 2, Wilson spoke before a joint session of Congress. A state of war already existed, he stated, because of acts by the German government. He made a sharp distinction between the German government, which had thrown away "all scruples of humanity," and the German people, for whom he expressed sympathy and friendship. For them and others, he said, "the world must be made safe for democracy." On April 4, 1917, the Senate voted 82 to 6 to declare war on Germany. The House followed on April 6 by a vote of 373 to 50.

This was the last straw, and the US entered war.

The Home Front

When the United States entered the war, Germany was on the verge of defeating both France and Britain. Although American leaders did not expect to send troops to fight in Europe, they recognized that an Allied victory depended on the ability of Americans to fortify the British and French with supplies immediately. The Overman Act, passed by Congress in 1918, delegated extensive power to Wilson for the duration of the crisis. He was to enforce wartime legislation and reorganize the government and the nation's resources for greater efficiency. Not since Lincoln had any chief executive exercised such vast authority and been so little subject to the traditional obligation to obtain congressional approval.

Mobilizing for War

The immense task of transforming a civilian nation into a massive war machine was assigned to federal agencies coordinated by the Council of National Defense, which was directly responsible to the president. Through these agencies the government acquired almost total control over areas of the economy that had seldom or never been touched by federal regulations before.

The United States now was required not only to feed its own people, but to produce enough extra food to supply its allies. As part of the government program to increase food production and place dis-

PART OF THE WAR MOBILIZATION EFFORT INVOLVED COLLECTING PEACH STONES TO MAKE LININGS FOR GAS MASKS.

6

INTERPRETING AMERICAN HISTORY

AMERICA'S ENTRY INTO WORLD WAR I Some historians, including Walter Mills and Charles C. Tansill, later disillusioned with American participation in World War I, have argued that the United States should never have become involved in the conflict. Basically, they blamed Wilson, claiming that he always wanted to enter the war on the Allied side. For this reason, they said, he allowed the British complete freedom in spreading their propaganda and in no way interfered with the expansion of trade and loans to the Allies. German submarine attacks were used as the pretext for a policy Wilson wished to pursue as soon as American public opinion was ready to support it.

Other historians, including Charles Seymour, Arthur Link, and E. R. May, have supported the theory that Wilson did not wish the United States to enter the conflict. They have emphasized the complexity of the factors that drew the president into the war. Wilson, they claimed, although a legalist and a moralist who was determined to protect America's rights as a neutral in wartime, was also a realist. The only reason he allowed American arms manufacturers to supply the Allies and not Germany, these historians claim, was that Britain controlled the seas. In their view, Wilson would have much preferred to maintain American neutrality so that he could mediate the conflict. These historians believe Wilson made every effort to stay neutral until German submarine warfare made such a position untenable. As late as February 1917 Wilson told Congress that he would accept the Germans' blockade, if they did not attack United States ships. According to this line of reasoning, it was Germany's gamble on complete victory that brought America into the war. Wilson then had no choice but to enter the conflict to save American honor, create a peaceful and orderly world in the future, and protect the Western Hemisphere from the possible consequences of a German victory in Europe.

Two interpretations of Wilson's motives have emphasized his concern for potentially conflicting ideas—on the one hand, the need to maintain world stability by preserving a balance of power among nations and, on the other hand, the desire for worldwide expansion of American trade. E. H. Buehrig has stressed international stability, citing Wilson's fear of a total German victory as a factor in America's entrance into the war. Likewise, the president's League of Nations proposal was based partly on the need for maintaining an equilibrium between nations in order to keep world peace. N. Gordon Levin, emphasizing economic expansion, believes that Wilson expected American participation in the conflict to aid in spreading free-trade capitalism along with the idea of political democracy. According to Levin, realism and idealism came together in the president's program of promoting a liberal-capitalist world order. After the war, Wilson believed, American enterprise would flourish in a world protected by international law.

---

tribution on a fair and effective basis, the Lever Act of 1917 established the country's first Food Administration, with the authority to fix food prices, license distributors, coordinate purchases, oversee exports, act against hoarding and profiteering, and encourage farmers to grow more crops. The bill had been hotly contested in Congress. Many felt that it was un-American to interfere with the freedom of farmers to produce the amount of crops they wanted.

The head of the Food Administration was one of the civilian heroes of the war, Herbert Hoover, who had been heralded for his effective administration of food relief in Belgium. His great accomplishment was persuading the American people to economize voluntarily on food. As his agency's slogans put it, he taught Americans to observe the "gospel of the clean plate" and to practice "the patriotism of the lean garbage pail." They followed his request for wheatless Mondays and Wednesdays, meatless

MANY AMERICANS, INCLUDING THESE CHILDREN, PLANTED VICTORY GARDENS TO HELP THE WAR EFFORT.

Tuesdays, and porkless Thursdays and Saturdays. They experimented with such foods as wheatless "victory bread," sugarless candy, vegetarian lamb chops, whale meat, and horsemeat. So successful was the policy that by 1918 America exported to the hard-pressed Allied countries three times the prewar quantities of wheat products, meat, and sugar.

By contrast, the mobilization of America's giant industries was initially much less vigorous. Finding that it was unable to coordinate the defense effort properly, the Council of National Defense created the War Industries Board in July 1917. The board, however, had little power to regulate the manufacture of munitions and other war goods until March 1918, when Wilson appointed Bernard Baruch, a wealthy business leader, to the post, and gave him broad authority. Baruch soon found, allocated, set priorities on, and fixed prices on some thirty thousand different items. He also initiated a standardization program to end the unnecessary use of vital materials and the duplication of products. This program proved its usefulness and continued into postwar industrial practice.

The newly created Fuel Administration concentrated on mining more coal for shipment over-

seas and using less at home. People patriotically observed "heatless Mondays," "lightless nights," and in the case of motorists, "gasless Sundays." Daylight saving time, introduced to conserve fuel, subsequently became a permanent feature of American life.

Railroads were essential to the war because they carried freight to the trans-Atlantic "bridge of ships" that supplied the Allies. In December 1917 Wilson placed the whole railroad network under a government Railway Administration, which operated at a tremendous loss in order to prevent delays in transporting raw materials to factories and munitions to ports.

Financing the War

Financing the war was an enormous problem. Besides asking the American people to reduce consumption, Wilson also had to contrive ways of paying private concerns for supplies that were sent to the Allies.

Some of the necessary funds came from increased taxes on individual and corporate incomes, taxes on excess profits, and higher luxury taxes on such items as theater tickets and tobacco. The bulk of the money, however, was raised by selling bonds. During the Civil War loans had been made by private, profit-making banking houses, but in World War I the government borrowed directly from the American people. Liberty and Victory bonds were issued in denominations as low as $50, and for 25¢ children could buy their own Thrift Stamps. In four massive Liberty Loan drives and a 1919 Victory Loan drive, citizens loaned the government over $21 billion. In all, the war cost the United States over $30 billion.

Suppressing Dissent

To mobilize American opinion behind the war, Wilson set up the Committee on Public Information under George Creel, an outspoken and imaginative journalist. Creel's approach was to "sell" the war as a crusade of good against evil—the forces of freedom and democracy against autocracy and militarism. Enlisting more than 150,000 painters, journalists, lecturers, poets, historians, actors, educators, photographers, and members of the clergy, Creel's committee flooded the country with posters, cartoons, editorials, pamphlets, speeches, and movies—all glorifying America's war aims and portraying the Germans as depraved, barbarian "Huns."

So effective was Creel's propaganda that the country was soon in a state of virtual hysteria. Enthusiasm for the war transformed into a demand for the suppression of all dissent. Among the groups that were perceived as potentially dangerous, the German-Americans, who numbered in the millions, caused the greatest concern. Many of them saw no contradiction in having a dual loyalty to Germany and to the United States. Thousands of Irish-Americans opposed intervention because of their historical enmity toward Britain. Pacifists, Progressives, and Socialists opposed the war on moral grounds. Now, among many Americans, it seemed that wartime "patriotism" was more important than the right of other citizens to express or even hold dissenting opinions.

As the Creel Committee moved to ensure conformity, vigilante groups began to appear around the country. These groups broke up Pacifist and Socialist meetings, lynched an organizer for the radical Industrial Workers of the World, and even denounced and hanged in effigy the eminent Progressive and opponent of the war, Senator Robert M. La Follette, in his home state of Wisconsin. They attacked all things German, mercilessly hounding people with German names, forcing schools to stop teaching the German language, throwing German books out of libraries, and banning German music and musicians from public performance. Even the language of daily life was censored; sauerkraut became "liberty cabbage" and hamburger was called "liberty sausage." In the face of this suppression of their civil liberties, the vast majority of German-Americans remained unswervingly loyal to the United States. Young German-American men joined the armed forces in great numbers and proved their patriotism on the battlefield. Their families at home contributed to the cause by buying Liberty Bonds.

In his eloquent speech before the Congress in April 1917, President Wilson had characterized America's purpose in entering the war as "the vindication of human right." Yet his conviction that the war was being fought for the highest purposes led him to perceive anyone who opposed or criticized American participation as a traitor to the future of humankind.

Legislative Measures The first legislative measure to curb dissent was the Espionage Act of June 1917, which placed penalties of up to twenty years in prison and a fine of $10,000 on anyone who willfully helped the enemy, obstructed the draft, or encouraged insubordination or mutiny in the armed forces. It also empowered the postmaster general to ban from the mails anything written or printed which might be helpful to the enemy or which seemed to call for action against the government.

Censorship increased when Congress passed the Trading-with-the-Enemy Act of October 1917. Primarily intended to prevent American supplies from reaching Germany, this measure also restricted publication of foreign-language newspapers and magazines. It had the effect of shutting off major outlets for "patriotic" expression as well as for possible dissent.

When these two laws failed to stop the antiwar activities of radical and pacifist groups, Congress passed the Sedition Act of May 1918, making it a

IN SPITE OF THE PREPAREDNESS CAMPAIGN, THE UNITED STATES IN 1917 WAS ILL-PREPARED TO FIGHT A
WORLD WAR. ITS TROOPS WERE INEXPERIENCED AND ITS EQUIPMENT OBSOLETE. THIS UPI PHOTO SHOWS
DRAFTEES TRAINING WITH WOODEN GUNS.

crime punishable by fine and imprisonment to discourage the sale of war bonds or to "utter, print,
write or publish any disloyal, profane, scurrilous or
abusive language about the form of government of
the United States, or the Constitution . . . or the
flag . . . or the uniform of the Army or Navy." The
Sedition Act was rigorously enforced, any criticism
becoming an invitation to arrest and imprisonment.
Over fifteen hundred persons were arrested by the
Justice Department for disloyal speech and sabotage.
Economic radicals were the chief victims. Small
Socialist magazines and newspapers were
suppressed, and when Eugene V. Debs publicly
argued against American participation in the war,
he was indicted for inciting resistance to the government and sentenced to ten years in a federal peni-
tentiary.

Judicial Measures The Supreme Court also lent its
support to restrictions on traditional liberties in wartime. In the case of *Schenck* v. *the United States*
(1919) a man had been arrested under the Espionage
Act for distributing antidraft leaflets to draftees.
Although Schenck maintained that the Espionage
Act violated the First Amendment, the Court ruled
that the act was constitutional because the right of
free speech was not absolute at any time. "Free
speech would not protect a man in falsely shouting
fire in a theatre, and causing a panic," Justice
Holmes wrote. Criticism which might be tolerated
during normal times should be suppressed in time of
war if it constituted a "clear and present danger" to
the nation. Yet according to Holmes, the Espionage
Act did not as a matter of course supersede the First
Amendment. A person's speech could be suppressed

DON'T WAIT for the Draft VOLUNTEER

only if it appeared likely to "bring about the substantive evils that Congress has a right to prevent."

Nevertheless, the *Schenck* decision was interpreted shortly thereafter as giving the government a free rein to compromise individual freedom during wartime. In *Abrams* v. *The United States* (1919), the Court upheld a man's conviction under the Sedition Act for publishing pamphlets which attacked the sending of an expeditionary force to Russia and called for a general strike. This time, however, Justices Holmes and Brandeis dissented, arguing that these actions presented no direct threat to the government and created no immediate danger to the war effort.

The Military Front

Raising an Army

Three weeks after the American declaration of war, French and British missions arrived in Washington to tell President Wilson that American ground troops would be essential to the winning of the war. The administration had not expected to send large numbers of American soldiers into battle, assuming that America's contribution would be in the form of money, shipping, and supplies. Although the armed forces quickly began the enormously complex preparations, well over a year passed before an American land force went into battle and became a significant factor in the war.

In response to the Allied plea for troops Congress passed the Selective Service Act of 1917. This draft law, the first such measure passed since the Civil War, aroused considerable opposition, for the United States had traditionally relied on a volunteer army. Still, to Wilson, Congress, and finally the whole country, nationwide conscription seemed to be the only means of raising a large army with sufficient speed. All men between the ages of eighteen and forty-five were required to register at local civilian draft boards. Of the twenty-four million who registered for the draft, 2.8 million were selected by numbers chosen through a nationwide lottery. An additional two million volunteered for service.

Some four hundred thousand black Americans served in the war to defend freedoms that to a great degree were still denied them. Discrimination continued unabated during this period, punctuated by particularly brutal race riots in East St. Louis, Missouri, and Houston, Texas, in 1917. The latter incident resulted in the hanging of thirteen black

Legend:

1916 Date of entry into the war
━━━━ Maximum advance of the Central Powers
- - - - Maximum Russian advance
·········· Line of the Brest-Litovsk Treaty Mar. 1918
─────── Armistice lines, eastern front Dec., 1917

0 ──────── 500
Miles

Central Powers
Allied Powers
Neutral nations

World War I • 1914 to 1918

soldiers who had retaliated against a vicious attack by killing seventeen whites. Racial discrimination was the norm in the army as well. Blacks served in segregated units, and a majority of them were relegated to menial jobs. The remainder served in combat units, some of which fought gallantly in France.

America's Naval Contribution

The first Americans to fight in the European war were sailors, for the navy was more quickly prepared for combat than the army. By the summer of 1917 the navy was playing a decisive role in antisubmarine warfare. American boats helped the British reduce losses from U-boat attacks to about one-third of the level reached early in 1917.

The United States contributed several strategies for dealing with the submarine threat. One plan, initiated by Assistant Secretary of the Navy Franklin D. Roosevelt, involved laying some seventy thousand mines in the North Sea between Scotland and Norway in order to enclose the German submarine fleet in the North Sea. A more successful effort was the system of armed convoys used to protect Allied shipping. The convoy system eventually brought the submarine menace under control and permitted British and American ships to transport some two million American troops to Europe in less than seven months in 1918, without the loss of a single troopship.

The Fledgling Air Effort

World War I saw the first use of the airplane as a weapon of war. Initially flown on reconnaissance flights across enemy lines, planes were soon armed with machine guns for fighting off enemy observers and for raids on German installations. Despite their contributions, however, airplanes were used on only a limited basis in World War I. It was on the ground that most of the action, and most of the casualties, occurred.

The American Expeditionary Force

The first American ground troops to reach the European front were members of the small American Expeditionary Force (AEF), which began arriving in France in the summer of 1917. These raw "Yank" recruits were commanded by General John J. Pershing, who had led the expedition against Pancho Villa in Mexico. A tenacious officer with a talent for organization, Pershing was one of the few American generals with any fighting experience. The Allied generals had planned to use the inexperienced Americans simply as reinforcements for the war-weary French and English troops, but Pershing insisted that the AEF should operate as a separate unit. His attitude reflected the desire of American troops to prove their mettle as an effective fighting force. For the time being, however, Pershing's efforts to convince the Allies met with little success.

President Wilson also favored a separate American effort, but for other reasons. He was aware that the Allies would seek to impose harsh peace terms against the Central Powers and wanted to leave the door open for making a separate, more generous peace if it became necessary. This prompted him to refer to the United States as an "associated" rather than an "allied" power.

Despite their inexperience, the doughboys of the AEF displayed an enthusiasm and a fighting spirit that surprised both the enemy and the Allied powers. Their arrival, although it had little initial impact on the fighting, succeeded in lifting Allied morale, badly depressed by a military stalemate.

The Last Years of War

The two sides had been involved in debilitating and deadly trench warfare for four years. After marching through Belgium, the Germans had been unable to push farther into France, and despite repeated attempts, the Allies had been unable to force them back more than a few miles. Both sides had dug themselves in. Between the two lines of trenches a no-man's land stretched for 450 miles, from the North Sea to Switzerland.

The battles fought from the trenches always followed the same futile pattern. They would begin with days of cannon fire. Then thousands of infantrymen, with shallow steel helmets their only armor, went "over the top," trying to overrun the enemy's trenches. "Bullets, millions of them, flying like raindrops," an American soldier wrote in his diary. "Rockets and flares in all directions. Shrapnel bursting the air and sending down its deadly iron. . . . Every minute looking to be gone . . . to

DOUGHBOYS STATIONED IN FRANCE
PEEL POTATOES WHILE ON K.P. DUTY.

the great beyond. A mad dash for fifty feet and then look for cover."

When American troops finally began arriving in substantial numbers in the spring of 1918, events favoring the Central Powers in Italy and Russia were about to end the long stalemate on the western front. In Italy, which had dissolved its prewar partnership with Germany and Austria-Hungary to side with the Allies, Austrian troops managed to shatter the Italian lines. This breakthrough forced a shift of Allied troops from the western front to Italy.

On the eastern front the Russian Revolution led to Russia's withdrawal from the war. The Bolsheviks, a radical minority led by Vladimir Ilyich Lenin, overthrew the liberal provisional government in November 1917 and began negotiating a unilateral peace agreement with Germany. In March 1918 the Bolsheviks signed the Treaty of Brest-Litovsk, agreeing to surrender Russian claims to Finland, Poland, the Ukraine, and the Baltic states and to remove Russia from the war. With Russia thus neutralized, seasoned German troops in the east were freed to fight on the western front.

At the same time, the Allies sent military expeditions to Russia to prevent German seizure of war materiel and facilities. Allied forces remained after the war ended, and some became involved in anti-Bolshevik resistance. American soldiers were sent to Archangel in northern Russia in June 1918 to support Allied efforts to cripple the Red Army and overthrow the Bolshevik regime. A year of fighting, during which the Americans suffered five hundred casualties and had to endure a bitter cold winter, left morale at a low ebb and United States forces were withdrawn. Another American detachment was sent to Siberia to rescue some fifty thousand anti-Bolshevik Czech soldiers from the Communists. An equally important aim, however, was to bolster the Open Door policy, which the United States had undermined in acquiescing to the Japanese in the Lansing-Ishii agreement. Now the American government sought to prevent Japan from gaining dominance over Siberia. Congressional pressure resulted in American withdrawal in 1920.

Stemming the German Tide With British and French forces weakened by transfers to the Italian-Austrian front and new German troops pouring in from the east, explosive action soon occurred on the previously stalemated western front. The Germans, five hundred thousand strong, were now determined to crash through the Allied line, take Paris, and crush the Allies. The first American troops began arriving just in time to help the hard-pressed Allies prevent a German victory.

The first important American assignment came at the end of May. In a powerful spring offensive the Germans had reached the west bank of the Marne

River near the town of Château-Thierry only fifty miles from Paris. Fewer than thirty thousand American troops launched a fierce four-day counterattack that drove the Germans back to the east bank of the river. In June American marines succeeded after a superhuman effort in forcing experienced German troops to retreat from a crucial stronghold in the Bois de Belleau near the highway to Paris.

The Germans made a desperate lunge toward Paris on July 15, in their last great offensive of the war. A force of eighty-five thousand American troops helped to hold the French lines. Three days later 270,000 Americans joined French and English troops in a counteroffensive that "turned the tide of the war," as Pershing put it. On July 15 Germany had confidently expected to receive peace overtures from the Allies. "On the 18th," the German chancellor wrote later, "even the most optimistic among us knew that all was lost. The history of the world was played out in three days."

The Allied Counteroffensive After this impressive American fighting alongside Allied units, French Marshal Foch, supreme commander of all the Allied forces, finally approved Pershing's plan for a separate American army. Its first assignment was to assault and wipe out the enemy's trench fortifica-

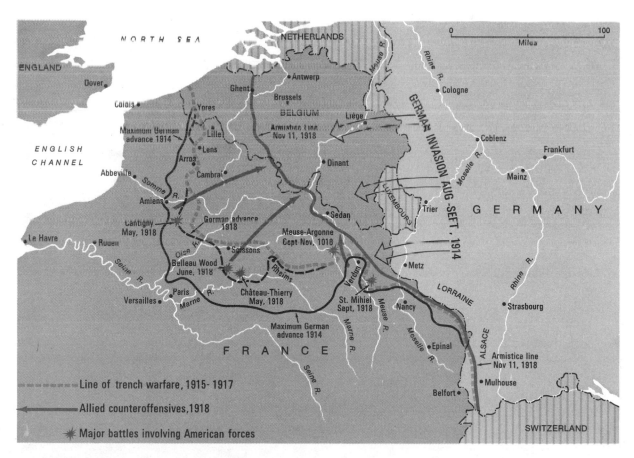

World War I • Western Front

tions at St. Mihiel, a vital railroad junction that the Germans had held since early in the war. In early September an American force numbering 550,000 men attacked and took the fortification in less than two days.

On September 26, the Americans joined the Allies in a gigantic offensive against German lines to the north. In one of the most savage battles of the war, over one million Americans in a twenty-four-mile line drove forward into the Argonne Forest, which Pershing described as a "vast network of un-cut barbed wire, . . . deep ravines, dense woods, myriads of shell craters and a heavy fog." As the Americans inched through the Argonne, units became hopelessly entangled and faced heavy fire from German artillery beyond the forest. Neverthe-less, small American platoons and companies managed independently to take German gun em-placements.

After forty-seven days of bloody battle, the Allied army regrouped, advanced through the Argonne, and broke the Hindenburg line, the main German defense on the western front. On November 7 the Allies reached the outskirts of Sedan, the goal of the long battle. There they cut the railroad line that supplied German troops at the front. On November 11, 1918, with the French and British armies advancing relentlessly along the rest of the front, Germany signed the armistice that ended the fighting.

The war had been a massive slaughter. More than one-half of the troops involved were killed,

ALLIED FORCES IN THE ARGONNE FOREST.

wounded, captured, or listed as missing. Battle deaths amounted to 1 out of every 28 people in the population of France, 1 out of every 32 in Germany, 1 out of every 57 in England, and 1 out of every 107 in Russia, for a total of 6.4 million. Although the Americans had been engaged in heavy fighting for only six months in 1918, their casualties included more than 50,000 killed in action, almost 63,000 dead from disease, 2,200 listed as missing in action, and about 206,000 wounded.

Wilson's Fourteen Points

Long before the carnage ended, President Wilson began trying to realize his dream of securing the benefits of democracy and independence for the people of Europe. This fondness for missionary diplomacy—the notion that the United States should not merely exemplify free government but should also actively bring it to others—had always been present in American history but had never been put into practice.

With American economic and military power to strengthen his position, Wilson began outlining a program that would foster the emergence of a new democratic world order. He believed that countries should end secret diplomacy, adopt constitutional governments similar to that of the United States, and undertake world disarmament. These steps would ensure that the world would never again suffer from war or imperialistic adventurism. Then, with the removal of trade barriers, countries would become economically interdependent. Wilson believed that on a practical level, American economic and strategic interests would be protected by this new order. His program was based on the Progressive view that individuals could solve international problems and end the need for bloodshed through rational planning. The United States would educate Europe on proper international conduct.

In January 1918, ten months before the armistice, the president outlined his vision of the postwar world in his famous Fourteen Points speech to Congress. The core of Wilson's new order lay in the first five points and the culminating point. He proposed that the warring nations agree to the following: open peace covenants, with no secret agreements permitted during the negotiations; freedom of the seas, in war as in peacetime; free trade between countries; disarmament; adjustment of colonial claims with respect for the just interests of native peoples in the British, German, and other empires; and a League of Nations to guarantee political independence and territorial integrity to all states. Several other points concerned the withdrawal of the Central Powers from territory taken during the war. The remainder upheld the rights of oppressed minorities—among them the Czechs, Poles, and Alsacians—to self-determination.

Coming at a time when the warring countries were weary of conflict, the Fourteen Points seemed to offer hope that lasting peace would follow the war. The Creel Committee spread word of the Fourteen Points by dropping millions of pamphlets and booklets behind enemy lines. By this means it hoped to sway public opinion against the German militarist regime and in favor of a quick end to the war.

People all over the world hailed Wilson's visionary plan. Even many Germans regarded the first five points as a promise that the establishment of a democratic German government would enable the country to rejoin the community of nations as an equal. But the Treaty of Brest-Litovsk, signed only two months after Wilson's speech, made it clear that the German government had no intention of retreating from its expansionist aims. His hopes for a peaceful end to the conflict dashed, Wilson now declared that the war must be won by "Force, Force to the utmost . . . Force which shall . . . cast every selfish dominion down in the dust." Nevertheless, he remained resolute in his determination to negotiate a peace based on the Fourteen Points.

Tactical Errors at Home

By the late fall of 1918, with the end of the war in sight, Wilson had demonstrated considerable strength both as a military leader and as a moral leader. The opportunity now lay before him to display his skills in pursuing a lasting peace. Unfortunately, the president's singleminded concern with global problems led him to make a number of serious political miscalculations which undermined his peace initiative.

Wilson wanted to be able to take his peace plan to Paris with the full support of the American people, and he urged Americans to vote for Democratic candidates in the congressional elections of November 1918 as a sign of confidence in his leadership. This infuriated those Republicans who had supported his war policies even more ardently than some Democrats. Such leading Republicans as Theodore Roosevelt urged the Senate to reject the Fourteen Points because Wilson had insulted the patriotic honor of the Republican party. The influential Republican Senator Henry Cabot Lodge of Massachusetts reversed his earlier support of an international organization for enforcing peace. When the Republicans narrowly won control of the House, 237 seats to 190, and carried the Senate by a two-vote majority, some politicians felt that the nation had rejected both Wilson and the ideals of his Fourteen Points.

Wilson's next mistake was to announce that he personally would head the United States delegation to the peace conference in Paris, apparently believing that he had a moral obligation to be physically present. Again Republicans protested. No previous president had ever traveled to Europe while in office. Wilson was accused of being an egotist. Moreover, Republicans insisted that he lacked the toughness to deal with the European leaders.

Finally, Wilson erred in his choice of peace commissioners to accompany him to Paris. The commission of five did not include a single senator, and the president had not consulted with any member of the Senate about the peace conference. To make matters worse, Wilson did not include any of the powerful and capable Republicans in the country, such as former Secretary of State Elihu Root, former President Taft, or Justice Hughes, all of whom favored a League of Nations and could have done much to create bipartisan support for the president's proposals. The only Republican in the delegation was a nonpolitical career diplomat, Henry White, who had been out of the government for nearly ten years.

The Paris Peace Conference

The Allied powers met in Paris from January to June 1919 to decide the terms of a formal treaty ending World War I. From the beginning, decision making rested with the leaders of the Big Four: President Wilson of the United States, Prime Minister David Lloyd George of England, Premier Vittorio Orlando of Italy, and Premier Georges Clemenceau of France. Although Wilson was hailed by the people of Europe as a prophet of a new world order, the feelings of the three Old World leaders were less than enthusiastic about the American's visionary plans. They had every intention of avenging themselves on Germany, protecting their security, and carving up the territorial spoils as they had arranged beforehand in secret treaties.

Wilson faced these issues of power politics with an idealistic dedication to the spirit of the Fourteen Points. Although his liberal peace plan had virtually no support among the Allied victors, Wilson had the advantage of seeking no territorial gains for the United States and the strength of speaking for the only country that came out of the war richer and more powerful than it had been in 1914. Against all odds, Wilson ultimately obtained a peace treaty which, if it offered a good deal less than he had hoped, was at least less vindictive than the one the Allies would have concluded without him.

Terms of the Treaty

The Allies were determined to punish the vanquished Germans by dividing up the German empire and crippling Germany economically as well as militarily. In the end Wilson had to accept the Allied terms, which imposed a strict reduction of the German army and navy, stripped Germany of all its colonies, and forced the German government to admit guilt for the war and to agree to pay for its cost.

To ensure the security of France, which had been overrun by German armies twice since 1870, Clemenceau demanded large areas of rich German land as a buffer zone between the two countries. Accordingly, France was awarded Alsace-Lorraine and given the right to occupy the Saar territory on the German border for fifteen years. Clemenceau gave up demands for French control of the German Rhineland area in return for its demilitarization and security treaties in which both England and the United States promised to defend France in case of a future German attack. The United States Senate, however, never even considered the security treaty.

For revenge, as well as to keep Germany weak, the Allies made Germany accept full responsibility for causing the war. Obviously, this was a gross

THE BIG FOUR AT VERSAILLES. FROM LEFT, PRIME MINISTER LLOYD GEORGE OF GREAT BRITAIN, PREMIER ORLANDO OF ITALY, PREMIER CLEMENCEAU OF FRANCE, AND PRESIDENT WILSON.

oversimplification of the complex sequence of events which had led to the conflict. At British insistence, the victors, over Wilson's strong protest, also demanded that Germany sign a "blank check" to cover all costs of the war. The German government was to pay not only for damage to civilian property but for indirect costs of the war, such as future pensions to Allied veterans. It was presented with an immediate bill for $5 billion and in 1921 with another bill for about $32 billion. The question of war reparations caused enormous international problems in the years following the war. Crushed by these war debts, some Germans blamed Wilson for their problems, calling him a "hypocrite" who had reduced their country to economic slavery by betraying his promises. German resentment over this issue played an important role in the eventual rise of Adolph Hitler.

Self-Determination One of Wilson's most cherished goals was political self-determination for the oppressed minorities of Europe. The final treaty did grant self-determination to several national groups within the German and Austrian empires by creating the countries of Poland, Yugoslavia, and Czechoslovakia. But complete self-determination was impossible to obtain because many regions in Europe contained mixed populations and the leading European diplomats were very interested in securing territorial gains for their own countries. Thus Italy received the Brenner Pass region of the Alps where two hundred thousand Austrians lived; Yugoslavia acquired the Italian-speaking port of Fiume; and Czechoslovakia received the Sudetenland where millions of Germans lived.

Distribution of Colonies In return for Japan's entering the war on the side of the Allies, England had promised the Japanese government the control of the Chinese peninsula of Shantung (formerly in German hands) as well as the German islands in the Pacific. Although President Wilson strongly opposed granting Japan control of these areas, he gave way when England insisted. Wilson did, however, persuade Japan to return the strategic peninsula to China at a later date, an agreement Japan kept in 1923.

Wilson also had a degree of success when the Allies began distributing the other German colonies in Africa and the Far East as well as the remains of the empire of Turkey, a wartime member of the Central Powers. He devised the so-called mandate system under which the Allies would hold certain colonies and territories in trust through the League of Nations. The trustees would give annual accounts of their supervision to the League and prepare the colonial populations for independence. Although the mandate system was very different from the self-determination Wilson had hoped for, it was better than the outright possession of lands and peoples envisioned by the Allies.

The League of Nations The one issue that outweighed all others in Wilson's mind was the establishment of the League of Nations. In calling for the League, the president sought to replace power politics with a worldwide alliance to maintain an orderly, peaceful world. For Wilson, the most satisfying outcome of the conference was his success in persuading the Allies to accept the League of Nations as part of the Treaty of Versailles. As he saw it, after the passions and prejudices of the war had been calmed, the League would correct the imperfections of the rest of the treaty.

The League was a remarkable innovation in international politics. It was founded on the idea that war and the acts leading to war are everybody's responsibility. It had no supreme authority, no armies, not even a way of forcing members to pay their financial dues. As an international forum for debate, the League's power depended entirely on the conscience of member nations. The League's potential for peacemaking lay in the hope that the habit of airing problems before they turned into armed conflicts, a growing success in settling disputes, and the common interests of its members would give the organization lasting strength.

The Covenant, or constitution of the League of Nations, called for an Assembly, a Council, and a permanent Secretariat headed by a secretary-general with headquarters in Geneva, Switzerland. With the exception of the defeated Central Powers and Communist Russia, all countries and self-governing members of the British Commonwealth (such as Canada) were eligible to join the League. Each member nation was to have one vote and equal representation in the Assembly. The nine-nation Council was to be made up of five permanent representatives from the victorious powers—the United States, Britain, France, Italy, and Japan —and four temporary members chosen by the Assembly. The Assembly was to control most of the

Europe after Versailles • 1919

internal operations of the League directly, but as far as international affairs were concerned, it could only investigate and advise. The more powerful Council was to decide whether to use force against a nation that had broken the peace.

Article X, which Wilson called "the heart of the Covenant," pledged the member nations "to respect and preserve against external aggression the territorial integrity and existing political independence" of all members of the League. If any country in or outside of the League threatened any other with aggression, or if there was any outside interference with the independence and self-government of the small nations, the Council of the League would confer on what measures to take. If any nations, violating their pledge to submit disputes to the League for arbitration, went to war to settle an argument, the Council could ask member nations to use economic, financial, or joint military pressure to stop the aggressor.

An International Labor Office was provided to investigate labor conditions, world health, and the international traffic in women, children, drugs, arms, and munitions. The Covenant also established a permanent court of international justice, the World Court, at The Hague in the Netherlands.

The Treaty Assessed

In June 1919, a defeated Germany signed the Treaty of Versailles. There have been many assessments of the treaty. Some writers have seen it as a triumph of self-determination for many nationalities; others have regarded it as an instrument of Allied vengeance that prepared the way for a future war. It has been argued that breaking up Austria-Hungary into small nations created a power vacuum in eastern Europe into which both Germany and Russia could later move. Some believe that the treaty's two worst features were the unlimited and unspecified war costs, which kept Germany resentful and financially unstable, and the disarmament clauses, which made that country incapable of self-defense. However, few people outside of Germany criticized either of these clauses at the time. If anything, France and Britain felt that they had already made more concessions than they cared to, for they had little sympathy with Wilson's views on self-determination and the importance of a League of Nations.

Defeat of the League

Partisan Attacks

When President Wilson left Paris in June 1919 to seek Senate ratification of the Treaty of Versailles, he faced opposition from all sides. Although a large majority of Americans favored the treaty, difficulties in securing its passage were accumulating. Many conservatives and nationalists strongly opposed the League of Nations, arguing that the League posed a threat to America's traditional isolation as well as to its sovereignty. Many Progressives argued that the terms of the treaty, instead of assuring a liberal peace, had enabled the forces of territorial acquisitiveness, nationalism, and vengeance to hold sway. Such a peace, they claimed, would create an atmosphere that might lead to a second world war. German-Americans protested that the severity of the conditions imposed on Germany was a gross betrayal of the Fourteen Points. Irish-Americans booed Wilson's name because he did not include the question of Irish independence in his negotiations. Italian-Americans were angry at Wilson's refusal to make sure that the port of Fiume was given to Italy. Finally, the Senate, dominated by the Republicans, was still smarting over Wilson's earlier slights.

In March 1919, with the president still negotiating in Paris, thirty-nine Republican senators openly opposed the League by signing a "round robin" warning that they would not approve a peace treaty containing the League Covenant as it was written. As a result, Wilson had to appeal to the Allies to accept changes that would ensure that the Covenant would not interfere with the Monroe Doctrine. He also persuaded them to accept other revisions the Senate wanted, including provisions that member countries could withdraw from the League after giving two years' notice, members could refuse mandates, and the League would have no jurisdiction over purely domestic issues. Many Republicans complained that even these concessions were insufficient.

Wilson, however, disdained the opposition of these senators because he was sure that public pressure for the League would force them to approve it. In private, he characterized them as "pygmy minded." He also declared arrogantly that "the Senate must take its medicine." Thus the stage was set for a fierce battle between an intransigent Democratic president and a bitter Republican majority in the Senate.

Wilson Versus Lodge

While almost all Democratic senators supported the president, Wilson's Republican opponents divided roughly into three groups. At one end of the scale was a small group of sixteen "irreconcilables," mostly Republicans, totally opposed to any treaty that included an international organization in any form. At the other end of the scale stood "mild" reservationists who approved the League in principle, but wanted to change the League Covenant in minor ways. The middle ground was occupied by a group of "strong" reservationists who would vote for the League only if American interests were fully protected, according to their standards, and only if it was made clear that Republicans had played a major part in creating the final version of the Covenant. The strategist for all these groups was the Chairman of the Senate Foreign Relations Committee, Henry Cabot Lodge.

Historians still debate why Lodge was so determined to defeat the League of Nations. He was probably motivated at least in part by political considerations, since both the Irish and the Italian votes were important in his state and enthusiasm for the League and the treaty would have cost him their support. Lodge did not oppose the League in principle and had even advocated such an organization during the war. Perhaps the most important element in his opposition was his political and personal animosity toward the president. Lodge was Wilson's intellectual peer. He had received Harvard's first Ph.D. in political science in 1876; Wilson had received an early Ph.D. from Johns Hopkins University. Both men had taken legal training and each had published extensively, but Lodge had left the academic world for politics earlier. Before Wilson had risen to prominence, Lodge had been considered the resident political intellectual.

Lodge was first and foremost a Republican politician, not an idealist. He disliked Wilson's legislative program and what he considered the president's autocratic manner, and he was angry at the personal rebuff he suffered in not being appointed to the peace commission. "I never expected to hate anyone in politics with the hatred I

feel towards Wilson," he said. Wilson's antipathy toward Lodge was equally intense.

Aware that there was broad support for the treaty, Lodge used parliamentary procedure to delay the debate. In addition, he proposed certain limitations on United States involvement with the League. There were fourteen Lodge reservations to match Wilson's Fourteen Points. The most important reservation struck at Article X, which Wilson had called "the heart of the Covenant." Lodge attacked the idea of committing the United States to action protecting the political independence and territory of League members without a congressional act or resolution authorizing it. Of course, the same procedure would have been followed even if Article X had been accepted in its original form.

Most Americans agreed with Lodge on this point. Although supporting the general concept of a world organization, they were not prepared to commit themselves to Article X as it stood. But the president was determined that the treaty would not be tampered with, especially by the Republicans. With Lodge leading the opposition, he was eager for a

WILSON DURING HIS TWENTY-TWO-DAY SPEAKING TOUR TO DRUM UP SUPPORT FOR THE LEAGUE OF NATIONS. EXHAUSTED BY YEARS OF CRISIS, WILSON FINALLY SUFFERED A STROKE.

Wilson and the League of Nations

"The United States entered the war . . . only because we saw the supremacy and even the validity of right everywhere put in jeopardy and free government likely to be everywhere imperiled by the intolerable aggression of a power which respected neither right nor obligation and whose very system of government flouted the rights of the citizen as against the autocratic authority of his governors. And in the settlements of the peace we have sought no special reparation for ourselves, but only the restoration of right and the assurance of liberty everywhere that the effects of the settlement were to be felt. We entered the war as the disinterested champion of right and we entered in the terms of peace in no other capacity . . . .

A league of free nations had become a practical necessity. Examine the treaty of peace and you will find that everywhere throughout its manifold provisions its framers have felt obliged to turn to the League of Nations as an indispensable instrumentality for the maintenance of the new order it has been their purpose to set up in the works,—the world of civilized men. . . ."

President Woodrow Wilson, 1919

Lodge Speaks against League of Nations

"I object in the strongest possible way to having the United States agree, directly or indirectly, to be controlled by a league which may at any time, and perfectly lawfully and in accordance with the terms of the covenant, be drawn in to deal with internal conflicts in other countries, no matter what those conflicts may be. We should never permit the United States to be involved in any internal conflict in another country, except by the will of her people expressed through the Congress which represents them. . . .

We may set aside all this empty talk about isolation. Nobody expects to isolate the United States or to make it a hermit Nation, which is a sheer absurdity. But there is a wide difference between taking a suitable part and bearing a due responsibility in world affairs and plunging the United States into every controversy and conflict on the face of the globe. By meddling in all the differences which may arise among any portion or fragment of humankind we simply fritter away our influence and injure ourselves to no good purpose. . . ."

Senator Henry Cabot Lodge, 1919

---

showdown. He had made many compromises in Paris, but would make none at home.

Wilson's Public Appeal   When after two months the treaty was still buried in Lodge's committee, Wilson set out on a cross-country speaking tour to appeal directly to the people, as he had done many times in the past. Never a robust man, his strength had been depleted by six years of constant crisis; he was in no condition to undertake such a venture and was warned against it by his doctor. At only sixty-three, he was pale, trembling, and exhausted as he traveled more than eight thousand miles in twenty-two days, making thirty-six speeches before enthusiastic audiences. On September 25 he collapsed after a speech at Pueblo, Colorado, and was hurried back to Washington. A few days later he suffered a severe stroke, which paralyzed his left side. For two

weeks he was near death. During the next six weeks his mind was clear, but he was still seriously ill. For more than six months he lived in seclusion, cut off from affairs of state, screened from contact with cabinet members and Congress, while Lodge maneuvered his fourteen reservations through the Senate.

Rejection of the Treaty

A coalition of Democrats and moderate Republicans could easily have passed the treaty. That it was voted down was as much Wilson's fault as the Republicans'. When it was time for the final roll call on November 19, a bitter and distraught Wilson ordered the Democrats to vote only for the unamended treaty without the Lodge reservations. Urged by his wife to reconsider, he answered,

"Better a thousand times to go down fighting than to dip your colors to dishonorable compromise." When the vote came, the thirteen "irreconcilables" were joined by forty-two Democrats obedient to Wilson's wishes, and the treaty with the reservations was defeated. In response to an outpouring of protest from the American public, the original treaty without reservations was again brought up for a vote. Thirty-eight senators, all but one of them Democrats, voted for it, but there were fifty-five votes against it. Again the treaty was defeated.

Dismayed, friends of the League of Nations —both Democrats and Republicans—forced another vote for the treaty with reservations in March 1920. Even then, given this last chance for the success of the most cherished work of his life, Wilson refused to compromise. Lodge, too, saw no reason to budge from his position. Although directed by the president to vote against ratification, this time half the Senate Democrats ignored him and voted for it. Nevertheless, at the final count the vote was forty-nine to thirty-five, seven votes short of the two-thirds majority needed for ratification.

The European response to American rejection of the treaty was one of shock. Britain and France felt betrayed and were convinced that they could not depend on the United States in the future. Contrary to Wilson's belief, both of these nations would have accepted the Lodge reservations in order to have ensured American membership in the League. Unrestrained, they now proceeded to deal harshly with Germany on war reparations, further embittering postwar European politics. Although the League was formed, it was ineffectual without the influence and power of the United States.

The United States formally ended the war with the Central Powers in July 1921, by a joint resolution of Congress. In August the United States signed separate treaties with Germany, Austria, and Hungary.

The War and America's Future

The impact of World War I on America's future was far-reaching. American economic power expanded enormously to meet the demands of war, as did government planning for the economic development of the country. The power of the president to conduct foreign affairs was given a tremendous boost by Wilson's wartime and postwar diplomacy. Congress was often ignored as the president unilaterally initiated and implemented policy. On the domestic scene patriotic conformity set the stage for curtailment of dissent during the next decade, and the demands of those who wanted to resume progressive reform were sidetracked by conservative administrations dedicated to a return to a laissez-faire economy.

Although Wilson's dream of a new international order had been shattered, the United States emerged as the unchallenged industrial and financial leader of the world. American companies expanded their opportunities in developing nations and the United States became Europe's creditor to the tune of $10 billion. But a crucial question remained: would American leaders have the wisdom, even without membership in the League of Nations, to want to help resolve the economic and political problems of the rest of the world that had resulted from the war?

Readings

General Works

Baldwin, Hanson W., *World War I*. New York: Harper & Row, 1962.

Buehrig, Edward H. (Ed.), *Wilson's Foreign Policy in Perspective*. Bloomington: Indiana University Press, 1957.

Coffman, Edward M., *The War to End All Wars*. New York: Oxford University Press, 1968.

Kuehl, Warren F., *Seeking World Order: The United States and International Organization to 1920*. Nashville, Tenn.: Vanderbilt University Press, 1969.

Link, Arthur S., *Wilson the Diplomatist*. Baltimore: Johns Hopkins Press, 1957.

May, Ernest R., *The World War and American Isolation*. Cambridge, Mass.: Harvard University Press, 1959.

Millis, Walter, *The Road to War*. New York: Fertig, 1969.

Notter, Harley, *The Origins of the Foreign Policy of Woodrow Wilson*. New York: Russell, 1965.

Pratt, Julius W., *Challenge and Rejection: The United States and World Leadership, 1900–1921*. New York: Macmillan, 1967.

Smith, Daniel M., *The Great Departure: The United States in World War I, 1914–1920*. New York: Wiley, 1965. (Paper)

Tuchman, Barbara, *The Guns of August*. New York: Macmillan, 1962.

Special Studies
Bailey, Thomas A., *Wilson and the Peacemakers*. Chicago: Quadrangle, 1963.

Cooper, John M., Jr., *The Vanity of Power: American Isolationism and the First World War, 1914–1917*. Westport, Conn.: Greenwood, 1969.

Devlin, Patrick, *Too Proud to Fight: Woodrow Wilson's Neutrality*. New York: Oxford University Press, 1975.

Fleming, D. F., *The United States and the League of Nations*. New York: Russell, 1968.

Gelfand, Lawrence E., *The Inquiry: American Preparations for Peace, 1917–1919*. New Haven, Conn.: Yale University Press, 1963.

Gilbert, Charles, *American Financing of World War I*. Westport, Conn.: Greenwood, 1970.

Levin, N. Gordon, *Woodrow Wilson and World Politics*. New York: Oxford University Press, 1968.

Link, Arthur S., *The Higher Realism of Woodrow Wilson and Other Essays*. Nashville, Tenn.: Vanderbilt University Press, 1971.

Livermore, Seward W., *Politics Is Adjourned*. Middletown, Conn.: Wesleyan University Press, 1966.

Luebke, Frederick C., *Bonds of Loyalty: German-Americans and World War I*. DeKalb: Northern Illinois University Press, 1974.

Maddox, Robert J., *The Unknown War with Russia: Wilson's Siberian Intervention*. San Rafael, Calif.: Presidio, 1977.

Mayer, Arno J., *Politics and Diplomacy of Peacemaking: Containment and Counterrevolution at Versailles, 1918–1919*. New York: Knopf, 1968.

Nelson, Keith, *Victors Divided: America and the Allies in Germany, 1918–1923*. Berkeley: University of California Press, 1973.

Parrini, Carl P., *Heir to Empire: U.S. Economic Diplomacy 1916–1923*. Pittsburgh, Pa.: University of Pittsburgh Press, 1969.

Perkins, Bradford, *The Great Rapprochement: England and the United States, 1895–1914*. New York: Atheneum, 1968.

Stone, Ralph, *The Irreconcilables: The Fight Against the League of Nations*. New York: Norton, 1973. (Paper)

Walworth, Arthur, *America's Moment: 1918, American Diplomacy at the End of World War I*. New York: Norton, 1977.

Primary Sources
Creel, George, *How We Advertised America*. New York: Harper, 1920.

Biographies
Garraty, John A., *Henry Cabot Lodge*. New York: Knopf, 1953.

Vandiver, Frank E., *BlackJack: The Life and Times of John J. Pershing*. College Station: Texas A&M University Press, 1977.

25 The 1920s: Prosperity and Cultural Change

The positive values of the 1920s may perhaps best be suggested in the phrase "useful innocence." In the decade two generations collaborated in an exhaustive review of America's past greatness and present status. The old generation . . . surveyed the weaknesses of a tradition that culminated in a war and an uneasy peace. The other generation . . . assumed the task of reviewing that culture, of making it over according to new principles . . .

Frederick J. Hoffman, author

Significant Events

Eighteenth Amendment to the Constitution (prohibition) Volstead Act [1919]

Wall St. blast [September 1920]

Farm Bloc organized in Congress [1921]

Sacco-Vanzetti case begins [1921]

Emergency Quota Act [1921]

Fordney-McCumber Act [1922]

National Origins Act [1924]

Scopes "Monkey Trial" [1925]

Charles Lindbergh crosses the Atlantic [May 1927]

Congress passes McNary-Haugen bill, but Coolidge vetoes it both times [1927 and 1928]

THE ZIEGFELD FOLLIES WERE POPULAR ENTERTAINMENT DURING THE "ERA OF WONDERFUL NONSENSE," THE 1920s.

The Postwar Transition

By the time the war had ended, Americans had grown weary of the regimentation of their private lives and of government restrictions on their personal freedom. Many citizens, disillusioned by the Treaty of Versailles and the bitter controversy over the League of Nations, rejected the idea that the United States should assume world responsibilities. The result was a massive reaction against the idealism of Wilson's international policy and the Progressive Era. Although some Progressive legislation was passed by Congress during the twenties, it was vetoed by presidents who were more in tune with public opinion. By and large, the American people favored a return to the laissez-faire economic policies of an earlier period.

Demobilization and Depression

Reflecting this prevailing mood, the federal government abruptly scrapped wartime programs and lifted wartime economic controls. Within a year of the armistice, most of the four million American troops stationed in Europe had been shipped home and discharged. The government, confident that private industry could easily convert to a peacetime economy, canceled all of its war contracts without making provisions for reconverting factories or re-employing the nine million workers whose jobs had depended on wartime production. Congress turned down Wilson's proposal for a public works program that would employ returning servicemen and defeated a plan to use them on reclamation projects in the western part of the country. A Vocational Rehabilitation Act (1918) placed several thousand men in schools but benefited only a small percentage of the total number of veterans disabled by the war. Nevertheless, many states established employment bureaus and welfare agencies and passed public works legislation in order to provide temporary relief to both unemployed civilians and returning servicemen. A boom in American business in 1919 made it easier for many to find jobs.

A national debate ensued over the continuation of government control of the railroads. While the railroad companies wanted Congress to restore private control, railway workers favored the continuation of public control begun during the war years.

In the Esch-Cummins Transportation Act of 1920, Congress legislated a compromise that returned the railroads to private ownership but increased government supervision of their operations. The act increased ICC control of the railroads' finances and authorized the commission to group the lines into a limited number of systems with financial assistance given to the weaker ones. The act was disappointing to labor both because it put railroads under private control and because the Railway Labor Board that it created proved ineffective.

The American economy was strong during the period immediately following the war. Released from wartime rationing of materials, the construction industry contributed to the postwar boom as did the European demand for American loans and exports, especially foodstuffs. Probably the most important factor in the nation's prosperity, however, was the tremendous increase in the purchase of consumer goods as buyers attempted to keep ahead of rapidly rising prices. Such buying fueled inflation by encouraging overproduction and overpricing of goods. Between 1918 and 1920, the cost of living rose 97 percent. Finally, toward the end of 1919, the Federal Reserve System began raising interest rates in an effort to reduce the money supply and thus cool down the economy. By mid-1920 the sharp reduction of the money supply coupled with the contraction of a greatly overexpanded economy contributed to a decline in prices and production which lasted over a year. Within a year the unemployment rate hit 10 percent. The recession was short-lived, however, and by the fall of 1921 business losses had been absorbed and employment and productivity once again began to rise.

Postwar Strikes

Inflation during 1919 and 1920 hurt most Americans. There were feelings of animosity between middle-class citizens living on fixed salaries and factory workers trying to meet the rising costs by striking for better pay. Public hostility toward striking workers was in part a reflection of the continuing influence of wartime propaganda. The public began to associate strikes with radicals, anarchists, and other subversive groups. This attitude became particularly widespread after a general strike in Seattle in February 1919 was reported to have been Communist-inspired. Given this atmosphere of suspicion, it was not surprising that several major strikes failed. In September 1919, steelworkers, who worked ten to fourteen hours a day for subsistence wages, struck for an eight-hour day, a six-day week, higher wages, and recognition of the union as their collective-bargaining agent. When the United States Steel Corporation refused to deal with the union, violence broke out at the Gary, Indiana, factory, and company heads blamed the trouble on Communist agitators. The company, backed by considerable public support and thousands of strikebreakers protected by state and federal troops, forced the workers to give in after a four-month struggle. Although President Harding finally persuaded the company to grant an eight-hour day in 1923, the company still refused to recognize the union.

In November 1919, almost four hundred thousand coal miners led by John L. Lewis walked out demanding a 60-percent wage increase, a six-hour day, and a five-day week. The attorney general, A. Mitchell Palmer, obtained an injunction against the union with the president's approval. Faced with the threat of government intervention, Lewis called off the strike. However, the miners refused to return to work until a government commission ordered the mining companies to grant an immediate 14-percent pay increase with an additional 27 percent to follow.

The cause of organized labor was hurt most by the Boston police strike of 1919. Longstanding grievances and the inability to keep up with the postwar cost of living prompted Boston police to secure a charter from the AFL and threaten a strike. Although a citizen's committee recommended meeting some of their demands, the police commissioner vetoed the suggestion and suspended nineteen policemen. Subsequently, the entire force went on strike. Looting and fighting broke out, Bostonians panicked, and the press further aroused public frenzy with false reports that the walkout had been incited by Communists. The mayor finally called in part of the National Guard. Then, three days later, Governor Calvin Coolidge sent in the rest of the troops, thereby breaking the strike. Coolidge also sent a telegram to labor leader Samuel Gompers that read: "There is no right to strike against the public safety by anybody, anywhere, any time."

The public's enthusiastic response to this statement brought Coolidge nationwide fame and significantly boosted his political career.

The Red Scare

Strikes alienated a public that craved stability. They also helped to create support for management's views that inflation was the result of wage increases and that "individualism" rather than unionization was "the American way." Corporate managers convinced the public that union demands were influenced by foreign radicals who had infiltrated labor's ranks. This argument seemed particularly persuasive in view of the fact that the Russian Revolution of 1917 had been followed by workers' strikes and uprisings throughout Europe. Bolshevik leaders of the Third (or Communist) International, an agency for world revolution, met in Moscow in March 1919 and expressed commitment to Communist victories all over the world, especially in the industrial countries of the West. Fearful of economic and political chaos, many Americans began to suspect that all movements for social and economic reform were instigated by international communism.

Yet the fact was that the American labor movement was strongly antagonistic to the small American Communist party, which was organized in 1919 under the leadership of foreign radicals. Whereas the homegrown Socialist movement advocated a gradual, peaceful redistribution of wealth, Communists called for the violent overthrow of the capitalist system. Only the more radical Industrial Workers of the World, or Wobblies, joined with the Communist party. Founded in 1905, the IWW's strongest support came from Western miners, lumberjacks, migratory workers, and unskilled immigrants in Eastern mill towns. Because it sometimes resorted to violence and sabotage, the IWW incurred considerable public antagonism.

Public hysteria over radicalism mounted steadily. Schoolteachers were required to sign loyalty oaths, professors under suspicion were dismissed, textbooks were censored, and workers who voiced unconventional economic ideas were harassed or fired. Some states enacted antiradical laws and made it illegal to display the "Red" flag. Five members of the New York state legislature who belonged to the Socialist party were expelled, although they had committed no crimes.

WALL STREET SOON AFTER THE EXPLOSION WHICH OCCURRED AT 11:59 ON SEPTEMBER 16, 1920. THIRTY-EIGHT WERE KILLED AND HUNDREDS WERE WOUNDED. THE PERSON DRIVING THE WAGON LOADED WITH DYNAMITE AND SCRAP IRON WAS NEVER CAUGHT.

The already jittery public was further alarmed when bombs were mailed in April 1919 to a number of prominent citizens, including John D. Rockefeller and Justice Oliver Wendell Holmes. Although the post office intercepted all but one of these bombs, there were other bombings in June. A bloody clash between the American Legion, a newly organized patriotic party, and IWW members during an Armistice Day parade resulted in the death of four legionnaires and the lynching of one IWW member. After these incidents, many Americans began to confuse their fear of wartime saboteurs with a fear of peacetime foreign radicals. Any alien of suspicious racial or national origin was regarded as likely to be a "Red." Accordingly a program of arrests, intimidation, and deportation, conducted primarily by Attorney General A. Mitchell Palmer, was initiated by the federal and state governments.

Working with the General Intelligence Division of the Justice Department under J. Edgar Hoover, Palmer ordered a series of raids on radical meetings and on the homes of suspected subversives. A large-scale raid in January 1920 led to the arrest of more than four thousand citizens in thirty-three cities. Most of these people were seized without warrants and herded into jails. Some of the arrests ultimately led to deportation, but most of them proved completely unfounded. Finally Palmer went too far when he warned of a conspiracy to overthrow the

United States government on May Day in 1920. The National Guard was called out, but when the day passed with no sign of bomb or bullet, Palmer began to look ridiculous.

The Red scare had waned by the summer of 1920. In September a wagon loaded with dynamite and scrap iron exploded on Wall Street killing thirty-eight persons and causing $2 million in damages. But the American public, although horrified, did not panic. The incident was accepted as the action of a deranged individual rather than the work of conspirators. Nevertheless, intolerance of those associated with radical ideologies continued unabated.

An example of the prevailing hostility directed against aliens and radicals was the case of Nicola Sacco and Bartolomeo Vanzetti, two Italian immigrants and self-declared anarchists. In 1921 Sacco and Vanzetti were convicted of murdering two payroll couriers in Massachusetts. Although the evidence against the defendants was inconclusive, the atmosphere of the time encouraged the belief that foreigners who spoke poor English and were self-confessed radicals also were likely to be robbers and murderers. Despite international attention and the fervent pleas of their supporters, who claimed that the two anarchists had not received a fair trial, Sacco and Vanzetti were executed in 1927. Although their cases were carefully reviewed by appellate courts, their imprisonment and subsequent execution caused a whole generation of American liberals to question the justice of the nation's legal system.

Restrictions on Immigration

After 1897 restrictions on immigration had eased and entrance to the country had been open to everyone except the insane, convicts, and, in 1917, persons over age sixteen who were not literate in any language. After the war, nativism manifested itself again in a further restriction of immigration. Labor leaders protested that they would lose recent wage gains if unlimited immigration continued. They were joined by narrowminded, old-stock Americans who protested that the nation was being flooded with inferior immigrants or radicals from southern and eastern Europe. In 1921 Congress passed the Emergency Quota Act, limiting the number of immigrants each year to 3 percent of the foreign-born of each national group living in the United States in 1910. The National Origins Act of 1924 was even more restrictive. It reduced the quota to 2 percent, based on the number of immigrants from each country in residence in the United States in 1890. Since 1890 predated the great wave of southern and eastern European immigration, the 1924 law clearly

favored admission of Scandinavians, Germans, Irish, and British. After 1929 a total of only 150,000 immigrants was to be admitted to the country each year with each national quota apportioned according to the national origins of the American people in 1920. The law established no quota for Japanese immigrants, however, and was perceived as a serious insult by the Japanese government, which for a long time had faithfully honored the terms of the Gentlemen's Agreement.

The Election of 1920

The election of 1920 was held in an atmosphere of nationwide disillusionment. The prevailing feeling was one of revulsion against the party and the policies that had led the nation into a costly war. As a result the Republicans, once again dominated by conservative leadership, were confident of victory.

Sources of Party Support The sources of party support in 1920 were substantially the same as in 1900. The Republicans continued to appeal to a broad coalition, including the middle class and the well-to-do, most farmers outside the South, and many workers and blacks. Old-line Republicanism dominated the politics of New England, the upper Middle West, and the Far West. The party platform favored a high tariff which would protect business and contribute to economic self-sufficiency. It condemned the League of Nations while at the same time calling for efforts among nations to preserve the peace.

Although the Democrats were backed by some business interests, their base of support lay in the rural Protestant South and among the growing number of immigrant groups, mostly Catholics and Jews, who resided in the large Northern cities. These Democratic supporters reflected the tensions rising between urban and rural ways of life in America during the 1920s. Ultimately, it was the urban/ethnic element which came to dominate the Democratic party after a decade of brutal intra-party battles. The party platform favored the League, tax reductions, and Philippine independence.

The Conventions The Republican party convened in Chicago in 1920 in a spirit of general elation. Confident of victory in November and seeking a candidate they could manage easily, the Old Guard

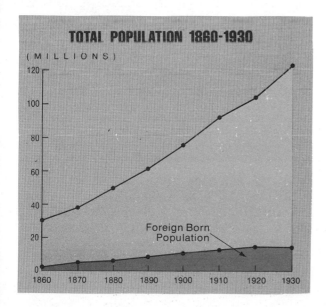

TOTAL POPULATION 1860-1930

(MILLIONS)

Foreign Born Population

DAPPER WARREN G. HARDING, A GENIAL SMALL-TOWN POLITICIAN WHO BECAME PRESIDENT, ONLY TO FIND THAT THE DEMANDS OF THE OFFICE WERE BEYOND HIS LIMITED ABILITY.

became deadlocked between Frank Lowden of Illinois and General Leonard Wood. Finally, after a long Saturday session, they settled on the genial but lackluster senator from Ohio, Warren G. Harding. Harding was nominated on the tenth ballot with Calvin Coolidge as his running mate.

Harding was a remarkably handsome man with an engaging personality. Beneath his surface polish was a small-town politician who possessed an undisciplined weakness for women, liquor, and cards. Nevertheless, he was hardworking and stubbornly loyal to the Republican party. His voting record was basically conservative. He had taken no definitive position on any important issue and could be counted on to leave the control of national politics to the congressional Republicans. In his genial manner he epitomized the small-town America of

his day. Folksy, unpretentious, and easygoing, he corresponded with many Americans' idea of a "regular fellow."

Harding followed the advice of his managers and made few speeches and took few stands on current issues. The general tone of his campaign was soothing and reassuring. He promised lower taxes, higher tariffs, immigration restriction, and assistance to farmers. He condemned the League of Nations but called vaguely for an international agreement to preserve the peace.

The Democratic party, by contrast, was in a state of confusion. Attorney General Palmer, highly favored for the nomination, had lost popularity after the May Day fiasco. William G. McAdoo was an able candidate, but as Wilson's son-in-law he ran the risk of being identified with the outgoing administration. Party bosses supported James M. Cox of Ohio, a proven votegetter and an opponent of prohibition. Although Palmer and McAdoo were closely matched, neither could gather the two-thirds majority necessary for the nomination. Finally, on the forty-fourth ballot, the convention nominated Cox. As his running mate they chose young Franklin D. Roosevelt, assistant secretary of the navy and a distant cousin of the late president.

In most campaigns Harding would have been an uninspiring candidate. In 1920 he had only to sit back and wait for the landslide against Wilson and the Democrats. The middle class, resentful of high taxes and labor strikes, had withdrawn from progressivism. Most Americans, even in the cities, were hostile to Wilson's foreign policies. These factors combined to produce a sweeping Republican victory. Harding received 61 percent of the popular vote and led Cox 404 to 127 in electoral votes. The Republicans won huge majorities in both houses of Congress. The voters had repudiated internationalism and government regulation of business in favor of a return to what Harding called "normalcy."

The Republican Ascendancy

The Harding Administration

Harding worked hard to demonstrate the good intentions of his administration. His relations with the press were excellent, and he made the public feel that their president was accessible to them again.

Nevertheless, he had serious limitations as a national leader. He lacked both superior intelligence and mental discipline, and the small-town attributes of generosity and blind loyalty to friends severely handicapped his effectiveness as an administrator. Harding's campaign slogan had been: "Less government in business and more business in government," and he promised to recruit "the best minds" in the country to serve in his administration. His own lack of expertise and perception led him to depend on his cabinet for the formulation of most policy. Only occasionally did he try to influence the headstrong Congress.

Treasury Policies

The president turned over most of the management of the domestic economy to Secretary of the Treasury Andrew Mellon, a multimillionaire who held the monopoly on aluminum production. Mellon believed that government was a business to be run according to strict principles of efficiency. In 1921 Congress passed the Budget and Accounting Act, aimed at streamlining government budgeting methods. The act created a director of the budget to assist the president in preparing the annual budget and a comptroller general to audit executive accounts. Mellon was very pleased with this legislation but he also wished to limit federal expenditures and reduce taxes on business. Arguing that taxing wealthy individuals and corporate profits inhibited business growth, he attempted to shift the primary tax burden from business to lower-income groups. His proposals were too drastic to win unqualified support from Congress. The House of Representatives was demanding tax cuts for lower-income groups, so Mellon constantly had to battle for his program between 1921 and 1925. In 1924 Congress did reduce taxes for lower-income brackets, but by 1926 Mellon had partially succeeded in his plan, and millionaires paid less than one-third of the taxes they had paid the year before. During the 1920s lowered tax rates saved the wealthy—including Mellon—almost $4 billion. Nevertheless, Mellon did balance the budget and he reduced the national debt by an average of over $500 million a year.

Protective Tariffs

The economic prosperity that characterized most of the decade of the 1920s never extended to the majority of the farm community. After the war rapid technological advances increased farm production, but the foreign demand for American farm produce dwindled. The result was an enormous crop surplus. In response, the Harding administration and Re-

publican congressional leaders set out to restore protective-tariff rates to prewar levels. They advocated a self-sufficient national economy, even though European nations depended on selling goods in the United States to pay their war debts. The Republicans were supported in this policy by the South, which had developed more industries, and by the farmers, who hoped higher tariffs would bring them greater profits. During the spring of 1921, Western and Southern congressional leaders formed the "Farm Bloc" to unite agricultural interests and secure the passage of desperately needed farm legislation. Although the Bloc strongly opposed Mellon's tax bill, they joined with business leaders in promoting the Emergency Tariff Act of 1921, which placed prohibitive duties on twenty-eight agricultural commodities, eliminated the excess-profits tax, limited the income tax on the wealthy, and gave low- and middle-income groups modest tax relief. Despite the work of the Farm Bloc, the new tariff legislation only succeeded in creating more crop surpluses.

Congress failed to understand basic agricultural problems, and they worsened throughout the decade. The Fordney-McCumber Act of 1922 raised tariff rates still further and created a tariff commission which was empowered to help the president determine the differences in production costs between the United States and other nations. It also granted the president the authority to raise or lower any rate by 50 percent. While this measure encouraged the consolidation of American business and protected it against competition, it greatly harmed foreign trade. Unfortunately, by making it almost impossible for Europeans to sell their goods in the United States, the act also discouraged them from buying American products, especially agricultural goods.

The Harding Scandals

Although by 1923 Harding was becoming a more assertive president, he was never able to come to grips with the offenses of the "Ohio Gang," a group of longtime companions and supporters to whom he had given important jobs in his administration. Uncertain of his own judgment, he often turned to these men for advice. "Ed" Scobey from Harding's hometown of Marion, Ohio, was director of the mint. "Doc" Sawyer was White House physician with the rank of brigadier general. Charles R.

Forbes, whom Harding had met by chance on a vacation in Hawaii, headed the Veterans Bureau. Albert B. Fall, a friend of Harding from the Senate, was secretary of the interior; and Harry M. Daugherty, an Ohioan who had promoted Harding's career, was attorney general. Harding's loyalty to his associates blinded him to their flaws. As a result, several instances of large-scale financial abuse in high government offices occurred, and the Harding administration was one of the most corrupt in American history. Yet when scandals implicating some of these men came to light, neither the press nor the public, imbued with postwar cynicism, voiced significant protest.

The first scandal to break involved Charles R. Forbes. While director of the Veterans Bureau, Forbes had personally pocketed a large portion of the agency's annual budget of $250 million through kickbacks and shady construction deals. In 1923, when Harding learned of the rumors about Forbes, he allowed him to resign and leave the country. Eventually Forbes was convicted and sent to prison, and a Senate committee investigation of the affair

THE TEAPOT DOME AFFAIR WAS ONLY ONE OF MANY SCANDALS THAT TARNISHED THE HARDING PRESIDENCY, AS THIS CARTOON SHOWS.

revealed that corruption and influence peddling were widespread.

Another scandal involved Thomas Miller, Harding's custodian of alien property. Miller had agreed to return American Metal Company bonds to German owners in return for a large bribe. The attorney involved in the transaction was John T. King, Republican national committee member, who received a fee of almost one-half million dollars in bonds. Fifty thousand dollars' worth of the bonds went to Miller. Two hundred thousand dollars' worth was deposited in an account managed by Attorney General Daugherty. Miller was finally tried and imprisoned, but two juries acquitted Daugherty in 1926.

The most notorious instance of corruption began in 1921, when Harding was persuaded by Secretary of the Interior Fall to transfer the naval oil reserves at Elk Hills, California, and Teapot Dome, Wyoming, to the Department of the Interior. After the transfer, Fall secretly leased drilling rights to private companies, one owned by Edward L. Doheny and the other by Harry Sinclair. In 1923 a Senate investigation showed that Doheny had "loaned" Fall $100,000 and that Sinclair had given him a herd of cattle, along with $330,000 in cash and bonds. Fall was convicted of bribery, fined, and sentenced to a year's imprisonment, the first cabinet officer to go to jail.

While Harding was not aware of the extent of the scandals, the betrayal of his so-called friends weighed heavily on him, and he felt oppressed by the burdens of his office. By mid-1923, even before the Teapot Dome scandal broke, he had grown disheartened and nervous. To take his mind off conditions in Washington, he traveled on a speaking tour through the Western states, only to learn of new disclosures of corruption. In Seattle he suffered an acute attack; one doctor diagnosed it as recurring indigestion, but others feared heart problems. On August 2, as his wife was reading to him in their San Francisco hotel room, Harding was seized by a sudden convulsion. Doctors could do nothing, and his subsequent death was attributed to a cerebral hemorrhage.

The Coolidge Administration

The new president, Calvin Coolidge, was a rural Yankee brought up to value the merits of hard work, frugality, and minding one's own business. The son of a Vermont storekeeper, he had worked his way through college and studied law in Northampton, Massachusetts, where he eventually entered politics. In time, he rose from city councilman to governor of the state. Twenty years after first winning public office, he finally achieved national prominence by ending the Boston police strike of 1919. This act prompted his nomination for the vice-presidency in 1920.

Shy, taciturn, and often awkward, Coolidge defied every stereotype of the successful politician. His dour expression led Alice Roosevelt Longworth, Theodore Roosevelt's daughter, to remark that Coolidge must have been "weaned on a dill pickle." However, conservative Republicans valued "Silent Cal's" shrewdness, integrity, and resistance to change. The press praised his diligence and caution, and the *Literary Digest* called him the "High Priest of Stability."

Although Coolidge chose not to meddle in most areas of the government, he did promise to cleanse it of corruption. To combat the Harding scandals, he selected two attorneys with reputations for absolute integrity to prosecute corrupt officeholders. His economic outlook was similar to Harding's. "The business of America is business," he declared. A man who revered wealth, Coolidge was awed by Andrew Mellon. In his first message to Congress he called for the continuation of conservative Republican domestic and foreign policies, Mellon's economic policies, and very limited aid for agriculture. He also reaffirmed the position that America should remain outside the League of Nations.

In general, Coolidge ignored the Congress, which only asserted itself on agricultural issues. However, he exercised executive power to veto every measure that conflicted with his own conservative philosophy. A firm believer in elitism, he relied on political appointments of business leaders to control the Republican party. Since the economy was healthy, he continued to rely on Mellon's policies, asserting that it was the responsibililty of the federal government to serve the interests of business.

The Election of 1924

By the time of the 1924 nominating convention, Coolidge had become a symbol of prosperity and had brought the Republican party machinery under control. He was nominated on the first ballot. A minority of Republicans, who dissented from the party's dominant conservative bloc, joined with some Democrats, farmers' groups, and Socialists to organize a new Progressive party. Attacking monopolies and promising reforms for farmers and laborers, they nominated the old Progressive, Robert La Follette.

The contest at the Democratic convention reflected the deep split between the party's rural Southern and urban Northern wings over prohibition and the Ku Klux Klan. William G. McAdoo, an ardent supporter of prohibition, and Alfred E. Smith, the Catholic governor of New York and an opponent of prohibition, battled for nine days, then withdrew when neither could win a two-thirds majority. Finally, on the one hundred third ballot the Democrats selected John W. Davis, a corporation lawyer of moderate views, as their candidate for president.

There was no real contest. Coolidge, with prosperity in his favor, polled 54 percent of the popular vote to Davis's 29 percent. He won in the electoral college with 382 votes to Davis's 136 and La Follette's 13.

An Era of Prosperity

The American economy reached maturity during the 1920s. Business groups, bankers, and agricultural producers were organized across the nation to accomplish more efficient planning and to increase profits. By the 1920s most important industries in the United States had become dominated by a few firms; therefore industrial planning involved coordinating the policies of only a handful of companies.

Finally, many small firms in the same line of business began to form voluntary trade associations which helped reduce unwelcome competition and made it easier for members to exchange information and to increase profits through cooperative planning.

The federal government was supportive of business, and the men who ran the new Federal

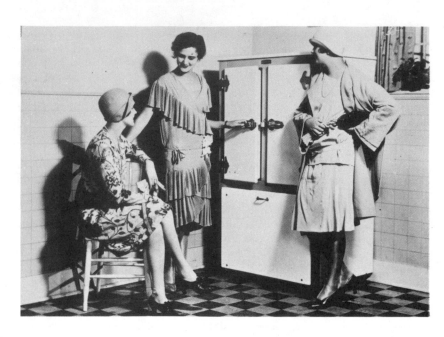

THE GROWING MARKET FOR CONSUMER GOODS DURING THE 1920s FOSTERED THE RISE OF ADVERTISING AS A BIG BUSINESS. SHOWN HERE, AN ADVERTISE-MENT FOR REFRIGERATORS.

Power Commission, the ICC, the FTC, and the Tariff Commission took the position that it was their duty to advise and aid business rather than to regulate it. Under Herbert Hoover, the most capable and creative thinker in the cabinet, the Commerce Department served as a clearinghouse for information, advising businesses on more efficient operating methods and on the standardization of their products. Hoover supported the voluntary-trade-association movement among small businesses, and his department sponsored conferences and issued statistical information useful to businesses.

Consumer's Paradise

With the end of the brief economic recession, the famous prosperity that marked the decade was under way. Between 1922 and 1929 the nation's industrial output doubled, and the productivity of labor rose 50 percent. These increases were aided by technological innovations in manufacturing and by improved mass-production techniques.

Except in the textile and coal industries, which remained depressed throughout the 1920s, unemployment became almost negligible. By 1928 real income, a measure of the dollar's buying power, was more than one-third higher than it had been

fourteen years earlier. With their wages higher than they had been before the war, workers were less eager to join labor unions. In turn, their increased purchasing power expanded the market for industrial products.

With more money in the consumer's pocket and more goods available, a mass market developed for durable goods and luxury items which workers had previously been unable to afford—refrigerators, washing machines, vacuum cleaners, cars, radios, and phonographs. Easy credit and installment-plan buying facilitated major purchases, including the purchase of homes. Nevertheless, by the end of the decade there were still many Americans—old people, farmers, seasonal workers, and minorities—who were excluded from the mainstream of free-spending consumers. Beneath the surface prosperity consumer purchasing power was not increasing sufficiently to meet the bloated volume of products entering the market.

One lasting phenomenon created by this mass market was the rise of the advertising industry. Since output was outstripping demand, businesses relied on carefully planned campaigns to foster the yearnings and illusions of the consumer. Advertising agencies helped make profitable businesses more profitable by convincing the American public that possession of the latest goods would transform their lives.

New Industries

Many new industries had been created or brought to maturity by the war. The use of airplanes in battle opened the door to an era of commercial aviation, which became a big business after Charles A. Lindbergh's successful flight across the Atlantic in May 1927. The handsome, clean-cut young flier was trying for the $25,000 prize offered for the first nonstop flight from New York to Paris. Equipped with five sandwiches and a quart of water, Lindbergh set out in a tiny monoplane, the *Spirit of St. Louis*, which could maintain an airspeed of just over one hundred miles an hour. Despite fog, ice, and a magnetic storm, he managed to cross two thousand unmarked miles of ocean and finally touched down in France 33½ hours after takeoff. Lindbergh was hailed as the greatest hero of the decade. A tumultuous welcome awaited him at home as well as abroad, and he was showered with awards from all over the world.

The war also gave impetus to the chemical industry. By 1929 the Allied Chemical, Union Carbide, and DuPont companies had outdistanced all foreign chemical firms in the production of new plastics and alloys. The use of new chemicals and the increased production of electricity revolutionized a number of other industries, including petroleum, steel, and the manufacture of electrical appliances. Electricity also increased the efficiency of the moving assembly line, which had become vital to mass production.

Although the radio industry had been founded in 1902 by the Italian inventor Guglielmo Marconi, it was not until the early 1920s that commercial production of radio sets for home use began. The sale of radio equipment skyrocketed from $10 million in 1921 to $411 million in 1929. The Westinghouse Company built America's first commercial broadcasting station, KDKA, in 1920 and began regular broadcasting on November 2, just in time to announce the Harding-Cox election returns. Shortly thereafter, nationwide broadcasting began with the establishment of the National Broadcasting Company in 1924 and the Columbia Broadcasting Company in 1927. In the belief that the airwaves should belong to the American people, Congress created the Federal Radio Commission in 1927 to control radio licenses and to set radio wave lengths and operating hours. The commercial and communication possibilities of radio were quickly recognized. As early as 1922 radio programming was subsidized by advertising from commercial sponsors. Hundreds of stations bombarded the public with slick slogans encouraging mass consumption, and by 1940 advertising was contributing almost $200 million to radio stations. Political parties were quick to take advantage of the new means for getting their message to the American people. In 1924 the national conventions of both parties were aired, and four years later stations across the country carried the campaign speeches of the presidential candidates.

The Automobile

Much of the decade's industrial growth was related to the automobile. Henry Ford and a few other innovators had begun to develop the automobile industry during the 1890s. By 1910 the number of companies had jumped to sixty-nine and the growing demand for cars dramatized the need for more efficient manufacturing techniques. In 1911 Ford opened an automobile plant in Highland Park, Michigan, which employed "systematized shop management," a term popularized by management expert Frederick W. Taylor. This system involved a continuous machine process in which raw materials entered a plant, went through numerous operations, and emerged as a finished product. Creating specialized tasks for workers and machines, Ford began turning out cars at an unheard-of rate.

Before Ford's Model T there was no sturdy, low-cost family car. By 1925, using assembly-line methods, Ford had brought the cost down to $260, a price within reach of the average American family. The "Tin Lizzie" was not an attractive or comfortable car, so competitors found a ready market for cars offering more glamour. From 1915 to 1929, automobile production increased fivefold and by 1929 some twenty-six million motor vehicles were registered across the nation. The industry was directly or indirectly responsible for employing over three million people.

General Motors, headed by William Durant, achieved prominence by catering to customers who demanded fashion and prestige. Nevertheless, Ford remained in first place for a long time and stub-

A MODEL-T ASSEMBLY LINE, 1913. THE BODY OF THE CAR IS DROPPED ONTO ITS CHASSIS.

bornly refused to change his basic model for the more attractive Model A until 1927. By that time he had sold fifteen million Model T's and the automobile had substantially altered economic and social life in the United States. As the auto industry grew, it brought prosperity to manufacturers of iron, steel, fabrics, glass, and tires. It created new businesses for sales and service. It was a major factor contributing to the growth of the oil industry, and its wages and profits became important financial supports for a building boom.

But the automobile had other unpredictable and far-reaching effects. Since urban workers could now live miles from their jobs, industry was able to expand into the suburbs. Wealthier families moved their permanent residences from the city to new suburban communities. Both these trends worked to deprive the cities of tax revenues. They also served to segregate Americans according to whether or not they had the economic means to relocate. An additional effect was that the quality of public transportation declined, restricting the mobility of those who remained in the city.

Land Development and Construction

The rapid growth of suburban areas was not accomplished without problems. As land developers exploited the demand for new homes they often looked more to immediate profit than to the future of either urban or suburban environments. Thus, much development was undertaken without adequate planning and careless buyers sometimes found that they had been cheated. The land boom reached a frenzied pitch in Florida where Northern buyers invested in thousands of acres of swamp and scrub, sight unseen. Many sites were located far inland or even underwater. However, some legitimate resort areas were developed, such as the famed Coral Gables, which was designed as a subtropical, middle-income Venice.

The prosperity of private construction was a key indicator of the nation's economic health during the 1920s. Houses, industrial buildings, and railroad facilities were built at a record rate. Road building was another indicator, as local, state, and federal budgets began to include enormous expenditures on paved roads to accommodate the rapidly increasing number of cars. Government spending on street and highway construction was a hidden subsidy, not only to the car industry, but to the entire economy as well. During the late 1920s, the slowdown in investments in road construction was an important symptom of weakness in the nation's economy.

Income Distribution

Despite overall prosperity, the strong tendency toward consolidation in industry contributed to a growing concentration of wealth in a few hands. Major firms, long aware of the value of administered, noncompetitive pricing, formed mergers to help control costs, prices, and output. By 1929, for example, over 25 percent of the nation's food, clothing, and general merchandise was being sold by chain stores. These chains bought on such a large scale that they could afford to undersell neighborhood stores, thus putting them out of business. One-half of all corporate wealth and 22 percent of all national wealth came to be owned by only two hundred corporations.

Uneven income distribution was caused by other factors as well. For example, stock dividends were increasing much more rapidly than wages. Although corporate leaders boasted that stocks were owned by a broad segment of the population, in fact, only one-third of one percent of the population received 78 percent of the dividends. Just before the crash of 1929, the combined income of one-tenth of one percent of the families at the top was equal to the combined income of 42 percent of the families at the bottom.

It was not only a matter of concentration of earnings but of concentration of savings. Only the well-to-do were able to put much aside. The richest 2.3 percent of families (those with incomes of $100,000 or more per year) held 66.6 percent of all personal savings, while those with incomes of under $2000 held only 1.6 percent. Corporations held 40 percent of the nation's total savings. Thus the great majority of Americans had no buffer against a possible economic downturn.

Agricultural Problems during the 1920s

The first two decades of the twentieth century had been prosperous ones for most farmers. By the 1920s, however, many were beginning to find their situation precarious. The war had created a large demand for foodstuffs, and farmers responded by increasing their output of various staples, including wheat, cotton, and livestock. Many went into debt in order to acquire additional land, livestock, and equipment, all purchased at inflated prices. After the war the European market contracted at almost the same time that wartime price supports were withdrawn. As demand decreased, prices fell, and farmers were left with huge crop surpluses and no way to pay their debts. The cotton market was depressed by the fashion for shorter dresses and by an increased use of rayon and silk fabrics. Staple farmers suffered so severely from costly mechanization, overproduction, and changing markets that from 1920 to 1925 they abandoned over thirteen million acres of farmland. In the course of the decade, the agricultural population dropped by three million people and there was a major migration to cities and towns. Almost half of the remaining farmers became tenants, and almost half of all landowners owned mortgaged property.

Farmers naturally struggled to improve their standard of living. Many again turned to organization to protect their interests by reactivating the Grange, forming the American Farm Bureau Federation, and reviving the Progressive party. In 1922, under pressure from the Farm Bloc, Congress exempted farm cooperatives from the antitrust laws. The following year it passed the Intermediate Credit Act, establishing twelve new farm banks which had the power to make short-term loans to producing and marketing cooperatives with farm produce as collateral. Although this act offered some assistance, it still did not solve the chronic problem of low prices for agricultural products. The tariff acts of 1921 and 1922, although designed to help farmers, were ineffective because the farmer's problem was due not to competition, but to a decline in the domestic market.

A new remedy was proposed by George N. Peek and General Hugh S. Johnson, both former administrators in the War Industries Board. They advocated a form of price supports for crops, whereby a government corporation would buy up surpluses at the fair-exchange value (based on farm income relative to the rest of the economy between 1910 and 1914). These surpluses would then be sold abroad at whatever price they would bring on the world market. To help make up for any loss, the government would charge American farmers an equalization fee on their entire crop. Although Congress passed the McNary-Haugen Bill twice, in 1927 and 1928, President Coolidge vetoed it both times on the grounds that it favored one interest group, sanctioned price fixing, and encouraged overproduction by not setting acreage restrictions.

Labor in the 1920s

During most of the 1920s the union movement suffered from unfavorable government policy. Because unionism was associated with radicalism, workers were threatened with federal injunctions or the use of federal troops if they tried to redress grievances by strikes or boycotts. Furthermore, federal courts consistently supported management's enforcement of "yellow dog" contracts which required workers to agree not to join a union.

Even so, workers did make some gains. In what has been characterized as welfare capitalism, many businesses adopted a more enlightened policy toward their workers in order to increase efficiency and morale. Aware that better pay helped keep workers from joining labor unions and expanded the market for consumer goods, management steadily increased wages, although wages never rose at the same rate as business profits. In addition, management reduced the number of working hours, offered paid vacations, provided recreation halls and cafeterias, and established more equitable hiring and firing procedures. Some businesses even encouraged workers to buy company stock and established company unions which elected representatives to confer with company officials. Of course, since these unions were under company control, their support by management depended on economic prosperity. They survived only as long as times were good.

The Jazz Age

The decade often called the Roaring Twenties was a paradoxical era. On the one hand, most people still accepted the same values that had served their forebears. They worked hard, raised families, attended church, paid their taxes, and obeyed the law. On the other hand, there was a tendency toward rebelliousness, pleasure seeking, and unrestrained individualism. The overall prosperity of the nation could not resolve the clash between old and new values nor the increasingly different outlooks of rural and urban communities.

Fundamentalism: The Scopes Trial

Most rural Americans, in particular, clung tenaciously to traditional social values and religious beliefs. Suspicious of any change, they were especially concerned about scientific discoveries and viewed modern science as the destroyer of Christian faith and moral standards. Sixty years after the publication of Darwin's *On the Origin of Species*, Protestant fundamentalists still rejected the idea of biological evolution and attacked those who taught it. In 1925 with the help of William Jennings Bryan, a devout fundamentalist, the Tennessee legislature outlawed the teaching of any theory of human

origins that contradicted a literal reading of the biblical account of creation. When the American Civil Liberties Union offered counsel to any Tennessee teacher who would test the law, John T. Scopes, a twenty-four-year-old high school teacher, agreed to lecture from Darwin's work in his classroom. Scopes was subsequently arrested, and in the famous "monkey trial" which ensued he was defended by the distinguished lawyer and skeptic, Clarence Darrow. The World Christian Fundamental Association retained Bryan for the prosecution. The trial reached its climax when Darrow pressed his examination of Bryan, who had taken the stand, and revealed his opponent's appalling ignorance of modern science. Shortly after the trial Bryan, now an old man, died of apoplexy brought on by strain and humiliation. Although Scopes was convicted and fined $100, the state supreme court later reversed the penalty on a technicality, thereby eliminating a conclusive test of the constitutionality of the law.

Changing Cultural Values

By the end of the decade less than 25 percent of the country's population lived on small farms, and the

DURING THE 1920s GREENWICH VILLAGE, THE CENTER FOR MANY ARTISTS AND BOHEMIANS, GAINED A REPUTATION FOR MORAL DECADENCE.

large metropolitan areas contained 48 percent of the population. Rapid urbanization and greater mobility had a profound impact on middle-class behavior and standards of conduct. Writer F. Scott Fitzgerald referred to this era, which witnessed the younger generation's rejection of long-accepted American values, as the jazz age.

Many young people saw themselves as survivors of a purposeless war to which they had been subjected by their elders. Their suspicion that the older generation had been wrong led them to question traditional social, sexual, and religious values. Rejecting the deprivation of the war years, they became increasingly preoccupied with material success and pleasure and with the physical comforts offered by the new mechanized, standardized, urban life-style.

This rebellious thinking was given further impetus by the psychoanalytical theory of Sigmund Freud. During the 1920s Freud became a popular prophet whose works were widely misquoted and seldom read firsthand. His new science of psychoanalysis fascinated a generation that was supremely self-absorbed. The application of psychoanalysis seemed to offer a way to resolve one's problems rather than having to learn to live with them. Freud's emphasis on unconscious motivation and the power of irrational impulses in directing behavior seemed to make sense of the war experience. And his assertion of the central importance of the sexual drive in human motivation was seized upon by young sophisticates eager to sample experiences that had formerly been restricted by social taboos. Going much farther than Freud, they advanced the notion that unlimited sexual freedom promoted mental health.

The urban environment also transformed the pattern of family living. In rural areas families tended to remain together, providing support, discipline, continuity, and a sense of belonging. In the city, on the other hand, families tended to be smaller, and the more impersonal environment weakened the bonds which held the family together. Divorces rose 50 percent between 1917 and 1922. Young people living in the city gained more social and sexual freedom, particularly the 12 percent who went to college.

Craze for Diversion

Prosperity created more leisure time, and the public craved diversion. Baseball and boxing, already popular, became national crazes, and for the first time mass journalism created national sports heroes such as the fabulous Babe Ruth who set a long-standing record of sixty home runs in a single season; heavyweight boxing champion, Jack Dempsey; and Gertrude Ederle, who swam the English Channel in 1926. Americans also took up golf and tennis and flocked to crowded beaches clad in scanty swimwear that shocked those with delicate sensibilities. When not attending sports events, the public enthusiastically pursued such amusements and fads as crossword puzzles, contract bridge, beauty contests, dance marathons, and flagpole sitting.

Every week millions of people of all ages lost themselves to the glamour and excitement of the silent screen. They delighted in identifying with the stereotyped demigods Hollywood offered: handsome Rudolph Valentino; saucy "It" girl, Clara Bow; comic genius Charlie Chaplin; and swashbuckling Douglas Fairbanks. Movies became big business, operating within set limits and formulas in which virtue always triumphed over evil, and vice—however alluring—was always punished. Then in 1927 Al Jolson's performance of *The Jazz Singer* became a sweeping success, and the era of talking pictures was born.

The number of city tabloids increased, satisfying a demand for sensational photographs, shocking crimes, and serialized comic strips. *Time*, first of the news magazines, caught the public's attention with its tough, telegraphic style. All these urban influences tended to standardize the country's thinking and behavior, displacing distinctive regional and ethnic traditions.

Flappers and Feminists

The smoking, drinking, rouged, and uncorseted flapper became the symbol of the decade's moral revolution. The combined product of the more relaxed moral climate of the early twentieth century and the prosperity of the 1920s, she aroused public fears that American society was in decline. Yet, the greater freedom symbolized by bobbed hair and short skirts, along with the revised standards of sexual behavior, were more superficial than actual changes for most women. Indeed, such surface changes only strengthened the persistent belief that although financial necessity might force women to work, their "natural" functions were those of wife and mother. A small band of feminists, who deplored the image of the new American woman as someone interested only in personal gratification, continued their fight for social justice. The Federation of Women's Clubs and the League of Women Voters formed the Women's Joint Congressional Committee to lobby for federal aid to maternal and health-care programs. Other organizations continued to press for legislation to protect working women. These efforts did not get far in the conservative atmosphere of the 1920s. Women themselves were divided over whether to support an equal rights amendment to the Constitution, for some believed such a provision would endanger legislation protecting women workers. By the end of the 1920s the women's movement had entered a period of decline.

Prohibition

Under pressure from the Women's Christian Temperance Union and the Anti-Saloon League, the drive against the consumption of alcoholic beverages gained momentum during the early twentieth century. Its proponents blamed strong drink for disease, crime, and broken homes. Support for prohibition was centered in rural America, and most state legislatures were controlled by representatives from farming districts. Consequently by 1916 two-thirds of the states had enacted prohibition laws. When the United States entered World War I, liquor was removed from the market as an economy measure. Temperance workers then demanded an amendment to the Constitution that would completely outlaw the use of hard liquor. Their

FLAPPERS RESIST ARREST FOR WEARING IMMODEST SWIMMING ATTIRE.

well-financed campaign paid off in 1919 with the enactment of the Eighteenth Amendment to the Constitution prohibiting the manufacture, transportation, and sale of alcoholic beverages. This article of legislation was one of rural America's last victories against the cities, and a shortlived triumph at best.

Nothing illustrates more clearly the tensions between urban and rural values than the difficulty encountered in enforcing the prohibition amendment. In October 1919, Congress overrode President Wilson's veto and passed the Volstead Act which outlawed the sale of all liquors containing more than one-half of one percent of alcohol. The enforcing agency, the Prohibition Bureau, was never given sufficient personnel, money, or supplies. In addition, its small force of agents was generally composed of third-rate political appointees who were

highly susceptible to bribery. In the end the act succeeded only in encouraging illegal traffic in alcohol. Public opinion, except in the rural South and Midwest, became increasingly hostile to the ban on liquor. Illegal whiskey was smuggled in from Canada and abroad, and only 5 percent of this contraband was intercepted by agents. In addition, thousands of domestic distillers produced foul-tasting, sometimes poisonous brew from industrial alcohol, moonshine stills, and home wine and cider makers. Prohibition encouraged the public to buy drinks at outrageous prices in private establishments. These "speakeasies" did business in every major city, frequently under the protection of corrupt local police. The result was a widespread contempt for the federal government, for the law was broken everywhere with the silent consent of public officials.

DURING PROHIBITION GOVERNMENT
AGENTS IZZY EINSTEIN (STOOPING) AND
MOE SMITH (RIGHT) CONFISCATED SOME
FIVE MILLION BOTTLES OF BOOZE AND
MADE NEARLY FIVE THOUSAND ARRESTS.

The enormous profits to be made from the illegal traffic in liquor sometimes brought city governments under the control of organized crime. While prohibition did not create organized crime, it provided the underworld with a profitable new market. In Chicago "Scarface" Al Capone established a multi-million dollar enterprise in whiskey, drugs, gambling, and prostitution. Backed by his private army of some one thousand gangsters, Capone was so powerful that not one conviction followed the 130 gang murders committed in Chicago between 1926 and 1927. To Capone this method of eliminating competition was merely good business. He once commented, "What's Al Capone done then? He's supplied a legitimate demand. Some call it bootlegging. Some call it racketeering. I call it a business. They say I violate the prohibition law. Who doesn't?"

Under President Hoover the Wickersham Commission was appointed to study the problems of enforcing prohibition. In 1931 the commission's report detailed the crime and corruption connected with the illegal liquor trade but recommended only that further efforts be made to enforce the ban.

Racial Problems

Another sign of tensions created by social change was the greater frequency of violent attacks on black Americans. The war had given some blacks a chance to break out of the rigid caste structure of the South. Many had served in the army, and others had been drawn to the urban centers of the North by the promise of better jobs. Although racism was less overt in the North, it was still present, and discrimination forced blacks to live in ghettos where they had to pay high rents for inferior housing. Often blacks were obliged to take low-paying jobs and to endure the hostility of white workers.

Educated by city experience, military service, and the "democratic ideal" preached in the war they had helped fight, blacks began to demand the rights long denied them, including higher wages, equal protection under the law, and equality of opportunity to vote and hold office. However, they made these demands at a time when racial fears were heightened among white Americans. Throughout the country white supremacists played on the fear of radicalism and communism in an attempt to prevent blacks from achieving their goals. In 1919 the North experienced the most severe race riots in its history. Among the worst were those in Washington, D.C., and in Chicago, where white mobs rampaged through black ghettos for thirteen days.

The Ku Klux Klan, long inactive, reemerged in Georgia in 1915. As during Reconstruction, it appealed to people's prejudices, racism, and fear. Its members claimed to be protecting America's pioneer heritage from the threat of blacks, radicals, Roman Catholics, Jews, and new immigrants. They struck at night dressed in disguise, using whippings, kidnappings, cross-burnings, arson, and homicide to terrorize entire communities. Composed of five million members at its peak, the Klan held the balance of political power in several Southern states and was very strong among the lower-middle class in small towns of the Midwest, Southwest, and Far West. In 1925 the Grand Dragon of Indiana was convicted of second-degree murder after a woman he had abducted and assaulted committed suicide. In subsequent years, the Klan's influence declined.

The NAACP continued to urge blacks to carry on the struggle for the passage of civil rights legislation. In 1919, along with other organizations, the NAACP began a campaign in support of the first antilynching bill. Although the House of Representatives passed such a measure, it was killed two years later by a Southern filibuster in the Senate.

A separatist organization for blacks was the Universal Negro Improvement Association. It was led by Marcus Garvey, and it claimed a membership of three million American blacks in 1922. Garvey, the son of a Jamaican peasant, encouraged blacks to return to Africa to establish a nation inhabited and governed by blacks. He succeeded in establishing a number of black businesses and he organized the largest mass movement of blacks that had ever existed. Nevertheless, his movement collapsed; most blacks simply were not interested in resettlement. Although Garvey had considerable appeal to many blacks, he alienated black leaders who were striving to create an integrated society, and the United States government considered him a radical.

Art and Rebellion

During the twenties American writers experienced bitter discontent. They were critical of the restrictiveness and intolerance of rural life and of the materialism and emptiness of popular urban culture. Sinclair Lewis spoke for these writers when he described the spiritual void characteristic of life in a small Midwestern town as "dullness made God."

An earlier generation of writers had responded to its perception of the deficiencies of American life with a spirit of reforming fervor, but writers in the twenties felt a sense of betrayal, disillusionment, and futility. They despised their culture less for its inequalities and injustice than for its smugness and the superficiality of its achievements. For the most part, they turned their backs on technological progress, economic prosperity, and aspiration for prestige. Their cynical view of politics was tersely expressed by drama critic George Jean Nathan: "I decline to pollute my mind with such obscenities." H. L. Mencken, editor and critic, contemptuously dismissed the notion of reform: "If I am convinced of anything," he remarked, "it is that doing good is in bad taste." Some writers fled to Europe, others to New York City's Greenwich Village, center of the nation's bohemian life.

Writers like F. Scott Fitzgerald and Ernest Hemingway created unforgettable images of the Jazz Age. In his first novel, *This Side of Paradise*, Fitzgerald portrayed the "sad young men" who had gone off to war with high ideals and come back painfully disillusioned. Shaken by the horrors of battle and repelled by the self-satisfaction of postwar American society, his characters were consumed with self-pity and engaged in a feverish search for pleasure. In his novels of the early thirties, particularly *Tender is the Night*, Fitzgerald looked back with regret on his own life and mourned the meaninglessness of the 1920s. In the collection of stories entitled *In Our Time* and in his novel *A Farewell to Arms*, Hemingway expressed the brutality of his own experience at the front, contrasting it with the idealization of war by the people back home.

Sinclair Lewis's *Main Street* and *Babbitt* were corrosive satires of small-town life in the Midwest.

BESSIE SMITH, ONE OF THE GREAT INTERPRETERS OF THE BLUES. THE BLUES, WITH ITS MELANCHOLY LYRICS OF LONELINESS AND LOST LOVE, WAS ONE OF THE FORERUNNERS OF JAZZ.

The characters in these novels were men and women whose lives revealed a blind craving for material success and a narrow, conventional morality. William Faulkner wrote of Southern life, describing a dying aristocracy, an ambitious and unprincipled middle class, and a lower class composed of poor blacks and whites alternating between resignation and violence.

The atmosphere of the 1920s deeply affected black writers and artists who congregated in the Harlem ghetto of New York City. They emphasized the contradiction between the national ideals of freedom and equality and the reality of black life. In what has been called the Harlem Renaissance, such writers and poets as James Welden Johnson (*Fifty Years and Other Poems*), Claude McKay, Langston Hughes, and Countee Cullen gave vivid expression to the black cultural experience.

Jazz, the popular music of the 1920s placed new emphasis on spontaneity, individualism, and sensuality. Free and uninhibited, jazz had sources deep in the experience of black life in America. Great jazz musicians, such as W. C. Handy, Joe "King" Oliver, "Jelly Roll" Morton, Bix Beiderbecke, and Louis Armstrong, made music that expressed their generation's disdain for convention and respectability. Although jazz was widely denounced as degenerate during its early years, it soon caught on, later finding its way into musical comedy and the works of classical composers such as George Gershwin. Eventually jazz was recognized all over the world as a distinctive contribution of black Americans to twentieth-century music.

The Election of 1928

Although he probably could have won the election of 1928, Coolidge announced, simply, "I do not choose to run." The Republicans then nominated Herbert Hoover on the first ballot and as a concession to the farmers gave the vice-presidential nomination to Senator Charles Curtis of Kansas. Hoover had neither the backing of farmers nor the enthusiastic support of professional politicians, who thought him too independent, but big business endorsed him without reservation. The Democrats nominated Alfred E. Smith for president on the first ballot and chose Senator Joseph T. Robinson of Arkansas as his running mate.

Hoover and Smith

The Republican and Democratic platforms did not seem to offer the voters much choice, although Hoover and Smith were strikingly different individuals. Hoover was a devout Quaker and a talented engineer, who was known for his expert management of the Commerce Department and his humanitarian administration of Belgian relief during World War I. He shared the view of the Progressives that government should rely on modern, scientific knowledge to assure efficient administration. His book *American Individualism* glorified enlightened capitalism. According to Hoover, the American economic system provided equal opportunity to all and rewarded each in proportion to merit. Hoover believed government should cooperate with business by preventing economic injustice without placing arbitrary restrictions on economic operations. He hoped that by limiting the power of the federal government and giving local governments more responsibility, political freedom and economic initiative would be protected.

During his campaign Hoover pledged to continue the high protective tariff, enforce the prohibition amendment, promote cooperative marketing as a method of controlling farm surpluses, and avoid affiliation with the League of Nations. He and his supporters pointed to the success of Republican policies in creating an unparalleled prosperity.

As governor of New York, Alfred E. Smith had a record for efficiency as impressive as Hoover's. He had reordered both the state's finances and the workings of its administration. He had promoted public health and recreation, workers' compensation, and civil liberties. His work for social legislation and his courageous stand against suppression of constitutional rights during the Red scare had damaged his standing with conservatives in his own party. During the campaign, however, Smith tempered his own liberalism in response to the mood of the times. He accepted the protective tariff, and even though he opposed prohibition and favored the control of liquor sales through state outlets, he went on record as opposing the return of the saloon. He even chose John J. Raskob, a Republican industrialist strongly identified with DuPont and General Motors, as his campaign manager. The Democratic platform was vague on farm relief and silent on the issue of American entry into the League.

Still, Smith was not a traditional presidential candidate. His nomination represented a breakthrough for urban forces that had been gathering momentum for several decades. The grandson of Irish immigrants, he was the first Roman Catholic to be nominated for the presidency by a national party. He had grown up on Manhattan's lower East Side and proudly identified himself with the city and its people. To many voters in villages and small towns, Smith epitomized the alien influences threatening rural America.

The Significance of the Election

The election was an impressive victory for Hoover, with Smith receiving only 87 electoral votes to Hoover's 444. Hoover received 58 percent of the popular vote compared to Smith's 41 percent. Economic prosperity was the decisive factor in the election. Hoover had only to point to the Republican record of business expansion and to the nation's high standard of living. Another important factor was anti-Catholic prejudice, which clearly drew many votes away from the Democrats. Nevertheless, a closer examination of the 1924 and 1928 election results reveals significant long-range political trends adverse to the Republican party. Smith had polled twice as many votes as John W. Davis, the Democratic presidential candidate in 1924. Former supporters of the Progressive party (many of whom had once been Republicans) had joined the Democrats, bringing the party additional strength that would prove significant in the years to come. This shift in loyalties helped reduce traditional Republican support from Western farmers. Even more impressive, Smith became the first Democratic candidate to carry Massachusetts as well as the twelve largest cities in the nation. He broke the Republican party's hold on the industrial centers, areas which the Republicans had carried handily in 1924. It was evident that many urban/ethnic voters, who had been alienated by Wilson's postwar diplomacy, were now solidly in the Democratic fold. The Democratic party was in the process of creating a base for a new majority coalition.

The Twenties Assessed

Despite the tensions between urban and rural America and the alienation of a small number of intellectuals, the spirit of the 1920s was generally one of confidence in the American way of life. The middle-class vision of progress had been confirmed by the economic well-being that characterized the decade and by the comforts made possible by many new inventions. If the pursuit of happiness was often viewed in material terms, it was still linked conceptually to the Jeffersonian ideals of freedom and the opportunity for hardworking individuals to better their position in life. Blinded by their inordinate admiration for the accomplishments of American business and its leaders, the majority of citizens were unaware of the serious flaws in America's economic and social system as a decade of prosperity drew to a close.

Readings

General Works

Allen, Frederick L., *Only Yesterday*. New York: Harper, 1931.

Baritz, Loren, *The Culture of the Twenties*. Indianapolis, Ind.: Bobbs-Merrill, 1970.

Braeman, John, *et al.* (Eds.), *Change and Continuity in Twentieth Century America: The 1920s*. Columbus: Ohio State University Press, 1968.

Burner, David, *The Politics of Provincialism: The Democratic Party in Transition, 1918–1932*. New York: Knopf, 1968.

Carter, Paul, *The Twenties in America*. New York: Crowell, 1968.

Faulkner, Harold, *From Versailles to the New Deal*. New York: U.S. Publishers' Association, 1963.

Furnas, J. C., *Great Times: Social History of the United States, 1914–1929*. New York: Putnam's, 1974.

Hicks, John D., *Republican Ascendency*. New York: Harper & Row, 1960.

Hoffman, Frederick J., *The Twenties*. New York: Viking, 1955.

Leuchtenburg, William E., *The Perils of Prosperity, 1914–1932*. Chicago: University of Chicago Press, 1958.

Preston, William, Jr., *Aliens and Dissenters: Federal Suppression of Radicals, 1903–1933*. New York: Harper & Row, 1963. (Paper)

Schlesinger, Arthur M., Jr., *The Crisis of the Old Order*. Boston: Houghton Mifflin, 1957.

Soule, George, *Prosperity Decade: From War to Depression*. New York: Harper & Row, 1968.

Wilson, Joan Hoff, *The Twenties: The Critical Issues*. Boston: Little, Brown, 1972.

Special Studies

Bernstein, Irving, *The Lean Years*. Boston: Houghton Mifflin, 1960.

Chafee, Zechariah, *Free Speech in the United States*. Cambridge, Mass.: Harvard University Press, 1941.

Chalmers, David M., *Hooded Americanism: The History of the KKK*. Garden City, N.Y.: Doubleday, 1965.

Clark, Norman H., *Deliver Us From Evil: An Interpretation of American Prohibition*. New York: Norton, 1976.

Ewen, Stuart, *Captains of Consciousness: Advertising and the Social Roots of the Consumer Culture*. New York: McGraw-Hill, 1976.

Fass, Paula S., *The Damned and the Beautiful: American Youth in the 1920s*. New York: Oxford University Press, 1977.

Furniss, Norman F., *The Fundamentalist Controversy, 1918–1931*. Hamden, Conn.: Shoestring, 1963.

Ginger, Ray, *Six Days or Forever?* Chicago: Quadrangle, 1969.

Huggins, Nathan, *Harlem Renaissance*. New York: Oxford University Press, 1971.

Kirschner, Don S., *City and Country: Rural Responses to Urbanization in the 1920s*. Westport, Conn.: Greenwood, 1970.

Lynd, Robert S., and Helen M. Lynd, *Middletown*. New York: Harcourt, Brace, 1929.

May, Henry, *The Discontent of the Intellectuals*. Chicago: Rand McNally, 1963.

Mowry, George (Ed.), *The Twenties: Fords, Flappers and Fanatics*. Englewood Cliffs, N.J.: Prentice-Hall, 1963.

Murray, Robert K., *The Harding Era*. Minneapolis: University of Minneapolis Press, 1969.

———, *The Politics of Normalcy: Government Theory and Practice in the Harding-Coolidge Era*. New York: Norton, 1973.

———, *The Red Scare*. Minneapolis: University of Minnesota Press, 1955.

Nielson, David Gordon, *Black Ethos: Northern Urban Negro Life and Thought, 1890–1930*. Westport, Conn.: Greenwood, 1977.

Noggle, Burl, *Into the Twenties: The United States from Armistice to Normalcy.* Urbana: University of Illinois Press, 1974.

Osofsky, Gilbert, *Harlem: The Making of a Ghetto.* New York: Harper & Row, 1966.

Silva, Ruth C., *Rum, Religion, and Votes: 1928 Reexamined.* University Park: Pennsylvania State University Press, 1962.

Sinclair, Andrew, *Prohibition: The Era of Excess.* Boston: Little, Brown, 1962.

Swain, D. C., *Federal Conservation Policy 1921–1933.* Berkeley: University of California Press, 1963.

Zieger, Robert H., *Republicans and Labor, 1919–1929.* Lexington: University Press of Kentucky, 1969.

Biographies

Best, Gary Dean, *The Politics of American Individualism: Herbert Hoover in Transition, 1918–1921.* Westport, Conn.: Greenwood, 1970.

Fox, Elton C., *Garvey: Story of a Pioneer Black Nationalist.* New York: Dodd, 1972.

Josephson, Matthew, and Hannah Josephson, *Al Smith: Hero of the Cities.* Boston: Houghton Mifflin, 1969.

McCoy, Donald R., *Calvin Coolidge: The Quiet President.* New York: Macmillan, 1967.

Nevins, Allan, and F. E. Hill, *Ford: The Times, The Man, The Company*, Vols. I–III. New York: Scribner's, 1954–1962.

Russell, Francis, *The Shadow of Blooming Grove.* New York: McGraw-Hill, 1968.

Primary Sources

Gatewood, Willard B., Jr. (Ed.), *Controversy in the Twenties: Fundamentalism, Modernism and Evolution.* Nashville, Tenn.: Vanderbilt University Press, 1969.

Leighton, Isabel (Ed.), *The Aspirin Age.* New York: Simon & Schuster, 1949.

Black Harlem

THE FIRST THIRTY YEARS

Folks, I come up North
Cause they told me de North was
fine. . . .
Been up here six months,
I'm about to lose my mind.
This mornin for breakfast
I chawed de mornin air. . . .
But this evenin' for supper,
I've got evenin' air to spare.[1]

Harlem is to black America what New York City is to the United States: an artistic, cultural, political, and intellectual center in which new movements are born and tested. In Harlem movements ranging from the Negro Renaissance to Black Nationalism have focused and flourished. Great black political, literary, and musical figures have gravitated to Harlem to find each other, develop their thinking, and expand their influences. Harlem has been a hub, a focal point of black culture in the urban North. It has reflected the achievements, dreams, horrors, and soul of ghetto America.

Now a dense urban community, Harlem was a sleepy rural shantytown just over a hundred years ago. Poor squatters had built an isolated village where most of the tiny shacks were constructed of barrels, tin cans hammered flat, and any other bits and pieces the inhabitants could find and use. But in the 1870s shanties, squatters, and goats were forced to make way for the construction of luxurious homes and apartment buildings. During the last thirty years of the nineteenth century, Harlem was to become a fashionable address for the rich and powerful.

[1] "Evenin' Air Blues" by Langston Hughes from *Shakespeare in Harlem.* Quoted in "The Literature of Harlem" by Ernest Kaiser in John Henrik Clarke (Ed.), *Harlem, A Community in Transition* (New York: The Citadel Press, 1964).

MARCUS GARVEY, 1922.

HARLEM CITIZENS MARCH TO PROTEST RACE RIOTS IN EAST ST. LOUIS, 1917.

The construction of subway routes to Harlem in the 1890s triggered a terrific wave of land speculation and development and Harlem was almost completely developed by 1904. New York land speculators and developers had gone wild in the late 1890s and early 1900s, anticipating that the new subway system would create fabulous real estate profits. Land had changed hands monthly and millions were made from the soaring prices. But land and housing prices had become inflated all out of proportion. The artificial boom in Harlem real estate led inevitably to a bust in 1904–1905.

Far too many houses and apartment buildings had been constructed. Overdevelopment and steep rents had resulted in a high vacancy rate. Faced with financial ruin, Harlem landlords

considered a desperate solution. It was a well established pattern that the only housing black Americans were ever offered was housing that white people had rejected. Inflated rents were also part of this pattern. Blacks had no control over housing—in fact, it was difficult for them to find any housing at all—and so they had no choice but to meet these high rents. Harlem landlords saw that rental to blacks was their only hope. Although there was a strong movement to keep blacks out of Harlem, the landlords' will to survive proved stronger.

Harlem was the first place in America where blacks had access to decent housing, and they rushed to fill whatever vacancies opened up. In response, whites began moving out in such numbers that by 1915 opposition

to black settlement there had ended. By 1917 Harlem was a predominantly black community and developed property could be bought for less than the value of the land alone. By 1920 nearly all of the major black institutions had moved from downtown New York City to Harlem.

Harlem quickly became the political and cultural capital for black people throughout the world. Though the community was poor and not without its problems, the 1920s were a uniquely vital and creative period in Harlem's history.

Black politics gained new focus, media, and momentum in Harlem during the 1920s. The community soon proved that it would be quick to respond—with marches, demonstrations, community action, and sometimes violence—to incidents of oppression against blacks. This responsiveness was due, in part, to the outdoor speakers who emerged in Harlem during the 1920s and who inspired many animated public discussions of political issues. Harlem's vigorous black press sprang up at the same time and black political leaders gravitated to the area.

In the early 1920s the political consciousness of black people reached a peak under the inspiration of Marcus Garvey. Garvey used Harlem as the base of a powerful international Africa for Africans campaign. He declared himself the provisional president of Africa and encouraged black Americans to "return" to Africa, where he envisioned the rebirth of a great civilization.

The value and meaning of Garvey's contribution is much debated to this day, but it is generally agreed that he did much to foster a sense of black identity. His charismatic, flamboyant personal style, romantic vision, and strong emphasis on black nationalism created a model for later popular black leaders such as Congressman Adam Clayton Powell and Black Muslim leader Malcom X. Garvey's movement helped broaden the popular base of future black national-

AMONG THE GREAT BLACK MUSICIANS TO EMERGE DURING THE JAZZ AGE WAS "DUKE" ELLINGTON, ONE OF THE TRULY ORIGINAL MUSICIANS OF THE TWENTIETH CENTURY. ELLINGTON'S BRILLIANT CAREER SPANNED ALMOST FIVE DECADES.
▼

ist movements—movements aimed, in one way or another, at achieving self-determination for black people.

Just as Garveyism was reaching its peak, there was a surge of black talent in literature and the arts. This movement, known as the Negro Renaissance, was also based in Harlem. In fact, it is often called the Harlem Renaissance. The Negro Renaissance was inspired by the publication of the *New Negro*, an anthology of essays, fiction, and poetry by or about Harlemites. With the publication of this book the largest black community in the world began to influence the wider American culture. Talented black writers such as Langston Hughes, Alain Locke, Countee Cullen, Claude McKay, and many others, suddenly came into the limelight. They addressed themselves to every aspect of the economic, social, and spiritual predicament of black Americans. They were also among the first black writers who succeeded in having their works published. The movement not only described, but gave impetus to the creation of the "new Negro"—a confident, self-defining human being. Never again would black Americans see themselves as whites saw them. They had found their own voice and their contribution to literature was enthusiastically hailed for its creativity and dynamic expression.

The 1920s were the beginning of a great musical era in Harlem, too. Jazz, which had been born and popularized in the South, found a home in Harlem, where it was developed into sophisticated, complex musical forms. Like black writers and political thinkers, black musicians gravitated to Harlem to collaborate on the development of new forms. From the late 1920s to the 1950s jazz greats such as Duke Ellington, Fats Waller, Count Basie, Charlie Parker, Miles Davis, John Coltrane, Dizzie Gillespie, Thelonius Monk, and Ornette Coleman met and grew in Harlem. Popular music had never before demanded such potency of expression on the part of each individual artist.

The 1930s marked the end of an era for Harlem. The intense poverty, suffering, and discouragement which the community experienced during the depression created a climate of apathy which the Negro Renaissance could not survive. Although Harlem has continued to produce writers, artists, and musicians of tremendous significance, the peak activity and glamor of the 1920s has never again been achieved.

By 1933 half of Harlem was unemployed and the other half was barely surviving. All the same, unskilled blacks continued to flock north from the American South, the Caribbean, and Central America, full of bright dreams and totally unprepared for the life which awaited them in Harlem and other Northern ghettos. Harlem's glaring problem was one which persists in the community to this day: white economic control of a non-white community. Harlem businesses, industries, housing, schools, health facilities, utilities, transportation, and entertainment facilities were white-owned, staffed, and controlled. In 1935 there were 2791 people working on 125th Street, Harlem's main shopping section, and only 13 were black.[2]

While these and other facts of ghetto life cut short the flowering of the 1920s, it would be a mistake to view black Harlem's first thirty years as a tale of glory and decline. The continuing traditions of urban black America are deeply rooted in the self-definition achieved in Harlem in the 1920s. The voice of a people who survived nearly 400 years of oppression was not to be silenced by new hardship. On the contrary, the 1920s have provided a source of continuing inspiration for urban black political and cultural movements. Present-day political figures, from community workers to militants, great modern writers such as Harlem-born James Baldwin, and accomplished musicians such as John Coltrane and Miles Davis owe a tremendous debt to the achievements of Harlem's earliest political and cultural leaders.

[2]Adam Clayton Powell, Jr., "Powell Says Men Can't Get Jobs," *New York Post*, March 27, 1935. Quoted in Allon Schoener, *Harlem on My Mind*, p. 136 (New York, Random House, 1968).

26 The Depression and the New Deal

We do not distrust the future of essential democracy. The people of the United States have not failed. In their need they have registered a mandate that they want direct, vigorous action. They have asked for discipline and direction under leadership. They have made me the present instrument of their wishes. In the spirit of the gift I take it.

Franklin D. Roosevelt
First Inaugural Address, March 4, 1933

Significant Events

Stock market crash [October 1929]

Hawley-Smoot Tariff [1930]

Reconstruction Finance Corporation [1932]

Emergency Banking Act [March 1933]

Civilian Conservation Corps [March 1933]

Agricultural Adjustment Act [May 1933]

Tennessee Valley Act [May 1933]

Silver Purchase Act [June 1933]

Federal Deposit Insurance Corporation [June 1933]

Glass-Steagall Banking Act [June 1933]

National Industrial Recovery Act [June 1933]

Gold Reserve Act [January 1934]

Securities and Exchange Act [June 1934]

Works Progress Administration [April 1935]

Public Utilities Holding Company Act [1935]

Wealth Tax Act [1935]

Social Security Act [1935]

Congress of Industrial Organizations formed [1937]

Agricultural Adjustment Act (second) [1938]

A VETERAN SELLS APPLES ON A CHICAGO STREET DURING THE GREAT DEPRESSION.

When Herbert Hoover entered the White House in 1929, the prevailing mood of the country was one of optimism, for during the twenties the United States had achieved an unparalleled standard of material well-being. The next four years were to be the climax of the "New Era" of prosperity and cooperation between government and business. But Hoover, although well prepared for the job in terms of experience, assumed office at the wrong time. Warning signals had already begun to appear, foreshadowing the worst economic disaster in the nation's history. Although the Great Depression crippled Europe as well as the United States, it was psychologically more disruptive to the American public because it was in such stark contrast to the pattern of continuous growth which had come before. The depression came about so rapidly that much of the country was plunged into a state of bewilderment and despair, and many began to question the soundness of American political and economic institutions.

The Beginning of the Great Depression

Efforts to Ease the Farm Problem

The 1920s had been marked by a steady decline in the prosperity of American farmers. Overproduction of agricultural products resulted in reduced prices which, in turn, caused a depression among large agricultural producers and further undermined the position of debt-ridden tenant farmers and sharecroppers. The farmers' reduced purchasing power contributed to the decline in the sale of manufactured goods, thus weakening the economy as a whole. As a result, Hoover, making good on a campaign promise, called a special session of Congress in 1929 to deal with the farm problem. At his request, Congress passed the Agricultural Marketing Act of June 1929. This measure created a Federal Farm Board with $500 million allocated for loans to farm cooperatives and for buying up farm surpluses. Although Hoover had agreed to permit the government to play a direct role in maintaining prices, he refused to support crop or acreage controls. Consequently, this innovative plan was only partially successful. Farmers increased production faster than surpluses could be purchased and shipped abroad. By 1932 the board had used up its resources, and prices had fallen anyway—in some cases as much as 50 to 75 percent. The government was left with a tremendous surplus of farm products and still no answer to the problem of overproduction.

The Hawley-Smoot Tariff Hoover also had promised to lend his authority to efforts to assist farmers through tariff legislation. During the special session of Congress he proposed a measure which would grant the president the authority to raise or lower tariff rates whenever advisable in order to protect domestic farm products and manufactured goods. Unfortunately, pressure from lobbyists resulted in a disastrous revision of his original proposal. The Hawley-Smoot Act of 1930 raised duties on a vast number of imports to over 55 percent, making it the highest protective tariff in peacetime history, but it did not give the president the authority he had desired. Exporters were appalled; and economists, who were concerned that the bill would encourage inefficiency at home and stifle world trade, petitioned Hoover to veto it. The president, after deliberation, responded to party pressure and accepted the bill.

The new tariff intensified the farm problem at home and contributed to the economic calamity that was spreading rapidly throughout the world. In the United States farmers had to pay higher prices for manufactured goods, and a number of industries which relied on export trade were forced to leave the country or go broke. In Europe the combination of the higher tariff and the earlier Fordney-McCumber Act further discouraged trade with the United States, which had declined precipitously throughout the 1920s, and prompted a number of countries to enact retaliatory tariffs.

The Downward Spiral

After World War I the United States had become the center of international finance. European governments were indebted to the United States for wartime loans. In order to pay reparations to the Allies, Germany had borrowed huge sums of money from America. In turn, Britain and France used the money Germany paid to them to pay their war debts to the United States. This income, along with a trade imbalance (resulting from the high American protective tariffs), led to an accumulation of gold in the United States.

The glut of capital in New York banking houses eventually led to rampant speculation in less stable industries. Yet despite rising stock prices, there were signs that all was not healthy in the economy. In addition to the weakness of American agriculture, boom industries, such as automobiles and steel, channeled the greater portion of their profits back into industrial expansion. Because too little money in the form of increased wages was returned to the workers, they became less able to purchase the growing volume of consumer goods. Eventually more goods were being produced than consumers were able to buy. As inventories filled manufacturers' warehouses, businesses closed down, workers were laid off, and the market for goods continued to shrink. Sensing that productivity was racing ahead of purchasing power, corporations and business leaders began decreasing those very investments that were vital to continued economic growth. Many businesspeople preferred to receive a smaller profit on high-priced goods in a diminishing market and to use these profits for stock-market speculation, rather than to reinvest in the production of more goods which could not be sold at current market prices.

The Coolidge administration was well aware of the rampant speculation sweeping the New York Stock Exchange but failed to take measures to control it. In fact, in 1927 the Federal Reserve Board contributed to the mania for speculation by lowering the interest rates to federal banks, thus making credit more easily obtainable. When the board later tried to retrench, it was too late to discourage the buying spree. "Buying on margin" became a popular form of investment for people with limited incomes. The buyer put up only part of the inflated price of the stocks priced above the earning power and productivity of the corporations they represented. Large commercial banks supplied much of the money to the brokerage houses which subsequently covered the balance needed to purchase the stock. Capital spent on stocks was, in effect, withdrawn from productive circulation in the economy. Thus, high market prices were a poor indicator of the nation's economic health.

The Wall Street Crash

When Herbert Hoover assumed the presidency he decided to act immediately to tighten credit. Although hesitant to ask Congress to intervene, he supported the Federal Reserve Board's warning against loans for speculation, and he approved the raise in the interest rate charged to member banks. The board's warnings were generally ignored, however, and speculation continued. Banks borrowed millions to cover their loans to speculators, investments continued to decline, and unemployment rose.

In September 1929 the stock market showed the first signs of instability. It fluctuated for over a month, and then on "Black Thursday," October 24, it plummeted disastrously. For a few days J. P. Morgan and a group of wealthy New York bankers stabilized the situation by purchasing stock, but their effort ultimately failed. On the following Tuesday, October 29, in an atmosphere of dread which hung over the New York Stock Exchange, more than sixteen million shares were dumped as the market fell forty points. Many people who had invested their life savings in securities faced financial ruin.

At first Hoover thought the crash would bring about a positive readjustment in the economy. He hoped the nation's two million investors would learn a lesson about the risks of speculation and begin putting their capital into more reliable enterprises. The problem was that a recession was already in progress before the crash occurred. Many people were in debt and did not have the money to reinvest. Overreacting to the crash, the Federal Reserve Board drastically cut back on all borrowing, thereby reducing the money supply and reinforcing the stagnation of the American economy. Many banks called in loans out of fear of bankruptcy when depositors demanded their money. Too often these deposits had been lent out and lost in stock speculation. The decline in purchasing power resulted in a further decline in production and in more unemployment which, in turn, produced even less purchasing power. As the downward spiral gathered momentum, panic swept the public. Secretary of the Treasury Mellon advised Hoover to let the situation readjust itself; however, although the market recovered briefly between January and June 1930, it turned down again.

CROWDS IN FRONT OF THE SUB-TREASURY BUILDING ON WALL STREET DURING THE STOCK MARKET CRASH OF 1929.

Hoover's Reaction While the crash itself did not cause the depression, the collapse of the stock market laid bare the weaknesses in the American economy and set the stage for the greatest depression of modern times. Hoover, believing the economic situation was merely a "crisis of confidence," issued a series of optimistic statements to rally public morale. At first he limited government action to a tax cut and conferences with prominent industrialists to whom he appealed for cooperative action in maintaining prices and wages and in employing as many workers as possible. He also called for the acceleration of public works programs, the lowering of interest rates to encourage business loans, and the expansion of local and state relief programs.

Although Hoover moved quickly to halt the decline, his policy of voluntary restraint on the part of the business community was short-lived. The depression gradualy overwhelmed many businesses, and by the fall of 1931 big companies which had tried to cooperate with the president were beginning to lay off workers. By 1932 approximately one-quarter of the working population was on relief. From 1929 to 1932 the national income dropped from $87 billion to $42 billion, and the liquidation of stocks and capital continued. Thousands of banks and small businesses failed.

Hoover's Relief Program

With conditions rapidly worsening, it soon became apparent that more concrete government policies were needed to restore economic stability. The president, however, believed that the depression had been brought about primarily by economic decline abroad rather than by domestic economic problems. Convinced that federal intervention might create a permanent dependence on the government and undermine local self-reliance, he hesitated to shift relief efforts away from state and local agencies. He also was apprehensive that large federal expenditures might result in budget deficits which would shake the confidence of businesses and encourage inflation. Nevertheless, it was clear that local agencies lacked sufficient resources to meet the needs of the destitute.

As late as 1932, New York City's poor were drawing a weekly support of $2.39, and Toledo, Ohio, could afford to give its poor only two cents a day for food. Black people and Mexican-Americans were among the hardest hit, for many local communities throughout the country offered even less relief money to minority groups than to white people.

Eventually Hoover was forced to supplement local relief efforts and boost employment through a program relying on an unprecedented degree of direct federal involvement. In 1930 he asked Congress to set up a standby fund of an additional $150 million to be allocated to public works projects. In the same year he created the Emergency Committee for Employment to help state and local governments with their public works programs. The committee was headed by Colonel Arthur Woods, who advocated federally assisted relief, such as slum clearance. But Hoover, firm in his belief that such programs should be run along established lines of local supervision, blocked many of Woods's suggestions. Woods finally resigned in 1931.

Although the congressional elections of 1930 left the Senate evenly divided between the parties, twelve progressive Republicans sided with the Democrats in calling for increased government action to deal with the crisis. The Democrats controlled the House, yet when the president offered a broadened legislative program in 1931, many of his proposals foundered. There was honest opposition to his proposals, but some politicians favored pork-barrel legislation over national welfare. In addition, some Democrats refused to support Hoover's program because they expected to win the upcoming election. The president's supporters charged them with thwarting legislation in order to capitalize on the popular notion that Hoover had not acted boldly in dealing with the country's hardships.

Most of the legislation enacted during Hoover's administration was aimed at aiding industries rather than individuals. Although critics charged that the new laws helped only those at the top of the economic pyramid, actually Hoover's proposals were broad. The Home Loan Bank Act of 1932 facilitated residential construction and decreased the number of foreclosures by creating special banks to extend emergency credit to people holding mortgages on private homes. Another measure passed by Congress was the Farm Loan Act which expanded the lending powers of the Federal Land Banks to extend more credit to farmers. The Glass-Steagall Act of February 1932 increased credit to those borrowing from the Federal Reserve System by diversifying the types of credit that could be used.

The most important creation of Hoover's administration was the Reconstruction Finance Corporation (RFC), formed in 1932 after bankers refused to make enough cash available to revive America's sinking industries. The RFC was essen-

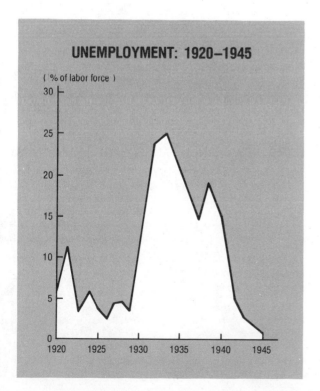

UNEMPLOYMENT: 1920–1945

(% of labor force)

tially a loan agency designed to serve banks, trust companies, railroads, insurance companies, and building and loan associations. Over a period of two decades, the agency loaned approximately $3 billion, backed by solid collateral, thereby alleviating the decline of businesses and forestalling many bankruptcies. Although the RFC was attacked for ignoring the farmers and the unemployed, without it the effects of the depression might have been worse.

The Social Impact of the Depression

As the depression deepened during the early 1930s, large segments of the population faced severe hardship, even starvation, and soup kitchens and breadlines were a common sight. Many tried to earn a pittance by shining shoes or selling apples from street corners. Families evicted from their homes gathered in ramshackle colonies called "Hoovervilles," where they erected shanties of wood, bits of corrugated iron, tarpaper, and packing boxes and cooked whatever they could scavenge over open fires. The public expressed its discontent with bitter humor, often with Hoover as its target. There was a rumor that when Babe Ruth refused to accept a salary cut of $10,000, a friend informed him that he was making more than the president. "So what?" Ruth retorted sharply, "I had a better season than he did."

Yet despite such desperate circumstances, outbursts of violence and social disorder were relatively few. There were occasional disturbances among farmers and workers. In Sioux City, Iowa, the Farmers' Holiday Association protested the low price of corn and wheat, which was not meeting the cost of production, and tried to stall mortgage foreclosures on farms until prices had time to rise. They picketed, punctured casks of milk, and blockaded railroad lines to keep produce from market, except in cases where food was en route to hospitals. They also gave away milk to the jobless. The movement was a failure, however, because the activities of the farmers' association were not sufficiently organized to produce positive results.

Veterans of World War I were another group that attempted to remedy their desperate situation. In 1932 some twenty thousand veterans staged a Bonus March, descending on the nation's capital to lobby the Congress to pass a bill that would give them their service bonuses before they fell due in 1945. When the Senate defeated the bill, the government offered the veterans their fares home. Unfortunately, many had no jobs to return to, and some five thousand took refuge near the Capitol in shanties and in deserted buildings. Their presence was a continual embarrassment to the Hoover administration and aroused the president's fear of social unrest. In July the police tried to remove some veterans from a building and a skirmish resulted. Hoover finally called in the army, and, although no shots were fired, two men were killed when troops, consisting of cavalry, infantry, six tanks, and a machine-gun squadron, attempted to disperse the crowd. Despite the lack of evidence, the administration charged that the Bonus Army was Communist-infiltrated and called the rest a "polyglot mob of tramps and hoodlums." Because of his ill-considered reaction, Hoover was assailed as a heartless leader who was willing to give big business what it wanted

AS THE DEPRESSION DEEPENED, FAMILIES SOUGHT REFUGE IN COLONIES OF RAMSHACKLE SHANTIES CALLED "HOOVERVILLES."

Federal Relief: Hoover's Position

"I should like to state to you the effect that . . . projection of government in business would have upon our system of self-government and our economic system. That effect would reach to the daily life of every man and woman. It would impair the very basis of liberty and freedom not only for those left outside the fold of expanded bureaucracy but for those embraced within it. . . .

I feel deeply on this subject because during the war I had some practical experience with governmental operation and control. I have witnessed not only at home but abroad the many failures of government in business. I have seen its tyrannies, its injustices, its destructions of self-government, its undermining of the very instincts which carry our people forward to progress. . . . I know the adoption of such methods would strike at the very roots of American life and would destroy the very basis of American progress."

Herbert Hoover, 1928

Federal Relief: The Position of the Unemployed

"In Washington Township there are more than 1,350 families on the county unemployed fund, and the heads of those families have been unemployed anywhere from eight months to more than a year. . . .

Our farmers have nothing. Our small merchants have gone bankrupt in trying to carry us. The banks have gone under, and there are only a few general stores.

I have heard the miners say, including myself, if it comes to the point where we must do it, we are going together and take over those general stores and take things we need to eat. We cannot let our families starve. Our country is practically broke. It has nothing to give us by way of relief. They have been giving some families as low as $8 whether the family consists of two or say, nine. . . . the children are the principal sufferers. I have known several cases where children collapsed in school, and that is the only time they would get relief from the county—when the child would collapse in school from hunger. . . ."

Joseph Rade, Fayette County, Pennsylvania, 1932

VETERANS GATHER ON THE STEPS OF THE CAPITOL BUILDING TO DEMAND LEGISLATION THAT WOULD AUTHORIZE EARLY PAYMENT OF THEIR SERVICE BONUSES.

but cared little for the average person suffering from the depression.

In many ways the depression years were stand-still years. While the indigent stood in breadlines or tried to find work as unskilled laborers, many middle-class Americans simply tightened their belts and waited for the economy to improve. Some independent businesspeople, such as grocers, druggists, and fuel dealers, were able to count on a small but steady income. A number of merchants whose businesses survived the early 1930s later took advantage of low prices and invested in real estate or stocks. As for the small percentage of the very rich—the least affected economic group—they continued to live in expensive houses, to wear the latest Paris fashions, and to winter in popular vacation spots in Florida and the Caribbean.

The traditional structure of the family was altered as poor relations moved in with more fortunate family members and as children were forced out of the house to work. Many couples postponed having children until better times, and the birthrate dropped dramatically. Most vulnerable were the elderly. With their life savings long since vanished, they faced their retirement years with uncertainty, worried about ill health and the likelihood of spending their last days in poverty.

Seeking relief from the pervasive atmosphere of gloom, Americans sought inexpensive leisure activities to help forget their problems. Card playing —especially contract bridge—monopoly, ping pong, and bingo all became immensely popular. Radio sets drew the nation together as people everywhere listened to broadcasts of popular tunes, big league games, and comedy shows. Those without jobs flocked to beaches, campsites, and parks. The trend toward individual sports, rather than family-oriented recreation, was illustrated by the public's enthusiasm for swimming, golf, and winter sports, particularly skiing and ice-skating.

The Failure of Good Intentions

Despite his genuine concern for the plight of America's needy and his sincere efforts to cope with the nation's economic crisis, Herbert Hoover was widely assailed for failing to take effective action. Convinced that the primary cause of the depression was economic decline abroad and that the federal government should limit its intervention, he concentrated instead on balancing the budget and restricting spending. His unshakeable belief that the American people could solve their problems through a cooperative community effort led him to assert that "Any organization by citizens for their own welfare is preferable to the same action by government." Yet, as the depression grew worse, his administration sponsored legislation that increased the federal government's role in the economy. Many historians agree that the RFC, the broadening of the powers of the Federal Reserve System, and the Agricultural Marketing Act anticipated the policies implemented during the first years of the New Deal.

Hoover himself contributed to the adverse reaction to his policies. Shy and stiff in public, he had no flair for dramatizing his program, and he reacted privately to criticism with resentment. Moreover, his admiration for experts and administrators and his dislike of politicians brought him into conflict with Congress. He had come to the presidency with humanitarian goals: to improve race relations, to advance prison reform and child welfare, to support women's rights, and to aid education. To his credit, he did succeed in redressing some long-standing abuses incurred by American Indians. Yet as historian David Burner pointed out, when Hoover left the White House, "No president . . . departed so caricatured as an enemy of the people since John Quincy Adams."

A "New Deal" for the American People

The Election of 1932

The delegates of the two major political parties came to their conventions in 1932 in completely different moods. The Democrats, confident that their time had come, drew up a platform which promised both a balanced budget and extensive new federal and state relief programs. On the fourth ballot they nominated as their presidential candidate Franklin D. Roosevelt, the governor of New York. Roosevelt called for "bold, persistent experimentation" and pledged himself to a "new deal for the American people." Although he defined his New Deal in only the vaguest terms, he promised a humanitarian program that would distribute the wealth of the nation more equitably and would build relief policies "from the bottom up not from the top down." Roosevelt's refusal to outline any specific plans prompted commentator Walter Lippman to write, "He is no enemy of entrenched privilege. He is a pleasant man who, without any important qualifications for the office, would very much like to be President."

The Republicans unenthusiastically nominated Hoover. The gloomy president warned Americans that Roosevelt's New Deal would be a dangerous departure from tradition, which would ruin the economy and put an end to political liberty.

The campaign of 1932 revolved primarily around economic issues. Since Roosevelt was not thoroughly versed in the intricacies of economics, he gathered around him a group of professorial advisers, dubbed the brain trust. This group helped Roosevelt with his campaign and, though its membership changed over the years, it continued to advise him during most of his presidency.

The election produced a Democratic landslide. FDR won by a margin of seven million popular votes and 472 to 59 in the electoral college, carrying all but six states. The Democrats swept the congressional elections as well. The depression brought about a significant shift in voting patterns. Many Northern blacks left the Republican fold and voted for Roosevelt. The Socialist and Communist parties gained new support, with Socialist candidate Norman Thomas polling almost nine hundred thousand votes and William Z. Foster, the Communist candidate, winning over one hundred thousand.

FDR Takes Office

Franklin D. Roosevelt shared with his distant cousin Theodore a conservative, wealthy, upper-class background. He completed his education at Harvard and Columbia Law School and a few years later joined a firm of New York lawyers. After serving in the New York Senate, Roosevelt was rewarded for his support of President Wilson in 1912 with an appointment as assistant secretary of the navy. Then in 1921, at the age of thirty-nine, he was stricken with infantile paralysis and paralyzed from the waist down. While battling courageously

against his illness, Roosevelt continued to strengthen his political contacts. In 1928 he was elected governor of New York where he established a record for creative reform by sponsoring programs for the unemployed.

Roosevelt's personal characteristics were an asset to his political career. Blessed with a genial, charming manner, he also possessed a keen understanding of human nature. Outgoing and self-confident, as well as shrewd and opportunistic, he was a pragmatic idealist who cared more about solving problems than about political theory. He got along well with congressional leaders, but at the same time knew when to apply pressure on them. As soon as he took office, FDR began to act decisively, and the White House was soon transformed into a dynamic center of ideas and experimental policies.

The Bank Crisis Before Roosevelt took office, he and Columbia University professor Raymond Moley, a central figure in the brain trust, met with

YOUNG FRANKLIN D. ROOSEVELT POSES WITH "BOBBIE" AT HIS HOME IN HYDE PARK, NEW YORK, JULY 1920.

Hoover to discuss the economy. Hoover wanted the president-elect to make a commitment to a balanced budget, an uninflated currency, and a scaling down of international debts owed to the United States. But Roosevelt refused to commit himself to a specific policy until he had taken up the reins of power. He disagreed with Hoover's analysis of the causes of the depression and his proposed remedies. Whatever the causes, in 1932 the economy was at its lowest point, and there was, as FDR said, an "unprecedented demand and need for undelayed action."

On the eve of Roosevelt's inauguration the nation's banking system was on the verge of total ruin. Controversy over whether the RFC was achieving the desired results had created a demand for a public airing of its records. However, when the names of RFC-supported banks were exposed, the agency's effectiveness was lost, for depositors began to make runs on the very banks the RFC had been designed to protect. Hoover blamed the crisis on the business community's fear of future Democratic policies, and, in fact, there may have been some truth to his charge: the uncertainty of Roosevelt's plans during the interim before he took office actually may have helped bring on the panic.

Government financial advisers expected a massive run on the banks and believed that the only way to prevent certain chaos was to declare a bank holiday for March 4. Neither Hoover nor Roosevelt was willing to take the responsibility, however. Finally on the evening of March 3 the governor of New York took action, ordering a two-day holiday for all New York banks. The governors of eighteen other states soon followed suit.

In his Inaugural Address, given on March 4, 1933, FDR spoke of his new vision, emphasizing creativity and achievement rather than the old "standard of success," material wealth. He blamed much of the economic crisis on the misconduct of incompetent business leaders and challenged his listeners to work to solve the depression, asserting that the nation had "nothing to fear but fear itself." Still, the precise details of Roosevelt's "new vision" remained unclear.

One thing was certain, however: Roosevelt believed in strong executive leadership and an active federal government. He claimed that the government's hands-off policy toward industrial concentration had become obsolete. The concentration of industrial power had destroyed the supply-and-demand cycle which was the foundation of a laissez-faire economic system. When modern corporations ceased to be competitive a free, competitive economy died. Roosevelt believed that concentrated business power had to be countered by increased federal regulation. Although the bank panic darkened his inauguration, President Roosevelt went right to work to stabilize the situation. He extended the bank holiday nationally and placed an embargo on gold exports. Then he called Congress into special session.

The "Hundred Days"

On March 9 Congress convened in a three-month session, during which it enacted a deluge of new legislation. In an atmosphere of crisis and improvisation bills were passed with unprecedented speed, and the session came to be known as the "Hundred Days." Roosevelt virtually had a free hand with Congress. The Emergency Banking Act, much of which had been drafted by the outgoing Hoover administration, was passed in a few hours. This bill approved Roosevelt's declaration of a bank holiday and permitted the RFC to provide necessary funds to banks. The measure was also intended to end hoarding by recalling all gold and gold certificates into the treasury. It provided for the inspection of banks and the reopening of those that were solvent and authorized "the twelve Federal Reserve banks to issue additional currency on good assets."

On March 12 Roosevelt gave his first "fireside chat" over the radio. The purpose of the talk was to explain the complex financial crisis to the American people and reassure them that the situation would soon improve. His methods of dealing with the emergency worked superbly. Within a short period of time, the banks were inspected and the majority declared solvent and reopened by March 15. Reversing his earlier opinion of Roosevelt, journalist Walter Lippmann declared, "In one week, the nation, which had lost confidence in everything and everybody, has regained confidence in the government and in itself."

The president next turned his attention to relief and reemployment and took steps to keep the budget balanced. The Economy Act of March 20 slashed salaries of government workers by 15 percent, slimmed down overgrown government agencies, and reduced veterans' pensions and allowances.

NEW YORKERS CELEBRATING THE REPEAL OF PROHIBITION IN 1933.

This last effort brought a new expedition of the Bonus Army to Washington, but this time the marchers were received hospitably, and the protest was defused.

Roosevelt also moved quickly to repeal prohibition in the hope of increasing government revenues through liquor taxes. Although the Twenty-First Amendment repealing prohibition was not passed until 1933, the President fulfilled a campaign promise on March 13 by asking Congress for immediate amendment of the Volstead Act to legalize light wines and beer. Such small attempts at economy had little effect in the wake of the extensive relief legislation that was enacted during the Hundred Days.

Going Off the Gold Standard The depression revived old silverite demands for inflation of the currency. Although Roosevelt did not advocate money inflation, he was determined to raise prices to ease the effects of the depression. On April 19 the United States abandoned the gold standard by ending all licenses for exporting gold, and in June Congress voided all contracts requiring payment in gold. As a result, the value of the dollar declined creating a rise in wholesale prices. At the same time, Roosevelt was concerned that the multination London Economic Conference then in session would produce a plan to stabilize international currencies by linking them to gold. Convinced that the distribution of wealth within the United States was more important than the theoretical value of the dollar compared to the pound or franc, he finally torpedoed the conference by withdrawing the American delegation.

Next, Roosevelt took action to devalue the dollar in hopes of maintaining its increased purchasing power and defusing the grumblings of farmers about low prices on agricultural produce. In June 1933 he reluctantly accepted the Silver Purchase Act which directed the Treasury to purchase silver until it reached one-third of the value of the federal government's huge gold reserves. This policy increased the money supply without causing excessive inflation. The administration also began buying gold at higher prices. In January 1934 the Gold Reserve Act formally took the country off the gold standard by abolishing gold coinage. The price of gold was set at $35 an ounce, with the effect of devaluing the dollar by about 40 percent. These measures had the support of leading bankers and in the long run aided the nation's economic recovery.

Protecting Public Investments While the Roosevelt administration was trying to increase the public's purchasing power, it was also concerned with protecting public investments. In June 1933 Congress established the Federal Deposit Insurance Corporation (FDIC) to guarantee individual bank accounts up to $2500 (by 1975, up to $40,000) and to reorganize insured banks that had failed. During the second phase of the New Deal the administration went further in its efforts to ensure sound banking practices. The Banking Act of 1935 reorganized the Federal Reserve System by creating a new Federal Reserve Board in Washington which would control the interest rate to member banks and the market operations of those banks. The government thus gained more authority over monetary policy.

Between 1932 and 1934 Senate investigations exposed extensive manipulations on the stock exchange. As a result, new legislation was passed to protect the public from fraud and misrepresentation in the sale of securities. All stocks for sale had to be listed with the Federal Trade Commission. The Securities Exchange Act of June 1934 set up a five-person Securities and Exchange Commission (SEC) to license stock exchanges, prevent pools and price manipulation, and require registration of securities listed on the exchange.

Aid to Farmers: The AAA The existence of a farm surplus was perhaps the greatest irony of the depression. Millions of urban dwellers were starving, yet farmers were impoverished because they produced more than they could sell. Voluntary crop reduction had not been successful because farmers feared they would be ruined if they did not compete for the existing market. Believing that overproduction was the most significant problem in the American economy, the administration set out to create a program that would curtail output in order to raise agricultural prices.

In the first few months of the New Deal there was a dispute over the type of program best suited to achieving this goal. Some, including small, poor farmers who disagreed with the policy of reducing production, advocated high prices at home and dumping the surplus abroad at cheaper world-market prices. Others, including Roosevelt's secretary of agriculture, Henry A. Wallace, advocated paying farmers to reduce production on the theory that planned scarcity would bring prices up. This plan was attractive to large farmers producing staple crops.

During the debate, agricultural discontent again erupted into violence. Small farmers, who had organized against foreclosures, nearly lynched an Iowa judge, and there were rumors of an agrarian revolt. The Farmers' Holiday Association threatened to strike unless the federal government offered direct aid to distressed farmers. The Farm Credit Act of 1933 gave them some relief by consolidating earlier farm boards and setting up an extensive system of loans for mortgages, production, marketing, and buying back property.

The more important Agricultural Adjustment Act (AAA) of May 1933 was essentially a variation of the Wallace plan and primarily aided large commercial farmers. The aim was to establish "parity," or price levels that would eventually restore the farmers' real purchasing power to its 1909–1914 level (years when farmers had earned a reasonably high fraction of the national income). Parity was to be achieved by buying and holding surpluses and by paying farmers to destroy excess crops and reduce their acreage under cultivation. The original list of farm produce covered by the act included cotton, wheat, corn, tobacco, rice, hogs, and milk, and it was later expanded. Farmers who agreed to reduce production were paid between $6 and $20 per nonproductive acre. Since money for the payments came from taxes on food processors, consumers ended up paying for the destruction of crops by buying food at higher prices.

The country's hog surplus was dealt with in a similar way. Hundreds of thousands of hogs were slaughtered, and some of the meat distributed to people on relief rolls. This approach, however, aroused public indignation. At a time when hunger was a serious national problem, it seemed absurd to destroy crop surpluses and animals merely to preserve the marketability of food. Leftists cited this as an example of capitalist madness. Yet over the next three years as production declined, farm income began to rise.

AAA policy was assisted by the widespread drought which struck the Plains states in 1934. Between 1933 and 1935 wheat output dropped by about 300 million bushels, and large numbers of livestock perished. When the Supreme Court ruled the AAA unconstitutional in 1936, the administration quickly persuaded Congress to pass the Soil

Conservation and Domestic Allotment Act which reimbursed farmers for diverting land from commercial crops to crops that would restore the soil's fertility. Although the dust-bowl tragedy and reduced crop acreages destroyed the livelihood of many sharecroppers and tenant farmers, agricultural income in general rose. By 1936 farm income had almost reached parity.

Industrial Planning: The NIRA

During World War I and throughout the 1920s, business and government had allied successfully to increase production. Some of Roosevelt's advisers thought a similar, government-directed alliance could help meet the new crisis. The administration was in general agreement that overproduction was the key problem of the depression and offered Congress a bill which proposed solving the problem by "organization of industry for the purpose of cooperative action among trade groups." The first part of the National Industrial Recovery Act, passed in June 1933, endeavored to stimulate industry while at the same time enhancing the position of labor. In return for exemption from antitrust laws, industries and trade associations were encouraged to cooperate in establishing codes of fair competition. These included quotas and prices that would take the public interest into account. The codes also would require common agreement on maximum hours and minimum wages for workers and an end to child labor. To further win the support of labor, Section 7a of the NIRA guaranteed workers the right to collective bargaining "free from restraint or coercion by employers." The codes were to include this provision as well.

Another section of the bill appropriated $3.3 billion for a Public Works Administration (PWA) that would put people to work building large public facilities such as dams, highways, post offices, courthouses, navy vessels, army camps, hospitals, schools, and parks.

In addition to the PWA, the NIRA established a second agency, the National Recovery Administration (NRA), which eventually set up a blanket code to which cooperating employers were to pledge themselves. Any industry or trade association which met the NRA's standards for fair competition and working conditions could display the NRA's symbol of compliance, the Blue Eagle. Under heavy pres-

sure from the NRA about 95 percent of industry ultimately became involved. The agency established codes providing for a thirty-five to forty-hour work week, a minimum wage of $.40 an hour, an end to child labor, and the right to collective bargaining between management and labor representatives under the supervision of a National Labor Board.

The NIRA's legacy was mixed. In theory it combined cooperation between government and business and national planning with industrial self-regulation, but in practice it increased the animosity between business and labor. Because the NIRA's antitrust provisions permitted industries to police themselves, the agency was accused of encouraging price fixing and the formation of monopolies. While the purpose of the NIRA was to increase purchasing power, administration appeals for moderate prices did not seem to work, and prices began to climb. Moreover, large corporations used various strategies to evade the collective-bargaining guarantees. Small businesses felt they were being victimized, for the National Labor Board, set up to mediate labor disputes, in practice showed little interest in collective bargaining. Union organizers, who had been encouraged by the passage of Section 7a, were enraged by corporate efforts to find loopholes and to prevent the organization of unions. Union members began calling the NRA the "National Run Around."

THE UBIQUITOUS BLUE EAGLE APPEARS ON THE BACKS OF SUN-BURNED HOLLYWOOD STARLETS. THE NRA, LAUNCHED WITH GREAT FANFARE IN MID-1933, PROVIDED JOBS, ESTABLISHED MINIMUM WAGES AND MAXIMUM HOURS FOR WORKERS, AND OUTLAWED CHILD LABOR DURING ITS BRIEF EXISTENCE.

Yet the NIRA did help stop deflation and it increased the nation's overall purchasing power. Moreover, it established the principle of government regulation of wages and hours, improved labor conditions, promoted labor's right to organize, and helped industry speed up production. Along with the AAA, it established the principle of government planning and intervention for the purpose of stimulating the national economy.

Relief and Conservation

The most popular actions of the first New Deal were those designed to give direct relief to people in need and to institute some federal ownership of public utilities. The Home Owners' Refinancing Act of 1933 established the Home Owners' Loan Corporation which saved more than one million families from eviction by refinancing home mortgages. The Federal Emergency Relief Act (FERA) of May 1933 provided extensive federal aid for state relief programs. It was a compromise between the old concept of local control and the need for federal revenue. By giving one dollar of federal money for every three raised by local funds, the FERA poured more than one-half billion dollars into local relief efforts.

More extensive than these acts were the Civilian Conservation Corps (CCC) and the Tennessee Valley Authority (TVA). Because the president was opposed to a dole, the CCC was created in 1933 to provide work for millions of jobless young people. From 1933 to 1942 young men between the ages of seventeen and twenty-five were hired on a temporary basis to work on forestry and park projects. They helped add over seventeen million acres of new forest to the American landscape. CCC employees also worked to prevent fires, control plant diseases and soil erosion, and improve fisheries and reservoirs. Although the program was not a major factor in reducing unemployment, FDR heralded it as a means of preserving the moral and physical fiber of the nation's youth.

The rescue and development of the seven-state Tennessee Valley area proved to be one of the New Deal's most successful efforts. During the First World War, a hydroelectric plant had been constructed on the Tennessee River at Muscle Shoals, Alabama. The facilities were run by the army, and during the 1920s Senator George W. Norris, who

wished to keep the operation under federal auspices, had sponsored a number of bills calling for government operation of the site. All of these bills had been vetoed by Republican presidents who would have preferred to turn the plant over to private interests. Roosevelt, however, believed the problems of the Tennessee Valley—including flooding, overcut forests, lack of electricity for many valley inhabitants, and poverty—should be targeted for a bold new experiment in social planning and conservation. He called upon Congress for the establishment of "a corporation clothed with the power of Government but possessed of the flexibility and initiative of a private enterprise," and in May 1933 the Tennessee Valley Authority was created.

The TVA was controversial because it was a long-range reform project, rather than a temporary relief measure. Under the TVA the government cleared the rivers, restocked the forests, and undertook flood control and the improvement of inland navigation. The board created by the act became involved in resettlement projects, industrial diversification, and the promotion of public health and cultural programs. In addition, the TVA built new dams on the Tennessee River and supplied electrical power at rates lower than those often charged by private utilities. Between 1934 and 1940 the number of Tennessee Valley farms receiving electricity more than quadrupled. Utility interests and conservative theorists denounced the TVA, calling it socialistic, unfair competition with private producers, and a violation of the Constitution. In 1936, however, in a test case, the Supreme Court ruled that the federal government had the right to build the dams under the war and commerce powers of the Constitution.

The TVA became one of the nation's largest utilities. It was unique in that it represented public control of a public utility, and it attempted regional planning that transcended state boundaries. Projects such as the Hoover Dam on the Colorado River and the Grand Coolee Dam on the Columbia River were completed at government expense. However, when Roosevelt proposed six similar projects in 1937, Congress refused to act.

The New Deal under Attack

Despite his earlier criticism of the "money changers," Roosevelt had been trying to halt the depression by the traditional methods of stimulating indus-

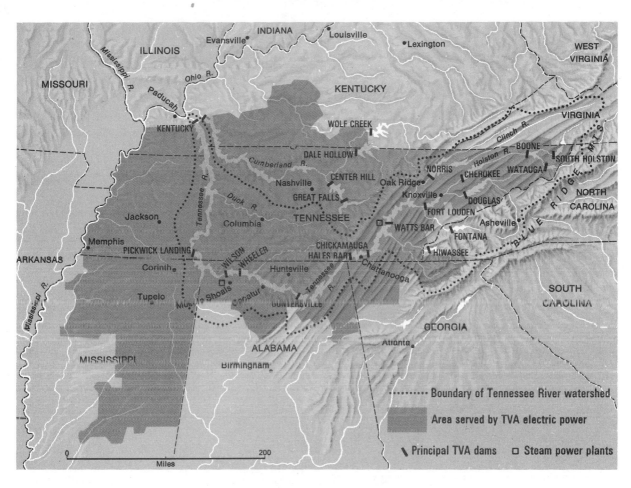

The map labels include:

INDIANA, Louisville, WEST VIRGINIA, Evansville, Lexington, ILLINOIS, Mississippi R., Ohio R., Paducah, KENTUCKY, MISSOURI, VIRGINIA, Clinch R., WOLF CREEK, KENTUCKY, Cumberland R., DALE HOLLOW, Holston R., BOONE, SOUTH HOLSTON, NORRIS, CHEROKEE, WATAUGA, CENTER HILL, Oak Ridge, NORTH CAROLINA, Nashville, Knoxville, DOUGLAS, GREAT FALLS, TENNESSEE, FORT LOUDEN, Jackson, Columbia, Asheville, WATTS BAR, Duck R., FONTANA, Memphis, PICKWICK LANDING, CHICKAMAUGA, HIWASSEE, ARKANSAS, Corinth, WILSON, WHEELER, HALES BAR, Tennessee R., Chattanooga, SOUTH CAROLINA, Huntsville, Tupelo, Mississippi R., Muscle Shoals, Decatur, GUNTERSVILLE, GEORGIA, ALABAMA, Birmingham, Atlanta, MISSISSIPPI, BLUE RIDGE MTS.

0 200
Miles

·········· Boundary of Tennessee River watershed
▮ Area served by TVA electric power
❭ Principal TVA dams   □ Steam power plants

The Tennessee Valley Authority • 1933 to 1945

try and creating public relief projects. For the most part he had relied on emergency legislation rather than on permanent reform measures. However, continued unemployment, increasing attacks on the New Deal by big business, the political threat from rising popular demagogic movements, and the Supreme Court's opposition to New Deal legislation led the president to search for more comprehensive methods of reform.

Business leaders and economic conservatives believed that the increasing number of federal agencies was turning the United States government into a bureaucratic maze and that centralization policies threatened the freedom of citizens to run their own lives. New York governor Al Smith, Roosevelt's ally in former years, eventually became one of the most bitter critics of the New Deal, labeling the many new federal agencies "alphabet soup." He joined with big-business leaders like DuPont in creating the American Liberty League which denounced Roosevelt's "radicalism." The president finally came to believe that the business community was myopic and that an alliance between government and big business was impossible. "I get more and more convinced that most of them can't see farther than the next dividend," he said privately.

Anti–New Deal Demagogues Among the most vocal critics of the New Deal were a number of demagogues whose schemes for getting the nation back on its feet led to mounting public unrest. Ironically, these individuals contributed to the New Deal by making the Roosevelt administration aware of the need for additional measures for relief and reform. Huey Long, who had forged a powerful dictatorial political machine in Louisiana, was one of the most notorious agitators. Under Long's authoritarian rule, Louisiana was modernized; hospitals, schools, and other public facilities were constructed. A combination Robin Hood and petty dictator, Long achieved national popularity with programs characterized by the slogans "Share the wealth" and "Soak the rich." He called for old-age pensions, free education, and a guaranteed annual minimum income of $5000 per family. Only his assassination in 1935 prevented a struggle with Roosevelt for control of the Democratic party, particularly its Southern wing. Roosevelt's reform legislation, though by no means simply a concession to Long, had the political value of defusing the threat of his popularity.

FATHER COUGHLIN, "THE RADIO PRIEST," HARANGUING THE DEMOCRATIC NATIONAL CONVENTION IN 1932.

Other American demagogues of the period supported programs with fascist overtones. Father Charles Coughlin, a Roman Catholic priest, spread his protofascist and racist ideas to some ten million radio listeners, earning the title "the radio priest." At first, Father Coughlin supported Roosevelt enthusiastically. By 1935, however, he was denouncing capitalism, the New Deal, Wall Street, Jews, and Communists as the causes of the depression. He was sympathetic to Italian fascism and favored the nationalization of industries and banks and the institution of a minimum wage. Like Huey Long, Coughlin had a large following among the lower-middle class.

Another challenger of New Deal policies was Dr. Francis E. Townsend, a retired physician who had lost his life savings. More benign and generous than either Long or Coughlin, Townsend proposed a pension plan granting all citizens over the age of sixty a monthly sum of $200—on condition that they spend the money within the month to keep the economy going. He established the Share-Our-Wealth Society, which received support from the elderly and those who were tired of competitive fervor and wanted more security. Although ridiculed at first, Townsend soon rallied millions of supporters. The resulting political pressure encouraged the passage of the Social Security Act in 1935.

Conservative Opposition: The Supreme Court New Deal measures such as the creation of the AAA and NIRA had helped large companies and improved the national economy. However, the Supreme Court, which was dominated by economic conservatives, began to overturn the legislation that had created these and some of the earlier New Deal programs. Most of the justices were opposed to the social philosophy of the New Deal and to the increase of federal powers at the expense of the states. The most important in a series of judgments, rendered in May 1935, was the case of *Schechter* v. *United States* (the so-called "sick-chicken" case) in which the Court overturned the NIRA. The Schechter brothers of Brooklyn had challenged the NRA's right to regulate the wages and hours of their employees and to prohibit the distribution of chickens allegedly diseased and unfit for consumption. The Court unanimously held that the establishment of a code of fair competition for the poultry industry constituted a regulation of agriculture, an area where the

Constitution left jurisdiction to the states. Furthermore the Court held that the NIRA was an improper delegation of legislative authority to the executive branch.

On the same day, the Court rebuked Roosevelt for illegally exercising his power of removal by dismissing a member of the Federal Trade Commission. Finally, the Court held that creditors had been unconstitutionally deprived of their property rights by the Frazier-Lemke Act of 1934, which had been designed to prevent foreclosures on farms.

Legislation of the Second New Deal

Evolution of the New Deal

The overall objectives of the New Deal were economic recovery, public relief, and social reform. During 1933 and 1934 (the first New Deal), planners had placed primary emphasis on the first two R's, recovery and relief. The federal government in cooperation with business and agriculture assumed responsibility for reducing overproduction through the regulation of supply and demand, an idea which ran counter to laissez-faire economics. Direct spending by the federal government to provide aid to those in desperate economic straits also increased.

With partial recovery under way, New Deal policies shifted toward firm opposition to concentrated business interests. Whereas federal planning had initially been used to aid and regulate business, during the second New Deal it was used to attack economic monopoly in an effort to restore equitable competition. In addition, social-welfare legislation was enacted, and government spending for public relief became an integral part of the economy. Such aid, which varied with the business cycle, was used to provide minimal economic security and became a substitute for reform of the American capitalist system.

The congressional elections of 1934 gave FDR the backing he needed. An even greater Democratic majority in Congress enacted new reform legislation—a second New Deal—that had a more extensive and more permanent effect than earlier legislation. The landmarks of the second New Deal were (1) permanent welfare legislation; (2) more effective guarantees of labor's right to collective bargaining; (3) heavier taxes on corporations and the wealthy; (4) further curbs on trusts and holding companies; (5) continued public projects; and (6) open acceptance of the policy of deficit spending.

The administration's original advisers, such as Raymond Moley and economist Rexford Tugwell, who had emphasized a working partnership with big business and agriculture, gradually disappeared from the Roosevelt inner circle. A new group came into prominence dedicated to reform of the capitalist system. Among its members were law professor Felix Frankfurter, professional social worker Harry Hopkins (who headed RFERA), and Chairman of the Federal Reserve Board Marriner Eccles. Eccles was chief advocate of a new policy which called for the deliberate creation of a deficit in the federal budget by the reduction of taxes and interest rates in order to stimulate public purchasing power and investments.

To a great extent the legislation of the second New Deal reflected the ideas of British economist John Maynard Keynes. Keynes's policies were designed to preserve economic freedom and at the same time eliminate the boom and bust of the business cycle. He believed that the way to achieve this was through carefully planned, flexible government intervention in the economy. When an economic crisis arose, government would increase spending and provide jobs until the crisis had passed. A number of Roosevelt's advisers, who saw the similarity between Keynesian economics and their own policies, embraced the philosophy after the fact.

The great legislative output of the second New Deal began in 1935. Congress appropriated $1.4 billion in April for the Works Progress Administration (later renamed the Works Projects Administration and known as the WPA), headed by Harry Hopkins. Hopkins believed WPA policy should emphasize providing relief with dignity through immediate employment. For the remainder of the decade the WPA employed millions of people on small-scale projects such as road building, flood-control dams, parks, playgrounds, schools, and libraries. The WPA provided many social services as well: adult-education classes, free lunches for children, and medical and dental clinics. A women's division created projects that put some five hundred thousand women to work. Sometimes accused of providing a haven for radicals, the WPA's most controversial activities involved projects in the arts which gave writers, photographers, theater groups, and others a chance to work. By 1941 the agency had spent about $11 billion on hundreds of thousands of projects.

Two other relief agencies were created in the same year. The Resettlement Administration aided tenant farmers, sharecroppers, and migrant laborers by extending credit to poor farm families and re-settling them on better land. It also sold farms on easy terms. Unfortunately, it was not as successful as had been hoped and remained in operation for only two years. The Rural Electrification Administration (REA) had a more far-reaching effect on farm life. It provided low-interest loans and relief labor to utility companies and farm cooperatives for spreading electrical power to farms not served by private utilities. By the 1930s nine out of ten American farms had electricity, mainly as a result of REA support.

Two additional acts passed in 1935 directly reflected the antimonopoly sentiment among Roosevelt's new advisers. The Public Utility Holding Company Act was a particularly important piece of legislation. It prohibited the formation of more than one holding company above the operating level for any public utility company. In the past there had been an instance of twenty-nine holding companies based on one operating company, an outrageous example of monopoly control. The Federal Power Commission was authorized to act as a watchdog over the rates, services, and financial operations of electric companies. The Wealth Tax Act, although watered down after a stiff debate in Congress, was an effort to tax the rich for social purposes. It included the graduated income tax, an excess-profits tax, and a higher estate tax. However, the act ultimately had no noticeable effect on the distribution of wealth in the country.

The Social Security Act signed by Roosevelt in 1935 was the landmark of his administration. It institutionalized government responsibility for the aged and jobless by providing a system of retirement pensions, unemployment insurance, and care for the dependent and disabled. The establishment of a federal pension fund required employers to match small deductions taken from their employees' wages. Federal and state contributions provided unemployment insurance. Over the years, the initial small benefits were extended, as were the categories of people covered. With this measure the government moved toward a position of permanent social welfare.

The Growth of Organized Labor

Soon after the Supreme Court killed the NRA, New Dealers produced new legislation to protect the unions. The National Labor Relations Act of 1935, or Wagner Act, ensured strong government protection of the exclusive right of labor unions to collective bargaining. It forbade management to interfere with the formation of unions, outlawed company unions, and created the National Labor Relations Board to hear complaints and issue cease-and-desist orders enforceable by federal courts. Many union organizers regarded the act as a turning point in the history of American labor.

Union membership grew rapidly during the 1930s, but not without conflicts within the labor movement itself. Up to then the AFL had dominated the movement, operating on the fundamental premises of trade and craft unionism. Under craft unionism, an industry was organized into as many unions as there were crafts involved in producing the product, rather than under a single union. As a result, large numbers of workers in the automobile, steel, and textile industries and on mass-production lines still had no union organization.

The Congress of Industrial Organizations A new labor movement seemed inevitable. In 1935 John L. Lewis, who believed in organizing by industry, not by craft, formed a rival labor federation, the Committee for Industrial Organization. The conservative leaders of the AFL opposed the new organization and in 1937 expelled all AFL members who had joined. Lewis's group then reorganized as the Congress of Industrial Organizations (CIO) and maintained a separate labor movement until 1955, when it merged with the AFL.

Lewis represented a leftward impulse in American unionism. The CIO attracted some Communist members and independent radicals who were seeking more sweeping changes than were being realized by the AFL and the New Deal. During the next few years, several unions left the AFL to join the CIO, and millions of previously unorganized workers, including many black Americans, became members. Some intellectuals and professionals, who preferred the industrial, mass-movement approach of the CIO, formed professional unions that were affiliated with it. During 1937 and 1938 a recession prompted Lewis to lead an unprecedented number of strikes in an effort to force giant corporations, particularly those in the automobile and steel industries, to recognize the union as a bargaining agent. A favorite tactic of CIO workers was the sit-down strike, in which they simply sat down and refused to work until they were granted the right of collective bargaining. The sit-down strike immobilized production and made it very difficult to hire strikebreakers. The United Automobile Workers (UAW) used the technique to win recognition from Chrysler and General Motors in 1937. However, Henry Ford fought the UAW with every means at his disposal, including the use of spies and hired thugs. He finally was forced to capitulate in 1941.

The steel industry suffered the worst labor crisis of the late 1930s. Less centralized than the automobile industry, steel was divided into two groups: "Big Steel," or United States Steel, and "Little Steel," such as Republic or Bethlehem. When United States Steel signed a contract with the Steel Workers' Organizing Committee in March 1937, Little Steel unexpectedly refused to follow suit. Bitter and violent strikes ensued. The police killed ten strikers outside Republic Steel's South Chicago plant. Despite reports claiming police brutality, a large segment of the public blamed the CIO's radical tactics for the violence. Little Steel did not sign any contracts with the union until 1941.

A PATROL WAGON STANDS READY AS VIOLENCE ERUPTS BETWEEN POLICE AND STRIKING STEEL WORKERS ON THE SOUTH CHICAGO FIELD, MAY 1937.

The End of the New Deal

The Election of 1936

Roosevelt's decisive moves in the second New Deal had created strong opposition among certain groups. The Republicans could now count on support from those who feared that big government would undermine individual freedom and who disliked higher taxes and labor unions. Launching a vast, well-funded attack, the Republicans worked to turn popular opinion against the New Deal by describing it in inflammatory terms as "a socialist state honeycombed with waste and extravagance and ruled by a dictatorship that mocks the rights of the States and the Liberty of the citizen." Most of the nation's newspapers supported this view.

Nevertheless, between 1934 and 1936 Roosevelt's policies had secured a new and formidable Democratic coalition. National income was up 50 percent, and substantial prosperity had returned even though eight million people were still unemployed. Having turned his back on big business, Roosevelt looked instead to the middle class and the underprivileged for support. He counted on widespread backing from organized labor, farmers, black Americans, young business and professional people, intellectuals, and urban groups of recent immigrant background. The CIO alone contributed $770,000 to the campaign. In addition, Roosevelt had the support of the Democratic political machines, backing not particularly to his taste, but politically essential.

The Republicans nominated Governor Alfred M. Landon of Kansas, in the hope that his Midwestern "folksy" aura would hold the farm vote. The Democrats renominated Roosevelt. Their platform countered Republican charges against big government by arguing that local governments were inadequate to meet the needs of a national crisis.

Roosevelt mounted a magnificent campaign. He toured the country, attracting record crowds wherever he went. Landon proved to be a disappointingly poor campaigner with little political glamour. Since he had the support of about 70 percent of the press, many people believed a straw poll predicting his victory. But after Huey Long's assassination in 1935, and with the popularity of the Socialist and Communist candidates diminished,

Roosevelt won every state except two. He had a margin of more than eleven million in the popular vote and won 523 to 8 in the electoral college. It was the greatest landslide in American history up to that time.

With the support of the new coalition, the Democrats were now the majority party for the first time since the mid-1890s. The realignment, which had begun along ethno-cultural lines during the late 1920s, was completed in 1936 along economic lines. Within the coalition the largest pro-Roosevelt group was the urban working class, many of whom were first- or second-generation Americans. In the nation's largest cities Democratic support among Roman Catholics and Jews rose 80 percent between 1932 and 1936. Black Americans, encouraged by the help they had received under the New Deal, had begun shifting their loyalty to the Democrats in 1932, and by 1936 the move was complete. The South, too, had benefited greatly from New Deal legislation and continued its traditional support of the Democratic party.

The party realignment on the whole reflected the outlook of a modern, urban, industrial society: a majority of Americans now believed that the nation's complex economy needed government direction to oversee its development. This new Democratic coalition lasted virtually unchanged until the 1970s.

Roosevelt Clashes with the Supreme Court

The sweeping victory of 1936 demonstrated Roosevelt's great popularity, but left the federal government deeply split ideologically. On one side was a reformist administration backed by tremendous popular approval; on the other side was the conservative Supreme Court.

The conservative majority in the federal judiciary seemed ready to overturn much of the major legislation passed during the second New Deal. The Court had continued to dismantle the legislation of the First New Deal when it overturned the AAA in 1936. In *United States* v. *Butler* it held that the government had improperly used its taxing power to regulate agriculture. The Court also declared a coal

ALL I SAID WAS "GIMME SIX MORE JUSTICES!"

ROOSEVELT'S ATTEMPT TO "PACK" THE SUPREME COURT LENT CREDENCE TO CHARGES THAT HIS AUTHORITY WAS DICTATORIAL.

conservation act unconstitutional and overruled a New York state minimum-wage law for women. Because of the Court's narrow interpretation of the Constitution, the future of laws such as the Social Security Act, the Wagner Act, and the Holding Company Act seemed uncertain.

In his Inaugural Address, FDR reminded the nation that poverty persisted despite a business upturn. "I see one-third of a nation ill-housed, ill-clad, and ill-nourished," he said. Hoping to complete the New Deal by correcting these conditions, he saw the Supreme Court as his only obstacle. Consequently, the first proposal of Roosevelt's new administration was not an article of welfare legislation, but a measure calculated to change the ideological complexion of the Court by forcing the older justices into retirement.

Of the nine justices on the Court in 1937, seven were Republican appointees. Four had consistently voted to restrict government regulation of business; three consistently supported it; and two "swing men" who had no consistent voting pattern often determined the majority ruling. Six were over

seventy years old. In order to change the Court's composition, Roosevelt proposed that each time a justice over seventy failed to retire, the president might appoint a new justice, allowing the Court to increase to as many as fifteen justices.

FDR's claim that it was necessary to increase the number of justices in order to ease the Court's workload and create more efficient administration was both clumsy and devious. By pretending his proposal was related to the problems of age and inefficiency, the president fooled no one but gave the appearance of trying to fool everyone. Moreover, he raised public fears that he was overstepping his Constitutional authority. Thus the Republicans' standard charge against him—that he was a would-be tyrant—in this case seemed to have some basis in fact. By the summer of 1937 public opinion had turned against the bill, and it died in the Senate Judiciary Committee, the only major defeat of Roosevelt's political career.

Ironically, the Supreme Court had been changing direction, thus inspiring the gibe "A switch in time saves nine." Although this reversal was in part

INTERPRETING AMERICAN HISTORY

THE NEW DEAL Given the innovative and sometimes conflicting features of the New Deal, it is not surprising that historians have viewed the 1930s from different perspectives. Roosevelt himself aroused intense feelings, and a discussion of the merits of the New Deal did not wait for the period to pass into history. FDR and his policies were debated widely throughout the 1930s.

Subsequently, liberal historians, such as Arthur Schlesinger, Jr., and Frank Freidel, writing in the last twenty-five years, have seen the New Deal as an extension of earlier conflicts between economic conservatives and economic liberals. It was a continuation of the struggle against monopoly and special interest. Arthur Schlesinger, Jr., in his multivolume *Age of Roosevelt* (1957–1960), discusses the New Deal as more than a response to the depression. It was a continuation of the liberal-conservative debate which had marked all of American history. It was a pragmatic and activist movement, which combined adherence to a modified capitalist system with personal freedom.

Other writers, however, have viewed the New Deal as an assault on individual freedom and competition. Following this line of attack are Edgar E. Robinson in *The Roosevelt Leadership* (1955) and John T. Flynn in *The Roosevelt Myth* (1956). These writers criticize New Deal legislation as the product of crisis planning which weakened the free-enterprise system. They also charge that state governments and Congress had been undermined by FDR's drive for personal power.

Richard Hofstadter in *The American Political Tradition* (1948) also sees the New Deal as a break with the past, but from a different perspective. He believes that past reform movements have been based on the concept that the government is solely a negative force, useful for destroying privilege. The New Deal, on the other hand, saw American society as needing changes that could be brought about only by positive federal action. New Dealers were interested in constructive government programs, not abstract moral positions. The New Deal, being piecemeal and nonideological, contained no rational government planning for the future.

Some neoconservative writers agree with Hofstadter that American history cannot be correctly interpreted on the basis of class conflict and ideological differences. Domestic struggles were

an effort to defeat Roosevelt's Court-packing plan, it was also a recognition by some justices that the judiciary could no longer block social change. In *NLRB* v. *Jones and Laughlin Corp.*, the Court upheld the constitutionality of the Wagner Labor Relations Act on the grounds that the government could regulate a manufacturing establishment if its products entered or affected interstate commerce. The Court also proved sympathetic to Social Security and minimum-wage legislation and gave the government a free hand in projects such as the TVA. In *West Coast Hotel* v. *Parrish*, a Washington state minimum-wage law was upheld as a valid use of the state police power.

Moreover, over the next few years retirements enabled Roosevelt to appoint new justices more to his liking. He appointed, among others, Hugo Black of Alabama, who had won recognition for his anti-trust activities; Felix Frankfurter, a Harvard professor and consultant on New Deal legislation; and William O. Douglas, a Yale law professor who had been chairman of the SEC. However, while the Supreme Court was beginning to sanction New Deal legislation, the New Deal itself was losing support. The fight with the Supreme Court marked a turning point in FDR's relationship with Congress. From then on the president was regarded with suspicion, and many of his proposals were defeated.

An Uncertain Legislative Program

Roosevelt's legislative program foundered after 1937. In that year a farm-tenancy law was passed, as was the first act ever passed by the federal government providing for low-income housing and slum clearance. But further legislative attempts over means, not ends. The New Deal was not a specific ideology, but rather a manifestation of the nation's attempt to solve its problems through politics instead of violence. And the New Deal proved America's institutions to be stable.

The 1960s brought new trends in interpreting the New Deal era. William E. Leuchtenberg advanced a partial synthesis of earlier views in *Franklin D. Roosevelt and the New Deal: 1932–1940* (1963). He sees the era as more than a period of improvisation. The New Dealers were practical administrators who believed that society could be improved by conscious, positive action. He calls it a "halfway revolution" that advanced justice for farmers, industrial workers, and ethnic groups. He admits, however, that sharecroppers, slum dwellers, and most blacks were not aided.

By the late 1960s, with the rediscovery of poverty in America, historians such as Barton Bernstein in *Towards a New Past* (1968) and Paul Conkin in *The New Deal* (1967) began stressing the limitations of New Deal reform. Bernstein argues that the Roosevelt administration could have done more to improve the inequitable distribution of income in the country, improve race relations, and even change the structure of power.

Conkin believes that given Roosevelt's intellectual limitations and the inertia of Congress, the Supreme Court, and the federal bureaucracy, it was impossible to accomplish more. As a result, the accomplishments of the New Deal were haphazard and small.

In one important rebuttal of these views Jerold Auerbach maintains that a majority of Americans received important benefits from the New Deal and did not want more radical solutions to economic problems ("New Deal, Old Deal, or Raw Deal: Some Thoughts on New Deal Historiography," *Journal of Southern History* XXXV, February 1969).

were blocked by a revival of conservatism in Congress. Many Southern Democrats disliked Roosevelt both for his statements against racism and for his expansion of federal legislative powers. Their alliance in Congress with the Northern Republicans reflected a changing national mood.

In 1937 the apparent economic recovery of 1935 and 1936 was suddenly checked by a recession. Roosevelt compounded the business slump by failing to continue his earlier economic policies. He reverted to trying to balance the budget and reduced welfare and reform expenditures by more than a billion dollars. Meanwhile, an increase in taxes, including those collected under the Social Security Act, resulted in the withdrawal of a substantial amount of money from circulation. Business confidence was low. The stock market declined again, and unemployment soared from six million to

ten million by 1938. Conditions were approaching those of the worst months of the early depression.

Indecision within the administration resulted in a debate over what course to follow. Conservatives, led by Secretary of the Treasury Henry Morgenthau, Jr., counseled Roosevelt against increasing government spending in order to end the economic decline. They argued that the business community, fearing deficit spending would lead to inflation and new taxes, had cut back their investments and production, thus bringing on the downturn in the economy. Harry Hopkins of the WPA and Marriner Eccles of the Federal Reserve, on the other hand, insisted that government reductions in spending had been the cause of the new decline. Only a resumption of deficit spending would reverse the trend.

Roosevelt resolved the debate by experimenting with both strategies. He waited to see if his budget-balancing policy would revive business confidence. When it did not, he quickly requested money from Congress for new public works projects. Within a year the recession had ended. Not until World War II, however, did genuine prosperity return.

The last New Deal legislation was passed in 1938. FDR finally secured a Fair Labor Standards Act, providing a minimum wage of $0.40 an hour and a forty-hour workweek. The act forbade employment of children under the age of sixteen and secured time-and-a-half overtime pay for union workers. In the same year, a new AAA continued the permanent soil-conservation program. It subsidized farmers who kept their production down to parity level and provided for removal of crop surpluses from the market and their storage by the government.

The New Deal ended with a broad antitrust campaign. Congress authorized a Temporary National Economic Committee which would exist for only three years. The committee's final report urged the strengthening of antitrust laws. Meanwhile, the Justice Department initiated antitrust suits in a drive against monopolies that continued until World War II.

New Political Coalitions

The Democrats suffered reversals in the congressional elections of 1938. Up to this time Roosevelt had worked with local and state Democratic politicians, regardless of their philosophical outlook, and had even strengthened some of the big-city bosses. Then he came up with an ill-considered plan to use his influence in local contests to eliminate conservative Democrats who opposed the New Deal. The plan was only partially successful because it overlooked the continuing commitment of Americans to the separation of national and state politics. When the elections were over, the Democrats still controlled Congress, but the Republicans had made important gains. Many of the conservative Democrats whom Roosevelt had opposed had been reelected. The conservative coalition of Northern Republicans and Southern Democrats continued to gain strength as the nation lost enthusiasm for the expansion of government bureaucracy and became increasingly disappointed over the New Deal's failure to create a drastic reduction in unemployment.

Women and Minorities in the 1930s

The 1930s brought few gains for American women. A few women were appointed to high government posts, and Eleanor Roosevelt became the most politically active First Lady in the nation's history. Nevertheless, in general, women's political power depended on their connections with influential men; they had no independent influence of their own. As in the past, working women were limited to domestic service, textile work, teaching, and nursing. If a woman went to work to enlarge a meager family income, her job was usually part-time, seasonal, or very much subject to layoffs. More women than men were out of work at the end of the 1930s, and women with college degrees had as much difficulty finding employment as those who were less skilled. Recent state and federal wage and hour legislation applied equally to men and women, and the new CIO recruited workers without regard to sex. Nevertheless, by 1939 many states still had no minimum-wage or maximum-hour laws and few women workers belonged to a union.

The New Deal had a mixed effect on the nation's minority groups. Millions of immigrant families were absorbed into the social structure, and some ethnic groups, such as Italians and Jews, began to exert more influence in public affairs. But black Americans made little progress. Blacks were helped by the WPA, PWA, and welfare agencies such as the CCC which provided temporary jobs. However, white liberals were primarily interested in aiding organized labor and curbing the power of business. Some New Deal programs, such as NRA, AAA, and TVA, even reinforced racial discrimination. Most New Dealers saw the problems of black Americans as problems faced by the lower class in general and not as problems resulting from discrimination. To make matters worse, blacks had little political strength because they lacked a united leadership and had not developed a cohesive organization.

Mexican-Americans, too, were hard-hit by the depression. Restrictions on European immigration in the 1920s had created a large demand for Mexican immigrants to work on farms in the Southwest and in industries in the big Northern cities. During the depression, however, Mexican workers were no longer welcome. Many who were destitute either returned to Mexico voluntarily or were deported. Those who stayed were often socially segregated; economically they barely subsisted and received only minimal relief from New Deal programs.

The Impact of Roosevelt and the New Deal

Like his illustrious cousin, Theodore, and like his fellow Democrat, Woodrow Wilson, Franklin Roosevelt used the presidency as a forum from which to lead and educate the American people. He brought the office of chief executive into the center of American politics after a decade of congressional dominance, a prestige which it maintained until the early 1970s. Unlike Wilson, however, Roosevelt was less an idealist motivated by high moral principles than a pragmatic politician with a strong social conscience. Although he lacked a consistent, long-range plan for refashioning the American capitalist system, he was sincerely concerned about the material well-being of the nation's citizens. If no one group could have all it wanted, then all groups deserved something from the New Deal.

Roosevelt's New Deal met the greatest economic upheaval in the nation's history with a combination of traditional and innovative policies. Much New Deal legislation had the stamp of traditional American optimism; it restored the country's faith in its ability to solve its own economic problems. It echoed the Jeffersonian idea of a government concerned with the welfare of *all* the people, the Jacksonian principle of providing every citizen the opportunity for economic betterment, and the Social Gospel's emphasis on action based on a concern for society. Economically, it carried on the Populist drive for monetary inflation and control of the stock market.

The New Deal drew heavily on precedents set by the Progressive movement and by the federal government's use of its emergency powers during World War I. Both Theodore Roosevelt's New Nationalism and the federal supervision of the economy that occurred during World War I were reflected in the first New Deal's conservation programs and its attempts to regulate big business and agriculture under the NRA and AAA. The second New Deal, characterized by FDR's support of labor and attempts to restore competition by breaking up monopolies, was closer to Wilson's New Freedom.

The New Deal did not bring full economic recovery to the nation. Moreover, the establishment of many new federal agencies increased government bureaucracy and subjected many formerly unregulated areas of American life to government control. No previous administration had ever accepted so much responsibility for meeting the daily needs of the people. Without trying to create a socialist society, as many critics charged, the New Deal superimposed a welfare state on top of a capitalist economic system.

Supporters of the New Deal claimed that only a strong federal government could protect the mass of the citizenry from exploitation by those with wealth and power. On the other hand, conservatives in both parties often opposed Roosevelt's policies on the grounds that they interfered with individual freedom and created economic dependence on the federal government. In fact, while the New Deal did not solve all of the nation's problems, it did boost the morale of a bewildered people. In establishing the principle that economic security for the country's citizens was the humanitarian responsibility of the national government, Roosevelt's program brought permanent changes to the American way of life.

Readings

General Works

Allswang, John M., *The New Deal and American Politics: A Study in Political Change.* New York: Wiley, 1978.

Conkin, Paul K., *The New Deal.* New York: Crowell, 1967. (Paper)

Degler, Carl N. (Ed.), *The New Deal.* New York: Watts, 1970. (Paper)

Fausold, Martin L., and George T. Mazuzan (Eds.), *The Hoover Presidency: A Reappraisal.* Albany: State University of New York Press, 1974.

Graham, Otis L., Jr., *An Encore for Reform*. New York: Oxford University Press, 1967.

Graham, Otis L., Jr. (Ed.), *The New Deal: The Critical Issues*. Boston: Little, Brown, 1971. (Paper)

Leuchtenburg, William E., *Franklin D. Roosevelt and the New Deal, 1932–1940*. New York: Harper & Row, 1963.

Rauch, Basil, *The History of the New Deal*. New York: Putnam, 1963.

Robinson, Edgar E., *The Roosevelt Leadership: 1932–1945*. Philadelphia: Lippincott, 1955.

Rothbard, Murray N., *America's Great Depression*. Freeport, N.Y.: Nash, 1973. (Paper)

Schlesinger, Arthur M., Jr., *The Age of Roosevelt*, Vols. I–III. Boston: Houghton Mifflin, 1957–1960.

Wolfskill, G., and J. A. Hudson, *All But the People: Franklin D. Roosevelt and his Critics*. New York: Macmillan, 1969.

Special Studies

Aaron, Daniel, *Writers on the Left*. New York: Avon, 1969.

Bernstein, Irving, *Turbulent Years: A History of the American Worker, 1933–1941*. Boston: Houghton Mifflin, 1971. (Paper)

Fusfeld, Daniel, *The Economic Thought of Franklin D. Roosevelt and the Origins of the New Deal*. New York: AMS Press, 1970.

Galbraith, John K., *The Great Crash*. Boston: Houghton Mifflin, 1965.

Hawley, Ellis W., *The New Deal and the Problem of Monopoly*. Princeton, N.J.: Princeton University Press, 1969.

Komisar, Lucy, *Down and Out in the USA: A History of Social Welfare*. New York: Watts, 1973. (Paper)

Lubove, Roy, *The Struggle for Social Security, 1900–35*. Cambridge, Mass.: Harvard University Press, 1968.

Moley, Raymond, *The First New Deal*. New York: Harcourt, Brace, 1966.

Patterson, James T., *Congressional Conservatism and the New Deal: The Growth of the Conservative Coalition in Congress, 1933–1939*. Lexington: University Press of Kentucky, 1967. (Paper)

Riesler, Mark, *By the Sweat of Their Brow: Mexican-American Labor in the United States, 1900–1940*. Westport, Conn.: Greenwood, 1976.

Romasco, Albert U., *The Poverty of Abundance: Hoover, the Nation, the Depression*. New York: Oxford University Press, 1965.

Schwarz, Jordan A., *Interregnum of Despair: Hoover's Congress and the Depression*. Urbana: University of Illinois Press, 1970.

Smith, Gene, *The Shattered Dream: Herbert Hoover and the Great Depression*. New York: Morrow, 1970.

Tugwell, Rexford G., *The Brain Trust*. New York: Viking Press, 1968. (Paper)

Witte, Edwin E., *The Development of the Social Security Act*. Madison: University of Wisconsin Press, 1962. (Paper)

Wolters, Raymond, *Negroes and the Great Depression: The Problem of Economic Recovery*. Stanley E. Kutler (Ed.). Westport, Conn.: Greenwood, 1970.

Primary Sources

Agee, James, and Walker Evans, *Let Us Now Praise Famous Men*. Boston: Houghton Mifflin, 1941.

Hoover, Herbert, *Memoirs: The Great Depression*. New York: Macmillan, 1915–1952.

Roosevelt, Eleanor, *This I Remember*. New York: Harper & Row, 1949.

Rosengarten, Theodore, *All God's Dangers: The Life of Nate Shaw*. New York: Knopf, 1974.

Terkel, Studs, *Hard Times*. New York: Avon, 1971. (Paper)

Biographies

Burner, David, *Herbert Hoover: The Public Life*. New York: Knopf, 1978.

Burns, James M., *Roosevelt: The Lion and the Fox*. New York: Harcourt, Brace, 1956.

Davis, Kenneth S., *FDR, The Beckoning of Destiny: 1882–1928, A History*. New York: Putnam's, 1972.

Freidel, Frank, *Franklin D. Roosevelt*, Vols. I–IV. Boston: Little, Brown, 1952–1956.

Williams, T. Harry, *Huey Long*. New York: Knopf, 1969.

Wilson, Joan Hoff, *Herbert Hoover: The Forgotten Progressive*. Boston: Little, Brown, 1975.

Fiction

Farrell, James T., *Studs Lonigan*. New York: Vanguard, 1935.

O'Connor, Edwin, *The Last Hurrah*. Boston: Little, Brown, 1956.

Steinbeck, John, *The Grapes of Wrath*. New York: Viking, 1939.

Warren, Robert Penn, *All The King's Men*. New York: Harcourt, Brace, 1946.

Wolfe, Thomas, *Of Time and the River*. New York: Scribner, 1935.

Wright, Richard, *Native Son*. New York: Harper & Row, 1969.

Babe Ruth and the Rise of National Sports

AS a nation changes so do its pastimes; indeed, sports and games tell us much about the values of a community's culture. A look at American sports magazines over the past seventy-five years reveals that the interests of American sports enthusiasts have undergone significant changes. Most striking has been the rapid growth of the sports industry during the twentieth century. It is ironic that the United States has become sports crazy when at one time in its history laws were on the books prohibiting all sports and other forms of "frivolous" entertainment.

For some two hundred and fifty years sports in America developed at a leisurely pace. America's first settlers regarded sports as an undesirable legacy handed down by the English gentry. However, as the proportion of non-Puritans in the colonies increased, a few public amusements began to appear. By the eighteenth century citizens in the more sophisticated cities of New York and Philadelphia were enjoying horse racing, bear baiting,

cock fighting, cricket, boat racing, and other contests measuring physical prowess. In the South, wealthy planters avidly pursued the sporting life and spent fortunes importing prize stock for horse racing, fox hunting, and the gamecock pits. But it was during the mid-1800s that the phenomenon of spectator sports began to come into its own. Thousands turned out for professional horse races, running events, and regattas. This surge of public interest was brought about by the growth of cities and by increased affluence and leisure time, both by-products of nineteenth-century industrialization.

Yet with the exception of horse racing there were no nationally organized sports and few team sports as we know them today. Basketball had not yet been invented. Football, founded at Yale early in the nineteenth century, was a crude version of soccer with few rules. Prize fighting was considered a brutal attraction for thugs and low-lifes and had been declared illegal in every state. Baseball, derived from the British game of rounders, was an amateur sport reserved for members of a few gentlemen's clubs. When the New York Knickerbockers challenged a team from the New York Club it was the first match ever played between two clubs. The game was played under the rules of the Knickerbocker Club's Game Book: the playing field was shaped like a diamond with bases spaced ninety feet apart, there were nine players on a team, and after three outs the opposing team came to bat. It seems doubtful that the participants could have foreseen that the game would become a national pastime and

that the New York rules would eventually be accepted throughout the nation. Baseball went commercial in the 1860s when towns began paying their players. By 1869 there were professional leagues, and the control of the sport had fallen into the hands of team owners, where to a great extent it remains to this day.

The extraordinary popularity of sports and its organization on a national scale between 1919 and 1930 was given impetus by the First World War. After the war, the public was tired of self-sacrifice and hungry for good times and entertainment. People took up golf and tennis, crowded the beaches in daring new swimwear, and flocked to tracks and stadiums to view their favorite events. This was the Golden Age of sports: an era of sports superstars, of outstanding performances and glittering prizes. Bobby Jones and Glenna Collett swept the major golf tournaments, poker-faced Helen Wills and dashing Bill Tilden dominated the tennis courts, the incomparable Man-O-War broke record after record on the race track, Jack Dempsey electrified boxing fans with his savage attacks, and Johnny Weissmuller garnered sixty-seven swimming records and defeated all rivals at any distance between fifty yards and a half-mile.

The athletes of the Golden Age had more than skill; they had color and personality, and there were talented sportswriters on hand to dramatize their achievements to a receptive audience. Leading these sports greats was an unbeatable showman who aroused frenzied adoration on the part of millions: the legendary "Sultan of Swat," Babe Ruth. It is difficult to realize the impact Ruth had in his time, partly because the significance of baseball in our culture has changed and partly because "the Babe" was a one-of-a-kind hero. With his natural athletic skill

and his flamboyant personality, he so dominated the world of baseball that his name has become synonymous with the game. And because baseball has long been regarded as America's national game, Ruth's stature assumes even greater symbolic significance.

Born in Baltimore in February 1895, George Herman Ruth was the son of a Maryland barkeeper. Before the age of ten he was exhibiting signs of delinquency and was placed in St. Mary's Industrial Training School where he learned to tailor shirts. At St. Mary's Ruth learned to play and to love baseball. One day Jack Dunn, owner of the Baltimore Orioles, spotted the talented young player in action and quickly signed him to a contract. After pitching a few games for Baltimore, the nineteen-year-old southpaw was sold to the Boston Red Sox, and for five years he was regarded as one of the best pitchers in the league. Before long, however, he developed his own batting style and began hitting the blistering home runs for which he became famous. His batting average was so sensational that in 1919 he was switched permanently to the outfield. About this time, the owner of the Red Sox decided to solve his financial problems by selling Ruth to the New York Yankees for a little over $100,000. Ruth's starting salary was $10,000 a year; by 1930 he was earning $80,000, an extraordinary sum during the depths of the Great Depression.

Babe Ruth transformed the game of baseball. Before he appeared on the scene, baseball had been considered a pitcher's game; with home runs an unusual occurrence, entire games were played for a single run. Between 1926 and 1931 the Babe averaged 50.3 home runs per year, setting distance records in almost every American League city. The crowds loved him. His popularity saved the game from the Black Sox scandal of 1919, and he brought base-

◄BABE RUTH SHOWS SOME YOUNG FANS HOW TO HOLD THE BAT.

ball to the level of the average citizen who could thrill at the sight of the Babe hammering another homer over the fence.

Like the decade itself, the New York Yankees in the 1920s were a wild, rowdy team, and Ruth outdid them all. His reputation for drinking, womanizing, and impulsive behavior became legendary. Possessed of a gargantuan appetite, he could gobble up dozens of hot dogs and down as many bottles of soda pop or brandy milk punches and still hit the ball. Journalist Jimmy Breslin recounts an incident when the Babe stormed into the barroom of the Bayside Golf Club in Queens and demanded one of his regular "heavens-to-Betsy drinks." The bartender proceeded to throw gin and ice into a big mixing glass which he then handed to Babe. Ruth said something about "how heavens-to-Betsy hot he was, and then he picked up the glass and opened his mouth, and there went everything. In one shot he swallowed the drink, the orange slice and the rest of the garbage, and the ice chunks too."*

As the years passed, Ruth settled down a little. In 1929 he married, and he and his wife had two daughters. But even living a quieter life he began to show signs of age. By 1933 his legs were failing him and his game was deteriorating. It had been his dream to become manager of the Yankees, but the club owner lacked confidence in his ability. Ruth requested and received an unconditional release and joined the Boston Braves as coach and outfielder in 1935. But the pace was too much for him and he retired a year later, returning only to play exhibition games. In later years, his health failing, Ruth worked to organize boys' baseball leagues. When he died of throat cancer

*James Breslin, *Can't Anybody Here Play This Game?* 1963, p. 19.

THE GLAMOUR AND SUCCESS OF INDIVIDUAL PLAYERS HELPED BASEBALL ATTAIN NEAR-MYTHICAL STATUS AS AMERICA'S NATIONAL GAME.

in August 1948, he left behind a lifetime record in baseball that has never been surpassed.

The Great Depression of the 1930s hurt many of the big team sports, particularly college football. Baseball, however, dominated by outstanding players like Babe Ruth, Lou Gehrig, and Joe DiMaggio, retained its status as America's number-one spectator sport. In 1932 the Winter Olympics at

Lake Placid started a new national craze—downhill skiing—and Sonja Henie, winner of three international gold medals, stirred the nation's interest in figure skating and ice shows. During the 1940s and 1950s popular participation in sports grew, as the construction of thousands of athletic fields, tennis courts, swimming pools, and playing grounds dramatically increased the opportunities for Americans to enjoy sports.

Educational institutions too, influenced the growth of sport by providing instruction in physical education. During World War I, physical examinations of draftees had revealed that as a nation Americans were physically unfit. As a result, gymnastic programs had gradually been transformed into full sports programs. This emphasis on health and physical fitness continued through World War II. After the war ended, regulatory agencies were set up to devise rules for interschool and intercollegiate competition, which had become increasingly popular. These regulations became crucial to amateur sports, especially college football, which entered the realm of big business.

The trend toward physical fitness and individual, participant sports continued into the 1970s; there was renewed interest in such activities as tennis, skiing, golf, sailing, camping, and most recently, running. In the area of spectator sports, the tempo increased to a point where many of the old games bore little resemblance to their modern counterparts. The demand for more violence, faster action, and higher and higher scores brought criticism from those who would prefer to see team sports played for skill, not thrills.

Clearly the broadcast media have had a tremendous impact on the sports explosion of recent decades. More Americans consume sports indirectly through the media than they do by either attending or participating in sports events. This has become especially true since the advent of television which, as some observers predicted, has diminished attendance levels at sports events. Although revenues lost at the gate have been more than compensated for by the sale of television rights to major games, television has gained enormous power over the sports industry because it is such a critical source of funds. Indeed the television industry now controls the very survival of certain games, including baseball. Perhaps it is true, as social commentator Marshall McLuhan has suggested, that those sports which lend themselves best to television have become the most popular, while those like baseball that do not televise well have lessened in popularity. Only a few years ago, Americans' perception of baseball as the national game was so strong that the baseball strike of 1972 was considered positively un-American and indicative of the decline of the nation.

Now football has replaced baseball as the public's favorite sport. Certainly it seems well-suited to the fast-paced, aggressive, competitive nature of contemporary American society.

From a cultural viewpoint it is worth noting that despite the influence of the media on the development of sports during this century, sports in themselves are a medium of communication, reflecting the values, tensions, and temperament of the societies in which they flourish. Will the current high interest in sports be sustained, and will the trend toward individual sports prevail? And what vision of a future America will be mirrored by the amusements of its citizens?

JOAN BENOIT, CAP ASKEW, CROSSES THE BOSTON MARATHON FINISH LINE IN THE RECORD TIME OF 2:35.15. LONT-DISTANCE RUNNING TYPIFIES THE TREND TOWARD PHYSICAL FITNESS AND INDIVIDUAL PARTICIPANT SPORTS WHICH BECAME INCREASINGLY POPULAR DURING THE 1970s.

27 From Isolation to Intervention

The experience of the past two years has proven beyond doubt that no nation can appease the Nazis. No man can tame a tiger into a kitten by stroking it. There can be no appeasement with ruthlessness. There can be no reasoning with an incendiary bomb. We know now that a nation can have peace with the Nazis only at the price of total surrender. . . .

I have the profound conviction that the American people are now determined to put forth a mightier effort than they have ever yet made to increase our production of all the implements of defense, to meet the threat to our democratic faith.

Franklin D. Roosevelt, 1940

Significant Events

Washington Naval Conference [1921–1922]

Kellogg-Briand Pact [1928]

Clark Memorandum to the Monroe Doctrine [1930]

Japanese invasion of Manchuria [1931]

United States recognizes Soviet Union [1933]

Reciprocal Trade Agreements Act [1934]

Platt Amendment abrogated [1934]

First Neutrality Act [1935]

Italy invades Ethiopia [1935]

Spanish Civil War [1936–1939]

Munich Agreement [1938]

Nazi-Soviet Pact [August 1939]

German invasion of Poland [September 1939]

German conquest of Holland, Belgium, and France [April–June 1940]

Battle of Britain [Summer–Fall 1940]

Lend Lease Act [March 1941]

Atlantic Charter [August 1941]

Japan attacks Pearl Harbor [December 7, 1941]

Philippines surrender to Japan [April 1942]

Battle of Coral Sea [May 1942]

Casablanca Conference [January 1943]

Allied forces invade Italy [September 1943]

Teheran Conference [November 1943]

Allied invasion of France [June 6, 1944]

Battle of the Bulge [December 1944]

Yalta Conference [February 1945]

Philippines retaken by United States forces [February 1945]

Germany surrenders [May 7, 1945]

Atomic bomb dropped on Hiroshima and Nagasaki [August 1945]

Japan surrenders [August 14, 1945]

FRENCH PEOPLE WEEP ON HEARING THE NEWS OF THEIR NATION'S DEFEAT BY THE NAZIS IN 1940.

In the first years after World War I the United States returned to its traditional isolationism. The American people had been stirred by Woodrow Wilson's dream of a new world order, but when that dream collapsed, they responded by turning inward. Yet it was not long before the American government began once again to play an important role on the world stage. In order to ensure the nation's security, the government actively promoted the peaceful settlement of international disputes. Treaties, conferences, and disarmament were the components of a policy that has been characterized as "independent internationalism." In the end, however, this approach to world affairs did not prevent American involvement in another world war.

Independent Internationalism

America and the World Court

Warren G. Harding interpreted his landslide victory in 1920 as a public repudiation of American membership in the League of Nations. At first Harding actually shut off all communication with the League, but eventually the American government sent unofficial observers to League meetings on issues that would not involve the United States in any commitments.

Membership in the World Court was another matter. Though it was joined to the League, its planners had specified that nations outside the League could participate in the Court on an equal basis. The role of the Court was to hear disputes involving international law and to present its decisions to the League. As it had no real power, the Court was more in tune with the American policy of independent internationalism than was the League of Nations. In 1923 at the urging of Secretary of State Charles Evans Hughes, Harding proposed American membership in the World Court to the Senate. To make his proposal more attractive to the conservative-dominated body he attached several qualifiers designed to ensure that the United States would maintain absolute control of its own affairs and to make it clear that American membership in the Court would not imply any commitment to the League. Even so, the Senate was extremely reluctant to act and only consented to apply for membership in 1926. The World Court, however, refused to accept the American demand that it never consider any question "in which the United States has an interest or claim" without the consent of the United States government. As a result, the nation did not join, and when Franklin Roosevelt tried to prod the Senate into approving membership in 1935 it narrowly defeated the proposal.

Efforts at Disarmament

During the war the United States, Japan, and Great Britain all had set in motion massive programs to build up their naval strength and in the early 1920s construction of warships by the three powers was proceeding apace. While naval rivalry with Great Britain concerned some Americans, Japan appeared to pose a more particular threat. With seventy-two thousand troops remaining in eastern Siberia, and with a foothold on the Shantung peninsula in China as well as in the German Pacific islands, it seemed clear that Japan would soon be in an ideal position to pursue further its expansionist aims. At the same time, two movements in the United States conflicted with a program of naval expansion: a strong desire to reduce taxes by cutting government expenses, and numerous proposals to bring about a limitation of armaments. Fortunately for the United States, both the British and the Japanese governments indicated a willingness to reduce naval building in order to cut expenses; and Great Britain was even willing to discuss modifications of its alliance with Japan (1901) to allay American fears of a possible military conflict with Britain if America and Japan should ever go to war.

The Washington Conference   Seizing the initiative, the Harding administration called for an international conference in Washington, D.C., toward the end of 1921 at which the United States made a dramatic unilateral move to stimulate disarmament. Secretary Hughes stunned the delegates by proposing an end to construction of big warships for ten years and offering to reduce the American navy by destroying thirty American battleships—provided that Britain and Japan would destroy thirty-six of theirs.

THE FIRST PHOTO TAKEN OF THE OFFICIAL UNITED STATES DELEGATES TO THE 1921 DISARMAMENT CONFERENCE HELD IN WASHINGTON, D.C. LEFT TO RIGHT: ELIHU ROOT, OSCAR UNDERWOOD, CHARLES EVANS HUGHES, HENRY CABOT LODGE, AND BASIL MILES.

To a war-weary world these proposals seemed bold and imaginative. Americans, Europeans, and Asians alike hailed the plan they hoped would ensure the peace. But negotiations were complex since the United States would not go through with its plan without abrogation of the Anglo-Japanese Alliance.

Accordingly, a Four-Power Treaty between Britain, Japan, the United States, and France was substituted for the Anglo-Japanese Alliance in December 1921. Under its terms the four nations agreed to respect each other's rights in the Pacific and to consult with each other if those rights were threatened by another power. This agreement cleared the way for specific limitations on shipbuilding established in the Five-Power Treaty, signed in February 1922. Joined by Italy, the countries now agreed to a ten-year moritorium on the building of large ships and to limit the number of heavy warships (such as battleships and aircraft carriers) to a ratio of 5:5:3 between the United States, Britain, and Japan and a ratio of 1.75:1.75 between France and Italy. Japan only accepted a smaller ratio than the United States and Great Britain when America agreed not to fortify its Pacific islands except Hawaii. The Nine-Power Treaty, signed the same day with four other nations (Belgium, Portugal, the Netherlands, and China), seemed to stabilize further the balance of power in Asia by eliciting solemn promises from all signatories to respect the Open Door policy in China. In addition, Secretary Hughes succeeded in extracting a pledge from the Japanese to withdraw their forces from eastern Siberia and leave the Shantung peninsula. Japan did, however, maintain economic control of the province.

These agreements created great optimism about the future of international peace. But their long-range significance in preventing aggression was limited. The right-wing military faction in Japan, already challenging the legitimacy of the liberal government in power, resented the fact that the agreements gave Japan fewer heavy warships than the United States and Great Britain. The Japanese never allowed the agreements to prevent them from rearming their home islands. The United States had voluntarily abdicated its potential superiority and only began to build up to the strength permitted by the Washington Conference in the mid-1930s.

Finally, the fact that the Washington Conference had achieved only partial disarmament left the door open for a different kind of naval buildup. Barred from the production of heavy warships, the major nations entered into an arms race involving lighter craft, including destroyers, cruisers, and submarines. Responding to this development, the United States participated in a number of conferences during the 1920s aimed at ending the worldwide arms race. In 1930 representatives of the United States, Great Britain, and Japan met in London and agreed to set limits on the lighter warships. The conference stipulated, however, that if a nation's security was endangered, the quotas could be exceeded. Thus the agreement in effect opened the door to a renewed arms buildup.

The Kellogg-Briand Pact The American peace movement, whose roots went back a hundred years, began to assert new influence after 1910 with the creation of the Carnegie Endowment for International Peace. By the 1920s Americans were flocking to the peace movement in hopes of preventing another war. Different groups tended to advocate different means of achieving the goal of preventing war. Some advocated isolationism, others disarmament, still others the idea of collective security, whereby nations would join together in a unified stand against potential aggressors. During the Coolidge administration a new idea began to gain widespread currency: that war could be prevented if nations would pledge to outlaw war "as an instrument of national policy." On a visit to Paris in 1927 the director of the Carnegie organization, James T. Shotwell, convinced the French Foreign Minister, Aristide Briand, of the merits of the idea. Briand then proposed to United States Secretary of State Frank B. Kellogg a bilateral pact permanently renouncing war between the two nations. More than he wanted to outlaw war, the French minister hoped to tie the United States to France in case of a national emergency. Irritated by the French initiative and fearful that the agreement might be construed as an alliance with France, the government at first ignored the proposal. Later, however, Kellogg suggested that the treaty be made multilateral. The Kellogg-Briand Pact of 1928, originally signed by fifteen nations, and eventually by over sixty, renounced war and called for a peaceful settlement of disputes. Unfortunately, since it was merely a sentimental declaration which entailed no actual restraints and provided no machinery for enforcement, it was cynically ridiculed at home and soon ignored abroad.

Foreign Trade between the Wars

Throughout the 1920s the American government attempted to further its foreign-trade advantage through advice to businesses and favorable tax laws. Already the world's leading manufacturer, exporter, and investor, America had doubled its exports between 1923 and 1929. Many large companies began moving into foreign countries where they built plants for the manufacture of goods and the extraction of minerals. American oil companies invested in the Middle East and American copper companies in Chile. Where competition for markets worked to its advantage, the American government encouraged it; where the United States already dominated trade and investment, such as in Latin America, the government did all it could to keep other countries out.

The Fordney-McCumber Act of 1922 had helped American business by raising the protective tariff. However, the prohibitive rates imposed by the bill made it virtually impossible for foreign nations to sell their imports in the United States. In retaliation, scores of countries began to adopt protective tariffs to restrict the importation of American products. Consequently the depression years of 1929–1933 saw a decline in world trade of 40 percent.

In 1933 Secretary of State Cordell Hull, who strongly supported a policy of international economic cooperation, began agitating to lower the tariff in order to stimulate foreign trade. In June 1934, with the backing of President Roosevelt, Congress passed Hull's plan, outlined in the Reciprocal Trade Agreements Act. This legislation provided that the president could lower tariffs by as much as 50 percent on specific imports from individual nations provided that the countries involved would reciprocate by lowering tariffs on American goods. Hull then began negotiating trade agreements with a number of foreign countries. By 1938 he had secured reciprocal agreements with sixteen nations, and American exports to these countries had jumped almost 40 percent.

The Problem of Debts and Reparations

The matter of war debts and reparations contributed to international tensions and economic problems between the wars. America's World War I allies resented the United States for its role as the major international creditor. Uncle Sam was dubbed "Uncle Shylock" by Europeans disgusted by America's insistence that the Allies repay war debts of $12.5 billion. They argued that the debts should be written off as part of the cost of the war for the United States, which had suffered far less damage than its European allies. The American public, however, strongly favored the repayment of the debt, thinking that repayment would inhibit rearmament. The United States government chose not to concern itself with the question of how the war debts were to be repaid in the face of the insurmountable tariff barriers that had been erected against European imports. Moreover, the government refused to acknowledge that the only way to raise the money was for the Germans to pay their reparations to the Allies, who in turn would use this money to pay the United States.

The issue of reparations had the most far-reaching repercussions in Germany. It had been assumed that the United States would chair the Reparations Commission under the League of Nations, thereby ensuring that Allied demands on Germany for payment of reparations would not be excessive. When the United States refused to join the League, the Allies, bent on revenge against Germany, demanded the outrageous sum of $33 billion. Such a sum victimized an economy already unstable and inflated, and it led to a French invasion of the Ruhr area when Germany defaulted on payments to France in 1923. Moreover, it fueled German resentment against the whole postwar settlement and fostered an atmosphere of hatred that facilitated the rise to power of Adolf Hitler.

In the fall of 1923 Britain and France agreed to Secretary Hughes's suggestion of an independent commission to study the German reparations problem. The Reparations Commission accepted the plan of an American banker, Charles G. Dawes, whereby Germany would receive an international loan of $200 million (mostly from American bankers) to stabilize its economy. In return Germany agreed to resume reparation payments on a scale parallel with the growth of its economy. For a few years the Dawes Plan worked. Germany paid the Allies $2 billion in reparations and the Allies in turn paid the American government about $2.6 billion in war debts.

By 1928 a new committee, headed by American banker Owen D. Young, prepared a plan accepted by Germany's creditors in 1930 to bring reparation payments to an end. It called for fifty-nine annual payments and reduced Germany's reparations by $9 billion. The stock market crash of 1929 ended American investment in Germany, however, and contributed in large measure to economic chaos in that nation. In 1931, to help relieve the world economic crisis, Hoover announced that all war-debt payments would be suspended for a year. From that point on the European countries defaulted.

The Good Neighbor Policy

The spirit of independent internationalism brought changes in American foreign policy in Latin America between the wars. United States intervention in the Caribbean had succeeded only in creating a climate of animosity and resentment in the nations to the south. In the late 1920s, in an effort to improve relations, the United States adopted a policy of nonintervention which under Herbert Hoover became known as the Good Neighbor policy. Difficulties remained, however: the end of military intervention was followed by more extensive economic penetration and support of stable dictatorships in Latin America.

The first major test of American sincerity about the policy of noninterference grew out of Mexican threats to nationalize American oil and mining investments. The Mexican constitution of 1917 had given that nation the right to expropriate properties formerly owned by foreign interests. In 1927 the quarrel came to a head, with Secretary of State Kellogg suggesting that there was Communist influence at work in Mexico and blustering about intervention. The Senate, however, holding fast to its noninterventionist stance, voted for mandatory arbitration of the disputed claims. Kellogg retreated.

President Coolidge also made clear his friendly intentions by appointing as ambassador to Mexico an old friend, banker Dwight D. Morrow, a man known to be sympathetic to the ideal of nonintervention in Latin American affairs. Morrow worked tactfully toward better relations; his efforts were given a boost when American aviation hero Charles Lindbergh visited Mexico in a gesture of goodwill. (Lindbergh subsequently married Morrow's daughter Anne.) In return for conceding Mexico's right to expropriate foreign holdings, the United States was able to salvage many of its oil investments. The compromise held until 1938 when Mexico expropriated the property of all foreign oil companies. President Roosevelt, eager to maintain good relations with Mexico, decided to negotiate. In 1941 Mexico agreed to partial compensation to American companies for the loss of their property.

When Herbert Hoover assumed the presidency in 1928 he was determined to evolve a consistent policy of nonintervention in Latin America. After his election Hoover spent ten weeks on a goodwill tour assuring Latin Americans that the United States intended to be "a good neighbor."

The most important statement of the new policy was contained in the unofficial Clark Memorandum of 1930, which stated that intervention in Latin America would now be considered justifiable only in those cases when the nation's "self-preservation" was at stake. At the same time, it specifically repudiated the Roosevelt corollary to the Monroe Doctrine. During the Hoover years the United States refrained from all military interventions in Latin America, despite the unstable conditions in the area, including some revolts during that four-year period. Under his administration troops were finally withdrawn from Nicaragua, where they had been stationed almost continuously since 1912, and partially withdrawn from Haiti (the remainder were pulled out in 1934).

When Franklin D. Roosevelt assumed office he adopted Hoover's "good neighbor" slogan, and in his first Inaugural Address he promised to respect the sanctity of "agreements in and with a world of neighbors." In addition to demonstrating American goodwill, the Good Neighbor policy under Roosevelt made sound strategic sense. With fascist dictatorships on the rise in Europe and Asia by the mid-1930s, Roosevelt embarked upon a program to enlist the support of Latin America to protect the Western Hemisphere against possible aggression.

At the Pan-American Conference in 1933 the United States signed a declaration publicly opposing intervention in Latin American affairs. When revolution broke out in Cuba in 1933, the United States did not send the marines. This was the first time in the twentieth century that the United States did not intervene in a Cuban crisis. The Platt Amendment, which had provided the legal justification for American intervention in Cuba since 1903, was officially abrogated in 1934. In addition, the United States withdrew all troops from Santo Domingo and in 1936 negotiated a treaty with Panama (ratified in 1939) that to some degree diminished American influence in that country.

Despite its policy of military nonintervention, the United States continued to exercise strong economic influence in Latin America throughout the 1930s. The Dominican Republic, Cuba, and Haiti, for example, were required to have the consent of the United States before borrowing foreign capital. The United States controlled the economy of Chile through its investment in and purchase of copper, and Central American countries such as Guatemala and Honduras were under the thumb of the American-owned United Fruit Company. One-third of United States foreign investments during the inter-war years were made in Latin America.

Although chafing under continued American economic dominance, Latin Americans were pleased with the policy of nonintervention and admired President Roosevelt and the New Deal. Representatives to a special Pan-American Conference in Buenos Aires in 1936 greeted Roosevelt's appearance with wild enthusiasm. Roosevelt first called for a permanent committee to consult on dangers to the Western Hemisphere. Although he was unable to achieve this, the president nevertheless reemphasized that the United States would not intervene in Latin America under any circumstances. In 1938, as war clouds gathered over Europe, the Latin American countries agreed that any country could call a special meeting of American foreign ministers if it feared a threat to the hemisphere. In September 1939 President Roosevelt called such a meeting in Panama. Coming together in the wake of the Nazi attack on Poland, the American republics announced a three-hundred-mile safety zone around the Western Hemisphere to keep the area isolated and neutral in the European conflict. While there was Nazi influence in Latin America, particularly in Uruguay and Argentina, the Roosevelt administration may have overreacted to its importance. Yet it is true that Hitler had made plans to use the merchant fleets of the defeated western European powers to take over Latin American trade as a preliminary to setting up a series of Nazi states in the Western Hemisphere.

In 1940 the American foreign ministers adopted the Act of Havana, a United States plan to take over French and Dutch colonies in the Western Hemisphere rather than allow them to fall into Ger-

Good Neighbor Policy

"I come to pay a call of friendship. In a sense I represent on this occasion the people of the United States extending a fellow greeting to our fellow democracies on the American continent. I would wish to symbolize the friendly visit of one good neighbor to another. In our daily life, good neighbors call upon each other as the evidence of solicitude for the common welfare and to learn of the circumstances and point of view of each, so that there may come both understanding and respect which are the cementing forces of all enduring society. This should be equally true amongst nations. We have a desire to maintain not only the cordial relations of governments with each other but the relations of good neighbors. Through greater understanding that comes with more contact we may build up that common respect and service which is the only enduring basis of international friendship. . . ."

Herbert Hoover, Address at Amapala, Honduras, 1928

Good Neighbor Policy

"1. That the American Nations, true to their republican institutions, proclaim their absolute juridical liberty, their unqualified respect for their respective sovereignties and the existence of a common democracy throughout America; 2. That every act susceptible of disturbing the peace of America affects each and every one of them, and justifies the initiation of the procedure of consultation provided for in the Convention for the Maintenance, Preservation and Reestablishment of Peace, signed at this Conference; and 3. That the following principles are accepted by the American community of nations: (a) Proscription of territorial conquest and that, in consequence, no acquisition made through violence shall be recognized; (b) Intervention by one State in the internal or external affairs of another State is condemned; (c) Forcible collection of pecuniary debts is illegal; and (d) Any difference or dispute between the American nations, whatever its nature or origin, shall be settled by the methods of conciliation, or unrestricted arbitration, or through operation of international justice."

Inter-American Conference for the Maintenance of Peace, 1936

man hands. In the Declaration of Havana the ministers also announced that an attack on one nation would be considered an attack on all. The Monroe Doctrine had finally become multilateral. In January 1942, after the United States had declared war on the Axis, eighteen Latin American countries (with only Chile and Argentina abstaining) joined the war on the side of the Allies. By the end of the war both Chile and Argentina had also sided with the United States.

Improved Relations with Russia

Following the death of Lenin in 1924, a titanic struggle for leadership ensued in the Soviet Union. Josef Stalin outmaneuvered his arch rival, Leon Trotsky, had him exiled and murdered, then insti-

tuted a rapid and forced program of industrialization. Under consecutive five-year plans in the late 1920s and the 1930s, the Soviet government succeeded, without the help of foreign capital, in expanding heavy industry. In addition, Stalin undertook a program of collectivization of Soviet agriculture. In the late 1930s Stalin also instituted massive purges within the Communist party to destroy any challenge to his own leadership. Russia had been turned into an industrialized police state.

Soviet-American relations had been tense ever since the United States, alarmed by constant Communist propaganda calling for world revolution, had refused to recognize the Soviet regime in the years following the 1917 revolution. For the next fifteen years or so American standoffishness had had little impact on the stability of the Communist government. But when the Japanese succeeded in setting up a puppet regime in Manchuria in 1932, their expansionist aims in the Far East became crystal clear. This development led Franklin Roosevelt to rethink America's relations with Russia. He believed that a Soviet-American bond might help curb Japanese aggression; in addition, the prospect of trade with Russia was alluring to America's business community.

Thus in 1933 Roosevelt opened talks with Russia. He agreed to recognize the Communist government in exchange for a series of verbal guarantees that the Soviet Union would discuss debts owed to Americans, would not foment unrest in the United States through its propaganda efforts, and would protect the legal rights and religious freedom of Americans within the Soviet Union. Although Soviet-American relations now had official sanction, the Russians continued their propaganda campaign, the debt question remained unsettled, and trade did not improve, primarily because the United States failed to grant an enormous loan that the Russians had expected.

The Threat of Totalitarianism

Fascism in Italy and Germany

The American government found it expedient to improve relations with the Soviet Union, but it remained aloof from the swiftly rising totalitarian regimes in Italy and Germany.

In Italy in the upheaval following the First World War, a movement known as fascism grew up, which called for a state in which business and labor would work together for the good of the nation. Ownership of private property and a capitalist economic system would continue under tight government regulation, but politically the state would be totalitarian, with only one ruling party and no opposition permitted. In 1922 Fascist leader Benito Mussolini, rushing in to fill a power vacuum, assumed control. In 1926 he declared himself dictator. Within ten years Mussolini, who cherished grandiose dreams of building a new Roman Empire, was actively pursuing a policy of foreign aggression.

In Germany Adolf Hitler and the small National Socialist Workers' Party (Nazi) began to maneuver for control. Hoping to capitalize on growing German resentment against the postwar settlement, Hitler staged an unsuccessful attempt to seize the government in Munich. Despite this setback, conditions in Germany were soon ripe for his emergence as dictator. With the onset of the depression, political weakness and division in Germany's leftist parties gave Hitler the chance he had been seeking. An electrifying orator, he roused audiences at Nazi rallies by playing on German resentment over the postwar settlement and the disastrous effects of depression and trumpeting the glorious history of the German race. Lending support to his rise were anti-Communist industrialists as well as middle-class people who were disillusioned with their economic condition but fearful of communism. Given this backing, the enthusiasm of the German army, and weak opposition, Hitler was appointed chancellor in January 1933. For the next two years he solidified his dictatorship through a reign of terror and suppression of civil liberties. Much of this effort was directed against the Jews, who Hitler claimed were racially inferior and who he blamed for the nation's economic woes. He routed them from the government, the professions, and the universities. In 1935 he denied them their civil and political rights and forbade marriages between Jews and those of "pure" Aryan blood. Jews were beaten, fined, and their businesses destroyed. They were allowed to leave Germany only after being deprived of all belongings. These actions were the prelude to a larger plan to exterminate Jews from the face of Europe.

In February 1932 a World Disarmament Conference opened in Geneva, Switzerland, a continuation of earlier efforts to reduce the threat of militarism. Hitler, preparing to embark on a campaign of aggressive territorial expansion, withdrew from the conference and from the League of Nations in 1934. In 1935 he denounced the Treaty of Versailles and undertook to rebuild the German army and air force.

The Rising Sun

During the 1920s the Japanese government fell increasingly under the sway of its military faction. Right-wing Japanese leaders believed that the country's prosperity and prestige in the world could be attained only through force. The first steps in the Japanese blueprint for conquest, outlined in the Tanaka Memorial of 1927, called for taking Manchuria, nominally a part of China, but 40 percent Japanese in population and vital to Japan's economy. With Manchuria under Japanese domination, the threat of expansion both by Russia and by the Nationalist Chinese under Chiang Kai-shek would be ended.

Frustrated by what they considered the discriminatory treatment of their country at international conferences and by the policies of the civilian government, the militarists in Japan took matters into their own hands. In September 1931 the Japanese army invaded Manchuria and by January 2, 1932, had secured complete control of the province. The victorious Japanese generals forced the moderate civilian government to accept the new territory by threatening Emperor Hirohito with assassination. In 1932 Manchuria was renamed Manchukuo and a puppet ruler was installed.

America's response to these open violations of the Kellogg-Briand Pact and the Nine-Power Treaty proved ineffective. Secretary of State Henry L. Stimson advocated economic sanctions against the Japanese in the hopes of forcing them out of Manchuria. But President Hoover, reflecting American public opinion, opposed a policy of economic pressure, fearing that it might lead to war. The resulting policy announced in a note to Japan on January 7, 1932, came to be known, ironically, as the Stimson Doctrine. Under this policy the United States refused to recognize any territorial changes in China which would impair American treaty rights or violate the Open Door policy or the Kellogg-Briand Pact. The American government had censured Japan before the rest of the world, but without the willingness to back up its position with force it could not end Japanese aggression. Three weeks later Japan invaded Shanghai.

Meanwhile, China appealed to the League of Nations for help. Early in 1933 the assembly of the League adopted a statement confirming Chinese sovereignty in Manchuria and calling for nonrecognition of the Manchukuo regime. Knowing that the League had no machinery to take military action, the Japanese ambassador walked out of the assembly. In 1935 Japan abrogated the Four-, Five-, and Nine-Power pacts and officially withdrew from the League of Nations.

Legislating Neutrality

A reexamination of American motives for entering World War I seemed to confirm the belief of much of the American public that the nation should avoid any possibility of involvement in another war. Books written since the end of World War I claimed that American bankers and munitions makers in pursuit of profits had caused American participation in the conflict. These arguments seemed to be confirmed in the years 1934 to 1936 by the reports of a Senate subcommittee headed by Gerald P. Nye, which greatly strengthened the belief that the so-called merchants of death had dragged the president and Congress into the European conflict.

The findings of the Nye Committee further convinced most Americans that the nation should follow the path of isolation and that the way to accomplish this was to legislate a policy of neutrality. Urged on by some prominent Americans as well as by college students and various women's groups, Congress passed the Neutrality Act of 1935 which provided for an arms embargo against all belligerents in time of war—a simple device that would make American war profiteering impossible. Roosevelt signed the bill reluctantly, for although he had found the Nye investigation convincing and nursed a sharp dislike for what he felt was business's narrow interest in profits, he favored legislation that would prohibit trading with aggressor nations only.

Additional legislation passed in 1936 and 1937 extended the earlier provisions. The 1936 act forbade loans to belligerents; the 1937 law prohibited travel by Americans on belligerent ships and provided that once the president determined that a state of war existed, warring nations could not receive nonmilitary supplies from the United States unless they paid cash and carried the goods away in their own ships (a provision which expired in two years without having been used). Despite the admirable motive of preventing war, the neutrality laws not only abandoned America's traditional assertion of the right to freedom of the seas but proved to be an aid to aggressive nations that had big navies, such as Japan. By 1939, as Germany and Japan increasingly pursued a course of territorial conquest, Roosevelt persuaded Congress to modify the existing legislation. A new neutrality act allowed the United States to extend credit to belligerents for ninety days, forbade American ships from entering zones designated by the president as areas of combat, and repealed the arms embargo by again permitting countries to buy military supplies from the United States on a "cash-and-carry" basis. This modification enabled Britain and France to secure arms from the United States.

The Road to War

When Roosevelt signed the first Neutrality Act in 1935, Mussolini, eager to build his new Roman Empire, had already invaded Ethiopia. Roosevelt had hoped that the arms embargo under the Neutrality Act would deter Italy. In fact, however, it hurt Ethiopia more; an agricultural country totally lacking modern weapons, Ethiopia was soon conquered.

Meanwhile, negotiations between Italy and Germany in 1936 resulted in secret agreements for military cooperation. Mussolini called the relationship between the two nations an "Axis" around which Europe would revolve. The new Rome-Berlin axis had its first test when civil war erupted in Spain in 1936. Fascist forces under General Francisco Franco were attempting to overthrow a weak Republican government. Hitler and Mussolini sent supplies and forces to aid Franco. Single-minded in their determination to avoid war, all of the democratic powers, including the United States, remained neutral. Only the Soviet Union made some effort to aid the Republicans. The United States Congress, under the neutrality laws, embargoed arms against both the Fascist forces and the Republicans, thus effectively destroying any chance of a Republican victory. Despite worldwide sympathy and the enlistments of private individuals in the Republican cause, by 1939 Franco's Fascist forces were victorious.

In July 1937 aggression flared again in the Far East, with the Japanese invasion of north China. American sympathy was with the Chinese, and Roosevelt, taking advantage of the fact that Japan had not declared war, refused to recognize that a state of war existed. This allowed him to continue shipping munitions to China in spite of the Neutrality Act. Unfortunately, however, it also meant that the Japanese could continue to benefit from American trade in many strategic raw materials.

In Chicago that October, Roosevelt, seriously concerned about the policy of naked aggression being undertaken by Italy and Japan, as well as by the potential for German aggression, declared in a speech that "the very foundations of civilization are seriously threatened" by "international lawlessness." He warned that the United States was inevitably involved, since it was the responsibility of peaceful nations to uphold law and order. This became known as the "quarantine-the-aggressor" speech, because Roosevelt compared Fascist aggression to a contagious disease. The way to do this, he implied, was by severing economic ties with the "diseased" nations. Reaction to this speech was extremely negative; given a new recession and

IN 1936 HITLER AND MUSSOLINI BECAME ALLIED IN THE ROME-BERLIN AXIS.

strong isolationist sentiment, the public was afraid that such ideas might lead to war.

Roosevelt firmly believed that the way to avoid war was through military preparedness. Despite persistent efforts, however, he was unable to persuade the public to his view. The American naval fleet had not been built up to the limits established under the London naval conference of 1930. It was not until 1938 that Congress finally passed legislation appropriating the funds to construct the vessels necessary to deter Fascist aggression.

In December 1937 an American gunboat, the *Panay*, was bombed and sunk by Japanese pilots while cruising in Chinese waters. It appeared to be a deliberate act, particularly since an American flag painted on the deck was clearly visible. Nevertheless, American anger was easily cooled by Japanese apologies and reparations. The mild response to the incident made it clear just how strong isolationist sentiment was in the United States.

Meanwhile, in Germany, Adolph Hitler had been building a powerful war machine in preparation for embarking on a step-by-step campaign to bring all of central Europe under Nazi domination. He planned to "relocate" Jews and other "non-Aryan" peoples and to take over their land to provide *Lebensraum* ("living space") for the Germans and to use it as a military and industrial base for his projected world conquest. His strategy of conquest was founded, in part, on the fact that ethnic and national boundaries in much of central Europe were unclear. The Treaty of Versailles had provided for an independent and demilitarized area west of the Rhine River. But in 1936 a rapidly rearming Germany marched into the Rhineland and reclaimed it, unopposed. The Treaty of Versailles had provided, too, that the German-speaking country of Austria was always to remain separate from Germany. But in March 1938 Hitler overthrew the Austrian government and annexed Austria to Germany. Great Britain and France, though profoundly disturbed by Hitler's expansionism, were mired in the economic and social problems of the depression. Determined to avoid war, they rationalized the takeover by saying that Austria had always been part of the German community.

Unfortunately their hopes that the German appetite would be satiated by the acquisition of Austria were soon dashed. In September 1938 Hitler demanded that the Sudetenland, an area of Czechoslo-

vakia populated by 3.5 million Germans, be turned over to Germany. The Czechs were willing to go to war to defend their territory, but the Western democracies, to whom they turned for help, were panicked by the thought of war and eager to appease the Germans. Prime Minister Neville Chamberlain of Great Britain and Prime Minister Edouard Daladier of France conferred with Hitler several times concerning the annexation, finally signing an agreement in Munich on September 29 which supported the German demands. In return Hitler pledged that this was his last territorial claim in Europe. The Czechs, who were not consulted and were in no position to fight Germany unaided, were forced to cede the Sudetenland. Six months later, in March 1939, Hitler broke his promise when he seized the rest of Czechoslovakia. The Western democracies were finally stunned into recognizing the folly of appeasement.

The other Axis power, Italy, continued its plans for conquest as well. In April 1938 the Italians invaded and conquered Albania. Europe stood on the brink of war.

Crisis over Poland

Early in 1939 Hitler demanded Danzig, a German-speaking port that had been declared a free city under the Treaty of Versailles. Poland, whose territory surrounded the city, refused the German demand. A new invasion was clearly imminent.

In March 1939, now fully aware of the extent of the German threat, France and Britain became formally allied and promised to come to the aid of Poland, Rumania, and Greece in the event of attack. President Roosevelt sent a message to the Axis in April, calling for a guarantee that over twenty nations, specified by name, would not be invaded. Hitler's reply was contemptuously noncommittal.

Since the new crisis centered in Poland, Americans hoped that Russia would join the Anglo-French alliance to help maintain Poland's neutrality as a buffer against German expansion. The traditional enmity between Germany and Russia was evident in Hitler's anti-Communist rhetoric and in the opposing positions the two countries had taken in the Spanish Civil War. Consequently, the world was stunned when a Russo-German nonaggression pact was announced at the end of August. The pact renounced war between the two powers and in-

A CARTOON FROM A BRITISH MAGAZINE IS CAPTIONED, "WHAT, ME? I NEVER TOUCH GOLDFISH!" THE TWO CATS (HITLER AND STALIN) ARE LICKING THEIR CHOPS OVER FISH LABELED BULGARIA, JUGO-SLAVIA, RUMANIA, AND GREECE.

cluded a secret protocol which stated that Russia and Germany would divide Poland between them in the coming weeks. The agreement with Russia meant that Germany would be free to attack Poland without Soviet interference. It also specified that the Soviet Union would dominate the Baltic states, recover part of Rumania lost in 1918, and stay out of a war between Germany and the Western democracies.

Having received a green light from Russia, Hitler was undeterred by the Anglo-French agreement guaranteeing Polish security. German troops marched into Poland on September 1, and the German *Luftwaffe* (air force) began a massive aerial bombardment. Great Britain and France declared war on Germany two days later, but there was little they could do to aid Poland. Poland was crushed under the Nazi heel in a matter of weeks and then occupied by German and Soviet armies. On September 3, Roosevelt spoke to the American people over the radio, promising that the United States would try to stay out of war, but adding that he could not "ask that every American remain neutral in thought." The United States proclaimed its neutrality on September 5.

War Begins

After the fall of Poland there was little fighting during the winter of 1939–1940, leading American isolationists to speak of the "phony war." The only major action involved Soviet efforts to continue to expand its territory. The Russians seized the Baltic states of Latvia, Lithuania, and Estonia and subsequently invaded Finland, which lost territory but maintained its independence.

In the spring of 1940 those who had sneered at the "phony war" had a chance to witness the real thing. In a rapid *blitzkrieg*, or "lightning war," Hitler invaded and defeated virtually every country in western Europe. Norway, aided by troops and naval forces from Britain and France, struggled valiantly, but was unable to defeat the German invaders.

In May, after the Germans had smashed through Holland, Belgium, and Luxembourg, they

Allied nations

Axis nations

Neutral nations

World War II • Alliances

struck at France. The invading German army trapped more than three hundred thousand British and French soldiers around Dunkirk on the northern coast of France. The slaughter of this enormously vulnerable force might have spelled Britain's defeat. But in one of the greatest retreats in military history, a motley cluster of small ships and commercial boats managed to evacuate most of the army. Neverthe-

less, Hitler's modernized army had pierced the Maginot Line, France's supposedly invulnerable wall of fortifications. In June France and Germany signed an armistice, and a French resistance movement was immediately established in London under General Charles de Gaulle.

Hitler was convinced that his defeat of France would now force the British to sue for peace. When

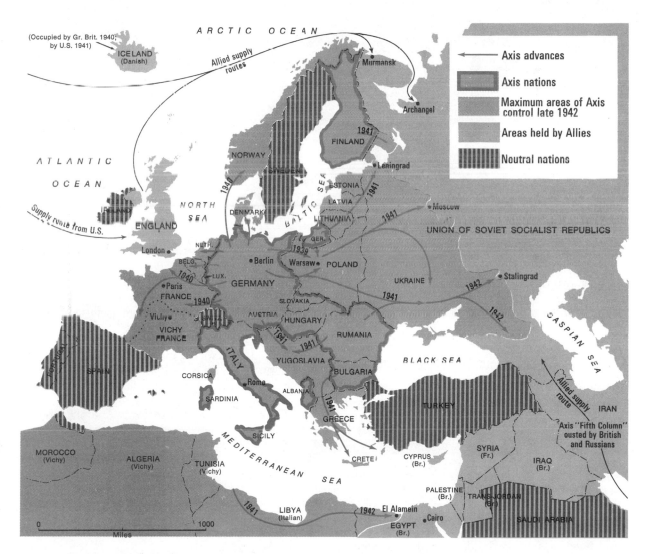

World War II • European Theater • 1939 to 1942

A GROUP OF ENGLISH CITIZENS TAKE REFUGE IN A LONDON UNDERGROUND USED AS
AN AIR-RAID SHELTER DURING HITLER'S BLITZ ON ENGLISH CITIES.

the new prime minister, Winston Churchill, refused, Hitler's *Luftwaffe* began relentless daytime
bombing raids on English cities as a prelude to an
invasion. The British Royal Air Force (RAF) destroyed so many German planes that the *Luftwaffe*
turned to night bombing. Night after night the English in industrial centers retreated into underground shelters. The blitz, although it caused enormous damage and suffering, did not succeed in
breaking the English spirit. The British people responded gallantly to Churchill's fervent appeals to
stand fast. Hitler finally abandoned his plan to invade England in 1940.

President Roosevelt, responding to continuing
requests from Churchill for destroyers to defend
British shipping vessels against German submarine
attacks, exchanged fifty World War I-vintage destroyers for ninety-nine-year leases on eight strategic
naval-base sites in Bermuda and the Caribbean
which would be invaluable to the United States in
case of attack. He accomplished this by presidential

agreement, thereby avoiding the possibility that his
opponents in Congress might attempt to block a step
he regarded as crucial. Although isolationists expressed loud disapproval, a majority of the American public, angered by the Nazi conquest of continental Europe and stirred by the plight of the British
as described in American news broadcasts from
London, were strongly in favor of aid to Great Britain.

The recognition of the threat to America should
Great Britain go under spurred Congress to take action toward military preparedness. The Burke-
Wadsworth Act of September 1940 instituted a
peacetime draft for the first time in American history. Congress also appropriated $37 billion to build
up the American navy and air force.

The Election of 1940

In the months preceding the election of 1940 a debate between those who favored American neutral-

ity in the war and those who advocated unlimited aid to the Allies gained momentum. The bipartisan America First Committee, with the support of such prominent people as Herbert Hoover and Charles Lindbergh, and the editorial backing of William Randolph Hearst, attacked as provocative Roosevelt's posture toward the Axis and Japan, called for confining America's armed defense to the Western Hemisphere, and advocated neutrality in Europe. The committee's position appealed to many loyal Americans but also attracted a small group of anti-Semites, pro-Nazi sympathizers, and Fascists. On the other side, the Committee to Defend America by Aiding the Allies, led by Kansas editor William Allen White, believed that American liberty would best be served by aiding the Allied effort, short of declaring war.

Since the Republican convention was held in June at the time of the fall of France, American national defense was a burning issue. In response to pressure from the party rank and file, the Republicans nominated Wendell Willkie, an interventionist and former Democrat who only lately had come over to the Republican Party. Willkie, although a newcomer to politics, had the sort of personal magnetism that could attract broad popular support.

On the Democratic side, Roosevelt believed that given the growing international crisis he should remain in the presidency. As a result, he decided to try for an unprecedented third term in office. The Democratic delegates, believing that only Roosevelt was more popular than Willkie, nominated him as their candidate.

Willkie waged a vigorous campaign, traveling across the country giving so many speeches his voice grew hoarse. On domestic issues he did not attack the New Deal as such but only its wasteful excesses. He characterized Roosevelt's leadership during his two terms as "dictatorial," and criticized him for running for a third term. In foreign affairs he differed little from the president. Although he charged that Roosevelt was leading the country into war, he nevertheless agreed with the president in advocating aid to the Allies and taking a tough stand against fascism.

Roosevelt, conducting much of his campaign from the White House, countered Willkie's attack by promising solemnly that American boys would not "be sent into any foreign wars." He defended the New Deal and continued to urge giving aid to America's European allies.

Ultimately the contest was more over leadership than over issues, and the people showed that they had continuing faith in Roosevelt's capacity to lead them during a crisis. Even so, Roosevelt's third victory was smaller than his others: in the popular vote he accumulated 27,244,160 votes to 22,305,198 for Willkie; in the electoral college the margin was substantial: 449 to 82.

Lend-Lease

Shortly after the election Churchill wrote to Roosevelt, outlining the extremity of the British position. The most urgent problem was that the British had run out of money to buy war materiel. He asked for an end to the "cash-and-carry" policy, because there was no money to pay for supplies and there were no ships available to carry them. Moreover, Churchill begged for arms with which to continue the fight against the Axis.

Roosevelt, now believing that American involvement in the war was inevitable, responded to Churchill's appeal by formulating the so-called Lend-Lease program. In a fireside chat to the American people on December 29, 1940, he prepared the American public for his aid plan by describing the Fascist menace to world democracy. Pointing to American industrial might, he argued that the United States "must be the great arsenal of democracy." Popular response to the speech was favorable. Thereupon Roosevelt proposed in the "Lend-Lease" bill that Congress appropriate $7 billion for the production of weapons and other war supplies, from airplanes to boots, and authorize the president to sell, lend, lease, or exchange these materials, as he saw fit, to any nation in danger whose security he determined was linked to that of the United States.

Isolationists vehemently opposed the measure, arguing that Lend-Lease would bring the United States closer to involvement in an undeclared war. Senator Burton K. Wheeler objected, "The Lend-Lease program is the New Deal's Triple A foreign policy; it will plow under every fourth American boy." Support for the measure, however, went across party lines and extended to a wide spectrum of the American public. While Lindbergh and others, including the historian Charles Beard, testified against the bill, Republican Wendell Willkie campaigned for it. Lend-Lease became law on March 11, 1941, and the United States eventually spent $54 billion for Lend-Lease aid to the Allies. However, the one-year selective-service system instituted in 1940 was renewed in 1941 by only one vote.

Alliance Building

The 1939 alliance between Germany and the Soviet Union had been an uneasy one, fraught with mutual suspicion. On June 22, 1941, Hitler, moving to extend his territorial gains and wipe communism from the face of Europe, suddenly turned on his ally, launching an all-out offensive deep into the Soviet Union.

Reaction from Washington was swift. Despite deep-seated anti-Communist sentiment among Americans, it was clear to many that the defeat of Russia, with its incredibly rich resources, would make it practically impossible to end the Nazis' systematic march toward world conquest. Cooperation with Russia's totalitarian government seemed a lesser evil than defeat by Nazi Germany. On June 24 Roosevelt promised assistance to the Soviet Union, and within a few months he extended $1 billion in

Lend-Lease aid. In the meantime, the president was already working closely with Churchill who, though fiercely anti-Communist, was more than happy to regard any of Hitler's foes as an ally. "If Hitler invaded Hell," Churchill remarked, "I would make at least a favorable reference to the Devil in the House of Commons."

The Atlantic Charter In August 1941 the Anglo-American bond was furthered by a secret meeting between Roosevelt and Churchill on a warship off the coast of Newfoundland. There they issued a joint statement which became known as the Atlantic Charter. The eight-point document, reminiscent of Wilson's Fourteen Points, expressed their goals for a peaceful world at the conclusion of the war. It opposed territorial expansionism, affirmed the right of peoples to choose their own governments and national boundaries (self-determination), and advocated free trade, disarmament of aggressor nations, freedom of the seas, and a new system of collective security. In addition, it included the humanitarian goal of "freedom from fear and want." The Atlantic Charter made it clear that the goals of the United States and Britain were inextricably linked.

FOUR MONTHS BEFORE THE UNITED STATES ENTERED THE WAR, ROOSEVELT AND CHURCHILL MET ABOARD A BATTLESHIP OFF THE NEWFOUNDLAND COAST WHERE THEY ISSUED A JOINT STATEMENT KNOWN AS THE ATLANTIC CHARTER.

The Undeclared War with Germany

Despite the fact that he was leading the nation toward a confrontation with Germany, FDR continued to maintain the pretense of American neutrality. Although he believed that the very existence of democracy was imperiled by Adolph Hitler, he was afraid that a direct statement of his conviction that America should enter the war would seriously divide the nation. Thus he continued quietly to increase American activities in support of the Allies. The American navy engaged in repairing British ships, seizing Axis vessels in American ports and turning them over to the Allies, and using United States ships to patrol the Atlantic.

The Lend-Lease Act had not provided for American vessels to escort British ships carrying war supplies to Britain. However, it was clear that with the British navy stretched to its limits the only way to assure the arrival of munitions was by convoy. In July 1941 Roosevelt ordered the navy to escort British vessels carrying lend-lease supplies to Iceland. In September a German U-boat fired two torpedoes that missed the American destroyer *Greer*, which had been tracking it for several hours and informing the British of its location. Although the *Greer* fired back, the German vessel was undamaged. Roosevelt, labeling the attack an act of piracy, gave orders to "shoot on sight" at German submarines in the waters between Iceland and North America. In October the destroyer *Kearney* was badly damaged and eleven navy men were lost in an engagement with German U-boats. Much worse was the sinking of the *Reuben James*, with the loss of some one hundred men. This incident seriously provoked the American public, who lent strong support to Roosevelt's efforts to persuade Congress to modify existing neutrality legislation to provide for the arming of American merchant ships. The new legislation, passed in November, also provided that merchant ships could carry war supplies to belligerent ports.

Negotiations with Japan

Meanwhile, the United States was almost as preoccupied with aggression in the Far East as with Axis attacks on shipping in the Atlantic. The Japanese military regime, having declared the Open Door policy an impediment to its expansionist goals, had continued its assault on China. At first the United States attempted to remain on good terms with Japan. Despite the opposition of many Americans who supported the Chinese nationalists under Chiang Kai-shek, the American government continued to supply Japan with aviation fuel, scrap iron, steel, and oil urgently needed by the Japanese military machine. In July 1939, however, Washington gave notice that the 1911 Treaty of Commerce and Navigation with Japan would be abrogated in six months, curtailing trade somewhat. The United States also loaned China $25 million and fortified Guam and Alaska. Sanctions finally were imposed in 1940 after Japan, taking advantage of the defeat of France, began insisting that the collaborationist Vichy government provide bases in Indochina and threatening to invade the oil-rich Dutch East Indies. The United States fleet was sent to Pearl Harbor in Hawaii in July 1940, and certain strategic materials such as aviation fuel and scrap iron and steel were placed under a strict licensing system.

The Japanese responded by moving into northern French Indochina and signing the Tripartite Pact with Germany and Italy in September 1940. This agreement pledged the three nations to aid each other if attacked by a fourth nation not then in the war. Since Japan's longtime foe, Russia, was already in the war, it was obvious that the provision was aimed specifically at the United States. The Axis powers hoped thereby to ensure American neutrality, since if the United States attacked in either theater it would be embroiled in a war on both oceans. The United States now imposed a complete embargo on the sale of all scrap iron and steel to Japan.

Still hoping to avoid hostilities, the Japanese made diplomatic overtures to the United States. Beginning in March 1941, the Japanese Ambassador, Admiral Nomura, began talks with Secretary Hull in an effort to end economic sanctions against Japan. Hull took a hard line, insisting that there were no grounds for negotiations as long as Japan maintained military operations in China, continued plans to expand into Indochina, and remain allied with the Axis.

The Japanese Prime Minister, Fuminaro Konoye, was eager to achieve his country's objectives in Asia without war, but militants in his cabinet forced his government to demand that France allow Japan to occupy southern Indochina. When France yielded, the United States retaliated in July by freez-

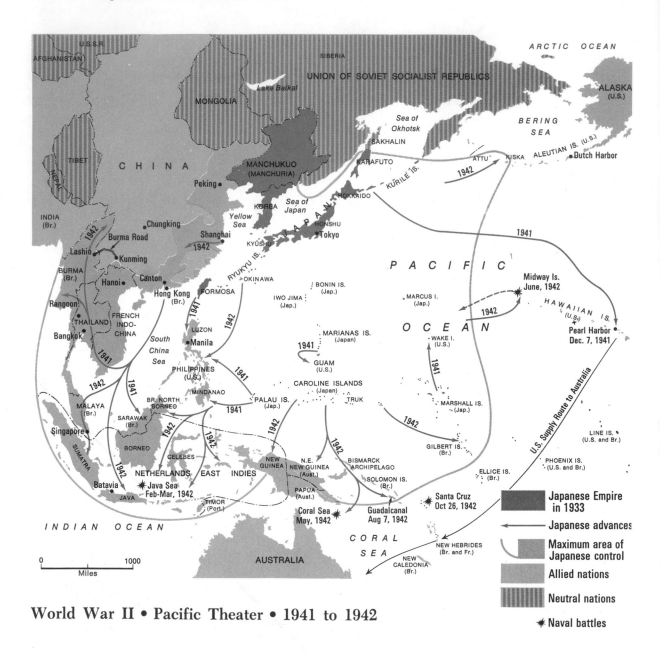

World War II • Pacific Theater • 1941 to 1942

ing all Japanese funds in the country, an action which meant the end of all trade with Japan, including oil, and closed the Panama Canal to Japanese ships. Now the moderate and militant factions in Japan furiously debated what course to pursue. When Premier Konoye's appeal for a summit con-

ference with the United States failed, he counseled accepting American terms in principle. Unable to overcome army resistance to even this concession, he resigned and was replaced on October 17 by General Hideki Tojo, an ardent militarist. War plans were formulated, and on November 5 the Japanese cabinet decided that the nation would go to war with the United States in an effort to break out of the economic stranglehold unless the Allies would stop aiding the Chinese and reinstate trade. On November 25 a fleet of ships secretly training in the Kurile Islands left for Hawaii, although it could be recalled if the United States agreed to Japan's offer.

Unaware of these plans, Ambassador Nomura and a special emissary, Saburo Kurusu, presented Japan's final proposals to the United States in mid-November. They would withdraw from Indochina and eventually from China in exchange for a renewal of trade with the United States. Because the offer made no provision for stopping hostilities against China and because the United States could not in conscience abandon China, Secretary Hull refused to consider it. Instead, he responded on No-

vember 26 with a Ten-Point Plan which restated in the most uncompromising terms American demands for a Japanese evacuation of China and Indochina and Japanese abandonment of the Axis alliance. The hard-line American proposal made war almost inevitable.

Pearl Harbor Events now moved rapidly. By late 1940 the American government had broken the Japanese code and had deciphered a voluminous amount of information from Japanese government sources. On the basis of this intelligence, Washington was sure that Japan was planning an attack somewhere in the South Pacific in mid-to-late November. On November 27 American forces in the Pacific received routine warnings to be on the alert. On December 6 the United States intercepted a mes-

THE JAPANESE ATTACK ON PEARL HARBOR, DECEMBER 7, 1941.

sage in which Tojo instructed his ambassadors who were still meeting in Washington to break with the United States the following day. Roosevelt knew that war was imminent, but on December 6 he sent one final appeal to Emperor Hirohito to avert war. The next morning Japan formally rejected the Ten-Point Plan.

Early that same fateful Sunday, December 7, the Japanese attacked the American fleet at Pearl Harbor, killing twenty-four hundred men, crippling the entire fleet, and destroying hundreds of planes. Despite later charges that Roosevelt had anticipated the attack and welcomed it as a dramatic and unifying excuse for entering the war, there is little doubt

that the site of the raid was a surprise. Because of the huge amount of conflicting intelligence information in its possession, the United States had anticipated an attack in the Philippines, not at Pearl Harbor.

On December 8 Roosevelt delivered a war message to Congress. He declared that December 7, 1941, was a day that would "live in infamy." Congress quickly passed a war resolution with only one dissenting vote in the House. On December 11 Germany and Italy declared war on the United States. The debate between isolationists and interventionists was now abandoned as American energies focused on crushing the Axis and on the unprecedented mobilization required to achieve victory.

American Mobilization

World War II triggered the greatest mobilization of physical and human resources ever undertaken by the United States. Sixteen million people served in the armed forces, including many women in the newly organized women's branches of the military. The war effort also created a new demand for labor on the home front, which erased unemployment and brought increasing numbers of blacks into industrial centers as factory workers. Mobilizing the domestic economy for total war created a fluid economic and social situation, which helped challenge traditional patterns and set the stage for postwar efforts by blacks, Mexican-Americans, and women to attain a position of equality in American society.

The government adopted several methods of financing the unparalleled military effort. Congress expanded the income tax to cover nearly all white-collar and industrial workers, but the tax was so steeply graduated that some of the wealthiest citizens paid as much as 90 percent of their income to the federal government. As in World War I, the administration conducted bond drives, calling for people to put aside 10 percent of their income for the purchase of war bonds. Free advertising for the drives was donated by every conceivable form of private enterprise, and the response was overwhelming. Over $40 billion of war bonds were sold.

Congress gave the president sweeping authority under the War Powers Act of December 1941 to unite the military and productive units of private industry into a coordinated whole. By the end of 1942 Roosevelt had created hundreds of wartime offices,

boards, and commissions. There was much overlapping and bureaucratic inefficiency, but the Office of Emergency Management under Harry Hopkins and the War Production Board under Donald Nelson created some semblance of order.

Nelson's enormous task included coordinating the allocation of materials for both industry and the

EMPLOYEES IN THE DOUGLAS AIRCRAFT PLANT ASSEMBLE THE SBD-2 DIVE BOMBERS, KNOWN AS THE WORKHORSES OF THE NAVAL AIR FLEET.

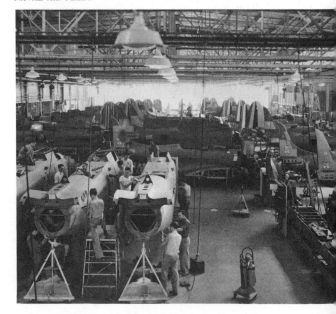

different branches of the armed service. Roosevelt had set very high production goals, and despite the board's inefficiency the goals were being substantially met by the end of 1942. By 1944 American factories were turning out twice as much as factories in the Axis nations.

One effect of this greatly increased production was that efficient big businesses were favored at the expense of small businesses. As the Senate Committee on Education and Labor pointed out: "Throughout the first two and one-half years of our effort, one hundred of America's largest corporations have received 75 percent of all war contracts by dollar value."

The Home Front

Just as the government allocated war materials for industry, a parallel system of controls on rents, wages, salaries, profits, rationing, and prices was developed for the civilian economy. Items such as sugar and gasoline were rationed, as the government again tried to sell the idea of self-denial to the American public. A pamphlet distributed by the Office of Civilian Defense emphasized that "conservation is a war weapon in the hands of every man, woman, and child." It advocated car pooling with the warning, "The empty seat is a gift to Hitler."

At the beginning of the war, higher food prices prompted workers to demand increased wages. Inflation continued until wages were stabilized in 1943 with the creation of the Office of War Mobilization and the Office of Price Administration.

Employment and income increased, and strikes were rare after the middle of 1943. When the war began, union leaders had pledged not to strike if there were reasonable guarantees against a cost-of-living inflation. This pledge was generally kept, although the United Mine Workers under John L. Lewis did strike during the war. Public indignation was so great that in June 1943 Congress passed the Smith-Connally War Labor Disputes Act providing for the government to take over plants involved in essential war industries in the event that they were struck.

Social Advances and Social Problems Although the high rates of unemployment during the Great Depression had driven many women out of the labor market and back into the home, the war emergency brought six million American women into the work force. Taking over jobs formerly held by men, they ran lathes, read blueprints, serviced airplanes, greased locomotives, and ran municipal bus lines. For the first time, their wages were increasing.

These advances, however, did not mean the end of discrimination and prejudice against working women. Enforcement of the uniform pay scales urged by the War Manpower Commission was lax. Some industries avoided paying equal wages by defining a job differently, depending on whether it was done by a man or a woman.

Discriminated against economically and hampered by the lack of day-care arrangements for their young children, many of the women who swelled the American work force during the war emergency were laid off when it ended. Employers wanted to make jobs available for returning veterans. Despite such setbacks, however, women remained in the work force in unprecedented numbers.

The acceleration of industrial output radically changed the lives of many black people, drawing more of them out of rural areas in the South and into industrial cities such as Chicago, Detroit, and Los Angeles. The growing presence of blacks in industry, like the increase of women workers, was largely the result of emergency needs rather than the lessening of prejudice. Pressure from blacks led by A. Phillip Randolph, president of the Brotherhood of Sleeping Car Porters, resulted in the creation in 1941 of the Fair Employment Practices Commission, which helped bring an end to segregation and discrimination in defense plants. At the same time, the huge influx of black workers into Northern urban centers brought an increase in racial tensions, particularly over the issue of segregation in housing and other facilities. The war years saw hundreds of racial conflicts, the worst of which was a bloody riot in Detroit in 1943 which resulted in thirty-four deaths, hundreds of injuries, and property damage estimated at over $2 million.

Segregation in the armed forces persisted despite black leaders' requests for integrated units. But progress was made in integrating some areas of the service. Black commissioned officers, for example, were at last sent to integrated officers' training camps. The navy changed its policy of using blacks as messmen only and enabled them to become sailors, assigning them to ships on a nonsegregated basis. Even so, it was not until a few years after the war that all branches of the military service were completely desegregated. Moreover, during the war social segregation continued in many forms. Separate black and white blood banks, for instance, continued to exist; ironically, it was a black physician, Dr. Charles Drew, who invented the process of storing blood plasma.

World War II also provided an opportunity for many Mexican-Americans to obtain jobs in war industries and to join the armed forces. Many served in combat divisions in Europe and the Far East, and seventeen won the Congressional Medal of Honor. Although social discrimination continued, in combat Mexican-Americans gained an equal place with other ethnic groups. Along with other veterans, many took advantage of government programs for veterans' education and job training after the war.

Japanese Internment For the most part the civil liberties of "hyphenated" Americans and radicals were respected during the war. Although some seventeen hundred Nazi sympathizers were rounded up by the FBI and a few of their leaders tried, the rabid anti-German feelings that characterized America during the First World War were little in evidence. Italian-Americans also were left alone, and Communists, who lauded Roosevelt for his aid to Russia, patriotically supported the war effort.

With respect to Japanese-Americans, however, the United States' record was dismal. Many Americans, especially on the West Coast, were paralyzed by fear of a Japanese invasion which they thought would be aided by a "fifth column" of secret support among Japanese-Americans. Moreover, the attack on Pearl Harbor brought to the surface long-standing resentment on the part of whites in California against successful Japanese-Americans who owned much rich farmland.

As a result of the atmosphere of hysteria, Roosevelt followed the advice of a United States Army report which characterized Japanese-Americans as "potential enemies of Japanese extraction." Areas with a high concentration of Japanese were placed under curfew, and more than one hundred thousand Japanese-Americans—two-thirds of them American-born citizens—were crowded into internment camps hundreds of miles from their homes. Although these actions were a blatant violation of civil liberties, the Supreme Court later upheld both the curfew and the relocation policies as justifiable means of preventing spying and sabotage during wartime. Even in the face of such treatment, most Japanese-Americans remained loyal to the United States. Those who served in the armed forces, particularly the 442nd unit from Hawaii, established a remarkable record fighting against the Axis powers in Europe.

The War in Europe

Allied Strategy

Shortly after the attack on Pearl Harbor, Winston Churchill met with Roosevelt in Washington. In a series of discussions the two leaders agreed on an overall strategy of "Europe first." This meant that top priority was to be given to defeating Germany, since Hitler appeared to be the primary threat. Although Japan was not to be ignored, efforts in Asia would be defensive.

The two leaders also focused on the formation of a "Grand Alliance" of anti-Axis nations. At a conference held in Washington in January 1942 (codenamed Arcadia), representatives of twenty-six nations signed the Declaration by the United Nations, a document which set the stage for expanding the Atlantic Charter into a new world organization.

Under the Declaration the signatories pledged acceptance of the principles outlined in the Atlantic Charter and agreed not to make separate peace treaties or armistices with the Axis powers. The same month, as noted previously, ministers of a number of Latin American nations issued a declaration that an Axis attack on one of the American nations would be viewed as an attack on all.

Despite their joint commitment to a "Europe-first" strategy, the Americans and the British disagreed over how to implement it. The Americans argued for building up the Allied armies in England in order to launch a major invasion of Europe across the English channel. The British, although agreeing with this plan in principle, had serious reservations about its feasibility. They argued that an invasion across the channel would require a massive buildup and careful preparations. In the meantime, there were already several fronts requiring immediate attention. They pressed for carrying out a series of attacks on the Axis periphery while building up the strength necessary for a major invasion of the Continent.

Although strategy questions created some tensions, relations between the United States and Britain remained close. Relations with Russia, by contrast, were precarious. Stalin was deeply mistrustful of the motives of his anti-Communist allies. Roosevelt and Churchill consistently tried to persuade him of their goodwill, and the United States supplied the Soviets with huge quantities of war materiel vital to Russian defense. Even so, Stalin never lessened his suspicions. To compound problems, the United States and Britain had promised to open up a "second front" in western Europe in 1942 intended to take the heat off Russian soldiers who, as Roosevelt reminded Churchill, were "killing more Germans and destroying more equipment than you and I put together." The delay of the second front until 1944 due to lack of Allied preparedness angered and exasperated the Soviets.

The Air-Sea War

While overall strategy was being debated, the Allied forces were engaged in an effort to stop the German submarine force, which was wreaking havoc on Anglo-American convoys in the Atlantic and disrupting trade in the Western Hemisphere. Air patrols were set up, scanning devices improved, and antisubmarine vessels and weapons developed; and by the end of 1943 the submarine menace had been substantially reduced. Meanwhile, Britain's Royal Air Force, assisted by the United States Air Force, began saturation-bombing raids on mass targets in Germany. Theoretically, the purpose of these raids was to cripple German industries by bringing cities such as Cologne to their knees. At least as important, however, was the objective of demoralizing the German population and seeking revenge for the blitz on Britain.

The North African Campaign

Allied plans for a counteroffensive against the Axis were finally worked out in the last months of 1942. The Americans, with reluctance, agreed to a British plan for an Anglo-American attack in North Africa where the German *Afrika Corps*, led by Field Marshal Erwin Rommel, was attempting to seal off the Suez Canal, a vital Allied supply route. Churchill finally succeeded in persuading Stalin of the advantages of an invasion of North Africa which would rout Rommel's forces and secure the area as a base for a northward assault on Italy. The second front, he explained, would open in 1943.

The North Africa campaign was commanded by General Dwight D. Eisenhower, a career officer skilled in administration who had been chosen by the chief of staff, General George C. Marshall. As assistant chief of staff Eisenhower had played a key role in developing a plan for the invasion of North Africa.

The counteroffensive got off to a slow start. For months British and German forces were stalled in a confrontation around El Alamein, located seventy-five miles from Alexandria, Egypt. In late October, however, the Germans were finally routed. In addition, the Allies had staged amphibious landings at three other key points in North Africa. Allied forces from the west and east now began converging on Rommel in Tunisia.

The Allies' African campaign was succeeding when Roosevelt and Churchill and their chiefs of staff met in Casablanca in January 1943 to discuss

AMERICAN RED CROSS WORKERS EN ROUTE TO THEIR STATIONS IN NORTH AFRICA WHERE THE ALLIES LAUNCHED A COUNTEROFFENSIVE IN 1942.

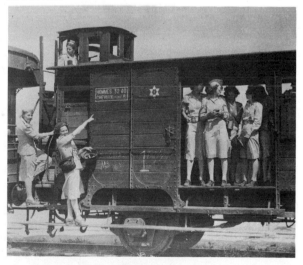

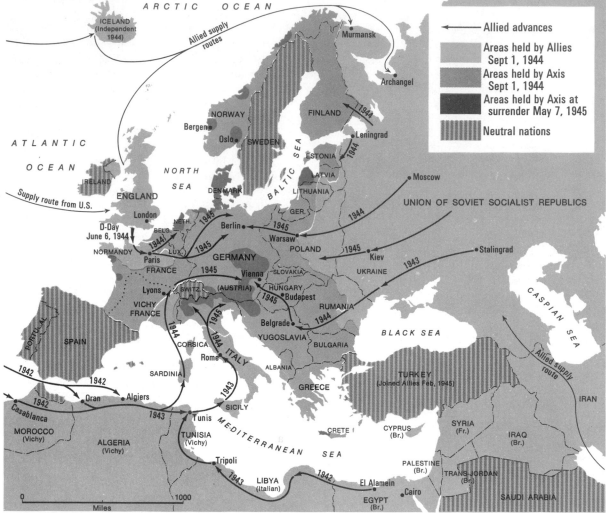

World War II • European Theater • 1942 to 1945

future strategy. The British favored attacking the Continent from the south through Sicily, with the aim of defeating Italy and forcing Hitler to draw large numbers of troops away from Russia to defend Italy and the Balkans. The Americans still favored a cross-channel invasion of the northern coast of France, but were persuaded of the merits of the British plan to attack from the south first. The two leaders also issued a statement that the war would be fought until unconditional surrender had been extracted from the Axis powers.

This policy was aimed at providing assurance that the nations that had signed the Declaration for the United Nations would remain unified in their efforts for victory and would not engage in separate maneuvering at war's end. It was also intended to reduce Soviet distrust of Allied intentions by avoiding any misunderstanding over the terms of surrender. Finally, such a policy would ensure that the Germans fully accepted their defeat—something they had not done after the First World War. The Allied policy of unconditional surrender has since been criticized as reinforcing Germany's determination to win, leaving no room for diplomatic maneuvering and prolonging the war.

Hitler did rush more troops to Tunisia, where several months of hard fighting culminated at last in Allied victory. With the southern Mediterranean thus recaptured by May 1943, the Allies now undertook the invasion of southern Europe.

The invasion of Sicily began on July 9, 1943. Despite initial American bungling, the Allies took the island in a matter of six weeks. With the fall of Sicily, the Italians overthrew Mussolini. The new government under Marshal Pietro Badoglio signed an armistice with the Allies in September and declared war on Germany the following month.

Meanwhile, Hitler moved large numbers of troops into northern Italy and dug in other units near Rome. Allied forces landed in southern Italy on September 9, 1943, one day after the official surrender. Their first beachhead, at Salerno, endured severe bombardment before they finally forced an agonizingly slow German retreat toward Rome. It took eight months for the Allies to fight their way to the capital. After an assault on the Anzio beachhead in which the Allies were almost beaten, the battered, exhausted Allied soldiers reached Rome on June 4, 1944, two days before the invasion of France.

The Invasion of Europe

In November 1943 Roosevelt, Churchill, and Stalin met in Teheran, Iran, to discuss plans for a second front, an invasion of Europe from the north. This was the first time the Big Three had all sat down together. Before this time Stalin had declined to meet, fearing to leave Russia while the Soviet military position remained precarious. During the critical winter months of 1942–1943, however, the Russian position improved considerably. At Stalingrad the Russians succeeded in surrounding and capturing a German army of a quarter million men. As the Russians pressed the offensive in 1943, Stalin became somewhat more flexible in his relations with his allies. The three leaders emerged from the conference apparently united, vowing to "work together in the war and in the peace that will follow." They reaffirmed plans for a massive invasion of France by the Western allies. Stalin would time an offensive from the east into Germany to coincide with the cross-channel assault. Churchill still feared that a second-front invasion might fail, but he gave it his full support. Stalin was deeply gratified that the northern invasion was at last about to begin and promised to enter the war against Japan after Hitler's defeat. Teheran marked the high point of cooperation among the Big Three.

On D-day, June 6, the largest amphibious operation in history (code-named Operation Overlord) was launched under the command of General Eisenhower. A slight advantage was gained by landing in Normandy, on the northwest coast of France, rather than farther north where Hitler's intelligence was persuaded the landing would take place. While fighter planes and ships offshore bombed the Nazi fortifications, an Allied force of 176,000 men poured from six hundred warships and four thousand smaller vessels. At the end of several days of terrible fighting the beachhead was secured. During the next month the Allies built up their forces and equipment in preparation for a sweep across France. After a ferocious struggle for each mile of territory, by mid-July the Allies had finally won control of a long stretch of coast, a base from which to move inland through France and on toward Germany. The Third Army under General George Patton now began a thrust eastward toward Germany. Simultaneously an Allied force launched an assault on southern France from bases on the African coast, and troops began working their way north. The converging Allied forces approached Paris, liberating the city on August 25 amid great rejoicing.

After the liberation of Paris, the Russians intensified their drive to push the Germans back on the eastern front. At an enormous cost in Russian lives, the Soviets forced the Germans to retreat. As it pushed toward Germany, the Red Army invaded or cooperated with resistance forces in Hungary, Yugoslavia, Rumania, Bulgaria, Czechoslovakia, and Austria, with important political consequences for the future.

Allied forces in France, stalled by problems of supply, now faced the most difficult phase of their assault, meeting stiff German resistance in their drive toward Germany. After a series of difficult and costly battles, the Allies reached the Rhine toward the end of 1944. Since their forces were stretched out over a long front, they were vulnerable to enemy attack.

Hitler attempted his last major counterattack in December 1944. The Allies had thought the Germans were very near defeat when Hitler suddenly launched a formidable surprise attack in the thinly defended Ardennes Forest of Belgium and Luxembourg. Heavily armed German troops and an enormous tank force tore a bulge forty-five miles wide in the Allied line of defense. The ensuing effort to force a German retreat was called the Battle of the Bulge. Allied reinforcements finally smashed through to the Ardennes, and after another month of fighting, the Germans were pushed back to the Rhine, their fighting strength finally sapped.

Crossing the Rhine to invade Germany involved another spectacular amphibious operation in March 1945. Allied aerial bombardment, which had already done so much damage to German cities, now intensified. Combined with a scorched-earth policy undertaken by German troops at Hitler's command, the Allied operation reduced Germany to rubble.

The Allied sweep across Germany and eastern Europe led to the discovery of concentration camps converted into extermination centers at Dachau, Auschwitz, Buchenwald, Bergen-Belsen, and numerous other locations. The Nazi persecution of the Jews had been known since the early 1930s, but the idea that Jews and other "undesirables" were being systematically exterminated in Germany and in Nazi-occupied countries was too horrifying to be

ALLIED FORCES LAND AT OMAHA BEACH ON THE NORMANDY COAST OF FRANCE, JUNE 6, 1944.

fully comprehended. The rigidity of American immigration laws had contributed to the Holocaust by preventing many Jews from fleeing Germany to the United States. So too had fear during the 1930s that a relaxation of quotas would bring in people who would take scarce jobs away from Americans. The real extent of the Nazi atrocity became apparent only when Allied forces liberated the camps and found mass graves where corpses were piled upon corpses, crematories, and gas chambers equipped with fake shower heads to delude victims. It has been estimated that six million Jews were exterminated along with large numbers of Slavs, gypsies, and other groups marked by Hitler for extinction.

The last months of the war brought chaos within the Third Reich. Many in the German high command had turned against Hitler, and there had been several attempts on his life. On April 30, with the Red Army entering Berlin, Hitler, rather than letting himself be captured, shot himself with a pistol in his bunker headquarters in Berlin. Two days before, Mussolini had been murdered by a mob of his countrymen and strung up by his heels. On May 7, 1945, the remnants of the German government surrendered unconditionally. The following day—which was proclaimed V-E day (victory in Europe)—was met with wild rejoicing in the United States and liberated Europe.

The Election of 1944

Even global war did not interrupt the American political process. Though Roosevelt was exhausted from the terrible stresses the war had placed on him, there was no opposition to his renomination in 1944. The fateful decision of the Democratic convention was to replace the liberal Henry Wallace with longtime party loyalist Senator Harry S Truman of Missouri as Roosevelt's running mate. The Republicans nominated the efficient governor of New York, Thomas E. Dewey, hoping his youth and vigor would draw support away from the fading president. They were wrong: Roosevelt easily won a fourth term by a margin of three and one-half million popular votes and an electoral vote of 432 to 99.

The Yalta Conference

In February 1945, three months before the German surrender, the Big Three met at Yalta in the Crimea to make final war plans, arrange the fate of Germany, and discuss proposals for organizing a successor to the League of Nations.

To induce the Soviet Union to enter the war against Japan after the defeat of Germany, Churchill and Roosevelt had granted Stalin a dominant commercial influence in Manchuria. This concession was contrary to an agreement made in 1943 at Teheran that Manchuria should come under Chinese control. In addition, the Soviets were to receive the Kurile Islands, the southern half of Sakhalin Island, and continue to control Outer Mongolia. Stalin also insisted on Germany's permanent and complete dissolution and asked for reparations of up to $20 billion in goods and services, with half going to the Soviet Union. The Western leaders would not accept any fixed sum; instead they accepted the proposal only as a basis for discussion by a Reparations Commission. They also resisted Stalin's demand for a territorial partition of Germany. The final agreement provided only for the country's temporary division into zones of military occupation by the Big Three powers and France.

Churchill and Roosevelt sought to forestall Russian dominance in eastern Europe after Germany's defeat. At Teheran the Big Three had secretly agreed that Russia would retain much of eastern Poland taken during the period of the Russian-German alliance. Poland was to be compensated with a comparable amount of territory inhabited by German-speaking peoples to the west. The crucial question at Yalta concerned the type of government that would be established in Poland. The Russians did not want the Polish government-in-exile in London or the Polish underground to share power with the present Soviet-influenced regime in Lublin. Nevertheless, Roosevelt and Churchill obtained Stalin's agreement to a provision specifying that the Polish government would be enlarged to include "democratic leaders from Poland itself and . . . Poles abroad." The degree of democratic representation was not specified. The new government was then to hold free elections based on "universal suffrage and secret ballot." As events would show, the Russian conception of free elections was vastly different from that of the Western democracies. Regarding the other countries in eastern Europe that had been liberated, the Great Powers agreed to the creation of interim governments and to free elections that would establish governments responsible to the people.

The agreements at Yalta were later criticized as "tragic blunders" because of postwar Soviet actions. But at the time the Allied leaders believed the conference had been a success. A protracted conflict with Japan was expected and the atomic bomb would not be ready for use for several months. The Big Three emerged from Yalta declaring their solidarity. Roosevelt and his advisers were hopeful that the postwar international climate would be truly peaceful. Some critics have pointed out that Roosevelt and his most important adviser, Harry Hopkins, were both ailing and tired. But neither Roosevelt, nor Hopkins, nor Churchill, saw themselves as ap-

peasing Stalin in eastern Europe or in the Far East. They believed they had worked long and hard to limit, on paper at least, the extent of Soviet influence in those areas. Compromises had been made, but Roosevelt felt he had done the best he could do.

Defenders of the agreements made at Yalta have pointed out that Roosevelt and Churchill could not have stopped Russian dominance in eastern Europe without a great sacrifice of human life. By the time of the Yalta conference, the Red Army was already in control of large sections of eastern Europe.

The War in the Pacific

Early in 1942, after their attack on Pearl Harbor, the Japanese had moved swiftly to round out their influence in Asia. They struck at the Philippines, destroying much of the American air force at Manila. Filipino and American troops, led by General Douglas MacArthur, fought desperately to defend the Bataan peninsula and the island fortress of Corregidor. Against hopeless odds, the Allied forces held out until April 1942. Their eventual surrender was followed by a fifty-five-mile forced march to a prison camp in which many of the 140,000 captured soldiers died. Roosevelt had already ordered MacArthur out of the Philippines because his military skills were needed in the defense of Australia, but the general vowed that he would return to the islands.

Step by step, Japan now took Thailand, British Malaya, the Netherlands East Indies, Hong Kong, Guam, the Gilbert and Solomon islands, and Wake Island. Having made vast territorial gains in only a few months, the Japanese might well have concentrated on consolidating and reorganizing their new empire. But in May 1942 the overconfident military leaders attempted to cut Australia off from the Allies. In the Battle of the Coral Sea, Japanese warships approached the Allied outpost at Port Moresby, New Guinea, and airplanes from the American carriers Lexington and Yorktown attacked, forcing the Japanese to retreat.

Still hoping to destroy the weak Pacific fleet before the United States had time to rebuild, the Japanese launched an attack on the American base at Midway Island in the mid-Pacific in early June 1942. However, the navy had intercepted Japanese transmissions and knew their strategy. As a result Admiral Chester W. Nimitz succeeded in turning the Japanese initiative into a massive defeat. Confident of victory, the Japanese had deployed a substantial part of their navy in the mid-Pacific, where it was routed by the smaller American force. Midway marked the turning point of the Asian war. After their defeat there, the Japanese fell into a defensive posture while they undertook repairs and reconstruction of their fleet.

Even without the benefit of priority status in supply allocations, the American forces in the Pacific were able to oust the Japanese from New Guinea and the Solomon Islands during the second half of 1942. The fighting for Guadalcanal in the Solomons lasted more than six months, but the Japanese finally retreated in February 1943.

Aid to the Chinese

In addition to the efforts against Japan, the United States had another objective in Asia: to prevent the collapse of China. Roosevelt believed in China's potential as a strong independent power and in the leadership of Generalissimo Chiang Kai-shek. He refused to recognize the country's weakness and the internal corruption and intrigue that characterized Chiang's regime.

American supplies flown from India over the Himalayas and General Claire Chennault's "Flying

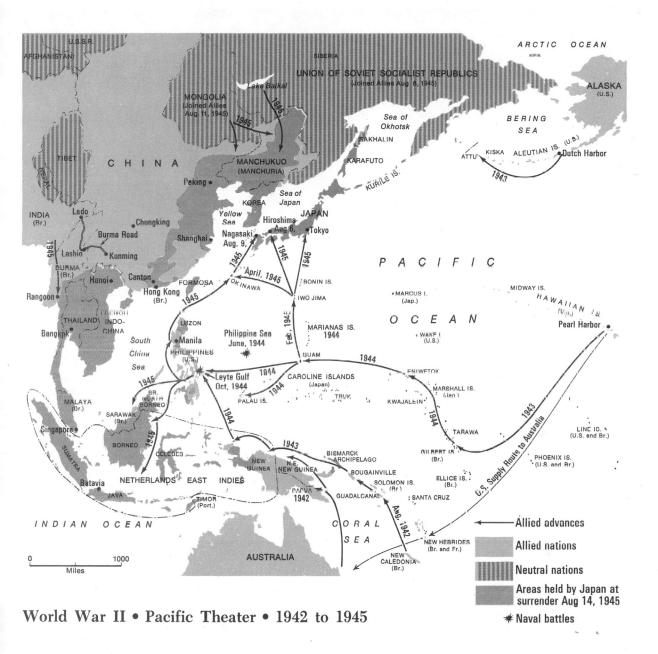

World War II • Pacific Theater • 1942 to 1945

Tigers" were all the support the United States could give China at first. But in 1942 the administration sent American troops under General Joseph Stilwell. Stilwell was able to build a road through northern Burma to facilitate the movement of supplies, but the rest of his mission was a failure. Chiang was more concerned about hoarding his supplies and troops for a future engagement with rising Chinese Communist insurgents in northwest China than with fighting the Japanese.

Stilwell warned the Joint Chiefs that the Generalissimo was undermining the war effort in China. In response, the administration asked Chiang to put Stilwell in command of the Chinese army, but the Generalissimo countered by asking for Stilwell's dismissal. Roosevelt decided to recall Stilwell in the fall of 1944 and send as his representative General Patrick J. Hurley. Hurley tried to forge a coalition between Chiang's government and the Communists led by Mao Tse-tung, but the Nationalist leader demanded that Communist forces be placed under his command, and the plan collapsed. China never played an important role in the war against Japan.

The Campaign against Japan

The United States was also planning a full-scale offensive against Japan. General MacArthur argued for an attack northward through the Philippines. However, his naval counterpart, Admiral Nimitz, favored an assault farther out in the Pacific against the Japanese bases in the Caroline and Mariana islands, and then Formosa and the China coast before attacking Japan. The result, like the two-front action against Hitler, was a decision in Washington to combine routes.

Between 1943 and 1945 the Americans inched toward Japan, suffering enormous casualties all along the way. MacArthur's forces staged complex amphibious landings to retake one island group after another, gradually moving northward toward the Philippines.

Nimitz carried on similar island-hopping actions in taking the Gilberts and Marshalls, using recaptured islands as bases for bombing raids to the north. After retaking Guam and the Marianas, he began to bomb Japan itself. A devastating new weapon, the fire bomb, was now introduced. By the end of the war 330,000 Japanese had perished in fire-bomb raids.

Despite heavy casualties among its civilian population, Japan continued to defend its shrunken empire. On October 20, 1944, MacArthur realized his long-cherished dream when he landed on the beach at Leyte Gulf in the Philippines declaring, "I have returned." The Japanese believed that this invasion was a key one and committed the bulk of their navy to trying to combat it. MacArthur managed to reach Manila by February 1945, but there were still months, perhaps years, of fighting ahead before the islands would be completely cleared of enemy troops.

Admiral Nimitz focused on trying to take tiny Iwo Jima, located only 750 miles from Tokyo. The Japanese-built airfields on the island would offer cover for American bombers bound for Japan and provide a landing place for crippled aircraft. The Japanese, however, had anticipated Nimitz's attack on the island and poured in vast numbers of troops and armaments. The battle for the island, which occurred in February 1945, resulted in a costly American victory. The Japanese fought so tenaciously that United States Marine casualties totaled over twenty thousand men. The capture of Iwo Jima facilitated the fire-bombing of Japan. In March a raid on Tokyo left eighty-three thousand people dead.

The final obstacle to an invasion of the main Japanese islands was Okinawa. The American assault that began on April 1, 1945 was met by desperate Japanese resistance on land and sea. Japanese suicide planes known as *kamikaze* ("divine wind") dove into Allied ships, sinking more than thirty of them and damaging hundreds. In the process the bulk of the Japanese air force was destroyed. When the battle was finally over in late June the Allies had lost fifty-thousand men and the Japanese over twice that number.

The Atomic Bomb On August 2, 1939, the physicist Albert Einstein had written to Roosevelt: "The element uranium may be turned into a new and important source of energy in the immediate future." Einstein warned that "watchfulness" and "quick action" were required. Roosevelt heeded the advice. The Manhattan Project, a secret wartime operation, placed a workable atomic bomb in the hands of the United States government in mid-summer 1945.

In the midst of the preparations for ending the war and dealing with the postwar world, President Roosevelt died of a cerebral hemorrhage at Warm Springs, Georgia, on April 12, 1945. Responsibility for handling the complexities of the situation now passed into the hands of Harry Truman.

Meeting in Potsdam, Germany, on July 26, the Allied leaders informed the Japanese that they would face total destruction if they refused to surrender at once. Churchill had given Truman his consent to use the new weapon should the Japanese

THE CENTER OF NAGASAKI, JAPAN, AFTER THE EXPLOSION OF THE ATOMIC BOMB

refuse. Moderate Japanese leaders believed that the war was lost and wanted to accept the Potsdam Declaration. Military leaders, however, were determined to fight to the bitter end. When Truman's deadline of August 3 had passed and the Japanese had not surrendered, he felt he had no alternative but to carry out his threat. On August 6 a single plane dropped an atomic bomb on Hiroshima, devastating the city. More than seventy-eight thousand people were killed and many more horribly burned, wounded, or doomed to suffer the terrible effects of radiation. Two days later Stalin, keeping the pledge he had made earlier, declared war on Japan and began an invasion of Manchuria. Still the Japanese made no move to surrender, and on August 9 the United States dropped a second bomb, this

time on the city of Nagasaki. Now fully aware of the shattering force of the atomic bomb and threatened by the looming presence of the Soviet Union in Manchuria, the Japanese surrendered on August 14.

The question of whether or not the United States should have used the atomic bomb has been hotly debated. Truman accepted the argument that dropping the bomb would hasten the end of the war by many months and save a million American lives. Moreover, he was persuaded that using the bomb would demonstrate American military might, thereby giving the government added diplomatic advantage in dealing with the Soviet Union. Specifically, the dropping of the bomb would reduce the possibility of Soviet influence in China and Japan after the war.

In retrospect, critics have argued that despite the unyielding position of its military leaders, the Japanese government was casting about for a way to accept the Potsdam ultimatum. Had Washington exhibited a little more patience, the Japanese moderates might have succeeded in their attempts to have the Potsdam Declaration accepted and Japan might have been spared the terrible losses due to the atomic bomb.

The War Ends The war in the Pacific ended three years and nine months after the attack on Pearl Harbor. On September 2 the formal terms of surrender were signed in Tokyo Bay by Allied and Japanese representatives aboard the United States battle-ship *Missouri*. They provided for Allied occupation of Japan under the command of General MacArthur and the creation of a new democratic government.

World War II was frightfully costly in terms of lives and resources. A total of some fourteen million fighting men and an even greater number of civilians died. American casualties exceeded one million. Much of Europe and Asia lay in ashes, and though the American mainland was untouched, America's resources had been stretched to the limit. The future posed the difficult and uncertain challenge of rebuilding the war-torn nations and finding a way to assure a more peaceful postwar world in a new atomic age.

Readings

General Works

Adler, Selig, *The Isolationist Impulse: Its Twentieth Century Reaction.* New York: Abelard-Schuman, 1957.

_____, *The Uncertain Giant: 1921–1941.* New York: Macmillan, 1969. (Paper)

Buchanan, A. Russell, *The United States and World War II*, Vols. I–II. New York: Harper & Row, 1964.

Churchill, Winston, *The Second World War*, Vols. I–VI. Boston: Houghton Mifflin, 1948–1953.

Dallek, Robert, *Franklin D. Roosevelt and American Foreign Policy, 1932–1945.* New York: Oxford University Press, 1979.

Ellis, L. Ethan, *Republican Foreign Policy 1921–1933.* New Brunswick, N.J.: Rutgers University Press, 1968.

Lingeman, Richard R., *Don't You Know There's a War On.* New York: Warner, 1971. (Paper)

Morton, Louis, *Strategy and Command* (1962). Washington: Office of the Chief of Military History, Dept. of the Army.

Offner, Arnold, *The Origins of the Second World War.* New York: Praeger, 1975.

Perrett, Geoffrey, *Days of Sadness, Years of Triumph: The American People, 1939–1945.* New York: Penguin, 1974. (Paper)

Toland, John, *The Rising Sun: The Decline and Fall of the Japanese Empire, 1936–1945.* New York: Random House, 1970. (Paper)

Wiltz, John E., *From Isolation to War, 1931–1941.* New York: Crowell, 1968. (Paper)

Special Studies

Ambrose, Stephen E., *The Supreme Commander: The War Years of General Dwight D. Eisenhower*, Sam Vaughan (Ed.). Garden City, N.Y.: Doubleday, 1970.

Beard, Charles A., *President Roosevelt and the Coming of the War.* Hamden, Conn.: Shoe String, 1968.

Borg, Dorothy, *The United States and the Far Eastern Crisis of 1933–1938.* Cambridge, Mass.: Harvard University Press, 1964.

Borg, Dorothy, and Shumpei Okomoto (Eds.), *Pearl Harbor as· History: Japanese-American Relations, 1931-41.* New York: Columbia University Press, 1973.

Clemens, Diana S., *Yalta.* New York: Oxford University Press, 1970.

DeConde, Alexander, *Herbert Hoover's Latin American Policy.* New York: Octagon, 1970.

Divine, Robert A., *Roosevelt and World War II.* New York: Penguin, 1970. (Paper)

Feis, Herbert, *Churchill, Roosevelt, Stalin.* Princeton, N.J.: Princeton University Press, 1967.

_____, *The Road to Pearl Harbor.* Princeton, N.J.: Princeton University Press, 1950.

Ferrell, Robert H., *American Diplomacy in the Great Depression.* Hamden, Conn.: Shoe String Press, 1969.

Girdner, Audrie, and Anne Loftis, *The Great Betrayal.* New York: Macmillan, 1969.

Kolko, Gabriel, *Politics of War: The World and U.S. Foreign Policy, 1943–1945.* New York: Random, 1968.

Langer, William L., and S. E. Gleason, *The Challenge to Isolation 1937–1940*. New York: Harper & Row, 1952.

———, *Undeclared War 1940–1941*. New York: Harper & Row, 1953.

Lash, Joseph P., *Roosevelt and Churchill, 1939–1941: The Partnership That Saved the West*. New York: Norton, 1976.

MacDonald, C. B., *The Mighty Endeavor: American Armed Forces in the European Theatre in World War II*. New York: Oxford University Press, 1969.

Morison, Samuel E., *The Two Arena War*. Boston: Little, Brown, 1963.

Munro, Dana, *United States and the Caribbean Republics, 1921–1933*. Princeton, N.J.: Princeton University Press, 1974.

Offner, Arnold A., *American Appeasement: United States Foreign Policy and Germany, 1933–1938*. Cambridge, Mass.: Harvard University Press, 1969.

Rappaport, Armin, *Henry L. Stimson and Japan: 1931–1933*. Chicago: University of Chicago Press, 1963.

Schaller, Michael, *The United States Crusade in China, 1938–1945*. New York: Columbia University Press, 1978.

Sherwin, Martin, *A World Destroyed: The Atomic Bomb and the Grand Alliance*. New York: Knopf, 1975.

Smith, Gaddis, *American Diplomacy during the Second World War: 1941–1945*. New York: Wiley, 1965. (Paper)

Weglyn, Michi, *Years of Infamy: The Untold Story of America's Concentration Camps*. New York: Morrow, 1976.

Wilkins, Myra, *The Maturing of Multinational Enterprise: American Business Abroad from 1914–1970*. Cambridge, Mass.: Harvard University Press, 1974.

Wilson, Joan Hoff, *American Business and Foreign Policy, 1920–1933*. Lexington: University Press of Kentucky, 1971.

Wohlstetter, Roberta, *Pearl Harbor, Warning and Decision*. Stanford, Calif.: Stanford University Press, 1962.

Primary Sources

Davies, John Paton, *Dragon by the Tail*. New York: Norton, 1972.

Loewenheim, Francis L., Harold D. Langley, and Manfred Jonas (Eds.), *Roosevelt and Churchill: Their Secret Wartime Correspondence*. New York: Dutton, 1975.

Pyle, Ernie, *Here's Your War: The Story of G. I. Joe*. Cleveland: World, 1945.

Biographies

Burns, James M., *Roosevelt: The Soldier of Freedom*. New York: Harcourt Brace Jovanovich, 1970. (Paper)

James, D. Clayton, *The Years of MacArthur*, Vols. I–II. Boston: Houghton Mifflin, 1970–1975.

Morison, Elting E., *Turmoil and Tradition: A Study of the Life and Times of Henry L. Stimson*. New York: Atheneum, 1964.

Pogue, Forrest, *George C. Marshall*, Vols. I–II. New York: Viking, 1963–1966.

Pratt, Julius W., *Cordell Hull*, Vols. I–II. New York: Cooper Square, 1964.

Tuchman, Barbara, *Stilwell and the American Experience in China*. New York: Macmillan, 1970.

Fiction

Heller, Joseph, *Catch Twenty-Two*. New York: Dell, 1961. (Paper)

Hersey, John R., *Hiroshima*. New York: Knopf, 1946. (Paper)

Jones, James, *From Here to Eternity*. New York: Scribner's, 1951.

Mailer, Norman, *The Naked and the Dead*. New York: New American Library, 1960.

I believe that it must be the policy of the United States to support free peoples who are resisting attempted subjugation by armed minorities or by outside pressures.

I believe that we must assist free peoples to work out their own destinies in their own way.

I believe that our help should be primarily through economic and financial aid which is essential to economic stability and orderly political processes. . . .

The free peoples of the world look to us for support in maintaining their freedoms.

If we falter in our leadership, we may endanger the peace of the world—and we shall surely endanger the welfare of our own nation.

Harry S Truman

Significant Events

Senate ratifies the United Nations Charter [1945]

Potsdam Conference [July 1945]

Full Employment Act [1946]

Committee on Civil Rights [1946]

Taft-Hartley Act [1947]

Truman Doctrine [1947]

Marshall Plan [1948]

Presidential Order desegregating the armed forces [1948]

Berlin Blockade [April 1948–May 1949]

North Atlantic Treaty Organization [1949]

Fall of China to Communists [1949]

Korean War [June 1950–July 1953]

McCarran Internal Security Act [1950]

Japanese-American peace treaty [1951]

General Douglas MacArthur dismissed as commander of Allied troops in Korea [April 1951]

Dennis et al. v. United States [1951]

A WARM WELCOME AWAITS GIs RETURNING HOME ABOARD THE QUEEN ELIZABETH. 1946.

When Roosevelt died in April 1945, Harry Truman seemed ill equipped to take his place. During his four months as vice-president he had remained outside the president's circle of trusted advisers. Although Roosevelt had been in poor health, he had not even informed Truman of the Manhattan Project. Truman was well aware of his lack of preparation for the office. The day after his inauguration he told reporters, "I felt like the moon, the stars, and all the planets had fallen on me."

Truman's early life was unconventional in terms of preparing him for a career in national politics. The son of a Missouri mule trader, he worked for the Santa Fe Railroad, farmed for twelve years, served as an artillery captain in World War I, and finally became a partner in an unsuccessful men's clothing store. Then he entered politics under the wing of Tom Pendergast, Democratic boss of Kansas City. Never personally implicated in the corrupt activities of the Pendergast machine, Truman was elected to the Senate in 1934 and reelected in 1940.

The new president possessed an interesting blend of human characteristics. Cocky and often prone to rash actions, he nonetheless brought to office a strong sense of dedication and responsibility and a record which revealed his concern for the public welfare. On his desk he kept a motto from Mark Twain, "Always do right. This will gratify some people, and astonish the rest." From the outset he was informal and accessible, far more concerned with solving the nation's problems than with the trappings of the office of the president. An honest and forthright man who enjoyed making decisions, Truman became increasingly confident of his ability to govern. His decision-making skills were soon put to the test.

Truman's most pressing domestic task was reconverting the nation to a peacetime economy. By 1945 five million service men and women had returned to civilian life and had to be reabsorbed into the economy. Truman spelled out his solution to this problem in a twenty-one point program that reflected his commitment to extend the policies of the New Deal. The president called for legislation to ensure full employment and advocated government support for low-cost housing, an increased minimum wage, price supports for agriculture, and a federally funded public works program. Later Truman recommended a health-insurance program and the expansion of social security. Despite Truman's vigorous efforts to see this program enacted, Congress, dominated by a coalition of conservative Republicans and Southern Democrats, ultimately defeated most of its major components. Nevertheless, the plan became the nucleus of the Fair Deal which Truman proposed in 1949.

Postwar Domestic Problems

The Economy

Because the war had stimulated production and spurred the economy, many people feared that the termination of hostilities would cause another economic decline. But for a variety of reasons the predicted postwar depression failed to materialize. Demand for many consumer goods which had been unobtainable in a war-oriented economy enabled factories to maintain high levels of production. Repeal of wartime taxes and the introduction of liberal credit policies pumped additional money into the economy. In addition, the Full Employment Act of 1946, based on one of Truman's twenty-one points, empowered the federal government to take action to promote a healthy economy although it did not specify the means which were to be employed.

As the fear of postwar depression began to subside, it was replaced by the fear of inflation. Truman favored the continuation of the Office of Price Administration (OPA), which had controlled wartime prices but was due to expire. The president feared that a sudden lifting of price controls, combined with an increased demand for consumer goods, would send prices spiraling upward. Congress, however, supported the demand of business and farmers to allow prices to rise. It voted to extend the OPA but so weakened its powers that Truman vetoed the bill. As a result, prices rose rapidly. Congress then passed another bill which the president signed reluctantly. But the damage had already been done. The cost of living, an indicator of the rate of inflation, jumped 25 percent between 1946 and 1948.

Labor

While the president was urging price controls, labor was pressing hard for wage increases to keep pace with rising prices. During 1946, demands for higher wages met determined resistance from employers and small businesspeople and led to several strikes. Truman found himself in an awkward position. Although he generally supported labor, he was concerned that strikes would be disruptive and that wage increases would produce additional inflation. Consequently, when a strike by the United Mine Workers resulted in a coal shortage, Truman declared a national disaster and ordered government troops to seize control of the mines. A compromise agreement was reached which increased miners' wages, improved safety regulations, and established a welfare fund for mine workers. When railroad workers struck a month later, Truman again intervened, threatening to draft the strikers into the army to keep the railroads running. Again the unions were forced to accept a compromise settlement. Infuriated labor leaders denounced the president's strike breaking tactics for weakening the workers' right to strike.

The Taft-Hartley Act In 1946 public discontent with the state of the economy and the directions in which it appeared to be heading led to the election of a Republican majority in Congress for the first time since the Hoover administration. The new Republican Congress cut government expenditures and taxes. It also passed the immensely controversial Taft-Hartley Act of 1947, which placed certain limitations on the conduct of labor in disputes with management. The act abolished the closed shop, whereby employers had been prohibited from hiring nonunion workers. Section 14(b) left intact the so-called right-to-work laws, which were state laws prohibiting agreements that would make union membership a condition for holding a job. The act authorized government injunctions forcing strikers to return to work for an eighty-day "cooling-off period" if the strike was considered a threat to the national welfare. In addition, it gave employers the right to sue unions for breach of contract, and prohibited unions from using coercion against nonunion workers. Finally, the act required unions to publish financial statements, forbade union contributions to political parties, and barred Commu-

nists from positions of union leadership. Concerned that the position of labor would be seriously undermined, Truman vetoed the bill; within a matter of days Congress overrode his veto.

Civil Rights

At the war's end the status of black Americans had improved little. Although discrimination in war-related industries had declined, the United States Army was still racially segregated. In many cities, North and South, blacks could not get accommodations at a hotel, eat at a lunch counter, or attend a movie downtown. In industries where they were employed, blacks were prevented from moving into management and sales positions and were often the first let go when business slowed down. Taking up the struggle to end discrimination against black Americans, Truman appointed a Committee on Civil Rights in 1946 to study existing patterns of discrimination and to suggest ways of eliminating them. Toward the end of 1947 the committee issued its findings and recommendations in a report entitled *To Secure These Rights*. The report examined discrimination in education, employment practices, housing, and public services and suggested bold legislative remedies. Eventually it became the basis of a series of proposals aimed at obtaining antilynching laws and securing voting and employment rights for blacks. Truman subsequently sent this program to Congress. When the conservative Congress failed to act, the president issued an executive order in 1948, desegregating the armed forces, civil service departments, and companies which did business with the government. He also called for the creation of a Civil Rights Division in the Justice Department. Although Truman's actions opened up the armed services and government employment to blacks, many private companies with government contracts continued their discriminatory practices.

The Election of 1948

As the 1948 election approached, Truman's chances for reelection seemed slim. He was opposed not only by the Republicans, but by a large number of disenchanted Democrats. During 1947 Truman had fired Secretary of Commerce Henry Wallace for criticizing the administration's vigorous anti-Communist foreign policy. Wallace responded by leaving the

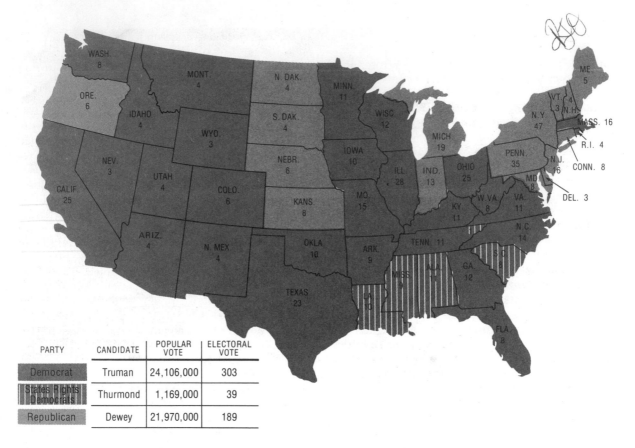

PARTY	CANDIDATE	POPULAR VOTE	ELECTORAL VOTE
Democrat	Truman	24,106,000	303
States Rights Democrats	Thurmond	1,169,000	39
Republican	Dewey	21,970,000	189

Election of 1948

Democratic party to form a new Progressive party, dedicated to seeking an accommodation with the Soviet Union on world problems. In addition, conservative Southern Democrats were disgruntled over Truman's civil rights proposals. When a strong civil rights plank, supported by Hubert H. Humphrey, then mayor of Minneapolis, was approved by the 1948 Democratic convention, many Southerners walked out. They formed the States' Rights Democratic party (often called the Dixiecrats) and nominated Governor Strom Thurmond of South Carolina for president. As if all this were not enough, moderate Democrats, convinced that Truman had no chance of winning, mounted a preconvention campaign to replace him with a more popular candidate

such as General Eisenhower. However, when Eisenhower refused to run, the president was unenthusiastically renominated.

With the New Deal coalition and the Democratic party apparently in ruins, the Republicans were confident of regaining the White House for the first time since 1928. To oppose Truman, they again nominated Thomas E. Dewey. While Dewey confidently conducted a low-key campaign and restricted his speechmaking to "glittering generalities," Truman embarked on a whirlwind "whistle-stop" campaign. Crisscrossing the country by train, the president made 356 speeches in thirty-five days, speaking mostly from the rear platform of his train to anyone who would listen. He decided to ignore predictions

Domestic
McCarthy

HAVING JUST DEFEATED DEWEY IN
THE 1948 PRESIDENTIAL ELECTION, A
BEAMING HARRY TRUMAN HOLDS UP
A COPY OF THE *CHICAGO DAILY
TRIBUNE*. THE NEWSPAPER HAD BEEN
CONVINCED DEWEY WOULD WIN,
ALTHOUGH TRUMAN LED IN THE
BALLOTING FROM THE START.

of failure in the public-opinion polls and to take his
case directly to the people. He stood frankly on his
record, lambasting the "do-nothing" Republican
Congress as the real cause of the nation's problems.
Crowds began to join in, shouting "Give 'em hell,
Harry!"

Against all the odds, Harry S Truman was
elected to serve a term of his own. In the four-way
contest, he received over twenty-four million popular votes to Dewey's twenty-two million and 303
electoral votes to a total of 228 for all his opponents.
The Democrats regained their majority in both
houses of Congress, riding into office on Truman's
coattails.

Historians are still analyzing Truman's surprising victory. Certainly the whistle-stop campaign
was an important factor, since it allowed him to
speak directly to large numbers of voters. Dewey's
overconfidence backfired, for in the closing days of
the campaign Truman made strong gains among
farmers, blacks, Jews, and workers who remembered his veto of the Taft-Hartley Act. Furthermore, many longstanding Democrats simply refused
to vote against the party of Roosevelt and the New
Deal.

The Fair Deal

Victory in the face of so many prophecies of defeat
boosted Truman's confidence and renewed his faith
in liberal social reform. In 1949 he submitted to
Congress a legislative plan based on his twenty-one-
point program. This program, called the Fair Deal,
encountered opposition from the Republican coalition and Southern Democrats that was strong
enough to defeat many of its provisions. Truman
did, however, secure congressional approval for
some measures: raising the minimum wage from
$.65 to $.75 an hour, expanding social security benefits to cover ten million more people, and providing
government funding for one hundred thousand low-
income public-housing units and for urban renewal.
But Congress defeated his provisions for civil rights
legislation and a health-insurance program. In addition, it refused his farm program which was designed to reduce agricultural surpluses, to support
farmers' incomes, and to place a price ceiling on
many farm products. The Agricultural Act of 1949
continued rigid price supports. When Truman tried
to keep a campaign promise to repeal the Taft-Hartley Act, Congress once again blocked his efforts.

Efforts to Forge a New Peace

International Organizations

For a brief period during the war, there was hope that past mistakes might be instructive and that the world would enter a new era of peace. American leaders believed that the nation's failure to deal responsibly with the war-debt crisis in Europe had encouraged the rise of European fascism. Subsequently, the United States took steps to prevent a similar state of economic instability from plaguing postwar Europe. In 1944 at Breton Woods, New Hampshire, forty-nine nations at war with the Axis met to create the International Monetary Fund and the International Bank for Reconstruction and Development (World Bank). The purpose of these new agencies was to stabilize international currency, to increase investment in underdeveloped areas, and to speed economic recovery of Europe.

In January 1942, the Arcadia conference had set the stage for the formation of an organization to replace the League of Nations. The groundwork was laid in Washington during the summer and fall of 1944 and in meetings at Yalta in early 1945. A conference in San Francisco in April 1945 worked out the United Nations Charter, and the Senate ratified United States membership in the organization later that year. Most Americans believed that the new United Nations was the best hope for world peace.

The United Nations was to be composed of a General Assembly, which would serve as a forum for discussion by representatives from all nations, and a Security Council, made up of six temporary members on a rotating basis and five permanent members: Great Britain, France, the Soviet Union, China, and the United States. Only the Security Council could take action on substantive issues through investigation, mediation, or other suitable measures. According to the UN charter, it could even employ armed forces supplied by member nations to enforce its decisions. A Secretariat, headed by a secretary-general, was to perform the organization's administrative work.

Although the major powers agreed to send representatives to the United Nations, they were unwilling to relinquish much of their own sovereignty. Both the United States and Russia insisted on restricting the Security Council's authority by granting a veto to each permanent member and by re-

quiring unanimous approval by the five permanent members for any action. During the first few years of the founding of the United Nations, the Soviet Union, in particular, repeatedly used its veto power to block measures which it opposed.

In 1946 the Russians vetoed an American proposal calling for an International Atomic Development Authority empowered to supervise the production of atomic energy throughout the world. The proposed agency would have been exempt from the permanent-member veto. Russia, however, was unwilling either to forgo development of the atomic bomb or to permit inspection of its atomic plants. In addition to retaining the veto, its counterproposal insisted on cessation of production and the elimination of nuclear stockpiles before controls were levied. The United States refused to accept these provisions.

The End to Allied Unity

The war had both immediate and long-range consequences throughout the world. Europe and Asia were left in a state of economic and political disarray. Thirty-five million Europeans, including Russians, had lost their lives, and millions more had been displaced. Both continents lay in physical ruin. As a result, the weakened European powers were unable to prevent the breakup of their colonial empires as new countries formed first in Asia and then in Africa. America and Russia emerged as two global superpowers with strong, clearly defined differences over how the peace should be organized. Russia was determined to be recognized as the great power it was. The United States was at its peak of military and economic might: its industrial capacity was unimpaired, and it possessed a seasoned, well-equipped army and navy as well as a terrible new weapon. American leaders rejected a return to isolationism and instead set about establishing a stable world community in which the United States would be the economic as well as the political leader. This policy was supported by two other developments which had resulted from the war: increased presidential power, and a close partnership between businesses hungry for defense contracts and the huge military establishment.

Origins of the Cold War

The wartime alliance between the Western democracies and the Soviet Union had been based not on trust, long-term mutual interests, or shared values, but on one necessity: opposition to a common enemy. With the approach of an allied victory, the need for cooperation began to diminish and American and Soviet differences became more apparent. These differences increased during the postwar period until America found itself facing the Soviet Union in a totally new kind of conflict, one which became known as the cold war.

Most Americans viewed communism as an ideology clearly opposed to the democratic way of life. Their mistrust was compounded by the Soviets' avowed intention of spreading communism throughout the world. As World War II neared its end, the cloud of rivalry and mutual suspicion shrouding the two global powers thickened.

The events immediately following the Yalta conference seemed to confirm long-held American suspicions regarding Russia's intention to spread communism. At Yalta, Stalin had promised the "earliest possible establishment, through free elections, of governments responsive to the will of the people." However, his participation in the Yalta conference was merely part of an overall Soviet strategy to work with the western powers toward the defeat of Nazi Germany. A few weeks after the conference, it became clear that Germany was close to defeat. Stalin then returned to his primary postwar concern, the creation of a power balance in Europe that would prevent another invasion of Russia in the future. Russia's battlefield casualties and the material damage to its territory had far exceeded Allied losses. Stalin was determined to create a buffer of friendly nations along Russia's western border as a means of securing his country against possible external attack. The desire of the peoples of eastern and central Europe for self-determination was irrelevant to this goal. After accusing Great Britain and the United States of preventing Soviet participation in negotiations for the surrender of Italy and of secret negotiations with Germany, Stalin quickly extended Russian dominance in eastern Europe by imposing Communist regimes on both Poland and Romania.

Roosevelt had left Yalta believing that cooperation between the United States and the Soviet Union after the war would be possible if the American government maintained a policy of patient firmness. Although anxious about Stalin's aggressive attitude and the turn of events in eastern Europe, he hoped to persuade "Uncle Joe," as he sometimes called Stalin, to modify his policy. Roosevelt perceived Stalin as a tough realist whose foreign policy was based not on a desire to spread communism throughout the world but rather on a desire to extend Russia's influence to peripheral territories in order to ensure its security.

After Roosevelt's death in 1945, Churchill tried to persuade Truman to send American and British troops deep into Germany in order to liberate Prague before the Russians arrived. Truman, however, believed such a move would alienate the Russians and tie up American troops in Europe at a time when they could better be used in the Far East against Japan. In addition, General Eisenhower advised the president that such a movement into central Europe was not a military necessity.

The new president was unfamiliar with the details of American foreign policy. While Truman initially seemed to believe he could work with Stalin, he was gradually persuaded by such advisers as George Kennan and W. Averell Harriman that Soviet expansion must be resisted and that Stalin could not be trusted. In May 1945 the United States abruptly terminated Lend-Lease after sidetracking a Russian request for a large loan. Such moves may have encouraged Soviet seizures of reparations from the Russian sector in Germany.

The Potsdam Conference

The Big Three met again to plan the final assault on Japan and to try to resolve their differences over the future of Germany and eastern Europe. When Truman, Churchill, and Stalin arrived for a meeting at Potsdam, Germany, in mid-July 1945, the president's primary objectives were to limit postwar Soviet expansion and to secure a reaffirmation of Stalin's promise to enter the war against Japan. Truman was aware, however, that if Russia entered the war in the Far East, Stalin would be in a stronger bargaining position in regard to eastern Europe. The Russian leader also would be in a better position to dominate Manchuria and to participate in the occupation government of Japan.

As the conference began, President Truman received news of the successful atomic-bomb test in New Mexico. With the ultimate weapon at his disposal, he judged that Soviet help against Japan was unnecessary. He told Stalin that the United States had a weapon that could end the war. The Russian dictator showed little interest; he may already have been informed about it by Russian intelligence. As noted earlier, before the Japanese surrendered, Russia declared war and quickly moved into Manchuria.

On the question of Germany, the Allies agreed that the defeated nations should be disarmed and demilitarized and the remaining Nazi leaders tried for war crimes. However, they were unable to reach an accord as to what type of political structure should be imposed. The United States wanted to revive the economy of western Europe, and Germany was a vital element in this plan. Eventually the Big Three reaffirmed the agreement reached at Yalta that Germany should be divided into four occupation zones—American, British, French, and Russian—but left as one economic unit.

While each country would control its own occupation zone, the affairs of Germany as a whole would be directed through participation in an Allied Control Center in Berlin. Berlin, located one hundred miles inside the Soviet sector, had no land corridor to the other zones. It was divided into four Allied occupation zones, but the Russians would not agree to a written guarantee of access to the city across the Soviet sector. Although the division and occupation of Germany were to be temporary, the Russians soon demonstrated their intent to establish a separate Communist government in the Soviet sector. The Russian zone was predominantly agricultural, and the Soviets withheld foodstuffs from the three other, largely industrial areas.

STALIN AND TRUMAN DURING AN INFORMAL MOMENT AT THE POTSDAM CONFERENCE.

A FAVORITE PLACE FOR YOUNG PEOPLE TO KILL TIME (MORE POPULARLY KNOWN AS "MESSING AROUND") WAS A LOCAL RECORD STORE LIKE THIS TEEN HANGOUT IN WEST GROVES, MISSOURI. (Nina Leen, Life Magazine © Time Inc.)

▲ AUTOS QUEUE UP BEFORE A GAS STATION IN
WASHINGTON, D.C., AT SEVEN IN THE
MORNING ON JULY 21, 1942, THE DAY BE-
FORE GAS RATIONING WENT INTO EFFECT.
(Reproduced from the collections of the Library of
Congress)

RIGHT: THE DAILY LIVES OF ALMOST ALL
AMERICANS WERE AFFECTED BY WORLD
WAR II. WOMEN'S SLACKS, WHICH MADE
THEIR APPEARANCE JUST BEFORE THE WAR,
GAINED GENERAL PUBLIC ACCEPTANCE
DURING THE 1940s WHEN MILLIONS OF
WOMEN ENTERED THE WORK FORCE, TAK-
ING OVER JOBS FORMERLY HELD BY MEN.
(National Archives)

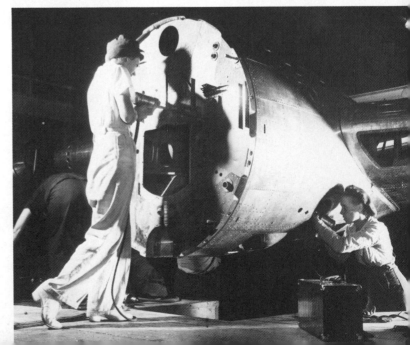

THE COLD WAR THREAT OF A POSSIBLE NUCLEAR
HOLOCAUST LED MANY AMERICANS TO CONSIDER
THE CONSTRUCTION OF HOME BOMB SHELTERS.
SOME COMPANIES OFFERED COMMERCIAL DESIGNS;
MANY HOMEOWNERS DESIGNED AND BUILT THEIR
OWN. (Loomis Dean, Life Magazine © 1951 Time Inc.)

A SHORT-LIVED FAD OF THE 1950s WAS THE 3-D
MOVIE. PATRONS ENTERING THE THEATER WERE
GIVEN A PAIR OF GLASSES THAT ENABLED THE
WEARER TO EXPERIENCE THE FILM'S SPECIAL
EFFECTS. (J. R. Eyerman, Life Magazine © 1952 Time Inc.)

MOVING VANS LINE THE STREETS OF ONE
OF THE MANY NEW HOUSING DEVELOP-
MENTS WHICH SPRANG UP DURING THE
1950s. (J. R. Eyerman, Life Magazine © 1953 Time
Inc.)

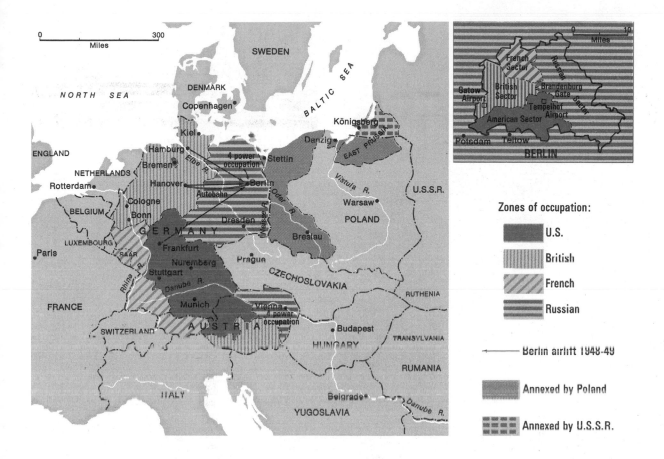

Occupation Zones • Germany and Austria • 1945 to 1950

Two other important agreements were reached at Potsdam. The Allies accepted the Communists' extension of Poland's western boundary to the Oder and Neisse rivers but left the final territorial decision to be concluded at the peace conference. In addition, a Council of Foreign Ministers was created to work out peace treaties for Italy, Austria, Hungary, Romania, Bulgaria, and Finland.

After the Potsdam conference, Soviet occupation troops enabled local Communist parties to take control in both Hungary and Bulgaria. Within two years, despite repeated protests by the United States, all of eastern Europe except Czechoslovakia was ruled by Communist governments either heavily supported by or dominated by Moscow. The one exception was the Communist government of Yugoslavia; under the leadership of Marshall Tito it successfully broke out of the Soviet orbit in 1948.

The events in eastern Europe complicated the often rancorous debates over peace treaties held in the Council of Foreign Ministers. Eventually treaties were concluded with Italy, Romania, Hungary, and Bulgaria in 1946 and Finland in February 1947. Soviet troops remained in Austria until 1955 when a treaty was worked out during the Eisenhower administration. A definitive peace treaty between the Allied and the Axis powers was never achieved.

Foreign Policy under Truman

In March 1946 Winston Churchill reviewed the international response to Russian aggression and declared that "From Stettin in the Baltic to Trieste in the Adriatic, an iron curtain has descended across the Continent. . . ." This was the first time the metaphor "iron curtain" was used, and the image struck a chord deep within the American consciousness. Even as Churchill spoke, the Soviets were expanding their influence, not only in eastern Europe, but also in the Mediterranean and the Middle East.

INTERPRETING AMERICAN HISTORY

THE ORIGINS OF THE COLD WAR Until the 1960s the historical interpretation of the development of antagonism between the United States and the Soviet Union following World War II was a reflection of the outlook of the State Department. According to this view the cold war resulted from efforts by the Soviet Union to pursue its prewar goal of spreading communism throughout the world. If the United States did not want to find itself isolated in a world dominated by a nation whose political and economic systems were diametrically opposed to its own, it would have to contain the spread of Soviet power. The validity of America's postwar foreign policy was well argued by Thomas A. Bailey in *America Faces Russia* (1950). Bailey contended that at the end of the war the prevailing attitude among Americans toward Russia was one of general good will, but that Stalin chose by his aggressive policies in eastern Europe and Germany to alienate rather than conciliate the United States, thus ending the possibility of American aid to rebuild the Soviet Union. Russia's crude and blustering tactics at the United Nations added fuel to the fire and turned America toward a program of preparedness for a possible conflict with its erstwhile ally. Bailey's interpretation of the cold war was mirrored in Joseph M. Jones's *The Fifteen Weeks: An Inside Account of the Genesis of the Marshall Plan* (1955) and Robert H. Ferrell's *George C. Marshall* (1966).

By the 1960s, however, several students of the period charged that the cold war had not been inevitable, that indeed the United States was more responsible than the Soviet Union for the development of international tensions. Influenced by a neo-Marxist analysis of American globalism, historians William A. Williams (*The Tragedy of American Diplomacy*, 1962), David Horowitz (*The Free World Colossus*, 1965), Walter LaFeber (*America, Russia, and the Cold War, 1945–1967*, 1967), and Gabriel and Joyce Kolko (*The Limits of Power*, 1972), emphasized American interventionism and Soviet moderation at the end of World War II. They argued that concern for the survival of its capitalist economy prompted the United States to pursue an imperialist foreign policy based on the acquisition of raw materials, markets, and outlets for overseas investments. Believing that the interest of the business community in an international "open-door" policy was endangered by a real or imagined Communist threat, Washington was persuaded to adopt the containment policy.

In *Atomic Diplomacy* (1965) Gar Alperovitz added to the revisionist argument the charge that the administration believed Soviet fear of American monopoly of atomic power would keep eastern Europe open to trade with the West. However, the threat of American atomic power did not deter the Soviet Union. Once Russia had achieved control of the Balkans, all of eastern Europe, as well as the Russian zone in Germany, became inaccessible to American trade.

Taking a more moderate revisionist line, Thomas G. Paterson in *Soviet-American Confrontation* (1973) stressed that Russia and the United States were equally responsible for the cold war. Hostile Soviet actions were matched by American determination to use its power to shape an American-oriented postwar world. In Paterson's analysis, the containment policy was an overreaction to a minimal threat in eastern Europe. Paterson

Although the Teheran conference in 1943 had provided for the freedom of Iran, Russian troops refused to leave northern Iran after the war. A revolt supported by Soviet arms broke out in that area in November 1945 and appeared to be a prelude to a Communist takeover. When protests to Moscow proved futile, the Iranian government took the matter to the United Nations where the Iranian position was backed by the United States. Confronted with a hostile world opinion, the Soviets withdrew their troops. However, Iran subsequently made an agreement with Russia in which the northern province was granted autonomy and a Russian-Iranian oil company was set up. Fearful that Iran

---

argued, for example, that while the Marshall Plan did bring about the rapid economic recovery of western Europe, it was also used to increase American economic influence there. In particular, the Marshall Plan fed Soviet animosity by rebuilding West Germany and drawing it economically into the western European orbit.

The first important reaction to cold war revisionism was contained in an article by historian Arthur M. Schlesinger, Jr. (*Foreign Affairs* "Origins of the Cold War" 46, Oct. 1967, 22–52). He argued that although the Soviets may not have been bent on world aggression, they were guided by a centuries-old desire to dominate eastern Europe and by an impulse to spread communism. At the end of World War II most American leaders advocated the Wilsonian dream of an international organization to guarantee world peace. But Russia had no faith in this concept and was determined to protect its national security by dominating eastern Europe. Mutual suspicion grew during 1945 with Soviet refusal to permit Western-style democracy to develop in the nations on its borders. Washington was apprehensive that western Europe would be the next target of Soviet expansion, while Moscow looked on American interest in the fate of eastern Europe as part of a worldwide capitalist threat to isolate the Soviet Union. The Soviet belief that there could be no peace between the capitalist and Communist economic systems and Stalin's deep, paranoic fear of the West further heightened tensions.

Two recent books on the cold war era also have challenged aspects of the revisionist thesis without returning to earlier interpretation of the origins of the conflict. In *The United States and the Origins of the Cold War, 1941–1947* (1972)

John Lewis Gaddis maintained that by 1946 two factors resulted in the development of the containment policy: the perception of the American government that Soviet actions in eastern Europe and Germany were aggressive in nature and pressure from Congress and the American public to make no more concessions to Russia. While conceding that the need to protect an "open door" for American trade and investment overseas played a role in the development of the containment policy, Gaddis argued that the political constraints created by American suspicions of Soviet motives made government opposition to Soviet policy in Europe almost inevitable. For his part, Stalin was preoccupied with maintaining his personal power, achieving national security, and spreading Communist ideology. Thus both nations bore responsibility for the creation of the cold war.

Finally, in *Shattered Peace* (1977) Daniel Yergin, while characterizing Soviet policy as clumsy and brutal, agreed with the revisionists that Russia's postwar aims did not include world domination. He viewed Soviet expansion immediately following World War II as based on a determination to protect its national borders. However, men of significant influence in the American government, such as George Kennan and James Forrestal, were suspicious of Soviet motives. They cautioned that the Soviet government was totalitarian and expansionist and that the United States must assert its military and economic power to secure Russian cooperation. Yergin argues that by 1947 advocates of this hard line had gained ascendency over more moderate members of the Truman administration who favored a cooperative approach to relations with Russia.

might be losing its independence, the United States extended aid, thus enabling Iran to reject the oil agreement and make military preparations against another Soviet threat.

At the same time Stalin heavily pressed Turkey and Greece in hopes of establishing military bases in the Turkish straits. Greece was in the throes of civil war, and although Stalin had not directly incited the revolt, the insurgents were dominated by Greek Communists and were receiving supplies from Russian satellites. Eventually British troops moved in to help the conservative, monarchist government. With their aid the monarchy was restored; however, guerrilla warfare continued in rural areas. By early 1947, the British could no longer afford the expense of maintaining an occupation force and began to withdraw.

The American government was alarmed at the possibility of an insurgent victory and the subsequent formation of a Communist government in a strategic Mediterranean country. Recognizing the inadequacy of the United Nations, which was paralyzed by Soviet vetoes, and unaware that Stalin had not been responsible for the uprising, the United States began formulating an independent policy for containing Soviet expansion. The new direction in policy—from attempts at cooperation to a stance of determined resistance—reflected America's belief that the Soviet Union represented a serious threat to world peace.

The Truman Doctrine

In March 1947 Truman proposed that Congress authorize economic and military aid to the embattled governments of Greece and Turkey. In his message he argued that: "The free peoples of the world look to us for support in maintaining their freedoms. If we falter in our leadership, we may endanger the peace of the world—and we shall surely endanger the welfare of our own nation." This concept that the United States was obligated to support any nation threatened by communism became known as the Truman Doctrine.

There were contradictions in the Truman Doctrine from the beginning. While the president called for support of peoples fighting to preserve their freedom, some of the governments which America aided, like those of Greece and Turkey, were not democracies. Some critics of the Truman Doctrine

characterized its application as self-serving or regarded it as a cynical bypassing of the authority of the United Nations. Others argued that American money would be better spent in feeding the world's poor, and they accused the United States of embarking on a worldwide crusade for ill-defined reasons. Nevertheless, even though the administration could not clearly demonstrate that Greece and Turkey were directly threatened with Soviet aggression, most Americans agreed with their president. The bill authorizing $400 million in aid for the two countries was swiftly passed, and by October 1949 American military and financial assistance had prevented the Communist takeover of Greece. The administration also called for international control of the Dardanelles, and the Soviets made no further moves against Turkey.

Containing Communism in Europe

Soon after Truman enunciated his doctrine, George Kennan, a member of the State Department and an authority on the Soviet Union, outlined the policy more thoroughly and gave it a new name—"containment." According to Kennan, the Soviets believed in the inevitable triumph of communism and, therefore, felt no need to take dangerous chances in order to bring about a quick victory. Although they would attempt to make gains wherever possible, they would stop short of war if met by resolute opposition. Accordingly, the United States would not risk war by opposing the Russians, since they could be expected to back down. The safest and most effective way to contain them was to "confront the Russians with unalterable counterforce at every point where they show signs of encroaching upon the interests of a peaceful and stable world."

The Marshall Plan Secretary of State George C. Marshall presented the economic equivalent of the containment policy in the commencement address at Harvard in June 1947. Called the Marshall Plan, his proposal advocated massive and systematic American economic aid to Europe. Its objective was to revitalize the devastated European economies. It was believed that an economically healthy Europe would be better able to withstand communism and to establish profitable trade with the United States. Although the United States had already extended vast economic aid ($9 billion) to Europe between

1945 and 1947 through the United Nations Relief and Rehabilitation Administration (UNRRA), Europe still faced a severe economic crisis.

While the policy of economic aid was received with great enthusiasm in Europe, some Americans opposed it as a handout. Even so, Congress overwhelmingly approved the Marshall Plan after the Communists seized control of Czechoslovakia early in 1948. By the end of Truman's presidency, Europe had received more than $13 billion in American aid and was well on the road to recovery. Increased prosperity diminished the threat of communism in western Europe and increased the influence of the European nations in international affairs.

Although the United States invited Communist participation in the Marshall Plan, the Soviet Union refused to participate or to allow its satellites to do so. Stalin was alarmed by the plan's potential for creating an economically strong Germany and by the attraction such an economic assistance program might have for Soviet-dominated nations in Europe. Therefore, in October 1947 Russia set up the Cominform (Communist Information Bureaus), a group of Communist agencies spread throughout eastern Europe for the purpose of ensuring conformity in the Soviet satellites. Communist parties in western Europe attempted to sabotage the Marshall Plan, primarily by fomenting labor strikes. In January 1949 Stalin announced a Soviet plan for economic assistance to eastern Europe.

Stalin was particularly apprehensive about the American effort to rebuild Germany's economy and to reunify the three zones of western Germany. After May 1946 the Soviets received no more reparations from the American zone, and in December 1946 the British and American zones were combined. By February 1947 the French zone had been integrated with the western zone and was to receive aid under the Marshall Plan. Stalin reacted by shoring up both the Communist regime in east Germany and the Soviet sector of Berlin.

In response, Great Britain, France, Belgium, the Netherlands, and Luxembourg formed the Brussels Pact in March 1948, a fifty-year alliance strongly supported by the United States. In June the alliance members joined with the United States to lay plans for the creation of a West German government which was to have control over domestic affairs but could not rearm. Currency reform was undertaken at this time to counter the inflation caused by the flow of east German money into the western zone.

The Berlin Blockade Stalin retaliated with the Berlin blockade. On April 1, 1948, Communist border guards began interfering with traffic to and from Berlin. Less than four months later the Russians halted all traffic and sealed off the city. American reaction was decisive. Together, the United States and Great Britain mounted an airlift to bring food and other supplies to the non-Communist sectors of the beleaguered city. The airlift, which was intended as a temporary solution, continued for nearly a year and became a dramatic symbol of the West's determination to stand firm against Soviet expansion. The Soviets were unwilling to enforce their blockade with military action. Seeing that the United States would not back down, the Russians ended the Berlin blockade in May 1949.

NATO The Soviet Union's response to the Marshall Plan as well as the Berlin blockade prompted the United States and western Europe to form a military alliance against Soviet expansion. With a clear bipartisan congressional mandate, the president formally proposed the establishment of the North Atlantic Treaty Organization with most of western Europe as well as Canada. Chartered in April 1949, and ratified by the Senate in July, this military alliance of eleven European nations and the United States is still in place. The charter stated that an attack on any one of NATO's members would be construed as an attack on all of them. An international military force, made up of the troops of member countries, was to provide the machinery for enforcing the provisions of the charter. The United States provided the bulk of the troops and equipment, and General Eisenhower became supreme commander of the NATO forces. In October 1949 the German Federal Republic was established at Bonn. The same month, the Soviets responded by forming the eastern zone into the Communist-dominated German Democratic Republic.

Conservatives like Senator Robert Taft of Ohio argued that the formation of the NATO pact was an aggressive action and the forerunner of an arms race. Others who believed it would drain American resources demanded to know what specific threat Russia posed. But fear of the Soviet Union was gen-

THE BERLIN AIRLIFT DEMONSTRATED BRITISH AND AMERICAN RESOLVE TO RESIST FURTHER SOVIET EXPANSION. A SIGNIFICANT OUTCOME OF THE AIRLIFT WAS THE FORMATION OF NATO.

erally strong, and proponents of the treaty claimed it would give Europe a sense of security and aid its economic recovery.

Containing Communism in Asia

China While the United States was occupied with the Soviet threat in Europe, momentous events were occurring in China. The *Kuomintang* (Nationalists) under Chiang Kai-shek had held the southwestern provinces ever since the Japanese retreat in World War II. Meanwhile, in the north, Communist insurgents under Mao Tse-tung were firmly entrenched

Driven to Taiwan

and steadily gaining support among the Chinese peasants. Except for a short period during 1945, the two factions had been in constant conflict since the late 1920s.

American policy during the Second World War had been to encourage the formation of a coalition government, thereby preventing all-out civil war. By 1946, however, two efforts by General George Marshall, at that time serving as the new ambassador to China, to arrange a settlement between Chiang and Mao had failed, and full-scale war had broken out. Before long Nationalist forces were taking a severe beating from the highly motivated, well-armed Communists. Russian troops which had entered Manchuria at the end of World War II withdrew, leaving that area as well in the hands of the Chinese Communists.

Continued shipments of American military supplies did not succeed in turning the tide in favor

THE CHINESE REVOLUTIONARY MAO TSE-TUNG (CENTER) POSES WITH CHOU EN-LAI (LEFT) AT THE COMMUNIST BASE AT YENAN, CHINA. IN DECEMBER 1949 MAO PROCLAIMED THE FORMATION OF THE PEOPLE'S REPUBLIC OF CHINA.

of the Nationalists. Although Chiang's supporters in Congress demanded more American aid, Truman and Marshall did not believe it would change the situation. Intervention in Greece had been manageable, but because China was so huge they calculated that billions of dollars and millions of American troops would be required to defeat the Communists. Equally important, the internal corruption and inefficiency of the Chiang regime, combined with its lack of broad-based support, convinced Truman that Chiang was incapable of defeating the Red Chinese forces.

Even though they received more than $2 billion in American aid from 1945 to 1949, the Nationalists steadily lost ground. In December 1949, Mao victoriously proclaimed the establishment of the People's Republic of China. Chiang and his followers fled to the island of Formosa where they set up a government-in-exile.

The immediate problem for the United States was whether to recognize the new Communist regime. Twenty-five nations had done so by 1950, and Mao eventually made an alliance with the Soviet Union. But the American people were antagonistic to such a move. Believing Communist China was now a Russian puppet, the administration refused to recognize the People's Republic. It blocked China's bid for UN membership and continued providing economic aid to Chiang in Formosa.

Japan Immediately after World War II, United States military forces under General Douglas Mac Arthur occupied Japan. Even though the Soviet Union had at last declared war on Japan, the United States saw to it that the Russians had no role in governing that nation. Although Japan was not forced to pay reparations, it was disarmed, demobilized, and deprived of all of its territories.

With the emergence of the Communist government in China in 1949, the United States took steps to strengthen Japan as an anti-Communist counterforce in the Pacific. Under a new constitution a democratic political system was set up, women were enfranchised, and the military was dismantled. The United States also helped to rebuild the Japanese economy. In 1951 the two nations signed a peace treaty ending American military occupation. Under the terms of this treaty Japan regained its sovereignty but continued to allow American troops on Japanese soil to provide for national defense.

Taft on China

"In China for some reason, the State Department has pursued a different policy from that followed throughout the rest of the world. There is not the slightest doubt in my mind that the proper kind of sincere aid to the Nationalist Government a few years ago could have stopped communism in China. But the State Department has been guided by a left-wing group who obviously have wanted to get rid of Chiang, and were willing at least to turn China over to the Communists for that purpose. They have, in effect, defied the general policy in China laid down by Congress. In recent months it has, of course, been very doubtful whether aid to the Nationalist Government could be effective, and no one desires to waste American efforts."

Senator Robert Taft
January 11, 1950

Acheson on China

"As I said, no one says that vast armies moved out of the hills and defeated him [Chiang Kai-shek]. To attribute this to the inadequacy of American aid is only to point out the depth and power of the forces which were miscalculated or ignored. What has happened in my judgment is that the almost inexhaustible patience of the Chinese people in their misery ended. They did not bother to overthrow this government. There was really nothing to overthrow. They simply ignored it throughout the country. . . .

The Communists did not create this condition. They did not create this revolutionary spirit. They did not create a great force which moved out from under Chiang Kai-shek. But they were shrewd and cunning to mount it, to ride this thing into victory and into power."

Secretary of State Dean Acheson
January 12, 1950

A Growing Mood of Isolationism

Although Congress and the American public shared the administration's opposition to communism, they also felt a growing desire to avoid foreign entanglements. After a long depression and a world war, Americans wanted to enjoy the benefits of peace and prosperity. Most hoped that America's possession of atomic weapons would be a sufficient deterrent to keep the peace and contain communism.

Truman was alarmed by the growing mood of isolationism for he feared the United States lacked the necessary resolve to stand up to the Communists. By the late 1940s his advisers were warning that the nation's military forces and planning were inadequate to meet its international responsibilities. In 1947 the president approved the National Security Act which created the cabinet post of Secretary of Defense. The secretary was charged with the task of overseeing the armed services. The act also created the Central Intelligence Agency (CIA) to handle intelligence gathering and the National Security Council (NSC) consisting of cabinet members and advisers who were to make recommendations to the president on the integration of foreign policy and national defense. The following year Congress again authorized a military draft.

In 1949 the administration had shown its further resolve to contain communism by the creation of NATO, but the defense appropriation bill to put muscle into the alliance was too small to adequately counter the power of the Red Army. Consequently, the real meaning of NATO was that it put the United States in a position of being able to use its bomber force and atomic weapons against Russia if the Soviets launched a ground attack on western Europe. In September 1949 Truman's new "intelligence community" reported to the president that an atomic explosion had occurred in the Soviet Union. The news shattered the sense of security which Americans had felt since Hiroshima. The United States was no longer the world's only atomic power. Although Truman soon announced plans for the development of the hydrogen bomb, the fact that the Soviets had the bomb sharply reduced American willingness to use atomic weapons.

Meanwhile, American conventional forces had declined. In 1950 the United States Army numbered only six hundred thousand. In April 1950 the NSC, stressing the need to combat what it perceived as a worldwide Communist conspiracy, recommended that the United States embark on a massive military buildup. Given public reluctance to spending vast sums of money on defense, such a program would have been impossible to implement if the United States had not immediately become involved in a major armed conflict. Between 1947 and 1950 military expenditures had declined from $14.4 billion to $13 billion, but after the beginning of the Korean War in 1950 the defense budget rose rapidly.

The Korean War

During World War II the Allies had agreed to establish a free and independent Korea, but once the war was over they were unable to agree on a form of provisional Korean government. Therefore the Americans and Russians decided to occupy the country jointly until an agreement was reached. Demarcation between the two zones was set at the thirty-eighth parallel with the Americans holding the south and the Russians controlling the north.

In Korea as in Europe, the Americans and the Russians were divided by conflicting interests. Each nation wanted to establish a Korean government ideologically friendly to its own. Accordingly, the Soviet Union established a Communist government in the north which was dominated by Soviet influence; the United States supported a government under Syngman Rhee in the south which, although pro-American, was corrupt and repressive.

In 1947 the United Nations voted to send a mission to Korea to hold a general election. The North Koreans, however, refused to accept the mission, and the general election of 1948 was held only below the thirty-eighth parallel. When it was over, Syngman Rhee presided over a Republic of Korea that covered only the southern half of the country. In 1949 Russian and American occupation forces withdrew, leaving Korea still divided.

Both North and South Korea sought control of the entire nation. Hostility between the two sectors rapidly escalated into border skirmishes and Communist-supported guerrilla warfare. Both governments developed large armies equipped with weap-

ons supplied by their respective backers. Then, on June 24, 1950, North Korean troops crossed the thirty-eighth parallel in a full-scale invasion of South Korea, whose forces collapsed under the assault. Within three days the North Koreans had gained control of the South Korean capital of Seoul.

As late as 1949 the Joint Chiefs did not regard South Korea as vital to American security. Military aid to the country had been limited, and in 1950 Secretary of State Dean Acheson stated that Korea was not within America's perimeter of defense. But when North Korea actually invaded South Korea, President Truman viewed the attack as yet another Moscow-inspired act of aggression. In fact, although the Russians were probably aware of the invasion plan, it is unlikely that they were directly responsible. Like the United States, the Soviet Union was preoccupied with Europe and had little interest in a confrontation that might lead to a large-scale land war in Asia. Russia gave little aid either to Korea or to China during the conflict. It now appears that the assault was initiated solely by the North Koreans in an effort to unify the country under Communist rule.

Truman moved immediately and decisively. Acting independently of Congress, he sent General MacArthur to assess the situation in Korea. He brought the matter before the Security Council at the United Nations on June 25. In the absence of the Russian delegate, Andrei Gromyko, the Security Council condemned North Korea for a "breach of the peace" and two days later called on member nations to go to the defense of South Korea. Although sixteen member nations sent troops to defend South Korea, the United States and South Korean troops comprised the main portion of the UN force.

Conduct of the War In the meantime, Truman, following MacArthur's recommendations—in what he called a "police action by the United Nations" —sent American air, naval, and ground troops to Korea. The first group of UN troops was unsuccessful in its attempt to repel the North Koreans, and American and South Korean forces withdrew to Pusan at the tip of the Korean peninsula. However, in September 1950, MacArthur took the enemy by surprise with a massive amphibious landing at Inchon near Seoul, cutting off the North Korean troops from their supply base and forcing a disorganized retreat. By October 1 American, South Ko-

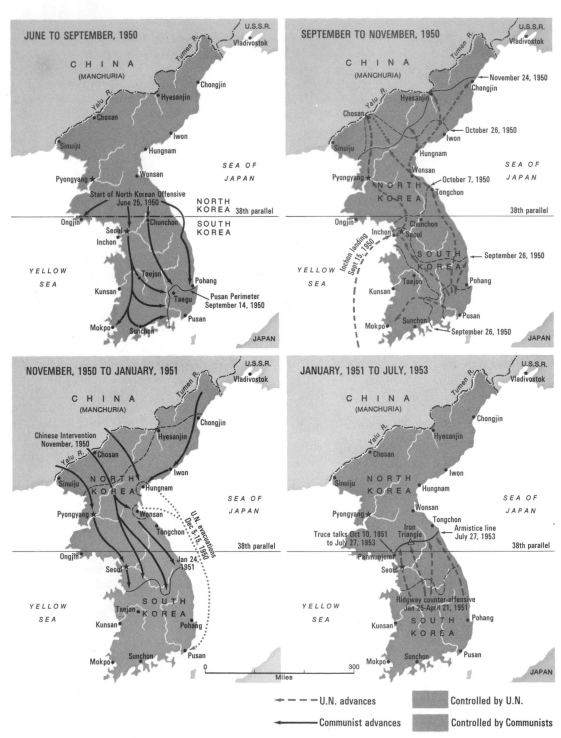

Korean War • 1950 to 1953

MacArthur too public

rean, and UN forces had pursued the North Koreans back across the thirty-eighth parallel.

The United States then had to decide whether to carry the war into North Korea. A halt in the fighting might give the North Koreans an opportunity to regroup for another attack. On the other hand, the Chinese had warned that they would intervene if North Korea were invaded. Influenced by a National Security Council plan to unite North and South Korea which had UN support and by a desire to halt Communist aggression, Truman decided to invade.

Disregarding warnings from Peking, MacArthur's troops crossed the thirty-eighth parallel in pursuit of the North Korean armies. On October 15 the general met with Truman at Wake Island and convinced the president that the Chinese threats were only a bluff. According to MacArthur, the war would be over by Thanksgiving.

MacArthur's assessment of the situation proved inaccurate. An invasion of North Korea was a threat China could not ignore. North Korea was the only buffer between China and the Japanese-American Pacific community. Moreover, the Chinese feared that the United States might try to overthrow their new Communist government and that a passive response to American military action in Korea might encourage such an attempt.

American and UN forces pushed deeper into North Korea toward the Chinese frontier, and MacArthur seemed confident that victory was within reach. But on November 26, 1950 a massive force of Chinese crossed the Yalu River which separated China from Korea. Joining with North Korean troops, the Communists smashed through MacArthur's advancing line, drove his forces back across the thirty-eighth parallel, and recaptured Seoul.

MacArthur's Dismissal After he was driven back, MacArthur pressed Truman for the authority to carry the war into China. At first, the general suggested bombing strategic supply and industrial bases in Manchuria, but as the war reached a stalemate near the thirty-eighth parallel, he demanded the right to use atomic weapons against China. Truman flatly rejected MacArthur's proposals. Despite the frustrations of waging a limited war, the United States was not prepared to provoke all-out war in Asia which might eventually lead to a nuclear war with Russia.

For his part, MacArthur felt the Korean War offered an opportunity to eradicate communism in Asia once and for all. He believed that lack of American military support to Chiang Kai-shek had been responsible for the emergence of a Communist regime in China. Exasperated by Truman's refusal to let him escalate the war, MacArthur became more vocal in expressing his disapproval of the president's policies. In a letter that became public, he wrote: "There is no substitute for victory." Finally, Truman felt that he had no alternative but to dismiss the general in order to maintain civilian control over the military. On April 4, 1951, he replaced MacArthur with General Matthew Ridgway.

Truman's dismissal of MacArthur was a courageous act performed with full knowledge of the criticism it would bring. Support for MacArthur's anti-Communist views was reflected in the emotional hero's welcome he received on returning home. Nevertheless, top military officials who testified before Congress disagreed with MacArthur's priorities. They believed the main Communist threat lay in Europe. As General Omar Bradley put it, MacArthur's projected war with China would have been "the wrong war at the wrong place at the wrong time with the wrong enemy."

President Truman continued the policy of limited war in Korea with the objective of retaking all territory to the thirty-eighth parallel. General Ridgway conducted successful military operations within the limits set by Washington. In June 1951 a ceasefire ended the heaviest fighting; however, peace talks, accompanied by sporadic raids, dragged on until July 1953.

The Korean War brought about a rapid expansion of America's military resources. Concern for defense was reflected in the fact that by 1952 the defense budget had reached $60 billion a year. During the ensuing years military spending continued to increase.

MacArthur @ Truman

Fear of Subversion

After World War II fear of subversion became a powerful force in American life. It was intensified by a lack of understanding about the causes of the Communist revolution in China, by Russia's development of an atomic bomb, and by the Korean conflict—all of which convinced many Americans that

GENERAL DOUGLAS MacARTHUR DEFENDS HIS ACTIONS BEFORE A JOINT SESSION OF CONGRESS, JUNE 19, 1951.

the Soviets were succeeding in their plan for world domination. In such a tense atmosphere, only a few people had the courage to declare that the fear of internal Communist subversion was largely imagined.

Truman's Loyalty Program

President Truman, although a militant anti-Communist, was not among those who believed the Communists posed an internal threat. However, in 1946 when the Canadian government uncovered a Communist spy ring involving "people in positions of trust" within their country, shock waves swept through the United States. The American public demanded an investigation of communism within the civil service, and the president took action in order to prevent the Republican Congress from making subversion a partisan political issue. In November

1946 Truman appointed a Temporary Commission on Employee Loyalty to conduct an investigation. Contrary to his expectations, the commission concluded that Communist infiltration was occurring and recommended that the government institute a tighter security system. Although the commission offered no tangible evidence for its findings, its recommendations were accepted.

In March 1947 Truman established a federal employee loyalty program. Under the program the FBI was to investigate all employees and forward any damaging information to a loyalty board in the suspected person's department. If found guilty, the individual was to be dismissed from the government. Eventually, a Loyalty Review Board was created with the power to review all dismissals and to maintain a master index of people and groups considered subversive. Potential disloyalty or mere opposition to American foreign policy was considered an adequate reason for dismissing a federal employee. Repercussions of the investigations were often unjust and harmful. By 1951 more than two thousand federal employees had been ordered to resign, and an additional 560 had been fired when they failed to comply.

The Hiss and Rosenberg Cases

Despite Truman's effort to avoid congressional involvement, Congress began its own investigation of subversion. The House Un-American Activities Committee had been created in 1938 as an instrument by which conservative members of Congress could attempt to ferret out New Deal radicals. Now the committee attained prominence in the fight against subversion. Using testimony of former Communist agents, HUAC turned up evidence of pro-Soviet activity high within government ranks. The most prominent person accused of being a Communist agent was Alger Hiss, a highly respected State Department official. In 1948 during HUAC investigations led by a young congressman from California, Richard M. Nixon, Hiss was accused of passing government secrets to the Communists. Although Hiss denied the charge, the body of available evidence against him was formidable. He was indicted, tried for perjury, and sent to prison. Because prominent Democrats, including President Truman and Secretary Acheson, had defended Hiss, his convic-

tion seriously damaged the administration's credibility on the issue of subversion.

Until 1949 the nation's major source of security lay in its belief that only the United States possessed the atomic bomb. Then Truman shattered American confidence by announcing the Russians' successful atomic test. In 1950 the British arrested Klaus Fuchs, a nuclear physicist once employed at the Los Alamos atomic facility, who confessed to having passed atomic secrets to the Russians. The Fuchs case led to an investigation of atomic spying in the United States. Before long Julius and Ethel Rosenberg were convicted of passing secrets to the Soviet Union. (Ethel's brother, David Greenglass, had been employed at Los Alamos and had pointed the finger at the Rosenbergs.) The Rosenbergs were sentenced to death, and after extensive appeals, were finally executed in June 1953, still proclaiming their innocence.

The Rise of McCarthyism

The hysteria created by the Hiss and Rosenberg cases contributed to the rise to prominence of Joseph R. McCarthy, a little-known Republican senator from Wisconsin. In February 1950 Senator McCarthy addressed a meeting of Republican women in Wheeling, West Virginia. He claimed to possess a list of 205 members of the State Department who were members of the American Communist party. Although McCarthy never produced the list, his speech marked the beginning of his infamous crusade against communism.

McCarthy had a genius for publicity, a desire for power, and a determination to use whatever tactics were necessary to further his career. He was able to build a strong following by linking communism with liberal intellectuals and internationalists. McCarthy's skill at demagoguery and intimidation enabled him to squelch many of his opponents. The mere threat of his wrath was often enough to silence many who might otherwise have spoken out against him. When Maryland Senator Millard Tydings investigated McCarthy's charges and pronounced them "a fraud and a hoax," McCarthy responded with a smear campaign that prevented Tydings's reelection in 1950. One of the few with the courage to oppose McCarthy was President Truman, who declared that the issue of subversion was a red herring.

Accusations of disloyalty within the government alarmed many Americans and gave rise to demands for new federal legislation to curb the Communist party. The result was the McCarran Internal Security Act of 1950, which required all Communist organizations and their members to register with the attorney general. The act also prohibited Communists from working in defense plants or from obtaining passports, provided for the internment of Communists in government "camps" in the event of war, and established a Subversive Activities Control Board to investigate loyalty cases. Truman vetoed the measure, declaring that "in a free country we punish men for the crimes they commit, but never for the opinions they have." Congress, however, overrode the veto, and the McCarran Act became law. The following year the Supreme Court, in *Dennis et al.* v. *United States*, upheld the conviction of eleven leading members of the Communist party for violating the Smith Act (1940), a law which forbade membership in any organization advocating the violent overthrow of the United States government. In 1952 Congress passed the McCarran-Walter Immigration and Nationality Act, again over the president's veto. While the act did set a small annual quota for Orientals, it also provided for the exclusion and deportation of naturalized citizens who had belonged to organizations considered disloyal to the American government.

The Republicans Return to Power

By 1951 the Democratic party and the Truman administration were under attack because of domestic inflation, fear of Communist expansion abroad, the perceived threat of internal subversion, and the Korean conflict. In addition, several instances of corruption in the administration dominated Washington headlines. The acceptance of a freezer by presidential aide General Harry Vaughan was publicized and condemned; Assistant Attorney General T. Lamar Caudle was caught in a tax-fixing scandal and sent to prison; and an investigation by Senator Estes Kefauver disclosed links between state and local Democratic bosses and leaders of organized crime. Added to all this was the fact that Democratic presidents had occupied the White House for twenty years, and voters felt it was time for a change. As the 1952 election approached, Truman measured the political mood and decided not to run. In his place, the Democrats nominated an articulate liberal intellectual, Governor Adlai Stevenson of Illinois. As his running mate Stevenson selected Senator John Sparkman of Alabama.

Sensing an opportunity for victory, moderate Republicans persuaded General Eisenhower to try for the presidential nomination, while the conservative wing of the party supported Ohio Senator

RICHARD NIXON AND DWIGHT D. EISENHOWER STAND WITH THEIR WIVES, PAT AND MAMIE, BEFORE THE REPUBLICAN NATIONAL CONVENTION AFER BEING CHOSEN AS THEIR PARTY'S VICE-PRESIDENTIAL AND PRESIDENTIAL CANDIDATES.

Robert A. Taft. Eisenhower won on the first ballot. Richard M. Nixon, well-known for his part in the Hiss case, became his running mate.

The real contest centered around the personalities of Eisenhower and Stevenson. An enormously popular war hero with a friendly grin and an unimpeachable character, "Ike" combined the appeal of military experience with grandfatherly warmth and wisdom. Amidst the apprehensions of the cold war and domestic suspicion, the image was overwhelmingly attractive. When Eisenhower promised that if elected, he personally would visit Korea to bring an end to the stalled peace talks, public response was enthusiastic.

Stevenson was fighting not only Eisenhower's popularity, but his own public image as well. Many

voters found him too much of an "egghead" who kept his distance from ordinary people. He was hampered, too, by the unpopularity of Truman, from whom he was unable to disassociate himself.

Eisenhower's momentum was temporarily halted when Nixon was accused of accepting contributions from businessleaders and putting the money into a private expense account. Although some party leaders urged Eisenhower to remove Nixon from the ticket, the general chose to let Nixon extricate himself from the scandal. Nixon succeeded in doing so through an emotional television address known as the "Checkers" speech because of a reference to his little cocker spaniel. Favorable public response persuaded Eisenhower to keep Nixon as his running mate. Even so, many people never believed

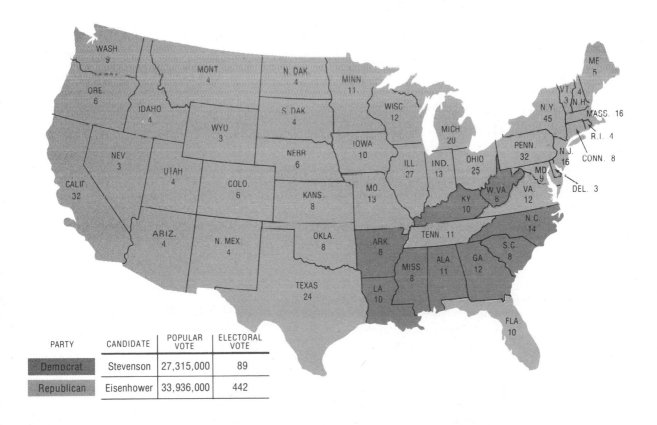

PARTY	CANDIDATE	POPULAR VOTE	ELECTORAL VOTE
Democrat	Stevenson	27,315,000	89
Republican	Eisenhower	33,936,000	442

Election of 1952

that Nixon had adequately answered the charges against him. Eisenhower won easily, amassing 442 electoral votes to Stevenson's 89 and gaining 6.5 million more popular votes than his opponent.

Readings

General Works

Ambrose, Stephen E., *Rise to Globalism: 1938-1970.* New York: Penguin, 1971.

Cochran, Bert, *Harry Truman and the Crisis Presidency.* New York: Funk and Wagnalls, 1973.

Donovan, Robert J., *Conflict and Crisis: The Presidency of Harry S Truman, 1945-1948.* New York: Norton, 1977.

Feis, Herbert, *From Trust to Terror: The Onset of the Cold War, 1945-1950.* New York: Norton, 1970. (Paper)

Halle, Louis, *The Cold War as History.* New York: Harper & Row, 1967.

Hamby, Alonzo L., *Beyond the New Deal: Harry S Truman and American Liberalism.* New York: Columbia University Press, 1973.

Horowitz, David, *The Free World Colossus.* New York: Hill and Wang, 1971.

Kolko, Joyce, and Gabriel Kolko, *The Limits of Power: The World and United States Foreign Policy, 1945-1954.* New York: Harper & Row, 1972.

Lubell, Samuel, *The Future of American Politics.* New York: Harper & Row, 1965.

Paterson, Thomas G., *Soviet-American Confrontation.* Baltimore, Md.: Johns Hopkins University Press, 1973.

Yergin, Daniel, *Shattered Peace: The Origins of the Cold War and the National Security State.* Boston: Houghton Mifflin, 1977.

Special Studies

Alperowitz, Gar, *Atomic Diplomacy: Hiroshima and Potsdam.* New York: Simon & Schuster, 1965.

Carr, Robert K., *The House Un-American Activities Committee, 1945-1950.* Ithaca, N.Y.: Cornell University Press, 1952.

Feis, Herbert, *The Atomic Bomb and the End of World War II.* Princeton, N.J.: Princeton University Press, 1966.

_____, *Between War and Peace: The Potsdam Conference.* Princeton, N.J.: Princeton University Press, 1960.

Fried, Richard M., *Men Against McCarthy.* New York: Columbia University Press, 1976.

Gaddis, John L., *The United States and the Origins of the Cold War: 1941-1947.* New York: Columbia University Press, 1972. (Paper)

Gimbel, John, *The Origins of the Marshall Plan.* Stanford, Calif.: Stanford University Press, 1976.

Harper, Alan D., *The Politics of Loyalty: The White House and the Communist Issue, 1946-1952.* Westport, Conn.: Greenwood, 1969.

Haynes, Richard F., *The Awesome Power: Harry S Truman as Commander in Chief.* Baton Rouge: Louisiana State University Press, 1973.

Iriye, Ahira, *The Cold War in Asia.* Englewood Cliffs, N.J.: Prentice-Hall, 1974.

LaFeber, Walter, *America, Russia and the Cold War: 1945-1971.* New York: Wiley, 1972. (Paper)

Parmet, Herbert S., *The Democrats: The Years After FDR.* New York: Macmillan, 1976.

Paterson, Thomas G. (Ed.), *Cold War Critics: Alternatives to American Foreign Policy in the Truman Years.* New York: Watts, 1971. (Paper)

Rees, David, *Korea, the Limited War.* Baltimore: Penguin, 1970.

Ross, Irwin, *The Loneliest Campaign: The Truman Victory of 1948.* New York: New American Library, 1968.

Primary Sources

Bernstein, Barton J., and Alan I. Matusow, *The Truman Administration: A Documentary Record.* New York: Harper & Row, 1968.

Chambers, Whittaker, *Witness.* New York: Random House, 1952.

Kennan, George F., *Memoirs.* Boston: Little, Brown, 1957.

Miller, Merle, *Plain Speaking: An Oral Biography of Harry S Truman.* New York: Putnam, 1974.

Stevenson, Adlai E., *Speeches.* New York: Random House, 1952.

Truman, Harry S, *Memoirs,* Vols. I-II. Garden City, N.Y.: Doubleday, 1955-1956.

Biographies

McLellan, David, *Dean Acheson: The State Department Years.* New York: Dodd, Mead, 1976.

Patterson, James T., *Mr. Republican: A Biography of Robert A. Taft.* Boston: Houghton Mifflin, 1972.

Rovere, Richard H., *Senator Joe McCarthy.* New York: World, 1959.

Steinberg, Alfred, *The Man from Missouri.* New York: Putnam, 1962.

Fiction

Ellison, Ralph, *The Invisible Man.* New York: Random House, 1952.

29 Eisenhower: The Politics of Moderation

There is, in world affairs, a steady course to be followed between an assertion of strength that is truculent and a confession of helplessness that is cowardly.

There is, in our affairs at home, a middle way between untrammeled freedom of the individual and the demands for the welfare of the whole nation. This way must avoid government by bureaucracy as carefully as it avoids neglect of the helpless.

In every area of political action, free men must think before they can expect to win.

President Dwight D. Eisenhower

Significant Events

Rio Pact [1947]

Creation of state of Israel [1948]

Armistice ending Korean War [July 1953]

Mutual Defense Treaty between United States and Formosa [1954]

Geneva conference on Indochina [1954]

Southeast Asia Treaty Organization (SEATO) [1954]

Brown v. Board of Education of Topeka [1954]

Merger of AFL and CIO [1955]

Baghdad Pact [1955]

German Federal Republic (West Germany) enters NATO [1955]

United States-Soviet summit conference in Geneva [July 1955]

Montgomery, Alabama, bus boycott [1955–1956]

Suez Crisis [October 1956]

Eisenhower Doctrine [1957]

Civil Rights Act [1957]

Inter-American Development Bank [1959]

Eisenhower-Khrushchev meeting at Camp David [1959]

St. Lawrence Seaway inaugurated [1959]

U-2 incident [1960]

AFTER THE WAR, AMERICANS TOOK ADVANTAGE OF THE NATION'S BOOMING ECONOMY AND SPENT FREELY ON THE GREAT VARIETY OF CONSUMER GOODS THAT FLOODED THE MARKET.

The predominant mood of the 1950s combined optimistic self-congratulation about the stability of American society with political and social conservatism. Americans were bone-weary of conflict and longed for respite from domestic and international controversy. While a few people were concerned about the nation's unresolved social crises—particularly race relations, poverty, and the decline of the cities—for the most part these festering ills were neglected. The great majority of Americans retreated from involvement in domestic reform and turned their attention instead toward building a comfortable, prosperous life.

The most important factor contributing to the elevation of the status quo as the American ideal was the great prosperity of the nation's economy. A large percentage of Americans, for whom memories of the Great Depression and the sacrifices of the war years remained all too fresh, were eager to obtain their share of the good life. The productivity of the next decade and a half gave them ample opportunity. By the 1950s the idea that the federal government should use its fiscal policy to maintain a healthy economy had been accepted by most of the leadership of both political parties. Secure in the knowledge that the government was willing to use its power to ensure against another depression, Americans continued freely spending the money they had saved during the war years. A great demand for new cars, electrical appliances, and other consumer

THE ADVERTISING INDUSTRY PLAYED A PROMINENT ROLE IN THE NEW AGE OF CONSUMERISM THAT FOLLOWED THE SECOND WORLD WAR.

goods of every conceivable description encouraged manufacturers to expand production rapidly.

The return of millions of veterans to their wives or sweethearts also had an important effect on the economy. Marriage and birthrates soared. In response to mounting demand, new housing developments sprang up. The flight of white Americans from the decaying inner cities influenced the growth of suburbs. Other shifts in the economy gradually resulted in reduced demand for farm and factory labor and greater opportunity for white-collar, technical, and professional workers. By the end of the decade the number of white-collar workers had surpassed that of blue-collar workers and millions of working-class Americans had moved up into the middle class.

After World War II, millions of women who had worked full time to aid the war effort again accepted the idea that the fulfillment of women lay in managing a home and rearing a family. Only in households that were hard-pressed financially did married women work. An increase in leisure time enabled many people to take up hobbies and many families to enjoy recreational activities and annual vacations. For middle-class Americans, the promise of the American Dream seemed close to being realized.

The Eisenhower Style

The Eisenhower years in American politics were the political counterpart of the satisfaction with the status quo that characterized the 1950s. While there were acrimonious feelings during the decade over McCarthyism, labor disputes, and the problems of agriculture, only the revolution in the expectations of black Americans began to shake the country before Eisenhower left office.

Dwight D. Eisenhower was born of middle-class parents in Denison, Texas, in 1890. He was raised in Abilene, Kansas, and in 1911 entered the United States Military Academy at West Point. One of the best-liked cadets at the academy, though not among the most scholarly, he was graduated in 1915. After receiving his commission Eisenhower served for twenty-five years in the United States Army. In 1942 "Ike" was made commander of the United States forces in Europe. His efforts against the Germans in the North African campaign revealed his ability to command and inspire, and he was subsequently sent to London to plan and direct the Allied invasion of Europe. The spectacular success of the Normandy invasion made him an international hero. After the war he served as Army chief of staff, president of Columbia University, and supreme commander of the NATO forces in Europe.

Eisenhower's landslide victory in the 1952 election reflected an immense personal appeal that was only partly due to his reputation as a war hero. He was a principled and forthright man whose grandfatherly appearance and congenial manner inspired confidence and trust.

Eisenhower came to the presidency with no political experience. He had never held elective office and was not a strong party man. He might easily have become the candidate of the Democrats instead of the Republicans; in fact, in 1948 the Democrats had considered nominating him instead of Truman. Once in office, however, Eisenhower developed a political philosophy he described as "modern Republicanism," a synthesis of conservative and moderate policies. Neither intellectual nor dogmatic, the president took a common sense approach to national problems. He was committed to preserving rather than reforming American society.

His moderation pleased neither conservative nor liberal politicians, however. Conservatives criticized him for continuing the New Deal trend toward increased government regulation of business and expanded government responsibility for social welfare. Liberals argued that he failed to go far enough in developing solutions for urgent national problems. However, his middle-of-the-road, nonpartisan philosophy appealed to the vast majority of voters. His winning personality and his even-handed approach suited the nation's desire for stability and a respite from the turmoil of the previous two decades.

Eisenhower's Attitude toward Executive Power

Eisenhower's administration reflected both his military training and his respect for the business community. He preferred not to exercise power directly, but instead to delegate authority to subordinates, reserving for himself final approval of their recommendations. In a controversy he listened to the arguments of opposing sides and then chose between them. Often his choice was a compromise. He was not a strong-willed and independent chief executive, but considered the president to be only one of the players on the executive team. He was a more skilled politician than was realized by many who were critical of his commonplace speeches and garbled syntax in press conferences.

The majority of Eisenhower's advisers and cabinet members were selected from the business community. Among them were some of the most successful men in America. Secretary of State John Foster Dulles had been an extremely successful corporation lawyer, and Secretary of Defense Charles E. Wilson was the former president of General Motors. The Departments of the Treasury, Interior, and Commerce and the Post Office were also headed by businessmen. To the post of secretary of labor Eisenhower appointed the president of the plumbers' union, Martin P. Durkin. When the Department of Health, Education, and Welfare was created in 1953, Eisenhower chose Mrs. Oveta Culp Hobby, former wartime commander of the WACS, to fill the new position. Democratic critics remarked irreverently that Eisenhower's cabinet consisted of "eight millionaires and a plumber."

Drawing on his military experience, Eisenhower administered the executive branch according to a chain of command which began with his chief of staff. His choice for this key position was Sherman Adams, a taciturn New Englander who after a successful business career had been governor of New Hampshire. "I don't want people springing things on me," Eisenhower said. The task of protecting him fell to Adams, who often frustrated members of the Congress and cabinet by deciding that their reasons for wanting to confer with the president were not sufficiently important.

Eisenhower's Effect on Party Politics

During the 1950s predictable party allegiances declined, and a large independent vote developed. This change reflected the emergence of a moderate majority that feared inflation and government spending but at the same time did not want to repeal the social-welfare legislation of the 1930s. Eisenhower's politics had great appeal to this new majority. In a time of fluctuating party loyalties, he was regarded as the primary source of political stability.

In the early years of the decade, the Republicans had a small majority in both houses of Congress. It was won as a result of Eisenhower's popularity, which brought the support of several blocs of traditionally Democratic voters. Blue-collar workers who were entering the middle class during the postwar economic boom, Roman Catholics who opposed communism, farmers concerned about inflation, and white, urban, middle-class Southerners angered by the Democrats' stance on civil rights, all moved to the Republican camp in 1952. By 1954, however, the Democrats regained some of these voters and were once again the majority party in Congress.

Even with a Democratic majority in Congress after 1954, relations between the legislature and the Republican president were generally amicable. The moderate consensus in Congress reflected the national mood, and a number of Democrats often crossed party lines to support Eisenhower's policies. The president himself contributed to this spirit by showing great deference to the legislative branch. Although he occasionally pressed hard for his programs, he considered the presidency an administrative rather than a policymaking position.

Domestic Issues

The Decline of McCarthyism

When Eisenhower took office, fear of subversion continued to trouble large numbers of Americans, and McCarthyism was still a powerful force in American life. McCarthy soon directed his attack at the new administration, calling Eisenhower's moderation in foreign policy "cowardly." Nevertheless,

FOLLOWING AN ANGRY EXCHANGE, ARMY COUNSEL JOSEPH N. WELCH (LEFT) LISTENS TO SENATOR JOSEPH McCARTHY'S TESTIMONY ON THE COMMUNIST PARTY ORGANIZATION IN THE UNITED STATES.

the president refused to stoop to McCarthy's level by using his influence against the senator or by confronting him directly. Instead, he set out to demonstrate to the American public that any internal subversion that did exist was being carefully monitored and controlled.

In April 1953 Eisenhower extended Truman's loyalty program, ordering the FBI to assemble files on all government employees. An additional twenty-two hundred government employees resigned or were dismissed as a result of these new investigations, although not a single one was proven to be a Communist. The most celebrated case involved Robert Oppenheimer, who had headed the laboratory in Los Alamos, New Mexico, that produced the first atomic bomb. Oppenheimer came under FBI scrutiny in 1950 when he opposed the development of a hydrogen bomb. In 1953 the FBI made available to President Eisenhower a report on Oppenheimer outlining his prewar associations with Communists and concluding that he was a security risk. As a result of government hearings, Oppenheimer was denied the security clearance he needed to continue his work as a consultant to the Atomic Energy Commission. (The Commission had been created in

1946 to oversee the research and production of atomic power.)

Eisenhower's efforts to demonstrate his vigilance against subversion did not satisfy McCarthy, who continued to make the same unsupported charges he had made against the Truman administration. One of McCarthy's standard accusations was that Roosevelt's advisers at Yalta were Communists or Communist sympathizers who had deliberately strengthened the Russians at the expense of American interests. Thus it was not surprising that he attacked Eisenhower for nominating Charles Bohlen, one of the Yalta advisers, as ambassador to Moscow. The president refused to withdraw the nomination. A Senate investigation led by Senator Taft cleared Bohlen, and he was confirmed.

McCarthy's downfall finally came when his anti-Communist crusade was turned against the United States Army. McCarthy's charges culminated in nationally televised Senate hearings which gave many Americans their first opportunity to see the senator in action. His "Red scare" had already been losing public support, but the hearings turned the tide, exposing McCarthy as a swaggering liar and bully. At last the president issued a statement criticizing McCarthy's tactics. In December 1954 the Senate condemned him for conduct unbecoming a senator. Stripped of his power and influence, he began to drink heavily and died in May 1957 of cirrhosis of the liver. *Deadbeat*

The Warren Court and the Right to Dissent

In sharp contrast to McCarthy's insidious efforts to destroy anyone whose attitudes did not conform to his peculiar brand of Americanism, the Supreme Court during the 1950s and well into the 1960s consistently supported the right to political dissent. This was due in great measure to Eisenhower's appointment late in 1953 of the three-time Republican governor of California, Earl Warren, to the position of chief justice. To Eisenhower's surprise, the Warren Court turned out to be perhaps the most activist and certainly the most controversial Supreme Court in the nation's history.

On June 17, 1957, the Court handed down two decisions which attempted to end judicial support for the suppression of dissent while still protecting the government's ability to defend itself from subversion. In *Yates* v. *United States* the Court made a sharp distinction between subversive words and subversive acts, stating that people advocating the forceful overthrow of the United States government could be convicted only if they advocated revolutionary action, and that the preaching of revolutionary doctrine alone was not a criminal act. In *Watkins* v. *United States* the Court upheld the right of a labor official, John T. Watkins, to refuse to reveal his past political associations to the House Un-American Activities Committee. The Court's opinion also noted that congressional power to investigate was not unlimited, especially when the aims of the investigation were excessively vague.

The Economy

By the time Eisenhower took office the country had successfully completed the massive reconversion to a peacetime economy that had begun in 1945. Factories, operating almost at capacity, produced more and better consumer goods, there was virtually full employment, wages were high, and construction of buildings and highways at federal expense progressed at record speed. The United States, which

had only 6 percent of the world's population, was producing and consuming more than one-third of the world's goods and services. Economic expansion had resulted partly from technological improvements in electronics, such as data-processing machines and computers, partly from research and development by scientists and engineers in all major industries. Increased government spending for goods and services as well as for defense was another factor in economic productivity. Even so, the years 1953–1960 were marked by boom and recession as well as a slow rate of economic growth—never more than 3 percent a year.

After decades of effort by reformers, American capitalism still tended toward consolidation. The steel and automobile industries, for example, were dominated by a few big corporations, and it was more and more difficult for small companies to compete with them. Under these conditions the emphasis was not on competitive pricing, but on advertising and packaging and on such intangibles as quality, style, and luxury. The day of the solitary business tycoon was gone. Company policy was usually determined by a team of managers, college-educated executives who had reached positions of power by climbing the managerial ladder. For them, good salaries, retirement benefits, and pride in their organizations were becoming more important than the accumulation of immense personal wealth.

The administration's economic policy was based on the belief that the government should interfere as little as possible in the conduct of business; its major responsibilities were to curtail inflation and balance the national budget even when this led to increased unemployment. When the economy slid toward recession in 1953–1954 following an $11 billion decline in government spending at the end of the Korean War, the administration moved to ease credit and lower taxes, hoping thereby to encourage increased spending and investment by the private sector, while at the same time avoiding the need for more government spending. This remedy proved successful, and by the summer of 1955 the economy was thriving again.

While higher steel production and automobile sales brought new prosperity to the country during 1955–1956, a number of wage increases in basic industries which exceeded gains in production gave rise to new fears of runaway inflation. The Federal

Reserve Board introduced new credit restraints to curb inflation, and this caused the economy to plunge into another serious recession during 1957–1958. Unemployment rose to 7.5 percent and a decrease in purchasing power produced a decline in consumer spending and a drop in production. Now the administration stepped up government spending, supporting larger appropriations for defense and public works, relaxing credit controls, and reducing down payments for housing. The problems of recession and unemployment continued during the later years of the Eisenhower administration, little affected by various prescriptions posed by economic experts.

Organized Labor

With the Republican-sponsored Taft-Hartley Act fresh in their memories, organized labor was concerned that under Eisenhower unions would lose the ground they had won during five consecutive Democratic administrations. This apprehension proved unfounded, however. During the Eisenhower years the union movement remained strong, comprising about 30 percent of the work force.

Organized labor's major objectives during the 1950s were to attain job security and to prevent the erosion, by inflation, of the real value of rising wages. Even before Eisenhower took office, workers had made significant progress toward these goals. In 1948 the United Auto Workers, led by Walter Reuther, won a major victory when General Motors agreed, in an "escalator clause," to automatic wage hikes which would be granted according to rises in the consumer price index (an economic index measuring the cost of living). By the middle of the decade many unions had made further progress in these areas under a plan originally proposed by Reuther providing for a guaranteed annual wage through a company fund that would be used to supplement state unemployment compensation if members were laid off.

Union gains, however, seemed to be endangered by expanding automation. Union workers believed that technological advances that would improve production efficiency would also deprive them of their jobs. In 1959 the steelworkers struck over this issue without success. As the decade ended, unions were beginning to seek new ways to protect their members from this threat. It is worth noting

that while automation did contribute to the problem of unemployment for unskilled workers, it created great numbers of jobs for skilled workers in new high-technology industries—the computer and electronics industries being among the most notable.

A momentous event for organized labor was the 1955 merger of the AFL and the CIO. The old rivalry between the two organizations ended with their unification under the leadership of George Meany of the AFL as president and Walter Reuther of the CIO as vice-president. This giant merger, which included all major unions except the United Mine Workers and the railroad workers, gave organized labor a powerful voice in national affairs.

Labor's strengthened position was undermined somewhat by the discovery of corruption in the leadership of the Teamsters' Union. In 1957 a Senate committee charged that high officials of the Teamsters had connections with organized crime and that Teamster President David Beck had misappropriated more than $320,000 in union pension funds. In his appearance before the committee Beck invoked the Fifth Amendment 209 times. He was later tried and found guilty of tax evasion and misusing union funds. To replace Beck as union president the Teamsters elected James R. Hoffa, who had also been a target of the Senate investigation. As a result, the Teamsters Union was expelled from the AFL-CIO. Largely in response to such instances of union corruption, Congress passed the Landrum-Griffin Act of 1959. The act placed tighter restrictions on picketing, included provisions to protect unions against criminal influence, and required unions to issue public financial statements.

Agricultural Problems

The agricultural sector was the major exception to the economic prosperity of the 1950s. Like business, agriculture was moving toward greater consolidation. Each year the number of farms diminished and the size of farms grew, as the family farm gave way to the larger commercial farm. In 1960 only 8.5 percent of the nation's labor force was employed in farming.

Even though the character of American farms was changing, the problems were the same as they had been in the 1920s. American farmers were producing more food than the nation could consume, and overproduction kept farm prices consistently low. President Eisenhower and Secretary of Agriculture Ezra Taft Benson proposed to reduce the surplus by instituting a more flexible price-support system aimed at helping farmers adjust their production to market demands. It was believed that with flexible supports prices would be lowered as production increased and raised as output declined. But the plan put into effect under the Agricultural Act of 1954 failed to reduce surpluses significantly, largely because without restrictions on the planting of crops overproduction continued in spite of declining prices.

In 1956 the administration tried another approach, called the "soil-bank" plan, which offered to pay farmers to turn part of their crop land into forest or pasture. This measure was no more successful than the earlier one, because as farmers began to cultivate fewer acres, their production on the remaining land became more efficient, increasing the per-acre yield. Finding that the surplus persisted, the government used some of it in a school lunch program and in shipments abroad.

The concept of government price subsidies went against Eisenhower's desire to free the economy of government regulation wherever possible. He realized, however, that although the system was imperfect, it prevented the agricultural depression that probably would have occurred without it.

Expansion of Government Services

"Along with the protection of freedom and maintenance of a strong and growing economy," Eisenhower wrote, "this administration recognizes a third great purpose of government—care for the human problems of our citizens." In line with this statement, the generally conservative president retained the social-welfare reforms of the New Deal. His success in this area resulted from Democratic support of measures opposed by conservative members of his own party. As noted earlier, in 1953 Eisenhower successfully engineered the creation of the cabinet Department of Health, Education, and Welfare. He also supported the extension of existing welfare programs. Between 1954 and 1956 Social Security benefits were extended to an additional ten million workers and unemployment compensation to an additional four million. Old-age pensions were

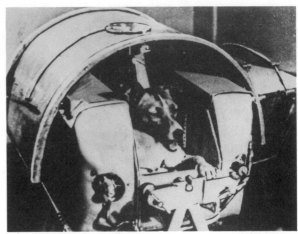

LAIKA, THE WORLD'S FIRST SPACE TRAVELLER, IS PHOTOGRAPHED IN HER AIR-CONDITIONED CABIN BEFORE BEING ROCKETED INTO SPACE ABOARD RUSSIA'S *SPUTNIK II.*

raised and the federal minimum wage was increased from $.75 to a dollar an hour.

In 1957, the Russians launched *Sputnik,* the first satellite sent into orbit from earth. This event unleashed a furor over the failure of the American educational system to keep pace with the Russians in the sciences. To make up this apparent educational lag, Congress in 1958 passed the National Defense Education Act, which allocated over a billion dollars in federal aid to education. Government dollars were spent on student aid, educational research facilities, improvements in the teaching of science and languages, and numerous other programs.

The administration also approved appropriations to aid home building and the construction of low-rent housing units. In 1956 the Interstate Highway Act made possible the largest road-building program in the nation's history. Despite opposition from rural America, during the next thirteen years the government spent more than $30 billion constructing over forty thousand miles of new highways.

Resource Development— Public Versus Private

In keeping with his preference for reduced government involvement in the economy, Eisenhower generally favored private development of power projects, a position his critics described as "the surrender of resources belonging to all the people." Public-power advocates criticized him when he made the damming of the Snake River at Hells Canyon, Idaho, into a private project and when he supported private development of offshore oil and natural-gas properties. In 1947 the Supreme Court had denied California ownership of the three-mile offshore area. But the 1953 Submerged Lands Act put offshore oil and natural gas under state control. When California, Texas, Louisiana, and Florida proceeded to pass the mineral rights on to private corporations, many advocates of public power protested. Eisenhower defended the states, arguing that private interests could develop the offshore resources more efficiently than the government.

The biggest controversy over private versus public development occurred in 1954, when the Tennessee Valley Authority announced plans to build a new generating plant. Eisenhower regarded further expansion of the TVA as "creeping social ism," supporting instead the construction of the plant by a private concern, Dixon-Yates. Outraged public-power advocates argued that the so-called Dixon-Yates plan would cost taxpayers several million dollars more per year than the public plan proposed by the TVA and that the government would be helping private companies to rake in sizable profits at the public's expense. When the city of Memphis offered to build the plant, Eisenhower was relieved and withdrew the plan.

On the St. Lawrence Seaway proposal the president demonstrated his pragmatism by reversing his earlier policies and supporting public construction of the seaway against the protests of private business interests. His position reflected his belief that the project was too large for private industry and could be completed only with the cooperation of both the Canadian and American governments. Congress agreed and the seaway was inaugurated in 1959.

The 1956 Election

Although he had suffered a serious heart attack in September 1955 and had undergone abdominal surgery in June 1956, Eisenhower was sufficiently recovered by the time of the Republican convention in August to win the unanimous endorsement of his party for a second term. Party support for Vice-President Richard Nixon, however, was considerably less enthusiastic. Nixon's critics especially deplored his ruthless exploitation of the fear of communism in the 1954 congressional elections. But when a "Dump Nixon" movement developed among party liberals, the president refused to support it since he thought Nixon was useful as a link between the moderate and conservative wings of the party. Party regulars and members of the business community defended Nixon, and he was renominated.

In a more boisterous Democratic convention, Senator Estes Kefauver challenged Adlai Stevenson for the presidential nomination. Although many Democrats believed that Stevenson could not win the election, he won the nomination and the convention chose Kefauver as his running mate. The election proved Stevenson's critics right. Eisenhower handed Stevenson an even greater defeat than the one he had suffered in 1952, carrying forty-one states and receiving thirty-five million popular votes to Stevenson's twenty-six million.

President Eisenhower was less effective during his second term than he had been in his first. After his heart attack and abdominal surgery, he was frequently ill. In addition, in the 1958 congressional elections the Democrats, supported by dissatisfied workers and farmers, increased their majority in Congress, and Eisenhower vetoed several measures aimed at solving domestic problems by increased government spending. Finally, the president lost his two most trusted advisers. In 1958 Sherman Adams was forced to resign as a result of charges that he had used his position to gain government favors for a friend; and in May 1959 Secretary of State John Foster Dulles died.

Civil Rights and Racial Equality

During the Eisenhower years, the struggle for civil rights became the nation's central domestic issue. As noted in the preceding chapter, Truman had failed in his attempts to push through legislation that would eliminate discrimination in employment and ensure the civil rights of blacks. Blocked from many areas of economic opportunity, black Americans focused their efforts on securing equal educational opportunity, as the black leadership had done in previous decades. The African independence movement against European colonialism provided inspiration and encouragement to the American civil rights movement. If black Africans could throw off the shackles of white oppression, activists felt, then black Americans could surely attain for themselves the freedom enjoyed by their white counterparts.

For their part, many white Americans supported equality in theory but were fearful of the turmoil the struggle for civil rights would bring. Others had had little or no contact with blacks and were largely unaware of the conditions they faced. Still others were motivated by deep-rooted racial animosity. Given the fundamental complacency of white middle-class Americans during the 1950s, it is not surprising that although President Eisenhower sympathized with the objectives of the civil rights movement, he wanted to avoid stirring up a potentially volatile situation.

Although he stated publicly that "there must be no second-class citizens in this country," he generally declined to take the initiative in promoting equal rights. The momentum within the government for civil rights reform during the 1950s came largely from the Warren Court.

Supreme Court Initiatives   In the _Plessy_ v. _Ferguson_ decision (1896) the Supreme Court had declared that the maintenance of separate facilities for blacks and whites was constitutional as long as those facilities were equal. This "separate-but-equal" doctrine had since become the legal rationale for racial segregation. In the 1940s, however, the Supreme Court began to undermine the 1896 decision by ruling against discrimination in the use of Pullman facilities on trains and against segregation on public buses in interstate travel. In 1950 a Court decision desegregated railroad dining-car facilities.

At the same time civil rights groups led by the NAACP were successful in their drive to convince the Supreme Court to compel universities in more than half a dozen states to admit black students. By

---

Race Relations: Integration

"In each of the cases, minors of the Negro race, through their legal representatives, seek the aid of the courts in obtaining admission to the public schools of their community on a nonsegregated basis. In each instance, they had been denied admission to schools attended by white children under laws requiring or permitting segregation according to race. This segregation was alleged to deprive the plaintiffs of the equal protection of the laws under the Fourteenth Amendment. . . .

We come then to the question presented. Does segregation of children in the public schools solely on the basis of race, even though the physical facilities and other "tangible" factors may be equal, deprive the children of the minority group of equal educational opportunities? We believe that it does. . . .

We conclude that in the field of public education the doctrine of 'separate but equal' has no place. Separate educational facilities are inherently unequal. . . ."

Brown v. _Board of Education of Topeka_, 1954

Race Relations: Segregation

"When the Constitution of the United States was enacted, a Government was formed upon the premise that people, as individuals, are endowed with the rights of life, liberty, and property, and with the right of local self-government. The people and their local self-governments formed a Central Government and conferred upon it certain stated and limited powers. All other powers were reserved to the states and to the people.

Strong local government is the foundation of our system and must be continually guarded and maintained. . . .

I stand here today, as Governor of this sovereign state, and refuse to willingly submit to illegal usurpation of power by the Central Government. I claim today for all the people of the State of Alabama those rights reserved to them under the Constitution of the United States. Among those powers so reserved and claimed is the right of state authority in the operation of the public schools, colleges, and universities. . . ."

Governor George C. Wallace, 1963

BLACK STUDENTS ASCEND THE STEPS OF LITTLE ROCK CENTRAL HIGH SCHOOL UNDER THE PROTECTION OF FEDERAL TROOPS, 1957.

1952 leaders of the civil rights movement were pressing the Supreme Court to overturn the "separate but-equal" doctrine for all schools.

In 1952 the case of *Brown* v. *Board of Education of Topeka* came before the Supreme Court. The case concerned an eight-year-old black child who lived only five blocks from the nearest school but who had to attend a black school two miles from her home. Arguments were presented beginning in late 1952 and again in late 1953 when the new chief justice, Earl Warren, was appointed. The Court's landmark ruling, delivered in May 1954, came down squarely against the "separate-but-equal" doctrine and against segregation in education: "In the field of public education the doctrine of 'separate but equal' has no place. Separate educational facilities are inherently unequal." The Court's decision was based on the equal-protection clause of the Fourteenth Amendment and on sociological evidence that segregation imposed a "feeling of inferiority" on black children. In another decision a year later, Chief Justice Warren, speaking for the Court, ordered school authorities to implement school desegregation "with all deliberate speed."

In the South, where school segregation was deeply entrenched, and to a considerable degree in the North, the Supreme Court order met stiff opposition. Ninety-six Southern representatives issued a declaration denouncing the decision as a violation of the Constitution and calling on the states to resist it "by all lawful means." Schools were closed and compulsory attendance abolished; some states even passed legislation giving indirect aid to private schools as an alternative to supporting integrated public schools. Resistance reached a climax in 1957, when Governor Orval Faubus of Arkansas mobilized the Arkansas National Guard to prevent black students from entering Little Rock's all-white Central High School.

Eisenhower was in an awkward position. He had felt that civil rights groups were demanding too much, too soon. Moreover, he had no wish to alienate white Southerners. But Faubus's actions were in clear defiance of a federal court order and a Supreme Court decision. Unable to avoid taking action, Eisenhower nationalized the Arkansas National Guard and sent one hundred army paratroopers to Little Rock to enforce the Court order and protect black students. His action marked the first government effort since Reconstruction to help black Americans in the South. While Eisenhower succeeded in desegregating the school, he incurred the wrath of countless Southerners. Even after the Little Rock incident, desegregation continued to encounter heavy resistance. In 1964, ten years after the Brown decision, only 1 percent of Southern black students were attending integrated schools.

Legislative Initiatives and Civil Disobedience
Although blacks were generally disappointed by Eisenhower's failure to use his moral authority more decisively to support civil rights, they applauded him for naming J. Ernest Wilkins, a black, as assistant secretary of labor and for supporting the Civil Rights Act of 1957. The act, passed after protracted debate, sought to put an end to practices that perpetuated discrimination. It established a Civil Rights Commission to investigate violations of voting rights and gave the attorney general authority to seek court injunctions to protect the voting rights of Americans, black or white. In 1960 Congress passed another Civil Rights Act despite a lengthy filibuster by the Southern bloc. The new act made interference with voting and school desegregation a federal offense.

Although legislation and court decisions were beginning to counteract racial discrimination, many blacks grew impatient with the slow rate of prog-ress. As the 1950s wore on, they increasingly turned from legislative and judicial efforts to other strategies, such as boycotts, sit-ins, and demonstrations. The event that crystallized this new phase in the civil rights movement occurred in December 1955 in Montgomery, Alabama. Rosa Parks, a black seamstress who was tired from a day's work, sat down in the front section of a bus—the section which by longstanding custom was reserved for whites. When told to move to the rear, Mrs. Parks, who had not anticipated the situation and who normally would have complied, refused to move. She had decided, as she later said, "never to move again." When she was subsequently arrested and sent to jail, Montgomery blacks rallied to her cause. Led by the Reverend Martin Luther King, Jr., a young black clergyman, they staged a year-long boycott of city buses, during which King and several followers were arrested and jailed. In December 1956 a federal court, acting on the earlier Supreme Court ruling against segregation on buses, ordered the desegregation of the Montgomery bus system.

Although the Congress of Racial Equality (CORE) had been carrying out nonviolent campaigns to end segregation since its creation in 1942, Martin Luther King now became the leader of the civil rights movement. He formed the Southern Christian Leadership Conference (SCLC), which stood at the center of the civil rights movement for the next ten years. King and the SCLC used techniques of passive resistance and civil disobedience successfully employed by Mahatma Gandhi, the great revolutionary who had led India to independence from Great Britain. When opponents charged that King was damaging the black cause by refusing to obey the nation's laws, he answered that people cannot be forced to obey unjust laws. A passionately religious man and a powerful and eloquent orator, he set an example of nonviolent action that was taken up by other black organizations such as the newly formed Student Nonviolent Coordinating Committee (SNCC).

Foreign Issues

Eisenhower, to a great extent, left the formulation of foreign policy to Secretary of State John Foster Dulles. A devout Presbyterian and a moralist by nature, Dulles was a more committed cold warrior than the president. He viewed the struggle against communism as a classic conflict between good and evil. Vowing to carry the anti-Communist crusade beyond Truman's policy of containment, he advocated a "rollback" policy to "liberate" nations which were already under Communist domination. Convinced that the Soviets would never negotiate in good faith, he asserted that the United States should use all the weapons at its disposal—from moral persuasion to military might—to counter Soviet power throughout the world.

In spite of Dulles's rhetoric, the Eisenhower administration generally followed the containment policy initiated by Truman. Militarily this meant relying on the NATO alliance as a deterrent to further Communist expansion in Europe and initiating the creation of new alliances in Asia and the Middle East to block Communist gains in those areas. Foreign aid became synonymous with military assistance to friendly foreign governments. Through the Mutual Security program, the government spent more than $3 billion a year providing aid to countries that declared their opposition to communism. Neutral nations, such as India, were considered pro-Communist and were therefore shunned. This rigid anti-Communist policy frequently placed the United States on the side of repressive and authoritarian regimes, such as those in Spain, Pakistan, and Brazil. The extent of the administration's concern over the spread of communism was evident, too, in the fact that the CIA was authorized to conduct covert actions to subvert governments considered hostile to the United States.

As a complement to its policy of military containment, the administration expanded its use of economic policy as a tool in attaining foreign-policy goals. The president and his advisers believed a more liberal trade policy would encourage the development of capitalism throughout the world. During the 1950s the reciprocal-trade agreements program was extended and the lending authority of the Export-Import Bank was expanded. American exports leaped from $15 billion in 1952 to $20 billion in 1960. And in 1954 Eisenhower launched the Food for Peace plan to dispose of America's agricultural surplus to needy peoples overseas. Under this program over $12 billion worth of farm goods were distributed abroad in the next ten years.

"Massive Retaliation"

Not far into Eisenhower's first term in office, Stalin died. His successor, Nikita Khrushchev, a gregarious and ebullient man, denounced the tyrannical excesses of Stalin's rule and, well-aware of the dangers of nuclear war, announced his desire for "peaceful coexistence" with the United States. He seemed determined to promote international communism without setting off a nuclear catastrophe. His weapons would be ideological. He was particularly active in trying to turn to Soviet advantage revolutionary nationalism in former colonial areas of Asia, the Middle East, and Africa.

Even with the apparent tempering of the Soviet position, Dulles remained distrustful. He continued to pursue the establishment of international alliances to protect vulnerable areas from Soviet military power. Yet neither Eisenhower nor Dulles believed that anti-Communist alliances would sufficiently protect United States interests and halt Communist aggression. They were determined that never again would the United States become embroiled in another indecisive war like the one in Korea. Accordingly, the administration proposed a new defense posture based on the strategy of "massive retaliation" with nuclear weapons. The Soviets were warned that if aggression were undertaken, the United States would retaliate with its full nuclear force against Russia itself. This policy, Dulles contended, would enable the nation to reduce the size of its costly standing army and conventional weapons systems while getting "more bang for a buck"—maximum destructiveness at minimum cost. As appealing as this "new look" in military policy sounded to an economy-minded public weary of international tensions, it had obvious drawbacks. Massive retaliation against Communist aggression anywhere in the world could precipitate world war, since by the middle of the decade the Soviet Union had nuclear weapons and a strong air force.

✳ The Far East ✳

Korea In December 1952, even before his inauguration, Eisenhower kept his campaign promise by going to Korea to seek a truce. While the death of Stalin the following March and the subsequent thaw in the cold war helped to facilitate negotiations, Eisenhower's threat to use atomic weapons against the North Koreans if they refused to resume negotiations was the most important factor in forcing them back to the bargaining table.

One of the stickiest issues in the talks concerned the repatriation of prisoners of war. In addition to thousands of North and South Koreans who refused

AMERICAN AND KOREAN POWs JOIN
THEIR COMMUNIST CAPTORS IN
SINGING AND WAVING FLAGS FOR A
COMMUNIST PHOTOGRAPHER. THE
PROBLEM OF REPATRIATION OF
SOLDIERS DELAYED THE SIGNING OF
AN ARMISTICE AGREEMENT UNTIL
JULY 1953.

to be repatriated, twenty-one American prisoners of war declined to return to their own country, setting off charges that they had been brainwashed. Eventually, the Communists agreed that all prisoners would be released and allowed to choose for themselves. The resolution of this problem opened the way for an armistice.

The armistice, signed in July 1953, ended hostilities, provided for troop withdrawals, and set the boundary between North and South Korea at the battle line, which would be demilitarized. For the most part, this line ran slightly north of the thirty-eighth parallel. Unfortunately, after the United States had lost thirty-three thousand lives and spent $22 billion, the Korean situation ultimately returned to what it had been before the war.

Indochina The threat of "massive retaliation" had little impact in Indochina, a French colony where Indochinese nationalists (the Vietminh) under [Ho Chi Minh] had been waging a war for independence since the end of World War II. After the Korean conflict, the insurgents, many of whom were also Communists, were aided indirectly by the Chinese Communists. As the nationalists continued to make substantial gains, the French, facing almost certain defeat, turned to the United States for help.

Although committed to the principle of self-determination, the United States feared that its opposition to French colonialism would alienate France and damage the NATO alliance. President Truman had tried to steer a middle course by supporting the French while urging that they eventually grant independence to Indochina. As the war progressed, however, support for French colonial policy became wholehearted as American leaders became convinced that the war was part of a larger pattern of Sino-Soviet efforts to dominate the Far East. Thus by 1954 the United States was paying 75–80 percent of the French cost of the war as well as supplying military equipment. When the French were still unable to defeat the anti-colonialists they asked for direct American intervention. Eisenhower, however, was opposed to intervention and Congress, fearing that the nation would become entangled in another Korea-type conflict, did not want to support military action. In May 1954 the French forces were decisively defeated at the isolated fortress of Dien Bien Phu.

With the weary, beaten French finally willing to negotiate, a peace conference was convened at Geneva. The agreement of July 1954 called for the partitioning of Indochina into three nations: Vietnam, Laos, and Cambodia. Vietnam was to be di-

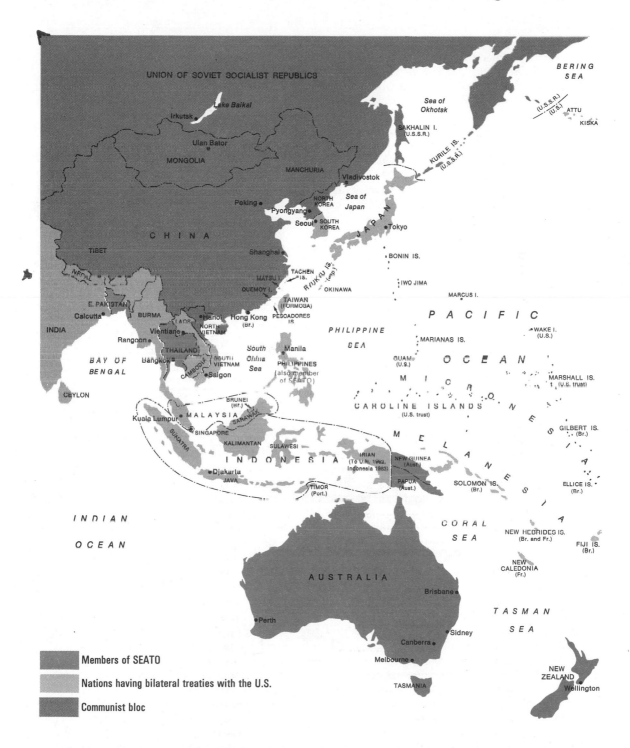

UNION OF SOVIET SOCIALIST REPUBLICS

BERING SEA

Sea of Okhotsk

(U.S.S.R.)
(U.S.)
ATTU
KISKA

Lake Baikal

Irkutsk •

SAKHALIN I.
(U.S.S.R.)

Ulan Bator •

KURILE IS.
(U.S.S.R.)

MONGOLIA

MANCHURIA

Vladivostok •

Sea of Japan

NORTH KOREA

Peking •

Pyongyang •

Seoul • SOUTH KOREA

• Tokyo

PACIFIC

C H I N A

Shanghai •

BONIN IS.

TIBET

IWO JIMA

MARCUS I.

TACHEN IS.

MATSU I.

QUEMOY I.

RYUKYU IS.

OKINAWA

O C E A N

NEPAL

TAIWAN (FORMOSA)

PESCADORES IS.

E. PAKISTAN

BURMA

Hanoi • Hong Kong (Br.)

PHILIPPINE SEA

MARIANAS IS.

WAKE I. (U.S.)

Calcutta •

LAOS

NORTH VIETNAM

GUAM (U.S.)

MARSHALL IS. (U.S. trust)

INDIA

Vientiane •

M I C R O N E S I A

Rangoon •

THAILAND

South China Sea

Manila

BAY OF BENGAL

Bangkok •

SOUTH VIETNAM

PHILIPPINES (also member of SEATO)

CAROLINE ISLANDS (U.S. trust)

CAMBODIA

• Saigon

GILBERT IS. (Br.)

CEYLON

BRUNEI (Br.)

M E L A N E S I A

Kuala Lumpur •

MALAYSIA

SARAWAK

SUMATRA

• SINGAPORE

KALIMANTAN

SULAWESI

IRIAN (To U.N. 1962, Indonesia 1963)

NEW GUINEA (Aust.)

SOLOMON IS. (Br.)

ELLICE IS. (Br.)

I N D O N E S I A

• Djakarta

JAVA

PAPUA (Aust.)

TIMOR (Port.)

INDIAN

OCEAN

CORAL SEA

NEW HEBRIDES IS. (Br. and Fr.)

FIJI IS. (Br.)

NEW CALEDONIA (Fr.)

A U S T R A L I A

• Brisbane

TASMAN SEA

• Perth

• Sidney

Canberra •

Melbourne •

NEW ZEALAND

TASMANIA

• Wellington

Members of SEATO

Nations having bilateral treaties with the U.S.

Communist bloc

Postwar Alliances • The Far East

vided temporarily into two parts. Ho Chi Minh, who presently had control of two-thirds of Vietnam, was to rule in the area north of the seventeenth parallel, while a French-backed regime would be established in the south. Internationally supervised elections would be held in 1956 to reunify the country under one government. The United States, determined not to be bound by any agreement that would bar it from preventing a Communist takeover of Indochina, refused to sign the Geneva agreement.

More determined than ever to contain the spread of communism, Secretary Dulles proposed an Asian alliance of non-Communist nations. The result was the formation in September 1954 of the Southeast Asia Treaty Organization (SEATO), which was modeled after NATO. Great Britain, France, Australia, New Zealand, Pakistan, the Philippines, Thailand, and the United States signed the agreement. South Vietnam, Laos, and Cambodia were prevented from joining by the Geneva agreement but were included in the region guarded by SEATO. All signatories agreed that an attack on one member nation would be construed as an attack on all. Unlike NATO, SEATO did not establish an international military force; its effectiveness would depend almost exclusively on American military power. The pact was weakened when the newly independent nations of India, Burma, and Indonesia refused to join, favoring instead a policy of neutrality. Their refusal demonstrated the unwillingness of many nations emerging from colonialism to become involved with their former colonial rulers or to be drawn into the cold war.

China Throughout the 1950s the United States continued to support the Chiang Kai-shek regime in Formosa as the legitimate government of China and to ignore the existence of the Communist People's Republic on the mainland. Late in 1954 the United States signed a mutual defense treaty with Formosa, and Dulles hinted at the American intention to defend the small islands of Quemoy and Matsu off the coast of China, which he considered vital to the defense of Formosa and which were not covered by the mutual-defense treaty. Communist shelling of the islands from the mainland in 1955 and 1958 was thought to be the first stage of a Communist invasion of Formosa. Nevertheless, when the United States' European allies indicated that they would not support an extensive American effort against the

Red Chinese, the administration pulled back and the Chinese turned their attention to other areas —most ominously, the new Indochinese nation of Laos. Thus the new foreign policy of massive retaliation had been exposed as ineffective in preventing the spread of Communist influence.

The Middle East

Before World War II American interest in the Middle East was minimal, reflecting only the investments of American oil companies. As the cold war developed, however, the area became the scene of strategic rivalry between the United States and the Soviet Union. Both to protect American oil interests and to curb Soviet influence, the United States sought the support of the Arab nations of the Middle East. This objective was complicated by two factors: American support for the newly created Jewish state of Israel—the focal point of Arab hostility—and the reluctance of the Arab states to become pawns in the cold war.

Israel In 1947 in the wake of the Nazi Holocaust, the United Nations General Assembly approved the creation of a Jewish homeland by ending the British mandate in Palestine and partitioning it into a Jewish state and an Arab state. The partition, however, was not accepted by the Arabs, who responded by initiating a guerrilla war. On May 14, 1948, the Jews proclaimed the state of Israel in what had been Palestine and, after a short but bloody war with the Arabs, gained control of the country. Half the Arab population fled and subsequently settled in refugee camps on Israel's borders. In 1949 an armistice was worked out by Dr. Ralph Bunche under UN auspices. (Bunche, the descendant of African slaves, won the Nobel Peace Prize in 1950 for his contribution.) Nevertheless, Arab raids continued and the Arabs bitterly refused to accept the existence of the state of Israel. Truman had extended diplomatic recognition to Israel immediately and Israel began to turn increasingly to the United States for aid against the much larger and more populous Arab states.

The Suez Crisis The Eisenhower administration, concerned about Soviet influence in the Middle East, sought to placate the Arabs in order to prevent their becoming dependent on the Russians. American efforts to quiet Arab rage focused on Egyptian strongman Gamal Abdel Nasser, self-appointed leader of the Arab nationalist movement. Dulles offered American economic aid, and Nasser accepted it for a time. But the United States angered him by refusing to supply Egypt with arms. Nasser was further alienated when the United States threw its support behind an alliance to counter Soviet influence in oil-rich Iran. While the United States was not a signatory, it stood behind the Baghdad Pact of February 1955, signed by Britain, Turkey, Pakistan, Iran, and Iraq. The purpose of the pact was to create a defense barrier on Russia's southern flank against the spread of communism. Nasser decried the pact as an attack on Arab unity and a threat to Egypt's leadership in the Middle East. In September 1955 Egypt and Russia made public an agreement whereby Nasser would receive an enormous quantity of arms from Czechoslovakia in return for Egyptian cotton.

The United States tried to regain a favorable position with Egypt by offering to help finance the construction of the Aswan Dam in central Egypt, a

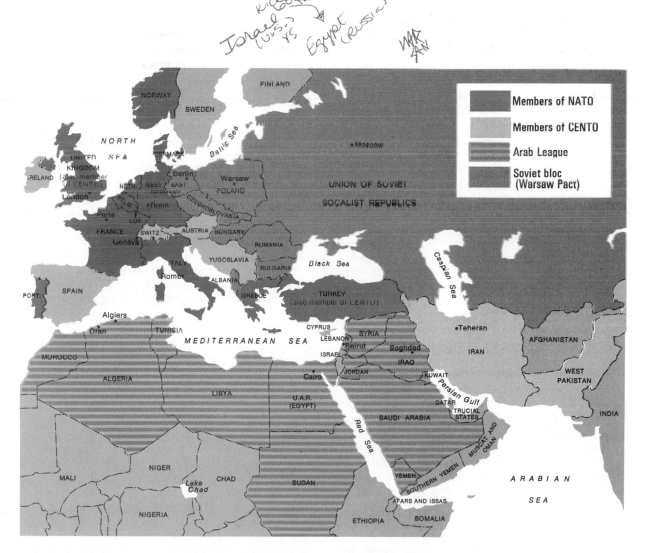

Postwar Alliances • Europe, North Africa, the Middle East

crucial part of an irrigation program that would aid Egyptian agriculture. However, congressional support for the offer was only lukewarm. American Jews opposed the strengthening of Egypt and Congress was reluctant to approve the necessary expenditures. Moreover, in 1956 Nasser recognized the People's Republic of China. As a result of congressional pressure, Dulles was forced to retract the American offer.

In July 1956, in response, Nasser seized and nationalized the Suez Canal Company, owned by Britain and France, and intensified Egyptian raids on Israel. The canal was of critical importance to British shipping and all of Europe depended on its use to acquire oil supplies. In an effort to occupy Suez and keep the canal open, Britain and France joined Israel in a military attack on Egypt in October 1956. The Egyptian army was quickly smashed and Nasser responded by blocking the canal with sunken ships. (The timing was fortuitous for the Soviets whose suppression of a 1956 revolt in Hungary drew much less world attention than it might have otherwise.)

Dulles and Eisenhower believed that the attacks on Egypt had no legal basis and were angered that the British and French had acted unilaterally. Subsequently, both the United States and Russia sponsored UN resolutions calling for a cease-fire. Britain and France vetoed the resolutions but could not prevent the passage of a resolution in the General Assembly calling for the immediate withdrawal of all foreign troops from Egypt. At the same time Russia threatened to send "volunteers" to Egypt and to use nuclear missiles against Britain and France. The two countries, faced with hostile world opinion, Russian threats, and the opposition of the United States, now decided to withdraw. A United Nations force was sent to Suez to supervise troop withdrawals and act as a peacekeeping force. Although the American response earned the United States grudging respect among anticolonial nations, it undermined relations with Britain and France and hurt the NATO alliance. Dulles's overall Mideast policy unfortunately succeeded only in drawing Egypt closer to Russia. (It was the Soviets who built the Aswan Dam.)

The Eisenhower Doctrine   The Eisenhower administration now believed that to prevent Soviet involvement in the Middle East, curb Nasser, and pro-

tect Israel, it would have to go it alone. In March 1957, Congress endorsed the so-called "Eisenhower Doctrine," which stated the United States' intention to act unilaterally if necessary to prevent any country "controlled by international communism" from violating the independence of any Middle East nation.

One month later the Eisenhower Doctrine was invoked to help King Hussein of Jordan put down Nasser-supported opposition to his rule. When a pro-Nasser rebellion broke out in Lebanon in 1958, Eisenhower dispatched American troops to prevent the eruption of full-scale civil war. By the end of the 1950s America's prestige in the Arab world was at a low ebb as a result of intervention under the Eisenhower Doctrine and America's strong support of Israel.

Latin America

Immediately following World War II pan-American relations appeared strong. The 1947 Rio Pact created a military alliance committing all the nations of the Western Hemisphere to collective defense. The following year at Bogotá the United States and Latin American countries established the Organization of American States to deal with problems of mutual interest.

By the 1950s, however, the relations between the United States and its southern neighbors had begun to deteriorate. Like the rest of the developing nations, the countries of Latin America were far more concerned with their own chronic economic and social problems than with the specter of international communism. Not surprisingly, they came to resent American pressure to join the anti-Communist crusade while the United States ignored their urgent problems of poverty, illiteracy, and overpopulation. In addition, the United States government was criticized for its support of military dictators in Latin America as well as for longstanding American economic dominance of some of the Latin countries.

Trouble in Guatemala   As noted earlier, Dulles's foreign policy called for the use of subversive tactics in Latin America as elsewhere in the world to prevent a leftist or Communist government from coming to power. In 1951, while Truman was in office, a left-wing government gained control in Guatemala. Although the United States feared that this would give communism a foothold in the Western Hemisphere, it took no action. Later, however, when the new government nationalized American businesses in Guatemala, offering the owners only partial compensation, American concern turned to open hostility. In 1954 the Eisenhower administration called an inter-American conference at Caracas and forced through a resolution declaring international communism a threat to the security of the Western Hemisphere.

The leftist Guatemalan government now turned to Russia for aid and received arms from Communist Czechoslovakia. Secretary of State Dulles responded by ordering the CIA to sponsor an invasion from Honduras. CIA-backed invading forces overthrew the pro-Communist government and seized power. The United States immediately recognized the new military regime and extended economic aid. These events not only caused further deterioration of America's position in Latin America, but brought a sharp rebuke from the NATO allies.

In 1958 Vice-President Nixon made a goodwill visit to South America that provided dramatic evidence of the growing disenchantment with the United States of its southern neighbors. Anti-Americanism was expressed throughout his tour in booing and shouted insults. Peruvian students threw stones at the vice-president, and Venezuelan protesters smashed his car windows and even threatened his life. These incidents shocked many Americans into realizing how poorly their nation was regarded in Latin America and forced the administration to begin a reevaluation of its Latin American policy. In an effort to demonstrate its concern for the progress of Latin America, the government in 1959 supported the creation of an Inter-American Development Bank.

The Cuban Revolution As the administration was pondering new ways to improve its relations with Latin America, its worst fears were realized in Cuba. A nationalist movement under Fidel Castro ended the tyrannical rule of the United States-supported dictator, Fulgencio Batista, and took control of the country. Eisenhower recognized the new regime and, eager to learn about the new Cuban leader, invited Castro to Washington for talks. When the visit ended, the president seemed satisfied that Castro was not a Communist. After he returned

to Cuba, however, Castro soon launched a series of diatribes against the United States and initiated a social revolution directed against foreign exploitation of Cuba. He developed a close relationship with Moscow and seized American property without compensation. When Cuba signed an economic pact with the Soviets in February 1960, the administration placed a retaliatory embargo on Cuban sugar imports to the United States. The lines were drawn even more clearly when Russia announced its support for the new Cuban regime by threatening to attack the United States if it tried to intervene in Cuban affairs. In January 1961 the United States severed diplomatic relations with the Castro government.

Europe: The Weakened NATO Alliance

Despite the American conviction that communism was a worldwide threat, Europe continued to be the main focus of concern. Although NATO had been established to shield Europe against Communist aggression, the organization was not as strong as United States policymakers would have liked. For one thing, American commitments throughout the world drained manpower and resources from the European alliance. For another, the French, still deeply suspicious of Germany, were angered when in May 1955 the German Federal Republic (West Germany), largely through Dulles's efforts, was granted independence, given the right to rearm, and brought into the NATO alliance. (To counter the NATO buildup the Soviets now formed a new military organization, known as the Warsaw Pact, with the nations of eastern Europe.) The slight thaw in Soviet-American relations following the death of Stalin undermined NATO somewhat by convincing many Americans that the Soviet threat in Europe was decreasing, making the need for a strong defense organization less critical.

Relations with Russia

With Khrushchev's rise to power in 1953, Soviet-American tensions seemed to ease for a time. Although both powers continued to use cold war rhetoric, they generally avoided actions that might endanger the tenuous improvement in their relations. Thus, although Secretary Dulles had vowed to liberate eastern Europe from Soviet domination, when Russia ruthlessly suppressed rebellions in East Berlin in 1953 and in Hungary in 1956, the United States, after registering its protest, stood by. In addition, over Dulles's objections, President Eisenhower, unlike his predecessor, was willing to negotiate with the Soviets. He agreed to a summit conference with Khrushchev at Geneva in July 1955. The conference produced no dramatic results, but the meetings were cordial and cultural exchanges followed.

The Soviet launching of *Sputnik* in 1957 as well as the firing of the first intercontinental ballistic missile (ICBM) had a profound impact on the American defense posture, causing a great flurry of concern. Angered by charges that he had allowed American defenses to slip, Eisenhower pressed Congress to appropriate vast sums for defense, especially for missiles and nuclear-powered submarines. The crisis was defused somewhat in November 1958 when the United States succeeded in firing its own ICBM.

The problem of Berlin, which had lain dormant for some time, was suddenly revived toward the end of 1958 when Khrushchev warned the United States of an impending cutoff of access to West Berlin. When Secretary Dulles died the following May, Eisenhower decided to invite Khrushchev to the United States, hoping that face-to-face diplomacy might help achieve a resolution of the problem and ultimately an end to the cold war. Khrushchev accepted and retreated from his ultimatum on Berlin. After touring the country, he met with the president for a round of talks at Camp David, Maryland, the presidential retreat. Both leaders emerged heartened over the amicable spirit of the talks—the "spirit of Camp David."

In 1960 they agreed to another summit conference. However, two weeks before the scheduled meeting in Paris, the Soviets shot down an American U-2 spy plane, capturing its pilot, Francis Gary

PREMIER NIKITA KHRUSHCHEV FORCEFULLY HAMMERS HOME HIS POINT TO THE UN ASSEMBLY. THE BURLY EX-COAL MINER WAS A MASTER SHOWMAN WHO DID NOT HESITATE TO RESORT TO TEMPER TANTRUMS AND BULLYING DENUNCIATIONS TO ACHIEVE HIS ENDS.

Powers. Unaware that the pilot had been taken alive, the State Department, President Eisenhower, and the CIA made a complete muddle of the situation, each offering a different explanation for the plane's flying deep into Soviet territory and, worse yet, telling it to the public and the Russians. In the end Eisenhower chose to accept personal responsibility for the spy mission. However, when Khrushchev demanded an apology, Eisenhower refused. The Russian premier promptly withdrew from the Paris talks, cancelled an invitation to Eisenhower to visit Russia, and humiliated the American president by putting Powers on trial. Khrushchev's strong response was designed to have maximum impact at home where he was encountering severe party criticism of his policy toward the United States. The net effect of the U-2 incident was to revive the cold war.

Readings

General Works

Alexander, Charles, *Holding the Line: The Eisenhower Era, 1952–1961.* Bloomington: Indiana University Press, 1975.

Lubell, Samuel, *The Revolt of the Moderates.* New York: Harper, 1956.

Miller, Douglas T., and Marion Nowak, *The Fifties: The Way We Really Were.* Garden City, N.Y.: Doubleday, 1977.

Osgood, Robert E., *et al.*, *America and the World: From the Truman Doctrine to Vietnam.* Baltimore: Johns Hopkins, 1970.

Potter, David M., *People of Plenty: Economic Abundance and the American Character.* Chicago: University of Chicago Press, 1954.

Riesman, David, *et al.*, *The Lonely Crowd: A Study of the Changing American Character.* New Haven, Conn.: Yale University Press, 1969.

Vatter, Harold G., *The U.S. Economy in the 1950s.* New York: Norton, 1963.

Whyte, William H., Jr., *The Organization Man.* New York: Simon and Schuster, 1956.

Special Studies

Baily, Samuel, *The United States and the Development of South America, 1945–1975.* New York: New Viewpoints, 1977.

Bartley, Numan V., *The Rise of Massive Resistance: Race-Politics in the South During the 1950s.* Baton Rouge: Louisiana State University Press, 1969.

Cook, Bruce, *The Beat Generation.* New York: Scribner, 1971.

Davies, Richard O., *The Age of Asphalt: The Automobile, the Freeway and the Condition of Metropolitan America.* Philadelphia: Lippincott, 1975.

Draper, Theodore, *Castro's Revolution: Myths and Realities.* New York: Praeger, 1962.

Eisenhower, Milton, *The Wine Is Bitter.* Garden City, N.Y.: Doubleday, 1963.

Finer, Herman, *Dulles over Suez.* Chicago: Quadrangle, 1964.

Hoopes, Townsend, *The Devil and John Foster Dulles: The Diplomacy of the Eisenhower Era.* Boston: Little, Brown, 1973.

Hurewitz, J. C., *Soviet-American Rivalry in the Middle East.* New York: Praeger, 1969.

Kurland, Philip B., *Politics, the Constitution and the Warren Court.* Chicago: University of Chicago Press, 1970.

Lomax, Louis E., *The Negro Revolt.* New York: Harper & Row, 1962.

Parsons, Talcott, and Kenneth B. Clark (Eds.), *The American Negro.* Boston: Beacon, 1966.

Rogin, Michael P., *The Intellectuals and McCarthy: The Radical Specter.* Cambridge, Mass.: MIT Press, 1969.

Thomas, Hugh, *The Suez Affair.* London: Weidenfeld and Nicolson, 1967.

Wilkinson, J. Harvie, III, *From Brown to Bakke, The Supreme Court and School Integration: 1954–1978.* New York: Oxford University Press, 1979.

Primary Sources

Eisenhower, Dwight D., *Mandate for Change.* Garden City, N.Y.: Doubleday, 1963.

Hughes, Emmet J., *The Ordeal of Power.* New York: Atheneum, 1963.

King, Martin Luther, Jr., *Stride Toward Freedom.* New York: Harper & Row, 1958.

Nixon, Richard M., *Six Crises.* New York: Pyramid, 1970.

Warren, Earl, *The Memoirs of Earl Warren.* Garden City, N.Y.: Doubleday, 1977.

Biographies

Davis, K. S., *The Politics of Honor.* New York: Putnam, 1967.

Guhin, Michael, *John Foster Dulles.* New York: Columbia University Press, 1972.

Lyon, Peter, *Eisenhower: Portrait of the Hero.* Boston: Little, Brown, 1974.

Martin, John B., *Adlai Stevenson of Illinois* (I) and *Adlai Stevenson and the World* (II). Garden City, N.Y.: Doubleday, 1976–1977.

Parmet, Herbert S., *Eisenhower and the American Crusades.* New York: Macmillan, 1972.

Weaver, John D., *Warren.* Boston: Little, Brown, 1967.

Fiction

Drury, Alan, *Advise and Consent.* Garden City, N.Y.: Doubleday, 1959.

Ellison, Ralph, *The Invisible Man.* New York: Random House, 1952.

Kerouac, Jack, *On the Road.* New York: Viking Press, 1957.

FEATURE ESSAY

The Age of Television

ON the evening of April 7, 1927, J. J. McCarty, vice-president of American Telephone and Telegraph Company, was standing in a television studio in Washington, D. C. As his face appeared on a TV screen in New York City over two hundred miles away, he spoke the first words ever carried on American television outside of an experimental laboratory:

I am instructed to make a little conversation while they are getting the loudspeaker ready. They are having a little power trouble.

From the studio in New York came the response of Walter Gifford, president of AT&T:

You screen well. You look more handsome over the wire.

Naturally interested in this observation, McCarty inquired:

Does it flatter me much?

This brief exchange came about by accident, and the reactions of the participants were completely spontaneous. Within moments the power

difficulty had been remedied, and the scheduled performer, Secretary of Commerce Herbert Hoover, made his prepared speech. But this casual conversation between the two phone-company executives brought to light a basic truth about television—that a difference exists between the television image and the "real thing." For one brief, unplanned moment there were two J. J. McCartys: the flesh-and-blood person in the Washington studio and the ten-inch miniaturized electronic version appearing on the New York screen. According to Gifford, the two were not the same. The ten-inch version was "more handsome."

In this particular instance the difference between television and real life

was only a matter of appearances, and the event was seen as something of a curiosity. AT&T claimed to have no idea of what might become of the new toy. Apparently no one could look ahead to the years immediately following World War II when television would begin to create a new social experience that would unite America into one big national neighborhood. Yet that phenomenon has occurred. Today events both at home and abroad are communicated instantaneously to all parts of the country, a fact which has drawn the nation together and had profound implications for many aspects of American life.

Commercial television was first introduced to the public over ten years after J. J. McCarty appeared on the small screen. On April 30, 1939, Franklin D. Roosevelt was televised opening the New York World's Fair, thus becoming the first American president to appear on TV. Television

THIS EARLY DEMONSTRATION OF TELEVISION TOOK PLACE ON JULY 30, 1935.

was a feature attraction of the fair. Hours of studio and on-location programming were telecast each day, drawing throngs of fascinated viewers. While the fair was in progress, the first television sets went on sale at prices ranging from $200 to $600. Only four hundred were sold in the first five months. With the entry of the United States into World War II, the experiment was suspended until more auspicious times. Commercial television had been born, but national television was still in the embryonic stages.

As soon as the war ended, the television industry began to expand rapidly. War-related research had produced many technological advances which were easily transferred to the peacetime market. On VJ day in August 1945, five American cities had TV and were broadcasting to some seven thousand homes, fifty-five hundred of them in New York City. Within a few months vastly improved black-and-white sets were available for sale to the public. Applications for station licenses poured into the Federal Communications Commission (FCC), and in less than three years the number of cities with television had increased to sixty-four, and there were a total of 108 operating stations. In 1948, generally considered the birth year of network television, several million sets already had been sold, and 140,000 new sets were being purchased each month.

Almost as important as the growing number of sets and stations was the telephone company's coaxial cable, which carried programs to each local station and allowed them to be viewed simultaneously in different cities. When the cable reached California early in 1951, television became available to fifty million people coast-to-coast. By the late 1970s that number had doubled. With television into its thirtieth year, about 97 percent of American homes owned one or more

JUDY GARLAND MAKES HER TELEVISION DEBUT IN SEPTEMBER 1955 ON THE "FORD STAR JUBILEE." SHE INSISTED ON A LIVE AUDIENCE INSTEAD OF CANNED LAUGHTER.

television sets. Nearly a hundred million Americans were regular television viewers, their sets on for an average of six hours a day. In fact, Americans were spending more time watching TV than participating in any other activity except sleeping. Today the average preschool child spends over fifty-four hours each week in front of the set, and the average adolescent logs some twenty-two thousand hours by the time he or she finishes high school. In other words, the typical American child spends a total of about three years watching TV!

The television audience—adults and children alike—was already hooked on many programs before the system became completely national. Four of the most popular shows appearing in 1947 and 1948—Milton Berle's *Texaco Star Theater*, Sid Caesar's *Your Show of Shows*, Ed Sullivan's *Toast of the Town*, and *The Kraft TV Theater*—were entertain-

ment forms which had evolved from radio. They gave little indication of the new experiences about to be made available by the television medium. Until the early 1950s TV was primarily "radio with a picture." Perhaps this is why the first great television event took the public so much by surprise.

In 1950 Senator Estes Kefauver's Subcommittee on Organized Crime began conducting a major investigation into the world of American crime. Almost as an afterthought, the subcommittee decided to permit television coverage of its hearings. These telecasts coincided with the completion of the transcontinental cable, which meant they were the first major live event to be broadcast to a national television audience.

The camera never lies. Or does it? The twenty million people watching the Kefauver hearings on their sets had a perfect view of the Senate subcommittee at work. They saw for them-

FRANK COSTELLO'S HANDS ON NATIONWIDE TELEVISION.

selves what was happening. They saw the truth—but not the whole truth. They were able to experience only what the camera showed and, therefore, what they saw was uniquely shaped by the presence of those same cameras. The hearing, which was supposedly an information-gathering session, became on television a public inquisition.

Television alone created the high point of the spectacle—the testimony of New York crime boss Frank Costello. Because he was unsure of himself in the new broadcast environment, Costello refused to allow his face to be televised. Instead, while his words were being picked up by the microphones, the cameras were focusing on his hands. And his hands instantly became the stars of the show. Constantly in motion, twitching nervously, they revealed an emotion which was instantly interpreted as guilt by every TV observer. To bring the point home more clearly, the telecasters repeatedly moved the cameras to show first the faces of the subcommittee members, then Costello's telltale hands. This was

an image available only to the TV audience, not to the spectators in the Senate gallery.

As a result of the televised Kefauver hearings, crime and political corruption became major issues in the 1952 presidential campaign, and Kefauver suddenly found himself a national figure. Television had done more than transmit the hearings, it had shaped the audience's perception of them and strongly influenced the results. Now that the power of television had been revealed, national events would never have the same impact. To some extent, things would always be staged for the cameras.

One year after the Kefauver hearings, the 1952 Democratic and Republican national conventions were televised, the first to be viewed by a large national audience and consciously designed to appeal to it. Television dominated both conventions, and it continued to affect national life in the areas of news, politics, and social change. The coverage of television news has magnified important political issues. The impact of the Watergate

hearings was so overwhelming because they were broadcast on TV. Audience response contributed in part to the decline of public support for President Nixon and helped create the pressure which brought about his resignation. The Vietnam War was the first one to be covered by television. It altered American perceptions of war, since both the conduct of the war and the nature of the protest against it were shaped and validated by television coverage.

Television has greatly influenced many other areas of American life as well. In recent years it has positively influenced the way races and sexes relate to each other by satirizing persistent stereotypes and giving more exposure to minority groups. On the other hand, many people believe that it has negatively influenced the health and personality development of American children. They argue that television creates passivity, or conversely that children may want to act out what they see. Some even contend that because of its powers of suggestion, television may be a contributing factor to juvenile delinquency. In a recent much-publicized trial, the defense blamed television for contributing to a teenage boy's commission of a murder.

Family relationships too, have been affected by television. For some parents, TV has become an easy alternative to interacting with children, a kind of electronic babysitter. Television has had a strong influence on American spending habits, as audiences are saturated with commercial messages telling them that the way to happiness is to buy new products.

In recent years a growing realization of the power of the video screen and concern over the poor quality of much of the programming has prompted the rise of consumer watch-dog groups such as Action for Children's Television. Public pressure resulted in the removal of cigarette advertising and a reduction in the level of violence permitted in "action" programs. The creation of a public television network provided an alternative to the offerings of commercial stations. A recent innovation has been the introduction of television critics whose reviews of forthcoming programs enable viewers to be more selective.

What is the future of television? With new technologies sweeping the industry, more options are becoming available to the public. Cable television now offers dozens of programs not provided by the major networks, including uninterrupted movies, sports, and other events. Video-cassette recorders have enabled people to record programs for later viewing. Some other innovations in progress include two-way television which will allow the viewer to vote on a referendum, to respond to a political speech, or to do the shopping; a 24-hour news channel; and a special children's network and a concert network.

The Age of Television is entering a new technological phase. But the changes it is undergoing affect only the type of viewing offered to the public, not the quality of that viewing. The power of the video screen is profound; it is up to the public to shape television to its needs, or if necessary, to turn off the set.

30 The 1960s: Years of Turmoil

We have waited for more than 340 years for our constitutional and God-given rights. The nations of Asia and Africa are moving with jetlike speed toward gaining political independence, but we still creep at horse-and-buggy pace toward gaining a cup of coffee at a lunch counter. Perhaps it is easy for those who have never felt the stinging darts of segregation to say, "Wait." But. . . there comes a time when the cup of endurance runs over, and men are no longer willing to be plunged into the abyss of despair. I hope, sirs, you can understand our legitimate and unavoidable impatience.

Reverend Martin Luther King, Jr.
Letter from Birmingham Jail
April 16, 1963

Significant Events

Alliance for Progress [March 1961]

Bay of Pigs invasion [April 1961]

Berlin Wall [August 1961]

Peace Corps [1961]

Civil rights demonstration, Birmingham, Alabama [April 1962]

Cuban Missile Crisis [October 1962]

Civil rights demonstration in Washington, D.C. [August 1963]

Test Ban Treaty [August 1963]

Office of Economic Opportunity [1964]

Civil Rights Act [1964]

Free Speech Movement [1964]

Tonkin Gulf Resolution [August 7, 1964]

Voting Rights Act [1965]

Medicare [1965]

Elementary and Secondary Education Act [1965]

Tet Offensive [January 1968]

MARTIN LUTHER KING, JR., ADVOCATE OF NONVIOLENT PROTEST,
LEADS A MARCH TO ORGANIZE SUPPORT FOR RACIAL EQUALITY.

The Election of 1960

The candidates in the election of 1960 offered two highly contrasting styles. The Republicans nominated Richard M. Nixon, Eisenhower's vice-president for eight years, who seemed to represent a continuation of the familiar policies of the 1950s. Henry Cabot Lodge, Jr., ambassador to the United Nations, was selected as Nixon's running mate. The Democratic nominee, Senator John F. Kennedy of Massachusetts, projected a vigorous, forward-looking image, but his religion and youth seemed to hamper his chances of winning the presidency. No Roman Catholic had ever become president, and if elected the forty-three-year-old Kennedy would be the youngest man ever to have held the office.

Senate majority leader Lyndon Baines Johnson of Texas was chosen as the Democratic vice-presidential nominee. Johnson had been a strong supporter of the New Deal, yet despite his social liberalism he had succeeded in gaining the support and respect of conservative Southerners. The Democrats were counting on him to carry the South.

Throughout the campaign Nixon identified himself with Eisenhower's record and promised only to enlarge on it, especially in the area of civil rights. Kennedy, on the other hand, launched a broad offensive against the Eisenhower administration. He promised to improve social and economic conditions for all Americans and to repair America's tarnished

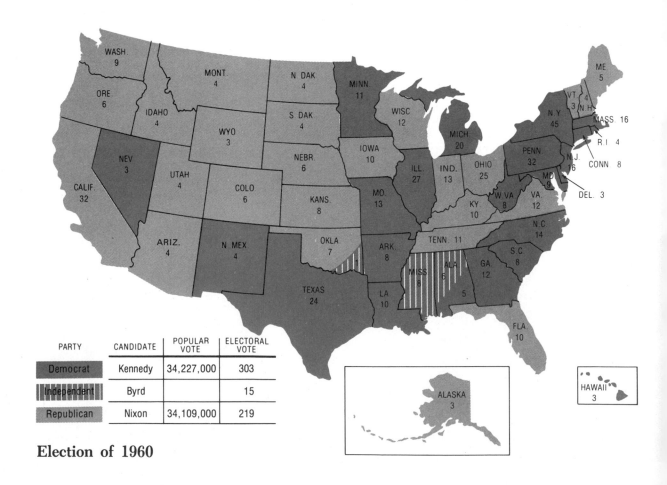

PARTY	CANDIDATE	POPULAR VOTE	ELECTORAL VOTE
Democrat	Kennedy	34,227,000	303
Independent	Byrd		15
Republican	Nixon	34,109,000	219

Election of 1960

reputation abroad. His most controversial charge concerned what he termed the "missile gap." Maintaining that the Soviet Union was ahead of the United States in the development of nuclear weapons, Kennedy stressed the importance of restoring the nation's military supremacy.

The most crucial element of the campaign was a series of television debates viewed by an estimated seventy million people. This unprecedented use of television launched a new era in political campaigning, giving candidates much broader exposure but also giving the advantage to those who could most effectively use the broadcast medium. In formal debating terms the contests were fairly equal, but the nationwide viewing audience reacted far more favorably to Kennedy's relaxed, confident style. Nixon, who had recently been ill, appeared tense and tired in front of the cameras. In the minds of many Americans Kennedy won the debates.

Election night created intense excitement across the nation. All night long Americans followed a race that could have gone either way, and it was not until noon the following day that Nixon conceded. Although both candidates had avoided the religious issue during the campaign, it was important in the final outcome. The Democratic strongholds were still the cities of the Northeast, where Kennedy's Catholicism worked in his favor, and the Deep South, which Johnson helped to win. By carrying the Midwest, the Far West, and the upper South, Nixon won more states than Kennedy and trailed in the popular vote by only 118,000 votes. Nevertheless, in the Electoral College, Kennedy collected 303 votes to 219 for Nixon. By the slimmest of margins, the American people had decided to reject continuity and face the challenges of the 1960s from a new perspective.

The Kennedy Years

KENNEDY—YOUTHFUL, HANDSOME, AND ELOQUENT—INSPIRED PUBLIC ADULATION WHICH IN EARLIER YEARS HAD BEEN RESERVED FOR SCREEN IDOLS RATHER THAN POLITICAL FIGURES.

John Fitzgerald Kennedy was the descendant of Irish families who had long been involved in Boston politics. In World War II he served in the Navy as a PT-boat commander in the South Pacific and was seriously injured in action. Returning home with a medal for bravery, it fell to him to carry on his family's traditional participation in politics. (His older brother, Joseph, had been killed in World War II.) Kennedy was elected to the House of Representatives in 1946 and to the Senate in 1952. His 1954 Pulitzer prize-winning study of American leaders, *Profiles in Courage*, displayed his developing liberal philosophy. By 1960, Kennedy was becoming a popular public figure with a reputation as an urbane, witty, and hard-fighting political liberal.

The New Frontier

From the beginning of his presidency Kennedy created an impression of dynamism. His Inaugural Address, which summoned the nation to embark on a New Frontier, inspired among many Americans a new sense of enthusiasm and optimism. Kennedy called on the nation to work to solve the continuing problems of poverty and unemployment, urban decay, poor housing, and inadequate health care.

The Kennedy style combined informality, accessibility, and an eagerness to meet new challenges. Kennedy disliked formal cabinet meetings and substituted more flexible sessions with small groups of political leaders and experts. He invited some of the most talented thinkers in the country to participate as informal advisers. More intellectual than his predecessor, Kennedy read and absorbed long reports, as well as numerous newspapers, magazines, and books. Through frequent speeches and press conferences he kept himself in the public eye.

Kennedy's cabinet and advisers were an extraordinarily self-confident group who, like the president, felt an urgency to solve the many problems they believed had been ignored during the previous decade. Douglas Dillon, a Wall Street banker, became secretary of the treasury; Robert S. McNamara, former president of Ford Motor Company, was named secretary of defense; and Dean Rusk, president of the Rockefeller Foundation, was appointed secretary of state. In his most controversial appointment, the president named his younger brother and closest confidant, Robert F. Kennedy, to the post of attorney general.

Despite his enthusiasm for the task, there were many difficult situations in store for the new president. Kennedy had never been a student of the legislative process and was at his best as an administrator and a speaker. Therefore, to steer his legislative programs through Congress he relied on the aging Speaker of the House, Sam Rayburn (who died in November 1961), and on Vice-President Johnson, probably the greatest modern master of congressional politics. Although there was a Democratic majority in Congress, the control of committees by Southern Democrats, often supported by Northern Republicans, seriously weakened the president's chances of getting his programs passed. Even so, Kennedy did manage to push through some important articles of legislation during his term in office.

Economic Policies

When Kennedy took office he inherited a downturn in the economy which had begun in 1960. More than 8 percent of the working population, some 5.7 million people, were unemployed. In addition, the Gross National Product (the total value of a nation's goods and services produced in a given year) was falling and the country was in the midst of its biggest recession since World War II. The president was concerned about the slow growth of the nation's economy, but he did not want to antagonize business by massive government spending. As a result, he was inclined to favor a system of social reform projects aimed at stimulating recovery by developing poverty-stricken areas and by putting money directly into the hands of the poor. On February 2, 1961, the president delivered an Economic Message to Congress, requesting specific new legislation of this nature. But since there was no emergency situation comparable to the conditions of 1932, the response was lukewarm. Nevertheless, about one-half of Kennedy's proposed legislation was passed, though often in altered form.

One of the most significant pieces of legislative measures was the Housing Act of 1961, which authorized federal loans or grants for construction of middle-income housing, mass transit, and preservation of city park areas. Another successful measure was the Area Redevelopment Act, which provided loans to new businesses and training for unemployed workers in chronically depressed areas. A minimum-wage law raising the minimum hourly wage from $1.00 to $1.25 and a liberalized social security law also were passed. By the end of 1961 the economy was on the upswing, although unemployment and inflation remained high.

Worried by the nation's continuing economic problems, Kennedy called on business and labor to hold wage and price increases in balance with gains in productivity. In 1962 the steelworkers accepted a contract that gave them only small pay increases. Shortly thereafter the steel industry, ignoring the request for price stability, declared large price increases. Enraged, Kennedy threatened antitrust suits and began intensive investigations of the steel industry. The companies finally backtracked and rescinded the increases.

In 1963 Kennedy proposed a large tax cut to counter the continuing recession. In this approach Kennedy was influenced by the advice of economist Walter Heller, who believed that tax cuts would encourage private spending and thus create higher corporate profits. The government would ultimately come out ahead because there would be more profits to tax. At the time of Kennedy's death, this issue was still being debated in the Senate, but the economy was already beginning to enter a long boom period, in part as a consequence of tax credits to business.

Civil Rights

Although Kennedy had not declared that the securing of civil rights for black Americans was among his priorities when he entered office, black resentment over continued discrimination prompted the president to move toward stricter enforcement of existing civil rights legislation. Asserting presidential leadership, he created the Committee on Equal Employment Opportunity to enforce nondiscriminatory hiring practices among businesses that had contracts with the federal government and appointed a large number of blacks to high federal positions. Under Robert Kennedy the Justice Department also made a strong commitment to desegregation. The attorney general used his office to aid school integration, force Southern election officials to conform to civil rights legislation, and end segregation of interstate transportation facilities.

In 1961, buoyed by the success of Martin Luther King, Jr., and the Southern Christian Leadership Conference (SCLC) in desegregating lunch counters, hotels, movie houses, and other public facilities in Southern cities, the Student Nonviolent Coordinating Committee (SNCC) and the Congress of Racial Equality (CORE) staged "freedom rides" in the South. Young civil rights workers, black and white, rode together on buses in an effort to open up interstate transportation facilities in accordance with federal legislation. The freedom riders met an angry, often violent response. Many of them were beaten by mobs, arrested, and their buses set ablaze. The Kennedy administration responded by dispatching federal troops to restore order and enforce the law.

In 1962 the University of Mississippi was desegregated when black student James Meredith, accompanied by federal troops, walked through a crowd of angry onlookers into the university. The Kennedy administration's use of the United States Army and the Mississippi National Guard to enforce the desegregation order intensified animosity among Southern segregationists.

Despite federal efforts, progress toward equality for black Americans remained slow. When 150,000 marchers, led by Martin Luther King, Jr., took part in peaceful demonstrations in Birmingham, Alabama, in April 1962, the city government under Police Chief Eugene "Bull" Connor responded by dispersing the crowds of men, women, and

UNITED STATES MARSHALS ESCORT JAMES MEREDITH TO HIS FIRST CLASS AT THE UNIVERSITY OF MISSISSIPPI IN OCTOBER 1962. FOUR YEARS LATER MEREDITH WAS WOUNDED BY A GUNSHOT BLAST WHEN HE RETURNED TO MISSISSIPPI TO PARTICIPATE IN THE TWO-HUNDRED-MILE MARCH AGAINST FEAR.

children with police dogs, electric cattle prods, and fire hoses. The spectacle of unresisting demonstrators being jeered by onlookers as they were hosed by police and dragged off to jail stunned Americans who watched these events on television. Yet, even in the face of such abuse the orderly demonstrations continued day after day.

The Birmingham incident was followed in June by an attempt by Governor George Wallace of Alabama to defy an order to desegregate the University of Alabama. Wallace personally stood in the doorway of the university to block the entrance of two black students. Shortly thereafter he was forced to back down. Now President Kennedy decided to appeal directly to the American people. Going on national television he called on the nation to "fulfill its promise" by providing first-class citizenship for black Americans. He then asked Congress for sweeping new civil rights legislation.

In August 1963 the civil rights crusade gained additional momentum through Martin Luther King, Jr.'s March on Washington. In an impressive and orderly demonstration, two hundred thousand people gathered in front of the Lincoln Memorial to hear King speak eloquently of his dream of an America where racial equality would someday be realized: "I have a dream that one day this nation will rise up and live out the true meaning of its creed: 'We hold these truths to be self-evident, that all men are created equal. . . . I have a dream that my four little children will one day live in a nation where they will not be judged by the color of their skin but by the content of their character." The march had a profound effect on public opinion and added strong impetus to congressional efforts, which finally resulted in the Civil Rights Act of 1964.

The Warren Court

Throughout the 1960s the activist Warren Court continued to provoke widespread anger among conservatives. Extremist groups, such as the right-wing John Birch Society, even posted signs on billboards calling for Warren's impeachment.

One of the Warren Court's most controversial decisions was *Engel* v. *Vitale* (1962) in which local and state laws requiring prayers in public schools were banned on the grounds that such laws were a violation of the First Amendment. Conservative opponents of the ruling recognized the principle of separation of church and state, but argued that the Founders of the nation had never meant to create a godless public order. Instead, they asserted, all forms of worship should be permitted, rather than none. They regarded the decision as part of a new decadence in American life that would eventually bring about the collapse of society. Supporters of the Court's ruling viewed it as a defense of religious freedom for children as well as of separation of church and state.

In *Baker* v. *Carr* (1962) the Supreme Court delivered a judgment that paved the way for reapportionment of state election districts. A longstanding problem of unequal representation had been aggravated by the growth of America's urban areas. In many states rural representatives dominated the legislature and prevented more populous urban areas, which were experiencing more and more problems, from receiving their fair proportion of state funds. The only way to change the balance of power would be to enforce a system of representation based on population—the principle of one man, one vote. Re-

luctantly, the Supreme Court accepted responsibility for dealing with this political crisis, ruling that under the equal-protection clause of the Fourteenth Amendment federal courts had jurisdiction in cases of alleged unfairness in apportionment of elected representatives within a state. Widespread redistricting soon followed.

Among the most controversial decisions of the Warren Court were those in the area of criminal law. In *Gideon* v. *Wainright* (1963) the Court held that under the Sixth Amendment states must provide defense counsel for indigent defendants in all cases. In *Escobedo* v. *Illinois* (1964) the Court ruled that convictions are invalid in cases where the police have denied a suspect legal counsel or failed to inform a suspect of the Fifth Amendment provision against self-incrimination. *Miranda* v. *Arizona* (1966) established rules regarding extracting confessions from individuals accused of crimes.

The Warren Court's efforts to safeguard the rights of suspects in criminal cases took place within the context of a rising crime rate. As a result, many detractors accused the Court of being too lenient toward criminals and of contributing to the increase in crime. Supporters of the Court's decisions, by contrast, believed that the rulings would help to secure for the poor and uneducated the same rights in criminal cases that were enjoyed by the middle class and the wealthy.

Foreign Policy

President Kennedy believed as strongly as had his predecessors that the Soviet Union posed a worldwide threat to American interests. The new administration, having inherited a renewal of cold war tensions, was determined to reassert American leadership throughout the world. Kennedy made this intention crystal clear in his Inaugural Address: "Let every nation know, whether it wishes us well or ill, that we shall pay any price, bear any burden, meet any hardship, support any friend, oppose any foe to assure the survival and success of liberty."

Once in office, Kennedy discovered that the "missile gap" that he had referred to during his campaign did not exist. America's nuclear arsenal was in fact superior to that of the Soviet Union. The United States did lag behind the Russians in the space race, however. In August 1961 a Russian cosmonaut had orbited the earth seventeen times. Six months later, American astronaut John Glenn succeeded in making a flight of only three orbits. To move the United States ahead in the space race, President Kennedy announced Project Apollo in 1961, asking Congress to appropriate approximately $20 billion over the next decade to put a man on the moon by 1970. The successful launching of communications and military observation satellites was encouraging, but American accomplishments in manned flights still lagged behind those of the Soviets during the Kennedy years.

Toward the end of his presidency Eisenhower had cautioned the nation to guard against the growing economic and political influence of the enormously powerful "military-industrial complex." When Kennedy assumed office, military spending amounted to one-half the federal budget and provided employment to over 3.5 million Americans. Yet the defense budget continued to swell during the next three years, in large part because of the perceived need to stay ahead of the Soviets. At the same time, however, the Defense Department, headed by Secretary McNamara, succeeded in bringing the armed services under tight civilian control. A new breed of expert, skilled in cost analysis and modern management techniques, began to assume authority over military officials at the Pentagon.

Kennedy shifted the emphasis in defense strategy away from massive retaliation with nuclear weapons and toward increasing the nation's capability to wage limited conventional wars. The earlier strategy had done little to contain the spread of communism, as the events in Indochina indicated. Kennedy was convinced that with the United States and Russia now in nuclear balance, it was the intention of the Soviets to pursue their expansionist aims by promoting "wars of national liberation." The administration deemed it essential, therefore, to ensure that American forces were trained in the techniques of counterinsurgency—jungle fighting and guerrilla warfare. In this way, the United States would be able to mount a "flexible response" to Communist aggression.

At the same time, Kennedy used America's economic strength to court the weak nations emerging from colonialism—the Third World. The administration offered assistance to these countries to help them overcome problems of poverty and to build their industrial base. Kennedy's aims were not purely humanitarian; he was hopeful that by extending the hand of friendship, the United States might be able to avert a Communist takeover in these struggling lands. The policy of refusing aid to neutral nations, which had been followed under Dulles, was now abandoned, and the administration accepted the fact that many Third World nations would welcome economic support from the Communist bloc as well as from the United States.

To further assist less developed countries, Kennedy established the Agency for International Development (AID). Its function was to coordinate various foreign-aid programs and find ways to make them more effective. The program that touched the most responsive chord at home was the Peace Corps, established in 1961. Thousands of idealistic young men and women considered it an honor to be selected to go abroad for two years (for very little compensation) to help train skilled workers and teachers and to initiate agricultural projects in remote areas of the world. The Peace Corps was young America's answer to Kennedy's challenge, "Ask not what your country can do for you—ask what you can do for your country."

The Alliance for Progress In line with Kennedy's policy of extending aid to emerging nations, the administration proposed the Alliance for Progress in March 1961, a $20 billion program of economic assistance for Latin America. The purpose of the venture was to improve standards of living, promote social reform, and build strong economies as a means of keeping Communist influence out of Latin America. The United States was to provide about half the financing over a period of ten years, the other half to come from private sources and international agencies.

As the decade wore on, the Alliance for Progress did not live up to its early promise. A major reason for this was America's insistence on land and tax reform before aid would be given. This demand met resistance from some Latin American governments and from landowners who opposed social change. Moreover, private interests did not want to invest in projects in such an unstable part of the world. Although a number of projects were completed, they had only a limited impact on the overwhelming problems of Latin America.

The Bay of Pigs Fiasco When Kennedy entered the White House, relations with Cuba were deterio-

THE FIRST SHIPMENT OF AN EIGHTY-
EIGHT-MILLION-POUND DONATION OF
POWDERED MILK TO BRAZIL UNDER
THE ALLIANCE FOR PROGRESS LEFT
THE COUNTRY IN MARCH 1962.

rating as Castro moved increasingly into the Soviet orbit. Under a project authorized by President Eisenhower, a large number of Cuban exiles were being organized, trained, and equipped in Central America by agents of the CIA for an invasion of Cuba. President Kennedy was faced with the decision of whether to continue the scheme or to open diplomatic talks with Castro on problems between the two nations. Military advisors and CIA planners assured him that the Cuban people resented Castro and would cooperate in his overthrow. Facing the certainty of criticism at home and abroad if the plan should fail, Kennedy authorized the invasion. He would not, however, agree to provide air support because such overt action would be perceived as American aggression.

On April 17, 1961, a force of about fourteen hundred invaders landed on the southern coast of Cuba in the *Bahia de Cochinos* (Bay of Pigs). Lacking air and naval support, the invaders were easily defeated by the Cuban army and air force. The projected popular uprising which was to accompany the invasion never took place. The disastrous failure

of this invasion underlined several serious problems in the conduct of American foreign policy. First, Kennedy had no real way of evaluating the intelligence estimates which the CIA had provided him. As a result, he let the agency execute a plan that was founded on a distorted picture of the Cuban scene. Second, in an effort to avoid charges of aggression, the United States did not provide the necessary air support, which virtually ensured failure. The upshot of this episode was that the United States' image was badly tarnished and Cuba became even more committed to its friendship with Russia. Castro could plausibly claim that his neighbors to the north were intent on pursuing an imperialist foreign policy.

Kennedy was deeply stung by the failure and by the public criticism the administration received. Within a few days he acknowledged his personal responsibility for the fiasco, and since he could easily have blamed others, this public admission won him considerable acclaim. Nevertheless, although the president became more wary of advice from the CIA and the military, he continued the economic embargo of Cuba, persuaded the OAS to remove Cuba from its membership, and refused to recognize the Castro regime. The CIA continued its covert activities in Cuba and even plotted to assassinate Castro.

The Berlin Wall The tensions created by the Cuban debacle led Kennedy to insist on a face-to-face encounter with the Soviet Union's Premier Khrushchev in Vienna in June 1961. Khrushchev, however, was unmoved by Kennedy's suggestion that the big powers should declare a moratorium on further maneuvering that would upset world stability. He declared that communism would continue to expand through wars of national liberation. Upon his return to Russia, Khruschev gave the Western powers six months to sign a peace treaty with Germany to bring an end to the four-power occupation of Berlin. If they refused to sign such a treaty, Khrushchev warned, the Soviet Union would sign a separate treaty with East Germany. Then the West would be forced to negotiate with a government they did not recognize for access to Berlin.

The situation was ominous. Soon Khrushchev increased the Soviet defense budget and announced that he would recognize the sovereignty of East Berlin by the end of the year. Kennedy responded by increasing American armed forces.

The success of the democratic West German economy was a crucial factor affecting Soviet actions during this period. Thousands of East Germans had escaped from the Soviet sector into West Berlin. Now, with this new crisis over Berlin, the number of refugees fleeing East Germany reached ten thousand a day, thereby depriving East Germany of great numbers of workers. Without warning, on August 13, 1961, Khrushchev suddenly closed the border between East and West Berlin and ordered the construction of the Berlin Wall, a barbed-wire and concrete barrier running through the divided city. Protests by the United States were to no avail. Tensions mounted, and the fear of war ran so high that federal and state governments called on the public to build fallout shelters for protection in case of nuclear war. By October, however, the pressure had begun to subside and Khrushchev had withdrawn his end-of-the-year ultimatum. West Berlin remained free, but the Soviets had succeeded in cutting off movement to and from East Berlin.

The Cuban Missile Crisis Less than one year after the Berlin crisis, Khrushchev tried another maneuver to seize the initiative in the cold war. In July 1962 the Soviets began pouring technicians and military equipment into Cuba. At first, American reconnaissance flights seemed to confirm Soviet assurances that no offensive missiles were coming in and no new missile sites were being built. Kennedy reported this intelligence to the public, at the same time warning that "significant offensive capability either in Cuban hands or under Soviet direction" would precipitate the "gravest" international crisis. However, Cuban refugees and secret intelligence sources disputed the first reports, and in October more extensive aerial reconnaissance of Cuba revealed that installations for short- and medium-range offensive missiles were hurriedly being completed.

Soviet offensive missiles in Cuba were simply unacceptable to the United States. While missiles launched from Russia would give a warning time of fifteen minutes, the Cuban sites reduced the margin to only two or three minutes, thus badly tipping the strategic balance in favor of the Soviets. Yet Kennedy realized the United States had to move with extreme caution. An overly aggressive action, such as an air strike on the missile sites, might set off a nuclear war. On the other hand, verbal protest alone might fail to oust the Soviet missiles. The idea of pursuing secret negotiations apparently was not considered out of concern that the Soviets would use the time to make the missiles operational and that they would perceive the American president as weak.

After a week's deliberation, on October 22 Kennedy made the crisis public and announced his plan. The United States would establish a naval quarantine of Cuba to prevent further Soviet shipments of military equipment from reaching the island. Moreover, Kennedy demanded that all bases currently installed in Cuba be removed. The Organization of American States approved the blockade the next day and the American navy encircled Cuba. A group of twenty-five Soviet vessels were bound for the island at the time, and no one knew what to expect when and if the ships met the blockade.

Kennedy and Khrushchev negotiated by cablegram for three days, but no progress was made. The Soviets continued to rush their new missile bases to completion, at the same time continuing to deny that they were introducing nuclear weapons into Cuba. American B-52 bombers, laden with nuclear missiles, were placed on alert and ICBM's and nuclear submarines were poised for attack. Finally, on October 24, the fleet of Soviet ships turned back. As Secretary of State Rusk described the unbearable tension that had preceded this break in the stalemate, "We're eyeball to eyeball, and I think the other fellow just blinked."

Two days later, on October 26, Kennedy received a letter from Khrushchev in which the Russian premier offered to remove the missiles and dismantle the bases if the United States would end the blockade and promise not to invade Cuba. But the following morning a second letter arrived that took a much different approach: the Soviets would remove their missiles from Cuba if the United States would remove its missiles stationed in Turkey. President Kennedy, on advice of his brother, Robert Kennedy, decided to ignore the second letter and accept the terms of the first. On October 28, Khrushchev agreed.

Kennedy's popularity in the United States skyrocketed. Although some critics believed that he had risked nuclear war, his firm stand had shown that the Soviet Union would back down in the face of a show of force. It was an American victory after the fiasco at the Bay of Pigs and the Soviet building of the Berlin Wall. The Russians removed their missiles and dismantled their missile sites, and American missiles were removed from Turkey. Furthermore, Khrushchev was soon ready to respond favorably to Kennedy's request for negotiations over nuclear testing. The Test-Ban Treaty signed in August 1963 prohibited tests in the water, in space, or in the atmosphere. A temporary thaw in cold-war tensions followed, but the Soviets then began a massive arms buildup in order to overtake the United States. In any event, hopes for a real accommodation between the two nations declined with a new escalation of American involvement in Southeast Asia.

More Involvement in Southeast Asia When Kennedy took office, nationalist movements in Southeast Asia were continuing to struggle for control. Although Kennedy felt that the United States should not become too involved in this area, his actual policy was determined by his acceptance of two ideas: (1) the "domino theory," first formulated by President Eisenhower, which held that if the Communists overran one part of Southeast Asia, the rest of the area would collapse like a row of dominoes; and (2) the belief that the Communist threat to these developing nations could be met through increased economic aid and the use of American counterinsurgency forces.

In Laos the Communist Pathet Lao guerrillas had long been engaged in skirmishes with the government. Eisenhower had poured millions of dollars into Laos in an effort to prevent it from going Communist. Moreover, he had counseled Kennedy to send American troops to Laos. Kennedy, however, was not eager to pursue a military course, particularly in light of the Bay of Pigs disaster. He favored instead a neutral Laos to be led by Prince Souvanna Phouma. In June 1962 under pressure from the United States, neutralist, pro-Western, and Communist factions met at Geneva and agreed to the formation of a coalition government and official neutrality. However, the North Vietnamese continued to use Laos as a supply route to aid the Communist infiltration of South Vietnam. The CIA, in turn, helped the coalition government. In 1963 the Communist faction withdrew from the government and the Pathet Lao, aided by the Soviet Union, resumed its activities, soon gaining control of almost two-thirds of the country.

In Vietnam, after the signing of the Geneva accords in 1954, a French-backed puppet regime under Bao Dai had been set up south of the seventeenth parallel in non-Communist South Vietnam. In 1955 Ngo Dinh Diem, leader of the powerful Roman Catholic minority, ousted Bao Dai and assumed the presidency. The following year Diem refused to allow the internationally supervised elections called for by the Geneva agreement, thereby ensuring the continued division of Vietnam. During his years in power Diem showed himself to be a corrupt, autocratic ruler who undermined self-government in the rural areas and ignored American pressure for political and economic reforms. Nevertheless, the United States continued giving Diem financial support, fearing that without American aid the nation would fall to the Communists.

Resistance to the Diem regime organized itself into the National Liberation Front (NLF). The NLF served as a political arm of a resistance group known as the Viet Cong (Viet Communists) originally formed in 1957 to overthrow Diem. The Viet Cong were mainly South Vietnamese who had been trained in Communist ideology and tactics in North Vietnam. They were well organized and used political indoctrination and guerrilla warfare effectively to undermine government control of most of the countryside. In addition to the more than two hundred thousand people associated with the Viet Cong, there were many other South Vietnamese who opposed the Diem regime—especially the Buddhist faction.

In 1961 Vice-President Johnson visited Saigon and reported back favorably on the South Vietnamese president. At the same time President Kennedy sent a small unit of crack Green Beret troops to train the South Vietnamese army in countering Viet Cong guerrilla activities. While he felt that the United States should not become directly involved in combat, he believed that military advisors could be of valuable assistance. By early 1962 American advisors were arriving; before long they were participating in combat as well.

Even so, the situation of the Diem regime was steadily deteriorating. Aware that much of the problem stemmed from Diem's inability to win the support of the Vietnamese people, Kennedy pressed him to make needed reforms. The inflexible Diem, however, urged on by his brother, Ngo Dinh Nhu, continued his repressive policies, particularly those directed against the Buddhists. By the late summer of 1963 American policymakers, finding Diem's corruption and abuses intolerable, had come to favor his removal. When a group of South Vietnamese army officers began to prepare for a coup, they were assured that Washington would support the new leadership. On November 1 Diem and Nhu were murdered. Far from stabilizing the situation, the overthrow of their regime plunged the country into even deeper trouble. By this time the United States had more than 16,700 American military "advisors" in South Vietnam, and almost six hundred Americans had been killed there.

The Assassination

In late 1963, President Kennedy's popularity was sagging in some parts of the country, especially in regions offended by his strong stand on civil rights enforcement. Looking ahead to the national election in 1964 and seeking to increase his popularity in Texas, where support for his policies among conservative Democrats was weak, Kennedy decided to tour the state.

On November 22, 1963, Kennedy, with the First Lady at his side, rode in an open car through cheering crowds in the city of Dallas. As the car slowed down to make a turn in front of the Texas School Book Depository in Dealey Plaza, a number of shots rang out, and the president was struck. Also wounded was Governor John Connally, who was sitting in the front seat of the president's car. President John F. Kennedy was pronounced dead shortly after arrival at Parkland Memorial Hospital. Vice-President Johnson, visibly shaken, was rushed to the presidential plane and immediately sworn in as president.

The Dallas police arrested Lee Harvey Oswald, charging him with the assassination of the president. Although much circumstantial evidence pointed to Oswald, he claimed that he was innocent. Then, before he could be brought to trial, he was murdered by a Dallas nightclub owner. Responding to the suspicion that Oswald was only a front for an elaborate conspiracy, President Johnson subsequently appointed Chief Justice Warren to head an investigatory commission. Although the Warren Commission concluded that Oswald had been acting alone, many people were unconvinced and conspiracy theories were put forward for years.

In the wake of the assassination, the country was swept with shock and grief. Although the young president had not enjoyed universal popularity, after his death the great majority of Americans experienced an acute sense of loss. The Kennedy assassination brought an end to the bright promise of the New Frontier and foreshadowed a period of violent upheaval in American society.

The Kennedy Legacy

A few months before his assassination Kennedy spoke at American University of the need to reexamine the assumptions on which the cold war was based, and called for greater efforts toward disarmament. But while his rhetoric stressed peace and disarmament, his actions were those of a cold warrior. During the almost three years Kennedy was in office, he had vigorously pursued the containment policy and even risked confrontation with the Soviet Union. His administration initiated the concept of aiding emerging nations in the Third World with both economic aid and counterinsurgency forces to thwart the efforts of leftist revolutionaries. Whether he would have averted the quagmire of Vietnam, we shall never know, but it seems clear that Kennedy's commitment of American troops laid the foundation for an increasing escalation of the conflict.

sympathy from Kennedy ☞ *reason for doing well* ☞

The Johnson Years *Very Powerful in Congress*

Lyndon Johnson came from a farm family in south central Texas, and worked his way through school. He entered the House of Representatives in 1937, and won a Senate seat in a close election in 1948. He was a shrewd bargainer and an effective politician who came to the presidency with almost twenty-five years of congressional experience. In 1954 he became Senate majority leader and is generally considered to have been the most effective individual to have held that post in modern times. Direct, earthy, sometimes crude in his manner, Johnson's only real interest was politics. Although not well-known to the American people, Johnson was well-known and well-liked on Capitol Hill. A man of great energy and determination, he succeeded magnificently in getting things done, but his secretiveness made it difficult for him ever to reach the public.

"Let Us Continue"

In the aftermath of the assassination, Congress offered little resistance to the late president's program. Partisan opponents who had once blocked Kennedy's proposals were suddenly willing to move them out of committee and onto the floor. Johnson made full use of the opportunity provided by this spirit of cooperativeness, and with the help of his own legislative genius, he was able to push through a great deal of legislation. Realizing that as yet he had no personal mandate, Johnson simply offered to complete the Kennedy program. "Let us continue," he said.

The Revenue Act that Kennedy had sought was passed early in 1964, reducing taxes by $11.5 billion. Soon, the longest economic boom in American his-

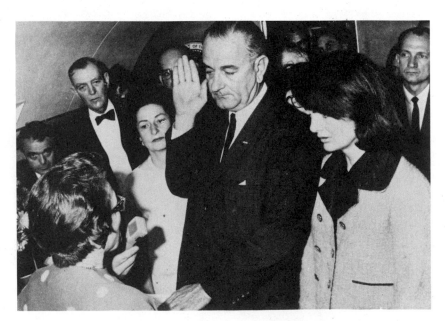

A SOMBER LYNDON JOHNSON TAKES THE OATH OF OFFICE ABOARD AIR FORCE ONE FOLLOWING THE ASSASSINATION OF JOHN F. KENNEDY.

tory was under way, and unemployment fell to 5 percent. Thus Johnson enjoyed a good relationship with both business and labor until the late 1960s.

President Johnson risked incurring the enmity of the Deep South by working for passage of a strong civil rights bill. After three months of filibuster by Southern senators and after demonstrations across the country by civil rights groups favoring the bill, the Civil Rights Act of 1964 was finally enacted. A landmark piece of legislation, this third civil rights act dramatically increased federal power in an attempt to ensure voting rights, end discrimination in the use of public facilities and accommodations, assure equal treatment by employers and unions, and end segregation in schooling. The new law also extended the life of the Civil Rights Commission and provided that programs receiving federal aid must end discriminatory practices or lose their funding.

Johnson's War on Poverty Perhaps the fundamental fact about Lyndon Johnson was his passion for social reform. A man who himself had experienced want as a child, Johnson was eager to use the powers of his office to ensure a better life for people in all segments of American society. Shortly after he took office Johnson announced his War on Poverty, a program aimed primarily at rescuing impoverished young Americans who otherwise seemed doomed to repeat the same hopeless pattern of illiteracy and despair as their parents. Public awareness of poverty in a supposedly affluent society had come about in part through government studies released in 1964, which showed that 18 percent of the population (some 34.1 million people) had incomes below the poverty line. Social criticism such as Michael Harrington's *The Other America* also did much to awaken Americans to the seriousness of the poverty problem.

Under the new Office of Economic Opportunity (OEO) a number of separate programs were launched. Head Start was created to help preschoolers gain skills required to succeed in school. The Job Corps, aimed at training inner-city youth, and the Youth Corps gave young people an opportunity to serve in their community. VISTA (Volunteers in Service to America) was a domestic Peace Corps that recruited young Americans, especially those between the ages of eighteen and twenty-five, to work on neighborhood projects in urban and rural poverty areas to reduce illiteracy and unemployment. Efforts were made to aid poor adults as well through such avenues as work programs and loans for starting small businesses.

The War on Poverty experienced some successes and encountered many difficulties. One serious obstacle was the opposition of conservative politicians. Republicans traditionally resisted spending public money to aid the poor. Southern Democrats, for their part, disliked the idea that so much attention was being lavished on blacks, who made up a large segment of the poor. To compound problems, black Americans were becoming increasingly militant, and Congress responded by tightening the purse strings. Perhaps most important was the fact that the War on Poverty did not have the broad base of middle-class support that was necessary to ensure that its goals could be met. Although some of the antipoverty programs instituted during the Johnson years are still in place, others fell by the wayside.

The Election of 1964

In 1964 President Johnson was overwhelmingly nominated by the Democrats to seek election in his own right. As his running mate, he chose a liberal senator from Minnesota, Hubert H. Humphrey.

On the Republican side, many conservatives disapproved of attempting to solve internal problems through increased federal action. Many of them opposed any policy of negotiation with the Communist bloc and believed that America's military posture was becoming too relaxed. This point of view was represented by Senator Barry Goldwater of Arizona, who won the Republican presidential nomination over the more moderate Governor Nelson Rockefeller of New York. Making no concession to Republican moderates, the party nominated William E. Miller, a conservative New York congressman, as Goldwater's running mate.

Throughout his campaign, Goldwater promised "a choice, not an echo." He vigorously attacked the expansion of the central government, the breakdown of traditional moral values, and programs of high government spending that concealed corruption. He demanded a stronger military commitment against world communism, argued that negotiations with the Soviet Union were useless, and charged that the Kennedy-Johnson administration had adopted a "no-win" policy in Vietnam. Goldwater believed that escalation of American involvement in

Vietnam was inevitable, and he advocated the use of tactical nuclear weapons at the discretion of field commanders—a position that most Americans found frightening.

Goldwater's arch-conservatism attracted many right-wing extremists. Their support, along with his tendency to make blunt, sometimes contradictory statements, worked to his disadvantage. Johnson, on the other hand, appeared benign, friendly, reassuring, and moderate. He presented himself as the peace candidate, promising that American soldiers would not be sent to Indochina. In the end he won one of the largest popular pluralities in American history, 61 percent of the vote, receiving wide support from business, labor, farm areas, the suburbs, and black Americans.

The Great Society

Johnson's landslide victory showed a general approval for the steps he had already taken on the domestic front. In addition, it strengthened his control over Congress, for a large number of Democrats were elected to the House and the Senate in 1964. As a result, conservatives found themselves unable to put together their traditionally effective coalition, and Johnson was able to proceed with a wide-ranging domestic program to build what he called the "Great Society."

The goals of the Great Society were to free Americans from poverty, discrimination, urban blight, environmental pollution, ignorance, and ill health. Johnson turned first to the areas of education and medical care. A bill for federal aid to education had been defeated under Kennedy because of the unresolved dispute over whether assistance to parochial schools was a violation of the principle of the separation of church and state. Johnson's solution was to reconstruct the federal-aid program so as to avoid this issue. The Elementary and Secondary Education Act of 1965 provided aid on the basis of the number of poor children in any school, whether public or private. Public grants were given for special programs and facilities but could not be used to meet overhead expenses. Another bill authorized federal expenditures to assist higher education. Over the next three years the Johnson administration saw enacted two dozen education-related bills and spent over $4 billion on federal aid to education.

A CARTOONIST'S VIEW OF PRESIDENT JOHNSON'S GREAT SOCIETY LEGISLATION.

Despite continued opposition from the American Medical Association, a Medicare program defeated under Kennedy was finally launched in 1965. Since the days of the New Deal, legislation had been proposed to deal with the economic suffering and health problems of the elderly. Now, Medicare allowances financed through Social Security provided for hospital and nursing-home care, doctors' bills, and prescription drugs.

The Appalachian Regional Development Act which had been rejected in 1964 was approved in 1965, making available $1.1 billion for projects in the impoverished Appalachian region. There were additional appropriations for public works, Youth Corps camps, and job-retraining programs.

The Great Society program contained new civil rights legislation as well. In the South there was continued resistance to allowing blacks to vote. A civil rights march from Selma to Montgomery, Alabama, was held in the spring of 1965 to protest qualifying tests which prevented blacks from registering to vote. Governor George Wallace refused to provide protection for the demonstrators. As a result, the peaceful marchers were viciously attacked by state police using clubs and tear gas. In the wake of this incident and the murder of several civil rights workers, Congress passed the Voting Rights Act of 1965, which abolished literacy and other qualifying tests for voting. The measure also authorized federal registrars to enroll eligible voters in many states where they had been refused registration and in states where less than one-half the voting-age population was registered. Thereafter the number of blacks registered to vote rose sharply.

In an effort to aid the urban poor, who for the most part were living in deplorable housing conditions, President Johnson promoted the creation of the Department of Housing and Urban Development. As its first secretary he appointed Robert C. Weaver, the first black to hold a cabinet post. Funds amounting to $7.8 billion were appropriated for urban-renewal projects, with the expectation that some 240,000 units of low-rent public housing would be built. Urban renewal was a mixed blessing, however. It often created more problems than it solved. Neighborhoods that had provided a vital sense of stability for many minority groups were broken up to make way for new projects, and efforts to relocate the victims of urban reconstruction were often haphazard.

Discrimination in immigration policy was finally ended by the Immigration Act of 1965. This measure terminated quotas based on national origin, substituting instead a system of hemispheric quotas with a total of 170,000 immigrants a year. Entrance requirements were to be based on skills and family ties. The result of the act was to greatly increase the number of immigrants from Asia, Latin America, the Mediterranean, and eastern Europe.

Johnson's concern for the quality of the environment led to the passage of measures to control water pollution, a highway-beautification program, and a token effort to reduce motor-vehicle exhaust fumes. In addition, the passage of the Wilderness Act of 1964 set aside millions of acres of land for preservation as wilderness areas.

By 1966 the momentum of Johnson's domestic program had slowed. Great Society projects were costly, and many of the available funds were being diverted to finance American military involvement in Southeast Asia. Furthermore, many people had reservations about the massive bureaucratic expansion needed to administer the far-flung efforts. But perhaps the greatest problem with the Great Society was that it simply did not seem to be working. Benefits were achieved in some specific areas, but on the whole America's domestic problems were still growing. The Great Society programs had failed to deal satisfactorily with many of the problems faced by black Americans, and repeated outbreaks of urban violence were the result. Moreover, the president and the country were increasingly preoccupied with the Vietnam War.

Foreign Policy

Lyndon Johnson applied the same energy to foreign as to domestic policy. He was a strong believer in Truman's policy of containment of global communism and Kennedy's policy of nation building through economic and military aid to emerging nations. He pursued these goals with an unrelenting and patriotic drive which would brook no dissent from subordinates. He never understood the domestic opposition that developed to what was considered his overcommitment and overextension of American power. He was bewildered, too, by the emergence of a more independent spirit among America's allies and among Third World nations.

Latin America Although Southeast Asia became the dominant area of concern during the Johnson administration, there were significant happenings in several other parts of the world. In Latin America the efforts that Kennedy had made to restore the nation's credibility as a good neighbor suffered a major setback as a consequence of the administration's response to events in the Dominican Republic. In 1961 longtime strongman Rafael Trujillo was assassinated, thus ending some thirty years of repressive dictatorship. The following year free, democratic elections were held and Juan Bosch became president. Bosch, a non-Communist leftist, proved unable to stabilize the nation, however, and in 1963 he was ousted in a right-wing military coup. When this regime proved weak as well, supporters of Bosch moved against the junta and the country was soon in a state of virtual civil war. In April 1965 President Johnson, acting on information that Bosch's group was infiltrated by Communists, sent twenty-two thousand marines to the island. Although at first he claimed that the forces had been sent to protect

American lives, Johnson later admitted that their purpose was to prevent another Communist take-over in the Western Hemisphere. Latin Americans and many liberals in the United States were furious, arguing that the administration never offered convincing proof of communist infiltration and failed to consult the Organization of American States before taking action. To end the unpopular intervention, the United States asked the OAS to send a peace-keeping force to the Dominican Republic. In 1966 new elections brought to power Joaquin Balaguer, a candidate acceptable to the United States. The incident seriously undermined Latin America's belief in the commitment of the United States to the policy of nonintervention.

The Middle East The United Nations had kept a peacekeeping force in the Middle East for some ten years. In 1967, at President Nasser's request, it was withdrawn, whereupon Egypt immediately called for a "Holy War" against the Jewish state. In the Six-Day War that followed, the Israelis struck first, rapidly defeating Egypt and gaining control of the Syrian border, West Jordan (including Jerusalem), and the entire Sinai peninsula. The war ended with a United Nations cease-fire, but real peace was as remote as ever. Israel refused to comply with a UN resolution calling for withdrawal from the occupied territories because the resolution, while recognizing Israel's right to secure boundaries, failed to guarantee this security. In the aftermath of the Six-Day War, the United States continued to pour military aid into Israel and the Soviet Union stepped up its support of Egypt.

Europe In its relations with Europe, the Johnson administration was unable to stem the movement led by General Charles de Gaulle of France away from American leadership. De Gaulle was angered by what he perceived as the American effort to play a decisive role in European economic organization and defense strategy. By 1966 he had removed all French naval forces and troops from NATO and was concentrating on building an independent nuclear capability for France. De Gaulle also succeeded in keeping Great Britain out of the Common Market, on the grounds that England was only a front for continued American political and economic domination of Europe. Faced with these setbacks, the Johnson administration devoted less and less atten-

tion to Europe as the nation became further embroiled in Vietnam.

Vietnam Just before the assassination of President Kennedy, reports on the situation in Vietnam had begun to take on an air of cautious optimism. For a brief time it appeared that Kennedy's plan (devised in the summer of 1962) for a phased withdrawal of all American troops by the end of 1965 was still feasible. By January 1964, however, new reports from American sources in Vietnam claimed that the Viet

Vietnam

CLINGING TO HER MOST VALUED POSSESSIONS, A VIETNAMESE WOMAN LEADS HER CHILDREN THROUGH A BARBED-WIRE BARRICADE IN AN ATTEMPT TO ESCAPE THE FIGHTING IN SAIGON'S CHOLON CHINESE SECTOR.

The White House insisted publicly that the raids, when reported, were conducted independently by the South Vietnamese. Then, on August 2, the American destroyer *Maddox* reported that it had been fired on by North Vietnamese torpedo boats. The United States claimed that the assault was unprovoked, but the North Vietnamese countered that the *Maddox* was a spy ship that had been providing protective cover for South Vietnamese sabotage units. On August 4 the *Maddox* was joined in the Gulf of Tonkin by another destroyer, the *C. Turner Joy*. The second ship reported that it had been attacked, a claim that sometime later was brought into serious question.

The administration used the incident as a pretext for increased American participation in the conflict. Within a few hours of the alleged August 4 attack, President Johnson announced retaliatory bombing raids on strategic North Vietnamese targets. On August 7, Congress, by a vote of 88 to 2 in the Senate and 416 to 0 in the House, passed what became known as the Tonkin Gulf Resolution, empowering the president "to repel any armed attack against the forces of the United States and to prevent further aggression." The resolution became in effect the legal basis for full-scale American military involvement in Vietnam, a development that many in Congress later said they had no intention of authorizing. The secret strategy pursued by the Johnson administration in 1964 also helped create what was later called the "credibility gap," a public recognition of the fact that reports on American progress, purpose, and involvement in the conflict were inaccurate and deceptive.

In reaction to reports that the South Vietnamese army was quickly losing ground, the United States early in 1965 hurriedly launched a military buildup. In February 1965 a Viet Cong attack on an American airfield at Pleiku caused the Americans to respond with regular aerial bombings of supply depots, army camps, and transportation lines in North Vietnam. By the end of the year the war had been "Americanized"; the total troop commitment was over 184,000.

In the view of American policymakers, the United States had to stay in Asia if it was to retain its credibility as a world power and as a guarantor of freedom. Washington continued to believe that the fall of Vietnam to Communist forces would inevitably lead to Communist takeovers throughout Asia

Cong had made swift progress and recommended expansion of the American military presence throughout Southeast Asia. Alarm over the rapidly growing numbers of Viet Cong forces and the instability of the Saigon government under a succession of military regimes prompted the United States to work with the South Vietnamese in carrying out spy missions, sabotage, and PT-boat bombardments of North Vietnamese coastal installations during 1964.

and ultimately in the free world as well. Vietnam came to be viewed as part of a vast strategy of aggression on the part of Communist China, which increased its arms supplies to the North Vietnamese as the United States expanded its aid to the regime in the South.

The American goal throughout 1966 was to force North Vietnam to the negotiating table by means of military pressure. American troop commitments had now reached 380,000, and new weapons, such as napalm and other chemicals—the use of which was partially concealed from the American public—had devastated vast areas of both North and South Vietnam. The South Vietnamese government, run by a Washington-supported military dictator, General Nguyen Van Thieu, received little popular support, and the war was essentially at a stalemate. During his years in office, President Johnson halted the bombing of North Vietnam several times, hoping to receive an acceptable response from Hanoi. He offered to pull out American troops, but only if North Vietnam would withdraw its forces first and only on condition that the Saigon government be left in place. These overtures were consistently rejected, as North Vietnam demanded a unilateral American withdrawal and the termination of all American bombing raids.

By the end of 1967 there were over 475,000 American troops in Vietnam. This was a larger United States military commitment than had been made at the peak of the Korean War. Many administration officials now began to doubt the wisdom of continuing to pursue the strategy of Americanization. Casualties among hapless Vietnamese civilians were mounting into the tens of thousands; American forces, too, were sustaining increasing losses. In the period from 1965 to 1967 American casualties rose from slightly over one thousand to almost seventy-five hundred. Furthermore, the escalation of the bombing had succeeded neither in "pacifying" the Viet Cong nor in halting North Vietnamese infiltration. Search-and-destroy missions against the Viet Cong only seemed to harden their resistance. Such missions frequently were frustrated by the ability of the enemy to blend in with the civilian population and by their thorough familiarity with the jungle terrain. In May 1967 Secretary of Defense McNamara expressed the feelings of many Americans when he stated that "the picture of the world's greatest superpower killing or seriously injuring a

thousand noncombatants a week, while trying to pound a tiny backward country into submission on an issue whose merits are hotly disputed, is not a pretty one."

Other factors, too, were contributing to growing national disillusionment with the war. In addition to the cost in human lives, the heavy American involvement in Vietnam was straining the economy. American taxpayers were footing a bill of $25 billion a year to finance the war. Although President Johnson promised that there would be both "guns and butter," the war produced drastic cutbacks in his Great Society programs.

Then, in January 1968 during Tet, the Vietnamese lunar New Year, the Viet Cong launched an attack on over thirty cities and towns in South Vietnam, including the capital, Saigon. They were repelled only after days of fierce fighting during which they suffered heavy casualties and after the total destruction of many of the cities they had held. After one village had been reduced to rubble in an attempt to root out the Viet Cong, an American officer explained, "It became necessary to destroy the town to save it." For many Americans who were growing increasingly disenchanted with the war, this statement epitomized the irrationality of the American effort.

The Peace Movement Before the Tet offensive, the majority of the American public had supported the escalation of United States involvement in Vietnam, accepting the government's official position that the nation had a moral responsibility to resist Communist aggression anywhere in the world. Even so, opposition to the war had been building since the spring of 1965 when the Students for a Democratic Society (SDS) organized "teach-ins" to educate college students on the conflict. The following November some thirty thousand protesters took part in an antiwar demonstration in Washington, D.C., and in October 1967 peace advocates two-hundred-thousand strong marched on the Pentagon. As the antiwar movement gained momentum, it began to attract influential supporters within the government itself. J. William Fulbright, the sharp-tongued chairman of the Senate Foreign Relations Committee, and Robert F. Kennedy, who was now a senator from New York, were among the most outspoken critics. Martin Luther King, Jr., brought his influence to the peace movement when he realized that

MILITARY POLICE ARMED WITH RIFLES BLOCK ATTEMPTS OF ANTIWAR DEMONSTRATORS TO PENETRATE SECURITY LINES OUTSIDE THE PENTAGON, OCTOBER 1967.

the war was drawing energy away from the struggle for civil rights.

Student involvement in the peace movement was sporadic until the government began restricting educational deferments in 1968. Now, faced with the real possibility of having to fight in Vietnam, college students responded by burning their draft cards, demonstrating, and picketing military recruiters on campuses. Some students fled to Canada or Sweden to avoid the draft and a few went to jail rather than be forced to serve. In the early years of American involvement the war had claimed the lives of poor blacks and whites—the first group to be drafted because they could not take advantage of student deferments. Now, as large numbers of middle-class youths began to be shipped to Vietnam, many middle-class parents began to question openly the validity of the American involvement.

Reasons for Opposition Critics of the war argued that the conflict in Vietnam was a civil war and that

the Viet Cong and its political arm, the NLF, were an indigenous, nationalist movement. It followed, then, that the United States was meddling in Vietnam's internal affairs. The reason the United States and South Vietnamese armies had few victories was that the "enemy" had the support of a majority of the South Vietnamese people. In response to the domino theory and the argument that the war was necessary to check the spread of Chinese influence, antiwar protesters pointed out that the Vietnamese had traditionally been hostile to the Chinese. The Vietnamese, peace advocates claimed, were committed to independence and would resist Chinese domination by themselves.

Critics also opposed the conflict on humanitarian grounds. They objected to the massive bombings and the use of napalm and other weapons of chemical warfare which left thousands of noncombatants dead or homeless every year. With television bringing scenes of destruction and cruelty into American living rooms night after night, the human cost of the war became impossible to ignore. Finally, the most radical opponents of the war went beyond strategic and moral considerations to attack what they regarded as blatant American imperialism. According to some, the war was worse than an unfortunate error of judgment; it was part of a deliberate administration policy to achieve world domination.

Rapid Change and Social Protest

The dominant feature of the tumultuous period 1963–1968 was rapid, virtually uncontrollable change. The initial optimism generated by the bold initiatives of the New Frontier and the Great Society gave way to a sense that the nation was coming apart. At times the United States seemed to be irrevocably divided within itself, torn by competing objectives and conflicting forces. In an era dominated by the television screen there could no longer be any isolated incidents, for a breakdown in one area produced shock waves throughout the entire system. As the nation became fragmented by American involvement in Vietnam, so too it was deeply divided in its response to new developments in the civil rights movement and to the cultural revolution among American youth.

From Nonviolence to Black Power

During the early part of the decade, civil rights activity was concentrated in the South. By 1965, however, the movement focused increasingly on the North. An important factor affecting this change had to do with the changing racial composition of the Northern cities. Throughout the 1950s agriculture in the South had become increasingly mechanized. As a result, large numbers of black sharecroppers and laborers were displaced from the land, and they moved North in search of jobs. In 1910 only 10 percent of the black population lived outside the South and only 25 percent lived in cities. By the 1960s, however, nearly 50 percent of black Americans were living outside the South and 70 percent of these had become urban dwellers. This trend was accompanied by the flight of many middle-class whites to the suburbs, leaving the new urban dwellers in isolated and economically deteriorating circumstances. Cities such as Los Angeles, Detroit, Washington, New York, Chicago, Gary, and Newark had expanding black ghettos, neighborhoods where high rents were charged for substandard housing, garbage went uncollected, schools were inferior, and economic opportunities were severely limited.

It was all too easy for Northern whites to express indignation at Southern racism while refusing to take action against, or even admit the existence of, very real forms of discrimination in their own communities. Northern schools were just as segregated as Southern ones because black and white communities were segregated. In neighborhoods where integration could have been accomplished, segregation was assured by districting ordinances. Schools in the black areas were often allowed to run down, equipment was poor and supplies sparse, and the attitudes of white administrators were frequently either hostile or defeatist.

To fight these conditions in Northern schools the black community turned first to boycotts. Demanding better educational opportunities, black parents simply kept their children out of school. During the boycotts, temporary classrooms were usually established. Some parents came to feel that these "freedom schools" were preferable to public schools; while others disagreed, the freedom schools were among the responses that helped to nurture a growing black pride.

Other peaceful strategies included picketing and economic boycotts. Blacks, often joined by sympathetic whites, refused to patronize stores that maintained discriminatory hiring practices. Construction sites where black workers were not employed were picketed. More militant blacks organized rent strikes to call attention to the living conditions in ghetto tenement housing.

Resistance to black demands came in the form of conservative "white backlash" led by "law-and-order" advocates whose real purpose was to keep blacks in their place. Increasingly frustrated in their efforts to secure social and economic equality, urban blacks began to question the philosophy of nonviolence put forward by Martin Luther King.

One of the most extraordinary figures to express the new black militancy was Malcolm X. Born Mal-

MALCOM X ADDRESSES A BLACK MUSLIM RALLY IN NEW YORK CITY IN 1963. HIS POSTHUMOUS *AUTOBIOGRAPHY* HELPED TO INFLUENCE THE "BLACK POWER" MOVEMENT.

colm Little in 1925, he moved as a youth to Boston and then to New York's Harlem where his involvement in narcotics and prostitution landed him in prison. There he developed a passionate allegiance to the Black Muslim movement led by Elijah Muhammad which preached separatism for black people. Malcolm X was the first important black leader to call for black control of the economic and political sources of power in black communities. If violence was necessary to achieve this goal, then it must be employed, he said. In February 1965 Malcolm X was assassinated, apparently by followers of the Elijah Muhammad faction, with which he had broken. His *Autobiography*, published posthumously, was widely read and had a significant influence on the younger black leadership.

Some months before the assassination of Malcolm X, waves of violence had begun to sweep the black ghettos of major cities. The eruption of rage proved beyond any doubt that the frustrations of black people were not just a Southern problem but a national one. The Harlem riots of June 1964 were followed rapidly by open rebellion in seven other cities over the next two months. In the summer of 1965 the violence continued, particularly in the

Watts section of Los Angeles, where thirty-four people died and damage to property was estimated at $35 million. That same year as well as the next, similar riots occurred again in Harlem and in Chicago, San Francisco, Cleveland, and other cities. In the summer of 1967 racial disturbances took place in no fewer than sixty-seven cities across the country. In Detroit federal troops were called in to restore order after days of violence. Trapped in urban slums all across the United States, blacks had vented their rage against white society.

The Report of the National Advisory Commission on Civil Disorder, published in 1968, placed the largest share of blame for the riots on the white population. "What white Americans have never fully understood—but what the Negro can never forget—is that white society is deeply implicated in the ghetto. White institutions created it, white institutions maintain it, and white society condones it." The commission made recommendations to Congress for a program to ensure equality and social justice. As a result, Congress passed an open-housing law in 1968 after a months-long protest in Washington by members of the SCLC, and President Johnson appointed Thurgood Marshall as the first black justice to the Supreme Court.

In the South, meanwhile, black efforts in the mid-1960s were aimed at securing enforcement of the new civil rights legislation. In June 1966 James Meredith returned to Mississippi for a two-hundred-mile March Against Fear. Meredith's goal was to show other blacks that they could walk into voting booths without fear, but shortly after beginning the march, he was wounded by a shotgun blast. Immediately, other civil rights activists, including Martin Luther King, Jr., Floyd McKissick of CORE, and Stokely Carmichael of SNCC, flew to Mississippi to continue the march. But repeated episodes of violence along the route began to bring out serious tactical differences among the black leadership.

"Black Power" The younger generation of black leaders, most notably McKissick and Carmichael, were growing increasingly frustrated with what they perceived as the failure of Martin Luther King's philosophy of brotherly love. In their view it was useless to continue to employ strategies of nonviolent civil disobedience, especially when such efforts often resulted in blacks getting beaten or killed. The answer they began to put forth was "black power."

Nonviolence and Black Power

"You may well ask: 'Why direct action? Why sit-ins, marches and so forth? Isn't negotiation a better path?' You are quite right in calling for negotiation. Indeed, this is the very purpose of direct action. Nonviolent direct action seeks to create such a crisis and foster such a tension that a community which has constantly refused to negotiate is forced to confront the issue. It seeks so to dramatize the issue that it can no longer be ignored. My citing the creation of tension as part of the work of the nonviolent-resister may sound rather shocking. But I confess that I am not afraid of the word 'tension.' I have earnestly opposed violent tension, but there is a type of constructive, nonviolent tension which is necessary for growth. Just as Socrates felt that it was necessary to create a tension in the mind so that individuals could rise from the bondage of myths and half-truths to the unfettered realm of creative analysis and objective appraisal, so must we see the need for nonviolent gadflies to create the kind of tension in society that will help men rise from the dark depths of prejudice and racism to the majestic heights of understanding and brotherhood."

Reverend Martin Luther King, Jr., 1963

Nonviolence and Black Power

"The seriousness of this situation must be faced up to. You should not feel that I am inciting someone to violence. I'm only warning of a powder-keg situation. You can take it or leave it. If you take the warning perhaps you can still save yourself. But if you ignore it or ridicule it, well, death is already at your doorstep. There are 22,000,000 African-Americans who are ready to fight for independence right here. When I say fight for independence right here, I don't mean any non-violent fight, or turn-the-other-cheek fight. Those days are gone. Those days are over.

If George Washington didn't get independence for this country non-violently, and if Patrick Henry didn't come up with a non-violent statement, and you taught me to look upon them as patriots and heroes, then it's time for you to realize that I have studied your books well. . . .

And the only way without bloodshed that this can be brought about is that the black man has to be given full use of the ballot in every one of the 50 states. But if the black man doesn't get the ballot, then you are going to be faced with another man who forgets the ballot and starts using the bullet."

Malcolm X, 1964

This slogan took on a variety of meanings. In one sense it referred to a new black pride and an emphasis on self-reliance. The idea was that blacks by their own efforts had to attain political and economic parity with the white population before effective integration could take place. In Stokely Carmichael's view, whites were no longer welcome in the civil rights movement. Black power also meant that white standards of beauty and social worth had to be rejected so that blacks might attain a new awareness of their unique identity. The slogan "Black is beautiful" became widespread as increasing numbers of young black Americans began wearing the Afro hair style and looking with pride on their African ancestry.

The most extreme advocates of black power used the phrase to mean that blacks must separate themselves entirely from white society and that white violence must be met with black violence. In 1966 the militant Black Panther party came into being. Led by Huey P. Newton, Bobby Seale, and Eldridge Cleaver (author of the remarkable book *Soul on Ice*), the organization's violent rhetoric alarmed moderate leaders like Martin Luther King, who believed that violence would only succeed in creating more violence.

The hopes of older, moderate black leaders like Whitney Young of the Urban League and Roy Wilkins of the NAACP that nonviolent tactics could still bring about equality were shaken in April 1968 when Martin Luther King, Jr., was assassinated in Memphis, Tennessee. His death from a sniper's bullet stunned blacks and whites alike and set off days of rioting in black ghettos across the country.

Youth in Revolt

The 1960s has been characterized as the "youth decade." As in the 1920s, youth was in revolt, and, to an even greater extent than in the 1920s, nationwide attention was focused on the activities of young people. Reasons for the youth rebellion were complex. One obvious factor was the shift in demographics. Children of the post–World War II "baby boom" were coming to maturity, and by 1964 teenagers comprised the single largest group within the population. Thus, their sheer numbers made their influence felt. Another cause was that, unlike their parents, most of these young, middle-class Americans had never experienced war or deprivation. Raised in security and affluence, they rejected the conformity and materialism which they believed dominated their parents' lives. In addition, they viewed the size, the centralization, and the impersonality of American government and big business as dehumanizing and alienating. Finally, the racist response generated by the efforts of blacks seeking equality and the increasing military involvement in Southeast Asia lent support to their assertions that American life was corrupt.

The Movement While many young Americans embraced the trappings of the youth revolt, only a small number can be described as genuine activists. This minority, which was composed mostly of university students, called itself "The Movement" and set out to reform the American system. In 1960 the Students for a Democratic Society (SDS) came into being. In its Port Huron statement of June 1962, the SDS outlined its intention to continue the struggle for racial equality, to work for world peace and break the hold of the military on American life, to put an end to anticommunism, and to resist the impersonality of powerful bureaucracies. The SDS hoped to establish "a democracy of individual participation" and to create a new sense of community among Americans.

One of the early targets of youthful dissatisfaction was the system of higher education. Since the Soviet launching of Sputnik in 1957, American education had tended to emphasize academic achievement as the way to meet the demand for new, specialized skills. More and more, a college degree had become an absolute prerequisite for a successful ca-reer. As a result, many students enrolled not so much out of choice as out of a sense of necessity. Moreover, the size of the college-age population was larger than before. Between 1960 and 1970 the number of students enrolled in college more than doubled. The vastly increased demand on the higher-education system forced it to expand tremendously, until many universities began to be seen as nothing more than huge diploma factories. Contact between undergraduates and professors was significantly diminished, and a sense of alienation gradually crept in.

The attitude of complacency that had prevailed in the 1950s gave way to growing discontent. In the opinion of many students, changes in the universities were not keeping pace with changes in the rest of society. Students objected to restrictions on their personal lives, and they were dissatisfied with the system of required courses, many of which they believed were no longer relevant to modern life. As a result, they began to demand a voice in governing their universities and determining school policies.

The first major outbreak of student unrest occurred in 1964 at the Berkeley campus of the University of California. Mario Savio, a white student activist who had worked in the civil rights movement in the South, led a protest which became known as the Free Speech Movement. The university had banned student radicals from using an off-campus area to give speeches and to organize political activities. It also had prohibited them from distributing political pamphlets on campus. The ensuing confrontation featured sit-in strikes in university buildings, a "dirty-speech campaign," and other forms of disruption over a period of months. When it ended, hundreds of students had been arrested, and the president of the University of California had been forced to resign.

The Berkeley uprising set the stage for student protests at universities all over the country. It was easier to disrupt a college campus than to put one's life on the line for racial equality in the South. Moreover, the protests usually paid off in reforms such as curriculum changes and the relaxation of regulations on personal conduct. But the universities resisted student demands that educational institutions be used as centers from which to attack government policies.

The escalation of the Vietnam War and the end of student deferments further radicalized many students. At Columbia University in 1968 a large group of SDS supporters and black students occupied university buildings and presented the administration with a series of "nonnegotiable demands." The blacks were protesting university relations with the neighboring minority communities, while antiwar activists called for an end to military research at the university. Similar strikes occurred in 1968 and 1969 at Stanford, Berkeley, San Francisco State, Harvard, Brandeis, and Cornell.

At its most extreme the Movement called for "Revolution Now!" The SDS's Weatherman faction (whose name was taken from a lyric by protest singer Bob Dylan which ran, "You don't need a weatherman to know which way the wind blows") engaged in terrorist tactics, including bombings and arson. At the University of Wisconsin a graduate student was killed when a bomb exploded at the Math Research Center. This episode brought forth a widespread sense of revulsion. The turning point finally came on May 4, 1970, at Kent State University, where the National Guard fired on students who were protesting the invasion of Cambodia. Four students died; ten others were wounded. The tragedy at Kent State, coming as it did when the war was winding down, the draft had ended, and racial protest had subsided, helped bring an end to campus violence.

The Hippies Another small segment of America's youth expressed its dissatisfaction with "establishment" values by dropping out. These were the "hippies," heirs to the 1950s "beat generation," represented by writers such as Jack Kerouac and Allen Ginsberg who rebelled against the repressive conformity of that period. During the mid-1960s, hippies gathered in the Haight-Ashbury district of San Francisco and formed a subculture of withdrawal based on drugs, communal living, sexual freedom, and rock music. These peaceful "flower children" were unified by their rejection of the traditional values and assumptions of Western society. They stressed emotion over reason, and some embraced Oriental philosophies and unorthodox diets which they believed would purify their bodies and free their minds. "Do your own thing," was the hippie credo. Their slogan on the war in Vietnam ran, "War is unhealthy for children and other living things."

The use of drugs was central to the hippie lifestyle. Marijuana, which formerly had been confined

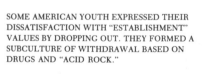

SOME AMERICAN YOUTH EXPRESSED THEIR DISSATISFACTION WITH "ESTABLISHMENT" VALUES BY DROPPING OUT. THEY FORMED A SUBCULTURE OF WITHDRAWAL BASED ON DRUGS AND "ACID ROCK."

to the lower classes and to hip musicians, came into widespread use. Those seeking greater self-awareness tried "tripping" on LSD (lysergic acid diethylamide). While some experienced pleasurable hallucinations on the drug, others suffered from depression, feelings of persecution, and even suicidal tendencies. The musical equivalent of LSD was "acid rock," a mind-blowing electronic sound that celebrated the joys of drugs and sex.

As the nation entered the 1970s, the hippie subculture—like the activist movement on college campuses—gradually dissolved, the victim of its own excesses. The communal experience provided by rock music, as epitomized by the successful Woodstock festival in New York (1969), gave way to the sense-

less violence that characterized the Altamont rock festival held the following winter. For a short time the Age of Aquarius portrayed in the rock musical *Hair* burned brightly before it was snuffed out.

The Election of 1968

In November 1967, Senator Eugene McCarthy of Minnesota, an outspoken opponent of the Vietnam War, announced his intention of competing in the upcoming Democratic primaries. Not a typical politician, McCarthy was quiet and introspective by nature, an intellectual who combined wit and intelligence. His candidacy was intended as a protest

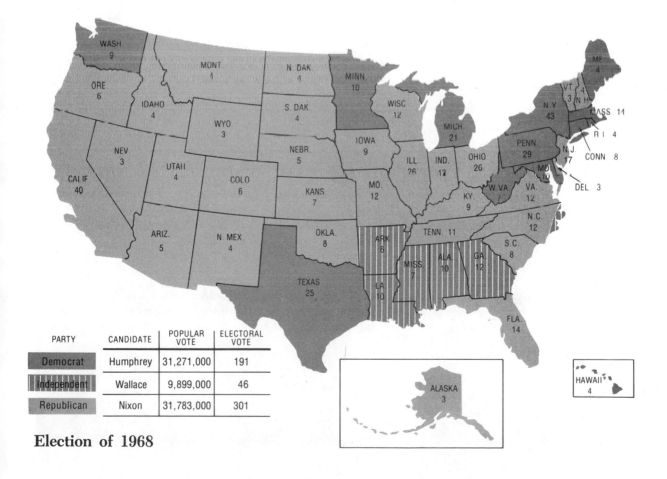

PARTY	CANDIDATE	POPULAR VOTE	ELECTORAL VOTE
Democrat	Humphrey	31,271,000	191
Independent	Wallace	9,899,000	46
Republican	Nixon	31,783,000	301

Election of 1968

against the war rather than a serious effort to win the presidency.

Contrary to all expectations, McCarthy began to gain considerable support, especially after the Tet offensive. Campaigning in New Hampshire, he suddenly became a formidable political figure. Hundreds of students and other volunteers canvassed the state and distributed leaflets on his behalf. McCarthy polled a startling 42 percent of the vote, a strong showing in a state often regarded as an indicator of national trends.

McCarthy's success in New Hampshire encouraged Robert Kennedy to join the race. Unlike McCarthy, Kennedy had a strong political organization and was well known to the public. Thus President Johnson now had two candidates from his own

A SMILING EUGENE McCARTHY TALKS TO CAMPAIGN WORKERS IN NEW HAMPSHIRE. HIS STRONG SHOWING IN THAT STATE'S DEMOCRATIC PRIMARY WAS ONE FACTOR IN PRESIDENT JOHNSON'S DECISION NOT TO RUN FOR REELECTION.

party lined up against him and was faced with the likelihood of defeat in the forthcoming Wisconsin primary and intense pressure from within his own administration to pull American forces out of Vietnam. On March 31, 1968, in a dramatic television appearance, Johnson, visibly exhausted, announced that he would not run for reelection. He promised to take major steps toward deescalation of the war, including a halt in air and naval bombing of North Vietnam, and called for peace talks to begin immediately with the aim of achieving a negotiated settlement. Hanoi responded favorably, and in May 1968 the long and arduous process of peace negotiations began in Paris.

With the incumbent out of the race, the mantle fell to Vice-President Hubert Humphrey. Humphrey's candidacy was hampered by his association with the Johnson administration and by the fact that he entered the race too late for the primaries. In the Kennedy-McCarthy contest, each candidate carried two primaries. Then Kennedy won the vital June 6 California primary by a small margin. Following his victory announcement that evening, the nation was stunned when Kennedy was shot and killed by Sirhan Sirhan, an Arab nationalist who was infuriated over Kennedy's support of Israel. The assassination of Robert Kennedy turned the tide in favor of Humphrey, since McCarthy had little standing in party circles.

The Democratic convention, held in Chicago, was a scene of bitterness, frustration, and violence. Thousands of antiwar activists descended on the city to protest the domination of the convention by what they viewed as the prowar "hawks." Throughout the convention, television cameras showed demonstrators being clubbed and gassed by Mayor Richard J. Daley's overzealous Chicago police. In the midst of this turmoil the Democrats nominated Humphrey, with the solid support of the White House and the party organization. Senator Edmund S. Muskie of Maine was chosen as Humphrey's running mate.

In contrast to the disorderly scene at the Democratic convention, the Republican convention was fairly serene; Richard Nixon was nominated on the first ballot. In 1962 Nixon's political career had seemed to be over when he was defeated in his bid for the governorship of California. Yet he remained politically active by campaigning for Republican candidates in the 1964 and 1966 elections. In 1968,

facing weak and belated opposition, he easily won the allegiance of a majority of the delegates. Nixon chose Spiro Agnew, the conservative governor of Maryland, as his running mate in hopes that Agnew would help consolidate Southern support for the Republican ticket. Nixon's campaign strategy was to promise an end to the Vietnam War and to emphasize his commitment to "law and order."

A third-party candidate also entered the race. The newly created American Independent party nominated Governor George Wallace of Alabama, who had a passionate following in his home state and in other bastions of conservatism. Although he refrained from outspoken expressions of racism, he had long been an active segregationist. During the campaign Wallace frequently called for decentralization of government with a return to states' rights, lower taxes, "law and order," and military victory in Vietnam. His candidacy thrived on the backlash against antiwar protest and civil rights activism, and his undeniable appeal was a threat to Nixon's drive for conservative support.

Hubert Humphrey faced a dilemma. On the one hand, he had loyally supported the administration for four years, so it would have been difficult for him to make an abrupt renunciation of Johnson's Vietnam policies. On the other hand, he needed the support of antiwar Democrats. Late in September he finally announced that if elected he would stop the bombing completely.

The final outcome was close, with Nixon topping his opponents by only one-half million votes out of over seventy-three million cast. Even so, the Republican ticket was victorious in the majority of states, so the electoral count was 301 to 191. Governor Wallace, with almost ten million popular votes and forty-six electoral votes, had carried most of the Deep South. Both houses of Congress remained under the control of the Democrats.

Nixon's victory suggested the emergence of a new alignment in American politics. The Republicans had cut deeply into the Southern white vote despite the Wallace candidacy. In addition, they had taken many votes from another Democratic stronghold, disaffected urban blue-collar workers. By adding these groups to the traditional middle- and upper-middle-class Republican support in the Midwest and Far West, Nixon believed that he was forging a new conservative coalition, which he called "the silent majority."

Readings

General Works

Berman, Ronald, *America in the Sixties: An Intellectual History.* New York: Harper & Row, 1970. (Paper)

Braden, William, *The Age of Aquarius: Technology and the Cultural Revolution.* Chicago: Quadrangle, 1970.

Burner, David, *et al., A Giant's Strength: America in the 1960s.* New York: Holt, Rinehart, and Winston, 1971.

Dickstein, Morris, *Gates of Eden: American Culture in the Sixties.* New York: Basic, 1977.

Evans, Rowland, and Robert Novak, *Lyndon B. Johnson: The Exercise of Power.* New York: New American Library, 1966.

Fitzgerald, Frances, *Fire in the Lake: The Vietnamese and the Americans in Vietnam.* New York: Random, 1972. (Paper)

Goldman, Eric F., *The Tragedy of Lyndon Johnson.* New York: Knopf, 1969.

Halberstam, David, *The Best and the Brightest.* New York: Fawcett World, 1973. (Paper)

Heath, Jim, *Decade of Disillusionment.* Bloomington: Indiana University Press, 1975.

O'Neill, William L., *Coming Apart: An Informal History of America in the 1960s.* New York: Quadrangle, 1973. (Paper)

Poole, Peter, *The United States and Indochina from FDR to Nixon.* Huntington, N.Y.: Krieger, 1973.

Sorenson, Theodore C., *Kennedy.* New York: Harper & Row, 1965.

Schlesinger, Arthur M., *A Thousand Days: John F. Kennedy in the White House.* Boston: Houghton Mifflin, 1965.

Special Studies

Buttinger, Joseph, *Vietnam: A Dragon Embattled,* Vols. I–II. New York: Praeger, 1967.

Dinnerstein, Herbert, *The Making of a Missile Crisis: October 1962.* Baltimore: Johns Hopkins University Press, 1976.

Fairlie, Henry, *The Kennedy Promise: The Politics of Expectation.* Garden City, N.Y.: Doubleday, 1973.

Gelfand, Mark I., *A Nation of Cities.* New York: Oxford University Press, 1975.

Hamilton, Charles V., *Black Power: The Politics of Liberation in America.* New York: Random House, 1967.

Hoopes, Townsend, *The Limits of Intervention.* New York: McKay, 1970.

Keniston, Kenneth, *Youth and Dissent: The Rise of a New Opposition.* New York: Harcourt, Brace, 1972.

Levinson, Jerome, and Juan de Onís, *The Alliance that Lost Its Way.* Chicago: Quadrangle, 1970.

Lipset, Seymour M., and Philip G. Altback (Eds.), *Students in Revolt.* Boston: Houghton Mifflin, 1969.

Manchester, William, *The Death of a President.* New York: Harper & Row, 1967.

Meier, August, and Elliott Rudwick (Eds.), *Black Protest in the Sixties.* New York: Watts, 1970.

Newman, Albert H., *The Assassination of John F. Kennedy: The Reasons Why.* New York: Potter, 1970.

Paper, Lewis J., *John F. Kennedy: The Promise and the Performance.* New York: Crown, 1975.

Schandler, Herbert Y., *The Unmaking of a President: Lyndon Johnson and Vietnam.* Princeton, N.J.: Princeton University Press, 1977.

Slater, Philip, *The Pursuit of Loneliness: American Culture at the Breaking Point.* Boston: Beacon, 1970.

Walton, Richard J., *Cold War and Counterrevolution: The Foreign Policy of John F. Kennedy.* New York: Viking Press, 1972.

White, Theodore H., *The Making of the President, 1960.* New York: Atheneum, 1961.

Wyden, Peter, *Bay of Pigs: The Untold Story.* New York: Simon & Schuster, 1979.

Primary Sources

Didion, Joan, *Slouching Towards Bethlehem.* New York: Farrar, Straus & Giroux, 1968.

Fulbright, J. William, *The Arrogance of Power.* New York: Random House, 1967.

Johnson, Lady Bird, *A White House Diary.* New York: Dell, 1971.

Johnson, Lyndon B., *Vantage Point: Perspectives of the Presidency.* New York: Holt, Rinehart, and Winston, 1971.

King, Martin Luther, Jr., *Why We Can't Wait.* New York: Harper & Row, 1964.

Biographies

Burns, James M., *John Kennedy: A Political Profile.* New York: Harcourt, Brace, 1959.

Kearns, Doris, *Lyndon Johnson and the American Dream.* New York: Harper & Row, 1976.

Lewis, David L., *King: A Critical Biography.* New York: Praeger, 1970.

Schlesinger, Arthur M., Jr., *Robert Kennedy and His Times.* Boston: Houghton Mifflin, 1978.

Steinberg, Alfred, *Sam Johnson's Boy.* New York: Macmillan, 1968.

Fiction

Vonnegut, Kurt, *Slaughterhouse Five.* New York: Delacorte, 1969.

In the long ironic history of America, events have kept unfolding contrary to the expectation of her greatest leaders and thinkers, but seldom has there been such an example of the irony and incongruity of political life as the case of Richard Milhous Nixon, who resigned the Presidency effective at noon August 9, 1974. . . .

It has been a terrible time, . . . but the long agony has not been without its advantages. It took a civil war to get rid of slavery, two apocalyptic world wars to put American power behind peace and order in the world, a wasting economic depression to reform the social structure of America, and Vietnam and Watergate to bring excessive Presidential power under control.

James Reston, Journalist
The End of a Presidency (1974)

Significant Events

Apollo II lands on moon [July 20, 1969]

Nixon Doctrine [July 1969]

American invasion of Cambodia [April 1970]

Kissinger's secret trip to Peking [July 1971]

Tonkin Gulf Resolution repealed [1971]

New York Times v. *United States* [June 1971]

Strategic Arms Limitation Agreement (SALT-I) [May 1972]

Watergate break-in [June 17, 1972]

Cease-fire in Vietnam War [January 1973]

Yom Kippur War [October 1973]

Five-month oil embargo announced by Organization of Petroleum Exporting Countries (OPEC) [1973]

Nixon resigns presidency [August 9, 1974]

North Vietnam defeats South Vietnam [April 1975]

Helsinki Accord [August 1975]

Investigation of FBI and CIA [1975–1976]

MEMBERS OF THE SENATE WATERGATE COMMITTEE CONFER WITH CHAIRMAN SAM ERVIN ABOUT THE INVOCATION OF EXECUTIVE PRIVILEGE REGARDING TAPE RECORDINGS MADE IN THE PRESIDENT'S OVAL OFFICE. (SURROUNDING ERVIN ARE, LEFT TO RIGHT: SEN. HOWARD BAKER; SEN. EDWARD GURNEY; H. WILLIAM SHURE, ASSISTANT MINORITY COUNSEL; RUFUS EDMISTEN, DEPUTY CHIEF COUNSEL; SEN. JOSEPH MONTOYA; AND SAM DASH, CHIEF COUNSEL.)

Richard M. Nixon was born in Yorba Linda, California, the second of five sons of a lower-middle-class Quaker family. The product of small-town America, he was serious, hard working, and determined to make his mark in life. After graduating from Duke University law school, Nixon practiced law and then served in the Navy during World War II. In 1946 he was elected to the House of Representatives. As a member of the House Un-American Activities Committee he achieved a national reputation with his investigation of Alger Hiss. In 1950 he was elected to the Senate. Two years later he became vice-president under Eisenhower, and after serving eight years in that capacity was narrowly defeated for the presidency in 1960. Although Nixon formally retired from politics after an unsuccessful bid for the governorship of California in 1962, he never really gave up his political ambitions. In 1968, in one of the most astounding comebacks in American political history, he won the Republican party nomination and defeated Hubert Humphrey for the presidency.

With a reputation for being a tough but flexible conservative on domestic issues and a hard-line anti-Communist on questions of foreign policy, Nixon entered the White House at a time when the effectiveness of his political philosophy would be severely tested. The economy was plagued with inflation as a result of government spending on the Vietnam War, and conservatives were demanding that the new administration cut taxes, eliminate many social-welfare programs, and wage a war on crime. Overseas, the United States was still mired in Vietnam. Moreover, domestic opposition to America's extensive

PRESIDENT-ELECT RICHARD M. NIXON BEAMS AS HE THANKS CAMPAIGN WORKERS IN HIS NEW YORK HEADQUARTERS.

commitments abroad as the self-appointed leader of the free world made it almost a necessity to seek better relations with China and the Soviet Union.

Nixon's Domestic Policy

The Economy

During Nixon's first term, the most pressing economic problem facing the nation was inflation. During his campaign Nixon had promised to stop the price spiral which had been caused by military spending and Johnson's easy-money policies without producing a recession. "Peace with prosperity" had been one of his key slogans.

To this end the new president cut back government spending. At the same time the Federal Reserve Board tightened the money supply in an effort to keep price levels constant. This strategy was predicated on a willingness to tolerate a relatively high level of unemployment in order to check rising prices. For two and a half years Nixon insisted that the strategy would work, and he consistently rejected the idea of imposing wage-and-price controls. Still, the nation's economy fell steadily into a deep recession. In the last half of 1969 interest rates soared to their highest levels in at least a century. Home mortgages were increasingly difficult to obtain; cities were unable to borrow money for municipal improvements; and corporate stock values fell sharply. Unemployment, which stood at slightly more than 3 percent when Nixon took office, reached 6 percent by the end of 1970. Meanwhile, prices continued to rise.

In August 1971 Nixon finally reversed his position and, announcing Phase I of a new economic initiative, declared a ninety-day wage-and-price freeze in hopes of containing the disastrous effects of inflation. Business leaders and consumers generally hailed the new initiative. But labor leaders, notably George Meany of the AFL-CIO, claimed that the freeze would hurt workers while leaving business profits and interest rates untouched. Furthermore, unemployment, particularly among minority groups, was unaffected by the new measures.

In November 1971, with the end of the freeze, the president introduced Phase II of his economic program, which aimed at limiting annual wage-and-price increases. A pay board was established to pass judgment on pay raises, and a price commission was created to rule on price increases in large businesses. Despite these measures, however, inflation and industrial stagnation continued. The term "stagflation" was invented to explain what had once been considered impossible: business stagnation and unemployment coupled with rising inflation. To make matters worse, grain crop failures overseas soon triggered a worldwide explosion in food prices.

Nevertheless, in January 1973 the president, convinced that Phase II had successfully brought inflation under control and that the recession was over, initiated Phase III, which was based on a decline in unemployment and an increase in production and consumer spending. Most mandatory wage-and-price controls were now abolished, but voluntary compliance with the guidelines did not work, and by the middle of 1973 inflation was on the rise again.

The Dollar under Attack The administration also faced an international monetary crisis. Since the end of World War II the dollar had been the international medium of exchange. But by 1971 America's favorable balance of trade had been upset by excessive spending on the military, imports, foreign aid, and tourism. Confidence in the value of the dollar was shaken. Demands for payment in gold instead of dollars reduced the country's gold reserves. At the same time, American goods were facing stiff competition in world markets from western European and

Japanese products, since domestic inflation made American goods more expensive than similar foreign products. Nixon responded by imposing a 10-percent surcharge on imports and allowing the value of the dollar to fluctuate according to world financial conditions.

Efforts at Reform

In some areas of domestic policy, Nixon undertook to institute reforms. In August 1969 he proposed a major and controversial innovation in the wasteful and inequitable national welfare system. Under the so-called family assistance plan, a family of four with no income would receive a guaranteed minimum annual income of $1600 or $2460 when food-stamp benefits were added. All welfare recipients who were deemed capable of working would be required to seek work. Conservatives objected to the increase in welfare costs under the plan and liberals to the low minimum-income figure. Although the measure was finally passed by the House in 1970, it was blocked by the Senate. The president also sought to turn over much of the responsibility for administering government programs such as job-training to the states, under a principle he labeled the "New Federalism." The keystone of the New Federalism was the concept of revenue sharing between federal and state governments. The intent was to increase local responsibility by allowing the states to administer more federally collected revenues. Congress approved the measure in 1972.

Relations with Congress

In addition to sponsoring legislation of its own, the Nixon administration supported some legislation initiated by Congress. There were increases in Social Security benefits, larger subsidies for low- and middle-income housing, and an expanded student-assistance program. An ambitious Tax Reform Act was passed in 1969 and the Twenty-sixth Amendment, granting eighteen-year-olds the right to vote, was ratified in July 1971. Yet even though there was some cooperation on legislation, Nixon's relations with Congress were seldom harmonious. Progressive legislators from both parties were angered over some of his vetoes. Moreover, by 1972 the war in Vietnam was generating strong support in Congress for curbing presidential power in the conduct of foreign policy. There was widespread resentment over the president's use of "executive privilege" to prevent his aides from testifying before congressional committees, his refusal to spend funds appropriated by Congress (a practice known as impoundment) in order to prevent laws from being carried out, and his remoteness, from Republican as well as from Democratic legislators.

Forging the New Majority

Slow-down on Civil Rights The president's desire to consolidate his base of support among the "silent majority," particularly in the conservative South, was most clearly demonstrated in his approach to the issues of civil rights and crime. When Nixon took office federal employment of minorities was increasing, and HEW Secretary Robert Finch announced his intention of withholding federal funds from schools where there was only token integration. But in August 1969 the efforts of HEW and the Justice Department to ensure that desegregation was moving forward as fast as possible began to be reversed. By October 1970 the United States Commission on Civil Rights reported "a major breakdown" in the enforcement of civil rights legislation.

A particularly controversial issue involved the busing of school children as a means of accomplishing integration. In April 1971 the Supreme Court ruled unanimously that cities could bus pupils out of their neighborhoods if busing was necessary to achieve integration. This decision provoked immediate protests in the North as well as the South.

Early in 1972, Nixon asked Congress for a moratorium on busing orders while new legislation was prepared. Congress had no more desire to become involved in this explosive issue than did the president, and it passed a weak bill prohibiting the implementation of court-ordered busing until the end of 1973.

Nixon's Anti-Crime Campaign During his first four years in office, Nixon waged an extensive war on crime. A keystone of his anticrime effort was the Omnibus Crime and Safe Streets Act of 1968 which established the Law Enforcement Assistance Administration (LEAA) within the Justice Department. Through LEAA state and local governments were given funds to improve and strengthen their law-enforcement capabilities, develop programs to reduce crime, and improve their systems of criminal justice. Under the Nixon administration LEAA became the fastest-growing agency of the federal government. Although the agency spent large amounts of money to carry out its program, the House Committee on Government Operations concluded in 1972 that LEAA had had "no visible impact on the incidence of crime in the United States." In the meantime, the administration sponsored other anticrime legislation including preventive detention in certain cases, court reform, wider use of wiretaps, and the right of police officers to enter dwellings without a search warrant in specified circumstances. Even with these measures the crime rate continued to rise.

Nixon's Foreign Policy

Throughout his administration President Nixon considered foreign affairs to be his main area of expertise. Although he dominated the field of foreign policy during his years in the White House, he also relied extensively on the advice of the brilliant and energetic Henry Kissinger. Kissinger—a former Harvard professor who had emigrated from Germany as a child—rapidly became one of the most powerful people in Washington. After serving as Nixon's national security adviser during his first term, Kissinger became secretary of state in 1973. He traveled widely, ignoring the State Department bureaucracy in favor of a form of diplomacy based

on personal interaction with world leaders. Witty and urbane, he enjoyed excellent relations with the news media until it was discovered toward the end of his term that he had wiretapped aides and journalists.

Détente with Russia and China

The major thrust of Nixon's foreign policy was a reversal of the militant anticommunism which had characterized his earlier career. While he never totally repudiated the hard line of strong military preparedness, he was a realist who believed that the

United States should not attempt to "roll back" communism as Dulles had advocated, but rather to reestablish a workable balance of power. His formula called for reducing America's global commitments, at the same time opening up negotiations with China and easing relations with the Soviet Union.

The Nixon-Kissinger world view was based on the concept of five centers of power rather than two: the United States, Russia, China, Japan, and Western Europe. Each should manage affairs in its own area, thus helping to achieve an international balance of power. This global strategy made no provision for an assertion of self-interest by the emerging Third World nations. Only toward the end of his tenure did Kissinger pay more than superficial attention to these areas.

In July 1969 at Guam the president proclaimed what has since been called the Nixon Doctrine, the central thesis of which was that the role of the United States in world politics would be that of a partner rather than the primary defender of the free nations of the world. Speaking before Congress in 1970, Nixon declared that "America cannot—and will not—conceive all the plans, design all the programs, execute all the decisions, and undertake all the defense of the free nations of the world." In practical terms this meant that the United States, while honoring its treaty obligations, would expect its allies to take a larger responsibility for their own development and security.

The policy of détente (relaxation of tensions) was given impulse by growing hostilities between China and the Soviet Union. In the latter half of the 1960s rivalry between the two powers had resulted in a number of serious military incidents along the Sino-Soviet border. Alarmed at the presence of Soviet troops along the Chinese frontier, the Chinese indicated an interest in secret talks with the United States. President Nixon realized that the long-standing American policy of nonrecognition of China was incompatible with his goal of improved world relations and he had been studying ways to reverse the policy. Recognition of China would help to secure the hoped-for power balance; moreover, it would enable the United States to seek the help of the Chinese in pressing the North Vietnamese to make peace. Finally, the prospect of a market for American goods in China was an enticing one.

Late in 1969 the president relaxed the embargo on American purchases of Chinese goods. Then in April 1971, the Chinese invited a team of American table-tennis players to compete in Peking. Shortly after this session of "ping-pong diplomacy," the process of détente began to accelerate. In July 1971 Henry Kissinger traveled secretly to Peking, where he discussed the situation in Vietnam and arranged for a later visit by the president. Simultaneously the State Department announced that it would no longer oppose the admission of the People's Republic of China to the United Nations. Finally, in February 1972 President Nixon visited Peking. Although the joint communiqué at the end of the visit was vague on areas of disagreement such as the status of Taiwan, the trip signaled a new commitment to friendly relations with China, and the two countries exchanged liaison representatives.

Concerned by American rapprochement with China as well as by China's nuclear potential, the Soviet Union was becoming more receptive to détente with the United States. The most pressing problem involved the need for limitation of nuclear armaments. After the Cuban missile crisis, the arms race between the two "superpowers" had acceler-

PRESIDENT AND MRS. NIXON TOUR THE SHANGHAI INDUSTRIAL EXHIBITION WITH CHINESE PREMIER CHOU EN-LAI IN FEBRUARY 1972.

ated, and now it had reached a point where each nation had the capability to destroy the other many times over. Of great concern, too, was the severe budgetary strain the arms race was imposing on each government. Both nations were designing an antiballistic missile (ABM) program to protect land-based ICBMs which were already in place. The idea was that the ABMs could be launched to destroy approaching enemy missiles before they could reach their target. Both nations were also testing a multiple warhead known as a MIRV (multiple, independently-targetable reentry vehicle) that could be fired from a missile in flight at several different targets. MIRVs could be attached to missiles already in the American arsenal, thereby helping to reduce the potential effectiveness of the Soviets' ABM system. In the United States the ABM and MIRV programs were supported by the Nixon administration; however, they met considerable opposition from legislators who saw them as a waste of money and believed that these weapons would probably be outmoded by the time the programs were completed. Nevertheless, Congress passed a modified ABM project in October 1969, by the narrow margin of one vote.

SALT–I In November a significant step toward ending the arms race was taken when the Soviets agreed to begin Strategic Arms Limitation Talks (SALT–I) in Helsinki, Finland. Progress was slow at first, but growing support for détente and the political need to show some results eventually led to agreements. In May 1972 President Nixon and Soviet Premier Leonid Brezhnev signed two significant arms accords. The first, a treaty, limited each country to two ABM sites. Compliance would be monitored by photo-reconnaissance satellites. The second was an interim agreement to put a five-year freeze on the number of offensive nuclear weapons both nations possessed, including ICBMs, submarine-launched missiles, and ballistic missile submarines. Since the agreements covered only the quantity of weapons that could be produced, they did not succeed in ending the arms race. Rather the United States and Russia turned to developing weapons systems not covered by the agreements.

Latin America

While the United States pursued détente with the Soviet Union and China, its relations with Latin America were troubled. Since the American economy was closely tied to Latin America by trade, the administration continued to support military regimes throughout the hemisphere in hopes of preventing leftist takeovers. At the same time, under pressure from the OAS the United States lifted the hemispheric economic blockade of Cuba in 1975 and permitted some travel between Cuba and the United States. But use of Cuban troops in Africa to aid leftist revolutionary groups precluded further efforts to improve relations.

Another trouble spot was Chile. When the CIA was unsuccessful in preventing the constitutional election of a Marxist, Salvador Allende, in 1970 Nixon ordered the agency to try to destabilize the Chilean economy. Washington cut off economic aid and big American companies doing business there cut back credit. Finally, viewing the American actions as a green light, the Chilean military overthrew and murdered Allende in 1973. He was replaced by a brutal dictatorship which put an end to civil liberties. The American involvement in this episode led to further deterioration of relations with Latin America.

The Moon Landing

In a period marked more by easing of tensions than by diplomatic victories, there was at least one clearcut American triumph. On July 20, 1969, the Apollo II space mission landed astronauts Neil Armstrong and Edwin Aldrin, Jr., on the surface of the moon. Other American moon landings followed in the next few years. Although critics charged that the $24 billion Apollo program represented a misuse of funds needed for domestic recovery, people all around the world, opponents and advocates alike, could not help but be impressed by the awesomeness of the great adventure. The moonwalk, as well as détente with the two major Communist powers, provided a few moments of welcome relief for a troubled world.

Southeast Asia

Vietnamization: 1968–1972 The Paris peace talks aimed at ending the war in Vietnam had barely begun before they bogged down. Although the North Vietnamese had begun some troop withdrawals in November 1968, President Johnson continued exert-

ASTRONAUT NEIL ARMSTRONG'S PHOTOGRAPH OF EDWIN ALDRIN'S FIRST STEP ON THE MOON. THE MOON LANDING WAS AN EXHILA-RATING ACHIEVEMENT DURING A TRYING PERIOD IN AMERICAN HISTORY.

wrong war wrong time

ing military pressure; the result was an end to the withdrawals. The Thieu government, for its part, exhibited little willingness to negotiate. By the time President Nixon entered the White House the talks had failed to move off center.

In the 1968 presidential campaign Nixon had promised to make every effort to end the war. Like his predecessor, however, he believed that the American withdrawal from Vietnam must be accomplished gradually if the nation were to achieve "a peace we can live with and a peace we can be proud of." Thus, during his first year in office he outlined a program of phased withdrawal of American forces, known as "Vietnamization." Under this program the South Vietnamese army was to take over the defense of the country, supported by massive use of American air power on North Vietnamese supply routes, military bases, and production centers. In April 1969 some 543,000 American ground troops were stationed in Vietnam. By Sep-

tember 1972 under Vietnamization, only 60,000 remained.

For a while after Nixon took office antiwar activists moderated their protests as they waited to see what policies the new president would pursue. When it became clear that little progress was being made toward ending the war, and that aerial bombing and defoliation were continuing to devastate Vietnam, the movement took action. On October 15, 1969, antiwar protesters—250,000 strong—gathered in Washington to march past the White House in a massive demonstration against the war. The president responded by going on television on November 3 to defend his Vietnamization policy, a strategy which had the desired effect of securing the support of the "silent majority." Vice-President Agnew contributed to a growing atmosphere of divisiveness when he characterized those who encouraged the protest as "an effete corps of impudent snobs who characterize themselves as intellectuals."

not really

In the first months of 1970 the story broke that American soldiers had massacred hundreds of civilians in the South Vietnamese hamlets of My Lai and Son My in 1968. These reports sparked intense debate about the morality of the war and about American atrocities. Then, in April 1970 the president ordered American troops into neutral Cambodia. (Unknown to Congress and the public, the military, acting on Nixon's orders, had secretly been bombing Cambodia since early in 1969.) The administration claimed that the invasion was necessary because Communist forces were using Cambodia as a staging area for raids into South Vietnam. Although the invasion resulted in the destruction of large quantities of supplies, no enemy sanctuaries were found.

The antiwar movement accepted neither Nixon's explanation of the need for the Cambodian operation nor his suggestion that it would shorten the conflict. Here, to them, was proof that the president was actually escalating the war. There was an immediate outburst of protest on an unprecedented scale. Students across the nation demanded that universities shut down in response to Nixon's war policies. As noted previously, at Kent State University four students were killed when the Ohio National Guard opened fire on demonstrators. Protests at a black college, Jackson State in Mississippi, resulted in two student deaths from police fire.

In addition to the public outcry against the Cambodian invasion congressional criticism was so intense that Nixon was soon forced to promise that all ground troops would be withdrawn from Cambodia within six weeks. Nixon's congressional critics were infuriated by his failure to consult with Congress before embarking on what was in essence a military invasion of a neutral country which did not present an immediate threat to American security. Longtime war opponent J. William Fullbright headed Senate efforts to limit the president's war-making power. In 1971 the Senate repealed the Tonkin Gulf Resolution which had been the official basis for American involvement in the Vietnam War.

The War Winds Down Despite Nixon's Vietnamization program the prospects for peace remained dim. In November 1970 full-scale bombing of North Vietnam was resumed, and in February 1971 Laos was invaded in what was called another "temporary incursion" to hasten the end of the war. The Laotian invasion was the first real test of the ability of the South Vietnamese army to continue the war on its own. It soon became clear that Vietnamization was failing miserably. On-the-scene reports told of South Vietnamese troops retreating on foot in complete disorganization, after suffering heavy casualties.

The invasion of Laos also brought on a new round of peace demonstrations. On May 3, 1971, police and military units in Washington, D.C., were called out in an attempt to frustrate antiwar efforts to close down government business. As many as twelve thousand demonstrators were arrested; these mass arrests, in turn, became the subject of intense criticism.

As time went on, Nixon's strategy for ending the war became clearer. American troop withdrawals continued, but the air war was expanded to include Laos and Cambodia. In April 1971 the president declared that he would continue the air raids until North Vietnam freed all American prisoners of war. The North Vietnamese responded with a promise to release the POWs if the United States would withdraw completely by the end of 1971.

As the election year of 1972 approached, efforts were intensified to break the four-year deadlock in the Paris negotiations and reach a settlement. Secretary Kissinger held a number of secret talks with the North Vietnamese in search of an acceptable formula for agreement. And then, in April 1972, North Vietnam launched a successful new offensive

throughout the south, which became a key element in the peace negotiations. Kissinger indicated that now the only American condition for a cease-fire would be the withdrawal of those North Vietnamese forces which had entered South Vietnam since the start of the offensive; the estimated one hundred thousand troops which had been in the south prior to the offensive could remain.

The administration increased military pressure to gain favorable terms. In May President Nixon ordered a blockade and the mining of major North Vietnamese harbors in order to cut off the flow of arms. The bombing missions were intensified, and by October the North Vietnamese were ready to respond to peace initiatives. Kissinger announced that "peace is at hand." The negotiations in Paris were still blocked by several disagreements, however, most notably the unwillingness of President Thieu to accept Kissinger's proposed terms. In December, when the talks again floundered, Nixon launched twelve days of saturation bombing of Hanoi and Haiphong. The apparent reason for this action was to win Thieu over by strengthening the military position of South Vietnam. Although Thieu continued to balk, American pressure finally forced him back to the bargaining table. On January 27, 1973, a cease-fire agreement was signed.

The Paris Accords called for an immediate cease-fire; the removal of all foreign troops from Vietnam, Laos, and Cambodia; and the release of American POWs over a sixty-day period. Two international truce teams would supervise the cease-fire, and a national election for a new South Vietnamese government was planned for the future.

Angered by Nixon's continuation of the American bombing of Cambodia after the cease-fire agreement was in effect, Congress set an August 15, 1973, deadline for ceasing all American military activity in Indochina. It also passed the War Powers Act, which provided that the president could not send American troops abroad for more than sixty days without congressional approval.

The Vietnam War Ends Almost immediately after the Paris Accords were signed violations occurred on both sides. The Saigon government refused to permit the North Vietnamese to exercise a role in the political settlement, as had been agreed upon at Paris. The North Vietnamese continued limited military efforts in the south. By early 1975 military activity throughout Southeast Asia intensified. Communist forces launched major offensives in Vietnam, Laos, and Cambodia, making rapid gains.

Responding to the deteriorating situation the new president, Gerald Ford, called on Congress to approve massive emergency military aid. Congress, however, had no stomach for another military effort in Southeast Asia and denied the president's request. Communist troops entered Phnom Penh, the capital of Cambodia, on April 17, 1975. Two weeks later, with Communist forces at the gates of Saigon, General Duong Van Minh announced the surrender of South Vietnam.

How Did It Happen?

The most unpopular war in American history was finally at an end. A million and a half Vietnamese had been killed and a third of the survivors had become refugees. Vietnamese society was left in disarray, defoliants had destroyed much valuable forest land; and American bomb craters pock-marked the countryside.

As for the effects on the United States, fifty-six thousand men had lost their lives and three hundred thousand more had been wounded. Far from being hailed as heroes, many returning veterans were reviled for their part in the conflict. Government efforts to help them readjust to civilian life were minimal at best. Witnessing the horror of the first "television war" had torn the country apart for eight years and had shattered Americans' idealism and self-confidence. To some, the war was deeply immoral, evidence that America, in spite of its professed ideals, was not immune to the tendency toward corruption inherent in the use of great power.

While most Americans wanted to forget the war, a few people sought to analyze its significance. Those who believed that America had entered the Vietnam conflict to halt Communist aggression argued that the United States should have used whatever force was necessary to win the war. Now they were concerned that the nation had sustained a severe blow to its credibility as a world power. Those in the military establishment who thought that even political problems had military solutions claimed that the war had been lost by a lack of nerve. In their view the use of more American fire power at the time of the Tet offensive would have secured victory. Other observers sought to place blame for the Vietnam experience either on the uniqueness of the situation in Southeast Asia or on the unchecked growth of presidential power. According to this view, Lyndon Johnson and Richard Nixon had bypassed congressional authority in order to carry out their own policies.

These assessments were challenged by more severe critics, some of whom argued that the war was the natural consequence of America's belief that it could control events through its superior moral and military power. Others viewed the Vietnam debacle as the result of an uncritical application of the containment doctrine to an area that was not vital to American security. The "elementary rule of playing power politics is not that you win some and lose some," wrote Ronald Steel in *Pax Americana*, "but that you should never confuse knights and bishops with pawns." Yet others maintained that the war had resulted from entrusting too much power to the national security bureaucracy in Washington and from permitting the business interests to pursue excessive expansion abroad in order to maintain profits at home. The proponents of this thesis argued that while the United States had not become embroiled in Vietnam specifically to obtain new markets and investments, defeat in Southeast Asia would weaken the American economic position in the rest of the Third World. In assessing this view it is worth noting that American sales and investments abroad were mainly in highly developed countries and that American business leaders as a group were not supporters of American intervention in Vietnam.

One lesson of Vietnam seemed to be that the American government would have to restrain its tendency to try to control events everywhere in the world. It seemed clear that future military commitments abroad should be undertaken with the utmost caution, for the American experience in Vietnam had shown that there were limitations on the effective use of military power, however great that power may be.

The Middle East

The other persistent trouble spot during the 1970s was the Middle East. The Israeli victory in the 1967 Six-Day War had two important results which

TANKS AND TRUCKS LOADED WITH TROOPS AND EQUIPMENT JAM THE MAIN SUPPLY ROAD FOR THE ISRAELI
ARMY FIGHTING AGAINST THE SYRIANS IN THE BATTLE OF THE GOLAN HEIGHTS, OCTOBER 1973.

seemed destined to make a resumption of hostilities almost inevitable. First, as noted previously, Egypt aligned itself more closely with the Soviet Union. The Soviets promptly dispatched military advisers and weapons to bring about rapid Egyptian rearmament. Second, the explosive Palestinian question came to a head. Some two million Palestinians had been displaced when Israel successfully repelled attacks by the Arab states in 1948 and 1949. Militant opposition to the existence of a Jewish state in what the Palestinians perceived as their own homeland led to the creation of terrorist groups such as the Palestine Liberation Organization (PLO).

When Egypt's President Nasser died in 1970 he was succeeded by Anwar el-Sadat. By the summer of 1972 Sadat had determined that his country's relationship with the Soviet Union was not yielding the anticipated dividends. Disillusioned and frustrated, he dismissed most of his Soviet advisers in

July and turned for support to other Arab states, particularly Saudi Arabia and the Persian Gulf sheikdoms which were accumulating huge quantities of unspent oil revenues. The strategy was successful. By August 1973 Arab states had pledged over $600 million in military aid to the Egyptians.

Two months later, on October 5, 1973, the Middle East erupted in another full-scale war. During the Jewish holy day Yom Kippur, Israel was attacked on two fronts: in the north by Syria and in the south by Egypt. For ten days the Israelis were in confusion. Then large airlifts of armaments and supplies from the United States helped them gain the upper hand. In the process of turning back the Egyptian army, they seized more Arab territory. President Nixon placed American nuclear forces on alert, although the reasons for this step are unclear. At the same time the administration worked with the Soviets on a UN resolution calling for an immediate cease-fire and peace negotiations. Although Secretary Kissinger finally succeeded in working out a cease-fire agreement, the basic issues dividing the combatants were no closer to resolution.

America's strong support of Israel during the October war strained its relations with the Soviet Union. Even more alarming, it produced economic retaliation from the Arab states. In the fall of 1973 the Organization of Petroleum Exporting Countries (OPEC), an international oil cartel dominated by an Arab majority, imposed a five-month embargo on shipments of oil to the United States and the European allies. This action introduced a new equation into world affairs. Third World nations that possessed resources vital to the West had realized that they could use them to tip the international balance of power in their favor. With the oil embargo the United States suffered the beginning of an energy crisis which has plagued the nation ever since.

The Nixon administration, recognizing America's growing vulnerability in the face of the oil weapon, focused intensive efforts on achieving a Mideast settlement. For two years Henry Kissinger shuttled back and forth between Cairo and Tel Aviv. His efforts finally resulted in a military truce in 1974. In 1975 Israel agreed to a pull-back of its troops in the Sinai and the creation of a buffer zone in that region to be supervised by American technicians at warning stations. Egypt, in turn, agreed to use peaceful means to resolve its differences with Israel. The agreement, however, left the Palestinian question unresolved. The PLO continued its terrorist activities, hoping thereby to bring pressure on Israel to relinquish control of the West Bank of the Jordan River. The Israelis, however, were convinced that the PLO's real goal was the destruction of the state of Israel. With a Palestinian presence on the West Bank, they argued, Israeli borders would be extremely vulnerable. Israel, therefore, pursued a policy of swift retaliation for every PLO attack. Groups of militant Israeli nationalists even began building settlements in the occupied West Bank.

The Growth of Presidential Power

Richard Nixon's first term in office demonstrated the alarming degree to which the power of the presidency had grown and revealed the extent to which Congress had abdicated its constitutional role. Although this trend toward the accumulation of power in the presidency had been developing for decades, it reached a peak during the Nixon years. Crucial decisions on foreign and domestic policy were made in the White House. In most instances Congress and the American public were informed only after the fact; sometimes they were not informed at all. A dangerous consequence of this concentration of power was the president's increasing unwillingness to tolerate any dissent from his policies. To an unprecedented degree, the Nixon administration used its authority to attack antiwar protesters and the news media.

The War on Dissent

The first group to feel the effects of the administration's crackdown on dissent was the antiwar movement. Although a 1970 CIA report stated that "radical movements were homegrown, indigenous responses to perceived grievances and problems that had been growing for years," the administration continually sought to discredit protest leaders personally or to convince the public that the antiwar movement was sponsored by Communists.

The Justice Department, under Attorney General John N. Mitchell, a former law partner of the president, sought to prosecute antiwar activists. The most widely publicized case was that of the Chicago Seven (1969–1970) in which seven radicals were convicted of conspiracy to cross state lines and incite riots during the 1968 Democratic National Convention. The convictions were later overturned on appeal. In another sensational case radical priest Philip Berrigan was charged along with six others of plotting to kidnap presidential adviser Henry Kissinger, plant bombs in heating ducts in federal buildings, and vandalize draft boards. The jury deadlocked and the government decided not to retry the case.

In the 1970 congressional elections the administration set out to court conservative backlash against the antiwar movement in an effort to return more Republicans to Congress. In their self-appointed role of guardians of law and order, those who spoke for the White House, especially Spiro Agnew, launched verbal attacks on Democratic liberals, black militants, peace demonstrators, and campus radicals. After the massive antiwar demonstration of October 15, 1970, Agnew told the nation that radical students should be "separated" from society "with no more regret than we should feel over discarding rotten apples from a barrel." Such attacks failed to achieve their objective; indeed, they succeeded only in further polarizing an already divided nation.

Agnew directed many of his verbal assaults toward the news media, charging that reporters did not reflect the views of the American majority and that coverage of the war in Vietnam was unfair and "misleading." The fact was that television and press coverage of the war had focused on some aspects of the war that undermined popular support for American involvement. In addition to covering the fighting, television news had reported on the human costs of the war—including the effects of napalm on humans, interviews with antiwar American soldiers, the increasing use of hard drugs by American service personnel, and incidents of "fragging" (using fragmentation grenades to kill hated superiors).

The president attempted to expand government control over the nation's news media by creating the Office of Telecommunications Policy (OTP) late in 1970. The OTP soon directed its attention to the Corporation for Public Broadcasting, which Congress had created in 1967 to provide a network for publicly owned television and radio stations. Convinced that the CPB was a tool of the "liberal media establishment," Nixon impounded funds for the system which had been voted by Congress.

In June 1971 another major battle erupted between the press and the administration when the New York Times published the first excerpts of what were soon to be called the Pentagon Papers, turned over to them by former Pentagon official Daniel Ellsberg. The Pentagon Papers created an outburst of criticism against the war with their detailed outline of the early stages of American involvement. Although the papers did not cover the policies of his administration, President Nixon was deeply angered, claiming that this was classified material that could undermine national security. The real problem was that the papers revealed the cynicism and deception that had long characterized American policy on Vietnam. For the first time in United States history, a presidential administration applied for an injunction against the newspapers to prevent the printing of further extracts. The attempt failed,

however; in New York Times Co. v. United States the Supreme Court ruled that the government had not shown sufficient justification for restraint of free expression, and publication continued.

The Supreme Court in the 1970s

During the 1960s the social activism of the Warren Court had antagonized many conservatives, including Richard Nixon. As president, Nixon sought to remedy what he viewed as the Court's leftist bias by adding "strict constructionists." When Earl Warren retired in 1969 the president appointed a conservative jurist, Warren Burger, to replace him as chief justice. When another seat became vacant, Nixon appointed three men before one was approved by the Senate. Nixon's first choice, Clement F. Haynesworth, Jr., of South Carolina, was rejected when a conflict of interest was revealed; and his second choice, G. Harrold Carswell of Florida, was rejected because of his mediocre record and his alleged racism. The president was infuriated but finally nominated a respected judge, Harry A. Blackmun of Minnesota, who was confirmed by the Senate in 1970. The following year justices Black and Harlan retired, and Nixon appointed two more conservative lawyers to the Court, William Rehnquist of Arizona and Lewis Powell of Virginia.

Although the new Supreme Court appointments were intended to make that body more conservative, the Court's ideological position proved difficult to pinpoint. Some of its early decisions in the field of criminal law chipped away at the absolute standard for the use of confessions established in the Escobedo and Miranda decisions. In Furman v. Georgia (1972), the Court ruled that the death penalty as it was currently applied was in violation of the Eighth Amendment, but it also held that the death penalty was not unconstitutional if applied uniformly.

The Court's decisions on cases concerning affirmative-action programs to eliminate racial discrimination in hiring also did not reveal a consistent philosophy. In a case alleging that seniority rules perpetuated discrimination against minorities in hiring, the Court held that seniority rules were not discriminatory under the terms of the 1964 Civil Rights Act. Then, in a complex "reverse-discrimination" case (University of California v. Bakke, 1978) the Court in a five-to-four decision affirmed the

GEORGE McGOVERN'S 1972 PRESIDENTIAL CAMPAIGN FALTERED SOON AFTER QUESTIONS AROSE CONCERNING THE MENTAL HEALTH OF HIS RUNNING MATE, THOMAS EAGLETON. AFTER HOLDING A PRESS CONFERENCE TO REITERATE HIS SUPPORT OF EAGLETON, McGOVERN ULTIMATELY DROPPED HIM FROM THE TICKET.

constitutionality of college-admissions programs that gave preference to minority applicants to help remedy past discrimination. At the same time the Court ruled that the plaintiff, Alan Bakke, had to be admitted to the University of California at Davis medical school on the grounds that the affirmative-action program at Davis was inflexibly biased against white applicants. While most black leaders regarded the decision as a retreat from affirmative action, they looked more favorably on a 1979 decision (*United Steelworkers of America* v. *Weber*) wherein the Court held that private employers could give preference to black workers in voluntary affirmative-action programs to eliminate "manifest racial imbalance" in jobs traditionally held by whites.

In other rulings the Court took steps toward narrowing the interpretation of the First Amendment guarantee of freedom of the press. In *Zurcher* v. *Stanford Daily* (1978) it sanctioned police searches of the files of news organizations if there was a "reasonable" belief that these files contained material that could be relevant in the investigation of a crime. In *Herbert* v. *Lando* (1979) the Court ruled that journalists defending their work against a libel suit could be required to disclose the opinions they held while preparing the material and their reasons for making specific news judgments. The Court also ruled in several cases that reporters had no constitutional right to protect the identity of their sources.

The Election of 1972

In 1972 a number of candidates vied for the Democratic presidential nomination. Although George Wallace made an impressive showing in the primaries and Hubert Humphrey eventually joined the contest, opposition to the Vietnam War helped consolidate support for Senator George McGovern of South Dakota. Recent Democratic party reforms that made it more difficult for party professionals to control the selection of candidates enabled McGovern to receive the nomination on the first ballot.

The Republican convention renominated Nixon and Agnew. The campaign was one-sided, with the Republicans leading two to one in the polls. Their "Southern strategy" of courting conservative Wallace supporters (Wallace dropped out of the contest after being crippled in an assassination attempt) drew many voters away from the Democrats. McGovern's troubles began immediately after he named Senator Thomas Eagleton of Missouri as his running mate. When it was disclosed that Eagleton had undergone electric-shock treatments during psychiatric therapy the ensuing publicity forced McGovern, after claiming to stand behind him

"1000 percent," to discard Eagleton and select R. Sargent Shriver, former head of the Peace Corps, to replace him. McGovern's campaign was seriously damaged by this incident. The widespread perception of him as a radical also harmed his chances. Finally, Henry Kissinger's announcement shortly before the election that "peace is at hand" in Vietnam robbed McGovern of his major campaign issue.

In an election that drew only 55 percent of eligible voters, President Nixon was reelected by a landslide, winning 61 percent of the popular vote and 521 of the 528 electoral votes. McGovern carried only one state, Massachusetts, and Washington, D.C. Nevertheless, the Democrats retained control of Congress.

Watergate

The Watergate Break-in

Early in the morning of June 17, 1972, five men equipped with cameras and electronic-surveillance devices were arrested after breaking into the Democratic National Committee headquarters in the Watergate apartment complex in Washington, D.C. It soon was discovered that the leader of the burglars, James McCord, was connected with the Committee to Reelect the President (CRP), a presidential campaign organization headed by former Attorney General Mitchell. This disclosure and the subsequent revelation of connections between the burglars and the CIA, the FBI, and presidential aides raised the question of White House involvement in the incident. At a press conference held late in August President Nixon vehemently denied this. "I can say categorically that the investigation indicates that no one in the White House staff, no one in this administration, presently employed, was involved in this bizarre incident," he announced.

The *Washington Post* Disclosures

On September 17, a federal grand jury returned an indictment against the Watergate burglars for conspiring to steal documents from and eavesdropping on the Democratic headquarters. Less than a month later the existence of a group of secret White House "plumbers" came to light. The plumbers unit had been established in 1971 after the release of the Pentagon Papers in an effort to "plug leaks" of sensitive information to the press. In addition to devising plans to install wiretaps on the telephones of prominent journalists and to infiltrate radical groups, the plumbers had burglarized the office of Daniel Ellsberg's psychiatrist in an effort to discover information that would damage Ellsberg's credibility. (A

government case against Ellsberg was dismissed in 1973 when the burglary was disclosed.) As the election of 1972 approached, the plumbers unit expanded its activities to include political "dirty tricks." The *Washington Post* revealed that the plumbers had been involved in forging damaging letters, disrupting campaign schedules, and searching for sensitive information on the private lives of Democratic candidates. In another story, the *Post* reported links between the Watergate episode, the "dirty-tricks" operation, and top Nixon aide H. R. Haldeman. Although McGovern angrily attacked the Nixon administration as "the most corrupt" in history, many voters believed his charges were politically motivated, and he won few votes in the 1972 election.

The Watergate Investigation

The trial of the Watergate defendants opened on January 8, 1973. In addition to the five burglars, two others had been indicted for their alleged involvement: former CIA agent E. Howard Hunt and one-time FBI agent and White House plumber, G. Gordon Liddy. The five burglars immediately pleaded guilty to conspiracy, burglary, and bugging, thus precluding any testimony. Only McCord and Liddy were left to stand trial, and they were quickly found guilty. One week later a Senate Select Committee under the chairmanship of North Carolina Democrat Sam Ervin was established to explore the Watergate affair further and to make recommendations for a new set of laws regulating political campaigns.

Following the trial, James McCord was initially the main source of information about the Watergate break-in. In a letter to Judge John J. Sirica he claimed that all the defendants had been under pressure to plead guilty and remain silent. He told the Ervin committee that highly placed government officials, including John Mitchell and White House counsel John W. Dean, III, knew of the wiretapping, bugging, and espionage operations.

Although the president promised to cooperate with the Senate Select Committee, he insisted that as a matter of "executive privilege" neither he nor his staff would be willing to testify. Reports of involvement by White House staffers continued, however, and by mid-April federal prosecutors believed that the White House was involved in a cover-up. Finally, when John Dean agreed to appear before the Ervin committee in return for immunity from prosecution, White House involvement was no longer a matter of serious doubt. On April 30 in a televised speech before the nation, President Nixon announced the resignations of H. R. Haldeman, John Ehrlichman, John Dean, and Attorney General Richard Kleindienst. He also repeated that he was personally unaware of the cover-up activities, and had learned of them only on March 21. The president appointed Massachusetts Republican Elliot Richardson as acting attorney general, and Richardson appointed Archibald Cox, a professor of law at Harvard, special Watergate prosecutor.

The Revelation of the Tapes

In the meantime, the Senate Select Committee began televised public hearings on May 17 which captivated audiences throughout most of the summer. In July the investigation took a dramatic new turn when presidential aide Alexander Butterfield revealed the existence of an electronic eavesdropping system in the White House which had been in place since February 1971 to record all presidential conversations. Both the Senate Select Committee and Special Prosecutor Cox immediately issued subpoenas for the tapes, believing that they would settle the question of presidential complicity once and for all. The president, however, refused access to the vital recordings, again claiming "executive privilege."

The Saturday Night Massacre

In August 1973 the ever-expanding web of scandal took in Vice-President Spiro Agnew, the advocate of law and order. Charged with having received payoffs and campaign donations for awarding state and federal contracts, Agnew at first denied the accusations. Then in October he pleaded "nolo contendere" ("I do not choose to contest") to the charge of falsifying his income-tax return in exchange for a dismissal of the more serious charges. Under the provisions of the Twenty-fifth Amendment (passed in 1967 to ensure smooth presidential and vice-presidential succession in the event of another catastrophe like the Kennedy assassination), the president named House Minority Leader Gerald Ford of Michigan as vice-president.

The Agnew resignation and the October war in the Middle East briefly distracted the nation's attention from the Watergate affair. In mid-October, however, one of the most controversial aspects of the entire Watergate episode returned the scandal to page one. Furious over Special Prosecutor Cox's continuing demand for the tape recordings, Nixon ordered Attorney General Richardson to fire him. Rather than do so, Richardson resigned, as did his deputy, William Ruckelshaus. Finally, Solicitor General Robert Bork, the next ranking official, carried out the presidential order. This incident was quickly dubbed the "Saturday Night Massacre." A fierce public outcry erupted and calls for the president's resignation appeared in the press. Faced with nationwide opposition, Nixon turned over the tapes. A well-known Texas lawyer, Leon Jaworski, was appointed to replace Cox.

The Road to Resignation

In December the House Judiciary Committee began an investigation to determine whether there was sufficient evidence to initiate impeachment proceedings. Among the issues considered were illegal campaign contributions, political-espionage activities, White House domestic surveillance, "dirty tricks" perpetrated by CRP, obstruction of justice through various "cover-up" schemes, and even alleged income-tax violations by the president himself. Despite the long list of corrupt and illegal practices, however, many members of Congress were reluctant to impeach the president. In April 1974 in an effort to secure direct evidence of Nixon's role in the cover-up, the House Judiciary Committee voted unanimously to subpoena forty-two more tapes of presidential conversations. Nixon countered by supplying the committee (and the public) with transcripts of a large number of tapes—none of which proved either his guilt or his innocence. The plot thickened, however, when it was discovered that key transcripts differed significantly from the original tapes in the committee's possession. Still the committee was divided over what constituted grounds for impeachment. Could a president be impeached for improper conduct in office or was it necessary to have specific evidence that he had committed a criminal act? Even without "the smoking gun" that would directly incriminate the president, the House Judiciary Committee, in a televised debate, voted three articles of impeachment in late

PRESIDENT NIXON EMBRACES HIS WEEPING DAUGHTER, JULIE, AFTER HIS RESIGNATION FROM OFFICE.

July. Nixon was charged with obstruction of justice, abuse of presidential powers, and contempt of Congress in willfully disobeying legally authorized subpoenas.

On August 5, after the Supreme Court ruled against Nixon's claim of executive privilege, three tapes were released proving his complicity in the Watergate cover-up from its inception. The tapes showed that Nixon had known about the cover-up since June 1972 and that he had actually ordered the use of the CIA to obstruct an FBI Watergate investigation. The president's remaining support in Congress evaporated. On August 9, 1974, in a nationally televised speech Richard Nixon became the first president in American history to resign from office.

What had destroyed the career of one of the ablest, shrewdest politicians in American history? Perhaps a partial answer may be found in the president's own words. The transcripts of the White House tapes showed him to be not the master of political events he appeared, but indecisive and unconcerned with the public welfare. In his public statements he called for a "new morality" and an end to divisiveness in the country, but the transcripts revealed him to be insecure and vindictive toward his political enemies as well as addicted to profane language. Most important, the tape of June 23, 1972, in which he ordered an end to the FBI investigation of the break-in clearly had exposed his complicity in the cover-up of the scandal. Through hard work and persistent effort Richard Nixon had risen from modest circumstances to the nation's highest public office, a classic example of the fulfillment of the American dream. Yet, having attained the pinnacle of political success, Nixon's ruthless attempts to keep the power he had gained regardless of the means destroyed his career and the careers of many of his closest associates.

Watergate Assessed

Although Nixon's resignation left many questions unanswered, it did spare the nation the agony of a House debate on impeachment and the possibility of a Senate trial followed by the imprisonment of a president. Most Americans were relieved that the long nightmare was finally at an end and that the American system of government had proved itself capable of weathering such a crisis and continuing to function.

The fact that more than forty members of the administration were criminally prosecuted, including two cabinet officers and twelve members of the White House staff, demonstrated the pervasiveness of corruption in the Nixon administration. Many believed that Watergate reflected a serious decline in the system of values prevailing in contemporary American politics. The president and the people with whom he surrounded himself had perceived of themselves as above the law that they so vociferously insisted the rest of the nation observe. The revelation of their total lack of ethics fed popular cynicism about the workings of government and politics.

After Watergate Congress finally took steps to reassert its constitutional authority and correct the imbalance between the branches of government. Legislation was enacted to limit the ability of the president to impound funds and to bring about partial federal financing of presidential campaign funding as well as limiting the amount of private contributions to an individual campaign. In 1975–1976 congressional investigations of the FBI and the CIA revealed that there had been extensive illegal activities performed by both agencies which produced demands for a curb on their powers. The states responded to increased public demand for government accountability by passing "sunshine laws" which would end the secrecy surrounding official decision-making.

Ford's Succession

Although he assumed the presidency in the wake of the worst political scandal in American history, Gerald Ford began his term in office with a high measure of public support. A representative from the state of Michigan for many years, Ford was an experienced, if undistinguished, political conservative with a genial, open temperament and a refreshing modesty. Soon after his succession, Ford named as his vice-president Governor Nelson Rockefeller of New York. For the first time in American history the offices of the president and vice-president were filled by men who had not been elected by the people. Although the country's initial response to the new president was quite positive, two of his early decisions badly eroded public confidence. One was his pardoning of Richard Nixon, who had gone into virtual seclusion since his resignation. Apparently motivated by awareness of Nixon's fragile physical condition (he had been suffering from phlebitis), and fearing the divisive effect of a public trial, President Ford granted the former president complete immunity from prosecution for any activities relating to Watergate. Ford's second controversial decision was his announcement of a program of conditional amnesty for draft evaders who had fled the country during the Vietnam War.

Public reaction to both of these steps was mixed. Although some people looked on the pardon as a positive step that would help to avoid further anguish over Watergate, many others felt that Nixon should have received the same treatment as the others who had been prosecuted for their participation in the affair. As for the amnesty program, some critics believed that the draft evaders had done nothing wrong in refusing to fight in the war and that the amnesty should not be conditional on performing two years of alternative government service. Others who had fought in the war or had lost a loved one in Vietnam were angered that those who had fled should be welcomed back.

Foreign Policy

Although President Ford made some changes in his cabinet, Henry Kissinger agreed to stay on as secretary of state. In the wake of the Communist takeover of South Vietnam, the administration sought to reassure America's allies that the United States would continue to support them. In May 1975 Communists seized an unarmed American cargo vessel, the *Mayagüez*. President Ford bypassed diplomacy and promptly sent a military force to rescue the small crew. Although this action was widely acclaimed at the time as a positive reassertion of America's will to defend its interests, critics viewed it as an overreaction against a small and weak country which resulted in unnecessary loss of American lives. To accomplish the rescue, American marines landed on an island off the Cambodian coast, American warships sank Cambodian gunboats, and American bombers struck an air base on the mainland.

Ford and Kissinger continued to pursue the policy of détente with the Soviet Union. Thirty-five countries, including Russia and the United States, signed an accord in Helsinki, Finland, on August 1, 1975, in which the two nations recognized the equality of states; agreed to find peaceful means for settling disputes; and endorsed human rights, international cooperation, and a freer exchange of peoples and ideas. While the ideals stated in the Helsinki Accord sounded appealing, they were mere platitudes impossible to enforce.

In spite of administration efforts, the policy of détente with Russia was in trouble at home and abroad. In 1974 the two countries had agreed that each side could build up to a maximum of 2400 strategic missiles and bombers. However, within a year negotiations for a new SALT agreement (SALT–II) deadlocked over whether to include the Soviet backfire bomber and the American cruise missile. The Soviets also made it clear that détente would not be allowed to interfere with their efforts to spread Marxism; nor would they permit open discussion of Western ideas in Russia. In the United States conservatives argued that the expansion of Soviet military power belied any real interest in relaxing tensions with America. They called for increased defense appropriations to meet the challenge. At the same time, liberals in Congress attacked Soviet suppression of human rights.

The Soviets made good their intention to expand their influence by aiding a leftist faction in a civil war in Angola. The administration requested funds to help the other side, but Congress, in no mood to support intervention abroad, refused. Now Kissinger turned his attention to a broader effort to aid developing nations and to combat Communist expansion in the whole of southern Africa. He promoted the establishment of a $1 billion International Resources Bank to assist development in poor countries and reduction of tariff barriers against their commodities. He also firmly committed the United States to the principle of black majority rule in southern Africa.

Economic Problems

President Ford spent much of his first year in office wrestling with the nation's economic woes. The problem of inflation had been compounded in late 1973 by the Arab boycott and the related staggering increase in the price of raw petroleum. The high cost of petroleum affected many other critical mate-

rials, and in 1974 the economy was suffering from an inflation rate of 12 percent a year.

Seeking a remedy, Ford asked Congress to reduce government spending and government regulation and enact a tax cut. But unemployment rose, and in the fall of 1974 the economy plunged into the steepest recession since the Great Depression. Responding to public demands, the Democratic-controlled Congress passed bills to increase government spending on agriculture, housing, education, health, and public works. These new measures in turn were vetoed by the president. Congress also refused to support Ford's plan to cut energy consumption by lifting controls from domestic oil prices. Instead, it moved to reduce the price of crude oil. Although many groups in the country were critical of Ford's efforts to return to a laissez-faire economic policy, by early 1976 the inflation rate had been cut in half. Even so, during 1976 economic growth slowed and unemployment remained high.

The Election of 1976

More than a year before the 1976 election, President Ford announced that he would seek to retain the presidency. Successfully countering a formidable challenge by the conservative ex-governor of California, Ronald Reagan, Ford finally secured the nomination by only fifty-seven votes. The president sought to accommodate the Reagan faction by choosing Senator Robert Dole of Kansas, a conservative, as his running mate.

On the Democratic side, the race for the nomination was won by a former governor of Georgia, Jimmy Carter. Although relatively unknown to voters, Carter took an early lead in the primaries, gradually building support throughout the country. He stressed that as an outsider who had never been part of the Washington power structure, he could restore honesty and efficiency to government. This strategy had widespread appeal and Carter was nominated without challenge at the convention. He chose Senator Walter Mondale of Minnesota, a highly respected liberal, as his vice-presidential running mate.

The campaign centered more on personalities than on issues. Because of a new law limiting campaign spending, both parties turned increasingly to television to reach the widest audience. For the first time since 1960, the candidates debated each other

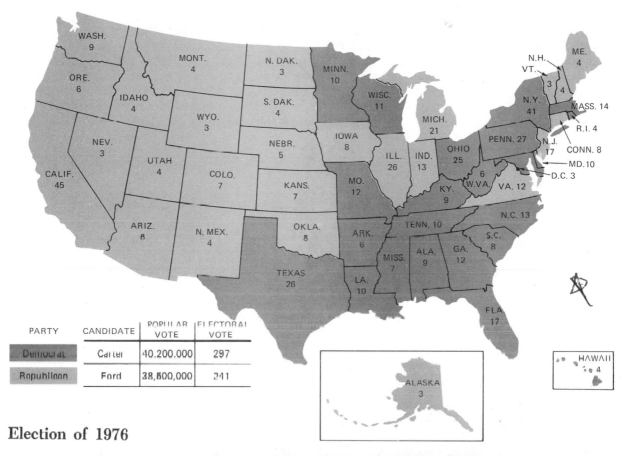

PARTY	CANDIDATE	POPULAR VOTE	ELECTORAL VOTE
Democrat	Carter	40,200,000	297
Republican	Ford	38,600,000	241

Election of 1976

GERALD FORD CAMPAIGNING WITH HIS
SONS DURING THE 1976 PRESIDENTIAL
RACE. FORD LOST BY A VERY NARROW
MARGIN.

on television. Although the debates produced no clear-cut advantage for either man, Ford gradually pulled up from behind in the polls until the race was considered a draw. In the closest presidential election in sixty years, Carter won with 51 percent of the popular vote and only a fifty-six-vote margin in the electoral college.

The American people could look back on the Ford presidency as a two-year period during which the executive had restored a sense of dignity and honesty to the nation's highest office. Ford's openness had helped renew the public trust in the political process. In attempting to deal with recession and inflation at the same time, he was only partially successful; but his administration did cut inflation, and the economy was healthier when he left office than when he entered it.

Readings

General Works

Bell, Daniel, *The Coming of Post-Industrial Society: A Venture in Social Forecasting.* New York: Basic, 1973.

Brandon, Henry, *The Retreat of American Power.* New York: Dell, 1974.

Evans, Rowland, Jr., and Robert D. Novak, *Nixon in the White House: The Frustration of Power.* New York: Random, 1971.

Hodgson, Godfrey, *America In Our Time.* New York: Vintage, 1976.

Osgood, Robert E., *et al., Retreat from Empire? The First Nixon Administration.* Baltimore: John Hopkins, 1973.

Safire, William, *Before the Fall: An Inside View of the Pre-Watergate White House.* Garden City, N.Y.: Doubleday, 1975.

Schell, Jonathan, *The Time of Illusion.* New York: Knopf, 1976.

Szulc, Tad, *The Illusion of Peace.* New York: Viking, 1978.

Special Studies

Cline, Ray S., *Secrets, Spies, and Scholars: Blueprint of the Essential CIA.* Washington, D.C.: Acropolis, 1976.

Funston, Richard Y., *Constitutional Counter-Revolution: The Warren Court and the Burger Court.* Cambridge, Mass.: Schenkman, 1977.

Friedland, Edward, Paul Seabury, and Aaron Wildavsy, *The Great Détente Disaster: Oil and the Decline of American Foreign Policy.* New York: Basic, 1975.

Kurland, Philip B., *Watergate and the Constitution.* Chicago: University of Chicago Press, 1978.

Lake, Anthony (Ed.), *The Vietnam Legacy.* New York: New York University Press, 1976.

Landau, David, *Kissinger: The Uses of Power.* New York: Apollo Editions, 1974. (Paper)

Marchetti, Victor, and John D. Marks, *The CIA and the Cult of Intelligence.* New York: Knopf, 1974.

Quant, William B., *Decade of Decisions: American Policy Toward the Arab-Israeli Conflict, 1967–1976.* Berkeley: University of California Press, 1977.

Rather, Dan, and Gary Gates, *The Palace Guard.* Boston: Harper & Row, 1974.

Reeves, Richard, *Convention.* New York: Harcourt, Brace, 1977.

Scheer, Robert, *America After Nixon: The Age of the Multinationals.* New York: McGraw-Hill, 1975. (Paper)

White, Theodore H., *Breach of Faith: The Fall of Richard Nixon.* New York: Atheneum, 1975.

_____, *The Making of the President, 1968.* New York: Atheneum, 1969.

Woodward, Bob, and Carl Bernstein, *All the President's Men.* New York: Simon & Schuster, 1974.

_____, *The Final Days.* New York: Simon & Schuster, 1976.

Primary Sources

Ford, Gerald R., *A Time To Heal.* New York: Harper & Row, 1979.

Kissinger, Henry, *White House Years.* Boston: Little, Brown, 1979.

New York Times, The End of a Presidency. New York: Bantam, 1974.

_____, *Watergate Hearings: Break-in and Cover-up.* New York: Bantam, 1973.

_____, *White House Transcripts: The Full Text of the Submission of Recorded Presidential Conversations to the Committee on the Judiciary of the*

House of Representatives by President Richard Nixon. New York: Viking Press, 1974.

Nixon, Richard, *RN: The Memoirs of Richard Nixon.* New York: Grosset & Dunlap, 1978.

Biography

Anson, Robert, and Sam Anson, *McGovern: A Political Biography.* New York: Holt, Rinehart & Winston, 1972.

Morris, Roger, *Uncertain Greatness: Henry Kissinger and American Foreign Policy.* New York: Harper & Row, 1977.

ter Horst, J. F., *Gerald Ford: Past . . . Present . . . Future.* New York: Third Press, 1974.

Willis, Garry, *Nixon Agonistes: The Crisis of the Self-made Man.* Boston: Houghton Mifflin, 1970.

32 America Enters Its Third Century

David Ryan, *The Boston Globe*

America no longer seems diverse so much as it seems split asunder into innumerable special interests. We read daily of gray power, gay power, red power, black power; Sun Belt and Frost Belt; environmentalists and hardhats; industrial groups, professional groups, educational groups. . . . When so many groups organize to protect their special interests, the politics of activism can become a politics of immobility, and we find ourselves unable to reach effective solutions for inflation, energy shortages, environmental issues, or other national problems. . . . Today, we still need specialized skills, but we now have an even greater need for able people who are not only expert in their chosen field but capable of helping different parts of the society to coexist more harmoniously, to work together in pursuit of common goals. . . .

Derek Bok, 1979
President of Harvard University

Significant Events

National Organization for Women (NOW) organized [1966]

Environmental Protection Agency [1971]

Consumer Product Safety Act [1972]

Panama Canal treaties [1977]

Camp David agreements between Israel and Egypt [September 1978]

United States establishes diplomatic relations with China [January 1979]

Nuclear accident at Three Mile Island power plant [March 1979]

Strategic Arms Limitation agreement (SALT-II) with Soviet Union [June 1979]

American embassy seized and hostages taken in Iran [November 1979]

A TANK-TRAILER DRIVER FOR THE EXXON CORPORATION DOES HIS BIT TO CONSERVE GASOLINE BY BICYCLING TO AND FROM WORK EVERY DAY—ABOUT TEN MILES ROUND TRIP.

Americans celebrated the bicentennial of their independence in 1976 with enthusiasm and immense good humor. Expressions of patriotism and national pride took the form of pageants, parades, fireworks, and even an awesome display of sailing vessels from all over the world in New York harbor on the fourth of July. Although beset with complex domestic and diplomatic challenges, over 215 million Americans from a variety of economic, ethnic, and racial backgrounds seemed for a short time to be united in reaffirming their past ideals before preparing to step into an uncertain future.

A Demographic Profile

As the United States entered its third century, the composition of the population was undergoing important changes. During the 1960s the largest population group was made up of teenagers and young adults in their twenties, born during the baby boom of the 1940s and 1950s. By the 1970s, however, this age group was growing much more slowly. The fer-

tility rate had declined to fewer than two children per couple, in part because more women were working and delaying marriage and in part because the availability of the birth-control pill gave couples a simpler means of controlling the size of their families. At the same time better diets and improved medical care were increasing people's life expectancy.

The mobility of Americans was as pronounced as ever, with the trend being a movement from the Northern and Eastern states to the "Sunbelt"—the South and Southwest region from Virginia to California. This area was growing almost 50 percent more rapidly than the rest of the country, and California replaced New York as the nation's most populous state. With their abundant raw materials, energy resources, and temperate climate, the Sunbelt states were very attractive to businesses as well as individuals. As the population of the Sunbelt grew its influence in national politics increased as well.

The shift of population from the cities to the suburbs and even to the countryside continued. By

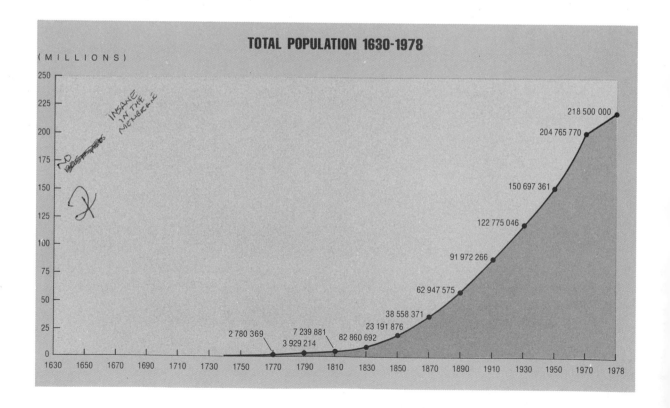

TOTAL POPULATION 1630-1978

(MILLIONS)

2 780 369
3 929 214
7 239 881
82 860 692
23 191 876
38 558 371
62 947 575
91 972 266
122 775 046
150 697 361
204 765 770
218 500 000

the 1970s more Americans lived in the suburbs than in urban centers, and suburban areas developed more diversity of population and took on to some degree the problems of the urban centers. The big cities, like New York, Los Angeles, Chicago, and Detroit, continued to be troubled by poverty and crime, the deterioration of public services, racial tensions, inferior educational facilities, drug addiction, and loss of community spirit. To compound these problems, many people who worked in the urban centers and enjoyed the cultural advantages available there lived in the suburbs and therefore made no financial contribution to the city's support. As people moved away from the cities, the tax base needed to finance efforts to solve urban problems contracted, and several metropolitan areas found themselves nearly bankrupt.

Dissenting Voices

TENNIS CHAMPION BILLIE JEAN KING AND SEVERAL COMRADES HOLD UP THE INTERNATIONAL WOMEN'S YEAR TORCH, WHICH HAD BEEN CARRIED BY SOME TWO THOUSAND RUNNERS FROM NEW YORK TO TEXAS IN CELEBRATION OF THE NATIONAL WOMEN'S CONFERENCE AT HOUSTON.

The Women's Movement

The tremendous outburst of protest which characterized the 1960s influenced the rise of new social movements. The struggle of black Americans in particular brought a growing realization by other ethnic and social groups that they, too, were being denied opportunities to participate fully in American economic and cultural life.

The social movement with perhaps the most far-reaching implications for American society as a whole was the women's movement. The early feminists had had some success in their drive to expand the legal rights of women, most notably in securing the right to vote. Nevertheless, although the suffragists had encouraged women to pursue a career, most professions remained the sole province of men and the social pressure on women to marry and raise a family remained as strong as ever.

In the 1940s this situation began to change. With many men serving in the armed forces, women filled their places in factories and offices. During the 1950s the trend was reversed, and growing economic prosperity was accompanied by a renewed emphasis on woman's role as wife and mother.

An important catalyst for the emergence in the 1960s of a new women's movement was the publication in 1963 of Betty Friedan's landmark book *The Feminine Mystique*. Friedan argued that women were being victimized by a sentimental and false perception on the part of men that woman's happiness lay only in the roles of wife and mother. Friedan's thesis was seized upon eagerly by educated women whose own efforts to seek opportunities outside these roles were being frustrated by the male-dominated society. Although in 1970 women comprised 51 percent of the population, fewer than 10 percent of the professional positions—university professors, doctors, and lawyers—were held by women. Women working in the civil rights and antiwar movements were infuriated that even there they were expected to play second fiddle to their male colleagues. In an effort to gain equal treatment, women activists picketed meetings of professional associations and demonstrated against large corporations, demanding equal pay for equal work. They forced their way into all-male clubs and stormed many other traditionally male bastions, challenging the notion that women could still be treated as second-class citizens.

From small "consciousness-raising" groups where women met to voice their frustrations and aspirations there developed organizations aimed at promoting women's issues. The most prominent of these, the National Organization for Women (NOW), was formed in 1966 and within a ten-year period had attracted sixty thousand members and many more sympathizers. The organization, which welcomed men as well as women into its membership, focused primarily on economic and social issues, including equal pay for equal work, the right to work in any job including traditionally all-male jobs, the right to birth control and abortion, passage of an equal rights amendment, freedom from sexual harassment on the job, and day-care for children.

The women's movement won notable victories in the legislative arena. The Civil Rights Act of 1964 prohibited sexual discrimination by employers; "affirmative-action" programs were set up under a 1965 executive order to ensure that more women and minorities would be hired in companies doing business with the federal government; and credit barriers that had made it difficult for women to achieve economic independence were eliminated.

The Supreme Court was less consistent in cases affecting women. On the one hand, the Court ruled that a woman could not be denied a job because she had small children, that women must receive equal pay for equal work, and that women could not be forced to retire at an earlier age than men. On the other hand, whereas the Court in 1973 upheld the right of women to obtain abortions, later decisions provided that states could deny medicaid payments for abortions and that states could refuse to perform abortions in publicly owned hospitals. The effect of these rulings was to undermine the ability of poor women to obtain safe abortions.

The civil rights movement had shown that equal participation in American society required political clout. Efforts to increase women's representation in politics gained impetus from the formation of the National Women's Political Caucus (NWPC) in 1971. By 1979 support by NWPC and NOW had helped elect women to various state offices: two women had become governor (Ella Grasso of Connecticut and Dixie Lee Ray of Washington) sixteen women were serving in the House of Representatives, and one was serving in the Senate (Nancy Kassebaum of Kansas). In addition, two women, Juanita Kreps and Patricia Roberts Harris, were appointed to President Carter's cabinet.

In 1972 Congress passed the Equal Rights Amendment (ERA) to the Constitution. First submitted in 1923, it stated simply that "equality of rights under the law shall not be denied or abridged by the United States or any state on account of sex." Its advocates believed that the amendment would help protect the legal gains already won by women as well as provide the legal basis for overturning the discriminatory laws that remained on the books. By mid-1979 the amendment needed ratification by only three more states to become the Twenty-seventh Amendment to the Constitution. Difficulties arose, however; the drive for ratification encountered a severe backlash of conservative opposition, particularly among women who believed that it threatened women's traditional role in American society. Although in 1979 Congress passed a three-year extension of the time period during which the amendment must be approved, opponents of the ERA had succeeded in slowing the drive for its ratification and casting doubt on its future.

Economic circumstances in the late 1970s brought a new focus to the women's movement. Whereas in the past many married women had worked to supplement the family income, now they were working to maintain, not improve, the family's standard of living. In 1970 43 percent of adult American women worked outside the home. By 1980 the figure had risen to 51 percent. In addition, 43 percent of married mothers with children under six were working outside the home. With working wives outnumbering housewives, the need for day-care and support systems to aid working mothers became a significant women's issue. "The agenda for the '80s," wrote Betty Friedan, "must be the restructuring of the institutions of home and work."

Black Americans

Although the murder of Martin Luther King, Jr., in 1968 unleashed a convulsion of black rage expressed in riots across the country, it was to be the last such outburst for over a decade. The civil rights movement had resulted in significant legislative gains for blacks, and life for many had improved noticeably. Between 1960 and 1970 the number of blacks in white-collar jobs rose from 16 percent to 28 percent. More blacks were entering the middle class, more were moving to the suburbs, and by 1974 almost one-fifth of black youngsters of college age were attending college. In addition, opportunities were opening up in the entertainment industry for black performers, and while this development affected only a tiny proportion of blacks, it had a beneficial effect in making black Americans visible as real human beings.

During the 1970s blacks clearly made their greatest gains in the political arena. After the passage of the Voting Rights Act of 1965 blacks began going to the polls in much larger numbers than in the past. Indeed, the black vote was crucial in the election of Jimmy Carter in 1976. By that year there were eighteen blacks in Congress, several hundred blacks in the state legislatures, and black mayors in a number of major cities, including Los Angeles, Atlanta, and Washington, D.C.

This progress, however, was undercut by the nation's growing economic difficulties. As the economy faltered, so did efforts to help the black poor. Without seniority in many union jobs, blacks suffered from the old problem of "last hired, first fired." The gap between whites and blacks in income, which had begun to close during the 1960s, began to expand again. In 1971 the median family income of blacks was about 63 percent of the income of whites; by 1977, it had dropped to 59 percent.

The black middle class was the exception to this trend. Although small, it was expanding to include well-paid blue-collar workers and middle-level managers as well as people in the professions. Well-educated black women were particularly in demand by employers as a result of affirmative-action programs. The percentage of blacks earning $25,000 to $50,000 a year more than doubled during the 1970s. One side effect was that the economic gains of the black middle class increased the differences in political and economic outlook between them and lower

class blacks. Black Americans in general faced an unemployment rate twice that of whites. It was alarmingly high among black youths, even those with more education than their white counterparts. In the late 1970s more than one young black person in three was unemployed, as opposed to about one in seven among whites. One cause of this problem was thought to be the swelling numbers of aliens and women who were competing for the low-paid, unskilled jobs once held by blacks. By the end of the decade it was becoming painfully apparent that the growing despair of young jobless blacks was threatening to create an entire generation of angry, dispossessed Americans.

Education remained a focal point for black activists in the 1970s. Since 1954 blacks had advocated integration of the nation's public schools as an important avenue toward racial equality. But after twenty-five years desegregation still had a long way to go. Gains were greatest in the South where by 1979 88 percent of black children were attending integrated schools. In the North, however, the number was under 70 percent.

Busing children to schools outside their neighborhoods became one of the most important and controversial methods of achieving school desegregation. Although busing seemed to work well in some communities, some urban centers such as Boston, with its tightly knit ethnic communities, adamantly resisted it. In all sections of the country, many white parents resented having to send their children to distant schools that they believed were of questionable safety and quality. Likewise, many black parents believed that the benefits to be derived from enrolling their children in schools integrated by forced busing were not worth the negative psychological effects that their children would suffer.

Widespread public resistance to busing caused educators to reassess its usefulness. Some experts claimed that mandatory busing was contributing to white flight to the suburbs, thereby leaving all-black inner-city schools to be supported by a shrinking tax base. Others began questioning the notion that the educational achievement of lower-class black children would improve if they attended schools with middle-class white children. It seemed clear that busing, while at times a useful instrument, was not the ultimate solution to the problem of achieving equal educational opportunity.

American Indians

The Dawes Act of 1887 established the policy of breaking up the reservations by dividing the land into individual farms of 160 acres, but most Indians preferred to stay on the reservations in order to maintain a tribal way of life. By staying on the reservations, however, they were subjected to the whims of frequently incompetent government administrators and denied the rights of citizenship which the act had promised to them. As a result, most Indians lived in conditions of hopeless poverty and many were illiterate and malnourished. Not surprisingly, the rates of alcoholism and suicide began to climb.

During the 1920s the situation slowly began to improve as Herbert Hoover took steps to redress some long-standing abuses. The management of the Indian Bureau was improved and funds were allocated for better educational facilities and agricultural assistance. Indians also were granted full rights as citizens in 1924. Under Franklin Roosevelt the government policy of "assimilation" through the breakup of tribal lands was reversed. The Indian Reorganization Act of 1934 provided for the revitalization of the tribal system as the basis for developing a renewed sense of community and self-government among the Indian people.

Such forward-looking policies were threatened, however, after World War II. The economic growth that accompanied the war helped farmers, cattle raisers, and lumber interests to expand their activities. As a result, these groups began casting a covetous eye on the remaining tribal lands. They lobbied Congress to adopt a policy of "termination" which would dismantle the reservations and the tribal system and end government services to the Indians. Although the government during the Eisenhower years moved toward termination by making available for sale over one and a half million acres of Indian land, the Kennedy, Johnson, and Nixon administrations firmly opposed termination. In 1970 President Nixon called for a policy of "self-determination without termination" whereby Congress would continue extending aid to native Americans while at the same time complying with Indian insistence that they supervise the administration of the aid themselves. To ensure that Indians would indeed be in charge of their own affairs, the president saw to it that the Indian Bureau would be made up predominantly of Indians.

Meanwhile, as the Indians were deprived of their lands during the 1950s, thousands of them were forced to move to the cities. By the 1960s some 40 percent of American Indians were urbanites. In 1968 militant young urban Indians, many of whom

INDIANS GATHER IN FRONT OF THE MAIN CELL BLOCK OF ALCATRAZ PRISON. YOUNG MILITANTS SEIZED THE ISLAND TO CALL ATTENTION TO PAST INJUSTICES AGAINST THE INDIAN PEOPLE.

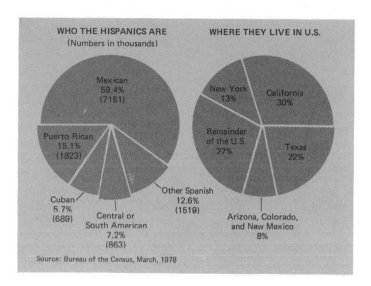

WHO THE HISPANICS ARE
(Numbers in thousands)

Mexican
59.4%
(7151)

Puerto Rican
15.1%
(1823)

Cuban
5.7%
(689)

Central or
South American
7.2%
(863)

Other Spanish
12.6%
(1519)

WHERE THEY LIVE IN U.S.

New York
13%

California
30%

Remainder
of the U.S.
27%

Texas
22%

Arizona, Colorado,
and New Mexico
8%

Source: Bureau of the Census, March, 1978

had been influenced by the black civil rights movement, formed the American Indian Movement (AIM) to promote Indian nationalism. Not satisfied with simply controlling their own reservations, and critical of the established Indian leadership, members of AIM called for a return of all ancestral lands and a revival of native American culture. In 1969 a group of Indian militants took over Alcatraz Island in San Francisco Bay, claiming that it should be returned to them in compensation for past white injustices. The publicity engendered by this incident resulted in more occupations of federal property, including the Bureau of Indian Affairs building in Washington, D.C., in 1972. The movement took a violent turn with the occupation of Wounded Knee village in South Dakota, the site of an 1890 army massacre of almost three hundred Dakota Sioux. The occupation, which lasted from March to May 1973, resulted in tremendous destruction of property and cost AIM the support of moderate Indians as well as the federal government.

Despite the harm done by Indian militants, by the late 1970s the Indian movement had achieved some significant victories on the legal front. The Narragansetts won a land-claims case in Rhode Island, as did the Sioux in North Dakota. Other favorable federal court rulings increased Indian control over taxation and administration of justice on tribal lands. Moreover, a number of cases involving water and mineral rights were under litigation. All these cases reasserted the concept embodied in old treaties with the United States that American Indians constituted a separate nation within a nation with dual citizenship and special rights.

Hispanic Americans

The fastest growing minority in the United States during the 1970s was the diverse group known as Hispanic-Americans. The March 1978 census report estimated that there were over twelve million Hispanics in the United States. Add to this the estimated eight to twelve million illegal aliens (or "undocumented," as they prefer to be described), and the total reached 10–12 percent of the American population. Almost 60 percent were Mexican, 15 percent were Puerto Rican, and 6 percent were Cuban. The remainder came from Central and South America or were of other Spanish origin.

Until the 1960s the Hispanic ethnic group was a "sleeping giant." Their rapidly growing numbers (one million Hispanics a year emigrate to the United States) and the example of other activist minorities roused them to action, however. Mexican-Americans in particular began to organize to improve their position in American society.

Chicanos People of Spanish origin had lived in New Mexico since the late sixteenth century, and Mexican settlement of Texas and California had begun in earnest when Mexico became independent of Spain. In the early twentieth century Mexican laborers crossed the border in large numbers to meet the need for agricultural workers. El Paso, Texas, became a way-station for these seasonal laborers. So convenient was this source of labor that when immigration from Europe and Asia was restricted in 1924, Latin Americans as a group were exempt. During the depression of the 1930s, however, the pendulum swung in the opposite direction and the United States government pressured Mexican-Americans and their American-born children to return to Mexico. Nearly one-third of the Mexican-American population was thus "removed."

During World War II another shift occurred as improved economic conditions again created a need for seasonal farm workers. A program administered jointly by the United States Department of Agriculture and the Mexican government was established to recruit temporary laborers who would come to the United States for seasonal employment, returning home when their tasks were completed. Between 1942 and 1964 some five million *braceros* (seasonal workers) were employed in the American Southwest. Although the *bracero* program had promised migrant workers suitable living conditions, adequate wages, and a minimum number of working days each season, they were in fact badly exploited, paid very low wages, and forced to live in shacks.

In an effort to improve economic conditions for Mexican-American workers, César Chávez formed the United Farm Workers Organizing Committee in 1962. Chávez, like Martin Luther King, was an advocate of nonviolent action. His major tactic, the strike, proved to be a powerful tool. Chávez's activities on behalf of California grape workers attracted the support of students, civil rights workers, religious leaders, and even Robert Kennedy. By 1968 Chávez's effort to organize a nationwide boycott of table grapes had succeeded, and in 1970 his union, the United Farm Workers (UFW), signed a three-year contract with table-grape growers. After additional years of conflict with the Teamsters Union over jurisdiction over farm workers, Chávez worked out an agreement with the Teamsters in 1977 which gave his union the right to organize field workers. By 1978 the UFW had concluded over one hundred contracts with growers.

Mexican-American activism was by no means confined to the rural communities. More and more

Mexican-Americans were becoming urban dwellers, and the young people among them were growing increasingly dissatisfied with their second-class status. This emerging generation of activists adopted a new term to emphasize their burgeoning cultural pride: "Chicano." Whereas the older leadership had worked toward assimilation through integrating schools in California and Texas, the Chicano movement of the late 1960s had a different purpose. Seeking to emphasize rather than to submerge their unique cultural identity, they demanded bilingual and bicultural education. Although Congress responded in 1968 by passing a bill providing for bilingual education, its original intent was to help non–English-speaking youngsters join the mainstream. As time passed such educational programs became a divisive issue across the country. While many non-Hispanics came to view the programs as delaying or even preventing assimilation, Hispanics by and large regarded any attempt to deny them bilingual education as an expression of racial prejudice.

In the early 1970s Chicanos began entering the political arena. In 1972 José Angel Gutiérrez helped to establish a national political party, *La Raza Unida*. After the party had won a few local elections in Texas, more Spanish-speaking citizens became politically active, even winning the governorships of Arizona and New Mexico and gaining a congressional seat in New York. In 1975 the Voting Rights Act of 1965 was extended to provide bilingual voting procedures in states that had large non–English-speaking populations.

Another important concern for Hispanics and non-Hispanics alike was the massive influx of illegal aliens, mostly from Mexico. The arrest and deportation of hundreds of thousands of Mexicans seeking to escape poverty in their native country created tensions with the United States' neighbor to the south. While some Americans complained that undocumented workers were displacing native-born workers, there was no hard evidence that this was happening. For the most part the newcomers worked at menial jobs that were abhorrent to a majority of Americans. Moreover, the argument that they were receiving welfare benefits was generally unsupported. Although the Carter administration proposed to grant amnesty to illegal aliens who had been in the United States since 1970, Congress failed to act on the proposal. In Texas a sensitive issue was

THE INFLUX OF CUBANS INTO MIAMI, FLORIDA, DURING THE 1960s REVITALIZED THE CITY'S SAGGING ECONOMY AND MADE IT A CENTER FOR CONDUCTING BUSINESS WITH LATIN AMERICA.

the acceptance of the children of undocumented workers in public schools. Local authorities ruled against it and took steps to enforce their ruling.

Puerto Ricans Puerto Ricans, as natives of a territory of the United States, have been American citizens since 1917. At the end of World War II they began emigrating in sizable numbers, until in 1978 Puerto Ricans on the American mainland numbered 1.8 million. The vast majority settled in New York City, although in recent years they have begun moving out over the Northeast.

Puerto Ricans encountered many of the same problems as blacks; discrimination on the basis of color (80 percent of Puerto Ricans are black), poverty, illiteracy, and high rates of unemployment. In addition, they came into political and cultural conflict not only with whites but with blacks as well. As economic conditions worsened during the 1970s, many Puerto Ricans began returning to Puerto Rico. Unfortunately, they found an economy there that was even worse.

A long-standing issue in the Puerto Rican community concerned independence from the United States. Although the majority appeared to prefer retaining their commonwealth status, a militant minority pushed for autonomy. In 1950 armed Puerto Rican nationalists gained entrance to the House of Representatives in Washington, wounding some members of Congress before being apprehended. In more recent years a small band of Puerto Rican terrorists has claimed responsibility for violent incidents aimed at forcing independence.

Cubans The experience of Cuban-Americans differed sharply from that of Chicanos and Puerto Ricans. Unlike these immigrant groups, who had come to the United States to escape poverty, the Cubans were political refugees fleeing the economic disruptions and political repression of the Castro regime in Cuba. The first exodus to Florida in the early 1960s was dominated by the upper layers of old Cuban society—supporters of Fulgencio Batista before the revolution, business leaders ousted by

Castro's takeover of industry, and upper-middle-class professionals whose livelihoods were threatened by communism. Later less affluent (although not poor) Cubans arrived: farmers, fishermen, industrial workers, and the like.

Non-Hispanics at first viewed this migration with alarm. The influx of Spanish-speaking Cubans threatened to overwhelm Miami's then-depressed economy. Blacks and union members feared the new competition for their jobs, and schools were ill-prepared to cope with children who could not speak English. To a great degree these fears proved unfounded. In the short period of only two decades the newcomers succeeded in transforming Miami into a thriving year-round city as opposed to a vacation town with a precarious seasonal economy. Still, blacks were displaced from many jobs in the hotel and other tourist industries, and this expe-

rience produced increasing tension toward the end of the decade.

The economic success of the Cubans was influenced by several factors. For one thing, the Cuban immigrants were largely middle class and well educated. In addition, 80 percent of them were white, which did much to reduce overt discrimination. Equally significant, the Cubans arrived in the United States ready to fight for economic gains by their own efforts rather than becoming dependent on charity and welfare. Yet the Cuban success story did not extend to all segments of their community. Elderly Cubans who could not speak English found loneliness and housing problems increasingly difficult to resolve. Many young people experienced adjustment problems and began dropping out of school: in the late 1970s the dropout rate for Miami's Cuban high school students exceeded that of blacks.

New Directions

A Permissive Society

The explosive events of the 1960s had a profound influence on the changing direction of American society. The demands of the civil rights and the women's liberation movements for a more egalitarian society and the hedonistic life-style of the counterculture changed the outlook of millions of Americans. By the mid-1970s many of the institutions that had given stability to people's lives were encountering serious challenges. The traditional values of the family, religion, the work ethic, even the democratic system itself, seemed to be under attack. As a result many people began to turn inward in their search for meaning. To a considerable degree, preoccupation with social reform was replaced by concern for individual self-fulfillment. Some observers came to characterize the 1970s as the "me decade" and to describe American society as the "culture of narcissism." The all-pervasive television commercials touting the importance of youth, beauty, and satisfaction of material desires reflected and intensified the trend.

The revolt against tradition took various forms. On a surface level it could be seen in the change in fashion. Long hair and casual dress proliferated. Blue jeans and T-shirts emblazoned with colorful slogans became the new uniform, not just for young people, but for many in the over-thirty generation as well. In a radical departure from their traditional conservative appearance, men began sprouting beards, sporting jewelry, and even going to beauty salons to have their hair styled. The new hedonism was expressed, too, in the widespread practice of smoking marijuana in public (its use was decriminalized in several states) and the increased use of all types of drugs.

On a deeper level, permissiveness was reflected in sexual mores. Premarital sexual activity became extremely widespread, extending even to youngsters just entering adolescence. Teenage pregnancies became an increasingly serious problem. The number of unmarried couples living together doubled during the decade; even some couples in their "golden years" began living together without marriage. Homosexuals who for years had kept their sexual preference a secret came "out of the closet" and demanded acceptance of the "gay" life-style as a legitimate alternative to "straight" behavior. While many Americans continued to maintain that homosexuality was immoral, there was increasing acceptance of the idea that homosexuals had a right to equal treatment under the law, particularly in the matter of employment. The themes of sex and violence pervaded the movies, books, and television shows.

For decades American society had been moving away from its traditional emphasis on the virtues of hard work, self-discipline, and self-denial. Now the desire to work less and enjoy life more produced a leisure boom made possible by rising personal income, increased vacation time, earlier retirement, higher Social Security benefits, and the creation by the federal government of five new three-day-weekend holidays. With spending for recreation jumping from $58.3 billion in 1965 to $160 billion in 1977, leisure-time activities became America's number-one industry.

A Religious Revival

While many people searched for satisfaction in various forms of self gratification, others sought meaning in traditional religious values. In the early nineteenth century, de Toqueville had remarked that "In arriving in the United States, the religious aspect of the country was the first thing that struck my attention." Despite the increasing secularization and materialism of American life, church membership in America remained relatively high over the next 150 years. Nevertheless, deep emotional commitment was frequently lacking, and by the 1960s the decline in membership was a matter of serious concern to established churches. Although churches attempted to make religion more "relevant" by supporting social and political reform movements, they still failed to attract large numbers of new adherents. In the 1970s, however, many people who were disturbed by the confusing lack of standards and growing materialism turned to traditional religion.

An important aspect of the new religious revival involved the spiritual healing of mind and body. It has been estimated that in the United States some ten million people, 7 percent of the population, were practicing faith healing. A number of Protestant churches that had not included spiritual healing in their services began to do so. In the Roman Catholic church over a thousand "charismatic renewal groups" were formed for the purposes of experiencing a renewal of faith and praying for the gift of spiritual healing. Among Jews the desire for religious and cultural renewal took the form of establishing fellowships known as *havurah* which represented a deeper commitment to Judaism through prayer and study.

Television played a significant role in the religious revival by airing the faith-healing services of Oral Roberts and other ministers. In the latter part of the 1970s, some religious leaders who established wide followings through their television programs began to make their political views a part of their preaching, urging their followers to support legislation and candidates that reflected their conservative political philosophy. In response to this development some civil libertarians expressed concern about the need to ensure a clear separation between the activities of church and state.

While it remains to be seen whether the religious revival will be a lasting phenomenon—and some theologians remain skeptical of its significance—many believe the renewed interest in religion is a hopeful sign in a chaotic world.

The Energy Crisis

During the 1970s the nation's economy was deeply affected by an intractable energy crisis brought into sharp focus by the oil embargo of 1973. For years American economic growth had depended on a massive, and constantly growing, consumption of cheap energy, especially oil. By the mid-1970s the nation was in a double bind. Domestic energy production was on the decline: production of coal began to decrease after World War II, production of oil dropped after 1970, and production of natural gas declined after 1974. At the same time, the demand for energy was rising. In the 1970s, with only 6 percent of the world's population, Americans were consuming one-third of the world's energy. The increasing demand resulted in a growing dependence on foreign oil, and after the oil embargo the price of imported oil began to climb rapidly.

Americans were being forced to recognize the fact that the nation was becoming dangerously dependent for its energy supply on a volatile area of the world. This, coupled with the growing awareness that energy resources were being used up at an astounding rate, led many within the federal government, including President Carter's two predecessors, to call for national energy self-sufficiency. President Ford had believed that this could be achieved by deregulating the price of oil, which had long been kept artificially low. He reasoned that if prices were to rise people would consume less. In addition, the higher profits generated would provide incentive to American oil companies to increase domestic production and develop alternative sources of fuel. While some members of Congress favored the Ford solution, others suggested other measures, such as taking action to break up the OPEC cartel. Although no steps were taken toward deregulation, it was generally accepted that the nation needed to conserve energy and to develop alternative energy sources.

Environmentalists vs. Proponents of Growth Since the 1960s, an environmental lobby had been gaining support in its efforts to secure legislation to protect the water, air, and soil. To meet the concerns of environmentalists Congress passed several new measures in 1970 aimed at protecting the remaining American wilderness and regulating the amount of pollutants that could "safely" be emitted into the air and water. (The most notable legislation was the Wilderness Act mentioned earlier.) In 1971 the Nixon administration established the Environmental Protection Agency which subsequently initiated dozens of lawsuits against cities and corporations for violating water and air quality standards. While oil slicks, irresponsible industrial-waste disposal, and smog were by no means eliminated, there was a significant decline in auto-exhaust emissions and the methods for disposing of sewage and manufacturing wastes began to improve.

The growing demands of consumers for protection against business practices that were harmful to the public resulted in the passage of the Consumer Product Safety Act in 1972. The act created an independent regulatory agency with the authority to test, regulate, and set standards for product safety as well as to initiate court action against violators. Since the passage of consumer-safety legislation, consumers have gained substantially more ability to influence the business practices that affect the public and private safety.

By the mid-1970s, the determination of environmentalists to protect the nation's ecological heritage came into conflict with increasing demands for the development of alternative sources of energy. The only form of energy that did not raise environmental problems was solar power. But for the immediate future, solar energy was impractical for many parts of the country and much expensive research would be required to make it widely applicable. Environmentalists objected to the idea of using

coal more extensively because of the emission of noxious fumes from coal burning, and they were opposed to extracting oil from coal shale because the strip-mining techniques required to extract the large amounts of shale needed would decimate the shale lands. The most promising immediate energy alternative was nuclear power, but many Americans considered it the most objectionable. By 1979 there were seventy-two nuclear plants producing 13 percent of the nation's energy, but nuclear reactors were expensive to build and almost no community wanted a nuclear facility constructed nearby because of the possible hazard to health of nuclear-radiation leakage and the difficulty of safely disposing of radioactive nuclear wastes. These fears increased dramatically in April 1979 when a serious nuclear accident occurred at the Three Mile Island power plant in a heavily populated area of Pennsylvania. Mechanical failure and human error combined to permit an escape of radiation over a sixteen-mile radius. In the aftermath antinuclear demonstrations proliferated, the Three Mile Island plant and several others were closed down, and construction of additional nuclear-power plants was halted until a thorough investigation of the safety of existing methods of construction could be made.

Carter's Response to the Energy Crisis When President Carter took office he appeared determined to meet the energy crisis head-on. In early 1977 he presented to Congress a wide-ranging energy program which emphasized conservation and sacrifice. Describing the massive effort needed to solve the energy crisis as the "moral equivalent of war," Carter called for an end to wasteful consumption through increased taxes on gasoline, domestically produced oil, and big-engine "gas-guzzler" automobiles. Under this program the price of natural gas (but not oil) would be deregulated, nuclear-energy development would be expanded, and tax credits would be given to Americans who installed insulating materials and other energy-saving devices, including solar equipment, in their homes.

While many people gave Carter credit for boldness, the program met considerable opposition. A large number of Americans did not really believe there was an energy crisis, and those who did had little idea what could be done to solve the problem. In addition, President Carter appeared to lack the political skills necessary to shepherd his program

COOLING TOWERS OF THE THREE MILE ISLAND NUCLEAR POWER PLANT OVER- SHADOW THE HOMES OF RESIDENTS IN HAR- RISBURG, PENNSYLVANIA. A SERIOUS ACCI- DENT AT THE PLANT IN THE SPRING OF 1979 SPARKED NEW DEBATES OVER THE DANGERS OF INCREASED USE OF NUCLEAR ENERGY.

through Congress. On a number of previous issues he had failed to consult with the congressional leadership or had proposed legislation that was po- litically unpopular in many key congressional dis- tricts. He had not established the kind of give-and- take with Congress that was necessary to make possible the enactment of such a significant pro- gram. Thus, although Congress created the new De- partment of Energy in 1977, the energy bill that fi- nally was passed in October 1978 was much diluted. Carter's plan to increase conservation through higher taxes on gasoline and domestic oil was re- jected by Congress. While Congress did provide for deregulation of the price of natural gas, this mea- sure did nothing to solve the much larger problem of wasteful oil consumption. The president's plan to give tax credits to homeowners who undertook con- servation measures was also passed.

Early in 1979 Carter changed his stance on de- regulation. He agreed to a gradual decontrol of oil prices over a two-year period, apparently acquiesc- ing in the view that the oil companies would use their increased revenues to search for new domestic oil. At the same time the administration sought to place a tax on the "windfall" profits being earned by the oil companies. Although Congress agreed to the decontrol of oil prices, it refused to grant the presi- dent standby authority to ration gas.

By the middle of 1979 the energy crisis had be- come acute. The decline in oil imports, due in large part to a revolution in Iran and oil-price increases by OPEC, resulted in long lines at the gas pumps in some parts of the nation in May and June. A brief nationwide shortage was aggravated in some areas by the complex and rigid allocation requirements of the Department of Energy and panic buying by motorists. This situation created a serious political crisis for the Carter administration. In July the president abruptly cancelled a new energy speech and went to Camp David for ten days of discussion with his advisers before addressing the American public. Although many Americans believed that Carter himself had contributed to the worsening en- ergy situation by his failure to pursue a consistent policy, in his speech he blamed the country's energy problems on a crisis of the American spirit. (In fact, it was the public's overconsumption of energy supplies that needed to be arrested.) He then set forth yet another plan to resolve the energy shortage which included the following elements: (1) limiting oil imports to 1977 levels, (2) establishment of an Energy Security Corporation to oversee development of alternative energy sources (a staggering cost of $140 billion over the next ten years would be financed from money gained from the windfall-profits tax on oil companies), (3) conversion to the use of coal by utility companies, (4) creation of an Energy Mobilization Board to coordinate conservation efforts, (5) granting gas-rationing authority to the president. In outlining this policy, Jimmy Carter chose the path of more government control over energy policy rather than the path of deregulation.

The Carter Administration

A renewal of religious commitment by millions of Americans coincided with the sudden emergence in national politics of Jimmy Carter, an outspoken adherent of the Baptist faith. The former naval officer and successful farmer served one term as governor of Georgia and then, thanks to an expertly managed campaign, was elected president. The first candidate from the Deep South to hold the office since Zachary Taylor, Carter entered the White House convinced of the need for more efficient government and a renewal of traditional moral values, but with little knowledge of the workings of Washington.

Domestic Policy

In the early months of his presidency Carter was extremely popular. Keenly aware of the importance of symbolism in politics, he made every effort to disassociate himself from the "imperial presidency" of Richard Nixon. He attended town meetings, donned a cardigan sweater for a televised fireside chat to the nation, and sent his daughter to an integrated public school. His popularity was short-lived, however, because of his inexperience in dealing with complex economic and foreign problems and because of his antagonistic relationship with Congress.

On the domestic front, Carter's first act as president was to pardon almost all the draft evaders of the Vietnam period. Although some criticized him for excluding deserters from the pardon, most Americans believed the gesture reflected the president's compassion and sincere desire to end the divisions created by the war.

Unemployment and Inflation When Jimmy Carter took office, inflation appeared to have been reduced to about 6 percent, but the nation faced other economic difficulties. Unemployment was hovering

WHILE FISHING ON HIS PROPERTY IN PLAINS, GEORGIA, DEMOCRATIC PRESIDENTIAL NOMINEE JIMMY CARTER DISPLAYS THE FOLKSY, DOWN-HOME STYLE WHICH APPEALED TO MANY VOTERS.

close to 8 percent; the housing industry was stagnant; and Detroit auto-makers were concerned about the costs of new environmental safety standards, the changing buying habits of the American consumer, and the directions the new president might take on energy policy. Thus President Carter focused initially on economic growth and unemployment as the nation's major economic priorities. His administration called for expanded government spending for public works and employment and job-training programs, combined with tax relief.

Carter's first tax proposal stressed modest rebates for individual taxpayers and a restoration of the investment credit for corporations, rather than a permanent tax cut. Although bills calling for the expansion of employment and training programs gained widespread support and easily passed through Congress, the administration's rebate plan faced stiff opposition, largely because its critics believed it would provide insufficient stimulus to the economy. Realizing that the rebate proposal lacked adequate congressional support and responding to advice from his economic advisers, Carter himself withdrew the plan. The bill that finally emerged included only a modest tax reduction and offered a few concessions to business and industry.

Before long, the problem of mounting inflation caused the president to shift the focus of his economic policies. In 1978 he introduced an antiinflation program based on holding down government spending, encouraging federal regulatory agencies to adopt antiinflation policies, and seeking the voluntary cooperation of business and labor to limit wage and price increases. These measures met resistance from various groups and seemed inadequate to combat ever-rising inflation. By early 1980, the annual rate of inflation reached 18 percent and a long-predicted recession began.

Diplomatic Initiatives

In contrast to Henry Kissinger, who had demonstrated a penchant for independently formulating and carrying out foreign policy, President Carter hoped to create a more open and cooperative approach by using the National Security Council as a channel for ideas from the State and other cabinet departments. As his national security adviser he appointed a Columbia University professor, Zbigniew Brzezinski, a man with hawkish views on American

policy toward the Soviets. By contrast, the president's choice for secretary of state was Cyrus Vance, a quiet lawyer-diplomat of long experience who proved to be a tireless negotiator in his efforts to continue the policy of détente with Moscow.

Carter's selection of foreign-policy advisers was a reflection of his basic diplomacy; it lacked a unified world view and a clear sense of priorities. As one observer wrote, administration policy "erupted in all directions . . . statements are issued on every subject, often confusing more than clarifying the complicated problems at hand."

The president's trumpeting of the importance of human rights in shaping America's relations with other nations illustrated the problem of basing diplomacy on public pronouncements rather than on quiet negotiation. His decision to criticize the Soviets openly for their suppression of dissidents succeeded only in hardening the resolve of the Communist leadership to silence internal opposition. Although Carter's attention to human rights pleased many Americans, it drew criticism from others who pointed out that the president was ignoring far worse violations of human rights in other parts of the world.

Yet Carter's inexperience in diplomacy did not prevent him from successfully securing passage of new treaties with Panama, establishing diplomatic relations with China, and prodding Israel and Egypt toward negotiating a treaty ending the state of war that had existed between them since Israel's founding in 1948.

The Panama Canal Treaties   Carter achieved a diplomatic breakthrough by resolving a long-standing conflict with Panama over control of the Panama Canal. In September 1977 the United States and Panama signed two treaties, the culmination of years of patient negotiations under four presidents. The agreements provided that the United States Canal Zone would cease to exist in October 1979 and that until the year 2000 the United States would pay Panama up to $50 million of the canal tolls each year and at least $10 million more every year to aid the operation of the canal. In return the United States was guaranteed a permanent right to protect the canal against a threat to the free passage of ships of all nations and the right to operate the canal (with increasing assistance from Panama) until the year 2000.

When the treaties came up for ratification, a number of conservative senators heatedly opposed relinquishing "sovereign rights and jurisdiction" over the canal, claiming that to do so would pose a threat to American security. Supporters of the treaty argued that ownership of the canal was not important as long as the United States had the right to use it to protect the national interest. The treaties would, they claimed, end an important source of resentment against the United States in Panama and, indeed, all of Latin America. The treaties were ratified in March and April 1978 by the same slim two-thirds majority (sixty-eight to thirty-two), but this was accomplished only after amendments had been attached which gave the United States the right to intervene militarily in Panama to keep the canal open and which gave American vessels the right to use the canal before anyone else in an emergency. While Panamanians were deeply unhappy with these amendments, they accepted them in order to secure control of the canal zone.

Diplomatic Recognition of China In another dramatic foreign-policy initiative, President Carter, building on the framework established by the Nixon administration, announced on December 16, 1978, that the United States and the People's Republic of China would establish diplomatic relations on January 1, 1979. At the same time the United States terminated the mutual-defense treaty with Taiwan and made plans for the withdrawal of American military personnel. While the administration accurately characterized diplomatic recognition of China as acceptance after thirty years of "simple reality," there were many Americans who echoed Senator Barry Goldwater's sentiment that the administration's move "stabs in the back the nation of Taiwan." Supporters of the Carter initiative were quick to point out that while Peking maintained that Taiwan was a part of China, the Communist Chinese made no threats to use armed force to take back the island or to interfere with its cultural and commercial ties with the United States. The Chinese even agreed that the United States could continue to supply Taiwan with "defensive" weapons. China's Deputy Prime Minister Teng Hsiao-ping was warmly welcomed by the American people during an eight-day visit to the United States early in 1979.

Breaking the Middle East Deadlock The major diplomatic initiative of the Carter administration was the president's efforts to bring about a Middle East peace settlement. At first the United States seemed more of a hindrance than a help in the negotiating process. In October 1977 the president joined with Moscow in calling for a conference in Geneva aimed at securing a comprehensive settlement which would resolve Arab-Israeli differences as well as provide for "the legitimate rights of the Palestinian people." This proposal outraged the Israelis, who immediately rejected it, and shocked many of Israel's American supporters as well. By alluding to the rights of the Palestinians, they argued, the president had undermined the Israeli position; moreover, the idea of including the Russians in any negotiations seemed fraught with danger.

A month later Egyptian President Anwar Sadat astounded everyone by ignoring the American initiative and offering to go directly to Jerusalem to talk with the Israelis. Israel's new conservative government, led by Menachem Begin, responded swiftly with an invitation to the Egyptian president. Sadat's visit to Israel in November 1977, during which he was welcomed by throngs of cheering Israelis, began the process which eventually led to agreements between the two nations.

At the insistence of both parties, the United States participated in the negotiations as an intermediary. The talks stalled temporarily over Israel's insistence on maintaining troops and settlements in the West Bank and Gaza strip, ostensibly to ensure Israel's security, but the impasse was finally broken in September 1978 when Carter, abandoning his goal of a comprehensive settlement, invited Begin and Sadat to Camp David for intensive discussions. After thirteen days of hard bargaining, the three leaders emerged with two agreements. The first provided for a phased return of the Sinai to Egypt in exchange for recognition of the state of Israel. The second set up a framework for a comprehensive peace predicated on a withdrawal of Israel from the West Bank over a five-year period and Palestinian and Jordanian participation in negotiations to determine the status of the area.

The initial response of most Arab governments was hostile. Viewing the agreements as a separate peace between Egypt and Israel, leaders of the more radical Arab states responded by isolating Egypt from the rest of the Arab community. Although Egypt and Israel began moving forward to fulfill the terms of the agreements, the Israeli government did

PRESIDENT CARTER LOOKS ON AS EGYPTIAN PRESIDENT ANWAR SADAT AND ISRAELI PRIME MINISTER MENA-CHEM BEGIN SIGN THE MIDEAST PEACE TREATY AT A CEREMONY HELD ON THE NORTH LAWN OF THE WHITE HOUSE.

little to prevent militant nationalists from continuing to build new settlements in the West Bank. This hard line tried Egyptian patience and was strongly opposed by the Carter administration as well as by moderate Israelis. It seemed clear that little progress would be made on the Palestinian question until the Israeli government moderated its position on the settlements.

Oil and the International Scene The hostility of the oil-producing Arab states to the Mid-East negotiations posed an indirect threat to America's oil supply. While there was no new embargo of oil, Arab pressure was felt in periodic increases in OPEC oil prices. From $3 a barrel in 1973 the price of oil skyrocketed to $23.50 a barrel by mid-1979. During the same period American dependence on oil increased and imports of oil from the Middle East rose from 22 percent in 1973 to 38 percent in 1978. Because United States government policies kept the price

charged to consumers for oil artificially low, Americans had little incentive to conserve, even with higher prices.

The overthrow of the Shah of Iran in January 1979 introduced an additional complicating factor into the oil situation. The authoritarian rule of the Shah (who had been strongly supported by the American government since World War II), most particularly his forced efforts to modernize Iran and his harsh repression of political opposition, led to a massive upheaval. The revolution that brought down his government instituted a conservative Moslem religious state whose leader, Ayatollah Ruhollah Khomeini, was virulently anti-American. A major cutback in the production of Iranian oil that followed close upon the revolution added new stresses to the international oil scene.

In November 1979 anti-American terrorists seized the American embassy in Teheran in angry response to a decision by the Carter administration to allow the Shah (who was then living in Mexico) to come to the United States for medical treatment. Outraged by this violation of international law, the American government impounded Iranian assets in the United States and announced that it would import no more Iranian oil. Ayatollah Khomeini then announced that Iran was cutting off its oil imports to the United States. The Carter administration refused to meet the unyielding demands of the militants to return the Shah to Iran for trial, declaring that under its democratic form of government it had no authority to return the Shah. The hostage situation, complicated by a number of additional factors, created an extraordinarily complex diplomatic challenge for the United States. As the hostage crisis dragged on it became clear that its resolution would require a great deal of patience on the part of the American government.

SALT-II Neither the crisis with Iran, nor Russian adventurism in Africa and the Middle East, nor sharp debate about America's military capability versus that of the Soviets deterred the administration from efforts to reach a new strategic arms limitation agreement (SALT-II) with Russia. The Soviet leadership, though they seemed genuinely interested in a new arms control agreement, refused either to restrain a Soviet military buildup or to end the use of Cuban troops in supporting Communist factions in such African countries as Angola and Ethiopia.

The road to SALT-II was a bumpy one, but in June 1979 President Carter and Soviet Premier Leonid Brezhnev signed an agreement in Vienna. Designed to be in force until 1985, the treaty would have limited each nation to 2550 strategic missiles and bombers by 1981. Under its terms the United States committed itself not to test long-range cruise missiles while the treaty was in effect and both sides agreed to reduce their arsenal of old weapons to the agreed-upon number by 1981. As had been the case with SALT-I, the treaty did not cover all types of missiles, which made it likely that both sides would continue to pursue the development of new missile systems. While the administration expected a long and acrimonious debate over the pact, all criticisms of it became academic when the Soviet Union invaded and took over the government of Afghanistan on its southern border early in 1980. In response the president decided to withdraw the treaty from consideration by the Senate.

The Carter Presidency Assessed

After two and a half years, the Carter presidency had been a study in contrasts. Carter's efforts to be accessible to the people, the fact that he was a Washington outsider, and his assertion of the need for a renewal of traditional values all contributed to his initial popularity. Yet within a few months of his inauguration, there began to be disturbing signs of the president's ineptitude in dealing with domestic and foreign-policy issues. Admittedly these problems were enormously complex and any proposed resolutions would surely antagonize some group or another. The ungovernably large Washington bureaucracy as well as innumerable special-interest lobbies did little to make his job easier. Moreover, although Congress was controlled by a Democratic majority, it had become more assertive since Vietnam and Watergate, and many of its younger members voted independently of the leadership. Even given these problems, Carter himself contributed to a growing public perception that he was inept. Although a Democrat, he failed to establish a congenial working relationship with a Democratic Congress. And whereas he seized the initiative in proposing new policies, when faced with opposition he began to waver. This tendency to change direction undermined his image as a strong leader with clear-cut priorities and led his critics to contend that he was trying to be all things to all people. Popular support for the president declined steadily after mid-1977.

The Challenge of the 1980s

By the end of the 1970s an uneasy mood of pessimism had developed among the American people. The country's prosperity was declining, and double-digit inflation was threatening the traditional ability of Americans to get ahead by hard work. It appeared to many that personal frontiers were closing and that the dream of improving one's living standard in order to be able to make a better life for the coming generation was unlikely to become a reality for most people.

The international position of the United States was uncertain as well. The Vietnam War, the growth of Soviet military power, and the increasing independence of America's allies and the Third World all contributed to a realization that the

United States was no longer in a position to impose its will on the rest of the world. Clearly the nation would have to resort to greater cooperation and negotiation with other nations to find solutions to world problems. The challenge facing the United States in the 1980s was to generate the resolve and the self-discipline necessary to preserve its high standard of living and at the same time defend the national ideals of individual freedom, equality of opportunity, and social justice.

Readings

General Works

Bell, Daniel, *The Cultural Contradictions of Capitalism*. New York: Basic Books, 1976.

Chafe, William H., *The American Woman: Her Changing Social, Economic and Political Roles, 1920–1970*. New York: Oxford University Press, 1974.

Cloward, Richard A., and Frances F. Piven, *The Politics of Turmoil: Essays on Poverty, Race, and the Urban Crisis*. New York: Pantheon, 1974.

Cronin, Thomas E., *The Presidency Reappraised*. New York: Praeger, 1977.

Gordon, Michael (Ed.), *The American Family: Past, Present, and Future*. New York: Random House, 1978.

Johnson, Haynes, *In the Absence of Power: Governing America*. New York: Viking, 1980.

Kennan, George, *The Cloud of Danger*. Boston: Little, Brown, 1977.

Levitan, S. A. *et. al.*, *Still a Dream: The Changing Status of Blacks Since 1960*. Cambridge, Mass.: Harvard University Press, 1975.

Meier, Matthew S., and Feliciano Rivera, *The Chicanos: A History of Mexican-Americans*. New York: Hill and Wang, 1972.

Wilkinson, J. Harvie, III, *From Brown to Bakke*. New York: Oxford University Press, 1979.

Special Studies

Friedan, Betty, *The Feminine Mystique*. New York: Norton, 1974.

Glazer, Nathan (Ed.), *Cities in Trouble*. New York: Watts, 1970.

Harrell, David E., Jr., *All Things Are Possible: The Healing and Charismatic Revivals in Modern America*. Bloomington: Indiana University Press, 1976.

Josephy, Alvin M., *Red Power: The American Indians' Fight for Freedom*. New York: American Heritage Press, 1971.

LaFaber, Walter, *The Panama Canal: The Crisis in Historical Perspective*. New York: Oxford University Press, 1978.

Lasch, Christopher, *The Culture of Narcissism*. New York: Norton, 1978.

Lewis, Oscar, *La Vida: A Puerto Rican Family in the Culture of Poverty, San Juan and New York*. New York: Random House, 1966.

Meister, Dick, and Anne Loftis, *A Long Time Coming: The Struggle to Unionize America's Farm Workers*. New York: Macmillan, 1977.

Morgan, Robin, *Sisterhood Is Powerful: An Anthology of Writings from the Women's Liberation Movement*. New York: Random House, 1970.

Yankelovich, Daniel, *The New Morality: A Profile of American Youth in the 1970s*. New York: McGraw-Hill, 1974.

Primary Sources

Carter, Jimmy, *Why Not the Best?* Nashville: Broadman, 1975.

Terkel, Studs, *Working*. New York: Avon, 1974.

Biography

Levy, Jacques, *César Chávez*. New York: Norton, 1975.

Wooten, James, *Dasher: The Roots and Rising of Jimmy Carter*. New York: Summit, 1978.

Appendix

Appendix

Further Readings

Chapter 15

Belz, Herman, *Emancipation and Equal Rights*. New York: Norton, 1978; Benedict, Michael L., *The Impeachment and Trial of Andrew Johnson*. New York: Norton, 1973; Brock, William R., *An American Crisis*. New York: St. Martin's, 1963; Buck, Paul H., *The Road to Reunion, 1865–1900*. Boston: Little, Brown, 1937; Carpenter, John A., *Sword and Olive Branch: Oliver Otis Howard*. Pittsburgh, Penn.: University of Pittsburgh Press, 1964; Current, Richard N., *Three Carpetbag Governors*. Baton Rouge: Louisiana State University Press, 1968; DuBois, William E. B., *Black Reconstruction in America, 1860–1880*. New York: Atheneum, 1969; Dunning, W. A., *Reconstruction, Political and Economic, 1865–1877*. New York: Harper & Row, 1968; Frederickson, George M., *The Black Image in the White Mind*. New York: Harper & Row, 1971; Gillette, William, *The Right to Vote: Politics and the Passage of the Fifteenth Amendment*. Baltimore: Johns Hopkins, 1965; Hershkowitz, Leo, *Tweed's New York—Another Look*. Garden City, N.Y.: Doubleday, 1977; Hesseltine, William B., *Lincoln's Plan of Reconstruction*. New York: Quadrangle, 1967 (Paper); Higgs, Robert, *Competition and Coercion: Blacks in the American Economy*. New York: Cambridge University Press, 1977; Holt, Thomas, *Black Over White: Negro Political Leadership in South Carolina During Reconstruction*. Urbana: University of Illinois Press, 1977; Hyman, Harold M. (Ed.), *New Frontiers of the American Reconstruction*. Urbana: University of Illinois Press, 1966; James, Joseph B., *The Framing of the Fourteenth Amendment*. Urbana: University of Illinois Press, 1956; Kirwan, Albert D., *The Revolt of the Rednecks: Mississippi Politics, 1876–1925*. Gloucester, Mass.: Peter Smith, 1964; Kousser, J. Morgan, *The Shaping of Southern Politics: Suffrage Restriction and the Establishment of the One-Party South, 1880–1910*. New Haven, Conn.: Yale University Press, 1974; Mantell, Martin E., *Johnson, Grant, and the Politics of Reconstruction*. New York: Columbia University Press, 1973; McFeely, William S., *Yankee Stepfather: General O. O. Howard and the Freedmen*. New Haven, Conn.: Yale University Press, 1968; Mohr, James C. (Ed.), *Radical Republicans in the North: State Politics During Reconstruction*. Baltimore, Md.: Johns Hopkins University Press, 1976; Perman, Michael, *Reunion Without Compromise: The South and Reconstruc-* *tion, 1865–1868*. New York: Cambridge University Press, 1973; Polakoff, Keith Ian, *The Politics of Inertia: The Election of 1876 and the End of Reconstruction*. Baton Rouge: Louisiana State University Press, 1973; Powell, Lawrence N., *New Masters: Northern Planters During the Civil War and Reconstruction*. New Haven: Yale University Press, 1980; Rabinowitz, Howard N., *Race Relations in the Urban South, 1865–1890*. New York: Oxford University Press, 1978; Ransom, Roger L., and Richard Sutch, *One Kind of Freedom: The Economic Consequences of Emancipation*. New York: Cambridge University Press, 1977; Rose, Willie Lee, *Rehearsal for Reconstruction: A Historical and Contemporary Reader*. New York: Random, 1964 (Paper); Simkins, Francis B., and Robert H. Woody, *South Carolina during Reconstruction*. Gloucester, Mass.: Peter Smith, 1932; Tindall, George B., *South Carolina Negroes, 1877–1900*. Columbia: University of South Carolina Press, 1970; Van Deusen, Glyndon, *Horace Greeley: Nineteenth-Century Crusader*. Philadelphia: University of Pennsylvania Press, 1953; Vaughn, William P., *Schools For All: The Blacks and Public School Education in the South*. Lexington: University Press of Kentucky, 1974; Wharton, Vernon L., *The Negro in Mississippi, 1865–1869*. New York: Harper & Row, 1965; Wiener, Jonathan M., *Social Origins of the New South*. Baton Rouge: Louisiana State University Press, 1978; Wiggins, Sarah Woolfolk, *The Scalawag in Alabama Politics, 1865–1881*. University: University of Alabama Press, 1977; Williamson, Joel, *After Slavery: The Negro in South Carolina During Reconstruction, 1861–1877*. Chapel Hill: University of North Carolina Press, 1965; Williamson, Joel R. (Ed.), *The Origins of Segregation*. Lexington, Mass.: Heath, 1968.

Chapter 16

Billington, Ray A., *America's Frontier Heritage*. New York: Holt, Rinehart and Winston, 1971; Durham, Philip, and Everett L. Jones, *The Negro Cowboys*. New York: Dodd, 1965 (Paper); Gray, John S., *Centennial Campaign: The Sioux War of 1876*. Fort Collins, Colo.: Old Army, 1976; Lamar, Howard R., *The Far Southwest, 1846–1912: A Territorial History*. New York: Norton, 1970 (Paper); Larsen, Lawrence H., *The Urban West at the End of the Frontier*. Lawrence:

The Regents Press of Kansas, 1978; McCracken, Harold, *George Catlin and the Old Frontier*. New York: Dial, 1959; Miller, David Harry, and Jerome O. Steffen (Eds.), *The Frontier: Comparative Studies*. Norman: University of Oklahoma Press, 1977; Priest, Loring Benson, *Uncle Sam's Stepchildren: The Reformation of United States Indian Policy, 1865–1887*. New York: Octagon, 1969; Sandoz, Mari, *Old Jules*. Lincoln: University of Nebraska Press, 1962; Skaggs, Jimmy M., *The Cattle-Training Industry: Between Supply and Demand, 1866–1890*. Lawrence: University Press of Kansas, 1973; Smith, Henry N., *Virgin Land*. Cambridge, Mass: Harvard University Press, 1950.

Chapter 17

Benson, Lee, *Merchants, Farmers and Railroads*. Cambridge, Mass.: Harvard University Press, 1955; Davis, Patricia J., *End of the Line. Alexander J. Cassatt and the Pennsylvania Railroad*. New York: Neale Watson, 1978; Diamond, Sigmund (Ed.), *The Nation Transformed: The Creation of Industrial Society*. New York: Braziller, 1963; Holbrook, Stewart H., *The Age of the Moguls*. Garden City, N.Y.: Doubleday, 1953; Ingham, John N., *The Iron Barons: A Social Analysis of an American Urban Elite, 1874–1965*. Westport, Conn.: Greenwood, 1978; Kirkland, Edward C., *Dream and Thought in the American Business Community, 1860–1900*. Ithaca, N.Y.: Cornell University Press, 1956; Lane, W. J., *Commodore Vanderbilt: An Epic of the Steam Age*. New York: Knopf, 1942; Lewis, Oscar, *The Big Four*. New York: Knopf, 1938; McCloskey, Robert G., *American Conservatism in the Age of Enterprise*. Cambridge, Mass.: Harvard University Press, 1951; Moody, John, *The Truth About the Trusts*. Westport, Conn.: Greenwood, 1960; North, Douglass C., *Growth and Welfare in the American Past: A New Economic History*. Englewood Cliffs, N.J.: Prentice-Hall, 1966 (Paper); Stover, John F., *American Railroads*. Chicago: University of Chicago Press, 1961; Stover, John F., *The Railroads of the South, 1865–1900*. Chapel Hill: University of North Carolina Press, 1955; Taylor, George R., and Irene D. Neu, *The American Railroad Network, 1861–1890*. Cambridge, Mass.: Harvard University Press, 1956; Wall, Joseph F., *Andrew Carnegie*. New York: Oxford University Press, 1970; Wyllie, Irvin G., *The Self-Made Man in America*. New York: Free Press, 1966 (Paper).

Chapter 18

Barth, Gunther, *Bitter Strength: A History of the Chinese in the United States, 1850–1870*. Cambridge, Mass.: Harvard University Press, 1964; Briggs, John W., *An Italian Passage: Immigrants to Three American Cities, 1890–1930*. New Haven, Conn.: Yale University Press, 1978; Bruce, Robert V., *Eighteen Seventy-Seven: Year of Violence*. New York: Watts, 1959 (Paper); Dulles, Foster Rhea, *Labor in America: A History*. New York: Crowell, 1966; Ginger, Ray, *Altgeld's America: The Lincoln Ideal Vs. Changing Realities*. New York: Watts, 1965 (Paper); Glazer, Nathan, *American Judaism*. Chicago: University of Chicago Press, 1972 (Paper); Golab, Caroline, *Immigrant Destinations*. Philadelphia: Temple University Press, 1977; Grob, Gerald, *Workers and Utopia: A Study of Ideological Conflict in the American Labor Movement, 1865–1900*. New York: Quadrangle, 1969 (Paper); Handlin, Oscar, *The Uprooted*. Boston: Little, Brown, 1951; Hawes, Joseph M., *Children in Urban Society: Juvenile Delinquency in Nineteenth-Century America*. New York: Oxford University Press, 1971; Hays, Samuel P., *The Response to Industrialism: 1885–1914*. Chicago: University of Chicago Press, 1957; Huggins, Nathan, *Protestants Against Poverty: Boston's Charities*. Westport, Conn.: Greenwood, 1970; Jick, Leon A., *The Americanization of the Synagogue, 1820–1870*. Hanover, N.H.: University Press of New England, 1976; Jones, Maldwyn A., *American Immigration*. Chicago: University of Chicago Press, 1960; Katzman, David M., *Seven Days a Week: Women and Domestic Service in Industrializing America*. New York: Oxford University Press, 1978; Kirkland, Edward C., *The Age of Enterprise: A Social History of Industrial America*. New York: Harper & Row, 1961; Linn, James W., *Jane Addams: A Biography*. Westport, Conn.: Greenwood, 1968; McLaurin, M. A., *Paternalism and Protest: Southern Cotton Mill Workers and Organized Labor, 1875–1905*. Westport, Conn.: Negro University Press, 1971; Miller, Randall N., and Thomas D. Marzik (Eds.), *Immigrants and Religion in Urban America*. Philadelphia: Temple University Press, 1977; Philpott, Thomas Lee, *The Slum and the Ghetto: Neighborhood Deterioration and Middle-Class Reform, Chicago, 1880–1930*. New York: Oxford University Press, 1978; Powderly, Terence U., *Thirty Years of Labor*. New York: Kelley, 1962; Rosenblum, Gerald, *Immigrant Workers: Their Impact on American Labor Radicalism*. New York: Basic, 1972; Schlesinger, Arthur M., *The Rise of the*

City, 1878–1898. New York: Macmillan, 1933; Solomon, Barbara, *Ancestors and Immigrants*. Cambridge, Mass.: Harvard University Press, 1956; Warner, Sam Bass, Jr., *Streetcar Suburbs, The Process of Growth in Boston, 1870–1900*. Cambridge, Mass.: Harvard University Press, 1962; Weber, Michael P., *Social Change in an Industrial Town: Patterns of Progress in Warren, Penn., From the Civil War to World War I*. University Park: Pennsylvania State University Press, 1976; Wolff, Leon, *Lockout*. New York: Harper & Row, 1965; Yans-McLaughlin, Virginia, *Family and Community: Italian Immigrants in Buffalo, 1880–1930*. Ithaca, N.Y.: Cornell University Press, 1971.

Chapter 19

Burchard, John E., and Albert Bush-Brown, *The Architecture of America*, Boston: Little, Brown, 1961; Condit, Carl W., *The Rise of the Skyscraper*. Chicago: University of Chicago Press, 1952; Cubberly, Ellsworth P., *Public Education in the United States*. Boston: Houghton Mifflin, 1919; Gilbert, James B., *Work Without Salvation: America's Intellectuals and Industrial Alienation, 1880–1910*. Baltimore, Md.: Johns Hopkins University Press, 1977; Goodrich, Lloyd, *Winslow Homer*. Greenwich, Conn.: New York Graphics Society, 1973; Hook, Sidney, *John Dewey*. New York: John Day, 1939; Morgan, Arthur E., *Edward Bellamy*. New York: Columbia University Press, 1944.

Chapter 20

Armstrong, William M., *E. L. Godkin: A Biography*. Albany: State University of New York Press, 1978; Buck, Solon J., *The Granger Movement*. Lincoln: University of Nebraska Press, 1963; Davison, Kenneth E., *The Presidency of Rutherford B. Hayes*. Westport, Conn.: Greenwood, 1972; DeSantis, Vincent P., *Republicans Face the Southern Question: The New Departure Years, 1877–1897*. Westport, Conn.: Greenwood, Reprint of 1959 edition; Durden, Robert F., *The Climax of Populism*. Lexington: University of Kentucky Press, 1965; Edmonds, Helen, *The Negro and Fusion Politics in North Carolina, 1894–1901*. New York: Russell, 1973; Gaither, Gerald H., *Blacks and the Populist Revolt: Ballots and Bigotry in the "New South."* University: University of Alabama Press, 1977; Ginger, Ray, *Age of Excess: The United States from 1877–1914*. New York: Macmillan, 1965 (Paper); Glad, Paul, *The Trumpet Soundeth: William Jennings Bryan and his Democracy, 1896–1912*. Gloucester, Mass.: Peter Smith, 1960; Hackney, Sheldon, *Populism to Progressivism in Alabama*. Princeton, N.J.: Princeton University Press, 1969; Hammarberg, Melvyn, *The Indian Voter: The Historical Dynamics of Party Allegiance During the 1870s*. Chicago: University of Chicago Press, 1977; Keller, Morton, *The Art and Politics of Thomas Nast*. New York: Oxford University Press, 1968; Knoles, George H., *The Presidential Campaign and Election of 1892*. New York: AMS Press, 1972; Koening, Louis W., *Bryan: A Political Biography of William Jennings Bryan*. New York: Putnam, 1971; Leech, Margaret, *In the Days of McKinley*. New York: Harper, 1959; Leech, Margaret, and Harry J. Brown, *The Garfield Orbit*. New York: Harper & Row, 1978; Logan, Rayford, *The Betrayal of the Negro: From Rutherford B. Hayes to Woodrow Wilson*. New York: Macmillan, 1965 (Paper); McKenna, George, *American Populism*. New York: Putnam, 1974 (Paper); McSeveney, Samuel T., *The Politics of Depression: Political Behavior in the Northeast, 1893–1896*. New York: Oxford University Press, 1972; Merrill, Horace S., *Bourbon Leader: Grover Cleveland and the Democratic Party*. Boston, Mass.: Little, Brown, 1965 (Paper); Nevins, Allan, *Grover Cleveland*. New York: Dodd, Mead, 1932; Pollack, Norman, *The Populist Mind*. New York; Bobbs-Merrill, 1967 (Paper); Ridge, Martin, *Ignatius Donnelly: Portrait of a Politician*. Chicago: University of Chicago Press, 1962; Simkins, Francis B., *Pitchfork Ben Tillman: South Carolinian*. Baton Rouge: Louisiana State University Press, 1967 (Paper); Tomisch, John, *A Genteel Endeavor: American Culture and Politics in the Gilded Age*. Stanford, Calif.: Stanford University Press, 1971; White, Leonard, *The Republican Era*. New York: Macmillan, 1958; Williams, T. Harry, *Romance and Realism in Southern Politics*. Baton Rouge: Louisiana State University Press, 1966 (Paper); Woodward, C. Vann, *Tom Watson: Agrarian Rebel*. New York: Macmillan, 1938; Youngdale, James, *Populism: A Psychohistorical Perspective*. Port Washington, N.Y.: Kennikat, 1975.

Chapter 21

Beisner, Robert L., *Twelve Against Empire*. New York: McGraw-Hill, 1968; Bemis, Samuel F., *The Latin American Policy of the United States*. New York: Norton, 1967; Campbell, Charles S., Jr., *Anglo-American Understanding, 1898–1903*. Baltimore: Johns Hopkins University Press, 1957; Cook, Adrian, *The Alabama Claims: American Politics and Anglo-American Relations, 1865–1872*. Ithaca, N.Y.: Cornell University Press, 1975; Dennett, Tyler, *John Hay*. Port Washington, N.Y.: Kennikat, 1963; Dulles, Foster R., *The Imperial Years*. New York: Apollo, 1960; Friedel, Frank, *The Splendid Little War*. Boston: Little, Brown, 1958; Griswold, A. Whitney, *The Far Eastern Policy of the United States*. New Haven: Yale University Press, 1938; Herman, S. R., *Eleven Against War: Studies in American Internationalist Thought, 1898–1921*. Stanford, Calif.: Hoover Institution Press, 1969 (Paper); James, Henry, *Richard Olney*. New York: Da Capo Press, 1969; Kushner, Howard I., and Anne H. Sherrill, *John Milton Hay: The Union of Poetry and Politics*. Boston: Twayne, 1977; McCormick, Thomas J., *China Market*. New York: Quadrangle, 1970 (Paper); Merli, Frank, and Theodore

A. Wilson (Eds.), *Makers of American Diplomacy*. New York: Scribner, 1974; Nevins, Allan, *Hamilton Fish*, Vols. I–II. New York: Ungar, 1957; Rickover, H. G., *How the Battleship Maine Was Destroyed*. Washington, D.C.: Department of the Navy, 1976; Rystad, Goran, *Ambiguous Imperialism: American Foreign Policy and Domestic Politics at the Turn of the Century*. Lund, Sweden: Scandinavian University Books, 1975; Schirmer, D. B., *Republic or Empire: American Resistance to the Philippine War*. Cambridge, Mass.: Schenkman, 1972; Sprout, Harold, and Margaret Sprout, *The Rise of American Naval Power*. Princeton, N.J.: Princeton University Press, 1943; Strong, Josiah, *Our Country*. Cambridge, Mass.: Harvard University Press, 1963; Werking, Richard Hume, *The Master Architects: Building the U.S. Foreign Service, 1890–1913*. Lexington: University Press of Kentucky, 1977; Wilkins, Mira, *The Emergence of Multinational Enterprise: American Business Abroad from the Colonial Era to 1914*. Cambridge, Mass.: Harvard University Press, 1970; Wolff, Leon, *Little Brown Brother*. Garden City, N.Y.: Doubleday, 1961; Young, George B., and John A. Grenville, *Politics, Strategy, and American Diplomacy*. New Haven, Conn.: Yale University Press, 1966.

Chapter 22

Aaron, Daniel, *Men of Good Hope*. New York: Oxford University Press, 1951; Adams, Larry T., *Walter Lippman*. Boston: Twayne, 1977; Bailey, Hugh C., *Liberalism in the New South: Southern Social Reformers and the Progressive Movement*. Coral Gables, Fla.: University of Miami Press, 1969; Burton, David H., *Theodore Roosevelt*. Boston, Mass.: Twayne, 1973; Chrislock, Carl H., *The Progressive Era in Minnesota, 1899–1918*. St. Paul: Minnesota Historical Society, 1971; Davis, Allen F., *Spearheads for Reform: The Social Settlements and the Progressive Movement, 1890–1914*. New York: Oxford University Press, 1967; Dittmer, John, *Black Georgia in the Progressive Era, 1900–1920*. Urbana: University of Illinois Press, 1977; Ebner, Michael H., and Eugene M. Tobin (Eds.), *The Age of Urban Reform: New Perspectives on the Progressive Era*. Port Washington, N.Y.: Kennikat, 1977; Forcey, Charles B., *The Crossroads of Liberalism*. New York: Oxford University Press, 1961; Goldman, Eric F., *Rendezvous with Destiny*. New York: Random House, 1956; Graebner, William, *Coal-mining Safety in the Progressive Period: The Political Economy of Reform*. Lexington: University of Kentucky Press, 1976; Hays, Samuel P., *Conservation and the Gospel of Efficiency*. Cambridge, Mass.: Harvard University Press, 1959; Holt, Laurence James, *Congressional Insurgents and the Party System, 1909–1916*. Cambridge, Mass.: Harvard University Press, 1967; Kaplan, Justin, *Lincoln Steffens*. New York: Simon & Schuster, 1974; Kennedy, David M., *Birth Control in America: The Career of Margaret Sanger*. New Haven, Conn.: Yale University Press, 1970 (Paper);

Kraditor, Aileen S., *The Ideas of the Woman Suffrage Movement, 1890–1920*. Garden City, N.Y.: Doubleday, 1971 (Paper); LaFeber, Walter, *The Panama Canal: The Crisis in Historical Perspective*. New York: Oxford University Press, 1978; Lippman, Walter, *Drift and Mastery*. Englewood Cliffs, N.J.: Prentice-Hall, 1961; Lubove, Roy, *The Professional Altruist: The Emergence of Social Work as a Career*. New York: Atheneum, 1969 (Paper); Mann, Arthur, *Yankee Reformers in the Urban Age*. New York: Harper & Row, 1966; Martin, Albro, *Enterprise Denied: Origins of the Decline of American Railroads, 1897–1917*. New York: Columbia University Press, 1971; McCullough, David, *The Path Between the Seas: The Creation of the Panama Canal, 1870–1914*. New York: Simon & Schuster, 1977; McKee, Delber L., *Chinese Exclusion Versus the Open Door Policy, 1900–1906: Clashes Over China Policy in the Roosevelt Era*. Detroit: Wayne State University Press, 1977; Mowry, George E., *The California Progressives*. Chicago: Quadrangle, 1963; Mowry, George E., *The Era of Theodore Roosevelt*. New York: Harper & Row, 1958; Neu, Charles E., *An Uncertain Friendship: Theodore Roosevelt and Japan, 1906–1909*. Cambridge, Mass.: Harvard University Press, 1967; Noble, David W., *The Paradox of Progressive Thought*. Minneapolis: University of Minnesota Press, 1958; Nye, Russel B., *Midwestern Progressive Politics*. East Lansing: Michigan State University Press, 1959; Olin, Spencer C., Jr., *California's Prodigal Son: Hiram Johnson and the Progressives*. Berkeley: University of California Press, 1968; Pringle, Henry, *Theodore Roosevelt*. New York: Harcourt, Brace, 1956; Rudwick, Elliot M., *W. E. B. DuBois: Propagandist of the Negro Protest*. New York: Atheneum, 1969; Quandt, Jean B., *From the Small Town to the Great Community: The Social Thought of Progressive Intellectuals*. New Brunswick, N.J.: Rutgers University Press, 1970; Roosevelt, Nicholas, *Theodore Roosevelt: The Man as I Knew Him*. New York: Dodd, Mead, 1967; Trani, Eugene P., *The Treaty of Portsmouth: An Adventure in American Diplomacy*. Lexington: University Press of Kentucky, 1969; Walsh, Mary Roth, *"Doctors Wanted: No Women Need Apply": Sexual Barriers in the Medical Profession, 1835–1975*. New Haven: Yale University Press, 1977; Weinberg, Arthur, and Leila Weinberg (Eds.), *The Muckrakers*. New York: Putnam, 1964; Weiss, Nancy, *The National Urban League, 1910–1940*. New York: Oxford University Press, 1974; Wiebe, Robert H., *The Search for Order, 1877–1920*. New York: Hill & Wang, 1967 (Paper).

Chapter 23

Anderson, Donald F., *William Howard Taft: A Conservative's Conception of the Presidency*. Ithaca, N.Y.: Cornell University Press, 1973; Brandeis, Louis D., *Letters of Louis D. Brandeis*, 3 Volumes. Melvin I. Urofsky and D. W. Levy (Eds.). Albany: State University of New York Press, 1972;

Calvert, Peter, *The Mexican Revolution 1910–1914: The Diplomacy of Anglo-American Conflict*. New York: Cambridge University Press, 1968; Cooper, John Milton, Jr., *Walter Hines Page: The Southerner as American, 1855–1918*. Chapel Hill: University of North Carolina Press, 1977; Finnegan, John Patrick, *Against the Specter of a Dragon: The Campaign for American Military Preparedness, 1914–1917*. Westport, Conn.: Greenwood, 1975; Gilderhus, Mark T., *Diplomacy and Revolution: U.S.—Mexican Relations Under Wilson and Carranza*. Tucson: University of Arizona Press, 1977; Grieb, Kenneth J., *The United States and Huerta*. Lincoln: University of Nebraska Press, 1969; Healy, David, *Gunboat Diplomacy in the Wilson Era: The U.S. Navy in Haiti, 1915–1916*. Madison: University of Wisconsin Press, 1976; Holt, Laurence James, *Congressional Insurgents and the Party System, 1909–1916*. Cambridge, Mass: Harvard University Press, 1967; Manners, William, *TR and Will*. New York: Harcourt, Brace, 1969; Penick, James, Jr., *Progressive Politics and Conservation: The Ballinger-Pinchot Affair*. Chicago: University of Chicago Press, 1968; Schmidt, Hans R., *The United States Occupation of Haiti, 1915–1934*. Brunswick, N. J.: Rutgers University Press, 1971; Scholes, Walter V., and Mary V. Scholes, *The Foreign Policies of the Taft Administration*. Columbia: University of Missouri Press, 1970; Urofsky, Melvin I., *Big Steel and the Wilson Administration: A Study in Business-Government Relations*. Columbus: Ohio State University Press, 1969; Walworth, Arthur C., *Woodrow Wilson*. Boston: Houghton Mifflin, 1965; Wilensky, Norman M., *Conservatives in the Progressive Era: The Taft Republicans of 1912*. Gainesville: University of Florida Press, 1965.

Chapter 24

Baldwin, Hanson W., *World War I*. New York: Harper & Row, 1962; Birdsall, Paul, *Versailles Twenty Years After*. Hamden, Conn.: Shoestring Press, 1962; Blakey, George T., *Historians on the Homefront: American Propagandists for the Great War*. Lexington: University Press of Kentucky, 1970; Cuff, Robert D., *The War Industries Board: Business-Government Relations During World War I*. Baltimore: Johns Hopkins University Press, 1973; DeWeerd, Harvey A., *President Wilson Fights His War*. New York: Macmillan, 1968; Gregory, Ross, *Walter Hines Page: Ambassador to the Court of St. James*. Lexington: University Press of Kentucky, 1970; Griffin, Frederick C., *Six Who Protested: Radical Opposition to the First World War*. Port Washington, N.Y.: Kennikat, 1977; Herman, Sandra, *Eleven Against War*. Stanford, Calif.: Hoover Institute Press, 1969; Hoover, Herbert, *The Ordeal of Woodrow Wilson*. New York: McGraw-Hill, 1958; Kennan, George F., *The Decision to Intervene*. Princeton, N.J.: Princeton University Press, 1958; Kennan, George F., *Russia Leaves the War*. Princeton, N.J.: Princeton University Press, 1956; Lane, Jack C., *Armed Progressive: General Leonard Wood*.

San Rafael, Calif.: Presidio, 1978; Livermore, Seward W., *Politics Is Adjourned*. Middletown, Conn.: Wesleyan University Press, 1966; Millis, Walter, *The Road to War*. New York: Fertig, 1969; Peterson, Horace C., and Gilbert C. Fite, *Opponents of War: 1917–1918*. Seattle: University of Washington Press, 1968 (Paper); Pratt, Julius W., *Challenge and Rejection: The United States and World Leadership, 1900–1921*. New York: Macmillan, 1967; Safford, Jeffrey J., *Wilsonian Maritime Diplomacy, 1913–1921*. New Brunswick, N.J.: Rutgers University Press, 1978; Simpson, Colin, *The Lusitania*. New York: Ballantine, 1974 (Paper); Stallings, Laurence, *The Doughboys*. New York: Harper & Row, 1963; Tillman, Seth P., *Anglo-American Relations at the Paris Peace Conference of 1919*. Princeton, N.J.: Princeton University Press, 1961; Thompson, John M., *Russia, Bolshevism, and the Versailles Peace*. Princeton, N.J.: Princeton University Press, 1966; Unterberger, Betty (Ed.), *American Intervention in the Russian Civil War*. Lexington, Mass.: Heath, 1969.

Chapter 25

Allswang, John M., *A House for All Peoples: Ethnic Politics in Chicago, 1890–1936*. Lexington: University Press of Kentucky, 1971; Ashby, Leroy, *The Spearless Leader: Senator Borah and the Progressive Movement in the 1920s*. Urbana: University of Illinois Press, 1972; Bagby, Wesley, *The Road to Normalcy*. Baltimore: Johns Hopkins University Press, 1962; Braeman, John, *et al.* (Eds.), *Change and Continuity in Twentieth Century America: The 1920s*. Columbus: Ohio State University Press, 1968; Chafee, Zechariah, *Free Speech in the United States*. Cambridge, Mass.: Harvard University Press, 1941; Galambos, Louis, *Competition and Cooperation: The Emergence of a National Trade Association*. Baltimore: Johns Hopkins University Press, 1966; Gustin, Lawrence R., *Billy Durant: The Creator of General Motors*. Grand Rapids, Mich.: Eerdmans, 1973; Hale, Nathan G., Jr., *Freud and the Americans: The Origin and Foundation of the Psychoanalytic Movement in America, 1876–1917*. New York: Oxford University Press, 1971; Handlin, Oscar, *Al Smith and His America*. Boston: Little, Brown, 1958; Harbaugh, William H., *Lawyer's Lawyer: The Life of John W. Davis*. New York: Oxford University Press, 1973; Hicks, John D., and Theodore Saloutos, *Twentieth Century Populism: Agricultural Discontent in the Middle West, 1900–1939*. Lincoln: University of Nebraska Press, 1964; Hoffman, Frederick J., *The Twenties*. New York: Viking, 1955; Jackson, Kenneth T., *The Ku Klux Klan in the City, 1915–1930*. Richard C. Wade (Ed.). New York: Oxford University Press, 1967 (Paper); Johnson, Donald, *The Challenge to American Freedoms*. Lexington: University of Kentucky Press, 1963; Joughin, Louis, and Edmund M. Morgan, *The Legacy of Sacco and Vanzetti*. Chicago: Quadrangle, 1964; Leighton, Isabel (Ed.), *The Aspirin*

Age. New York: Simon & Schuster, 1949; Lemons, J. Stanley, *The Woman Citizen: Social Feminism in the 1920s.* Urbana: University of Illinois Press, 1973; Levine, Lawrence W., *Defender of the Faith: William Jennings Bryan, The Last Decade, 1915–1925.* New York: Oxford University Press, 1965; Levy, Eugene, *James Weldon Johnson: Black Leader, Black Voice.* John H. Franklin (Ed.). Chicago: University of Chicago Press, 1973; Lowitt, Richard, and George W. Norris, *The Persistence of a Progressive, 1913–1933.* Urbana: University of Illinois Press, 1971; Martin, Tony, *Race First: The Ideology and Organizational Struggles of Marcus Garvey and the Universal Negro Improvement Association.* Westport, Conn.: Greenwood, 1976; Murray, Robert K., *The Harding Era.* Minneapolis: University of Minnesota Press, 1969; Noggle, Burl, *Teapot Dome: Oil and Politics in the 1920s.* New York: Norton, 1965; Peace, Otis, *The Responsibility of American Advertising.* New Haven, Conn.: Yale University Press, 1958; Preston, William, Jr., *Aliens and Dissenters: Federal Suppression of Radicals, 1903–1033.* New York: Harper & Row, 1963 (Paper); Prothro, J. W., *The Dollar Decade: Business Ideas in the 1920s.* Baton Rouge: Louisiana State University Press, 1954; Rice, Arnold S., *The Ku Klux Klan in American Politics.* New York: Haskell, 1972; Rochester, Stuart I., *American Liberal Disillusionment in the Wake of World War I.* University Park: The Pennsylvania State University Press, 1977; Schlesinger, Arthur M., Jr., *The Crisis of the Old Order.* Boston: Houghton Mifflin, 1957; Sherman, Richard B., *The Republican Party and Black America: From McKinley to Hoover, 1896–1933.* Charlottesville: University Press of Virginia, 1973; Sinclair, Andrew, *The Available Man: The Life Behind the Masks of Warren Gamaliel Harding.* New York: Quadrangle, 1969 (Paper); Sinclair, Andrew, *Prohibition: The Era of Excess.* Boston: Little, Brown, 1962; Soule, George, *Prosperity Decade: From War to Depression.* New York: Harper & Row, 1968; Swain, D. C., *Federal Conservation Policy 1021–1033.* Berkeley: University of California Press, 1963; Tuttle, William M., Jr., *Race Riot: Chicago in the Red Summer of 1919.* New York: Atheneum, 1970 (Paper); Wik, Reynold M., *Henry Ford and Grass-Roots America.* Ann Arbor: University of Michigan Press, 1972.

Chapter 26

Allen, Frederick L., *Since Yesterday.* New York: Harper & Row, 1940; Blum, John M., *Roosevelt and Morgenthau.* Boston: Houghton Mifflin, 1972 (Paper); Braeman, John, *et al.* (Eds.), *The New Deal,* Vols. I and II. Columbus: Ohio State University Press, 1975; Bunche, Ralph J., *The Political Status of the Negro in the Age of FDR.* Dewey W. Grantham (Ed.). Chicago: University of Chicago Press, 1973; Conrad, David E., *The Forgotten Farmers.* Urbana: University of Illinois Press, 1965; Daniel, Pete, *The Shadow of Slavery: Peonage in the South, 1901–1969.* Urbana: University of Illinois Press, 1972; Daniels, Roger, *The Bonus March: An Episode of the Great Depression.* Westport, Conn.: Greenwood, 1971; Dorsett, Lyle W., *FDR and the City Bosses.* Port Washington, N.Y.: Kennikat, 1977; Draper, Theodore, *The Roots of American Communism.* New York: Viking, 1957; Dubovsky, Melvyn, and Warren Van Tine, *John L. Lewis.* New York: Scribners, 1976; Ekirch, Arthur A., Jr., *Ideologies and Utopias: New Deal and American Thought.* New York: Quadrangle, 1971 (Paper); Fine, Sidney, *The Automobile Under the Blue Eagle.* Ann Arbor: University of Michigan Press, 1963; Gould, Jean, and Lorena Hickok, *Walter Reuther: Labor's Rugged Individualist.* New York: Dodd, 1971; Huthmacher, J. Joseph, *Senator Robert F. Wagner and the Rise of Urban Liberalism.* New York: Atheneum, 1971 (Paper); Kennedy, Susan E., *The Banking Crisis of 1933.* Lexington: University Press of Kentucky, 1973; Koskoff, David E., *Joseph P. Kennedy: A Life and Times.* Englewood Cliffs, N.J.: Prentice-Hall, 1974; Lash, Joseph P., *Eleanor and Franklin.* New York: New American Library, 1973 (Paper); Lash, Joseph P., *Eleanor: The Years Alone.* New York: Norton, 1972; McConnell, Grant, *The Decline of Agricultural Democracy.* Berkeley: University of California Press, 1953; McCoy, Donald R., *Angry Voices: Left-of-Center Politics in the New Deal Era.* Lawrence: University of Kansas Press, 1958; McCoy, Donald R., *Landon of Kansas.* Lincoln: University of Nebraska Press, 1966; McCraw, Thomas K., *TVA and the Power Fight, 1933–1939.* Philadelphia: Lippincott, 1971 (Paper); Mann, Arthur, *La Guardia: A Fighter Against His Time.* Chicago: University of Chicago Press, 1969; Marcus, Sheldon, *Father Coughlin: The Tumultuous Life of the Priest of the Little Flower.* Boston: Little, Brown, 1973; Parrish, Michael E., *Securities Regulations and the New Deal.* New Haven, Conn.: Yale University Press, 1970; Patterson, James T., *The New Deal and the States: Federalism in Transition.* Princeton, N.J.: Princeton University Press, 1969; Pells, Richard H., *Radical Visions and American Dreams: Culture and Social Thought in the Depression Years.* New York: Harper & Row, 1973; Perkins, Van L., *Crisis in Agriculture: The Agricultural Adjustment Administration and the New Deal.* Berkeley: University of California Press, 1969; Sherwood, Robert E., *Roosevelt and Hopkins.* New York: Harper & Row, 1950; Smith, Gene, *The Shattered Dream: Herbert Hoover and the Great Depression.* New York: Morrow, 1970; Stave, Bruce M., *The New Deal and the Last Hurrah: Pittsburgh Machine Politics.* Pittsburgh: University of Pittsburgh Press, 1970; Stein, Herbert, *The Fiscal Revolution in America, 1931–1962.* Chicago: University of Chicago Press, 1969 (Paper); Stein, Walter J., *California and the Dust Bowl Migration: Contributions in American History.* Westport, Conn.: Greenwood, 1973; Sternsher, Bernard, *The Negro in Depression and War: Prelude to Revolution.* New York: Watts, 1969 (Paper); Stott, William, *Documentary Expression and Thirties America.* New York: Oxford University Press, 1973; Swanberg, W. A.,

Norman Thomas: The Last Idealist. New York: Scribners, 1976; Tindall, George B., *The Emergence of the New South: 1913–1945.* Baton Rouge: Louisiana State University Press, 1967; Tugwell, Rexford, *In Search of Roosevelt.* Cambridge, Mass.: Harvard University Press, 1972; Warren, Harris G., *Herbert Hoover and the Great Depression.* New York: Oxford University Press, 1959; Williams, T. Harry, *Huey Long.* New York: Knopf, 1969; Witte, Edwin E., *The Development of the Social Security Act.* Madison: University of Wisconsin Press, 1962 (Paper).

Chapter 27

Adams, Frederick C., *Economic Diplomacy: The Export-Import Bank and American Foreign Policy, 1934–1939.* Columbia: University of Missouri Press, 1976; Adler, Selig, *The Isolationist Impulse: Its Twentieth Century Reaction.* New York: Abelard-Schuman, 1957; Beard, Charles A., *President Roosevelt and the Coming of the War.* Hamden, Conn.: Shoe String, 1968; Bennett, Edward, *Recognition of Russia.* Waltham, Mass.: Blaisdell, 1970; Bishop, James, *FDR's Last Year, April 1944–April 1945.* New York: Morrow, 1974; Blum, John M., *From the Diaries of Henry Morgenthau,* Vols. I–II. Boston: Houghton Mifflin, 1959–1967; Bowles, Chester, *Promises to Keep: My Years in Public Life, 1941–1969.* New York: Harper & Row, 1972 (Paper); Bradley, Omar N., *A Soldier's Story.* New York: Popular Library, 1970; Buckley, Thomas H., *The United States and the Washington Conference, 1921–1922.* Knoxville: University of Tennessee Press, 1970; Calcott, Wilfrid H., *The Western Hemisphere: Its Influence on United States Policies to the End of World War II.* Austin: University of Texas Press, 1968; Chatfield, Charles, *For Peace and Justice: Pacifism in America, 1914–1941.* Knoxville: University of Tennessee Press, 1971; Cohen, Warren, *America's Response to China.* New York: Wiley, 1971; Cole, Wayne S., *Charles A. Lindbergh and the Battle Against American Intervention in World War II.* New York: Harcourt Brace Jovanovich, 1974; Current, Richard N., *Secretary Stimson: A Study in Statecraft.* Hamden, Conn.: Shoe String, 1970; Dalfiume, Richard M., *Desegregation of the United States Armed Forces: Fighting on Two Fronts, 1939–1953.* Columbia: University of Missouri Press, 1969; Dingman, Roger, *Power in the Pacific: The Origins of Naval Arms Limitation, 1914–1922.* Chicago: University of Chicago Press, 1976; Eisenhower, Dwight D., *Crusade in Europe.* Garden City, N.Y.: Doubleday, 1948; Farnsworth, Beatrice, *William C. Bullitt and the Soviet Union.* Bloomington: Indiana University Press, 1967; Feis, Herbert, *The Road to Pearl Harbor.* Princeton, N.J.: Princeton University Press, 1967; Friedman, Saul S., *No Haven for the Oppressed: United States Policy toward Jewish Refugees, 1938–1945.* Detroit: Wayne State University Press, 1973; Gardner, Lloyd, *Economic Aspects of New Deal Diplomacy.* Madison: University of Wisconsin Press, 1964; Girdner, Audrie, and Anne Loftis, *The Great Betrayal.* New York: Macmillan, 1969; Green, David, *The Containment of Latin America.* Chicago: Quadrangle, 1971; Grew, Joseph C., *Turbulent Era,* Vols. I–II. Freeport, N.Y.: Books for Libraries, 1970; Hogan, Michael J., *Informal Entente: The Private Structure of Cooperation in Anglo-American Economic Diplomacy.* Columbia: University of Missouri Press, 1977; Iriye, Akira, *After Imperialism: The Search for a New Order in the Far East, 1921–1931.* Cambridge, Mass.: Harvard University Press, 1965; Kahn, E. J., Jr., *The China Hands.* New York: Viking, 1975; Kimball, Warren F., *The Most Unsordid Act: Lend-Lease, 1939–1941.* Baltimore: Johns Hopkins University Press, 1969; Levering, Ralph B., *American Opinion and the Russian Alliance.* Chapel Hill: University of North Carolina Press, 1976; MacArthur, Douglas, *Reminiscences.* New York: McGraw-Hill, 1964; Maddox, Robert J., *William E. Borah and American Foreign Policy.* Baton Rouge: Louisiana State University Press, 1969; Melosi, Martin V., *The Shadow of Pearl Harbor: Political Controversy Over the Surprise Attack, 1941–1946.* College Station: Texas A&M University Press, 1977; Morison, Elting E., *Turmoil and Tradition: A Study of the Life and Times of Henry L. Stimson.* New York: Atheneum, 1964; Morison, Samuel E., *The Two-Ocean War.* Boston: Little, Brown, 1963; Neu, Charles E., *The Troubled Encounter: The United States and Japan.* New York: Wiley, 1975; O'Connor, Raymond G., *Diplomacy for Victory: FDR and Unconditional Surrender.* New York: Norton, 1971 (Paper); Offner, Arnold A., *American Appeasement: United States Foreign Policy and Germany, 1933–1938.* Cambridge, Mass.: Harvard University Press, 1969; Polenberg, Richard, *War and Society: The United States, 1941–1945.* Philadelphia: Lippincott, 1972 (Paper); Pratt, Julius W., *Cordell Hull,* Vols. I–II. New York: Cooper Square, 1964; Smith, Gaddis, *American Diplomacy during the Second World War: 1941–1945.* New York: Wiley, 1965 (Paper); Smith, Richard Harris, *OSS: The Secret History of America's First Intelligence Agency.* Berkeley: University of California Press, 1972; Smith, Robert F., *The United States and Revolutionary Nationalism in Mexico, 1916–1932.* Chicago: University of Chicago Press, 1972; Sontag, Raymond, *A Broken World: 1919–1939.* New York: Harper & Row, 1971; Steward, Dick, *Trade and Hemisphere: The Good Neighbor Policy and Reciprocal Trade.* Columbia: University of Missouri Press, 1975; Stoler, Mark A., *The Politics of the Second Front: American Military Planning and Diplomacy in Coalition Warfare, 1941–1945.* Westport, Conn.: Greenwood, 1977; Thorne, Christopher, *Allies of a Kind: The United States, Britain, and the War against Japan, 1941–1945.* New York: Oxford University Press, 1978; Thorne, Christopher, *The Limits of Foreign Policy: The West, the League, and the Far Eastern Crisis of 1931–1933.* New York: Putna, 1973 (Paper); Traina, Richard P., *American Diplomacy and the Spanish Civil War.* Bloomington: Indiana University Press, 1968; Varg, Paul, *The Closing of the Door: Sino-American Relations, 1936–1946*. East Lansing: Michigan State University Press, 1973; Wilson, Theodore A., *The First Summit: Roosevelt and Churchill at Placentia Bay, 1941*. Boston: Houghton Mifflin, 1969; Wood, Bryce, *The Making of the Good Neighbor Policy*. New York: Columbia University Press, 1961.

Chapter 28

Acheson, Dean, *Present at the Creation*. New York: Norton, 1969; Alperowitz, Gar, *Atomic Diplomacy: Hiroshima and Potsdam*. New York: Simon & Schuster, 1965; Aron, Raymond, *The Imperial Republic: The United States and the World, 1945–1973*. Englewood Cliffs, N.J.: Prentice-Hall, 1974; Bailey, Thomas A., *The Marshall Plan Summer: An Eyewitness Report on Europe and the Russians in 1947*. Stanford, Calif.: Hoover Institute Press, 1977; Belknap, Michael R., *Cold War Political Justice: The Smith Act, the Communist Party, and American Civil Liberties*. Westport, Conn.: Greenwood, 1977; Bernstein, Barton J. (Ed.), *Politics and Policies of the Truman Administration*. New York: Watts, 1970; Block, Fred L., *The Origins of International Economic Disorder: A Study of International Monetary Policy from World War II to the Present*. Berkeley: University of California Press, 1977; Caridi, Ronald J., *The Korean War and American Politics: The Republican Party as a Case History*. Philadelphia: University of Pennsylvania Press, 1969; Davis, Lynn E., *The Cold War Begins*. Princeton, N.J.: Princeton University Press, 1974; Detzer, David, *Thunder of the Captains: The Short Summer in 1950*. New York: Crowell, 1977; Divine, Robert A., *Second Chance: The Triumph of Internationalism in America During World War II*. New York: Atheneum, 1971 (Paper); Eckes, Alfred E., Jr., *A Search for Solvency: Bretton Woods and the International Monetary System, 1941–1946*. Austin: University of Texas Press, 1975; Fairbank, John K., *The United States and China*. New York: Viking, 1971; Feis, Herbert, *The Atomic Bomb and the End of World War II*. Princeton, N.J.: Princeton University Press, 1966; Ferrell, Robert H., *George C. Marshall*. New York: Cooper Square, 1966; Freeland, Richard M., *The Truman Doctrine and the Origins of McCarthyism, 1946–1948*. New York: Knopf, 1972; Gaddis, John L., *Russia, The Soviet Union and the United States: An Interpretive History*. New York: Wiley, 1978; Gardner, Lloyd C., *Architects of Illusion: Men and Ideas in American Foreign Policy, 1941–1949*. New York: Watts, 1972 (Paper); Goldman, Eric F., *The Crucial Decade—and After: America 1945–1960*. New York: Knopf, 1960; Griffith, Robert, *The Politics of Fear: Joseph B. McCarthy and the Senate*. Lexington: University Press of Kentucky, 1971 (Paper); Herring, George, *Aid to Russia, 1941–1946*.

New York: Columbia University Press, 1973; Hofstadter, Richard, *The Paranoid Style in American Politics and Other Essays*. New York: Knopf, 1965; Horowitz, David, *The Free World Colossus*. New York: Hill and Wang, 1971; Kennan, George F., *American Diplomacy 1900–1950*. Chicago: University of Chicago Press, 1951; Kuklick, Bruce, *American Policy and the Division of Germany: The Clash with Russia Over Reparations*. Ithaca, N.Y.: Cornell University Press, 1972; Latham, Earl, *The Communist Controversy in Washington*. Cambridge, Mass.: Harvard University Press, 1966; Lee, R. Alton, *Truman and Taft-Hartley*. Lexington: University Press of Kentucky, 1966; Lubell, Samuel, *The Future of American Politics*. New York: Harper & Row, 1965; Markowitz, Norman D., *The Rise and Fall of the People's Century: Henry A. Wallace and American Liberalism, 1941–1948*. New York: Free Press, 1973; Matusow, Allen J., *Farm Policies and Politics in the Truman Years*. Cambridge, Mass.: Harvard University Press, 1967; Mee, Charles L., Jr., *Meeting at Potsdam*. New York: Evans, 1975; Merli, Frank, and Theodore A. Wilson (Eds.), *Makers of American Diplomacy*. New York: Scribners, 1974; Miller, Merle, *Plain Speaking: An Oral Biography of Harry S Truman*. New York: Putnam, 1974; Neustadt, Richard E., *Presidential Power*. New York: Wiley, 1960; Paterson, Thomas C. (Ed.), *Cold War Critics: Alternatives to American Foreign Policy in the Truman Years*. New York: Watts, 1971 (Paper); Patterson, James T., *Mr. Republican: A Biography of Robert A. Taft*. Boston: Houghton Mifflin, 1972; Phillips, Cabell, *The Truman Presidency*. New York: Macmillan, 1966; Purifoy, Lewis McC., *Harry Truman's China Policy: McCarthyism and the Diplomacy of Hysteria, 1947–1951*. New York: New Viewpoints, 1976; Rose, Lisle A., *After Yalta: American Political Culture and the Cold War*. New York: Scribner, 1973; Rose, Lisle A., *Roots of Tragedy: The United States and the Struggle for Asia, 1945–1953*. Westport, Conn.: Greenwood, 1976; Smith, Gaddis, *Dean Acheson*. Robert H. Ferrel (Ed.). New York: Cooper Square, 1972; Spanier, J. W., *The Truman-MacArthur Controversy and the Korean War*. Cambridge, Mass.: Harvard University Press, 1959; Steel, Ronald, *Pax Americana*. New York: Viking Press, 1970 (Paper); Stevenson, Adlai E., *Speeches*. New York: Random House, 1952; Theoharis, Athan, *Seeds of Repression: Harry S Truman and the Origins of McCarthyism*. New York: Quadrangle, 1971; Truman, Margaret, *Harry S Truman*. New York: Morrow, 1973; Tsou, Tang, *America's Failure in China: 1941–1950*. Chicago: University of Chicago Press, 1963; Tucker, Robert W., *The Radical Left and American Foreign Policy*. Baltimore: Johns Hopkins, 1971 (Paper); Ulam, Adam B., *The Rivals: America and Russia Since World War II*. New York: Viking Press, 1972 (Paper); Walker, J. Samuel, *Henry A. Wallace and American Foreign Policy*. Westport, Conn.: Greenwood, 1976; Walton, Richard, *Henry Wallace, Harry Truman and the Cold War*. New York: Viking, 1976.

Chapter 29

Adams, Sherman, *Firsthand Report*. New York: Harper & Row, 1961; Adams, Walter, and Horace M. Gray, *Monopoly in America: The Government as Promoter*. New York: Macmillan, 1955; Albertson, Dean (Ed.), *Eisenhower as President*. New York: Hill & Wang, 1963; Bass, Jack, and Walter DeVries, *The Transformation of Southern Politics: Social Change and Political Consequence Since 1945*. New York: Basic, 1976; Bell, Daniel, *The End of Ideology*. New York: Macmillan, 1960; Benson, Ezra T., *Crossfire: The Eight Years with Eisenhower*. Garden City, N.Y.: Doubleday, 1962; Berger, Raoul, *Government by Judiciary*. Cambridge, Mass.: Harvard University Press, 1977; Blaustein, Albert P., and Clarence C. Ferguson, Jr., *Desegregation and the Law: The Meaning and Effect of the School Segregation Cases*. New Brunswick, N.J.: Rutgers University Press, 1957; Bryson, Thomas A., *American Diplomatic Relations and the Middle East, 1784–1975*. Netuchen, N.J.: Scarecrow, 1977; Childs, Marquis, *Eisenhower: Captive Hero*. New York: Harcourt Brace, 1958; Clark, Thomas D., *The Emerging South*. New York: Oxford University Press, 1968; Cochrane, Williard W., and Mary E. Ryan, *American Farm Policy, 1948–1973*. Minneapolis: University of Minnesota Press, 1976; Cox, Archibald, *The Warren Court: Constitutional Decision as an Instrument of Reform*. Cambridge, Mass.: Harvard University Press, 1968; Dayton, E. L., *Walter Reuther*. New York: Devin-Adair, 1958; Donovan, Robert J., *Eisenhower: The Inside Story*. New York: Harper & Row, 1956; Dozer, Donald M., *Are We Good Neighbors? Three Decades of Inter-American Relations, 1930–1960*. Gainesville: University of Florida Press, 1959; Eulau, Heinz, *Class and Party in the Eisenhower Years*. New York: Free Press, 1962; Finer, Herman, *Dulles over Suez*. Chicago: Quadrangle, 1964; Frier, D. A., *Conflict of Interest in the Eisenhower Administration*. Ames: Iowa State University Press, 1969; Galbraith, John K., *The Affluent Society*. Boston: Houghton Mifflin, 1969; Gerson, Louis L., *John Foster Dulles*. New York: Cooper Square, 1967; Gorman, Joseph B., *Kefauver: A Political Biography*. New York: Oxford University Press, 1971; Graebner, Norman, *The New Isolationism*. New York: Ronald, 1956; Hughes, Emmet J., *The Ordeal of Power*. New York: Atheneum, 1963; Kennan, George F., *Russia, the Atom, and the West*. Westport, Conn.: Greenwood, 1974 (Reprint 1958 edition); Kinnard, Douglas, *President Eisenhower and Strategy Management*. Lexington: University Press of Kentucky, 1977; Larson, Arthur, *Eisenhower: The President Nobody Knew*. New York: Scribner, 1968; Lewis, Anthony, *The New York Times, Portrait of a Decade: The Second American Revolution*. New York: Random, 1964. Lomax, Louis E., *The Negro Revolt*. New York: Harper & Row, 1962; Lyon, Peter, *Eisenhower: Portrait of the Hero*. Boston: Little, Brown, 1974; Mills, C. Wright, *The Power Elite*. New York: Oxford University Press, 1959 (Paper); Mills, C. Wright, *White Collar: American Middle Classes*. New York: Oxford University Press, 1956; Noble, Bernard G., *Christian A. Herter*. New York: Cooper Square, 1970; Osgood, Robert E., *Alliances and American Foreign Policy*. Baltimore: Johns Hopkins, 1968 (Paper); Osgood, Robert E., *et al.*, *America and the World: From the Truman Doctrine to Vietnam*. Baltimore: Johns Hopkins University Press, 1970; Pusey, Merlo J., *Eisenhower: The President*. New York: Macmillan, 1956; Rovere, Richard, *The Eisenhower Years: Affairs of State*. New York: Farrar, Straus, 1956; Safran, Nadav, *From War to War: The Arab-Israeli Confrontation, 1948–1967*. Indianapolis: Pegasus, 1969; Sayler, Richard H., Barry B. Boyer, and Robert E. Gooding, Jr. (Eds.), *The Warren Court: A Critical Analysis*. New York: Chelsea, 1968; Schapmeier, Edward L., and F. H. Schapmeier, *Ezra Taft Benson and the Politics of Agriculture: The Eisenhower Years, 1953–1961*. Danville, Ill.: Interstate, 1975; Shannon, David A., *The Decline of American Communism: A History of the Communist Party of the United States Since 1945*. New York: Harcourt, Brace, 1959; Soth, Lauren, *Farm Trouble in an Age of Plenty*. Princeton, N.J.: Princeton University Press, 1957; Stein, Herbert, *The Fiscal Revolution in America*. Chicago: University of Chicago Press, 1969; Tindall, George B., *The Disruption of the Solid South*. New York: Norton, 1972 (Paper); Trebing, Harry M. (Ed.), *The Corporation in the American Economy*. New York: Watts, 1970 (Paper); Widick, B. J., *Labor Today*. Boston: Houghton Mifflin, 1964.

Chapter 30

Abel, Elie, *The Missile Crisis*. Philadelphia: Lippincott, 1965; Allison, Graham T., *Essence of Decision: Explaining the Cuban Missile Crisis*. Boston: Little, Brown, 1971 (Paper); Anderson, Walt (Ed.), *The Age of Protest*. Pacific Palisades, California: Goodyear, 1969 (Paper); Baldwin, James, *The Fire Next Time*. New York: Dial, 1963; Baldwin, James, *Nobody Knows My Name*. New York: Dial, 1961; Barnet, Richard, *The Roots of War: The Men and Institutions Behind U.S. Foreign Policy*. New York: Penguin, 1973 (Paper); Bell, Daniel, and Irving Kristol (Eds.), *Confrontation: The Student Rebellion and the Universities*. New York: Basic Books, 1969; Bishop, James A., *The Days of Martin Luther King, Jr.* New York: Putnam, 1971; Branyan, Robert L., and Lawrence Larsen, *Urban Crisis in Modern America*. Lexington, Mass.: Heath, 1971; Brown, Claude, *Manchild in the Promised Land*. New York: Macmillan, 1965; Chester, Lewis, *et al.*, *An American Melodrama: The Presidential Campaign of 1968*. New York: Viking Press, 1969; Conot, Robert, *Rivers of Blood, Years of Darkness*. New York: Bantam, 1967; Cooper, Chester L., *The Lost Crusade: The U.S. in Vietnam*. New York: Dodd, Mead, 1970; Divine, Robert A., (Ed.), *The*

Cuban Missile Crisis. New York: Watts, 1971; Donald, Aida DiPace (Ed.), *John F. Kennedy and the New Frontier*. New York: Hill & Wang, 1966; Draper, Theodore, *Abuse of Power*. New York: Viking, 1967; Epstein, Edward J., *Inquest*. New York: Viking, 1966; Fall, Bernard, *The Two Vietnams*. New York: Praeger, 1964; Feuer, Lewis S., *The Conflict of Generations*. New York: Basic, 1969; Fifield, Russell H., *Americans in Southeast Asia: The Roots of Commitment*. New York: Crowell, 1973; Fitzsimons, Louise, *The Kennedy Doctrine*. New York: Random, 1972; Galloway, John, *The Gulf of Tonkin Resolution*. Cranbury, N.J.: Fairleigh Dickinson, 1970; Garrow, David J., *Protest at Selma: Martin Luther King, Jr., and the Voting Rights Act of 1965*. New Haven: Yale University Press, 1978; Gettleman, M. E., and David Mermelstein, *Failure of American Liberalism after the Great Society*. Gloucester, Mass.: Smith, 1970; Geyelin, Philip L., *Lyndon B. Johnson and the World*. New York: Praeger, 1966; Goldman, Peter, *The Death and Life of Malcolm X*. New York: Harper & Row, 1974 (Paper); Graff, Henry, *The Tuesday Cabinet: Deliberation and Decision on Peace and War under Lyndon B. Johnson*. Englewood Cliffs, N.J.: Prentice-Hall, 1970; Graham, Hugh D., and Ted R. Gurr, *A History of Violence in America: Historical and Comparative Perspectives*. New York: Praeger, 1969; Heller, Walter, *New Dimensions of Political Economy*. Cambridge, Mass.: Harvard University Press, 1969; Hilsman, Roger, *To Move a Nation*. Garden City, N.Y.: Doubleday, 1967; Johnson, Lady Bird, *A White House Diary*. New York: Dell, 1971, Levinson, Jerome, and Juan de Onís, *The Alliance that Lost Its Way*. Chicago: Quadrangle, 1970; Kennedy, Robert F., *Thirteen Days: A Memoir of the Cuban Missile Crisis*. Richard Neustadt and Graham Allison (Eds.). New York: New American Library (Paper); Kennedy, Rose Fitzgerald, *Times to Remember*. Garden City, N.Y.: Doubleday, 1974; Levitan, Sar A., and Robert Taggart, *The Promise of Greatness*. Cambridge, Mass.: Harvard University Press, 1976; Lord, Donald C., *John F. Kennedy: The Politics of Confrontation and Conciliation*. Woodbury, N.Y.: Barron's, 1977; Lowenthal, Abraham F., *The Dominican Intervention*. Cambridge, Mass.: Harvard University Press, 1972; Mailer, Norman, *Miami and the Siege of Chicago*. New York: New American Library, 1968; Malcolm X, *The Autobiography of Malcolm X*. New York: Grove Press, 1966; Mehnert, Klaus, *Twilight of the Young: The Radical Movements of the 1960s and Their Legacy*. New York: Holt, 1976; Meier, August, and Elliot Rudwick, *CORE*. New York: Oxford University Press, 1973; Miroff, Bruce, *Pragmatic Illusions: The Presidential Politics of John F. Kennedy*. New York: McKay, 1976; Moulton, Harland B., *From Superiority to Parity: The United States and the Strategic Arms Race, 1961-1971*. Westport, Conn.: Greenwood, 1973; Muse, Benjamin, *The American Negro Revolution: From Non-violence to Black Power, 1963-1967*. Bloomington: Indiana University Press, 1968 (Paper: Citadel, 1970); New York Times

Editors, *Report of the National Advisory Commission on Civil Disorders*. New York: Dutton, 1968; Power, Thomas, *The War at Home*. New York: Grossman, 1973; Reedy, George E., *The Twilight of the Presidency*. New York: New American Library, 1971 (Paper); Reich, Charles, *The Greening of America: How the Youth Revolution is Trying to Make America Liveable*. New York: Random, 1970 (Paper: Bantam, 1971); Rogers, William D., *The Twilight Struggle: The Alliance for Progress and the Politics of Development in Latin America*. New York: Random, 1967; Roszak, Theodore, *The Making of a Counter-Culture*. Garden City, N.Y.: Doubleday, 1969 (Paper); Ruiz, Ramon E., *Cuba: The Making of a Revolution*. Amherst: University of Massachusetts Press, 1968 (Paper: Norton, 1970); Salinger, Pierre, *With Kennedy*. Garden City, N.Y.: Doubleday, 1966; Sidey, Hugh, *John F. Kennedy, President*. New York: Atheneum, 1963-1964; Steinberg, Alfred, *Sam Johnson's Boy*. New York: Macmillan, 1968; Sundquist, James L., *Politics and Policy: The Eisenhower, Kennedy, and Johnson Years*. Washington: Brooks Institute, 1968; Vanden Heuvel, William, and M. Gwirtzman, *On His Own: Robert F. Kennedy, 1964-1968*. Garden City, N.Y.: Doubleday, 1970; Viorst, Milton, *Fire in the Streets: America in the 1960s*. New York: Simon & Schuster, 1980; Warner, Sam Bass, Jr., *The Urban Wilderness*. New York: Harper & Row, 1972; Waskow, Arthur I., *From Race Riot to Sit-in*. Garden City, N.Y.: Doubleday, 1900; Whalen, Richard J., *The Founding Father: The Story of Joseph P. Kennedy*. New York: New American Library, 1964; White, Theodore H., *The Making of the President, 1964*. New York: Atheneum, 1965; White, William S., *The Professional: Lyndon B. Johnson*. Boston: Houghton Mifflin, 1964; Wicker, Tom, *JFK and LBJ: The Influence of Personality upon Politics*. New York: Morrow, 1968.

Chapter 31

Anson, Robert, and Sam Anson, *McGovern: A Political Biography*. New York: Holt, Rinehart and Winston, 1972; Barnaby, Frank, and Ronald Huisken, *Arms Uncontrolled*. Cambridge, Mass.: Harvard University Press, 1975; Barnet, Richard J., and Ronald Muller, *Global Reach: The Power of the Multinational Corporations*. New York: Simon & Schuster, 1974; Brzezinski, Zbigniew, *Between Two Ages: America's Role in the Technetronic Era*. New York: Viking, 1971 (Paper); Burke, Vincent J., and Vee Burke, *Nixon's Good Deed: Welfare Reform*. New York: Columbia University Press, 1974; Chester, Lewis, Godfrey Hodgson, and Bruce Page, *An American Melodrama: The Presidential Campaign of 1968*. New York: Viking, 1969; Cohen, Richard M., and Jules Witcover, *A Heartbeat Away*. New York: Bantam, 1974 (Paper); Cronin, Thomas E., *The Presidency Reappraised*. New York: Praeger, 1977; Davies, Peter, *The Truth About Kent State: A Challenge to the American Conscience*. New

York: Farrar, Straus & Giroux, 1973 (Paper); Drury, Allen, *Courage and Hesitation: Notes and Photographs of the Nixon Administration.* Garden City, N.Y.: Doubleday, 1971; Evans, Rowland, Jr., and Robert D. Novak, *Nixon in the White House: The Frustration of Power.* New York: Random, 1971; Frady, Marshall, *Wallace.* New York: World, 1968; Gardner, Lloyd C. (Ed.), *The Great Nixon Turnaround.* New York: New Viewpoints, 1973; George, Alexander L., and Richard Smoke, *Deterrence in American Foreign Policy.* New York: Columbia University Press, 1975; Goldwater, Barry, *The Conscience of a Majority.* New York: Pocket Books, 1971 (Paper); Graubard, Stephen R., *Kissinger, Portrait of a Mind.* New York: Norton, 1974 (Paper); Hart, Gary W., *Right From the Start.* New York: Quadrangle, 1973; Hsiao, Gene T. (Ed.), *Sino-American Détente and Its Policy Implications.* New York: Praeger, 1974; Jaworski, Leon, *The Right and the Power.* New York: Reader's Digest Press, 1976; Kalb, Marvin, and Bernard Kalb, *Kissinger.* Boston: Little, Brown, 1974; Kendrick, Alexander, *The Wound Within: America in the Vietnam Years, 1945–1974.* Boston: Little, Brown, 1974; Labovitz, John R., *Presidential Impeachment.* New Haven: Yale University Press, 1978; McCloskey, Robert G., *The Modern Supreme Court.* Cambridge, Mass.: Harvard University Press, 1972 (Paper); McGinniss, Joe, *The Selling of the President, 1968.* New York: Trident, 1969; Magruder, Jeb S., *An American Life.* New York: Atheneum, 1974; Mazlish, Bruce, *In Search of Nixon: A Psychohistorical Inquiry.* New York: Basic, 1972; Mazo, Earl, and Stephen Hess, *Nixon: A Political Portrait.* New York: Harper & Row, 1968; Packard, Vance, *A Nation of Strangers.* New York: McKay, 1972 (Paper: Pocket Books, 1974); Sale, Kirkpatrick, *SDS: Ten Years Toward a Revolution.* New York: Random, 1973; Scammon, Richard M., and Ben J. Wattenberg, *The Real Majority: How the Silent Center of the American Electorate Chooses Its President.* New York: Coward, 1970. Schlesinger, Arthur M., Jr., *The Imperial Presidency.* Boston: Houghton Mifflin, 1973; Shawcross, William, *Sideshow: Kissinger, Nixon, and the Destruction of Cambodia.* New York: Simon & Schuster, 1979; Sheehan, Edward R. F., *The Arabs, Israelis, and Kissinger.* New York: Reader's Digest Press, 1976; Sirica, John J., *To Set the Record Straight.* New York: Norton, 1979; Sroessinger, John, *Henry Kissinger: The Anguish of Power.* New York: Norton, 1976; Sussman, Barry, *The Great Coverup: Nixon and the Scandal of Watergate.* New York: Crowell, 1974; ter Horst, J. F., *Gerald Ford: Past . . . Present . . . Future.* New York: Third Press, 1974; Vestal, Bud, *et al.*, *Jerry Ford, Up Close.* New York: Coward, 1974; White, Theodore H., *The Making of the President, 1972.* New York: Atheneum, 1969; Witcover, Jules, *The Resurrection of Richard Nixon.* New York: Putnam, 1970.

Chapter 32

Carson, Rachel, *The Silent Spring.* Boston: Houghton Mifflin, 1962; Commoner, Barry, *The Closing Circle: Nature, Man and Technology.* New York: Knopf, 1971; Decter, Midge, *The New Chastity.* New York: Coward, McCann, and Geoghegan, 1972; Evans, Sara, *Personal Politics, The Roots of Women's Liberation in the Civil Rights Movement and the New Left.* New York: Knopf, 1979; Gornick, Vivian, and Barbara K. Moran, *Woman in Sexist Society: Studies in Power and Powerlessness.* New York: Basic, 1971; Harrington, Michael, *Decade of Decision, The Crisis of the American System.* New York: Simon & Schuster, 1980; Harris, Fred R., and J. V. Lindsay, *The State of the Cities.* New York: Praeger, 1972; Lasch, Christopher, *Haven in a Heartless World: The Family Beseiged.* New York: Basic, 1977; Matthiessen, Peter, and Sal Si Puedes: *César Chávez and the New American Revolution.* New York: Random, 1969; McLuhan, Marshall, *The Medium is the Massage.* New York: Bantam Books, 1967; Meyer, Peter, *James Earl Carter: The Man and the Myth.* Kansas City: Sheed Andrews & McMeel, 1978; Robinson, Paul, *The Modernization of Sex.* New York: Harper & Row, 1976; Wooten, James, *Dasher: The Roots and Rising of Jimmy Carter.* New York: Summit, 1978; Yates, Gayle G., *What Women Want: The Ideas of the Movement.* Cambridge Mass.: Harvard University Press, 1975.

The Declaration of Independence

When in the Course of human events, it becomes necessary for one people to dissolve the political bands which have connected them with another, and to assume among the Powers of the earth, the separate and equal station to which the Laws of Nature and of Nature's God entitle them, a decent respect to the opinions of mankind requires that they should declare the causes which impel them to the separation.

We hold these truths to be self-evident, that all men are created equal, that they are endowed by their Creator with certain unalienable Rights, that among these are Life, Liberty and the pursuit of Happiness. That to secure these rights, Governments are instituted among Men, deriving their just powers from the consent of the governed, That whenever any Form of Government becomes destructive of these ends, it is the Right of the People to alter or to abolish it, and to institute new Government, laying its foundation on such principles and organizing its powers in such form, as to them shall seem most likely to effect their Safety and Happiness. Prudence, indeed, will dictate that Governments long established should not be changed for light and transient causes; and accordingly all experience hath shown, that mankind are more disposed to suffer, while evils are sufferable, than to right themselves by abolishing the forms to which they are accustomed. But when a long train of abuses and usurpations, pursuing invariably the same Object evinces a design to reduce them under absolute Despotism, it is their right, it is their duty, to throw off such Government, and to provide new Guards for their future security.—Such has been the patient sufferance of these Colonies; and such is now the necessity which constrains them to alter their former Systems of Government. The history of the present King of Great Britain is a history of repeated injuries and usurpations, all having in direct object the establishment of an absolute Tyranny over these States. To prove this, let Facts be submitted to a candid world.

He has refused his Assent to Laws, the most wholesome and necessary for the public good.

He has forbidden his Governors to pass Laws of immediate and pressing importance, unless suspended in their operation till his Assent should be obtained; and when so suspended, he has utterly neglected to attend to them.

He has refused to pass other Laws for the accommodation of large districts of people, unless those people would relinquish the right of Representation in the Legislature, a right inestimable to them and formidable to tyrants only.

He has called together legislative bodies at places unusual, uncomfortable, and distant from the depository of their public Records, for the sole purpose of fatiguing them into compliance with his measures.

He has dissolved Representative Houses repeatedly, for opposing with manly firmness his invasions on the rights of the people.

He has refused for a long time, after such dissolutions, to cause others to be elected; whereby the Legislative Powers, incapable of Annihilation, have returned to the People at large for their exercise; the State remaining in the mean time exposed to all the dangers of invasion from without, and convulsions within.

He has endeavoured to prevent the population of these States; for that purpose obstructing the Laws of Naturalization of Foreigners; refusing to pass others to encourage their migration hither, and raising the conditions of new Appropriations of Lands.

He has obstructed the Administration of Justice, by refusing his Assent to Laws for establishing Judiciary powers.

He has made Judges dependent on his Will alone, for the tenure of their offices, and the amount and payment of their salaries.

He has erected a multitude of New Offices, and sent hither swarms of Officers to harass our People, and eat out their substance.

He has kept among us in times of peace, Standing Armies without the Consent of our legislature.

He has affected to render the Military independent of and superior to the Civil power.

He has combined with others to subject us to a jurisdiction foreign to our constitution, and unacknowledged by our laws; giving his Assent to their acts of pretended Legislation:

For quartering large bodies of armed troops among us:

For protecting them, by a mock Trial, from punishment for any Murders which they should commit on the Inhabitants of these States:

For cutting off our Trade with all parts of the world:

For imposing taxes on us without our Consent:

For depriving us in many cases, of the benefits of Trial by Jury:

For transporting us beyond Seas to be tried for pretended offences:

For abolishing the free System of English Laws in a neighbouring Province, establishing therein an Arbitrary government, and enlarging its Boundaries so as to render it at once an example and fit instrument for introducing the same absolute rule into these Colonies:

For taking away our Charters, abolishing our most valuable Laws, and altering fundamentally the Forms of our Governments:

For suspending our own Legislature, and declaring themselves invested with Power to legislate for us in all cases whatsoever.

He has abdicated Government here, by declaring us out of his Protection and waging War against us.

He has plundered our seas, ravaged our Coasts, burnt our towns, and destroyed the lives our people.

He is at this time transporting large Armies of foreign Mercenaries to compleat the works of death, desolation and tyranny, already begun with circumstances of Cruelty & perfidy scarcely paralleled in the most barbarous ages, and totally unworthy the Head of a civilized nation.

He has constrained our fellow Citizens taken Captive on the high Seas to bear Arms against their Country, to become the executioners of their friends and Brethren, or to fall themselves by their Hands.

He has excited domestic insurrections amongst us, and has endeavoured to bring on the inhabitants of our frontiers, the merciless Indian Savages, whose known rule of warfare, is an undistinguished destruction of all ages, sexes and conditions.

In every stage of these Oppressions We have Petitioned for Redress in the most humble terms: Our repeated Petitions have been answered only by repeated injury. A Prince, whose character is thus marked by every act which may define a Tyrant, is unfit to be the ruler of a free People.

Nor have We been wanting in attention to our British brethren. We have warned them from time to time of attempts by their legislature to extend an unwarrantable jurisdiction over us. We have reminded them of the circumstances of our emigration and settlement here. We have appealed to their native justice and magnanimity, and we have conjured them by the ties of our common kindred to disavow these usurpations, which, would inevitably interrupt our connections and correspondence. They too have been deaf to the voice of justice and of consanguinity. We must, therefore, acquiesce in the necessity, which denounces our Separation, and hold them, as we hold the rest of mankind, Enemies in War, in Peace Friends.

We, therefore, the Representatives of the united States of America, in General Congress, Assembled, appealing to the Supreme Judge of the world for the rectitude of our intentions, do, in the Name, and by Authority of the good People of these Colonies, solemnly publish and declare, That these United Colonies are, and of Right ought to be Free and Independent States; that they are Absolved from all Allegiance to the British Crown, and that all political connection between them and the State of Great Britain, is and ought to be totally dissolved; and that as Free and Independent States, they have full Power to levy War, conclude Peace, contract Alliances, establish Commerce, and to do all other Acts and Things which Independent States may of right do. And for the support of this Declaration, with a firm reliance on the protection of divine Providence, we mutually pledge to each other our Lives, our Fortunes and our sacred Honor.

The Constitution of the United States

We the people of the United States, in Order to form a more perfect Union, establish Justice, insure domestic Tranquility, provide for the common defence, promote the general Welfare, and secure the Blessings of Liberty to ourselves and our Posterity, do ordain and establish this CONSTITUTION for the United States of America.

Article 1

Section 1 All legislative Powers herein granted shall be vested in a Congress of the United States, which shall consist of a Senate and House of Representatives.

Section 2 The House of Representatives shall be composed of Members chosen every second Year by the People of the several States, and the Electors in each State shall have the Qualifications requisite for Electors of the most numerous Branch of the State Legislature.

No Person shall be a Representative who shall not have attained to the Age of twenty-five Years, and been seven Years a Citizen of the United States, and who shall not, when elected, be an Inhabitant of that State in which he shall be chosen.

Representatives and direct Taxes shall be apportioned among the several States which may be included within this Union, according to their respective Numbers, which shall be determined by adding to the whole Number of free Persons, including those bound to Service for a Term of Years, and excluding Indians not taxed, three-fifths of all other Persons. The actual Enumeration shall be made within three Years after the first Meeting of the Congress of the United States, and within every subsequent Term of ten Years, in such Manner as they shall by Law direct. The Number of Representatives shall not exceed one for every thirty Thousand, but each State shall have at Least one Representative; and until such enumeration shall be made, the State of New Hampshire shall be entitled to chuse three, Massachusetts eight, Rhode-Island and Providence Plantations one, Connecticut five, New-York six, New Jersey four, Pennsylvania eight, Delaware one, Maryland six, Virginia ten, North Carolina five, South Carolina five, and Georgia three.

When vacancies happen in the Representation from any State, the Executive Authority thereof shall issue Writs of Election to fill such Vacancies.

The House of Representatives shall chuse their Speaker and other Officers; and shall have the sole Power of Impeachment.

Section 3 The Senate of the United States shall be composed of two Senators from each State, chosen by the Legislature thereof, for six Years; and each Senator shall have one Vote.

Immediately after they shall be assembled in Consequence of the first Election, they shall be divided as equally as may be into three Classes. The Seats of the Senators of the first Class shall be vacated at the Expiration of the second Year, of the second Class at the Expiration of the fourth Year, and of the third Class at the Expiration of the sixth Year, so that one-third may be chosen every second Year; and if Vacancies happen by Resignation, or otherwise, during the Recess of the Legislature of any State, the Executive thereof may make temporary Appointments until the next Meeting of the Legislature, which shall then fill such Vacancies.

No Person shall be a Senator who shall not have attained to the Age of thirty Years, and been nine Years a Citizen of the United States, and who shall not, when elected, be an Inhabitant of that State in which he shall be chosen.

The Vice President of the United States shall be President of the Senate, but shall have no vote, unless they be equally divided.

The Senate shall chuse their other Officers, and also a President pro tempore, in the absence of the Vice President, or when he shall exercise the Office of the President of the United States.

The Senate shall have the sole Power to try all Impeachments. When sitting for that purpose, they shall be on Oath or Affirmation. When the President of the United States is tried, the Chief Justice shall preside: And no person shall be convicted without the Concurrence of two thirds of the Members present.

Judgment in Cases of Impeachment shall not extend further than to removal from Office, and disqualification to hold and enjoy any Office of honor, Trust, or Profit under the United States: but the Party convicted shall nevertheless be liable and subject to Indictment, Trial, Judgment, and Punishment, according to Law.

Section 4 The Times, Places and Manner of holding Elections for Senators and Representatives, shall be prescribed in each state by the Legislature thereof; but the Congress may at any time by Law make or alter such Regulations, except as to the Places of Chusing Senators.

The Congress shall assemble at least once in every Year, and such Meeting shall be on the first Monday in December, unless they shall by Law appoint a different Day.

Section 5 Each House shall be the Judge of the Elections, Returns and Qualifications of its own Members, and a Majority of each shall constitute a Quorum to do Business; but a smaller number may adjourn from day to day, and may be authorized to compel the Attendance of absent Members, in such Manner, and under such Penalties, as each House may provide.

Each House may determine the Rules of its Proceedings, punish its Members for disorderly Behaviour, and, with the Concurrence of two-thirds, expel a Member.

Each House shall keep a Journal of its Proceedings, and from time to time publish the same, excepting such Parts as may in their Judgment require Secrecy; and the Yeas and Nays of the Members of either House on any question shall, at the Desire of one-fifth of those Present, be entered on the Journal.

Neither House, during the Session of Congress, shall, without the Consent of the other, adjourn for more than three days, nor to any other Place than that in which the two Houses shall be sitting.

Section 6 The Senators and Representatives shall receive a Compensation for their Services, to be ascertained by Law, and paid out of the Treasury of the United States. They shall in all Cases, except Treason, Felony, and Breach of the Peace, be privileged from Arrest during their Attendance at the Session of their respective Houses, and in going to and returning from the same; and for any speech or Debate in either House, they shall not be questioned in any other Place.

No Senator or Representative shall, during the Time for which he was elected, be appointed to any civil Office under the Authority of the United States, which shall have been created, or the Emoluments whereof shall have been increased, during such time; and no Person holding any Office under the United States shall be a Member of either House during his continuance in Office.

Section 7 All Bills for raising Revenue shall originate in the House of Representatives; but the Senate may propose or concur with Amendments as on other Bills.

Every Bill which shall have passed the House of Representatives and the Senate, shall, before it become a Law, be presented to the President of the United States; If he approve he shall sign it, but if not he shall return it, with his Objections, to that House in which it shall have originated, who shall enter the Objections at large on their Journal, and proceed to reconsider it. If after such Reconsideration two-thirds of that House shall agree to pass the Bill, it shall be sent, together with the Objections, to the other House, by which it shall likewise be reconsidered, and if approved by two-thirds of that House, it shall become a Law. But in all such Cases the Votes of both Houses shall be determined by Yeas and Nays, and the Names of the Persons voting for and against the Bill shall be entered on the Journal of each House respectively. If any Bill shall not be returned by the President within ten Days (Sundays excepted) after it shall have been presented to him, the Same shall be a Law, in like Manner as if he had signed it, unless the Congress by their Adjournment prevent its Return, in which case it shall not be a Law.

Every Order, Resolution, or Vote to which the Concurrence of the Senate and House of Representatives may be necessary (except on a question of Adjournment) shall be presented to the President of the United States; and before the Same shall take Effect, shall be approved by him, or being disapproved by him, shall be repassed by two-thirds of the Senate and House of Representatives, according to the Rules and Limitations prescribed in the Case of a Bill.

Section 8 The Congress shall have Power To lay and collect Taxes, Duties, Imposts and Excises, to pay the Debts and provide for the common Defence and general Welfare of the United States, but all Duties, Imposts and Excises shall be uniform throughout the United States;

To borrow money on the credit of the United States;

To regulate Commerce with foreign Nations, and among the several States, and with the Indian Tribes;

To establish an uniform Rule of Naturalization, and uniform Laws on the subject of Bankruptcies throughout the United States;

To coin Money, regulate the Value thereof, and of foreign Coin, and fix the Standard of Weights and Measures;

To provide for the Punishment of counterfeiting the Securities and current Coin of the United States;

To establish Post Offices and post Roads;

To promote the Progress of Science and useful Arts, by securing for limited Times to Authors and Inventors the exclusive Right to their respective Writings and Discoveries;

To constitute Tribunals inferior to the Supreme Court;

To define and punish Piracies and Felonies committed on the high Seas, and Offenses against the Law of Nations;

To declare War, grant Letters of Marque and Reprisal, and make Rules concerning Captures on Land and Water;

To raise and support Armies, but no Appropriation of Money to that Use shall be for a longer Term than two Years;

To provide and maintain a Navy;

To make Rules for the Government and Regulation of the land and naval forces;

To provide for calling forth the Militia to execute the Laws of the Union, suppress Insurrections and repel Invasions;

To provide for organizing, arming, and disciplining the Militia, and for governing such Part of them as may be employed in the Service of the United States, reserving to the States respectively, the Appointment of the Officers, and the Authority of training the Militia according to the discipline prescribed by Congress;

To exercise exclusive Legislation in all Cases whatsoever, over such District (not exceeding ten Miles square) as may, by Cession of particular States, and the acceptance of Congress, become the Seat of Government of the United States, and to exercise like Authority over all Places purchased by the Consent of the Legislature of the State in which the Same shall be, for the Erection of Forts, Magazines, Arsenals, dock-Yards, and other needful Buildings;—And

To make all Laws which shall be necessary and proper for carrying into Execution the foregoing Powers, and all other Powers vested by this Constitution in the Government of the United States, or in any Department or Officer thereof.

Section 9 The Migration or Importation of such Persons as any of the States now existing shall think proper to admit, shall not be prohibited by the Congress prior to the Year one thousand eight hundred and eight, but a tax or duty may be imposed on such Importation, not exceeding ten dollars for each Person.

The privilege of the Writ of Habeas Corpus shall not be suspended, unless when in Cases of Rebellion or Invasion the public Safety may require it.

No Bill of Attainder or ex post facto Law shall be passed.

No Capitation, or other direct, Tax shall be laid unless in Proportion to the Census or Enumeration herein before directed to be taken.

No Tax or Duty shall be laid on Articles exported from any State.

No Preference shall be given by any Regulation of Revenue to the Ports of one State over those of another: nor shall Vessels bound to, or from, one State, be obliged to enter, clear, or pay Duties in another.

No Money shall be drawn from the Treasury, but in Consequence of Appropriations made by Law; and a regular Statement and Account of the Receipts and Expenditures of all public Money shall be published from time to time.

No Title of Nobility shall be granted by the United States: And no Person holding any Office of Profit or Trust under them, shall, without the Consent of the Congress, accept of any present, Emolument, Office, or Title, of any kind whatever, from any King, Prince, or foreign State.

Section 10 No State shall enter into any Treaty, Alliance, or Confederation; grant Letters of Marque and Reprisal; coin Money; emit Bills of Credit; make any Thing but gold and silver Coin a Tender in Payment of Debts; pass any Bill of Attainder, ex post facto Law, or Law impairing the Obligation of Contracts, or grant any Title of Nobility.

No state shall, without the Consent of the Congress, lay any Imposts or Duties on Imports or Exports, except what may be absolutely necessary for executing its inspection Laws: and the net Produce of all Duties and Imposts, laid by any State on Imports or Exports, shall be for the Use of the Treasury of the United States; and all such Laws shall be subject to the Revision and Control of the Congress.

No State shall, without the Consent of Congress, lay any duty of Tonnage, keep Troops, or Ships of War in time of Peace, enter into any Agreement or Compact with another State, or with a foreign Power, or engage in War, unless actually invaded, or in such imminent Danger as will not admit of delay.

Article II

Section 1 The executive Power shall be vested in a President of the United States of America. He shall hold his Office during the Term of four Years, and, together with the Vice President, chosen for the same Term, be elected, as follows:

Each State shall appoint, in such Manner as the Legislature thereof may direct, a Number of Electors, equal to the whole Number of Senators and Representatives to which the State may be entitled in the Congress: but no Senator or Representative, or Person holding an Office of Trust or Profit under the United States, shall be appointed an Elector.

The Electors shall meet in their respective States, and vote by Ballot for two persons, of whom one at least shall not be an Inhabitant of the same State with themselves. And they shall make a List of all the Persons voted for, and of the Number of Votes for each; which List they shall sign and certify, and transmit sealed to the Seat of the Government of the United States, directed to the President of the Senate. The President of the Senate shall, in the Presence of the Senate and House of Representatives, open all the Certificates, and the Votes shall then be counted. The Person having the greatest Number of Votes shall be the President, if such Number be a Majority of the whole Number of Electors appointed; and if there be more than one who have such Majority, and have an equal Number of Votes, then the House of Representatives shall immediately chuse by Ballot one of them for President; and if no Person have a Majority, then from the five highest on the List the said House shall in like Manner chuse the President. But in chusing the President, the Votes shall be taken by States, the Representation from each State having one Vote; a quorum for this Purpose shall consist of a Member or Members from two-thirds of the States, and a Majority of all the States shall be necessary to a Choice. In every Case, after the Choice of the President, the Person having the greatest Number of Votes of the Electors shall be the Vice President. But if there should remain two or more who have equal votes, the Senate shall chuse from them by Ballot the Vice President.

The Congress may determine the Time of chusing the Electors, and the Day on which they shall give their Votes; which Day shall be the same throughout the United States.

No person except a natural-born Citizen, or a Citizen of the United States, at the time of the Adoption of this Constitution, shall be eligible to the Office of President; neither shall any Person be eligible to that Office who shall not have attained to the Age of thirty-five Years, and been fourteen Years a Resident within the United States.

In Case of the Removal of the President from Office, or of his Death, Resignation, or Inability to discharge the Powers and Duties of the said Office, the same shall devolve on the Vice President, and the Congress may by Law provide for the Case of Removal, Death, Resignation, or Inability, both of the President and Vice President, declaring what Officer shall then act as President, and such Officer shall act accordingly, until the Disability be removed, or a President shall be elected.

The President shall, at stated Times, receive for his Services a Compensation, which shall neither be increased nor diminished during the Period for which he shall have been elected, and he shall not receive within that Period any other Emolument from the United States, or any of them.

Before he enter on the Execution of his Office, he shall take the following Oath or Affirmation:—"I do solemnly swear (or affirm) that I will faithfully execute the Office of President of the United States, and will, to the best of my Ability, preserve, protect, and defend the Constitution of the United States."

Section 2 The President shall be Commander in Chief of the Army and Navy of the United States, and of the Militia of the several States, when called into the actual Service of the United States; he may require the Opinion, in writing, of the principal Officer in each of the executive Departments, upon any subject relating to the Duties of their respective Offices, and he shall have Power to Grant Reprieves and Pardons for Offences against the United States, except in Cases of Impeachment.

He shall have Power, by and with the Advice and Consent of the Senate, to make Treaties, provided two-thirds of the Senators present concur; and he shall nominate, and by and with the Advice and Consent of the Senate, shall appoint Ambassadors, other public Ministers and Consuls, Judges of the supreme Court, and all other Officers of the United States, whose Appointments are not herein otherwise provided for, and which shall be established by Law: but the Congress may by Law vest the Appointment of such inferior Officers, as they think proper, in the President alone, in the Courts of Law, or in the Heads of Departments.

The President shall have Power to fill up all Vacancies that may happen during the Recess of the Senate, by granting Commissions which shall expire at the End of their next Session.

Section 3 He shall from time to time give to the Congress Information of the State of the Union, and recommend to their Consideration such Measures as he shall judge necessary and expedient; he may, on extraordinary occasions, convene both Houses, or either of them, and in Case of Disagreement between them, with respect to the Time of Adjournment, he may adjourn them to such Time as he shall think proper; he shall receive Ambassadors and other public Ministers; he shall take Care that the Laws be faithfully executed, and shall Commission all the Officers of the United States.

Section 4 The President, Vice President and all civil Officers of the United States, shall be removed from Office on Impeachment for, and Conviction of, Treason, Bribery, or other high Crimes and Misdemeanors.

Article III

Section 1 The judicial Power of the United States, shall be vested in one supreme Court, and in such inferior Courts as the Congress may from time to time ordain and establish. The Judges, both of the supreme and inferior Courts, shall hold their Offices during good Behaviour, and shall, at stated Times, receive for their Services, a Compensation, which shall not be diminished during their Continuance in Office.

Section 2 The judicial Power shall extend to all Cases, in Law and Equity, arising under this Constitution, the Laws of the United States, and Treaties made, or which shall be made, under their Authority;—to all Cases affecting Ambassadors, other public Ministers and Consuls;—to all Cases of admiralty and maritime Jurisdiction;—to Controversies to which the United States shall be a Party;—to Controversies between two or more States;—between a State and Citizens of another State;—between Citizens of the same State claiming Lands under Grants of different States, and between a State, or the Citizens thereof, and foreign States, Citizens or Subjects.

In all Cases affecting Ambassadors, other public Ministers and Consuls, and those in which a State shall be Party, the supreme Court shall have original Jurisdiction. In all the other Cases before mentioned, the supreme Court shall have appellate Jurisdiction, both as to Law and Fact, with such Exceptions, and under such Regulations as the Congress shall make.

The trial of all Crimes, except in Cases of Impeachment, shall be by Jury; and such Trial shall be held in the State where the said Crimes shall have been committed; but when not committed within any State, the Trial shall be at such Place or Places as the Congress may by Law have directed.

Section 3 Treason against the United States, shall consist only in levying War against them, or in adhering to their Enemies, giving them Aid and Comfort. No Person shall be convicted of Treason unless on the Testimony of two Witnesses to the same overt Act, or on Confession in open Court.

The Congress shall have power to declare the Punishment of Treason, but no Attainder of Treason shall work Corruption of Blood, or Forfeiture except during the Life of the Person attainted.

Article IV

Section 1 Full Faith and Credit shall be given in each State to the public Acts, Records, and judicial Proceedings of every other State. And the Congress may by general Laws prescribe the Manner in which such Acts, Records and Proceedings shall be proved, and the Effect thereof.

Section 2 The Citizens of each State shall be entitled to all Privileges and Immunities of Citizens in the several States.

A Person charged in any State with Treason, Felony, or other Crime, who shall flee from Justice, and be found in another State, shall on demand of the executive Authority of the State from which he fled, be delivered up, to be removed to the State having Jurisdiction of the crime.

No Person held to Service or Labour in one State, under the Laws thereof, escaping into another, shall, in Consequence of any Law or Regulation therein, be discharged from such Service or Labour, but shall be delivered up on Claim of the Party to whom such Service or Labour may be due.

Section 3 New States may be admitted by the Congress into this Union; but no new State shall be formed or erected within the Jurisdiction of any other State; nor any State be formed by the Junction of two or more States, or parts of States, without the Consent of the Legislatures of the States concerned as well as of the Congress.

The Congress shall have Power to dispose of and make all needful Rules and Regulations respecting the Territory or other Property belonging to the United States; and nothing in this Constitution shall be so construed as to Prejudice any Claims of the United States, or of any particular State.

Section 4 The United States shall guarantee to every State in this Union a Republican Form of Government, and shall protect each of them against Invasion; and on Application of the Legislature, or of the Executive (when the Legislature cannot be convened) against domestic Violence.

Article V

The Congress, whenever two-thirds of both Houses shall deem it necessary, shall propose Amendments to this Constitution, or, on the Application of the Legislatures of two-thirds of the several States, shall call a Convention for proposing Amendments, which, in either Case, shall be valid to all Intents and Purposes, as part of this Constitution, when ratified by the Legislatures of three-fourths of the several States, or by Conventions in three-fourths thereof, as the one or the other Mode of Ratification may be proposed by the Congress; Provided that no Amendment which may be made prior to the Year One thousand eight hundred and eight shall in any Manner affect the first and fourth Clauses in the Ninth Section of the first Article; and that no State, without its Consent, shall be deprived of its equal Suffrage in the Senate.

Article VI

All Debts contracted and Engagements entered into, before the Adoption of this Constitution, shall be as valid against the United States under this Constitution, as under the Confederation.

This Constitution, and the Laws of the United States which shall be made in Pursuance thereof; and all Treaties made, or which shall be made, under the Authority of the United States, shall be the supreme Law of the Land; and the Judges in every State shall be bound thereby, any Thing in the Constitution or Laws of any State to the Contrary notwithstanding.

The Senators and Representatives before mentioned, and the Members of the several State Legislatures, and all executive and judicial Officers, both of the United States and of the several States, shall be bound by Oath or Affirmation to support this Constitution; but no religious Test shall ever be required as a qualification to any Office or public Trust under the United States.

Article VII

The Ratification of the Conventions of nine States shall be sufficient for the Establishment of this Constitution between the States so ratifying the same.

Done in Convention by the Unanimous Consent of the States present the Seventeenth Day of September in the Year of our Lord one thousand seven hundred and Eighty seven, and of the Independence of the United States of America the Twelfth. In Witness whereof We have hereunto subscribed our Names.

Articles in Addition to, and Amendment of, the Constitution of the United States of America, Proposed by Congress, and Ratified by the Legislatures of the Several States, Pursuant to the Fifth Article of the Original Constitution.

Amendment I [1791]

Congress shall make no law respecting an establishment of religion, or prohibiting the free exercise thereof; or abridging the freedom of speech, or of the press; or the right of the people peaceably to assemble, and to petition the Government for a redress of grievances.

Amendment II [1791]

A well regulated Militia, being necessary to the security of a free State, the right of the people to keep and bear Arms, shall not be infringed.

Amendment III [1791]

No Soldier shall, in time of peace, be quartered in any house, without the consent of the Owner, nor in time of war, but in a manner to be prescribed by law.

Amendment IV [1791]

The right of the people to be secure in their persons, houses, papers, and effects, against unreasonable searches and seizures, shall not be violated, and no Warrants shall issue, but upon probable cause, supported by Oath or affirmation, and particularly describing the place to be searched, and the persons or things to be seized.

Amendment V [1791]

No person shall be held to answer for a capital or otherwise infamous crime, unless on a presentment or indictment of a Grand Jury, except in cases arising in the land or naval forces, or in the Militia, when in actual service in time of War or public danger; nor shall any person be subject for the same offence to be twice put in jeopardy of life or limb; nor shall be compelled in any criminal case to be a witness against himself, nor be deprived of life, liberty, or property, without due process of law; nor shall private property be taken for public use, without just compensation.

Amendment VI [1791]

In all criminal prosecutions, the accused shall enjoy the right to a speedy and public trial, by an impartial jury of the State and district wherein the crime shall have been committed, which district shall have been previously ascertained by law, and to be informed of the nature and cause of the accusation; to be confronted with the witnesses against him; to have compulsory process for obtaining witnesses in his favor, and to have the Assistance of Counsel for his defence.

Amendment VII [1791]

In Suits at common law, where the value in controversy shall exceed twenty dollars, the right of trial by jury shall be preserved, and no fact tried by a jury, shall be otherwise re-examined in any Court of the United States, than according to the rules of the common law.

Amendment VIII [1791]

Excessive bail shall not be required, nor excessive fines imposed, nor cruel and unusual punishments inflicted.

Amendment IX [1791]

The enumeration in the Constitution, of certain rights, shall not be construed to deny or disparage others retained by the people.

Amendment X [1791]

The powers not delegated to the United States by the Constitution, nor prohibited by it to the States, are reserved to the States respectively, or to the people.

Amendment XI [1798]

The Judicial power of the United States shall not be construed to extend to any suit in law or equity, commenced or prosecuted against one of the United States by Citizens of another State, or by Citizens or Subjects of any Foreign State.

Amendment XII [1804]

The Electors shall meet in their respective States and vote by ballot for President and Vice President, one of whom, at least, shall not be an inhabitant of the same States with themselves; they shall name in their ballots the person voted for as President, and in distinct ballots the person voted for as Vice President, and they shall make distinct lists of all persons voted for as President, and of all persons voted for as Vice President, and of the number of votes for each, which lists they shall sign and certify, and transmit sealed to the seat of the government of the United States, directed to the President of the Senate; —The President of the Senate shall, in the presence of the Senate and House of Representatives, open all the certificates and the votes shall then be counted;—The person having the greatest number of votes for President, shall be the President, if such number be a majority of the whole number of Electors appointed; and if no person have such majority, then from the persons having the highest numbers not exceeding three on the list of those voted for as President, the House of Representatives shall choose immediately, by ballot, the President. But in choosing the President, the votes shall be taken by states, the representation from each state having one vote; a quorum for this purpose shall consist of a member or members from two-thirds of the states, and a majority of all the states shall be necessary to a choice. And if the House of Representatives shall not choose a President whenever the right of choice shall devolve upon them, before the fourth day of March next following, then the Vice President shall act as President, as in the case of the death or other constitutional disability of the President.—The person having the greatest number of votes as Vice President, shall be the Vice President, if such number be a majority of the whole number of Electors appointed, and if no person have a majority, then from the two highest numbers on the list, the Senate shall choose the Vice President; a quorum for the purpose shall consist of two-thirds of the whole number of Senators, and a majority of the whole number shall be necessary to a choice. But no person constitutionally ineligible to the office of President shall be eligible to that of Vice President of the United States.

Amendment XIII [1865]

Section 1 Neither slavery nor involuntary servitude, except as a punishment for crime whereof the party shall have been duly convicted, shall exist within the United States, or any place subject to their jurisdiction.

Section 2 Congress shall have power to enforce this article by appropriate legislation.

Amendment XIV [1868]

Section 1 All persons born or naturalized in the United States, and subject to the jurisdiction thereof, are citizens of the United States and of the State wherein they reside. No State shall make or enforce any law which shall abridge the privileges or immunities of citizens of the United States; nor shall any State deprive any person of life, liberty, or property, without due process of law; nor deny to any person within its jurisdiction the equal protection of the laws.

Section 2 Representatives shall be apportioned among the several States according to their respective numbers, counting the whole number of persons in each State, excluding Indians not taxed. But when the right to vote at any election for the choice of electors for President and Vice President of the United States, Representatives in Congress, the Executive and Judicial officers of a State, or the members of the Legislature thereof, is denied to any of the male inhabitants of such State, being twenty-one years of age, and citizens of the United States, or in any way abridged, except for participation in rebellion, or other crime, the basis of representation therein shall be reduced in the proportion which the number of such male citizens shall bear to the whole number of male citizens twenty-one years of age in such State.

Section 3 No person shall be a Senator or Representative in Congress, or elector of President and Vice President, or hold any office, civil or military, under the United States, or under any State, who, having previously taken an oath, as a member of Congress, or as an officer of the United States, or as a member of any State legislature, or as an executive or judicial officer of any State, to support the Constitution of the United States, shall have engaged in insurrection or rebellion against the same, or given aid or comfort to the enemies thereof. But Congress may by a vote of two-thirds of each House, remove such disability.

Section 4 The validity of the public debt of the United States, authorized by law, including debts incurred for payment of pensions and bounties for services in suppressing insurrection or rebellion, shall not be questioned. But neither the United States nor any State shall assume or pay any debt or obligation incurred in aid of insurrection or rebellion against the United States, or any claim for the loss or emancipation of any slave; but all such debts, obligations, and claims shall be held illegal and void.

Section 5 The Congress shall have the power to enforce, by appropriate legislation, the provisions of this article.

Amendment XV [1870]

Section 1 The right of citizens of the United States to vote shall not be denied or abridged by the United States or by any State on account of race, color, or previous condition of servitude—

Section 2 The Congress shall have power to enforce this article by appropriate legislation.

Amendment XVI [1913]

The Congress shall have power to lay and collect taxes on incomes, from whatever source derived, without apportionment among the several States, and without regard to any census or enumeration.

Amendment XVII [1913]

The Senate of the United States shall be composed of two Senators from each State, elected by the people thereof, for six years; and each Senator shall have one vote. The electors in each State shall have the qualifications requisite for electors of the most numerous branch of the State legislatures.

When vacancies happen in the representation of any State in the Senate, the executive authority of such State shall issue writs of election to fill such vacancies: *Provided*, That the legislature of any State may empower the executive thereof to make temporary appointments until the people fill the vacancies by election as the legislature may direct.

This amendment shall not be so construed as to affect the election or term of any Senator chosen before it becomes valid as part of the Constitution.

Amendment XVIII [1919]

Section 1 After one year from the ratification of this article the manufacture, sale, or transportation of intoxicating liquors within, the importation thereof into, or the exportation thereof from the United States and all territory subject to the jurisdiction thereof for beverage purposes is hereby prohibited.

Section 2 The Congress and the several States shall have concurrent power to enforce this article by appropriate legislation.

Section 3 This article shall be inoperative unless it shall have been ratified as an amendment to the Constitution by the legislatures of the several States, as provided in the Constitution, within seven years from the date of the submission hereof to the States by the Congress.

Amendment XIX [1920]

The right of citizens of the United States to vote shall not be denied or abridged by the United States or by any State on account of sex.

Congress shall have power to enforce this article by appropriate legislation.

Amendment XX [1933]

Section 1 The terms of the President and Vice President shall end at noon on the 20th day of January, and the terms of Senators and Representatives at noon on the 3d day of January, of the years in which such terms would have ended if this article had not been ratified; and the terms of their successors shall then begin.

Section 2 The Congress shall assemble at least once in every year, and such meeting shall begin at noon on the 3d day of January, unless they shall by law appoint a different day.

Section 3 If, at the time fixed for the beginning of the term of the President, the President elect shall have died, the Vice President elect shall become President. If a President shall not have been chosen before the time fixed for the beginning of his term, or if the President elect shall have failed to qualify, then the Vice President elect shall act as President until a President shall have qualified; and the Congress may by law provide for the case wherein neither a President elect nor a Vice President elect shall have qualified, declaring who shall then act as President, or the manner in which one who is to act shall be selected, and such person shall act accordingly until a President or Vice President shall have qualified.

Section 4 The Congress may by law provide for the case of the death of any of the persons from whom the House of Representatives may choose a President whenever the right of choice shall have devolved upon them, and for the case of the death of any of the persons from whom the Senate may choose a Vice President whenever the right of choice shall have devolved upon them.

Section 5 Sections 1 and 2 shall take effect on the 15th day of October following the ratification of this article.

Section 6 This article shall be inoperative unless it shall have been ratified as an amendment to the Constitution by the legislatures of three-fourths of the several States within seven years from the date of its submission.

Amendment XXI [1933]

Section 1 The eighteenth article of amendment to the Constitution of the United States is hereby repealed.

Section 2 The transportation or importation into any State, Territory, or possession of the United States for delivery or use therein of intoxicating liquors, in violation of the laws thereof, is hereby prohibited.

Section 3 This article shall be inoperative unless it shall have been ratified as an amendment to the Constitution by conventions in the several States, as provided in the Constitution, within seven years from the date of the submission hereof to the States by the Congress.

Amendment XXII [1951]

No person shall be elected to the office of the President more than twice, and no person who has held the office of President, or acted as President, for more than two years of a term to which some other person was elected President shall be elected to the office of the President more than once.

But this Article shall not apply to any person holding the office of President when this Article was proposed by the Congress, and shall not prevent any person who may be holding the office of President, or acting as President, during the term within which this Article becomes operative from holding the office of President or acting as President during the remainder of such term.

Amendment XXIII [1961]

Section 1 The District constituting the seat of Government of the United States shall appoint in such manner as the Congress may direct:

A number of electors of President and Vice President equal to the whole number of Senators and Representatives in Congress to which the District would be entitled if it were a State, but in no event more than the least populous State; they shall be in addition to those appointed by the States, but they shall be considered, for the purposes of the election of President and Vice President, to be electors appointed by a State; and they shall meet in the District and perform such duties as provided by the twelfth article of amendment.

Section 2 The Congress shall have power to enforce this article by appropriate legislation.

Amendment XXIV [1964]

Section 1 The right of citizens of the United States to vote in any primary or other election for President or Vice President, for electors for President or Vice President, or for Senator or Representative in Congress, shall not be denied or abridged by the United States or any State by reason of failure to pay any poll tax or other tax.

Section 2 The Congress shall have the power to enforce this article by appropriate legislation.

Amendment XXV [1967]

Section 1 In case of the removal of the President from office or his death or resignation, the Vice President shall become President.

Section 2 Whenever there is a vacancy in the office of the Vice President, the President shall nominate a Vice President who shall take the office upon confirmation by a majority vote of both houses of Congress.

Section 3 Whenever the President transmits to the President pro tempore of the Senate and the Speaker of the House of Representatives his written declaration that he is unable to discharge the powers and duties of his office, and until he transmits to them a written declaration to the contrary, such powers and duties shall be discharged by the Vice President as Acting President.

Section 4 Whenever the Vice President and a majority of either the principal officers of the executive departments, or of such other body as Congress may by law provide, transmit to the President pro tempore of the Senate and the Speaker of the House of Representatives their written declaration that the President is unable to discharge the powers and duties of his office, the Vice President shall immediately assume the powers and duties of the office as Acting President.

Thereafter, when the President transmits to the President pro tempore of the Senate and the Speaker of the House of Representatives his written declaration that no inability exists, he shall resume the powers and duties of his office unless the Vice President and a majority of either the principal officers of the executive departments, or of such other body as Congress may by law provide, transmit within four days to the President pro tempore of the Senate and the Speaker of the House of Representatives their written declaration that the President is unable to discharge the powers and duties of his office. Thereupon Congress shall decide the issue, assembling within forty-eight hours for that purpose if not in session. If the Congress, within twenty-one days after receipt of the latter written declaration, or, if Congress is not in session, within twenty-one days after Congress is required to assemble, determines by two-thirds vote of both houses that the President is unable to discharge the powers and duties of his office, the Vice President shall continue to discharge the same as Acting President; otherwise, the President shall resume the powers and duties of his office.

Amendment XXVI [1971]

Section 1 The right of citizens of the United States, who are eighteen years of age or older, to vote shall not be denied or abridged by the United States or any state on account of age.

Section 2 The Congress shall have the power to enforce this article by appropriate legislation.

Presidential Elections

Year	Candidates	Party	Popular vote	Electoral vote
1789	**George Washington**			69
	John Adams			34
	Others			35
1792	**George Washington**			132
	John Adams			77
	George Clinton			50
	Others			5
1796	**John Adams**	Federalist		71
	Thomas Jefferson	Democratic-Republican		68
	Thomas Pinckney	Federalist		59
	Aaron Burr	Democratic-Republican		30
	Others			48
1800	**Thomas Jefferson**	Democratic-Republican		73
	Aaron Burr	Democratic-Republican		73
	John Adams	Federalist		65
	Charles C. Pinckney	Federalist		64
1804	**Thomas Jefferson**	Democratic-Republican		162
	Charles C. Pinckney	Federalist		14
1808	**James Madison**	Democratic-Republican		122
	Charles C. Pinckney	Federalist		47
	George Clinton	Independent-Republican		6
1812	**James Madison**	Democratic-Republican		128
	DeWitt Clinton	Federalist		89
1816	**James Monroe**	Democratic-Republican		183
	Rufus King	Federalist		34
1820	**James Monroe**	Democratic-Republican		231
	John Quincy Adams	Independent-Republican		1
1824	**John Quincy Adams**	Democratic-Republican	108,740	84
	Andrew Jackson	Democratic-Republican	153,544	99
	Henry Clay	Democratic-Republican	47,136	37
	William H. Crawford	Democratic-Republican	46,618	41
1828	**Andrew Jackson**	Democratic	647,231	178
	John Quincy Adams	National Republican	509,097	83
1832	**Andrew Jackson**	Democratic	687,502	219
	Henry Clay	National Republican	530,189	49
	William Wirt	Anti-Masonic	33,108	7
	John Floyd	National Republican		11
1836	**Martin Van Buren**	Democratic	761,549	170
	William H. Harrison	Whig	549,567	73
	Hugh L. White	Whig	145,396	26
	Daniel Webster	Whig	41,287	14

Year	Candidates	Party	Popular vote	Electoral vote
1840	**William H. Harrison** **(John Tyler, 1841)**	Whig	1,275,017	234
	Martin Van Buren	Democratic	1,128,702	60
1844	**James K. Polk**	Democratic	1,337,243	170
	Henry Clay	Whig	1,299,068	105
	James G. Birney	Liberty	62,300	
1848	**Zachary Taylor** **(Millard Fillmore, 1850)**	Whig	1,360,101	163
	Lewis Cass	Democratic	1,220,544	127
	Martin Van Buren	Free Soil	291,263	
1852	**Franklin Pierce**	Democratic	1,601,474	254
	Winfield Scott	Whig	1,386,578	42
1856	**James Buchanan**	Democratic	1,838,169	174
	John C. Frémont	Republican	1,335,264	114
	Millard Fillmore	American	874,534	8
1860	**Abraham Lincoln**	Republican	1,865,593	180
	Stephen A. Douglas	Democratic	1,382,713	12
	John C. Breckinridge	Democratic	848,356	72
	John Bell	Constitutional Union	592,906	39
1864	**Abraham Lincoln** **(Andrew Johnson, 1865)**	Republican	2,206,938	212
	George B. McClellan	Democratic	1,803,787	21
1868	**Ulysses S. Grant**	Republican	3,013,421	214
	Horatio Seymour	Democratic	2,706,829	80
1872	**Ulysses S. Grant**	Republican	3,596,745	286
	Horace Greeley	Democratic	2,843,446	66
1876	**Rutherford B. Hayes**	Republican	4,036,572	185
	Samuel J. Tilden	Democratic	4,284,020	184
1880	**James A. Garfield** **(Chester A. Arthur, 1881)**	Republican	4,449,053	214
	Winfield S. Hancock	Democratic	4,442,035	155
	James B. Weaver	Greenback-Labor	308,578	
1884	**Grover Cleveland**	Democratic	4,874,986	219
	James G. Blaine	Republican	4,851,981	182
	Benjamin F. Butler	Greenback-Labor	175,370	
1888	**Benjamin Harrison**	Republican	5,444,337	233
	Grover Cleveland	Democratic	5,540,050	168
1892	**Grover Cleveland**	Democratic	5,554,414	277
	Benjamin Harrison	Republican	5,190,802	145
	James B. Weaver	People's	1,027,329	22

Year	Candidates	Party	Popular vote	Electoral vote
1896	**William McKinley**	Republican	7,035,638	271
	William J. Bryan	Democratic; Populist	6,467,946	176
1900	**William McKinley**	Republican	7,219,530	292
	(Theodore Roosevelt, 1901)			
	William J. Bryan	Democratic; Populist	6,356,734	155
1904	**Theodore Roosevelt**	Republican	7,628,834	336
	Alton B. Parker	Democratic	5,084,401	140
	Eugene V. Debs	Socialist	402,460	
1908	**William H. Taft**	Republican	7,679,006	321
	William J. Bryan	Democratic	6,409,106	162
	Eugene V. Debs	Socialist	420,820	
1912	**Woodrow Wilson**	Democratic	6,286,820	435
	Theodore Roosevelt	Progressive	4,126,020	88
	William H. Taft	Republican	3,483,922	8
	Eugene V. Debs	Socialist	897,011	
1916	**Woodrow Wilson**	Democratic	9,129,606	277
	Charles E. Hughes	Republican	8,538,221	254
1920	**Warren G. Harding**	Republican	16,152,200	404
	(Calvin Coolidge, 1923)			
	James M. Cox	Democratic	9,147,353	127
	Eugene V. Debs	Socialist	919,799	
1924	**Calvin Coolidge**	Republican	15,725,016	382
	John W. Davis	Democratic	8,385,586	136
	Robert M. LaFollette	Progressive	4,822,856	13
1928	**Herbert C. Hoover**	Republican	21,392,190	444
	Alfred E. Smith	Democratic	15,016,443	87
1932	**Franklin D. Roosevelt**	Democratic	22,809,638	472
	Herbert C. Hoover	Republican	15,758,901	59
	Norman Thomas	Socialist	881,951	
1936	**Franklin D. Roosevelt**	Democratic	27,751,612	523
	Alfred M. Landon	Republican	16,681,913	8
	William Lemke	Union	891,858	
1940	**Franklin D. Roosevelt**	Democratic	27,243,466	449
	Wendell L. Willkie	Republican	22,304,755	82
1944	**Franklin D. Roosevelt**	Democratic	25,602,505	432
	(Harry S Truman, 1945)			
	Thomas E. Dewey	Republican	22,006,278	99
1948	**Harry S Truman**	Democratic	24,105,812	303
	Thomas E. Dewey	Republican	21,970,065	189
	J. Strom Thurmond	States' Rights	1,169,063	39
	Henry A. Wallace	Progressive	1,157,172	

Year	Candidates	Party	Popular vote	Electoral vote
1952	**Dwight D. Eisenhower**	Republican	33,936,234	442
	Adlai E. Stevenson	Democratic	27,314,992	89
1956	**Dwight D. Eisenhower**	Republican	35,590,472	457
	Adlai E. Stevenson	Democratic	26,022,752	73
1960	**John F. Kennedy** **(Lyndon B. Johnson, 1963)**	Democratic	34,227,096	303
	Richard M. Nixon	Republican	34,108,546	219
1964	**Lyndon B. Johnson**	Democratic	43,126,233	486
	Barry M. Goldwater	Republican	27,174,989	52
1968	**Richard M. Nixon**	Republican	31,783,783	301
	Hubert H. Humphrey	Democratic	31,271,839	191
	George C. Wallace	Amer. Independent	9,899,557	46
1972	**Richard M. Nixon** **(Gerald R. Ford, 1974)**	Republican	47,169,911	521
	George S. McGovern	Democratic	29,170,383	17
1976	**James Earl Carter**	Democratic	40,827,394	297
	Gerald R. Ford	Republican	39,145,977	241

Date of Statehood

Delaware	December 7, 1787	Michigan	January 16, 1837
Pennsylvania	December 12, 1787	Florida	March 3, 1845
New Jersey	December 18, 1787	Texas	December 29, 1845
Georgia	January 2, 1788	Iowa	December 28, 1846
Connecticut	January 9, 1788	Wisconsin	May 29, 1848
Massachusetts	February 6, 1788	California	September 9, 1850
Maryland	April 28, 1788	Minnesota	May 11, 1858
South Carolina	May 23, 1788	Oregon	February 14, 1859
New Hampshire	June 21, 1788	Kansas	January 29, 1861
Virginia	June 25, 1788	West Virginia	June 19, 1863
New York	July 26, 1788	Nevada	October 31, 1864
North Carolina	November 21, 1789	Nebraska	March 1, 1867
Rhode Island	May 29, 1790	Colorado	August 1, 1876
Vermont	March 4, 1791	North Dakota	November 2, 1889
Kentucky	June 1, 1792	South Dakota	November 2, 1889
Tennessee	June 1, 1796	Montana	November 8, 1889
Ohio	March 1, 1803	Washington	November 11, 1889
Louisiana	April 30, 1812	Idaho	July 3, 1890
Indiana	December 11, 1816	Wyoming	July 10, 1890
Mississippi	December 10, 1817	Utah	January 4, 1896
Illinois	December 3, 1818	Oklahoma	November 16, 1907
Alabama	December 14, 1819	New Mexico	January 6, 1912
Maine	March 15, 1820	Arizona	February 14, 1912
Missouri	August 10, 1821	Alaska	January 3, 1959
Arkansas	June 15, 1836	Hawaii	August 21, 1959

Population of the United States

1790	3,929,214		1890	62,947,714
1800	5,308,483		1900	75,994,575
1810	7,239,881		1910	91,972,266
1820	9,638,453		1920	105,710,620
1830	12,860,692		1930	122,775,046
1840	17,063,353		1940	131,669,275
1850	23,191,876		1950	150,697,361
1860	31,443,321		1960	179,323,175
1870	38,558,371		1970	204,765,770
1880	50,155,783		1978	218,500,000 (approx.)

Chief Justices of the United States Supreme Court

John Jay, N.Y. 1789–1795
John Rutledge, S.C. 1795
Oliver Ellsworth, Conn. 1795–1799
John Marshall, Va. 1801–1835
Roger B. Taney, Md. 1836–1864

Salmon P. Chase, Ohio 1864–1873
Morrison R. Waite, Ohio 1874–1888
Melville W. Fuller, Ill. 1888–1910
Edward D. White, La. 1910–1921
William H. Taft, Ohio 1921–1930

Charles E. Hughes, N.Y. 1930–1941
Harlan F. Stone, N.Y. 1941–1946
Fred M. Vinson, Ky. 1946–1953
Earl Warren, Calif. 1953–1969
Warren E. Burger, Minn. 1969

Presidents, Vice-Presidents, and Cabinet Members

President	Vice-President	Secretary of State	Secretary of Treasury	Secretary of War
1. **George Washington** 1789–1797 Federalist	John Adams 1789–1797	Thomas Jefferson 1789–1794 Edmund Randolph 1794–1795 Timothy Pickering 1795–1797	Alexander Hamilton 1789–1795 Oliver Wolcott 1795–1797	Henry Knox 1789–1795 Timothy Pickering 1795–1796 James McHenry 1796–1797
2. **John Adams** 1797–1801 Federalist	Thomas Jefferson 1797–1801	Timothy Pickering 1797–1800 John Marshall 1800–1801	Oliver Wolcott 1797–1801 Samuel Dexter 1801	James McHenry 1797–1800 Samuel Dexter 1800–1801
3. **Thomas Jefferson** 1801–1809 Republican	Aaron Burr 1801–1805 George Clinton 1805–1809	James Madison 1801–1809	Samuel Dexter 1801 Albert Gallatin 1801–1809	Henry Dearborn 1801–1809
4. **James Madison** 1809–1817 Republican	George Clinton 1809–1813 Elbridge Gerry 1813–1817	Robert Smith 1809–1811 James Monroe 1811–1817	Albert Gallatin 1809–1814 George Campbell 1814 Alexander Dallas 1814–1816 William Crawford 1816–1817	William Eustis 1809–1813 John Armstrong 1813–1814 James Monroe 1814–1815 William Crawford 1815–1817
5. **James Monroe** 1817–1825 Republican	Daniel D. Tompkins 1817–1825	John Quincy Adams 1817–1825	William Crawford 1817–1825	George Graham 1817 John C. Calhoun 1817–1825
6. **John Quincy Adams** 1825–1829 National Republican	John C. Calhoun 1825–1829	Henry Clay 1825–1829	Richard Rush 1825–1829	James Barbour 1825–1828 Peter B. Porter 1828–1829
7. **Andrew Jackson** 1829–1837 Democrat	John C. Calhoun 1829–1833 Martin Van Buren 1833–1837	Martin Van Buren 1829–1831 Edward Livingston 1831–1833 Louis McLane 1833–1834 John Forsyth 1834–1837	Samuel Ingham 1829–1831 Louis McLane 1831–1833 William Duane 1833 Roger B. Taney 1833–1834 Levi Woodbury 1834–1837	John H. Eaton 1829–1831 Lewis Cass 1831–1837 Benjamin Butler 1837

Secretary of Navy	Postmaster General	Attorney General
	Samuel Osgood 1789–1791 Timothy Pickering 1791–1795 Joseph Habersham 1795–1797	Edmund Randolph 1789–1794 William Bradford 1794–1795 Charles Lee 1795–1797
Benjamin Stoddert 1798–1801	Joseph Habersham 1797–1801	Charles Lee 1797–1801
Benjamin Stoddert 1801 Robert Smith 1801–1809	Joseph Habersham 1801 Gideon Granger 1801–1809	Levi Lincoln 1801–1805 John Breckinridge 1805–1807 Caesar Rodney 1807–1809
Paul Hamilton 1809–1813 William Jones 1813–1814 Benjamin Crowninshield 1814–1817	Gideon Granger 1809–1814 Return Meigs 1814–1817	Caesar Rodney 1809–1811 William Pinkney 1811–1814 Richard Rush 1814–1817
Benjamin Crowninshield 1817–1818 Smith Thompson 1818–1823 Samuel Southard 1823–1825	Return Meigs 1817–1823 John McLean 1823–1825	Richard Rush 1817 William Wirt 1817–1825
Samuel Southard 1825–1829	John McLean 1825–1829	William Wirt 1825–1829
John Branch 1829–1831 Levi Woodbury 1831–1834 Mahlon Dickerson 1834–1837	William Barry 1829–1835 Amos Kendall 1835–1837	John M. Berrien 1829–1831 Roger B. Taney 1831–1833 Benjamin Butler 1833–1837

Presidents, Vice-Presidents, and Cabinet Members

President	Vice-President	Secretary of State	Secretary of Treasury	Secretary of War
8. **Martin Van Buren** 1837–1841 Democrat	Richard M. Johnson 1837–1841	John Forsyth 1837–1841	Levi Woodbury 1837–1841	Joel R. Poinsett 1837–1841
9. **William H. Harrison** 1841 Whig	John Tyler 1841	Daniel Webster 1841	Thomas Ewing 1841	John Bell 1841
10. **John Tyler** 1841–1845 Whig and Democrat		Daniel Webster 1841–1843 Hugh S. Legaré 1843 Abel P. Upshur 1843–1844 John C. Calhoun 1844–1845	Thomas Ewing 1841 Walter Forward 1841–1843 John C. Spencer 1843–1844 George M. Bibb 1844–1845	John Bell 1841 John C. Spencer 1841–1843 James M. Porter 1843–1844 William Wilkins 1844–1845
11. **James K. Polk** 1845–1849 Democrat	George M. Dallas 1845–1849	James Buchanan 1845–1849	Robert J. Walker 1845–1849	William L. Marcy 1845–1849
12. **Zachary Taylor** 1849–1850 Whig	Millard Fillmore 1849–1850	John M. Clayton 1849–1850	William M. Meredith 1849–1850	George W. Crawford 1849–1850
13. **Millard Fillmore** 1850–1853 Whig		Daniel Webster 1850–1852 Edward Everett 1852–1853	Thomas Corwin 1850–1853	Charles M. Conrad 1850–1853
14. **Franklin Pierce** 1853–1857 Democrat	William R. King 1853–1857	William L. Marcy 1853–1857	James Guthrie 1853–1857	Jefferson Davis 1853–1857
15. **James Buchanan** 1857–1861 Democrat	John C. Breckinridge 1857–1861	Lewis Cass 1857–1860 Jeremiah S. Black 1860–1861	Howell Cobb 1857–1860 Philip F. Thomas 1860–1861 John A. Dix (1861)	John B. Floyd 1857–1861 Joseph Holt 1861
16. **Abraham Lincoln** 1861–1865 Republican	Hannibal Hamlin 1861–1865 Andrew Johnson 1865	William H. Seward 1861–1865	Salmon P. Chase 1861–1864 William P. Fessenden 1864–1865 Hugh McCulloch (1865)	Simon Cameron 1861–1862 Edwin M. Stanton 1862–1865

Secretary of Navy	Postmaster General	Attorney General	Secretary of Interior
Mahlon Dickerson 1837–1838 James K. Paulding 1838–1841	Amos Kendall 1837–1840 John M. Niles 1840–1841	Benjamin Butler 1837–1838 Felix Grundy 1838–1840 Henry D. Gilpin 1840–1841	
George E. Badger 1841	Francis Granger 1841	John J. Crittenden 1841	
George E. Badger 1841 Abel P. Upshur 1841–1843 David Henshaw 1843–1844 Thomas Gilmer 1844 John Y. Mason 1844–1845	Francis Granger 1841 Charles A. Wickliffe 1841–1845	John J. Crittenden 1841 Hugh S. Legaré 1841–1843 John Nelson 1843–1845	
George Bancroft 1845–1846 John Y. Mason 1846–1849	Cave Johnson 1845–1849	John Y. Mason 1845–1846 Nathan Clifford 1846–1848 Isaac Toucey 1848–1849	
William B. Preston 1849–1850	Jacob Collamer 1849–1850	Reverdy Johnson 1849–1850	Thomas Ewing 1849–1850
William A. Graham 1850–1852 John P. Kennedy 1852–1853	Nathan K. Hall 1850–1852 Sam D. Hubbard 1852–1853	John J. Crittenden 1850–1853	Thomas McKennan 1850 A. H. H. Stuart 1850–1853
James C. Dobbin 1853–1857	James Campbell 1853–1857	Caleb Cushing 1853–1857	Robert McClelland 1853–1857
Isaac Toucey 1857–1861	Aaron V. Brown 1857–1859 Joseph Holt 1859–1861 Horatio King (1861)	Jeremiah S. Black 1857–1860 Edwin M. Stanton 1860–1861	Jacob Thompson 1857–1861
Gideon Welles 1861–1865	Horatio King (1861) Montgomery Blair 1861–1864 William Dennison 1864–1865	Edward Bates 1861–1864 James Speed 1864–1865	Caleb B. Smith 1861–1863 John P. Usher 1863–1865

Presidents, Vice-Presidents, and Cabinet Members

President	Vice-President	Secretary of State	Secretary of Treasury	Secretary of War
17. **Andrew Johnson** 1865–1869 Unionist		William H. Seward 1865–1869	Hugh McCulloch 1865–1869	Edwin M. Stanton 1865–1867 Ulysses S. Grant 1867–1868 John M. Schofield 1868–1869
18. **Ulysses S. Grant** 1869–1877 Republican	Schuyler Colfax 1869–1873 Henry Wilson 1873–1877	Elihu B. Washburne 1869 Hamilton Fish 1869–1877	George S. Boutwell 1869–1873 William A. Richardson 1873–1874 Benjamin H. Bristow 1874–1876 Lot M. Morrill 1876–1877	John A. Rawlins 1869 William T. Sherman 1869 William W. Belknap 1869–1876 Alphonso Taft 1876 James D. Cameron 1876–1877
19. **Rutherford B. Hayes** 1877–1881 Republican	William A. Wheeler 1877–1881	William M. Evarts 1877–1881	John Sherman 1877–1881	George W. McCrary 1877–1879 Alexander Ramsey 1879–1881
20. **James A. Garfield** 1881 Republican	Chester A. Arthur 1881	James G. Blaine 1881	William Windom 1881	Robert T. Lincoln 1881
21. **Chester A. Arthur** 1881–1885 Republican		F. T. Frelinghuysen 1881–1885	Charles J. Folger 1881–1884 Walter Q. Gresham 1884 Hugh McCulloch 1884–1885	Robert T. Lincoln 1881–1885
22. **Grover Cleveland** 1885–1889 Democrat	T. A. Hendricks 1885	Thomas F. Bayard 1885–1889	Daniel Manning 1885–1887 Charles S. Fairchild 1887–1889	William C. Endicott 1885–1889
23. **Benjamin Harrison** 1889–1893 Republican	Levi P. Morton 1889–1893	James G. Blaine 1889–1892 John W. Foster 1892–1893	William Windom 1889–1891 Charles Foster 1891–1893	Redfield Procter 1889–1891 Stephen B. Elkins 1891–1893
24. **Grover Cleveland** 1893–1897 Democrat	Adlai E. Stevenson 1893–1897	Walter Q. Gresham 1893–1895 Richard Olney 1895–1897	John G. Carlisle 1893–1897	Daniel S. Lamont 1893–1897

Secretary of Navy	Postmaster General	Attorney General	Secretary of Interior	Secretary of Agriculture
Gideon Welles 1865–1869	William Dennison 1865–1866 Alexander Randall 1866–1869	James Speed 1865–1866 Henry Stanbery 1866–1868 William M. Evarts 1868–1869	John P. Usher 1865 James Harlan 1865–1866 O. H. Browning 1866–1869	
Adolph E Borie 1869 George M. Robeson 1869–1877	John A. J. Creswell 1869–1874 James W. Marshall 1874 Marshall Jewell 1874–1876 James N. Tyner 1876–1877	Ebenezer R. Hoar 1869–1870 Amos T. Akerman 1870–1871 G. H. Williams 1871–1875 Edwards Pierrepont 1875–1876 Alphonso Taft 1876–1877	Jacob D. Cox 1869–1870 Columbus Delano 1870–1875 Zachariah Chandler 1875–1877	
R. W. Thompson 1877–1881 Nathan Goff, Jr. 1881	David M. Key 1877–1880 Horace Maynard 1880–1881	Charles Devens 1877–1881	Carl Schurz 1877–1881	
William H. Hunt 1881	Thomas L. James 1881	Wayne MacVeagh 1881	S. J. Kirkwood 1881	
William E. Chandler 1881–1885	Thomas L. James 1881 Timothy O. Howe 1881–1883 Walter Q. Gresham 1883–1884 Frank Hatton 1884–1885	B. H. Brewster 1881–1885	Henry M. Teller 1881–1885	
William C. Whitney 1885–1889	William F. Vilas 1885–1888 Don M. Dickinson 1888–1889	A. H. Garland 1885–1889	L. Q. C. Lamar 1885–1888 William F. Vilas 1888–1889	Norman J. Colman 1889
Benjamin F. Tracy 1889–1893	John Wanamaker 1889–1893	W. H. H. Miller 1889–1893	John W. Noble 1889–1893	Jeremiah M. Rusk 1889–1893
Hilary A. Herbert 1893–1897	Wilson S. Bissel 1893–1895 William L. Wilson 1895–1897	Richard Olney 1893–1895 Judson Harmon 1895–1897	Hoke Smith 1893–1896 David R. Francis 1896–1897	J. Sterling Morton 1893–1897

Presidents, Vice-Presidents, and Cabinet Members

President	Vice-President	Secretary of State	Secretary of Treasury	Secretary of War*	Secretary of Navy*
25. **William McKinley** 1897–1901 Republican	Garret A. Hobart 1897–1901 Theodore Roosevelt 1901	John Sherman 1897–1898 William R. Day 1898 John Hay 1898–1901	Lyman J. Gage 1897–1901	Russell A. Alger 1897–1899 Elihu Root 1899–1901	John D. Long 1897–1901
26. **Theodore Roosevelt** 1901–1909 Republican	Charles Fairbanks 1905–1909	John Hay 1901–1905 Elihu Root 1905–1909 Robert Bacon 1909	Lyman J. Gage 1901–1902 Leslie M. Shaw 1902–1907 George B. Cortelyou 1907–1909	Elihu Root 1901–1904 William H. Taft 1904–1908 Luke E. Wright 1908–1909	John D. Long 1901–1902 William H. Moody 1902–1904 Paul Morton 1904–1905 Charles J. Bonaparte 1905–1906 Victor H. Metcalf 1906–1908 T. H. Newberry 1908–1909
27. **William H. Taft** 1909–1913 Republican	James S. Sherman 1909–1913	Philander C. Knox 1909–1913	Franklin MacVeagh 1909–1913	Jacob M. Dickinson 1909–1911 Henry L. Stimson 1911–1913	George von L. Meyer 1909–1913
28. **Woodrow Wilson** 1913–1921 Democrat	Thomas R. Marshall 1913–1921	William J. Bryan 1913–1915 Robert Lansing 1915–1920 Bainbridge Colby 1920–1921	William G. McAdoo 1913–1918 Carter Glass 1918–1920 David F. Houston 1920–1921	Lindley M. Garrison 1913–1916 Newton D. Baker 1916–1921	Josephus Daniels 1913–1921
29. **Warren G. Harding** 1921–1923 Republican	Calvin Coolidge 1921–1923	Charles E. Hughes 1921–1923	Andrew W. Mellon 1921–1923	John W. Weeks 1921–1923	Edwin Denby 1921–1923
30. **Calvin Coolidge** 1923–1929 Republican	Charles G. Dawes 1925–1929	Charles E. Hughes 1923–1925 Frank B. Kellogg 1925–1929	Andrew W. Mellon 1923–1929	John W. Weeks 1923–1925 Dwight F. Davis 1925–1929	Edwin Denby 1923–1924 Curtis D. Wilbur 1924–1929

*Lost cabinet status in 1947.

Postmaster General	Attorney General	Secretary of Interior	Secretary of Agriculture	Secretary of Commerce	Secretary of Labor
James A. Gary 1897–1898 Charles E. Smith 1898–1901	Joseph McKenna 1897–1898 John W. Griggs 1898–1901 Philander C. Knox 1901	Cornelius N. Bliss 1897–1898 E. A. Hitchcock 1898–1901	James Wilson 1897–1901		
Charles E. Smith 1901–1902 Henry C. Payne 1902–1904 Robert J. Wynne 1904–1905 George B. Cortelyou 1905–1907 George von L. Meyer 1907–1909	Philander C. Knox 1901–1904 William H. Moody 1904–1906 Charles J. Bonaparte 1906–1909	E. A. Hitchcock 1901–1907 James R. Garfield 1907–1909	James Wilson 1901–1909	George B. Cortelyou 1903–1904 Victor H. Metcalf 1904–1906 Oscar S. Straus 1906–1909	
Frank H. Hitchcock 1909–1913	G. W. Wickersham 1909–1913	R. A. Ballinger 1909–1911 Walter L. Fisher 1911–1913	James Wilson 1909–1913	Charles Nagel 1909–1913	
Albert S. Burleson 1913–1921	J. C. McReynolds 1913–1914 T. W. Gregory 1914–1919 A. Mitchell Palmer 1919–1921	Franklin K. Lane 1913–1920 John B. Payne 1920–1921	David F. Houston 1913–1920 E. T. Meredith 1920–1921	W. C. Redfield 1913–1919 J. W. Alexander 1919–1921	William B. Wilson 1913–1921
Will H. Hays 1921–1922 Hubert Work 1922–1923 Harry S. New 1923	H. M. Daugherty 1921–1923	Albert B. Fall 1921–1923 Hubert Work 1923	Henry C. Wallace 1921–1923	Herbert C. Hoover 1921–1923	James J. Davis 1921–1923
Harry S. New 1923–1929	H. M. Daugherty 1923–1924 Harlan F. Stone 1924–1925 John G. Sargent 1925–1929	Hubert Work 1923–1928 Roy O. West 1928–1929	Henry C. Wallace 1923–1924 Howard M. Gore 1924–1925 W. M. Jardine 1925–1929	Herbert C. Hoover 1923–1928 William F. Whiting 1928–1929	James J. Davis 1923–1929

Presidents, Vice-Presidents, and Cabinet Members

President	Vice-President	Secretary of State	Secretary of Treasury	Secretary of War*	Secretary of Navy*
31. **Herbert C. Hoover** 1929–1933 Republican	Charles Curtis 1929–1933	Henry L. Stimson 1929–1933	Andrew W. Mellon 1929–1932 Ogden L. Mills 1932–1933	James W. Good 1929 Patrick J. Hurley 1929–1933	Charles F. Adams 1929–1933
32. **Franklin Delano Roosevelt** 1933–1945 Democrat	John Nance Garner 1933–1941 Henry A. Wallace 1941–1945 Harry S Truman 1945	Cordell Hull 1933–1944 E. R. Stettinius, Jr. 1944–1945	William H. Woodin 1933–1934 Henry Morgenthau, Jr. 1934–1945	George H. Dern 1933–1936 Harry H. Woodring 1936–1940 Henry L. Stimson 1940–1945	Claude A. Swanson 1933–1940 Charles Edison 1940 Frank Knox 1940–1944 James V. Forrestal 1944–1945
33. **Harry S Truman** 1945–1953 Democrat	Alben W. Barkley 1949–1953	James F. Byrnes 1945–1947 George C. Marshall 1947–1949 Dean G. Acheson 1949–1953	Fred M. Vinson 1945–1946 John W. Snyder 1946–1953	Robert P. Patterson 1945–1947 Kenneth C. Royall 1947	James V. Forrestal 1945–1947

				Secretary of Defense	
				James V. Forrestal 1947–1949 Louis A. Johnson 1949–1950 George C. Marshall 1950–1951 Robert A. Lovett 1951–1953	
34. **Dwight D. Eisenhower** 1953–1961 Republican	Richard M. Nixon 1953–1961	John Foster Dulles 1953–1959 Christian A. Herter 1959–1961	George M. Humphrey 1953–1957 Robert B. Anderson 1957–1961	Charles E. Wilson 1953–1957 Neil H. McElroy 1957–1961 Thomas S. Gates 1959–1961	
35. **John F. Kennedy** 1961–1963 Democrat	Lyndon B. Johnson 1961–1963	Dean Rusk 1961–1963	C. Douglas Dillon 1961–1963	Robert S. McNamara 1961–1963	

Postmaster General	Attorney General	Secretary of Interior	Secretary of Agriculture	Secretary of Commerce	Secretary of Labor	Secretary of Health, Education and Welfare
Walter F. Brown 1929–1933	J. D. Mitchell 1929–1933	Ray L. Wilbur 1933–1945	Arthur M. Hyde 1929–1933	Robert P. Lamont 1929–1932 Roy D. Chapin 1932–1933	James J. Davis 1929–1930 William N. Doak 1930–1933	
James A. Farley 1933–1940 Frank C. Walker 1940 1945	H. S. Cummings 1933–1939 Frank Murphy 1939–1940 Robert Jackson 1940–1941 Francis Biddle 1941–1945	Harold L. Ickes 1933–1945	Henry A. Wallace 1933–1940 Claude R. Wickard 1940–1945	Daniel C. Roper 1933–1939 Harry L. Hopkins 1939–1940 Jesse Jones 1940–1945 Henry A. Wallace 1945	Frances Perkins 1933–1945	
R. E. Hannegan 1945–1947 Jesse M. Donaldson 1947–1953	Tom C. Clark 1945–1949 J. H. McGrath 1949 1952 James P. McGranery 1952–1953	Harold L. Ickes 1945–1946 Julius A. Krug 1946–1949 Oscar L. Chapman 1949–1953	C. P. Anderson 1945–1948 C. F. Brannan 1948–1953	W. A. Harriman 1946–1948 Charles Sawyer 1948–1953	L. B. Schwellenbach 1945–1948 Maurice J. Tobin 1948–1953	
A. E. Summerfield 1953–1961	H. Brownell, Jr. 1953–1957 William P. Rogers 1957–1961	Douglas McKay 1953–1956 Fred Seaton 1956–1961	Ezra T. Benson 1953–1961	Sinclair Weeks 1953–1958 Lewis L. Strauss 1958–1961	Martin P. Durkin 1953 James P. Mitchell 1953–1961	Oveta Culp Hobby 1953–1955 Marion B. Folsom 1955–1958 Arthur S. Flemming 1958–1961
J. Edward Day 1961–1963 John A. Gronouski 1963	Robert F. Kennedy 1961–1963	Stewart L. Udall 1961–1963	Orville L. Freeman 1961–1963	Luther H. Hodges 1961–1963	Arthur J. Goldberg 1961–1962 W. Willard Wirtz 1962–1963	A. H. Ribicoff 1961–1962 Anthony J. Celebrezze 1962–1963

Presidents, Vice-Presidents, and Cabinet Members

President	Vice-President	Secretary of State	Secretary of Treasury	Secretary of Defense	Postmaster General*	Attorney General
36. **Lyndon B. Johnson** 1963–1969 Democrat	Hubert H. Humphrey 1965–1969	Dean Rusk 1963–1969	C. Douglas Dillon 1963–1965 Henry H. Fowler 1965–1968 Joseph W. Barr 1968–1969	Robert S. McNamara 1963–1968 Clark M. Clifford 1968–1969	John A. Gronouski 1963–1965 Lawrence F. O'Brien 1965–1968 W. Marvin Watson 1968–1969	Robert F. Kennedy 1963–1965 N. deB. Katzenbach 1965–1967 Ramsey Clark 1967–1969
37. **Richard M. Nixon** 1969–1974 Republican	Spiro T. Agnew 1969–1973 Gerald R. Ford 1973–1974	William P. Rogers 1969–1973 Henry A. Kissinger 1973–1974	David M. Kennedy 1969–1970 John B. Connally 1970–1972 George P. Shultz 1972–1974 William E. Simon 1974	Melvin R. Laird 1969–1973 Elliot L. Richardson 1973 James R. Schlesinger 1973–1974	Winton M. Blount 1969–1971	John M. Mitchell 1969–1972 Richard G. Kleindienst 1972–1973 Elliot L. Richardson 1973 William B. Saxbe 1974
38. **Gerald R. Ford** 1974–1977 Republican	Nelson A. Rockefeller 1974–1977	Henry A. Kissinger 1974–1977	William E. Simon 1974–1977	James R. Schlesinger 1974–1975 Donald H. Rumsfeld 1975–1977		William B. Saxbe 1974–1975 Edward H. Levi 1975–1977
39. **Jimmy Carter** 1977– Democrat	Walter F. Mondale 1977–	Cyrus R. Vance 1977–1980 Edmund S. Muskie 1980–	W. Michael Blumenthal 1977–1979 G. William Miller 1979–	Harold Brown 1977–		Griffin Bell 1977–1979 Benjamin R. Civiletti 1979–

*On July 1, 1971, the Post Office became an independent agency. After that date, the Postmaster General was no longer a member of the Cabinet.

Secretary of Interior	Secretary of Agriculture	Secretary of Commerce	Secretary of Labor	Secretary of Health, Education and Welfare*	Secretary of Housing and Urban Development	Secretary of Transportation
Stewart L. Udall 1963–1969	Orville L. Freeman 1963–1969	Luther H. Hodges 1963–1965 John T. Connor 1965–1967 Alexander B. Trowbridge 1967–1968 C. R. Smith 1968–1969	W. Willard Wirtz 1963–1969	Anthony J. Celebrezze 1963–1965 John W. Gardner 1965–1968 Wilbur J. Cohen 1968–1969	Robert C. Weaver 1966–1968 Robert C. Wood 1968–1969	Alan S. Boyd 1966–1969
Walter J. Hickel 1969–1971 Rogers C. B. Morton 1971–1974	Clifford M. Hardin 1969–1971 Earl L. Butz 1971–1974	Maurice H. Stans 1969–1972 Peter G. Peterson 1972 Frederick B. Dent 1972–1974	George P. Shultz 1969–1970 James D. Hodgson 1970–1973 Peter J. Brennan 1973–1974	Robert H. Finch 1969–1970 Elliot L. Richardson 1970–1973 Caspar W. Weinberger 1973–1974	George W. Romney 1969–1973 James T. Lynn 1973–1974	John A. Volpe 1969–1973 Claude S. Brinegar 1973–1974
Rogers C. B. Morton 1974–1975 Stanley K. Hathaway 1975 Thomas D. Kleppe 1975–1977	Earl L. Butz 1974–1976 John A. Knebel 1976–1977	Frederick B. Dent 1974–1975 Rogers C. B. Morton 1975 Elliot L. Richardson 1975–1977	Peter J. Brennan 1974–1975 John T. Dunlop 1975–1976 W. J. Usery 1976–1977	Caspar W. Weinberger 1974–1975 Forrest D. Mathews 1975–1977	James T. Lynn 1974–1975 Carla A. Hills 1975–1977	Claude S. Brinegar 1974–1975 William T. Coleman 1975–1977
Cecil D. Andrus 1977–	Robert S. Bergland 1977–	Juanita M. Kreps 1977–1979 Philip M. Klutznick 1979–	F. Ray Marshall 1977–	Joseph Califano 1977–1979 Patricia Roberts Harris 1979–	Patricia Roberts Harris 1977–1979 Moon Landrieu 1979–	Brock Adams 1977–1979 Neil E. Goldschmidt 1979–
				Secretary of Energy†	Secretary of Education‡	
				James R. Schlesinger 1977–1979 Charles W. Duncan, Jr. 1979–	Shirley M. Hufstedler 1979–	

*In 1979 HEW was renamed the Department of Health and Human Services.   †Created in 1977.   ‡Created in 1979.

Photo Credits

Index

Index